(Continued on back endsheets)

Twentieth-Century British Literary Biographers

Dictionary of Literary Biography® • Volume One Hundred Fifty-Five

Twentieth-Century British Literary Biographers

Edited by
Steven Serafin
Hunter College of the City University of New York

A Bruccoli Clark Layman Book
Gale Research Inc.
Detroit, Washington, D.C., London

Printed in the United States of America

Published simultaneously in the United Kingdom
by Gale Research International Limited
(An affiliated company of Gale Research Inc.)

The paper used in this publication meets the minimum requirements
of American National Standard for Information Sciences–Permanence
Paper for Printed Library Materials, ANSI Z39.48-1984. ∞ ™

Library of Congress Cataloging-in-Publication Data

Twentieth-century British literary biographers / edited by Steven Serafin.
    p. cm. – (Dictionary of literary biography; v. 155)
"A Bruccoli Clark Layman book."
Includes bibliographical references and index.
ISBN 0–8103–5716–X (alk. paper)
    1. English prose literature – 20th century – Bio-bibliography. 2. English prose literature – 20th century – Dictionaries. 3. Biographers – Great Britain – Biography – Dictionaries. 4. Biography as a literary form – Bio-bibliography. 5. Biography as a literary form – Dictionaries. 6. Authors, English – Biography – Dictionaries. I. Serafin, Steven. II. Series.
PR756.B56T84   1995
820.9'492 – dc20   95–21105
                                                                      CIP

10 9 8 7 6 5 4 3 2 1

Contents

Plan of the Series

. . . Almost the most prodigious asset of a country, and perhaps its most precious possession, is its native literary product – when that product is fine and noble and enduring.

Mark Twain*

The advisory board, the editors, and the publisher of the *Dictionary of Literary Biography* are joined in endorsing Mark Twain's declaration. The literature of a nation provides an inexhaustible resource of permanent worth. We intend to make literature and its creators better understood and more accessible to students and the reading public, while satisfying the standards of teachers and scholars.

To meet these requirements, *literary biography* has been construed in terms of the author's achievement. The most important thing about a writer is his writing. Accordingly, the entries in *DLB* are career biographies, tracing the development of the author's canon and the evolution of his reputation.

The purpose of *DLB* is not only to provide reliable information in a convenient format but also to place the figures in the larger perspective of literary history and to offer appraisals of their accomplishments by qualified scholars.

The publication plan for *DLB* resulted from two years of preparation. The project was proposed to Bruccoli Clark by Frederick C. Ruffner, president of the Gale Research Company, in November 1975. After specimen entries were prepared and typeset, an advisory board was formed to refine the entry format and develop the series rationale. In meetings held during 1976, the publisher, series editors, and advisory board approved the scheme for a comprehensive biographical dictionary of persons who contributed to North American literature. Editorial work on the first volume began in January 1977, and it was published in 1978. In order to make *DLB* more than a reference tool and to compile volumes that individually have claim to status as literary history, it was decided to organize volumes by topic, period, or genre. Each of these freestanding volumes provides a biographical-bibliographical guide and overview for a particular area of literature. We are convinced that this organization – as opposed to a single alphabet method – constitutes a valuable innovation in the presentation of reference material. The volume plan necessarily requires many decisions for the placement and treatment of authors who might properly be included in two or three volumes. In some instances a major figure will be included in separate volumes, but with different entries emphasizing the aspect of his career appropriate to each volume. Ernest Hemingway, for example, is represented in *American Writers in Paris, 1920–1939* by an entry focusing on his expatriate apprenticeship; he is also in *American Novelists, 1910–1945* with an entry surveying his entire career. Each volume includes a cumulative index of the subject authors and articles. Comprehensive indexes to the entire series are planned.

With volume ten in 1982 it was decided to enlarge the scope of *DLB*. By the end of 1986 twenty-one volumes treating British literature had been published, and volumes for Commonwealth and Modern European literature were in progress. The series has been further augmented by the *DLB Yearbooks* (since 1981) which update published entries and add new entries to keep the *DLB* current with contemporary activity. There have also been *DLB Documentary Series* volumes which provide biographical and critical source materials for figures whose work is judged to have particular interest for students. One of these companion volumes is entirely devoted to Tennessee Williams.

We define literature as the *intellectual commerce of a nation:* not merely as belles lettres but as that ample and complex process by which ideas are generated, shaped, and transmitted. *DLB* entries are not limited to "creative writers" but extend to other figures who in their time and in their way influenced the mind of a people. Thus the series encompasses historians, journalists, publishers, and screenwriters. By this means readers of *DLB* may be aided to perceive literature not as cult scripture in the keeping of intellectual high

*From an unpublished section of Mark Twain's autobiography, copyright by the Mark Twain Company

priests but firmly positioned at the center of a nation's life.

DLB includes the major writers appropriate to each volume and those standing in the ranks immediately behind them. Scholarly and critical counsel has been sought in deciding which minor figures to include and how full their entries should be. Wherever possible, useful references are made to figures who do not warrant separate entries.

Each *DLB* volume has a volume editor responsible for planning the volume, selecting the figures for inclusion, and assigning the entries. Volume editors are also responsible for preparing, where appropriate, appendices surveying the major periodicals and literary and intellectual movements for their volumes, as well as lists of further readings. Work on the series as a whole is coordinated at the Bruccoli Clark Layman editorial center in Columbia, South Carolina, where the editorial staff is responsible for accuracy of the published volumes.

One feature that distinguishes *DLB* is the illustration policy – its concern with the iconogra-

phy of literature. Just as an author is influenced by his surroundings, so is the reader's understanding of the author enhanced by a knowledge of his environment. Therefore *DLB* volumes include not only drawings, paintings, and photographs of authors, often depicting them at various stages in their careers, but also illustrations of their families and places where they lived. Title pages are regularly reproduced in facsimile along with dust jackets for modern authors. The dust jackets are a special feature of *DLB* because they often document better than anything else the way in which an author's work was perceived in its own time. Specimens of the writers' manuscripts are included when feasible.

Samuel Johnson rightly decreed that "The chief glory of every people arises from its authors." The purpose of the *Dictionary of Literary Biography* is to compile literary history in the surest way available to us – by accurate and comprehensive treatment of the lives and work of those who contributed to it.

The *DLB* Advisory Board

Introduction

"For better or worse," Richard D. Altick writes in *Lives and Letters: A History of Literary Biography in England and America* (1965), "literary history is the essence of innumerable biographies." Extending from the mid eighteenth century to the present, the evolution of biography from craft to genre serves to affirm the emerging status of the literary figure within society and to accentuate the relationship between an individual's life and his or her creative process. The popularity of biography is in part the result of a pronounced interest by the reading public in the lives of other people and, more important, in the biographer's artistry in telling the story of the subject's life. When the subject is a writer, the biographer allows the reader insight into the personal, as well as the literal, development of the individual and in so doing provides an imaginative means to visualize the transformation of actual into fictional experience. In this way the biographer influences not only our perception and understanding of a literary figure but our appreciation and appraisal of literature itself.

With the advent of modernism in the late nineteenth and early twentieth centuries, biographical writing in Great Britain evolved as one of the most accessible and exemplary forms of literary expression. The commemorative "life and times" favored by Victorian biographers that often suppressed or distorted information under the guise of truthfulness was gradually replaced with authorial integrity and objective scholarship, exemplified by authors such as E. V. Lucas, Charles Harold Herford, Percy Lubbock, Sir Sidney Colvin, P. P. Howe, and Hugh Kingsmill, among others. Unquestionably, the most significant event in redefining the concept and practice of biography was the publication in 1918 of Lytton Strachey's *Eminent Victorians*. Incorporating shifts in narrative techniques with innovative strategies toward structure and design to explore the complexities of character, Strachey was instrumental in establishing biography as an art of introspection as well as illumination. Strachey helped to elevate biography to a position of critical stature, and as summarized by Michael Holroyd, "After Strachey, no good biographer has dared to be less than an artist."

The development of twentieth-century biography was further enhanced by the appearance of new theories and schools of psychology, which drastically revised man's view of himself and opened vast new fields of speculation. As a result of Freudianism, the biographer became increasingly concerned with examining and understanding the inner forces that shape the life of a subject in order to present a more complete and satisfying interpretation. Existing data had to be reexamined and evaluated for significance that had been previously unrecognized or misinterpreted. In relation to literary biography, the quest for the personality of the subject is magnified by the need to explore the relationship between the writer and his or her body of work. As such, the process of presenting a life becomes a journey of discovery for both the biographer and the reader.

The demands placed on biography from psychology and other social sciences in conjunction with those from the reading public in general have been directly responsible for revolutionizing the genre. As a result, there is now renewed interest both in the history of biography and in the creative process of the biographer. The comparative nature of biography enables each configuration of a life to serve as the biographer's version of the individual. As a genre, Ira Bruce Nadel writes in *Biography: Fiction, Fact and Form* (1984), "biography continually unsettles the past, maintaining its vitality through its continual correction, revision and interpretation of individual lives. Each new life is a provocation to reassess all past lives of that subject. Versions of a life are necessary stages in the evolution of the genre as well as in the understanding of the subject." If one perceives the multiplicity of lives as an inherent strength of biography, then the appearance of a "new" version of a life can enlarge our appreciation of the subject as well as the genre. Often the biographer's purpose in re-creating a life is to incorporate newly discovered or released information, exemplified by Julian Symons's life of his brother, *A. J. A. Symons* (1950); Nigel Nicolson's dual biography of his parents, Harold Nicolson and Vita Sackville-West, *Portrait of a Marriage* (1973); and P. N. Furbank's two-volume life of his friend and colleague, *E. M. Forster* (1977, 1978). However, accentuating the fact that biography can never be completely objective, the process of demythologizing a subject simultaneously necessitates that the biographer create a revised mythical identity. Biography is also used to revive public esteem for the author's work, exemplified by Angus Wilson in his lives of Emile Zola (1952), Charles Dickens (1970), and Rudyard Kipling (1977); Georgina Battiscombe's *John Keble* (1963); and Edward Chitham's *A Life of Anne Brontë* (1991). It is crucial that the need for reassessment be shared by biographer and reader alike and pertain to historical as well as modern subjects. Historical subjects whose popularity extends into the twentieth century continue to demonstrate the demand for reassessment: George Gordon, Lord Byron, is the subject of numerous biographical treatments, notably by Peter Quennell (1934), Iris Origo (1949), and Elizabeth Longford (1976); Dickens has been treated by Angus Wilson, Symons (1951), Peter Ackroyd (1990), and in part by Claire Tomalin (1990); Charlotte Brontë is the subject of biographies by Winifred Gerín (1967), Tom Winnifrith (1988), and Lyndall Gordon (1994). Similarly, the need to assess the lives of twentieth-century authors has produced biographies of critical importance, notably the lives of Robert Graves by Martin Seymour-Smith (1956; revised edition, 1965; revised again, 1970), Virginia Woolf by Quentin Bell (1972) and Gordon (1984), W. Somerset Maugham by Anthony Curtis (1977), Evelyn Waugh by Martin Stannard (1986, 1992), George Bernard Shaw by Holroyd (1988–1992), Graham Greene by Norman Sherry (1989, 1994), and C. S. Lewis by A. N. Wilson (1990).

One of the most distinguished biographies of the twentieth century is George D. Painter's two-volume *Marcel Proust* (1959, 1965), which is recognized for its breadth of scholarship as well as its artistic merit. It is also representative of the penchant of British biographers for non-British literary subjects, further exemplified by Angus Wilson's *Emile Zola;* Ronald Hayman's lives of Antonin Artaud (1977), Franz Kakfa (1982), Bertolt Brecht (1983), Jean-Paul Sartre (1986), and Thomas Mann (1995), among others; Ian Hamilton's *Robert Lowell* (1982); A. N. Wilson's *Tolstoy* (1988); and Furbank's *Diderot* (1992). Similar to Painter, who in addition to *Marcel Proust* has written a biography of André Gide (1951), both Ronald Hingley and Michael Meyer have established their reputations by association with other national literatures. Drawn to nineteenth- and twentieth-century Russian authors, Hingley has written lives of Anton Chekhov (1976), Fyodor Dostoyevsky (1978), and Boris Pasternak (1983); Meyer, on the other hand, has written pre-

dominantly on Scandinavian authors, producing lives of Henrik Ibsen (1967, 1971) and August Strindberg (1985).

Although biography is archival by nature, hybrid forms of biographical writing have transformed the genre by expanding the function and role of the biographer in presenting his or her interpretation of a life. As conventional methodology and practice governed by chronology and the linear development of detail has become less satisfying both to the writer and to readers in general, biography has responded by becoming more diversified in form and stylistic presentation. There is now more comprehensive interaction between biography and other literary genres, exemplified by authors such as Margaret Forster and Ackroyd, who view biography as an extension of fiction and successfully incorporate narrative techniques to enhance their relationships with their readers. In *William Makepeace Thackeray: Memoirs of a Victorian Gentleman* (1978), Forster presents Thackeray's life as a fictional autobiography. Ackroyd, on the other hand, admits to searching for "a new way to inter-animate biography and fiction," exemplified perhaps most effectively by interspersing fictional interludes within his life of Dickens. The imaginative identification between the biographer and his subject has enabled Richard Holmes to view biography as a process of rediscovery and to write a form of metabiography that merges biography and autobiography. The need for reassessment of women writers encouraged narrative experimentation by such authors as Forster in her lives of Elizabeth Barrett Browning (1988) and Daphne du Maurier (1993); Glendinning in her lives of Sackville-West (1983) and Rebecca West (1987); Francis Spalding in her life of Stevie Smith (1988); and Tomalin in her lives of Mary Wollstonecraft (1974) and Katherine Mansfield (1987). There is also continued interest by biographers in the writing of dual and group biographies, notably by Nicolson with *Portrait of a Marriage,* Holmes with *Dr. Johnson & Mr. Savage* (1993), and Humphrey Carpenter with *The Inklings: C. S. Lewis, J. R. R. Tolkien, Charles Williams, and Their Friends* (1978), *Geniuses Together: American Writers in Paris in the 1920s* (1987), and *The Brideshead Generation: Evelyn Waugh and His Friends* (1989). Infused with imaginative and psychological insight, scholarship, and creativity, the many forms of biographical writing have rejuvenated the genre with a renewed sense of purpose and expectation that further enhances the relationship of the biographer with both his or her subject and his or her reader.

Within the twentieth century, biography has emerged as a distinct literary endeavor, and the contribution of the professional biographer is widely acknowledged. In the tradition of nineteenth-century men of letters such as John Forster, John Morley, Leslie Stephen, Edmund Gosse, and Hesketh Pearson, contemporary biographers such as Carpenter, Glendinning, Hayman, Longford, Holmes, and Holroyd are recognized as writers of scholarly purpose and artistic merit. Interestingly, literary biography has consistently attracted as practitioners authors known primarily as creative writers, including novelists such as Ackroyd, Margaret Drabble, and A. N. Wilson; mystery writer Symons; and poet John Wain. As a consequence of "Strachey's psychologizing, candour and stylistic energy" and as a reaction to new forms of fictional expression, twentieth-century biography has become more aware of how it tells its story, as evident in Symons's *Thomas Carlyle* (1952), Wain's *Samuel Johnson* (1974), Drabble's *Arnold Bennett* (1974), Ackroyd's *T. S. Eliot* (1984), and Carpenter's *A Serious Character: The Life of Ezra Pound* (1988). "Relations not facts establish significance," Nadel observes, and biography "recognizes the importance of this quality as it becomes more aware of the value of narrative design, structure and style, as well as the position of the reader and the subject in the text."

As a literary art, biography is a creative process involving selectivity and synthesis of data that provides an interpretation of a life through language. The form of biographical expression is invented by the biographer both to shape the life of his or her subject and to orchestrate the reader's response and appreciation of the individual. Transforming fact into literary reality, the biographer uses rhetorical strategies and narrative techniques to maintain point of view as well as unity in creating the story. The structure and organization of story is essentially determined by the arrangement of factual information. Since the details of a person's life are presented by the biographer through linguistic elements, the form of their presentation in the evaluation of contemporary biography has become an issue of increasing importance. Through the use of language, the biographer provides access to his or her conception of a life, merging imaginative vision with reader sensibility and understanding.

As a storyteller, the biographer in much the same way as a novelist relies on narration to provide balance and cohesiveness to the story. Depending on figurative as well as referential language to invent the subject in the mind of the reader, the interpretive narrator creates a broader vision of the subject while expanding the literary possibilities of the genre. For the contemporary biographer, the texture and contiguity of biography is fused by linguistic modes that actualize the experience of the subject's life for both the writer and the reader. It is through language that the biographer's presence and purpose is felt within the text, engaging the reader's imagination in the biographical process. Interpretative biography also incorporates what Holmes has called a "kind of rhythm, almost like someone breathing in and out." "The breath-ins are when there's a scene or a person or group of people held in a close-up," Holmes adds, "and you get a physical sense of their immediate presence. Then there should be a moving away to the other thing which biography can do so well, setting that person or group in a much wider historical perspective."

Twentieth-Century British Literary Biographers introduces the lives and works of those individuals who have influenced the development of the genre from the early twentieth century to the present. Recognized primarily as writers on literary subjects, the biographers included in the volume represent the establishment of literary biography as an artistic endeavor of critical importance. The volume is designed to provide an analysis of the methods and techniques of these biographers in the practice of their craft and in the exploration of their art. As observed by Altick, "Whatever its services to an enlarged comprehension of the human mind and the ways of society and culture, the primary importance of literary biography continues to lie in its quest for a deeper and more accurate understanding of the mind that produces a poem, a play, or a novel, and hence of the work itself. By continuing to seek new information and to reinterpret the old, by destroying legends and prejudices and misconceptions, by applying to the data of history the techniques of modern cultural and psychological analysis, the biographer strives for a fairer estimate of the author and his creation."

– Steven Serafin

Acknowledgments

This book was produced by Bruccoli Clark Layman, Inc. Karen L. Rood is senior editor for *The Dictionary of Literary Biography* series. James W. Hipp was the in-house editor.

Production coordinator is James W. Hipp. Photography editor is Bruce Andrew Bowlin. Photographic copy work was performed by Joseph M.

Bruccoli. Layout and graphics supervisor is Penney L. Haughton. Copyediting supervisor is Laurel M. Gladden. Typesetting supervisor is Kathleen M. Flanagan. Systems manager is George F. Dodge. Julie E. Frick is editorial associate. The production staff includes Phyllis A. Avant, Charles D. Brower, Ann M. Cheschi, Melody W. Clegg, Patricia Coate, Denise Edwards, Joyce Fowler, Stephanie C. Hatchell, Jyll Johnston, Rebecca Mayo, Margaret Meriwether, Kathy Lawler Merlette, Jeff Miller, Pamela D. Norton, Laura S. Pleicones, Jessica Rogers, Emily R. Sharpe, William L. Thomas Jr., Allison Trussell, Jonathan B. Watterson, and Jane M. J. Williamson.

Walter W. Ross and Robert S. McConnell did library research. They were assisted by the following librarians at the Thomas Cooper Library of the University of South Carolina: Linda Holderfield and the interlibrary-loan staff; reference-department head Virginia Weathers; reference librarians Marilee Birchfield, Stefanie Buck, Cathy Eckman, Rebecca Feind, Jill Holman, Karen Joseph, Jean Rhyne, Kwamine Washington, and Connie Widney; circulation-department head Caroline Taylor; and acquisitions-searching supervisor David Haggard.

Dictionary of Literary Biography® • Volume One Hundred Fifty-Five

Twentieth-Century British Literary Biographers

Dictionary of Literary Biography

Peter Ackroyd
(5 October 1949 –)

Glen M. Johnson
Catholic University of America

BOOKS: *Ouch* (London: Curiously Strong Press, 1971);

London Lickpenny (London: Ferry Press, 1973);

Notes for a New Culture: An Essay on Modernism (London: Vision Press, 1976; New York: Barnes & Noble, 1976);

Country Life (London: Ferry Press, 1978);

Dressing Up: Transvestism and Drag: The History of An Obsession (London: Thames & Hudson, 1979; New York: Simon & Schuster, 1979);

Ezra Pound and His World (London: Thames & Hudson, 1981; New York: Scribners, 1981);

The Great Fire of London (London: Hamish Hamilton, 1982; Chicago: University of Chicago Press, 1988);

The Last Testament of Oscar Wilde (London: Hamish Hamilton, 1983; New York: Harper, 1983);

T. S. Eliot (London: Hamish Hamilton, 1984; New York: Simon & Schuster, 1984);

Hawksmoor (London: Hamish Hamilton, 1986; New York: Harper, 1986);

The Diversions of Purley and Other Poems (London: Hamish Hamilton, 1987);

Chatterton (London: Hamish Hamilton, 1987; New York: Grove, 1988);

First Light (London: Hamish Hamilton, 1989; New York: Grove Weidenfeld, 1989);

Dickens (London: Sinclair-Stevenson, 1990; New York: HarperCollins, 1990);

Introduction to Dickens (London: Sinclair-Stevenson, 1991; New York: Ballantine, 1991);

English Music (London: Hamish Hamilton, 1992; New York: Knopf, 1992);

The House of Doctor Dee (London: Hamish Hamilton, 1993);

Dan Leno and the Limehouse Golem (London: Sinclair-Stevenson, 1994); published as *The Trial of*

Peter Ackroyd

Elizabeth Cree: A Novel of the Limehouse Murders (New York: Doubleday, 1995).

OTHER: "The Inheritance," in *London Tales,* edited by Julian Evans (London: Hamish Hamilton, 1983);

PEN New Fiction, edited by Ackroyd (London: Quartet Books, 1984);

Dickens' London: An Imaginative Vision, introduction by Ackroyd (London: Headline, 1987);

Frank Auerbach, *Frank Auerbach: Recent Works,* introduction by Ackroyd (New York: Marlborough, 1994).

SELECTED PERIODICAL PUBLICATION –
UNCOLLECTED: "Autobiography of a House,"
House and Garden, 164 (May 1992): 36–39.

"Biographers are simply novelists without imagination": in one of the fanciful interchapters of his biography *Dickens* (1990), Peter Ackroyd imagines hearing this sentiment from Charles Dickens. The statement illuminates the challenge biography holds for Ackroyd, who considers novel writing his profession. While working on *Dickens,* Ackroyd told an interviewer for *Publishers Weekly* (25 December 1987), "I hate being called a biographer": the term was "not only an insult but also untrue" in terms of his "time spent or vocation." But in 1992 he told an audience at a public "conversation" that he found the combination of novel writing and biography "fruitful." By that time he had also changed his mind about making *Dickens* his last biography and was researching the life of William Blake.

As his career has developed, Ackroyd has sought "a new way to interanimate" biography and fiction. All of his novels have historical elements, and four have biographical titles: *The Last Testament of Oscar Wilde* (1983), *Hawksmoor* (1986), *Chatterton* (1987), and *Dan Leno and the Limehouse Golem* (1994). Historical persons have long been accepted as characters in novels, whereas a claim that fiction can animate biography is certain to be controversial. For Ackroyd, the claim arises from the genre's nature: a biographer is continuously aware of "just how much cannot be known," yet "the uncertainty principle" is "quite impossible to build into biography." The novelist's tools can help to "make the narrative coherent." In part, Ackroyd admits, this involves what he calls cheating: deliberately confusing the biographer's "act of interpretation" with the novelist's ability to "insist that things happen the way they ought to happen." But in a more fundamental sense, Ackroyd's approach involves identification with history: "I realized I was able to understand the past in a kind of concrete way, think myself back into it." The primary means of this is language: "the only way of getting a grip on the past . . . was to write the language of the past" – in biography, to identify with the literary style of the subject and with the milieu that formed it. This notion of imaginative identification is visionary – to cite the characteristic Ackroyd believes his fictional and biographical protagonists share – but it provides the motivating tension of his writing in both genres.

Ackroyd was born 5 October 1949, the only child of Graham and Audrey Whiteside Ackroyd, who separated early in Ackroyd's life. Ackroyd was raised by his mother and grandparents in West London council housing. Later Ackroyd came to see his interest in London visionaries as a product of his family's Roman Catholicism and of his upbringing in the metropolis. He writes in *Dickens* that "cities do not change over the centuries. . . . Their atmosphere, their tone, remain the same." He showed talent early and at ten was, as he says, "lifted out" of the working-class environment by a scholarship to Saint Benedict's, a public school in Ealing. In 1968 he went from Saint Benedict's to Clare College, Cambridge, and after graduating in 1971 he spent two years at Yale University as a Mellon fellow. Returning to London, he was associated for eight years with the *Spectator* magazine, first as literary editor and then as joint managing editor. Beginning in 1981 he devoted himself to writing novels and biographies; since 1986 he has served as chief book reviewer for the London *Times.* With Brian Kuhn, his companion since his years at Yale, he divides his time between London and a country house in Devon.

Before 1981 Ackroyd concentrated on poetry, reviews, and nonfiction, including *Notes for a New Culture: An Essay on Modernism* (1976), a polemic against the English realist tradition and in favor of Continental literary theory, and *Dressing Up* (1979), a history of transvestism and "drag" culture. Poetry was his earliest literary ambition, with volumes in 1971, 1973, and 1978 and collected poems in 1987; but once Ackroyd began writing novels his poetry was "transformed into another context. I don't suppose I'll ever go back to writing poetry." The turn to fiction and to full-time writing in 1981 began a period of extraordinary productivity that continues. By 1995 Ackroyd, at forty-six, had published eight novels and three literary biographies.

Ackroyd's first biographies were of two great modernist poets: *Ezra Pound and His World* (1981) and *T. S. Eliot* (1984). *Ezra Pound* was one of a series of short illustrated biographies published by Thames and Hudson; Ackroyd's contribution was biographical text to run alongside the illustrations. The result (Ackroyd has called it "a long essay") is necessarily concise but distinctive. Ackroyd's main interest is in the poetry and how it, along with Pound's aggressive support for other modernists, "created the taste of an entire literary generation." Ackroyd's critical comments are apt and frequently provocative: he champions *The Cantos* (1948), and especially later installments like *Section: Rock-Drill: 85–95 de los Cantares* (1956), for "rather coarse, but genuine, mysticism" and "a stupendous affirmation of the imagination and of the visionary powers of poetry." The connection of the poetry to the life of Pound is somewhat vague in this context. And in fact Ackroyd devalues the works that are most often interpreted biographically, *Hugh Selwyn Mauberley* (1920) and the *Pisan Cantos* (1948). The main quality Ackroyd finds in Pound's life is his sense of being an outsider. Pound called himself "alien," and for Ackroyd the key is a "mythical America from which he imagined he had come." Though his concept is valid in terms of the interest of some of the cantos in American history, Ackroyd's shaky sense of that history renders it less than convincing as an explanation of Pound. To cite one example, Ackroyd says that Pound's birth in 1885 was to an American "race before the flood of European immigrants who were to transform American life in the new century."

Pound's fascism tests, as starkly as with any twentieth-century writer, the relationship among biographical acts, paraphrasable content, and evaluation of literature. For Ackroyd, Pound's acts and statements (including some in the poetry) are undeniable and not to be excused: he "directly implicated himself, through his writings, in the horrors" that included Auschwitz; "His temperament . . . had become a divining rod of the age's character — reflecting its darkest sides as well as its brighter." Nevertheless, Ackroyd holds out a value that transcends both "the divisive tendencies of the age, and the obsessive weaknesses of [Pound's] own character." This "visionary view of the world that the world itself could hardly understand" is Pound's value for Ackroyd. Although Ackroyd does not clarify how "mysticism" and the "visionary" transcend more overt statements and actions, his position here is a version of the modernist distinction between artist and artwork — what Eliot thought should be a perfect separation between "the man who suffers and the mind which creates."

Separation between biography and creative artifact is especially problematic when applied to Eliot himself, who called poetry an "escape from personality" but whose "personality and experience" are, in Ackroyd's words, "branded in letters of fire upon his work." Ackroyd remembers that the idea of writing Eliot's biography came from his publisher and that he was soon drawn to challenge the project's difficulties. Primary among those difficulties was the uncooperativeness of Eliot's estate, following desires expressed in the poet's will: the biographer could see nothing not in public collections and could quote only briefly from published works and not at all from unpublished works or correspondence. The restriction on quoting un-

published writings had led many scholars to assume that such materials were unavailable, but Ackroyd found "more than enough" in library collections. Still, the inability to quote created a "need to be much more inventive about how I brought him to life": "Most biographers are . . . able to quote a lot of letters and other material and then leave it to the reader to make up their minds about what kind of person their subject was, but I had to do all that work myself, to internalize the material and then present it in my own way." One result of this internalization was a fair approximation by Ackroyd to Eliot's prose style — noticed by a few reviewers but less striking than a similar attempt in *Dickens* would be, perhaps because Eliot's continuing influence had made his a dominant prose style in British letters.

Reviews of *T. S. Eliot* typically began by calling it fair and broad-minded; Christopher Ricks, in the 1 November 1984 *London Review of Books,* went further to call it "benign" and "decent." Such praise reflects, in large part, Ackroyd's refusal to impose on the facts of Eliot's life a unitary thesis or theoretical preconceptions. To the extent that Ackroyd finds some general explanation for Eliot, it is similar to the one he found for Pound. Each developed a "sense of being an alien in America," "estranged from the country itself" during a "time of great ethical and social confusion." Ackroyd's brief description of the America of Eliot's youth cites *The Education of Henry Adams* (1918) — a peculiar connection, since Adams's childhood preceded Eliot's by a half century. Still, comparing Eliot and Adams forwards Ackroyd's emphasis on an attenuated New England character that both are assumed to share: Ackroyd speaks, without apparent irony, of "that clean-cut listlessness which is characteristic of young and well-bred Americans." John Updike, writing in *The New Yorker* (25 March 1985), found Ackroyd's ignorance of America both irritating — he has the Massachusetts coast extending to Canada — and silly: "he tends to see us as little Puritan dears far across the sea: [for Ackroyd] America is 'marked by a vague spirituality and an inchoate civilization.' " The best one can say about Ackroyd's notion of American culture is that the looseness of his generalizations keeps them from imposing much rigidity on the narrative.

Ackroyd is on surer (that is, English) ground in analyzing the two biographical events that dominated Eliot's adult life and influenced the course and the content of his mature poetry: his failed first marriage to Vivien Haigh-Wood and his conversion to Anglican Christianity. The "terrible disaster" of

Dust jacket for Ackroyd's biography of T. S. Eliot, which Christopher Ricks calls "benign" and "decent"

the marriage is analyzed in detail by Ackroyd, with tact and sensitivity that are all the more noticeable since *T. S. Eliot* was published while a popular play, *Tom and Viv,* was sensationalizing the same materials. Ackroyd's most interesting suggestion is that the Eliots' marital agonies, increasingly played out before others, had an "element of willed drama": "Eliot and Vivien were quite aware of their nervous predicament, recognizing the effect which it had upon themselves and others, and were . . . inclined to make a kind of game out of it." The effect of his marriage on Eliot's poetry, particularly *The Waste Land* (1922), has long been acknowledged by critics; Ackroyd's sensitive reading of the facts of the marriage adds subtlety to that line of interpretation.

Those primarily interested in Eliot's poetry have tended to see his religious conversion as a loss of nerve. Ackroyd insists that it was no dramatic reversal but "the culmination of a lengthy and consistent process." He adds significantly to the understanding of Eliot's Christianity by discussing the decades after his baptism in 1927. For one thing, though Eliot accepted orthodoxy, "his stance within the English Church was critical and combative," and his need for Christian rituals – "the rite *qua* rite" – "came from a much deeper source" than his

doctrinal allegiances. Such suggestions lead naturally to a discussion of poetry, where, says Ackroyd, "belief need play no part." At this point Ackroyd returns, eloquently if once again vaguely, to a mystical notion: "Within Eliot's own work, the structure of orthodox faith and the language of devotion are broken apart in order to make room for something much stranger and more tenuous, like the sound of someone crying in an empty church."

"Belief need play no part," but obviously it does at some level. Ackroyd seems to be suggesting that what distinguishes great poetry is some deep quality that transforms belief into art. Just what constitutes this quality in Eliot (or Pound's "visionary power") is never directly addressed by Ackroyd. Ackroyd speaks of "Eliot's genius" when describing his stance of "scepticism and relativism." A conception of genius also seems involved in the second sentence of Ackroyd's chapter 1, where he suggests that "In symbolic representations of [Eliot's] birth, the forms of Tennyson and Poe, Browning and Whitman, might have been depicted as struggling for mastery over the eventual direction of the infant poet." Genius, then, or the something strange and tenuous that distinguishes great poetry, seems to be an intellectual gift that makes a born poet. A reader of Ackroyd should not take his verbal flourishes too seriously; nevertheless, a mystical notion of poetic creation is clearly central here. "Genius," "mystery," "mysticism," and "visionary power" are some of Ackroyd's terms for "those hidden perceptions or experiences that run alongside the observable life but may not necessarily touch it." This notion enables the biographer to jump the gap between individual and poem. Thus, regarding Eliot's visit to Little Gidding, an experience that led to the conclusion of *Four Quartets* (1943), Ackroyd comments: "The events themselves can be known but not the experiences which they provoked, so we cannot hope to understand Eliot as he knelt in that chapel. . . . We cannot reach into the mystery of Eliot's solitude."

One test of the hidden relationship of man and creation involves Eliot's political attitudes, particularly his anti-Semitism. The connection between modernism and right-wing politics has been a concern of biographers and critics at least since the controversy in 1949 over the awarding of the Bolingen Prize to Pound's *Pisan Cantos*. (Eliot was on the jury that chose the recipient of the award.) At the time when Ackroyd's *T. S. Eliot* appeared, the rise of sociological and materialist criticism was putting renewed emphasis in literary evaluation on an artist's political views. Ackroyd's is probably the last book on Eliot that can devote only a single paragraph to "examining the evidence" of anti-Semitism. This is not to say that Ackroyd denies Eliot's prejudice against Jews. He cites "two egregious instances" in the published poetry and four references in correspondence. He then quotes Leonard Woolf, "himself a Jew": "I think T. S. Eliot was slightly anti-Semitic in the sort of vague way which is not uncommon." Ackroyd adds a suggestion that Eliot's "distrust of Jews and women was the sign of an uneasy and vulnerable temperament. . . . This is an explanation, however, and not a justification."

Two published critiques of Ackroyd's *T. S. Eliot* focus on issues related to the gap between describing the man and evaluating the poetry. Anthony Hecht, in the 9 December 1984 *Washington Post Book World,* notes significant instances of anti-Semitism ignored by Ackroyd, calling the claim of only six examples "flatly ridiculous. . . . He is being cunning or slipshod." Barbara Everett, in the *London Review of Books* (24 January 1985), focuses specifically on the significance for literary biography of Ackroyd's strange something that is sensed in the work but perhaps not detectable at all in the life. From that viewpoint, biographical origins are likely to be so transformed in poetry that studying the

facts may be useless. For Everett this gap is "dangerous." To illustrate, she points to Ackroyd's handling of Eliot's visit to Burnt Norton in 1935, accompanied by Emily Hale — whom Ackroyd says "he might conceivably have married if his wife were not alive" — and the reflection of this visit in the poem "Burnt Norton" (1936). As Everett puts it, "having set up 'Burnt Norton' as a biographical event, the localisation of something like a secret love affair, [Ackroyd] then finds that he cannot read the poem. He therefore draws a conclusion" that any meaning in "Burnt Norton" has been "concealed" within formal unity. For Everett, Ackroyd's shift "make[s] of the poet something very like a liar, and of the poem an obscurely indecent or crooked secret."

Hecht's and Everett's reviews make clear the conceptual difficulty of literary biography that accepts the modernist belief in the impersonality of great poetry. The solution, Everett suggests, would be to reverse Ackroyd's process and work backward from the poems through the experiences they perpetuate to the "now lost 'events' of the life." This technique was adopted by William H. Pritchard in his *Lives of the Modern Poets* (1980), which includes both Eliot and Pound. Almost all reviews of *T. S. Eliot* were mixed, perhaps inevitably since Ackroyd's subject, dead less than twenty years, was personally known to, or at least directly influential on, many of the reviewers. Still, most reviewers were more willing than Hecht and Everett to accept what Rosemary Dinnage, in the *New York Review of Books* (20 December 1984), called a "satisfactorily mysterious" sense that Eliot's work "eludes biography." A. Walton Litz summarized Ackroyd's achievement in the 16 December 1984 *New York Times Book Review:* "Peter Ackroyd has written as good a biography as we have any right to expect. . . . We should be grateful for this energetic and scrupulous account of Eliot's life." *T. S. Eliot* received England's Whitbread Prize and the Heinemann Award of the Royal Society of Literature.

Only six years separated *T. S. Eliot* from the publication of *Dickens,* a period during which Ackroyd also published three novels. Ackroyd remembers that he saw Dickens as "another challenge" after Eliot — yet the challenge was quite different. A fiction writer rather than a poet, enormously productive compared to Eliot's small canon, vastly popular but never the cultural icon Eliot became, Dickens was also the subject of thirty-six previously published full-length biographies. The most recent, by Fred Kaplan, was published in 1988, just as Ackroyd began to write. Ackroyd's challenge was both to manage an immense amount of primary and secondary material and to present the biography in some original way. Dickens, whom Ackroyd considers the greatest English novelist, provided an opportunity on the largest scale to develop the "interanimation" of biography and fiction that has been Ackroyd's ambition.

A dense book of more than eleven hundred closely printed pages, *Dickens* includes a prologue, a self-interview concerning the writing of the book, and "Notes on Text and Sources," which clarify Ackroyd's intentions. He also discussed his work with interviewers widely and was the subject of an article in the *New York Times Magazine* (22 December 1991) when *Dickens* was published in the United States. Several early decisions affected the eventual nature of the biography. Ackroyd was determined to have no documentation at all. In the book itself he calls footnoting a "derelict and now often farcical practice, established upon the nineteenth-century illusion that scholarship can fulfill the demands of a science." Nevertheless, Ackroyd says that during the final stages of composition "my nerve failed," and he wrote fifty-eight pages of "Notes on Text and Sources," which expand upon his eleven-page bibliography but do not locate origins of specific quotations. John Sutherland, reviewing *Dickens* in the *London Review of Books* (27 September 1990), took Ackroyd to task for his attitude toward previous scholarship: "Citing [others'] efforts is . . . common honesty. . . . The reason [academics] acknowledge each other's efforts in footnotes and annotate sources is . . . a recognition that theirs is a professional team effort." Sutherland suggests that Ackroyd's attitude comes from an assumption that biographers, like novelists, should be "solitary geniuses, like Dickens or Ackroyd."

Chapter 1 of *Dickens* speaks of "the chemistry of genius." In a positive way, something like Ackroyd's mystical notion (applied to Dickens *and* Ackroyd) inspired his method of preparing to write the biography. Ackroyd read "all the books *about* Dickens" and collated a day-to-day chronology of the novelist's life. But the crucial method was to read "at least three times" everything Dickens wrote that was still available – fiction, journalism, and correspondence. This years-long immersion in Dickens's words obviously relates to Ackroyd's belief, as he put it in the 1987 interview with *Publishers Weekly,* that he can "think myself back into" a past era, so that the key themes of his books "somehow just emerge." This notion can be tested only in what it produces on the printed page. Most striking in *Dickens* is Ackroyd's way of "getting a grip on the past

[by] writing in the language of the past." One effect is Ackroyd's reproduction, usually at the beginnings of chapters, of Dickens's abrupt syntax. For example, the opening of Ackroyd's third chapter – "London. The Great Oven. The Fever Patch. Babylon. The Great Wen. In the early autumn of 1822 the ten-year-old Charles Dickens entered his kingdom" – is comparable to the first words of *Bleak House* (1852–1853): "London. Michaelmas Term lately over, and the Lord Chancellor sitting in Lincoln's Inn Hall. Implacable November weather." But Ackroyd's stylistic pastiche goes beyond this specific tic, aiming at a rambling, jerky prose that is strikingly different from the orderly style of *T. S. Eliot.* As might be expected, reviewers' taste for such experimentation varied markedly. John Sutherland quoted Anthony Trollope – "No young novelist should ever dare to imitate the style of Dickens" – and concluded that "It doesn't come off here and Ackroyd shouldn't have done it." At the opposite extreme, the novelist Anthony Burgess reported in the *Independent* that he found the "immense book" so compelling in its presentation that he lost "two nights' sleep" reading straight through it.

Ackroyd goes beyond pastiche in segments where he writes fiction into the biography. These fictional flourishes are not merged into the narrative of Dickens's life but are confined to seven short sections between chapters, identified with roman numerals and printed with wide margins. Ackroyd's table of contents does not locate these interchapters, so they turn up more or less unexpectedly, like interludes in a stage show. One such interlude is the self-interview on the practice of biography, which seems like a misplaced foreword. The other six imaginative segments are all narratives: Charles Dickens enters his own novel and talks with Little Dorrit; a group of Dickens characters converse as they journey to Greenwich Fair; a "questioner" (presumably representing Ackroyd) meets Dickens on the street twice; Ackroyd recounts the only dream he has had of Dickens. The wittiest interchapter is the third, where Thomas Chatterton, Oscar Wilde, Dickens, and Eliot – all subjects of Ackroyd's writing – talk about themselves and literature and wait for Blake, who "will be joining us shortly." Ackroyd mischievously titles this imaginary colloquy of historical persons "A true conversation between imagined selves." Burgess thought the interludes "charming," but most reviewers found them arch if not arrogant. The narrative interchapters are clever without being particularly informative or funny; still, they are few in number, short, and placed so as to be minimally disruptive.

*Dust jacket for Ackroyd's biography of the Victorian novelist,
which attempts to imitate Dickens's style*

Ackroyd's narrative of Dickens's life, assembled from published sources, contains little new information. In interpretation he accepts, as have all major biographers, the focus of Dickens's own "autobiographical memorandum" as well as of *David Copperfield* (1849–1850) on childhood traumas: like previous biographers John Forster (1874), Edgar Johnson (1952), and Fred Kaplan (1988), Ackroyd emphasizes Dickens's time as a child laborer in a blacking factory and at the Marshalsea Prison where his father was incarcerated for debt. Using his novelistic talents to great effect, Ackroyd (whose first novel, *The Great Fire of London* [1982], features the Marshalsea) brings these places vividly to life: "Around this whole area was of course the high wall, with the spikes upon it. It was not a large place, and it would have been crowded, noisy, squalid and malodorous; a dank and desperate reality, indeed, the despair seeping into its bricks, its stone staircases and unswept floors." Ackroyd con-

stantly interanimates the life and the novels – not just in obvious ways like citing descriptions from *Little Dorrit* (1855–1857) of the Marshalsea as seen by a child's eyes but also more subtly: "A bell was rung at ten in the evening, warning visitors that the gates were about to be locked for the night. (Greetings and partings are very important in Charles Dickens's fiction – it is as if at this point his characters become most real, caught in that charmed temporary light in which we can see their true feelings.) After the bell had been rung those like the young Dickens who did not have to reside in this place would walk out into the night, into the grimy streets of the Borough fitfully illuminated by oil lamps."

The most distinctive feature of *Dickens* as biography is how Ackroyd emphasizes, even more than he did in *T. S. Eliot,* what cannot be known. This is a motif throughout the book: "There is something in Dickens's infancy, something which cannot now be recovered or understood, some primal fear–";

"How is it possible now to guess at what was passed by mouth, by the sudden expression or by the unintentional phrase? The whole meaning of a life may be evoked in such moments which cannot now be reclaimed – like the life itself disappeared utterly"; "But, even if by a feat of the historical imagination we stand upon the same pavements and see the old buildings and gates rising up once more, they would still not be the same places which Dickens saw." At such times the biographer is "like an archaeologist . . . field walking over the life of his subject, looking for those faint traces and furrows which indicate the presence of a time long gone." (A year before *Dickens* Ackroyd published his novel *First Light,* wherein archaeologists uncover an ancient tomb holding a body deep within the earth.) This notion of "forgotten culture" and events is only superficially at variance with Ackroyd's claim to be able to think himself back into history. His books make clear that this is a verbal identification that recovers the style of the subject and the mood of his era. The biographer then has insight – again the word *visionary* seems appropriate – into a past individual's ways of thinking and modes of feeling. But Ackroyd insists that the biographer cannot in this way reproduce lost events or "experiences" that were not verbal, like Eliot kneeling at Little Gidding or Dickens working in the front window of Warren's Blacking Warehouse. The imagination can make hypotheses to fill the gaps, but the biographer must accept uncertainty: "When we observe his life and his work in continuous motion and combination, will these biographical certainties remain or will they dissolve?"

Dickens chronicled his age, but he also "stood apart." In recounting Dickens's personality and actions, Ackroyd accentuates their strangeness. He extends farther than previous biographers the suggestion of the autobiographical memorandum that the sufferings of childhood lay behind the adult Dickens's often inexplicable behavior. In fact, Ackroyd's prologue begins by describing Dickens in death with a phrase from *Oliver Twist* (1837–1838) connecting "the rigid face of the corpse and the calm sleep of the child." Without giving any specific source for a childlike expression on the dead Dickens's face, Ackroyd proceeds to suggest that death brought peace to a man on the verge of insanity by moving him back before the childhood traumas that produced the strange adult: "This connection between death and infancy is one that had haunted him: sleep, repose, death, infancy, innocence, oblivion." Another line of interpretation emphasizes the influence on Dickens of the histrionic nineteenth-century theater which so engaged him as actor, impresario, and performer of his own works in legendary public readings. One of Ackroyd's chapters contains a suggestive discussion of this influence; another finds the radical politics of Dickens and other contemporaries to be rooted in theatrical gesture, explaining why Dickens could treat down-and-out fictional characters with such sympathy but, in life, take "a notoriously unsentimental attitude towards prisoners, prostitutes, and other 'liberal' causes."

More-extreme examples of Dickens's strangeness Ackroyd leaves mysterious. For example, Dickens recounted the death of a doomed character named Dora in *David Copperfield* shortly after his own daughter Dora was born; and in the article "A Poor Man's Tale of a Patent" (1850) he gave the protagonist a son who has died in India – this written shortly after arrangements were made for Dickens's own son Walter to go there. Ackroyd declines to believe in some subconscious death wish of the father for his children; he points out, without suggesting any significance beyond irony, that Dora Dickens died suddenly in infancy and that Walter Dickens died in India. Instead, he holds it "likely that [Dickens] did not know *what* he was doing" in such matters. "One is tempted to use Betsy Trotwood's words on David Copperfield, that character himself so strange a simulacrum of Dickens – ' . . . blind, blind, blind!' "

The strangest of all episodes in Dickens's life was his relationship of more than a dozen years with the actress Ellen Ternan. The affair was so secret that it reached print only in Thomas Wright's 1935 biography of Dickens. Previous biographers of Dickens – as well as Claire Tomalin's work on Ellen Ternan, *The Invisible Woman* (1990) – have assumed that the affair was adulterous, differing only in guessing when it became sexual and to what extent Ternan was initially resistant. There were rumors of a child, but so far no major biography has adopted them. Ackroyd has no new facts, but his interpretation is characteristic – for Ackroyd – in that it makes the strange affair even stranger. Ackroyd theorizes that Dickens and Ternan never consummated the relationship sexually. Ackroyd's explanation, which was tentatively anticipated by Michael Slater's *Dickens and Women* (1983), seems far-fetched but intriguing. First, Dickens was "decidedly odd. . . . We should not fall into the trap of expecting him to behave in a conventional way [that is, sexually] with Ellen Ternan." Ackroyd goes on to "remember the idealism in which all his most fervent expressions about love are couched" and to note Dickens's continuing to call Ternan "my dear girl," a salutation Ackroyd thinks unlikely to be used with a mistress. In the fiction he cites Arthur Clennam's "innocent" and "affectionate" love for Little Dorrit and in Dickens's writings in general an emphasis on "sexless marriage between brother and sister, or father and daughter." Ackroyd's most intriguing suggestion is that the model for Dickens's relationship with Ternan was set many years earlier in his affection for his wife's sister, Mary Hogarth, who died at eighteen (Ternan's age when Dickens met her) and to whose death Dickens had a sentimentally "hysterical reaction" – preserving her clothes and meditating on them, longing to be buried with her, and so on. For Ackroyd the behavior toward Mary Hogarth was odd enough to predict an equally odd sexless devotion to Ellen Ternan and, further, to suggest that it became for him "the very pattern of idealized love." So, Ackroyd asks, "is it too fanciful or extravagant to suppose that his love for [Ternan] was all along as pure as it was obsessive?" The question mark indicates Ackroyd's willingness to leave the matter open; in his "Notes" he adds, "The present writer knows well enough that he might be quite mistaken . . . but he offers his interpretation of the evidence in the belief that it is the most plausible because it is the one most compatible with all he has learned about Dickens's life and character." Most reviewers were willing to allow Ackroyd's interpretation without necessarily accepting its plausibility. James R. Kincaid, in *The New York Times Book Review* (13 January 1991), found this the "oddest explanation yet" for the affair to be the "best of all" of Ackroyd's suggestions about Dickens: "he reinvests Dickens, that familiar figure of hearth and home, with an alien, slightly repellent mystery." One vigorous dissenter was John Sutherland, in the *London Review of Books* (27 September 1990), who felt that Ackroyd's "hunches" produced a "psycho" Dickens, "a kind of Norman Bates whose secret object of desire was a mummy with whom he could play little boy games."

Unlike Edgar Johnson, whose two-volume *Charles Dickens* interpolates chapters of criticism on the novels, Ackroyd was determined to avoid what he calls "the orthodox 'life and work' divide in most biographies" and to provide little "conventional literary criticism." Nevertheless, the novels are continuously present in *Dickens* because Ackroyd freely jumps from the events of the life to suggestive parallels in the work. "To see . . . the incidents of his existence shaping his fiction just as his fiction alters his life, the same pattern of emotion and imagery . . . is to turn biography into an agent of true

knowledge, even as we remember that the greatness of his fiction may lie in its absolute *difference* from anything which the life may show us." To cite three examples among many: Ackroyd notes the prevalence of characters bearing the name of Dickens's sister Fanny and suggests that "the platonic bond between brother and sister" became his model for idealized relationships, including of course the one with Ellen Ternan. He notes how often Dickens's characters "track" the same London streets that Dickens did as a child and goes from Forster's remark about young Dickens looking at the cross on Saint Paul's Cathedral to noting three novels and an autobiographical story where the cross or dome serves as "the very symbol of London, of its grimy and labyrinthine ways." And he counters the charge of sentimentality by noting that the emphasis on child deaths in Dickens's fiction was "no more than the simplest truth" in a city where almost half the funerals were of children under ten; Dickens's younger brother Alfred and his daughter Dora both died in infancy.

Dickens was a best-seller in England and a selection of the Book of the Month Club in the United States. But reviews were extraordinarily mixed. That of Kincaid in *The New York Times Book Review* mixed negatives and positives in an extreme example of the general critical response. Kincaid criticized the book's length, finding Ackroyd "a bore and a nag . . . droning on for so long that the reader may start to root for death to come to Dickens just to get it over with." He found Ackroyd's "personal opinions" to be "bubble-headed" and his imaginative interludes "quite ghastly" and mocked his "smugness" and "preposterously narrow" field of vision. The biography "waddles along like a maudlin elephant that has attached itself to us against our will." Nevertheless, "Mr. Ackroyd's 'Dickens' demands our attention" because "it is so open to the peculiarity of its subject. By refusing to shoo away the strangeness in his subject . . . he provides for us a variety of possibilities for understanding that are engaging just because they remain uncontrolled, even unexplained." For examples, Kincaid cited not only Ackroyd's treatment of Ellen Ternan but also his accounts of Dickens's ambiguous relationships with his mother and his wife. Ackroyd gives the reader facts, "all that exist, one supposes"; but he also insists that "still we do not *know,* and that not knowing," said Kincaid, "paradoxically, keeps us from closing off the issue with easy judgments." All in all, "one is haunted by the book and its images of oddity," though Kincaid added that "whether the estranging is worth the price extracted from us is a question I cannot answer."

Ackroyd's ability to provoke such extreme reactions – and humorous critical rhetoric – from academics like Kincaid and Sutherland is a measure of his power as a writer. *T. S. Eliot* showed his ability to write literary biography in the standard mode, even under the extraordinary liability of not being able to quote the subject's own words. But *Dickens,* along with such biographical novels as *Chatterton,* more clearly exemplifies Ackroyd's ambitions as a writer. The inclination toward difficult biographical projects, the interanimation of biographical and novelistic techniques, the belief in kinds of visionary experience perhaps available to the biographer through imaginative identification rather than through research, the biographer's own turns upon the stage of his book, the acceptance of uncertainty and the cultivation of strangeness in the subject, stylistic pastiche and a willingness to risk ridicule for one's imaginative flourishes – all these constitute Ackroyd as a biographer. And he intends to continue his imaginative experiments in literary lives. He acquired an eighteenth-century house in Devon at least partly, he says, because he wanted to work on Blake in a building that was standing during the poet's era. He has said that he thought about writing his biography of Blake as a first-person narrative interspersed with historical description. "I never doubt I can *do* anything. But . . . I'm in a constant state of agony over whether I'm any good or not."

Peter Ackroyd continues the productivity that has marked his career. When he visited the United States in 1995 to promote his novel *The Trial of Elizabeth Cree: A Novel of the Limehouse Murders,* his biography of Blake was being prepared for publication. Ackroyd was already at work on two new projects: a biography of Thomas More and a fantastical novel that brings the poet John Milton to colonial North America.

Interviews:

Amanda Smith, "Peter Ackroyd," *Publishers Weekly,* 232 (25 December 1987): 59–60;

Walter B. Ross, "CA Interview," in *Contemporary Authors,* volume 127 (Detroit: Gale Research, 1989), pp. 3–5.

Reference:

Laura Leivick, "Following the Ghost of Dickens," *New York Times Magazine,* 22 December 1991, pp. 27–36.

Georgina Battiscombe

(21 November 1905 –)

David Hopkinson

BOOKS: *The Mantle of Prayer,* as Gina Harwood, with A. W. Harper (London: Mowbray, 1931);

Haphazard, as Gina Harwood (London: Mathews & Marrot, 1932);

Charlotte Mary Yonge: The Story of an Uneventful Life (London: Constable, 1943);

Two on Safari: A Story of African Adventures (London: Muller, 1946);

English Picnics (London: Harvill, 1949);

Mrs. Gladstone: A Portrait of a Marriage (London: Constable, 1956; Boston: Houghton Mifflin, 1956);

John Keble: A Study in Limitations (London: Constable, 1963; New York: Knopf, 1964);

Christina Rossetti (London: Longmans, Green, 1965);

Queen Alexandra (London: Constable, 1969; Boston: Houghton Mifflin, 1969);

Shaftesbury: A Biography of the Seventh Earl (London: Constable, 1974); published as *Shaftesbury: The Great Reformer, 1801–1885* (Boston: Houghton Mifflin, 1975);

Reluctant Pioneer (London: Constable, 1978);

Christina Rossetti: A Divided Life (London: Constable, 1981; New York: Holt, Rinehart & Winston, 1981);

The Spencers of Althorp (London: Constable, 1984).

OTHER: Arthur Ransome, *The Soldier and Death,* foreword by Battiscombe (London: Ward, 1962);

"How It All Ended," in *A Chaplet for Charlotte Yonge,* edited by Battiscombe and Marghanita Laski (London: Cresset, 1965), pp. 118–124;

"The Aylesford Affair," in *Society Scandals,* edited by Harriet Bridgeman (Newton Abbot: David & Charles, 1977), pp. 86–99;

"Exile from the Golden City," in *The Cool Web,* edited by Margaret Meek, Aidan Warlow, and Griselda Barton (London: Bodley Head, 1977), pp. 284–290;

Queen Alexandra's Christmas Gift Book, edited, with an introduction, by Battiscombe (London: National Trust, 1984);

Georgina Battiscombe (photograph by Bassano Limited)

Charlotte M. Yonge, *The Clever Woman of the Family,* afterword by Battiscombe (London: Virago, 1985);

Yonge, *The Daisy Chain,* afterword by Battiscombe (London: Virago, 1988);

Winter Song, compiled and introduced by Battiscombe (London: Constable, 1992).

   As a married woman with a young child and with her husband serving for a second time as a soldier in a world war, Georgina Battiscombe wrote her first biography, *Charlotte Mary Yonge: The Story of an Uneventful Life,* published in 1943. The book achieved success partly because it dealt with the intensely industrious but wholly peaceful life of a lady living in times far removed in every way from the perils of World War II. On this initial success, Battiscombe built up a reputation for serious, original, and highly readable books, choosing as her subjects the lives and works of important nineteenth-century characters not always widely known.

Born Georgina Harwood on 21 November 1905, Battiscombe's family ties and affections were always to be of great importance. It is significant that her longer, more demanding books are all dedicated to members of her family, two to her husband and the others to brother, sister, daughter, and son-in-law. Her father, George Harwood, was a master cotton spinner and a member of Parliament for the town in which his mills were situated, Bolton in Lancashire. Her mother was Ellen Hopkinson Harwood, eldest daughter of another Lancastrian, Sir Alfred Hopkinson, scholar, teacher, lawyer, and politician who resigned his seat in Parliament to become first vice chancellor of the University of Manchester. Her parents were public-spirited, practical, and idealistic. They were devoted members of the Church of England. Their eldest daughter inherited this faith and sense of social duty. Principles, values, and attachments took shape from early experiences and formed the pillars of her house, neither overturned nor updated by friends, tutors, or pastoral guides but strengthened, during her lifetime, by her mother's eldest brother, an Anglican priest who possessed vision combined with common sense. Moreover he had a flair for writing. He prepared his niece for confirmation, and after her father's death in 1913 he came to fill the paternal role in her life.

Georgina Battiscombe's earliest ambitions were to be married and to write. She was educated at an Anglican convent school in Oxford, which taught her the elements of how to learn. Reading for pleasure had always come naturally, but her ability to read for knowledge, which could be synthesized and manipulated to serve a purpose, was built slowly on that foundation. Her education was continued at Lady Margaret Hall College, Oxford, where she obtained a degree in modern history. She enjoyed herself, made many good friends, wrote for Oxford magazines, and indulged in much political activity in connection with the University Liberal Club. Her mother had married again and bought a large country house near Oxford where there was much entertaining and sophisticated conversation. Her stepfather was a scholar but also a politician, who later became principal of University College,

Exeter. Battiscombe later wrote biographies of five brilliant women who earned distinction for a variety of different qualities and achievements but who had in common the fact that not one of them received any kind of formal, institutionalized higher education. Three of them were compensated, if compensation were needed, by social and financial security in a contented, intellectual, and public-spirited home rooted in strong religious conviction. Battiscombe's home life in the formative years provided her with much the same conditions that some of her future biographical subjects had enjoyed.

The interests and the essential influences that later informed her writing were now developing. She owed to her mother in the first place the inspiration she drew from the church and a secure Christian faith. She grasped the hallowed sacramental nature of the bonds that united her parents in their comparatively short married life. In her approach to religion, reason and emotion were present, but both could be bypassed, with all the problems they created, because everything she knew and loved pointed in the one and only possible direction. In later years she saw it as inconceivable to deviate from loyalty to the church because it admitted women to the priesthood or took any other administrative or organizational steps – insignificant compared with that unassailable reality of which one was spiritually conscious. The Protestant tradition, strong in the Hopkinson family, had a place in the makeup of Anglo-Catholics. The inner voice was what mattered, and probability all that they could count on in this life.

Religion and the Anglican Church as it had developed under the influence of venerated spiritual leaders, such as John Keble, John Henry Newman, and Dean Church, gave direction and purpose to the first phase of Battiscombe's work, but her outlook and literary activities were also influenced by her own and her extended family's concern with politics and the exercise of social responsibilities. Her father, her grandfather, two uncles, and her stepfather had all been members of Parliament at one time or another. Her Oxford friends included two men who were to play distinctive roles in future Parliaments as vigorous and independent reformers. Harwood family tradition steered her into the Liberal camp from which she campaigned in elections and was ready to submit herself for adoption as a candidate for Bolton. But though she enjoyed public speaking and was responsive to the claims of public service, her simple early ambitions – to marry and to write – remained, and they were to win out.

In 1932 she married Christopher Battiscombe, who came from a south country family, landed and military, which was very different from her own. He was conservative by temperament and in politics. These differences never disturbed an exceptionally happy marriage. Her husband had joined the Colonial Service in 1914, but before taking up an overseas appointment he received a commission in the Grenadier Guards and so fought through the war, receiving a severe wound but surviving it. Though at first declared medically unfit for a government appointment, he eventually returned to the Colonial Service. At the time of his marriage he was serving as secretary to the sultan of Zanzibar, a Muslim state under British protection. This location fulfilled his wife's early yearning, excited by her reading of Rudyard Kipling, for exotic lifestyles in colorful regions. She wrote articles on life in East Africa and found that she could sell them to magazines in England. Later she considered this time in Africa the best years of her life. When they returned it was to the north of England and a home close to the cathedral in the ancient university city of Durham. The society of neighbors in the area around the cathedral and in the university was valued by them both. He could now pursue his archaeological, and she her literary, interests. They were a devoted couple. Battiscombe's verve, her readiness to go into action without inhibitions, was matched by her husband's warmth and steady good humor. He was by far the most important element in her life throughout her most productive years. A daughter, Aurea, was born to them. When World War II began in 1939 Christopher Battiscombe was recalled to the army.

With her husband away, no immediate prospect of a wartime job, and a young child, Battiscombe, by nature not immune to boredom, turned to serious writing. There was time enough to spare, even though much less than that of Charlotte Mary Yonge, the Victorian lady to whose life and work her mind had turned. An endless vacancy of spare time was spread out before most young ladies of that period, but Yonge filled it throughout her life with a continuous output of writing that took many forms. Her novels, now little read, retained a place in the folk memory of countless middle-class families up to and beyond World War II. She wrote stories of family life for the honor and glory of the Church of England, stories designed to make goodness attractive and badness ugly. As Battiscombe points out, she possessed "a simplicity so obvious that it leaves the complicated mind of the average man gasping with unbelief." The secret of Yonge's

phenomenal success lay in her power to live and move in settings as solid and familiar as the homes of her numerous, patient readers. Families were large, and reading aloud in the family circle was a common practice.

For the modern reader the attractions of Battiscombe's biography lie first in its vivid picture of a style of life that has nothing in common with the present. Its author is not uncritical and certainly not sentimental about this vanished world. She admits that affection for the novels may become a little crazed, and she compares Yonge unfavorably with Jane Austen and Louisa May Alcott, noting that while Austen observed Hampshire society on the lookout for humor, eccentricity, and good sense, Yonge had an eye only for religion and romance. But her aims and ambitions were heroic. She meant to turn the Byronic hero into a devout churchgoer, faithful and unselfish – and all this without loss of his romantic appeal. Published on coarse paper in the grim year of 1943, *Charlotte Mary Yonge* was well received. A period of total war had produced a remarkable increase in the demand for books, and a well-written study of a different era, full of life, and particularly of family life, was much welcomed.

Two issues of particular interest to students of the nineteenth century emerge from this biography. From the age of twelve, Yonge came under the spiritual guidance of John Keble, who had left Oxford to become vicar of the Hampshire parish where she lived. Keble was already famous as a poet and a potent influence in a great Oxford effort to restore the authority and influence of the Anglican Church and to inspire it with fervor and a new sense of direction. Keble prepared Yonge for confirmation and until his death gave her continuous advice and encouragement. If not the greatest of those associated with the Oxford Movement, Keble was certainly the most revered by Anglicans. Though religious doubts became more widespread, the churches played a highly significant part in social change as the century proceeded.

The position of women in society is also something that historic-minded readers of the biography are led to consider. Yonge's aim was not so much to improve woman's place in society as to improve women through education, religious observance, and enhanced spiritual awareness. She expected her readers to employ their energies outside the home as well as within, but the first charge to a woman was to be a good wife and helpmate. To this end education, according to one's station in life, was important. She believed that home education under the inspection and encouragement of sensible fathers was the best arrangement for girls, but later, when approached for support at Oxford, she conceded that a women's college could be a valuable training ground for Christians, whether as educators or as mothers of families. To educate women was not to remedy injustice but to add to the sum of human happiness in man, woman, and child.

Many people in the 1940s regarded William Ewart Gladstone as the greatest of nineteenth-century prime ministers. A monumental, multivolume biography, written by his friend John Morley, had appeared in 1903, but no shorter study of his whole life and work existed. Battiscombe contemplated the enormous task of meeting this need, although the Gladstone papers constituted by far the largest archive of any British statesman while the great mass of family and private papers were at the Gladstone home, Hawarden Castle in North Wales, and his voluminous journal was in the library of Lambeth Palace. The long-awaited modern biography was, however, already in the hands of another writer, Philip Magnus. Battiscombe took on a lesser, but important, figure in British history, Catherine, the wife and protector of the "Grand Old Man" for nearly sixty years.

In a foreword to *Mrs. Gladstone: A Portrait of a Marriage* (1956) Battiscombe asks why matrimony, "by far and away the most popular of feminine careers, goes unhonoured and unsung." Even the Christian Church, she observes, has consecrated far more virgin saints than "godly matrons." Her book is perhaps more a portrait of a woman, and a remarkable woman, in the married state than the portrait of the marriage as such. In the book Catherine Gladstone is endowed with glowing vitality. Gladstone himself remains a somewhat baffling and distant figure. Since the publication of the biography much has changed both in attitudes to marriage and in public knowledge of Gladstone.

As a young woman Catherine Gladstone was admired for her beauty, her wit, her social vitality, her kindness, and her strong will; she was unmethodical, uncalculating, outspoken, and delightfully spontaneous. In temperament the young couple must have seemed strangely incompatible, and Catherine had nothing approaching her husband's intellectual powers; but in letters, if she had anything to add to the domestic and family matters with which they normally dealt, she could express herself as forcibly as her husband and without his prolixity. Battiscombe cleverly brings out those matters on which she differed from him and tried to bring him round to act, as she thought, more wisely. One example, where her success might have had

Dust jacket for the American edition of Battiscombe's biography of the British politician and social reformer

historical importance, was in relation to Queen Victoria. Unavailingly, Catherine had beseeched her husband to modify the solemnity of his approach to the sovereign; that relationship grew more icy than ever, but in some of their meetings in his last term as prime minister, the queen, as Gladstone pathetically told his wife, inquired after her with "perhaps a touch of warmth." Indeed the queen's affection for Catherine, important in the early years of Victoria's widowhood, remained to the end. There were occasions when Catherine tried to use her influence in directions that could have brought no possible good to either of them. These arose from Catherine's conviction that, even at the age of eighty-two, no one else but her husband could be thought fit to run the country.

Whatever their differences, they were absolutely united in giving primacy to matters of conscience. He could no more keep her out of cholera wards than she could keep him from his efforts to rescue prostitutes from the London streets. The rescue effort is a subject that Battiscombe was little able to explore, writing when she did, but the mind must dwell on its singular, ever likely to be unique, appearance on a prime minister's agenda. By contrast with a certain thinness at some points, this book contains many revealing vignettes, one of which is the description of Catherine's joy in the weekly walk to church on Sunday mornings, wherever the couple happened to be, and "the surprised signs of recognition" they perceived.

As Battiscombe clearly knew her way through the intricacies of Victorian society, its politics, its literature, and, above all, its enthusiasm for religion, she found herself with a steady flow of reviewing for the London *Times* and the *Times Literary Supplement*. She wrote always as someone well informed, respectful of hard facts but presenting them well macerated and seasoned with irony. She had behind her two enterprising and highly readable Victorian books and a recognized talent for clear, lively, and well-constructed biographical writing. She was ready for work on a large scale.

A strong reaction against Victorian values and Victorian intellectual preoccupations had now spent itself. It had been usual for lengthy memoirs or even lengthier "Life and Letters" of great Victorian statesmen and pundits to appear within a few years of their deaths, often followed by short popular accounts of their lives and works. By the middle of the present century a distinct lack of recent biographies was evident. The publication in 1963 of *John Keble: A Study in Limitations* filled one of these gaps, but Battiscombe here accomplished something more than an up-to-date biography of distinction.

Keble was an Anglican clergyman, friend, and associate of Newman but unchanging in allegiance to his church and living a relatively tranquil life in a country parish. He was a minor poet whose work won a large, enthusiastic public in the middle years of the nineteenth century. But it was with the Oxford Movement that his name came to be associated, because as its initiator and as one who made his whole life an exemplar of its tenets, he seems to reflect its spirit more truthfully than any other of its leading figures. The Oxford Movement, as its name implies, was scholarly in origin. Historians have adopted as its starting point a sermon preached by Keble in Oxford in 1833. This was twelve years before Newman announced his conversion to Roman Catholicism. Battiscombe observes that those within the inner circle of the Oxford Movement saw Keble as its leader, however dubious he himself

might have felt about that supposition. But as Newman's reputation grew, Keble's seemed to decline. Battiscombe believed that this was neither right nor just. She is, of course, an admirer of Keble, but not to the point of idolatry. In controversy she invariably remains cool and well mannered but not lacking in the confidence to employ sharp and positive expressions. She demolishes some of those to whom leadership of the Oxford Movement in its later stages has been attributed. Newman is not her favorite among the great interpreters of Christian doctrine and guides to Christian living. She could not accept Sir Geoffrey Faber's assertions in his influential *Oxford Apostles* (1936) that Keble's ascendancy is almost inexplicable and that his poetry is beneath contempt. Keble, she concludes, "stamped the imprint of his personality deeply and firmly upon the Oxford Movement," but she describes his limitations in full detail and shows how they, as much as his flowing virtues, have subsequently affected the nature of Anglicanism. Keble's judgment was fallible, and for all his saintliness and the love and devotion he attracted and inspired, he was without the power to look ahead.

In this book for the first time the author lists sources in considerable detail and supplies references as well as the usual index. In a private letter John Betjeman, who shared Battiscombe's love and knowledge of the church, and especially its flowering in terms of architecture, art, and artifacts in the Victorian age, wrote of the book, "One of the best biographies I have ever read, subtle, humane, humorous, compassionate and INSPIRING." It received the James Tait Black Prize.

Before publication of her next book, *Queen Alexandra* (1969), the Battiscombes moved to Windsor Castle. There they took possession of a romantic but highly inconvenient home, Henry III Tower. Her husband worked at Cumberland Lodge, a conference center in Windsor Park, and she waited for permission to produce the first biography of Queen Alexandra. Battiscombe now had access to one of the nation's greatest and best-organized archives. In addition she had access to the papers of families who had served the court in two reigns, and she had opportunities to obtain personal recollections of the queen from members of the Royal family and others. The correspondence between husband and wife had been destroyed, but the queen's correspondence with King George V and his wife, Queen Mary, had survived. All Alexandra's letters to her family in Denmark had disappeared or been withheld. A surprising source of material was located in Moscow. From 1867 to 1917 Alexandra had poured out her thoughts in letters to her sister, the Russian empress; they were in Danish and written in an almost indecipherable hand. Battiscombe was able to read only one of the forty volumes among the exhibits sent to the Anglo-Russian Exhibition of 1967. Alexandra's devotion to her family in Denmark was so intense as to earn Queen Victoria's disapproval on several occasions. Alexandra's devotion to Denmark was matched with her violent hatred of the Germans who had invaded her country and consequent refusal to speak German, a refusal that Queen Victoria resented.

Battiscombe had shown herself well able to deal with complex ideas, unusual personalities, and great institutions, like the Church of England or the British government, as they had evolved in the nineteenth century. A royal biography was a different matter, especially when it concerned a queen with a limited span of attention, neither intellectual nor artistic, whose interest in affairs of state was fleeting and restricted. She possessed exceptional, if somewhat inanimate, beauty and a certain touching innocence. Ever seeking to relate a character to the main currents of change in the culture of that character's time, Battiscombe suggests that "the very mediocrity of her mind, flitting butterfly-like, made her the more typical of her generation." Much that is of human interest colors the book as well as social and domestic detail. Anecdotes and sometimes the spice of period gossip are used effectively. There exist some singular aspects of Alexandra's character, and quaintly charming incidents in her life can be observed. The narrative is vigorous and spirited throughout a book that does not seem too long for the subject's relatively uneventful life. There are some points at which Alexandra's native common sense was of service both to the monarchy and to the state. As a biographer Battiscombe is invariably open and honest toward her readers. There is no shirking of the inevitable questions: How warm was Alexandra's affection for her husband? How deeply did she feel his repeated infidelities? The biographer makes no claim to certainty but will not let the reader get away with any cheap, unhistorical answer. "The pattern of her marriage was a common one in her day. . . . Wives put up with the unfaithfulness in a husband much as they put up with meanness or bad temper or any of the other disagreeable qualities for which the law offered no redress." Alexandra found her fulfillment in her children, whose best interests she served not only with unfailing devotion but also with an astonishing measure of good sense.

A curious bond united the biographer to this lovable, unlettered queen; the writer and her subject both suffered from progressive deafness for a large part of their lives. The writer, with the assistance of modern aids, made light of the handicap, which in a less resourceful person would have been a severe one. The queen, whose kindness and concern for others had been conspicuous, became increasingly isolated and self-centered. What consolation she might find for a sad widowhood lay in her religion and in her son, King George V.

Her next biography was of the earl of Shaftesbury, a politician and social reformer whose name has become legendary in British history. *Shaftesbury: A Biography of the Seventh Earl* was first published in 1974. It was the longest and most labor-intensive of Battiscombe's books, a work of careful scholarship, valuable to the student but enjoyable to the general reader. There were obstacles to be overcome with such a subject; a whole mythology had built itself up around the figure of the great, benevolent nobleman who devoted his life to good works and died in debt and disappointment but with a name known all over the world. As always, the biographer's problem is to disentangle from legend such truth as can be revealed by evidence from the subject himself and his contemporaries. Shaftesbury was a strange young man who had suffered a desolate childhood. Clever and serious-minded, he entered Parliament as a Tory at the age of twenty-five. With his appointment to a select Committee on the Lunacy Laws and Asylums, he began his lifetime's work on behalf of the poor and disadvantaged.

It could not have been easy to present an entirely exceptional range of parliamentary and pressure-group activities in the cause of social welfare and to retain the reader's interest throughout. Prolonged struggles to secure effective regulation of the conditions under which women and children might be employed in mines and factories do not readily slip into elegant, smooth-flowing prose. Over fifty years on the front line of such battles constitute the main body of the biography. It would seem too that Shaftesbury's own personality, with its tendencies to depression and self-pity, must have presented an additional problem. His crusading spirit was not a glorious one. He was an unstable character, but he remained dogged in pursuit of ends to which God had pointed the direction. The greatest of the author's difficulties was, however, the one most triumphantly overcome. Shaftesbury became a household name in his own day; his aristocratic background, his Tory politics, his paternalism, the intensity of his introspection, and above all his evangelical religion are foreign to the present age, where his opinions and his motivating influences are almost entirely unrepresented. There seem to be contradictions not easily resolved, and thus to bring Shaftesbury's outlook and character within reach of a modern mind presents serious problems. He was bewildered and often passionately distressed by the opposition he encountered because of the absolute conviction that God was on his side. He thus veered between a manic excitement aroused by doing God's work and dire depression on finding it obstructed here on earth. His diary is clearly the most important of a biographer's sources, but Battiscombe points out that with such a man a diary must be used with the utmost discretion. States of depression give rise to long, unhappy entries, while happiness and success are treated briefly. Her virtuosity in achieving command of so recondite a figure makes this perhaps the finest of her biographical works.

Reluctant Pioneer (1978) was occasioned by a request from her college for a biography of its first principal, who was the daughter of a bishop and great-niece of William Wordsworth. Feminist members of the college, past and present, might well have been startled by the Battiscombe opening sentence. "Elizabeth Wordsworth is one of the greatest figures in the women's movement, a cause in which she took not the faintest interest." From her study of church leaders and the ideology of the Oxford Movement Battiscombe possessed a knowledge not only of Elizabeth Wordsworth's own family and the religious tradition in which she was raised but also of a whole group of families to which she was closely attached – the Gladstones, the Lyttletons, the Moberleys, the Bensons, the Talbots – families from whom leaders in church and state were drawn. Through her parents, and through her friendship with Charlotte Mary Yonge, Elizabeth Wordsworth was influenced by Keble. She is seen by her biographer as "a Miss Yonge heroine come to life." The biography is short, high-spirited, and often funny.

The zest for life, the warm affection, and the personal eccentricities of her subject seem to delight the author no less than the centrality of her religion and her irreverent attitude to the women's movement. The book seems calculated to disturb shallow opinions about the struggle for the higher education of women in its early years. Conventional stereotypes of sanctimonious Victorian spinsterhood are challenged by such evidence as the brisk reply of the principal to an earnest student who confessed that she had lost her faith and ought perhaps to leave the college. "All right, my dear, stay on, of

Dust jacket for the American edition of Battiscombe's biography of the British poet who was a product of both the Oxford Movement and the Pre-Raphaelite Brotherhood

course, but do brush your hair and don't be late for breakfast." It was said that she kept her students constantly on the edge of laughter and that in her "the supreme quality of the unexpected" was a determinant feature of her success as a principal. She was determined that the college should hold its own within the university but worried not at all about academic achievement. Her aim was to know her students individually and thereafter to help them grow to maturity, which she did with cheerful, unfussy affection. She was a classical scholar, a poet, and a compulsive writer. She was one of the most original, unorthodox heads that any college ever had. Never forced or overemphatic in her praise, *Reluctant Pioneer* turns Wordsworth into a heroine.

The life of the poet Christina Rossetti was dominated by the cruel demands of her passionately held religious beliefs. Her attachment to her family came second, but a close second. Her poetry was as much controlled by those two influences as was her life. In 1965 Battiscombe wrote a pamphlet on her life and work for a series published for the British Council and the National Book League, which covered the most important British writers from Geoffrey Chaucer to Dylan Thomas. Her full-scale life of Christina Rossetti was published in 1981.

Christina Rossetti formed her beliefs from what she learned from her mother in childhood and from John Keble. The strongest subsequent influence was that of her elder brother, the poet and artist Dante Gabriel, and the friends who accepted him as their leader in a revolutionary aesthetic movement calling itself the Pre-Raphaelite Brotherhood. Tragic love affairs and debilitating illness slowly destroyed her brother's life but not before his originality and power as poet and artist had aroused great admiration and some fierce hostility. Through many testing events, Christina held firmly to her own convictions and ideals expressed with an extraordinary freshness and originality in poems that won instant acclaim. Battiscombe suggests that the force behind her poetry came more from her brother and the Pre-Raphaelites than from the Oxford Movement's profound effect on her life and character. There seem to be contradictions in the active expression of Christina's Christianity. In character she was austere and reserved, but in poetry an opposite strain in her nature came uppermost. Essays on her work by Maurice Bowra and Virginia Woolf place her at the center of a second flowering of the romantic imagination in nineteenth-century poetry. Battiscombe finds her poetry full of tensions, the work of a passionate woman, part English and part Italian, caught between the sensuousness of Pre-Raphaelitism and the asceticism of the Oxford Movement, almost overwhelmed by the final, searing conflict between human and divine love. Above this turmoil her best poems sing with an astonishing vocal purity. Battiscombe may have found it hard to accept that the life of so devoted and enlightened a Christian should have been so sad, so fraught with anxiety. The anxiety of "agonising sweetness" in Christina's verse may have eluded her, but she is a clear guide through the intricate complexities of an extraordinary life. It is also apparent that the author's familiarity with the disciplines and the idealism of the Anglo-Catholics enabled her to interpret the relationship between the cloudy vision of the Pre-Raphaelites and the stern self-immolation that bound Christina to her Anglo-Catholic inheritance. Her religious sense was that of the Oxford Movement's early years — austere, rigid, but possessed with all the fervor of a romantic revival. Battiscombe's cool, objective biographies add up to make her one of the most significant interpreters of this tradition and its later history.

Attention focused on an English family with a long history of service to the state when Prince Charles married Diana, the daughter of Earl Spencer of Althorp. At the suggestion of her publisher, Battiscombe wrote an account of the family, and a lavishly illustrated book was published in 1984. It was characteristic of the author who had to deal briefly with many Spencers that the two who most appealed to her were Lord Althorp, leader of the House of Commons at the time of the great Reform Bill of 1832 and subsequently third earl, and the Reverend George Spencer, an independent-minded Christian who ended as Father Ignatius of Saint Paul.

Her most recent publication is an anthology of poems on old age entitled *Winter Song* (1992). Similar to her creative impulse as a biographer, the anthology is characterized by the creation of a firm historical background to her subjects' lives and achievements. Her introduction begins by noting the changing attitudes of English poets to age and aging. Until the eighteenth century few poets survived into what would now be regarded as old age. Battiscombe points out that as expectations of life increased, poets tended to romanticize this phase of human development. Even as a young man Wordsworth was obsessed by the subject, combining deep pity with strong feelings of reverence. The Victorians followed him in adopting a benevolent attitude to the old and stressing the serenity of old age. Only in the twentieth century did the ugly details of the aging process find their way into poetry, and even then that innovative tendency was offset by the two poets whom Battiscombe regards as the greatest of the moderns, W. B. Yeats and T. S. Eliot. She chooses from Eliot the Christian resignation of his "A Song for Simeon" (1928) and from Yeats several great prayers and utterances in which he challenges in an intensely personal manner the harsh realities of old age. Half a century after Constable had accepted her first book, the firm published *Winter Song,* a testament to her own longevity as a literary figure.

Quentin Bell

(19 August 1910 –   )

Charles Calder
University of Aberdeen

BOOKS: *On Human Finery* (London: Hogarth Press, 1947; New York: Wyn, 1949; revised and enlarged edition, London: Hogarth Press, 1976; New York: Schocken, 1976);

Those Impossible English (London: Weidenfeld & Nicolson, 1952; New York: Crown, 1952);

The True Story of Cinderella (New York: Barnes & Noble, 1960);

Ruskin (Edinburgh: Oliver & Boyd, 1963; New York: Braziller, 1978);

Roger Fry: An Inaugural Lecture (Leeds: Leeds University Press, 1964);

Victorian Artists (London: Routledge & Kegan Paul, 1967; Cambridge, Mass.: Harvard University Press, 1967);

Bloomsbury (London: Weidenfeld & Nicolson, 1968; New York: Basic, 1969);

Virginia Woolf: A Biography, 2 volumes (London: Hogarth Press, 1972; New York: Harcourt Brace Jovanovich, 1972);

The Art Critic and the Art Historian (London: Cambridge University Press, 1974);

A Demotic Art (Southampton: University of Southampton Press, 1976);

Vanessa Bell's Family Album (London: Norman & Hobhouse, 1981);

A New and Noble School: The Pre-Raphaelites (London: Macdonald, 1982);

Techniques of Terracotta (London: Chatto & Windus, 1983);

The Brandon Papers (London: Chatto & Windus, 1985; San Diego: Harcourt Brace Jovanovich, 1985);

Charleston: Past & Present (London: Hogarth Press, 1987; San Diego: Harcourt Brace Jovanovich, 1987);

Bad Art (London: Chatto & Windus, 1989; Chicago: University of Chicago Press, 1989).

OTHER: Julian Bell, *Essays, Poems and Letters,* edited by Bell (London: Hogarth Press, 1938);

The Diary of Virginia Woolf, 5 volumes, edited by Anne Olivier Bell, introduction by Bell (London: Hogarth Press, 1977–1984; New York: Harcourt Brace Jovanovich, 1977–1984);

Virginia Bell's Family Album, compiled by Bell and Agelica Garrett (London: Norman & Hobhouse, 1981);

Virginia Woolf: A Centenary Perspective, edited by Eric Warner, with a foreword by Bell (London: Macmillan, 1984; New York: St. Martin's Press, 1984).

Quentin Bell, younger son of Clive and Vanessa Bell, has been not only a biographer but also a painter, sculptor, and art critic. Uniquely qualified for understanding and interpreting the world of Bloomsbury, his superlative two-volume biography of his aunt Virginia Woolf appeared in 1972; it succeeds both as a narrative and as an evocation of the Bloomsbury milieu. Bell is a craftsman in words; he writes with clarity, intimacy, and an appealing sense of the absurd.

Quentin Claudian Stephen Bell was born on 19 August 1910 at 46 Gordon Square, London. His elder brother, Julian, who died in 1937, had been born two years earlier. Bell was educated at Leighton Park. He showed early talent as a painter. His first exhibition was held in 1935. He worked in the Political Warfare Executive from 1941 to 1943. After the war Bell continued to exhibit, while developing his capacities as a scholar and teacher. He was appointed lecturer in art education at King's College, University of Newcastle-upon-Tyne, in 1952, becoming senior lecturer four years later. He has held several professorships, including the Slade Professorship in Fine Art at Oxford from 1964 to 1965 and the Ferens Professorship of Fine Art at the University of Hull from 1965 to 1966. He is now emeritus professor of the history and theory of art at Sussex University. Bell married Anne Olivier Popham on 16 February 1952; they have three children.

such a marriage, a marriage between an elderly man and an invalid girl, one of them almost certainly impotent, the other poised upon the brink of insanity, could have been happy may well be doubted."

But Bell's prime interest lies in Ruskin's work. And here he shows the same virtues of patient examination and judicious comment as in his dealings with the troubled personal life of his subject. He notes that Ruskin was the first Englishman to make art criticism a major prose form: "our grandfathers turned to Ruskin in matters of art as we turn to the A.B.C. in search of a train." Bell identifies three modes of Ruskinian style: early, middle, and late. The *Praeterita* chapter pays tribute to the stylistic achievement of that work – tempered, matured, limpid in its simplicity. But Bell also recognizes the force and urgency of the mode deployed in *Modern Painters* (1843–1860). He makes the reader aware that the writings of early Ruskin is full of "literary" artifice; but what matters is the "desperate sincerity" of the writer, which makes it possible for the reader "to enjoy the sheer gusto and exuberance."

A pleasing aspect of *Ruskin* is its author's admission of the debt he owes his subject. "At the risk of sounding immodest I would say that whatever positive virtues there may be in my own style, whatever skills I have acquired and later used in the writing of biography are due to a year's immersion in Ruskin. And yet I do not think that my style is Ruskinian. He taught me that writing is not just a matter of exactitude, clarity and discretion, important though these qualities certainly are; writing is tremendous fun . . . a business in which one needs, not only a steering wheel and a good strong brake but a good strong engine as well." Bell's readers would no doubt agree with these sentiments. For his writing, at its best, combines discipline and zest. There is control and exactitude; but there is also a generous enthusiasm and (his own word) gusto. These qualities find their happiest expression in the two-volume *Virginia Woolf: A Biography* (1972).

Bell makes it plain in his foreword to the first volume that the title means what it says. His aim is to present facts "which hitherto have not been generally known and by providing what will, I hope, be a clear and truthful account of the character and personal development of my subject." To achieve this end, Bell drew upon three collections of material in particular: the Berg Collection of the New York Public Library; the Charleston Papers, deposited in the library of King's College, Cambridge; and a group of documents he christened "the Monk's House Papers." This adds up to a rich assortment of primary material. The Berg Collection

Anne Olivier Bell and Quentin Bell, 1990

Bell's first book was *On Human Finery* (1947; revised and enlarged, 1976). His study of John Ruskin appeared in 1963, being part of the Writers and Critics series published by Oliver & Boyd. The Writers and Critics format places a premium on economy; the critic has to deal with the essentials. *Ruskin* accommodates a good deal of matter in its small compass. Bell treats Ruskin as critic and social theorist, considers his private life, and makes excellent observations on Ruskin's stylistic variety. A chapter is devoted to *Praeterita* (1885–1889), Ruskin's uncompleted autobiography. Bell is a judicious admirer of his subject. He writes with conspicuous good sense about the vexed question of Ruskin's marriage – or nonmarriage – to Effie Gray. He notes that some admirers of Ruskin have criticized Gray for writing such a frank account of her former husband's inadequacies in reply to an inquiry from the mother of Rose La Touche. Still, as Bell observes, "she knew what it was like to be married to Ruskin and we do not; if she believed a half of what she wrote, she had a strong moral case for doing her best to prevent another young woman from sharing her experience. Undoubtedly her letter did more than anything else to stop the match [between Ruskin and Rose La Touche]. Whether

of English and American Literature contains the twenty-seven manuscript volumes of Virginia Woolf's diaries (1915–1941) as well as eight early notebook diaries and letters from Virginia Woolf to Vanessa Bell, Violet Dickinson, Vita Sackville-West, and Ethel Smyth. This was a source of first importance. The only portions of the diaries then in print were the extracts published by Leonard Woolf under the title *A Writer's Diary* (1953). The Charleston Papers contain letters and papers of Clive Bell, Vanessa Bell, and Duncan Grant; the correspondence between Vanessa Bell and Roger Fry is part of this collection. The Monk's House Papers consist of letters and manuscripts that Leonard Woolf made available to Quentin Bell to assist him in producing the biography. In addition to these sources, Bell made use of material relating to the Stephen family, for example, copies of the "Hyde Park Gate News," the weekly "newspaper" that was produced by the young Virginia for her family's entertainment.

The biography is therefore securely based on authentic sources. Bell uses this material with skill and judgment in constructing his narrative. A prime quality of Bell is his reliance on evidence – his refusal to present speculation as fact. He conceives it as his duty to assemble and exhibit the evidence and to establish facts and dates. This is no small undertaking. With the help of his wife, Anne Olivier Bell, he produced a detailed chronology of Virginia Woolf's life; this is printed in the appendixes and is an invaluable feature of the biography. The Bell chronology underpins the Nigel Nicolson–Joanne Trautmann edition of Woolf's letters (1975–1980).

"Biographers pretend they know people," Woolf complained in a diary entry for 4 September 1927, to which Bell replied: "They don't, or at least they ought not to. All that they can claim is that they know a little more than does the public at large and that, by catching at a few indications given here and there in recollections or writings, they can correct some misconceptions and trace, if they are very skilful or very lucky, an outline that is consistent and convincing, but which, like all outlines, is but tenuously connected with the actual form of the sitter in all lights, poses, moods and disguises." This seems, in its modesty and realism, an admirable statement of the case. Borrowing Bell's metaphor, the outline he traces is indeed consistent and convincing. The tact and scrupulousness of the biographer give authority to the portrait.

The author is thoroughly at home, not just in the Bloomsbury of Lytton Strachey and Duncan Grant but in the intellectual world of the previous

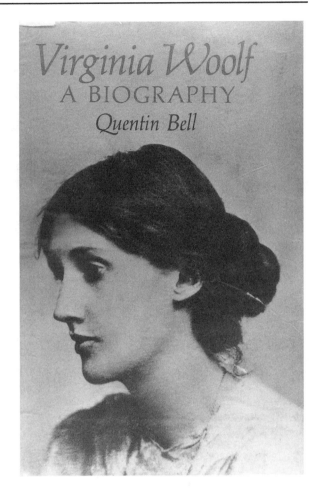

Dust jacket for Bell's biography of his aunt

generation. For Virginia Woolf, as Bell reminds us on his first page, was the daughter of Leslie Stephen. Bell is therefore careful to explore the social and literary nexus of the late Victorian period. Bell brings to life for us the Stephens, Pattles, and Fishers who populated Woolf's early life. In particular, there is the figure of her father. Bell captures the admirable features of Stephen: the industry, the application, the concern for truth – attributes that were to distinguish Virginia herself. Bell also notes the domestic failings and failures that made life difficult for the inhabitants of 22 Hyde Park Gate. "A complete and self-effacing devotion was what [Leslie] demanded and this [Vanessa] was not ready to provide."

Bell memorably depicts the consolations which the sisters experienced. Thus, he writes of Vanessa's absorption in art. "In the life-room, in that blessed peace which is broken only by the gentle scrape of charcoal upon paper, in that pleasant atmosphere of hard work and turpentine, she could for a time enjoy an existence which must have seemed utterly remote from Hyde Park Gate." And

*Dust jacket for the American edition of Bell's biographical study
of the Victorian art and social critic*

just as Vanessa applied herself to art, so Virginia applied herself to her apprenticeship as a writer. "Virginia would go upstairs . . . to tackle Sophocles or Euripides or to write letters and essays. This she did in the old nursery at the top of the house. Here she accumulated a great many books and here she sometimes received friends or teachers. . . . Her manner of working was unusual. She had a desk standing about 3 feet 6 inches high with a sloping top; it was so high that she had to stand to her work." Bell suggests that the motive behind this strange method of operation was the desire to emulate Vanessa by making the practice of writing as arduous as that of painting. In any event, these hours in the nursery were put to good use; the claims of "society" could be forgotten in the pursuit of her occupation – the craft of words.

Bell is extremely good at capturing the texture of daily life, particularly the petty disasters and humiliations suffered by the Stephen sisters as they struggled to accommodate themselves to the requirements of "good society." Virginia recorded plaintively in a letter to Emma Vaughan (8 August 1901): "The truth of it is, as we frequently tell each other, we are failures. Really, we can't shine in Society. I don't know how it's done. We aint popular – we sit in corners & look like mutes who are longing for a funeral." Bell presents vividly the embarrassments the eighteen-year-old Virginia suffered in the ballroom – "miserable humiliating evenings when she couldn't find a partner, ghastly meaningless conversations which got bogged down and left her blushing and wordless." To make matters worse, her mentor on these dismal occasions was her half brother, George Duckworth, a tyrannical combination of "censor and . . . chaperone" who did not allow his concern for public propriety to prevent him from making overtures to Virginia in private. The confusion and misery of this period of Virginia's life are made abundantly clear.

The move from Hyde Park Gate to 46 Gordon Square made possible a new phase of liberation. Bell establishes 16 February 1905 as the date on which Bloomsbury was inaugurated. This was the first of Thoby Stephen's "Thursday Evenings," a sufficiently inauspicious beginning, since the occasion attracted only the taciturn Saxon Sydney-Turner: "he and his host and the dog Gurth formed the entire company." But soon there appeared on the scene those other friends of Thoby who were to figure prominently in the saga of Bloomsbury. Bell conveniently characterizes the Gordon Square visitors, suggesting that "they can perhaps be divided into a central core, the mute circle of seekers after truth who sat puffing their pipes around the discreet shrine of G. E. Moore – Saxon Sydney-Turner, Leonard Woolf, and Lytton Strachey – and an outer circle, more worldly and more garrulous, which . . . would include Thoby himself, Clive Bell, and Desmond MacCarthy who, though a thorough Mooreist, was never taciturn." Bell takes the opportunity to supply economical sketches of these young men who, after Thoby's death, would play such a significant part in Virginia's life. One is aware of the skill with which the author, like a musical composer, introduces motifs that will later be developed and amplified.

The death of Thoby in 1906 and the decision to accept Leonard Woolf's proposal of marriage in 1912 are the cardinal events of volume one. "Thoby's death was a disaster from which Virginia could not easily recover . . . even after twenty years it still seemed to her that her own continuing life was no more than an excursion without him, and that death would be no more than a return to his company." Their common loss brought Lytton Strachey and Virginia together; Bell depicts with sympathy the seriocomic episode that resulted in their (very brief) engagement and rapid disengagement. The first volume ends, fittingly, on the eve of Virginia's marriage. Her acceptance of Leonard Woolf's proposal was, as Bell puts it, "the wisest decision of her life." In effect, Leonard Woolf is the hero of volume two; it is therefore satisfying for the reader to be given such a convincing portrait of him in the final chapter of volume one. Bell's deft comparisons help to establish the contrasting characters of Strachey and Woolf – close friends at Cambridge and after, and devoted adherents of Moore. Bell comments succinctly that Strachey ought, perhaps, to have gone out to Ceylon (as was suggested from time to time). "Lytton never got that slight baptism of fire . . . which fate provided for Gibbon. . . . Would Lytton have given a sharper edge – a

slightly deeper note of comprehension to Gordon and to Florence Nightingale if he had sat amidst the flies and dirt of Jaffna and Hambantota? It is hard to say, and hard to imagine Lytton visiting, let alone ruling, a province." In Leonard's case, Bell notes, the arrogance of the Cambridge intellectual was tempered, his understanding enlarged, by his experiences as a colonial servant.

Volume two covers the years of Virginia Woolf's literary achievement. There is a large cast of characters; Bell contrives to present a living portrait of Woolf in her surroundings in those crowded years. The original Cambridge – Bloomsbury figures such as Lytton Strachey, Desmond MacCarthy, and John Maynard Keynes – are joined by a younger Bloomsbury generation. The trials involved in running the Hogarth Press naturally occupy a prominent place in the narrative. The most striking of the new characters is Vita Sackville-West. Bell devotes some well-considered pages to the relationship between Woolf and Sackville-West. His handling of this topic shows Bell at his best – sympathetic, tactful, unwilling to erect speculation into assertion. What is the term to use of the relationship, he wonders. "The word 'friendship' has a coy look on this page and I would use the word 'affair' if I were perfectly certain of not being misunderstood. But, in fact, I myself know too little." Bell suggests that this was an affair of the heart that presented no threat to Leonard. The charm, beauty, good nature, and aristocratic command of Vita made a powerful appeal (as we can see from Woolf's diary entries); but Virginia "could not really love without feeling that she was in the presence of a superior intellect."

Bell abandons his chronological method at the beginning of chapter 5. Here he pauses in the narrative sequence in an attempt to examine Woolf's mind at work. This abandoning of chronology is in the event justified. Bell does not pretend to "know" or to "explain" his central character. He has, mercifully, no psychological key to personality. He proposes interpretations but does not insist on them. In dealing with the diary entries that record Woolf's mental state in the period 1925–1928, he shows an appealing delicacy of touch. The first four pages of this chapter provide, in their combination of modesty and intimacy with the subject, a model for biographical procedure.

Volume two records loss and grief, notably the deaths of Lytton Strachey and Roger Fry. But it is a celebratory volume too, in that it depicts the joys and miseries that went into the making of the novels. And throughout, Leonard is a reassuring presence. Leonard and Vanessa emerge as the constants in Virginia's life, lavishing on her the "maternal protection which . . . I have always most wished from everyone."

Bell makes good use of the diary material. He notes the importance of the diary to its author as an outlet for her feelings, as a source for a possible autobiography, as a mode of spontaneous composition that gave practice in the art of writing. Bell also recognizes that the diary does not necessarily concern itself with those matters that were of the greatest importance to her at the time. "Virginia's mind was so constituted that it is very hard to know what would have been supremely important to her . . . her acquisition . . . of a green glass jar from a chemist — one of those great flagons that flow or used to glow in pharmacy windows — was for her . . . an event possibly as important as Katherine Mansfield's friendship or the German air raids." Bell points out that in her entries for autumn 1917 Woolf says nothing about the project that was more important to her than Mansfield or the jar — the writing of *Night and Day* (1919).

Bell has an eye for absurdity. He is adept at realizing the comic possibilities of his material. An episode from the second volume reveals his mastery of an understated comic manner. Leonard and Virginia are returning from a fancy-dress party for which the guests had attired themselves as characters from the Alice books (Roger Fry, as the White Knight, was the star attraction). On the way home, the Woolfs become involved in a distressing scene of injustice. A tipsy old woman is on the point of being arrested for disturbing the peace, although the real instigators are two men who had jeered at her. Leonard pleads eloquently in her favor; the policeman relents; a small crowd watches approvingly.

Among the observers is Lydia Keynes, gazing with amazement at the proceedings. "Mrs. Keynes had good reason to be amazed, for not only was the scene unusual, but it was made more so by the fact that Leonard was still in his party dress. He was Lewis Carroll's Carpenter, complete with paper hat, green baize apron and chisels, while Virginia wore the paws and ears of the March Hare."

Virginia Woolf: A Biography presents a life set richly in its context. Together with Michael Holroyd's *Lytton Strachey* (1967–1968), these generously proportioned works make up a formidable biographical exploration of the Bloomsbury world. The publication, in recent years, of those primary documents, the diary and the letters of Virginia Woolf, allows us to supplement the biographical studies and to gain a richer appreciation than before of Woolf and her world.

Quentin Bell retired from his Sussex chair in 1975, but this did not signal any decline in literary activity. In addition to writing on art, he has published a novel, *The Brandon Papers* (1985). He contributed a substantial introduction to volume one of *The Diary of Virginia Woolf* (1977), which is much more than a mere condensing of the biography. Bell provides a fresh and precisely observed account of the Victorian professional upper middle class that produced Virginia Woolf. A highlight of the introduction is Bell's evocation of a representative gathering of Mr. and Mrs. Leslie Stephen's friends. This is social history at its best — not dull, plodding, and tendentious but enlivened by intimate knowledge and elegance of execution. Biography is an ancient literary mode that has an honorable history. *Virginia Woolf: A Biography* will continue to be regarded as a classic contribution to the form.

Edmund Blunden

(1 November 1896 – 20 January 1974)

John Henry Raleigh
University of California, Berkeley

See also the Blunden entries in *DLB 20: British Poets, 1914–1945* and *DLB 100: Modern British Essayists: Second Series.*

BOOKS: *Poems 1913 and 1914* (Horsham, U.K.: Price, 1914);

The Barn (Uckfield, U.K.: Privately printed, 1916);

The Silver Bird of Herndyke Mill; Stane Street; The Gods of the World Beneath (Uckfield, U.K.: Privately printed, 1916);

The Harbingers (Uckfield, U.K.: Privately printed, 1916);

Pastorals: A Book of Verses (London: Macdonald, 1916);

The Waggoner and Other Poems (London: Sidgwick & Jackson, 1920; New York: Knopf, 1920);

The Appreciation of Literary Prose: Being One of the Special Courses of the Art of Life (London, 1921);

The Shepherd and Other Poems of Peace and War (London: Cobden-Sanderson, 1922; New York: Knopf, 1922);

Old Homes, A Poem (Clare, U.K.: Ward, 1922);

The Bonadventure: A Random Journal of an Atlantic Holiday (London: Cobden-Sanderson, 1922; New York: Putnam, 1923);

Dead Letters (London: Printed for Holbrook Jackson at the Pelican Press, 1923);

To Nature (London: Beaumont Press, 1923);

Christ's Hospital: A Retrospect (London: Christophers, 1923);

Masks of Time (London: Beaumont Press, 1925);

The Augustan Books of Modern Poetry: Edmund Blunden (London: Benn, 1925);

English Poems (London: Cobden-Sanderson, 1926; New York: Knopf, 1926; revised edition, London: Duckworth, 1929);

More Footnotes to Literary History (Tokyo: Kenkyusha, 1926);

On Receiving from the Clarendon Press (Oxford: Clarendon Press, 1927);

On the Poems of Henry Vaughn: Characteristics and Imitations, with His Principal Latin Poems Carefully

Edmund Blunden

Translated into English Verse (London: Cobden-Sanderson, 1927; Folcroft, Pa.: Folcroft Library Editions, 1974);

Lectures in English Literature (Tokyo: Kodowkan, 1927);

Retreat (London: Cobden-Sanderson, 1928; Garden City, N.Y.: Doubleday, Doran, 1928);

Japanese Garland (London: Beaumont Press, 1928);

Winter Nights (London: Faber & Gwyer, 1928);

Undertones of War (London: Cobden-Sanderson, 1928; Garden City, N.Y.: Doubleday, Doran, 1929; revised edition, London: Cobden-Sanderson, 1930); reprinted, with a new introduction by Blunden (London: Collins, 1964);

Leigh Hunt's "Examiner" Examined (London: Cobden-Sanderson, 1928; New York & London: Harper, 1931);

Nature in English Literature (London: Hogarth Press, 1929; New York: Harcourt, Brace, 1929);

Shakespeare's Significances: A Paper Read before the Shakespeare Association (London: Oxford University Press, 1929; Folcroft, Pa.: Folcroft Library Editions, 1974);

Near and Far: New Poems (London: Cobden-Sanderson, 1929; New York & London: Harper, 1930);

Leigh Hunt: A Biography (London: Cobden-Sanderson, 1930; New York & London: Harper, 1932);

De Bello Germanico: A Fragment of Trench History (Hawstead, U.K.: G. A. Blunden, 1930);

A Summer's Fancy (London: Beaumont Press, 1930);

The Poems of Edmund Blunden (London: Cobden-Sanderson, 1930; New York & London: Harper, 1932);

Votive Tablets: Studies Chiefly Appreciative of English Authors and Books (London: Cobden-Sanderson, 1931; New York & London: Harper, 1931);

To Themis: Poems on Famous Trials with Other Pieces (London: Beaumont Press, 1931);

Constantia and Francis: An Autumn Evening (Edinburgh: Privately printed, 1931);

In Summer: The Rotunda of the Bishop of Derry (London: Privately printed, 1931 [i.e. 1932]);

The Face of England in a Series of Occasional Sketches (London, New York & Toronto: Longmans, Green, 1932);

Fall In, Ghosts: An Essay on a Battalion Reunion (London: White Owl Press, 1932);

Halfway House: A Miscellany of New Poems (London: Cobden-Sanderson, 1932; New York: Macmillan, 1933);

We'll Shift Our Ground; or, Two on a Tour, by Blunden and Sylva Norman (London: Cobden-Sanderson, 1933);

The Epilogue for King John: Presented by the O.U.D.S. February 25th, 1933 on the Occasion of the Closing of the New Theatre Oxford (Oxford: Holywell Press, 1933);

Charles Lamb and His Contemporaries: Being the Clark Lectures Delivered at Trinity College, Cambridge, 1932 (Cambridge: Cambridge University Press, 1933; New York: Macmillan, 1933);

The Mind's Eye: Essays (London: Cape, 1934);

Choice or Chance: New Poems (London: Cobden-Sanderson, 1934);

Edward Gibbon and His Age (Bristol: University of Bristol Press, 1935; Folcroft, Pa.: Folcroft Library Editions, 1975);

Keats's Publisher: A Memoir of John Taylor (1781–1864) (London: Cape, 1936; Clifton, N.J.: Kelley, 1975);

Verses to H.R.H. the Duke of Windsor (Oxford: Privately printed, 1936 [i.e. 1937]);

An Elegy and Other Poems (London: Cobden-Sanderson, 1937);

On Several Occasions (London: Corvius Press, 1939);

Poems 1930–1940 (London: Macmillan, 1940 [i.e. 1941]; New York: Macmillan, 1940 [i.e. 1941]);

English Villages (London: Collins, 1941; New York: Hastings House, 1941);

Thomas Hardy (London: Macmillan, 1941; New York: Macmillan, 1942);

Cricket Country (London: Collins, 1944);

Shells by a Stream: New Poems (London: Macmillan, 1944; New York: Macmillan, 1945);

Shelley: A Life Story (London: Collins, 1946; New York: Viking, 1947);

Shakespeare to Hardy: Short Studies of Characteristic English Authors Given in a Series of Lectures at Tokyo University (Tokyo: Kenkyusha, 1948; Folcroft, Pa.: Folcroft Library Editions, 1973);

Two Lectures on English Literature (Osaka: Kyoiku Tosho, 1948);

After the Bombing and Other Short Poems (London: Macmillan, 1949; New York: Macmillan, 1949);

Addresses on General Subjects Connected with English Literature Given at Tokyo University and Elsewhere in 1948 (Tokyo: Kenkyusha, 1949);

Sons of Light: A Series of Lectures on English Writers (Hosei: Hosei University Press, 1949; Folcroft, Pa.: Folcroft Library Editions, 1974);

Poetry and Science and Other Lectures (Osaka: Osaka Kyoiku Tosho, 1949);

Hamlet, and Other Studies (Tokyo: Yuhodo, 1950);

Eastward: A Selection of Verses Original and Translated (Kyoto: Benrido, 1950);

Influential Books: Lectures Given at Waseda University in 1948 and 1949 (Tokyo: Hokuseido, 1950);

Favourite Studies in English Literature: Lecture Given at Keio University in 1948 and 1950 (Tokyo: Hokuseido, 1950);

A Wanderer in Japan (Tokyo: Asahi-shimbun-sha, 1950);

Reprinted Papers, Partly Concerning Some English Romantic Poets: With a Few Postscripts (Tokyo:

Kenkyusha, 1950; Norwood, Pa.: Norwood Editions, 1977);

Records of Friendship: Occasional and Epistolary Poems Written during Visits to Kyushu, edited by T. Nakayama (Kyushu: Kyushu University Press, 1950);

John Keats (London, New York & Toronto: Longmans, Green, 1950; revised 1954; revised, 1959);

Edmund Blunden: A Selection of His Poetry and Prose, edited by Kenneth Hopkins (London: Hart-Davis, 1950; New York: Horizon, 1951);

Chaucer to "B.V.": With an Additional Paper on Herman Melville (Tokyo: Kenkyusha, 1950; Norwood, Pa.: Norwood Editions, 1977);

Sketches and Reflections (Tokyo: Eibunsha, 1951);

Essayists of the Romantic Period, edited by Ichiro Nishizaki (Tokyo: Kodokwan, 1952);

The Dede of Pittie: Dramatic Scenes Reflecting the History of Christ's Hospital and Offered in Celebration of the Quatercentenary 1953 at the Fortune Theatre (London: Christ's Hospital, 1953);

Charles Lamb (London, New York & Toronto: Longmans, Green, 1954; revised, 1964);

Poems of Many Years (London: Collins, 1957);

War Poets 1914–1918 (London: Longmans, Green, 1958; revised, 1964);

Three Young Poets: Critical Sketches of Byron, Shelley, and Keats (Tokyo: Kenkyusha, 1959; Folcroft, Pa.: Folcroft Library Editions, 1970);

A Wessex Worthy: Thomas Russell (Beaminster, U.K.: Toucan Press, 1960);

English Scientists as Men of Letters (Hong Kong: Hong Kong University Press, 1961);

A Hong Kong House: Poems 1951–1961 (London: Collins, 1962);

William Crowe (1745–1829) (Beaminster, U.K.: Toucan, 1963);

A Corscambe Inhabitant (Beaminster, U.K.: Toucan, 1963);

Guest of Thomas Hardy (Beaminster, U.K.: Toucan, 1964);

A Brief Guide to the Great Church of the Holy Trinity, Long Melford (Ipswich, U.K.: East Anglian Magazine, 1965);

Eleven Poems (Cambridge: Golden Head, 1965 [i.e. 1966]);

A Selection of the Shorter Poems (Long Melford, U.K.: White, 1966);

Poems on Japan, Hitherto Uncollected and Mostly Unprinted: Compiled and Edited in Honour of His Seventieth Birthday, edited by Takeshi Saito (Tokyo: Kenkyusha, 1967);

Blunden (seated at right) with a group of fellow officers, circa 1917

A Few Not Quite Forgotten Writers? (London: English Association, 1967);

The Midnight Skaters: Poems for Young Children, edited by C. Day Lewis (London, Sydney & Toronto: Bodley Head, 1968);

A Selection from the Poems, edited by Jim White (Long Melford, U.K.: Restoration Fund Committee of the Great Church of the Holy Trinity, 1969);

John Clare: Beginner's Luck (Wateringbury, U.K.: Bridge Books, 1971).

OTHER: *John Clare: Poems Chiefly from Manuscript,* edited by Blunden and Alan Porter (London: Cobden-Sanderson, 1920; New York: Putnam, 1921);

Christopher Smart, *A Song to David with Other Poems,* edited by Blunden (London: Cobden-Sanderson, 1924);

John Clare, *Madrigals and Chronicles,* edited by Blunden (London: Beaumont Press, 1924);

A Hundred English Poems from the Elizabethan Age to the Victorian: To Which Are Added Specimens of Son-

nets, Ballads, Epigrams, & c.; and of the Principal American Poets, edited by Blunden (Tokyo: Kenkyusha, 1927; revised, 1949);

The Autobiography of Leigh Hunt, introduction by Blunden (Oxford: Oxford University Press, 1928);

Great Short Stories of the War, edited by Blunden (London: Eyre & Spottiswoode, 1930);

The Poems of Wilfred Owen, edited by Blunden (London: Chatto & Windus, 1931; New York: Viking, 1931);

Charles Lamb: His Life Recorded by His Contemporaries, compiled by Blunden (London: Hogarth Press, 1934);

Coleridge: Studies by Several Hands on the Hundredth Anniversary of His Death, edited by Blunden and Earl Leslie Griggs (London: Constable, 1934; Folcroft, Pa.: Folcroft Library Editions, 1973);

"Sussex," in *English Country: Fifteen Essays by Various Authors,* edited by H. J. Massingham (London: Wishart, 1934), pp. 43–60;

"Home Thoughts on Kent, 1844–1944," in *Eastes & Loud Ltd Centenary Souvenir* (Ashford, U.K.: Eastes & Loud, 1945 [i.e. 1944]), pp. 5–19;

"The Rural Tradition," in *The Natural Order: Essays in the Return to Husbandry,* edited by Massingham (London: Dent, 1945), pp. 21–30;

Christopher Smart, *Hymns for the Amusement of Children,* edited by Blunden (Oxford: Blackwell, 1948 [dated 1947]);

The Christ's Hospital Book, edited by Blunden and others (London: Hamilton, 1953; revised, 1958);

Ivor Gurney, *Poems Principally Selected from Unpublished Manuscripts,* edited by Blunden (London: Hutchinson, 1954);

Percy Bysshe Shelley, *Selected Poems,* edited by Blunden (London: Collins, 1954);

John Keats, *Selected Poems,* edited by Blunden (London & Glasgow: Collins, 1955);

Alfred, Lord Tennyson, *Selected Poems of Tennyson,* edited by Blunden (London, Melbourne & Toronto: Heinemann, 1960);

Wayside Poems of the Seventeenth Century: An Anthology, edited by Blunden and Bernard Mellor (Hong Kong: Hong Kong University Press, 1963);

Wayside Poems of the Early Eighteenth Century: An Anthology, edited by Blunden and Mellor (Hong Kong: Hong Kong University Press, 1964);

Wayside Sonnets, 1750–1850: An Anthology, edited by Blunden and Mellor (Hong Kong: Hong Kong University Press, 1971).

Edmund Charles Blunden was born in London on 1 November 1896 to Charles and Georgina Tyler Blunden, but his family moved to the village of Yalding, Kent, in 1900, providing Blunden with one of the more enduring aspects of his poetry, the love of the English countryside. His family was always in straitened financial circumstances, but he was a bright and promising student and was admitted in 1909 to Christ's Hospital, a venerable and famous school that subsidized gifted students from poor families. The Christ's Hospital experience was one of the most profound and lasting influences on Blunden's life, memory, and imagination. By 1914 he was the ranking student at Christ's, meaning that he would be subsidized to study in a university. He enrolled in Queen's College, Oxford; in 1915 he left school to join the Eleventh Royal Sussex Regiment, which in 1916 was sent to the front lines in France. He saw much action in World War I, won the Military Cross, and was gassed but survived. At the Battle of Passchendaele in 1917, with the British undergoing horrendous casualties, two of the four fellow officers who had been Christ's Hospital students were killed in action. A decade later Blunden published what was to become his best-known work, *Undertones of War* (1928), one of the best of the many memoirs of the World War I experience.

In 1919 he returned briefly to Queen's College before moving with his new wife, Mary Davies, to Boar's Hill, where he began to write poetry. From that time his creative life was very active and multiple: poetry, literary criticism, biographies of (usually) Romantic writers, editing, reviewing, and teaching. He also led a peripatetic life. He was professor of English literature at Tokyo University from 1924 to 1927; from 1947 to 1950 he was once more in Japan with the United Kingdom Liaison Mission, in which capacity he lectured extensively on English literature and culture; and from 1953 to 1963 he was professor of English literature at the University of Hong Kong. He was much honored for his Asian career, being elected to the Japan Academy in 1950 and inducted into the Order of the Rising Sun, Third Class, in Japan in 1963. His years in England were marked by the variety of roles and tasks that he performed. Besides his brief time at Queen's College, Oxford, in 1919, he was elected in 1931 to Merton College, Oxford, as fellow and tutor and served there for the next decade. In 1940, during World War II, he began service as a staff member of the Oxford Senior Training Corps. In 1966 he was elected professor of poetry at Oxford. In addition to this considerable honor, he had won the Hawthornden Prize for poetry with

Blunden with his family in 1953 (Hulton Deutsch)

The Shepherd in 1922; was made a Commander of the British Empire in 1951; and was awarded the Queen's Gold Medal for Poetry in 1956. In 1961, for his sixty-fifth birthday, there was published *Edmund Blunden: Sixty-Five,* a collection of tributes by fellow writers, colleagues, friends, and students. In addition to his academic career in England, he was also a general man of letters, serving once as an assistant editor for the *Atheneum.* During World War II he lived in London and did extensive book reviewing for the *Times Literary Supplement,* where all reviews were anonymous (although many of Blunden's pieces have been identified), and other London literary journals. In 1964, after his return from Hong Kong, he retired to his residence in Suffolk, where he died on 20 January 1974.

As a writer Blunden was immensely prolific; the bibliography compiled by Brownlee Jean Kirkpatrick in 1979 runs to 725 pages. The sections on his contributions to periodicals alone contain 3,370 entries, and the total for his entire corpus is 3,830 entries. He was an intensely bookish man, a type

that perhaps in the present age no longer exists. Not only did he reread often the books of the writers of the past, he was a haunter of book shops, especially interested in the out-of-the-way or what he thought were neglected authors of the past. His most substantial contribution in this realm was the rediscovery of John Clare, a rural laborer with a talent for verse, thought of by some scholars as an English equivalent to Robert Burns. Several books of Clare's poetry were published during his lifetime, but by the end of the nineteenth century he had fallen into obscurity. Blunden began researching Clare when he was at Merton College, Oxford, and had access to some manuscripts by Clare.

Two of the dominant interests and influences on Blunden's mind were the Romantic writers, principally Leigh Hunt, Charles Lamb, and Percy Bysshe Shelley, about whom he wrote biographies; and Christ's Hospital, which Hunt, Lamb, and Samuel Taylor Coleridge, another poet and thinker of great interest to Blunden, had all attended. Blunden's preoccupation with the Romantic writers is explained by several considerations. First, the Romantics were often lovers and celebrators of the English countryside and landscape, which was one of the great loves of Blunden's life. Secondly, he seems to have been attracted to the Romantic age, which represents one of the most sweeping eras of change in English culture. Blunden wrote no single description of the Romantic era, but in some of the remarks that he made in connection with his various chosen authors one can discern some of the attitudes of that age which attracted him. Blunden admired Shelley extravagantly, whom he saw as embodying the great idealism of the revolt by creative writers against the status quo. History itself was galvanized by powerful forces breaking the crusts of old settlements and arguments, and Blunden thought that Shelley's *Prometheus Unbound* (1820) was a prime document in dramatizing these seismic shifts, one of which was the struggle for freedom. Subtle, abstract, delicate, and difficult to comprehend, *Prometheus Unbound* was the classical embodiment of the Promethean figure of the Romantics, an outline of which had first appeared in the early writings of Johann Wolfgang von Goethe. That Shelley's poem embodied the stirrings of his age was confirmed, according to Blunden, by the fact that Henry Fuseli's painting "The Deliverance of Prometheus" was exhibited at the Royal Academy exhibition in June 1821; that in 1820 Ludwig van Beethoven's "Overture to Prometheus" was performed in London and Shelley heard it just before leaving London; and that Beethoven himself was composing his "Choral Symphony" at the same time that Shelley in Italy was composing his "Prometheus."

And, of course, the actual historical events of the period – the American Revolution, the French Revolution, the Napoleonic Wars – provided great subjects for ambitious dramatic talents. According to Blunden, the two great poetic literary documents for the history of the Romantic era were George Gordon Byron's *Don Juan* (1819–1824) and Thomas Hardy's *The Dynasts* (1904, 1906, 1908). Blunden did not care for Byron but admired Hardy immensely, regarding him as a belated Romantic writer. But any effort of any writer on the history of this period is dwarfed by *The Dynasts,* the finest literary dramatization of the era in English, and analyzed in detail by Blunden in his *Thomas Hardy* (1941). The Romantic age, thought Blunden, expected "mighty visions" from its authors and worshiped the long poem (Shelley again would be a prime example of both tendencies). But it was also an era in which creative talents from the poor and obscure social classes could write literature and even be

published. His prize example was John Clare; he thought that John Keats – along with Shelley, his favorite Romantic poet – was an instance of a first-rate poetic talent appearing from nowhere, at least according to the standards and expectations of the educated elite of early-nineteenth-century England.

Blunden also, of course, commented upon the purely literary developments in the age of the late eighteenth and early nineteenth centuries. Besides announcing the onset of Romanticism by listing the usual historical names – Jean-Jacques Rousseau; William Godwin; Henry Mackenzie, author of *The Man of Feeling* (1771); and Edmund Burke, among others – Blunden also more narrowly tries to encapsulate its spirit as it is exhibited by his chosen set of authors, most of whom he had discussed somewhere in his own works: Lamb, Hunt, William Wordsworth, Shelley, Keats, Coleridge, Robert Southey, William Hazlitt, and T. N. Telford. It is by no means an accident that his most considered observations on these matters were made in connection with Lamb, the favorite Romantic writer of his heart, outranking, all things considered, even Shelley and Keats. In *Charles Lamb and His Contemporaries* (1933) Blunden writes:

> What change or discovery did they make? One may almost say, that as critics they discovered or rediscovered the soul. They pointed out greatness or want of it by an unfamiliar expectancy and delicacy of response to life and letters. Their manner of estimating genius was not to estimate it, in the former measurement of principles observed or neglected, but instead by an antiphonal beauty to transmit its effect on their spirits.

They had no academy or ordinances or precepts and dealt in subtle discriminations rather than methodical disquisition. Their interest was in the total impression or atmosphere of a work rather than the detached appearance of one detail or another. This was all, said Blunden, a rebellion against the eighteenth-century idea of "correctness." He added that neither the eighteenth-century concept of limitation nor Romantic boundlessness was free of faults. Lamb best exemplified this new critical spirit: his business was to commend, and he only discommended by way of silently rejecting. His method of commendation was the seemingly simple one of catching the spirit of his authors and speaking for them at the height of that experience. Much of Blunden's description of the Romantic "spirit" sounds like a description of Blunden himself, and he did say that he thought his own world of critical discourse in the twentieth century was still in the Romantic period, as indeed he was anyway.

Blunden's predilection for the Romantic period and for certain Romantic writers had its roots, probably, in his own Christ's Hospital experience, about which he published a book in 1923, *Christ's Hospital: A Retrospect*. First of all, he cherished his days in the ancient institution, and his book closes with an ecstatic, impressionistic description of his own time there – an experience of "harmonious sweetness," just like "a new Jerusalem in England's green and pleasant land." In terms of his own career, it was Christ's Hospital that provided the route to Oxford and his academic career. Like so many Englishmen of his time, Blunden venerated institutions founded in the past which had survived into the modern age. Christ's Hospital was such an institution, and Blunden provides a brief history of it. In 1546, after the suppression of the monasteries, Henry VIII gave to the city of London the Grey Friar's Church, the original cluster of buildings which were to be named Christ's Hospital. Edward II established these buildings, for the first time called Christ's Hospital, as a shelter for the poor, the indigent, and the crippled. On 23 November 1552 the first children were admitted to the school there. From the beginning Christ's Hospital produced illustrious graduates: Edmund Campion, William Camden, and George Peele, among others. Endowments were established to give the brightest students access to a university, while those less bright went most often into business, the clergy, the navy, and other occupations. In later times Isaac Newton, John Locke, and Christopher Wren were all associated with the school.

In Blunden's school days the boys wore blue coats and yellow stockings and were henceforth known as Old Blues, and some wrote memoirs. Blunden mentions especially Benjamin Templeman's *The Fortunate Blue-Coat Boy* (1770), about Templeman's experiences at Christ's Hospital forty years earlier. There were more formal histories as well. (Blunden lists twenty-six authorities in his bibliography.) Blunden regarded the late eighteenth-century period as "the golden one, the brilliant episode" in Christ's Hospital's long life, for it was the time when Lamb, Coleridge, and Hunt were students. Lamb, of course, wrote two essays on Christ's Hospital, and Blunden regards those as the most important memoirs of the institution, although Coleridge and Hunt also wrote about it. The nineteenth century, says Blunden, had many distinguished graduates, but the "true greats" were those of the eighteenth.

And it was perhaps Lamb most of all whom Blunden cherished as the very spirit and epitome of old Christ's Hospital. In his preface to *Christ's Hospital: A Retrospect* Blunden names the book as a memorial to Lamb's life and writings. He also mentions a volume issued in 1835 which contains tributes to Lamb by Old Blues.

There was a final irony for Blunden in all this. By the time he arrived there in 1909, the school had been moved to the country, to West Horsham in Sussex. He never had the London experience of Christ's Hospital and thought he had missed something: the dress remained the same, there was a little left of the distinctive dialect or slang of the London school, and pride of place persisted. What was missing was "the sense of the past as an impulse, a treasure." However, there were buildings named after Lamb and Coleridge and other illustrious graduates, and nearby was "Shelley Wood." Though he did not know whether this applied to Percy, Shelley had lived as a boy only a mile or two away from the school.

Still another way in which his chosen host of writers appealed to Blunden was the fact that most of them had known one another, had socialized and visited with one another – talking endlessly – and were often published in the same journals or by the same publisher. To read a letter or memoir or biography of one was always to encounter some of the others. They cast light, both bright and indirect, upon one another. Most of Blunden's critical and biographical endeavors in his long life were spent in their company. Further, Blunden had given over the years, especially the years in Asia, literally hundreds of lectures, and virtually all of them had been about these same Romantic writers. In the words of Thomas Mallon:

> The same subjects and the same names occur again and again in his lectures and books, and are recited almost in the manner of a lover. The sense of intimacy and regard between subject and explicator is unusual and impressive.

Finally, in the consideration of why certain Romantic writers so appealed to Blunden, there is a grimmer or more dark aspect, although he seldom mentions this. Often Blunden's favorite writers suffered from some kind of disability or weakness or underwent a tragic fate. Clare was given to drinking and suffered from progressive mental instability; in 1836 he was declared insane and spent his many remaining years in an asylum. Hunt, though he lived long, was always in debt, surviving on loans (he was caricatured as Harold Skimpole in Charles Dickens's *Bleak House* [1852–1853], not the only time he was abused by a contemporary), often ill and had an alcoholic wife and at least one son who deserved the name of "blackguard." Shelley, whose first wife committed suicide in mysterious circumstances while they were separated and who lost several children, died in a boating accident at age thirty, and Keats died of tuberculosis at twenty-six. Charles Lamb was shadowed by tragedy. Some strain of mental instability in his family eventuated in a bout of derangement once for him in his early life (though this is not mentioned by Blunden) and dominated the life of his sister Mary, who in a fit of madness had stabbed their mother to death. She was given over to the charge of her brother, who took care of her for many years despite regular recurrences of her mental problems. A lesser note, one of pathos, is added to Lamb's disabilities by the fact that he evidently had a speech impediment. Thus, while he was an outstanding student at Christ's Hospital, he was not selected, as was his brilliant fellow student Coleridge, to be sent to a university but was rather dispatched to commercial life as a clerk in the East India Company at age seventeen. Lamb once proposed marriage to an actress whom he admired and was turned down. Finally, Lamb was overfond of drink, as all who knew him remarked, sometimes with much disdain, as did Thomas Carlyle. When Lamb died as the result of a fall in 1834 at age fifty-nine, it was rumored that he was drunk at the time.

Blunden's heart likely went out to the underdog and the handicapped, those who endured and created despite debilitating circumstances. He was always quick to defend the character of his favorite writers against the aspersions of their contemporaries, as he did especially with Hunt and Shelley. But the singular fact of Blunden's biographical career is that Thomas Hardy was the only one of Blunden's biographical subjects who lived a long and successful life, free, relatively, of unpleasant or tragic aspects. Blunden's biographies are not conventional scholarly productions; there are no footnotes attributing the many quotations, usually from letters or memoirs; only the biography of Hunt has a bibliography. Given these drawbacks, it is still not at all difficult to see that Blunden prodigiously read letters, memoirs, biographies, journals, published records, and reminiscences. He liked especially to explore the out-of-the-way, the untraveled, the neglected sources that illuminate an author's writing career. He liked to investigate the actual writing and publishing conditions of that time. Two examples of this type of work are *Leigh Hunt's "Examiner" Examined* (1928) and *Keats's Publisher: A Memoir of*

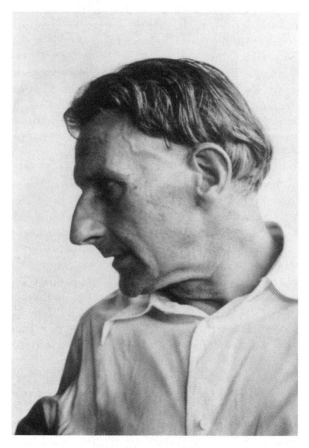

Blunden in 1955

John Taylor (1781–1864) (1936). In *Leigh Hunt's "Examiner" Examined* Blunden read the whole file, from 1810 to 1825, of the journal that Hunt, along with his brother John, edited and contributed to on a massive scale. *Keats's Publisher: A Memoir of John Taylor (1781–1864)* tells the story of how Keats, and many other Romantics, were first published by virtue of the good taste and sense of John Taylor.

The most problematic biography by Blunden was *Leigh Hunt: A Biography* (1930). Hunt has never been considered by most observers, Blunden excepted, a first-rate writer or a particularly admirable man. As a creative writer, Hunt was most well known for his poem *The Story of Rimini* (1816), based on a passage in Dante. Later in his life he had one play produced, and he continued to write plays, with all of them being turned down by producers. He wrote countless pages of criticism, some of it good, little of it first-rate. The book generally thought to be his best was his *Autobiography* (1850). Hunt's life was beset by difficulties, and family, financial, and medical problems. In Blunden's words Hunt's life was "long and careworn" and marked by an "excess of misfortune, obstructions, and estrangements." But the whole substance and tone of Blunden's biography is very positive about Hunt the man and writer. In short this is what might be called a "defensive" biography, seeking to replace negatives with positives. For example, about Hunt's finances, always borrowing, seldom repaying, Blunden says much of the borrowing was done without Hunt's knowledge by his wife and son, who are the villains of Blunden's book.

Blunden's affection, for it can only be called that, for Leigh Hunt was based on several aspects of Hunt's life. First, Hunt was a political hero, who was willing to suffer for his beliefs in a reactionary and authoritarian age. In 1812 the Hunts published in *The Examiner* a powerful attack upon the character and person of the Prince of Wales, who was at that time the prince regent. They were accused by the government of libel, tried, convicted, and fined five hundred pounds each and sentenced to prison for two years, during which time they were able to continue to produce *The Examiner*.

Second, Hunt had been at one time or another a friend and close acquaintance with most all of the Romantic writers who were Blunden's favorites. For example, when Hunt was imprisoned he brought his family to live with him, established a kind of prison suite, complete with a little garden in the jail yard, and set up an open house. The many visitors included the Lambs, Maria Edgeworth, Byron, Thomas Moore, and James Mill, among other artistic and intellectual luminaries. After his release the Hunts settled in Hampstead, and to their new residence came Shelley, Keats, Byron, and others. In fact, Shelley and Keats first met at the Hunts'. Blunden asserts that "the chief life of Leigh Hunt is in the wealth of his friendships."

Other reasons for the attraction of Blunden for Hunt come readily to mind. Hunt exemplified for Blunden one of the prime qualities he admired in writers. Reacting against T. S. Eliot's influential doctrine of "impersonality" in creative art, Blunden believed that the author's personality should always show through. Of *The Story of Rimini* Blunden writes that "There is personality here. The composition is stamped with the author's image." Blunden prizes Hunt's versatility, enthusiasm, and generosity as a critic – using as an example his rhapsodic and seemingly knowledgeable appreciation of Mozart's *Don Giovanni*. Of his theatrical criticism Blunden says he was easily pleased and entertained but adds somewhat defensively that Hunt was capable of condemnation, citing a very negative review by Hunt of George Lillo's *George Barnwell* (1731).

Hunt's never-failing optimism, whatever his personal disasters, was for Blunden a positive characteristic. And so in *Leigh Hunt's "Examiner" Examined* Blunden asked the rhetorical question: "If he Hunt preferred as he grew older to descant on the excellences and the happy evolution of humanity, is that a reason for treating him as so many idlers in literature treat him – like a shallow hedonist, a pious fraud?" Hunt's most famous short expression on the benignity of the universe was uttered to the young Coventry Patmore sometime around 1840. In a letter to Sir Edmund Gosse, Patmore described his visit. With a letter of introduction, Patmore came to call on Hunt. After a two-hour wait in Hunt's parlor the door opened:

> . . . a most picturesque gentleman, with hair flowing nearly or quite to his shoulders, a beautiful velvet coat and a Vandyck collar of lace about a foot deep, appeared, rubbing his hands and smiling ethereally, and saying, without a word of preface or notice of having waited so long, 'This is a beautiful world, Mr. Patmore!'

Patmore, who lived for many more years, confessed to never having forgotten this.

> Blunden's Hunt is an attractive man, yet always in one's memory are Byron's scathing remarks about the Hunts or Dickens's Harold Skimpole. Nothing can make Hunt a writer of stature and Blunden does not attempt to do so, although once claiming that he is just below that level. Blunden is to be commended for a full-scale picture of an interesting man and life.

Blunden's *Shelley: A Life Story* (1946) was a labor of love for the author since he was most enthusiastic about Shelley, at least when he wrote *Shelley*. Later on he may have tempered that enthusiasm a little; in 1959 Blunden published *Three Young Poets: Critical Sketches of Byron, Shelley and Keats,* in which Keats emerges as the favorite. *Shelley* is composed in the usual Blunden style – no footnotes for the many quotations and no bibliography. In his preface Blunden discusses his sources, saying they were overabundant in some respects, scarce in others, and often unreliable, if not outright forgeries. He does not explain how he sorted them out.

The form of *Shelley* is simple: a straightforward narrative of Shelley's life, from his boyhood on his father's estate to his tragic drowning in a boat accident at age thirty in 1822. The swift-moving story is interrupted by comments on the poetry. Blunden made two comments on Shelley's life that epitomize it, at least for him. The first comment was on its complexity: "Of all the complicated lives of which we have word Shelley's was the most complicated; of all swift hopes and felicities his changed most rapidly into remorse." Blunden was referring to the complexity both of Shelley's inner life and the complexity of his outer life, his relations with others, the two wives and other women, and the many men, in often volatile relations to Shelley. The second generalization that Blunden made of Shelley's life was when he referred to "one of those semitragic incidents in which Shelley was so often involved." The major tragic event in Shelley's life was the suicide by drowning of his first wife, Harriet, when the two were estranged. There are many unanswered questions about this affair. Some have felt that Shelley in some indirect way was partially responsible for the tragedy. Blunden, with his customary positive outlook on his subjects, did not think so, and he expressed rapturous sentiments about the supposed character of Harriet herself – "a woman of deepest generosities, unforced abilities" – although in truth we know rather little about her.

The biography was written out of admiration for the man and the poet. This admiration extended to Shelley's physical person. Blunden was always interested in the physiognomy and general appearance of his subjects, and throughout *Shelley* there are descriptions of the poet by his contemporaries – tall, slim, blue-eyed, with classical features and brown hair, altogether pleasing to the eye. The character is equally prepossessing and many-sided: scientist, philosopher, theologian, explorer, statesman, ambassador; perpetually outspoken, a rebel against injustice; a constant reader and scholar of both ancient and modern literature; tireless walker always on the move; and someone with a winning way with children, not to mention most adults. He even insists, on the basis of not much evidence, that Shelley had a sense of humor. Blunden regards Shelley as "the most ardent idealist in the length of English poetry." Blunden praises Shelley's first major poem, *Queen Mab* (1813), as social document, a protest against the rottenness of society. He also describes in detail its wealth as an intellectual document, placing in its sources Robert Southey, James Thomson, Alexander Pope, William Cowper, Lucretius, Ecclesiastes, Edward Gibbon, Isaac Newton, Francis Bacon, Baruch Spinoza, David Hume, and William Godwin. Besides being a compendium of thinkers, Blunden sees the poem as a blend of ideas – divinity, science, nature worship, romance, and social and political aspiration. Blunden believes that *Prometheus Unbound* was Shelley's greatest achievement, so difficult to understand and yet so powerful and profound as a symbol of human his-

tory at the opening of the nineteenth century, with its titanic struggles for human freedom. *Prometheus Unbound* was published in a volume with "Ode to the West Wind" and other shorter poems, and Blunden called this volume "One of the most illustrious single collections of verse ever issued in England." Of Shelley's "The Cloud" he remarked on its originality and how in it Shelley becomes "the humorist of the sky."

Shelley presents two other tendencies of Blunden the biographer. First, he was a great believer in human potential and thus in "might-have-beens," especially about such a short life as Shelley's. He believed that had Shelley, the inveterate traveler, lived he might have visited the whole globe and composed poetry about it. The second tendency was to put a positive face on things. When Shelley died he left unfinished an extensive fragment, "The Triumph of Life," which was one of the saddest poems that Shelley ever wrote. But Blunden thought that Shelley, had he lived, would have finished the poem and closed it on a positive note.

Thus, Blunden's Shelley is a composite: idealist, social critic, encyclopedic repository of the culture of Western civilization, mythmaker, an authentic original, both easily grasped and difficult to understand. Blunden prized the individual and unique presence of the person of the poet in the poem. Blunden summarizes Shelley's career by saying that "the great and final achievement is that he creates whatever he strives for with a personal originality. And none of our poets could say with greater truthfulness of his work, 'This is my book.'"

Blunden never wrote a full biography of Lamb on the scale of his work on Hunt and Shelley, although he had once planned to. But he did publish three works on Lamb. The first and largest was called *Charles Lamb and His Contemporaries* (1933), given as the 1932 Clark Lectures at Trinity College, Cambridge. In 1934 *Charles Lamb: His Life Recorded by His Contemporaries,* compiled by Blunden, was published. *Charles Lamb,* a brief sketch of Lamb's life and works written for the British Council and National Book League, appeared in 1954. For this same series he did the forty-page monograph *John Keats* in 1950.

Of course, Blunden does tell of Lamb's life in its major outlines. Lamb was born in 1775, the son of John Lamb, a clerk with literary interests. There follows the by-now-familiar story: the acceptance to Christ's Hospital along with Coleridge, who remained a lifelong friend; the clerkship, to last his working lifetime, in the East India Company; the murder of their mother by his sister; the many

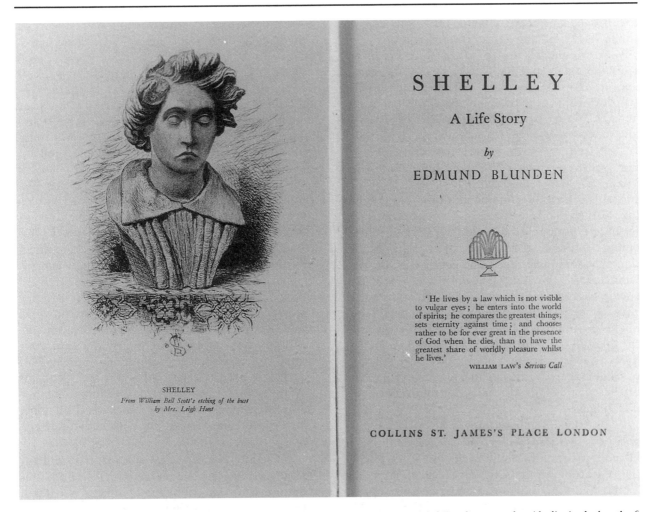

SHELLEY

A Life Story

by

EDMUND BLUNDEN

'He lives by a law which is not visible
to vulgar eyes; he enters into the world
of spirits; he compares the greatest things;
sets eternity against time; and chooses
rather to be for ever great in the presence
of God when he dies, than to have the
greatest share of worldly pleasure whilst
he lives.'
WILLIAM LAW's *Serious Call*

COLLINS ST. JAMES'S PLACE LONDON

SHELLEY
*From William Bell Scott's etching of the bust
by Mrs. Leigh Hunt*

*Frontispiece and title page for Blunden's biography of the British Romantic poet he regarded "as the most ardent idealist in the length of
English poetry"*

years of creative activity by both him and his sister and their rich social life with many friends; and, finally, the retirement in 1825, becoming "The Superannuated Man," the declining years, and death in 1835. Blunden has his usual affection for his subject, especially so for Lamb.

Blunden prizes Lamb for his fidelity and fortitude in caring for his mentally unstable sister and for his sociability and conviviality with his many friends and their epic conversations, featuring puns (Lamb was an inveterate punster), endless dilations on writers of the past, epic displays of erudition, sharp verbal sparring, and general high spirits. *Charles Lamb: His Life Recorded by His Contemporaries* is full of interesting and amusing encounters, featuring the usual cast of Romantics – Coleridge, Wordsworth, Hazlitt, Godwin, and many others. Blunden takes up the subject of Lamb's drinking, not to condemn it but to let Lamb explain its source in inner conflicts and nervous tortures, an explanation first put forth by Lamb in 1813 in "Confessions

of a Drunkard." According to one observer, Lamb, though friendly to all, had a different manner for each of his many friends: with Hazlitt he talked on equal terms; with Leigh Hunt he exchanged repartees; with Wordsworth he was almost respectful; with Coleridge he was sometimes jocose, sometimes deferring; with Martin Burney fraternally familiar; with Manning affectionate; and with Godwin merely courteous. Many of these individuals thought that only he really knew Lamb. Blunden says that none of them really did, there being so many wheels-within-wheels in Lamb's elaborate character, so simple and winning on the surface.

As for Lamb the writer, Blunden prizes his versatility: poetry, theater criticism, prose and verse for children (with his sister), literary criticism with a constant effort to define greatness in art, and his greatest achievement, *Essays of Elia* (1823). Blunden was always interested in thwarted talent or potential, and Lamb's first creative impulse had been poetic. He began by writing sonnets. Coleridge had encouraged him to write verse (later on, Wordsworth was to tell him he had the makings of a good novelist). Blunden's idea is that Lamb had great potential as a poet and could possibly have become a peer of Wordsworth and Coleridge. But after the murder of his mother he burned all his verses, to dedicate himself henceforth to the care of his sister and to less-exalted literary pursuits.

It was Lamb the essayist that Blunden most highly prized. Indeed he named him, along with Michel Montaigne and Bacon, as one of the three superior practitioners of the mode in Western culture. Blunden liked things to be cozily, quirkily, meanderingly English but with real wit and considerable erudition – and Lamb's essays fit the description. The first important Lamb essays were on William Hogarth and William Shakespeare. The Shakespeare essay included the famous declaration that *King Lear* was impossible to stage and that Shakespeare's plays generally were best enacted in the mind of the reader and not observed and heard by eye and ear. These, and other remarks of Lamb on Shakespeare, made him in Blunden's estimation the best critic of Shakespeare, not equaled even by Coleridge.

But the crowning achievement of Lamb's essayistic career was the *Essays of Elia,* beginning with "Recollections of the South Sea House," "Oxford in the Vacation," and "Christ's Hospital Five and Thirty Years Ago" and continuing to cover a great range of subjects, many of them reminiscences. He liked to use archaic words and to quote (and misquote) from past literature, especially of the seventeenth century. The essays, according to Blunden, move through a series of modes: wild and sweet, grave and subdued, clear and practical, sumptuous and sonorous. In *Charles Lamb,* Blunden makes the claim for Lamb's great importance as an expander of the range of English prose: "It was Lamb who more than anyone brought about an imaginative treatment of English prose. . . . he rejoiced in a far larger spectrum of prose style than he first found in use." Given all the praise that Blunden bestows on Lamb's literary accomplishment, he places Lamb the man as more important (he does in fact once say this) and quotes with approval in *Charles Lamb and His Contemporaries* Coleridge's tribute: "Charles Lamb has more totality and individuality of character than any man I know or have ever known." So, in a sense, at the top of the apex of Blunden's pyramid of the Romantic writers stands the person of Charles Lamb.

Thomas Hardy was the only non-Romantic writer about whom Blunden wrote a book and is the only one who was living during a good part of Blunden's life. It is not a biography in the sense that Blunden's *Hunt* and *Shelley* are, for *Thomas Hardy* (1942), while mentioning events in Hardy's life, is mainly concerned with his writings. In characteristic fashion Blunden is highly admiring of both the man and the work, calling Hardy "the kindest and brightest of men." As Blunden was always interested in the physical appearance of his subjects, *Thomas Hardy* offers intermittent descriptions of his subject's appearance during the span of his life. Blunden notes that James Russell Lowell was reported to have written a very demeaning description of how Hardy looked, but Blunden says this could not have been Lowell and that it sounded more like Julian Hawthorne, who was quite capable of such cruelties. Again in *Thomas Hardy,* Blunden shows great interest in the potentialities of the paths not followed. Of Hardy he says that the poet-novelist could have been a great classical scholar or an eminent divine or an outstanding man of action. As a former warrior himself Blunden approved of Hardy's descriptions of soldiers in several of his novels and in *The Dynasts.* Among writers contemporary to Blunden, only Hardy and Rudyard Kipling provided "genuine characterizations" of English soldiers.

In many respects *Thomas Hardy* is Blunden's best-sustained piece of literary criticism. First, it is discriminatory and judicious, pointing out flaws, which he does not usually do, as well as virtues; second, the literary criticism is often very specific, pointing out, for example, the specific words Hardy used for obtaining his effects. In Hardy's poetry, Blunden said, "So long as they are words that strike, bite in, caress, disturb, unveil the truth, quicken the curiosity, they will suit him."

Blunden's evaluation of Hardy's prose and verse is discriminating and subtle and therefore difficult to summarize, but some sense of the major points can be mentioned. Typical of Blunden, he de-emphasizes the popular conception of Hardy as a pessimist (a concept which Hardy himself denied). He was, says Blunden, a proponent of "evolutionary meliorism." Blunden also says Hardy was no "coarse and clotted" realist. He admitted that Hardy in some of his work was often given to crudities, lapses, monotonies, inconsequences, and other faults. But at least six of his novels are masterpieces; *The Dynasts* is incomparable for its scope and sweep and poetry. Viewed as a whole, his vast oeuvre ranks with the accomplishment of Gibbon and John Milton in that "It is a vast work of study in the school of our planetary life, comprising a multitude of memoranda and of imaginative or meditative exercises upon them, varying widely not only in the forms in which they are embodied and the apparent importance, seriousness, diligence which attaches to them, but still forming an extraordinary continuous volume of inspired industry in this ancient scene of inquiry."

Hardy often gets compartmentalized. There are books on his novels, and there are books on his poetry. *The Dynasts* usually receives great respect but little critical examination. Blunden's *Thomas Hardy* is an admirable treatment and consideration of the whole corpus. Blunden as a literary biographer has some drawbacks, usually overdefending his subjects's characters against slurs, sometimes overenthusiastic about their works or silent about their flaws. But these drawbacks are certainly outweighed by his detailed and intimate knowledge of the lives of his chosen, mostly Romantic, writers, and his often acute and insightful observations on their lives and works. Above all, his unflagging enthusiasm for his large cast of characters and their creations is infectious and commendable, especially in the present age, in which such enthusiasm is lacking.

Interviews:

Ichiro Nishizaki, Interview with Blunden, *Youth's Companion,* 7 (July 1949): 28–32;

Nishizaki, "On Life and Reading," *Study of English,* 52 (November 1963): 4–9;

Dom Moraes, "A Dream of Violence among the Spires: Edmund Blunden," *Nova* (London) (May 1966): 128–129, 131.

Bibliography:

Brownlee Jean Kirkpatrick, *A Bibliography of Edmund Blunden* (Oxford: Clarendon Press, 1979).

References:

L. Aaronson, "Edmund Blunden," *Nineteenth Century and After,* 129 (June 1941): 580–585;

Chau Wah Ching, Lo King Man, and Yung Kai Kin, eds. *Edmund Blunden: Sixty-five* (Hong Kong: Hong Kong Cultural Enterprise, 1965);

Alec M. Hardie, *Edmund Blunden,* revised edition (London: Longmans, Green, 1971);

Massao Hirai and Peter Milward, eds., *Edmund Blunden: A Tribute from Japan* (Tokyo: Kenkyusha, 1974);

Thomas Mallon, *Edmund Blunden* (Boston: Twayne, 1983);

Barry Webb, *Edmund Blunden: A Biography* (New Haven: Yale University Press, 1990).

Papers:

The Harry Ransom Humanities Research Center, University of Texas at Austin, has a collection of Edmund Blunden's letters, as well as the manuscripts of *Undertones of War* and poems; the Department of Manuscripts, British Library Reference Division, and the Berg Collection, New York Public Library, have manuscripts of poems.

Vincent Brome

(14 July 1910 –)

Robert Calder
University of Saskatchewan

BOOKS: *Europe's Free Press* (London: Feature
Books, 1943);
Clement Attlee (London: Lincolns-Prager, 1949);
H. G. Wells (London & New York: Longmans,
Green, 1951);
Aneurin Bevan: A Biography (London & New York:
Longmans, Green, 1953);
The Last Surrender (London: Dakers, 1954);
The Way Back (London: Cassell, 1957; New York:
Norton, 1958);
Six Studies in Quarrelling (London: Cresset Press,
1958);
Sometimes at Night (London: Cassell, 1959);
Frank Harris (London: Cassell, 1959);
Acquaintance With Grief (London: Cassell, 1961);
We Have Come a Long Way (London: Cassell, 1962);
The Problem of Progress (London: Cassell, 1963);
Love in Our Time (London: Cassell, 1964);
Four Realist Novelists (London: Longmans, Green,
1965);
The International Brigades (London: Heinemann,
1965; New York: Morrow, 1966);
The World of Luke Simpson (London: Heinemann,
1966);
Freud and His Early Circle (London: Heinemann,
1967; New York: Morrow, 1968); published
as *Freud and His Disciples* (Dover, N.H.:
Caliban Press, 1984);
The Surgeon (London: Cassell, 1967); published as
The Operating Theatre (New York: Simon &
Schuster, 1968);
The Revolution (London: Cassell, 1969);
Confessions of a Writer (London: Hutchinson, 1970);
The Brain Operators (London: Cassell, 1971);
Reverse Your Verdict: A Collection of Private Prosecutions
(London: Hamish Hamilton, 1971);
The Embassy (London: Cassell, 1972); published as
The Ambassador and the Spy (New York: Crown,
1973);
The Day of Destruction (London: Cassell, 1974);
The Happy Hostage (London: Cassell, 1976);

Vincent Brome

Jung: Man and Myth (London: Macmillan, 1978;
New York: Atheneum, 1978);
Havelock Ellis: Philosopher of Sex (London: Routledge
& Kegan Paul, 1978; Boston: Routledge &
Kegan Paul, 1979);
Ernest Jones: Freud's Alter Ego (London: Caliban
Press, 1983; New York: Norton, 1983);
The Day of the Fifth Moon (London: Gollancz, 1984);
J. B. Priestley (London: Hamish Hamilton, 1988);
The Other Pepys (London: Weidenfeld & Nicolson,
1992).

OTHER: *My Favourite Quotation: An Anthology,* edited
by Brome (London: Methuen, 1934);
"Confessions of a Biographer," *Encounter,* 61 (November 1983): 35–40.

No one who has regularly conducted research
under the great dome of the Reading Room of the
British Library in the past forty years will be un-

aware of Vincent Brome. Whether at his desk, quietly exchanging literary gossip in a corner, or advising a succession of young readers over tea in the coffee room, he has been a fixture in what he calls "the Intelligence Nerve Centre of scores of international scholars and writers." One of the last of a vanishing breed – the man of letters earning his living by his pen – he has used the Reading Room as his workplace to produce an impressive number of novels, histories, essays, articles, radio and television talks, and, in particular, biographies.

Herbert Vincent Brome was born in Streatham, a south London suburb, on 14 July 1910 to Emily Maud Brome and Nathaniel Gregory Brome, a clerk in the London office of an American meat-canning company. His early years were spent in Streatham, where he attended Streatham Grammar School, Elleston School, and, for a year, a private school called Freeways. Shortly thereafter, having discovered a love of language and literature, and under the influence of an extensive reading of H. G. Wells, he fled Streatham and an apprentice job in a tea company to pursue a writing career in London.

As he describes in his autobiography, *Confessions of a Writer* (1970), the life he had chosen was difficult and, in the beginning, not very remunerative. During the early 1930s he eked out a living by writing brief pieces for the *Manchester Guardian* newspaper, occasional short stories, cultural articles commissioned by the British Council, and book reviews for the British Broadcasting Corporation. In 1934 *My Favourite Quotation: An Anthology,* which he edited, was published. During World War II he wrote propaganda for the Ministry of Information, worked in its Photograph Division, and later came to control a section. One product of this work was *Europe's Free Press,* which was published in 1943.

During the 1930s Brome joined the Fabian Society, sympathetic to its socialist aims and excited by the vigorous crossfire of ideas launched from the mouths and pens of Wells, George Bernard Shaw, Harold Laski, and G. D. H. Cole. Like many other intellectuals of his generation, he flirted with, and ultimately rejected, communism in the 1930s. He did have a sympathy for the political Left and worked for the Labour Party. Surprising for a professional writer, Brome seems to have had a personal affinity for the subjects of many of his books, an association so close that occasionally in his autobiography he will describe himself in nearly identical terms he had earlier used to describe, for example, Wells or Frank Harris. Given his political convictions, it is hardly surprising that two of his earliest biographical studies were of Labour politicians: *Clement Attlee* (1949) and *Aneurin Bevan* (1953).

Brome's first major book, however, was *H. G. Wells* (1951), a biography of the great influence of his adolescence. Having met Wells by chance in Regent's Park early during World War II, he soon began collecting material. The final product of his study is informed, but not overwhelmed, by several interviews Brome conducted with Wells in the years before Wells's death in 1946. Moreover, it is enlivened by conversations with Shaw, Dorothy Richardson, and one of Wells's mistresses, Moura Budberg.

Despite this contact with many of the principals in Wells's life, Brome is circumspect about the author's sexual affairs, many of which deeply affected him and influenced his fiction. The source of this reticence was undoubtedly the living presence of most of Wells's mistresses in 1951 and the biographer's concern, if not for taste, certainly for the law. His liaisons with Moura Budberg and Odette Keun are not mentioned, and Amber Reeves, with whom Wells had an intense affair and a child, is hinted at only obliquely as an American student who may have borne Wells a child. More important, having been told by reliable sources that the formidable Rebecca West would certainly seek an injunction to prevent publication, Brome says nothing of her lengthy relationship with Wells or the birth of their son, Anthony West. As a result, a more complete portrait of Wells had to wait until later biographers had not only the freedom to publish but, as in the case of Norman and Jeanne MacKenzie in 1973, the cooperation of many of these essential figures.

What Brome does offer is an eminently readable, careful, and thoughtful analysis of Wells as artist, scientist, and social agitator. He grounds his interpretation on Kingsley Martin's comment that "Wells was the logical outcome of the long curve which ran from the Renaissance through the Encyclopaedists to Huxley, a curve sustained by the conviction that man was a rational being, that once enlightened education had become universal and scientific techniques widely accepted, hunger, want and war could be controlled." In his fiction written before 1920, Wells was able to convey this vision artistically, with moments of original genius. Thereafter, "the world-maker blustered in," and the remainder of his work is marred by a heavy didacticism. Taken as a whole, however, Wells was "one of the creators of modern man."

Brome's biography was greeted by a particularly caustic review by Desmond MacCarthy in the London *Sunday Times,* who wrote that it was "a flashy, credulous, untidy book, full of poor sentences and doubtful intuitions." It was, moreover, based on no new information. In general, though, the notices were favorable. Sir Compton Mackenzie called it "nothing less than brilliant . . . a profoundly moving experience," and Malcolm Muggeridge praised its "steady common sense" and "basic affection for its subject."

Wells appears again in Brome's *Six Studies in Quarrelling* (1958), which examined his famous debates with George Bernard Shaw, Henry James, and Hilaire Belloc, as well as those between Shaw, Henry Arthur Jones, G. K. Chesterton, and G. G. Coulton. The book is a lively treatment of an age of ideological ferment in which the public venerated the ideas of writers, who would often match wits and ideas with each other in vigorous public confrontations.

Brome's next full literary biography was *Frank Harris* (1959), in which he undertook the difficult task of sifting the elements of truth in the life of a writer widely known to have been a pathological liar. Recognizing Harris as "an exquisite actor" who could adopt any role he thought would please a listener, and in the face of the many obvious fabrications in his autobiography *My Life and Loves* (1923–1929), Brome presents what he calls an "impressionistic, interim portrait."

In his *Frank Harris* (1970), Robert B. Pearsall states that Brome's *Frank Harris* is a destructive biography emphasizing the "weaknesses and peculiarities of Harris," but Brome's evenhanded and careful weighing of often contradictory evidence is persuasive. Harris, Brome argues, was a poor critic, an indifferent novelist, a fairly skilled short story writer, and a remarkable editor. His tragedy was that he wasted his considerable talents on "the tawdry, the sordid and the second-rate."

Between literary biographies, Brome produced a considerable body of work in a wide range of genres. He continued to work as a journalist, writing for a wide variety of newspapers and journals, including the London *Times,* the London *Sunday Times,* the *New Statesman,* the *New Society, Encounter,* the *Spectator,* the *Times Literary Supplement, The Listener, The New York Times Book Review, London Magazine,* the *Nation,* the *New Republic,* and the *International Psycho-Analytic Journal.*

In 1954 Brome published his first novel, *The Last Surrender,* and followed this with *Sometimes at Night* (1959), *Acquaintance With Grief* (1961), *Love in*

Our Time (1964), *The World of Luke Simpson* (1966), *The Surgeon* (1967), *The Revolution* (1969), *The Brain Operators* (1971), *The Embassy* (1972), *The Day of Destruction* (1974), *The Happy Hostage* (1976), and *The Day of the Fifth Moon* (1984). Among histories he has written *The Way Back* (1957), which describes the World War II Resistance exploits of Dr. Albert Marie Guerisse, and *The International Brigades* (1965). *We Have Come a Long Way* (1962) and *The Problem of Progress* (1963) are excursions into social history that investigate whether the life of the ordinary working person had improved during the past two centuries.

Brome has long had an interest in psychology, which has been evident in the occasional use of psychological analysis in his biographies. Four of his biographies have taken psychological figures as their subjects: *Freud and His Early Circle* (1967), *Jung: Man and Myth* (1978), *Havelock Ellis: Philosopher of Sex* (1978), and *Ernest Jones: Freud's Alter Ego* (1983). In 1965 he wrote *Four Realist Novelists* for the British Council, a useful pamphlet about a quartet of late-Victorian writers: Arthur Morrison, Edwin Pugh, Richard Whiteing, and William Pett Ridge. In 1970 Brome attempted to sum up his life and work in *Confessions of a Writer,* which is both a remarkably candid account of his personal life and a detailed picture of the obstacles facing the professional author in general and the biographer in particular: elusive biographical subjects, obstructive literary executors, lethargic agents, myopic publishers, and vindictive critics.

In the mid 1980s Brome found a subject for a literary biography around whom there were few of these impediments, and he produced the work for which he is most likely to be remembered. On 14 August 1984 the British author J. B. Priestley died at the age of ninety, and within a year Brome was invited to write his life. Jacquetta Hawkes, Priestley's wife during his last thirty-one years, cooperated fully, talking openly about her relationship with Priestley and allowing Brome to use his many letters to her. Moreover, Priestley's children of several marriages; his stepdaughter, Angela Wyndham Lewis; several mistresses; and many of his friends contributed important, if often contradictory, evidence. Added to this were Brome's own records of conversations with Priestley when they were members of the Savile Club, as well as those Brome had had years earlier with such witnesses as Wells, Bertrand Russell, and Ralph Richardson. Careful mining of the Priestley papers held at the Harry Ransom Humanities Research Center at the University of Texas at Austin and in the Beinecke

Library at Yale give to the book a scholarly substance that is perhaps lacking in his earlier literary biographies.

Michael Holroyd has said that biography is a form of collaboration between the biographer and his subject (even if dead), and in many ways Brome was admirably suited to re-create Priestley in print. Coming from a working-class background in Bradford, Yorkshire, and attending Cambridge on an educational grant, Priestley always saw himself as a man of the common people, speaking for those not empowered by birth or income; Brome had come from suburban London and achieved his literary position through hard work rather than privilege. Priestley had been a lifelong socialist, incurring the displeasure of the British government with his common-man radio broadcasts during World War II and helping start the famous CND marches in the 1950s; Brome had absorbed Fabianism as a youth and never lost his left-wing views. Priestley had been a prolific and versatile writer, producing novels, plays, essays, reviews, articles, travel books, histories, memoirs, radio talks, and war propaganda; Brome, though less prolific, has also had a diversified literary career. Finally, Priestley always held academic scholars in contempt; Brome views literary critics in general, particularly those sitting in comfortable tenured positions, as parasites on the living body of literature.

Because Priestley was so enormously prolific, Brome concentrates on his life rather than his writing, though he offers brief, periodic explications of the more important works and a balanced summing up of his career. Priestley, he argues, is an old-fashioned essayist, novelist, playwright, and journalist deriving as much from the Edwardians like Wells as from his own generation. As a novelist he is a superb entertainer whose verbal exuberance, social commentary, and strong evocations of time and place create worlds that are "fundamentally warm . . . full of belief in simple values." An "eloquent prophet" of the divide between northern, industrial England and the more economically and politically powerful south, Priestley ranges across the lower and middle classes, effectively isolating the upper classes. Though not an innovator in fiction, he experimented with drama, with mixed success.

Brome's real purpose in *J. B. Priestley* (1988) is to deconstruct the public persona of Priestley – that of the bluff, down-to-earth, pipe-smoking Yorkshireman – that he had built around himself. As he had done with Wells and Harris, Brome presents his subject as a man of many roles. The novelist, playwright, broadcaster, psychologist, politician, social agitator, secular preacher, husband, father, and lover are all subjected to scrutiny and reconciled within one man. The biographer's own interest in Jungian psychology enables him not only to understand Priestley's own commitment to it but also to attempt cautious and sensitive interpretations of Priestley's personality and emotional life. In this area the testimony of various people is often contradictory, and Brome wisely offers the opposing views for the reader's judgment rather than forcing them into a strained and artificial synthesis. The result, as Anthony Burgess noted in the *Times Literary Supplement* (21 October 1988), is "total candour of portraiture." *J. B. Priestley* is not only the best of Brome's work but the best example of his strengths as a biographer: intelligence, common sense, and lively, readable prose. While not perhaps matching the achievements of Richard Ellmann, Michael Holroyd, or A. N. Wilson, he has illuminated the lives of important literary figures of our time for a great many general readers.

Humphrey Carpenter

(29 April 1946 –   )

Jason Berner
Marymount College

BOOKS: *A Thames Companion,* by Carpenter and Mari Prichard (Oxford: Oxford Illustrated Press, 1975);

The Joshers; or, London to Birmingham with Albert and Victoria: A Story of the Canals (London: Allen & Unwin, 1977);

J. R. R. Tolkien: A Biography (London: Allen & Unwin, 1977); published as *Tolkien: A Biography* (Boston: Houghton Mifflin, 1977);

The Captain Hook Affair (London: Allen & Unwin, 1979);

The Inklings: C. S. Lewis, J. R. R. Tolkien, Charles Williams, and Their Friends (London: Allen & Unwin, 1979; Boston: Houghton Mifflin, 1979);

Jesus (Oxford: Oxford University Press, 1980; New York: Hill & Wang, 1980);

W. H. Auden: A Biography (London: Allen & Unwin, 1981; Boston: Houghton Mifflin, 1981);

The Oxford Companion to Children's Literature, by Carpenter and Prichard (Oxford & New York: Oxford University Press, 1984);

Mr. Majeika (London: Viking Kestrel, 1984);

Secret Gardens: A Study of the Golden Age of Children's Literature (London: Allen & Unwin, 1985; Boston: Houghton Mifflin, 1985);

OUDS: A Centenary History of the Oxford University Dramatic Society (Oxford & New York: Oxford University Press, 1985);

Mr. Majeika and the Music Teacher (London: Viking Kestrel, 1986);

Geniuses Together: American Writers in Paris in the 1920s (London: Unwin Hyman, 1987; Boston: Houghton Mifflin, 1987);

Mr. Majeika and the Haunted House (London: Viking Kestrel, 1987);

A Serious Character: The Life of Ezra Pound (London: Faber, 1988; Boston: Houghton Mifflin, 1988);

Mr. Majeika and the Dinner Lady (London: Viking Kestrel, 1989);

The Brideshead Generation: Evelyn Waugh and His Friends (London: Weidenfeld & Nicolson, 1989; Boston: Houghton Mifflin, 1990);

Further Television Adventures of Mr. Majeika (London: Puffin, 1990);

Mr. Majeika and the School Play (London: Viking, 1991);

Wellington and Boot (London: Macmillan, 1991);

Benjamin Britten: A Biography (London: Faber, 1992; New York: Scribners, 1992);

Mr. Majeika and the School Book Week (London: Viking, 1992);

What Did You Do at School Today? (London: Orchard, 1992);

Charlie Crazee's Teevee (London: Pan, 1993);

Mr. Majeika and the School Inspector (London: Viking, 1993);

Mr. Majeika's Postbag (London: Viking, 1994);

Mr. Majeika and the Ghost Train (London: Viking, 1994);

Shakespeare Without the Boring Bits (London: Viking, 1994).

OTHER: *The Letters of J. R. R. Tolkien,* edited by Carpenter and Christopher Tolkien, with an introduction by Carpenter (London: Allen & Unwin, 1981; Boston: Houghton Mifflin, 1981);

"Excessively Impertinent Bunnies: The Subversive Element in Beatrix Potter," in *Children and Their Books: A Celebration of the Work of Iona and Peter Opie,* edited by Gillian Avery and Julia Briggs (Oxford: Clarendon Press, 1989).

SELECTED PERIODICAL PUBLICATION –
UNCOLLECTED: "Poor Tom: Mary Trevelyan's View of T. S. Eliot," *English,* 38 (Spring 1989): 37–52.

Throughout his distinguished literary career, Humphrey Carpenter has produced work in a wide variety of genres – literary criticism, children's literature, magazine and newspaper journalism, and, primarily, literary biography. He has thus far, however, never attempted a novel. Nevertheless, in a 1983 interview for the *Contemporary Authors: New Revision Series,* Carpenter declared that he "would love to be a novelist," continuing, "I think the novel, when it comes off – and sometimes even when it doesn't quite come off – is such a wonderfully satisfying thing. There's nothing else quite like it." And what distinguishes the work of Carpenter from that of other literary biographers is a prominent use of techniques that are generally associated with fiction and that might be shunned by the "pure" biographer. Through careful attention to details of setting; through the portrayal of authors as literary characters whose own stories (as well as those of their fictional creations) are worth recounting; and even through an occasional indulgence in pure fiction – extrapolating known information into imaginary days and conversations in the lives of his "characters" – Carpenter has created a noteworthy body of biographical work.

Humphrey William Bouverie Carpenter was born in Oxford, England, on 29 April 1946. He attended Keble College at Oxford University, where he received his M.A. in education. He subsequently worked as a radio producer and broadcaster for the British Broadcasting Corporation (BBC) before commencing a full-time writing career in the late 1970s. Carpenter is married to Mari Prichard, with whom he has two daughters.

His time at Oxford clearly influenced his literary career: if Carpenter can be considered a "novelistic" biographer, then Oxford University and its environs are, throughout a significant portion of his oeuvre, his primary setting. Taken together, *J. R. R. Tolkien: A Biography* (1977); *The Inklings: C. S. Lewis, J. R. R. Tolkien, Charles Williams, and Their Friends* (1979); and *W. H. Auden: A Biography* (1981), along with the later books *OUDS: A Centenary History of the Oxford University Dramatic Society* (1985), *The Brideshead Generation: Evelyn Waugh and His Friends* (1989), and portions of *Secret Gardens: A Study of the Golden Age of Children's Literature* (1985), give a rather complete portrait of Oxford University life from the late Victorian period through the first half of the twentieth century that is in many ways as rich and in-depth as William Faulkner's depiction of Yoknapatawpha County or James Joyce's of Dublin.

Carpenter began his portrait of Oxford in his first full-length biography, a life of British fantasist J. R. R. Tolkien. Tolkien's fame as an author rests primarily on his epic fantasy trilogy *The Lord of the*

Dust jacket for the American edition of Carpenter's biography of the British fantasist and linguist

Rings (1954–1956) and its "prologue," *The Hobbit* (1938); but Tolkien himself was, in Carpenter's words, "an obscure Oxford professor whose specialization was the West Midland dialect of Middle English, and who lived an ordinary suburban life bringing up his children and tending his garden." Carpenter's achievement in this biography is, therefore, considerable. Despite the unspectacular nature of his subject's life, Carpenter's biography does not deteriorate into a stagnant chronicle of mundane events. This is due in large measure to Carpenter's novelistic techniques.

Carpenter prefaces the biography with an account of a visit he paid the elderly Tolkien at his Bournemouth home in the late 1960s. The tone of the introduction is reminiscent of a fairy tale, with Carpenter depicting Tolkien as a "tubby, pipe-smoking, rumpled old man with eyes surrounded by wrinkles and folds that change with and emphasize each mood." Readers who note something hobbitlike in Carpenter's description of the author are not far off the mark; Carpenter himself explicitly draws the picture of Tolkien as a sort of hobbit toward the end of the biography.

From the outset Carpenter emphasizes Tolkien's intellectual preoccupations. One of the more intriguing aspects of the biography is its description of Tolkien's image of himself as more of a historian than a creative artist. In the introduction, for example, Carpenter describes Tolkien "talking about his book not as a work of fiction but as a chronicle of actual events"; when revising his writing "he seems to see himself not as an author who has made a slight error that must now be corrected or explained away, but as a historian who must cast light on an obscurity in an historical document." Elsewhere Carpenter illustrates Tolkien's almost obsessive scholarliness. In constructing his mythical worlds, Tolkien would base the names of his fantastic characters upon linguistic principles of languages that he himself had invented. When, in the heat of writing, Tolkien dashed off a name that he later deemed inappropriate, he would, rather than simply changing the name, attempt to determine the linguistic principles on which the name was "necessarily" – albeit without Tolkien's conscious knowledge – based. While nonscholars might consider such beliefs deranged, Carpenter ascribes them to Tolkien's profound love of languages and philology.

The first half of *J. R. R. Tolkien: A Biography* is essentially straightforward biography. It presents a brief description of Tolkien's parents and describes the author's youth and the first stirrings of his mythological imagination. Carpenter narrates Tolkien's growing interest in philology and his early academic triumphs in this field, as well as his experiences in World War I.

In the second half of the biography, however, Carpenter indulges in more-creative techniques. He begins this section by explaining that, after being appointed professor at Oxford, Tolkien did not, in fact, do much more than teach and write, living a long and quiet life in the English suburbs. Thereafter, the biography becomes somewhat more investigative in tone, as if Carpenter is attempting to determine how this quiet man managed to create one of the richest worlds of fantasy in all of literature. In what becomes something of a trademark technique, Carpenter engages in an extended description of an imaginary day in his subject's life, envisioning Tolkien's morning routines, his lecturing style, and his social personality (as a member of the literary group the Inklings, whom Carpenter profiled in his next book). Carpenter justifies this technique, certainly surprising from a biographical

purist's point of view, by explaining that these imaginary elements "expressed the general truths about [his subjects] much more succinctly than chapter after chapter of all sorts of lists of what they did in one week or another, and where they spent Christmas and so on." Through this narrative technique, Carpenter generates interest in Tolkien's life, effectively transforming the novelist into a character whose life is described by an omniscient author-narrator. Carpenter also creates excitement in the biography through an in-depth, dramatic description of the evolution of *The Lord of the Rings,* metamorphosing as it did from a children's book (a sequel to *The Hobbit*) into a major fantasy epic. In his narration Carpenter provides a compelling description of Tolkien's unique composition technique: first writing quickly, almost unconsciously, and then, during the revision process, attempting to find linguistic and historical "justification" for the fictional events and characters. Readers of *Tolkien* are thereby provided with a convincing account of the intellectual and creative processes of this supremely imaginative author.

Carpenter's next biography was *The Inklings: C. S. Lewis, J. R. R. Tolkien, Charles Williams, and Their Friends,* a "group biography" of the eponymous Oxford literary club. In this book Carpenter's distinctive biographical style continues to manifest itself. *The Inklings* is neither a pure biography of one person – although C. S. Lewis does, in fact, become the central figure – nor is it pure literary criticism. Carpenter admits this in his preface when he says the book sometimes "strays" from the one realm into the other. Ultimately the book is reminiscent of a philosophical novel with real people for its primary characters.

Carpenter chooses Lewis as his "protagonist," arguing in his introduction and throughout the book that the Inklings owed their existence as a group almost entirely to Lewis. Lewis thus becomes the dominant personality – a main character who strongly affects and is affected by those around him and whose development we observe through the course of the narrative. Like Tolkien, Lewis is perhaps best known for his works of fantasy. His trilogy – *Out of the Silent Planet* (1940), *Perelandra* (1943), and *That Hideous Strength* (1945) – and his Chronicles of Narnia series are classics of the genre. In *The Inklings* Carpenter recounts the evolution of Lewis's preoccupation with religion – specifically Catholicism – through his interactions with Tolkien, Williams, and other members of his cultural milieu. *The Inklings* thus becomes as much a character study of Lewis as a work of literary criticism. To portray his subjects more accurately, Carpenter again experiments with fiction, presenting a lengthy speculative conversation between members of the Inklings. Granted, as Colman O'Hare argues in *Canadian Forum* (June–July 1979), this conversation is "contrived"; one must nevertheless appreciate Carpenter's attempt to breathe life into his subjects and display them as real people who engaged in real interactions. In this book Carpenter also continues his evocation of Oxford University life in the early twentieth century.

Carpenter received generally favorable reviews for *The Inklings*. Writing in *The New York Times Book Review* (8 April 1979), Christopher Ricks, who agreed with Carpenter's assessment of Lewis as "the hub of this self-fanning club," says, "Carpenter is open-minded and open-handed, and he has a fresh eye for the small comedies and the even smaller tragedies of university life, of college collusion and faculty fracas." Kingsley Amis, himself no novice to the description of university life, praised *The Inklings* in the *New Statesman* (20 October 1979) as "a triumph of skill and tact . . . in which there is not one dull or slack sentence." The biography won the Society of Authors' Somerset Maugham Award for 1979. This technique of group biography – in which an entire literary circle is examined with specific emphasis on one major writer – is one that Carpenter uses again in *Geniuses Together: American Writers in Paris in the 1920s* (1987) (focusing on Ernest Hemingway) and *The Brideshead Generation* (focusing on Evelyn Waugh).

Tolkien and Lewis, as well as Williams and other members of the Inklings, in addition to being prolific writers of fantasy, were also religious philosophers and devout Christians. It seems somehow appropriate, therefore, that Carpenter followed *The Inklings* with a brief study of Jesus Christ, *Jesus* (1980). This short book, a critical study of Jesus as an intellectual (as opposed to a religious or messianic) figure, opens with a statement of the inevitable uncertainty of any scholarly account of Jesus' intellectual activities, since, as Jesus himself produced no written documents, all accounts of his teachings are necessarily secondhand. In addition, there are doubts as to the historical authenticity of many events in Jesus' life. Thus, there is necessarily a certain fictional quality to any description of Jesus' life, which no doubt made him an appealing subject for Carpenter.

Carpenter's study portrays Jesus the intellectual figure as a careful reasoner who combined different modes of argumentation in explicating his theories. For example, Carpenter describes Jesus'

Dust jacket for the American edition of Carpenter's biography of the modernist poet

justification to the scribes of plucking ears of corn on the Sabbath as "a blend of [the scribes'] own method, of a precept made on his own authority, and of a statement about the nature of that authority." Carpenter's style throughout this short book is clear, concise, and mildly irreverent:

> No doubt that people thought that, while the kingdom of God was something that would certainly arrive one day, only a foolish man would predict that its coming was certainly very near. On the other hand there must have been fanatics, just as there are on street corners today, who made a loud parade of their belief that the long awaited event was about to happen – "The end of the world is at hand!"

> By this criterion, John the Baptist and Jesus were fanatics.

It is this style that led David Caute to praise *Jesus* in the *New Statesman* (4 April 1980) as "a short book of great charm and interest."

Carpenter's next biography, which firmly established his reputation as a major literary biographer, was *W. H. Auden: A Biography*. Auden, like the subjects of Carpenter's first two biographies, was associated with Oxford University and, peripherally – as a student of Tolkien and a devotee of Williams – with the Inklings. But *W. H. Auden: A Biography* also represented something of a departure for Carpenter. Auden is a vastly different character type from Carpenter's earlier subjects. The British expatriate poet's life was more eventful than either Tolkien's or Lewis's, and Carpenter attempts to explain Auden's poetic production by relating it to the events of his life. According to Carpenter, a great deal, if not all, of Auden's poetry can be understood through reference to events in the poet's life: an unconsummated homosexual attraction toward a school friend, Robert Medley, inspired the poem "To a Toadstool" (1922); Auden's experiences during the Spanish civil war led to the poems of *Spain* (1937); and his profound questioning of his own spirituality, combined with the German invasion of Poland, generated the somber reflections of "September 1, 1939" (1939). These, as well as other events of greater or lesser significance, provided the primary impetus for major poetic production. While it is certainly reasonable to assume that events in a poet's life will inspire literary production, and while Carpenter's thorough scholarship adequately supports his assertions about Auden's poetic sources, this insistence on the influence of the poet's life upon his work tends to frustrate some readers. Alan Brownjohn complained in *Encounter* (September 1981) that "Auden's poetry has been unwittingly diminished. . . . When the poems are unimportant, the references make no difference. When they are well known and more important, they are a distraction." His dissatisfaction notwithstanding, however, Brownjohn went on to praise the book as "a fascinating account of a creative life that was immensely poignant and still puzzling." In the *Times Literary Supplement* (3 July 1981) Peter Porter writes that "Carpenter's book amounts almost to an official biography: It is very thorough and, while sympathetic to Auden, does not gloss over his many peculiarities and occasional nastiness." And Paul Fussell in *The New York Times Book Review* (4 October 1981) sums up both the book's critical shortcomings and its biographical merits, calling *W. H. Auden* "fascinating, wonderfully readable, funny and touching at once. If it makes no new friends for Auden's poetry, it will make many for the man." The biography received the E. M. Forster Award and was also nominated for both the 1981 *Los Angeles Times* award for best biography and the Whitbread Award for biography.

After the publication of *W. H. Auden* Carpenter took a brief hiatus from literary biography, turning his attention to another of his chief interests. His next book, written in collaboration with his wife, Mari Prichard, was *The Oxford Companion to Children's Literature* (1984), which was followed in the next year by his own critical work, *Secret Gardens: A Study of the Golden Age of Children's Literature*. In these two books Carpenter provides a general overview of children's literature. In *Secret Gardens* he focuses on late-Victorian and Edwardian literature. This was a flourishing era for children's literature, during which many established classics of the genre were published – *Alice in Wonderland* (1865), *The Wind in the Willows* (1908), and *Peter Pan* (1911). In *Secret Gardens* Carpenter sets out to answer the question of what possessed the late Victorians and the Edwardians to create a whole new genre of fiction. Whereas in the Auden biography Carpenter explains a great deal of the artist's creative production through reference to events in the poet's life, in *Secret Gardens* he resists the temptation to ascribe the creative explosion strictly to the individual/psychological attributes of the writers. In a deadpan introductory comment, he states that "I had begun to realize [while writing the book] that the important thing [these writers] had in common, whatever it might be, was not simply warped private lives." Through a discussion of various children's writers from this period, Carpenter concludes that the main unifying element in their works was a search for Arcadia, the enchanted "secret garden" of the book's title. Carpenter's interest in juvenile literature is further apparent in the juvenile titles in his own oeuvre, among them *The Joshers; or, London to Birmingham with Albert and Victoria: A Study of the Canals* (1977), *The Captain Hook Affair* (1979), and the Mr. Majeika books (1984–   ).

In his next book Carpenter returns to the group-biography technique employed in *The Inklings. Geniuses Together: American Writers in Paris in the 1920s* is, in Carpenter's words, "the story of the longest-ever literary party, which went on in Montparnasse, on the Left Bank, throughout the 1920s." Ernest Hemingway is the main character of the book (although he does not dominate it to the same extent that Lewis dominates *The Inklings* or that Evelyn Waugh dominates *The Brideshead Generation*), and perhaps the most interesting aspect of the book is Carpenter's extensive description of the actual people and events behind Hemingway's classic novel *The Sun Also Rises* (1926). *Geniuses Together* is evocative of Paris in the 1920s in much the same way as Carpenter's other books are of Oxford, providing a rich portrait of the literary and intellectual life of the region. Overall, however, the book is not a major addition to the scholarship on this literary subculture. As John Taylor writes in *The New York Times Book Review* (31 January 1988), this book is a "professionally written remake" of other studies of American expatriates of the 1920s, and as such it is probably most useful as a layman's introduction to some of the major figures of this era, particularly Hemingway and Gertrude Stein.

Another of the central figures of *Geniuses Together,* Ezra Pound, is the subject of Carpenter's most ambitious biography, *A Serious Character: The Life of Ezra Pound* (1988). Given Carpenter's novelistic and narrative leanings, Pound is a perfect subject. As Carpenter says in the opening paragraph of *A Serious Character,* "If Ezra Pound had not existed, it would be hard to invent him. On the other hand, somebody stumbling across the facts of his life for the first time might suppose him to be an exotic character in fiction or drama, rather than a real historical person."

Pound lived a long and eventful life – by far the most eventful life of any of Carpenter's biographical subjects. Born in Idaho, Pound grew up in Pennsylvania, where he acquired some of the ideas and prejudices he was to hold throughout his life (notably his questionable economic theories and his anti-Semitism). He relocated to Europe in the early part of the twentieth century and joined the intellectual circle described in *Geniuses Together.* Pound became a major figure in Paris intellectual life, adopting a variety of roles: a literary impresario, championing the early efforts of such future giants of modernism as Joyce, Hemingway, and T. S. Eliot; a literature, art, music, and, ultimately, social critic, serving as foreign correspondent for several American periodicals; and, of course, a blossoming poet in his own right. But Pound also had a "dark side": an unabashed admiration for the Fascist government of Benito Mussolini and outspoken views on the "international Jewish conspiracy" that he felt was at the root of the world's economic problems. During World War II, he broadcast radio programs from Italy, which ultimately led to a trial for treason in the United States after the war and his eventual committal to Saint Elizabeth's mental hospital, after which he was allowed to return to Italy, where he died in 1972.

Carpenter does not attempt to excuse Pound's moral shortcomings. On the whole the book is more of an attempt to understand Pound, the human being rather than Pound the literary figure. Considering the fact that the biography is more than nine

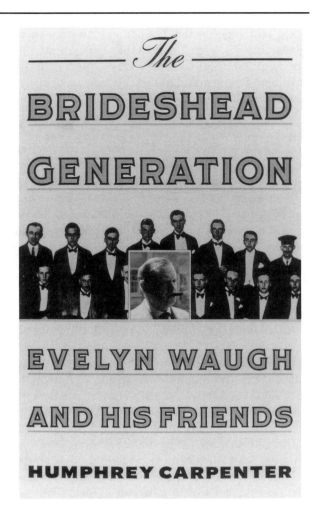

Dust jacket for the American edition of Carpenter's group biography of literary figures associated with Oxford University in the 1920s

hundred pages long, there is not a great deal of critical comment on Pound's poetry. What explication there is tends, as in the Auden biography, to explain the poetry through reference to events and preoccupations in Pound's life. And the image of Pound by the end of the biography is emphatically not that of a great literary artist; Pound may have been a "serious character," but it remains unclear whether he was a great artist. "Mr. Carpenter," writes Phoebe-Lou Adams in the *Atlantic* (January 1989), "considers his subject, Ezra Pound, a man of many masks, but this superb biography suggests that the dominant person was the know-it-all spoiled brat, arrogantly confident of the validity of his opinions and certain of his ability and his right to do whatever he pleased, from composing an opera to reforming world fiscal habits." Carpenter sums up his subject (with a quote from one of Pound's Cantos about Sigismundo Malatesta) as "a failure worth all the successes of his age." This suggests that Carpenter views Pound as something of a tragic figure, a man who set out – in his own highly idiosyncratic way – to change the world but whose accomplishments were, ultimately, questionable at best.

Carpenter next produced another group biography, *The Brideshead Generation: Evelyn Waugh and His Friends*. In this book Carpenter returns once again to the familiar confines of Oxford University, picking up his narrative of university life where he left off at the end of *The Inklings*. The cast of this work consists to a large extent of students of the Inklings: notably Waugh, Graham Greene, and John Betjeman. Waugh is, as the subtitle suggests, the central figure, ultimately dominating the book with a personality that is almost as forceful, in its own way, as Pound's.

The "Brideshead Generation" shares many features with the "Inklings Generation": a tug-of-war between the Catholic Church and the Church of England; an apparent distrust of women and a consequent development of strong ties of male friendship; and of course a significant corpus of literary work. Between the eras of the two literary circles, however, there has apparently occurred a major shift in values. The members of the Inklings, notably Tolkien and Lewis, were mythmakers; despite their fervent beliefs in God and religion, there was something almost iconoclastic in their vivid creations of alternate realities. The Brideshead Generation, in contrast, sought somehow to validate old traditions; and its members frequently endorsed – or at times seemed to mourn the passing of – time-honored, aristocratic institutions in their works. It is as if, according to Carpenter, Oxford University, as great a symbol of British tradition as Buckingham Palace or London Bridge, is a microcosm of twentieth-century English society – and perhaps the world at large. The optimism of the early 1900s, embodied at Oxford by the youthful members of the Inklings, gave way, with the rapid rate of progress and the horrors of worldwide war, to a sense of uncertainty and fear and a consequent desire to return to a familiar stability. As Carpenter comments on Waugh's *Vile Bodies* (1930), "Any contact with the Absolute, however ludicrous the circumstances, is better than the chaos of arbitrary values," and he goes on to say of Waugh and Betjeman that both were in their writing "attempting to identify what was individual and enduring in a world that seemed to have lost touch with permanent values."

Carpenter's most recent biography, *Benjamin Britten: A Biography* (1992), narrates a life of the twentieth-century British composer. An ardent admirer of Britten as well as a lover of music in general (Carpenter plays the tuba and, in 1983, founded a band, Vile Bodies, named after the Waugh novel), Carpenter enthusiastically accepted a commission to write this book when it became apparent that Donald Mitchell, a longtime friend and associate of the composer and the man designated by Britten to be his biographer, would be unable to undertake the assignment. As in his literary biographies, Carpenter here seems concerned with developing Britten more as character than as composer, although one cannot help but notice that his extensive analyses of Britten's compositions are more indepth than his earlier explications of the poetry of Auden or Pound.

Carpenter has said, in an interview with Jean W. Ross, that "a biography must be, if possible, a work of literature in itself . . . as well and carefully shaped and planned as any other literary work." In Carpenter's estimation biographies are not generally considered literary works, an idea borne out by the fact that authors are routinely praised by scholars and laypeople alike for an ability to write biographies that "read like novels." A good biography should convey a subject's life with a pace and dramatic structure that is usually (and solely) attributed to works of fiction. This is what distinguishes "lively" biographies from dry, scholarly explications of a subject's life and work or simple chronological records of dates and events. The subjects of successful biographies are treated as literary characters, and their surroundings are described in rich detail. By all these criteria, Humphrey Carpenter has striven to write biographies that are as readable as works of fiction. And more often than not, he succeeds.

Interview:

Interview with Jean W. Ross, *Contemporary Authors: New Revision Series,* volume 13 (Detroit: Gale Research, 1984): 100–102.

References:

Roger Lewis, "Et in Arcadia Ego: Demons in Neverland," *Encounter,* 65 (September–October 1985): 54–59;

William McNaughton, "Kingdoms of the Earp: Carpenter and Criticism," *Pnidenma,* 21 (Winter 1992): 9–40.

Lord David Cecil

(9 April 1902 – 1 January 1986)

A. R. Jones
University of Wales

BOOKS: *Cans and Can'ts,* by Cecil and Cynthia Asquith (London: Hutchinson, 1927);

The Stricken Deer, or The Life of Cowper (London: Constable, 1929; New York: Oxford University Press, 1935);

William Cowper (London: English Association, 1932);

Sir Walter Scott (London: Constable, 1933);

Early Victorian Novelists: Essays in Revaluation (London: Constable, 1934);

Jane Austen (Cambridge: Cambridge University Press, 1935);

The Young Melbourne and the Story of His Marriage with Caroline Lamb (London: Constable, 1939);

The English Poets (London: Collins, 1941);

Hardy, the Novelist: An Essay in Criticism (London: Constable, 1943; Indianapolis & New York: Bobbs-Merrill, 1946);

Anthony and Cleopatra (Glasgow: Jackson, 1944);

Two Quiet Lives: Dorothy Osborne, Thomas Gray (London: Constable, 1948; Indianapolis & New York: Bobbs-Merrill, 1948);

Poets and Story-Tellers: A Book of Critical Essays (London: Constable, 1949; New York: Macmillan, 1949);

Reading as One of the Fine Arts (Oxford: Oxford University Press, 1949);

Hatfield House: An Illustrated Survey of the Hertfordshire Home of the Cecil Family (Derby: English Life Publications, 1952);

Lord M.: or the Later Life of Lord Melbourne (London: Constable, 1954);

Walter Pater: The Scholar-Artist (Cambridge: Cambridge University Press, 1955);

The Fine Art of Reading and Other Literary Studies (London: Constable, 1957; Indianapolis & New York: Bobbs-Merrill, 1957);

Max: A Biography (London: Constable, 1964; Boston: Houghton Mifflin, 1965);

Visionary & Dreamer: Two Poetic Painters, Samuel Palmer & Edward Burne-Jones (London: Constable,

1969; Princeton: Princeton University Press, 1970);

The Cecils of Hatfield House (London: Constable, 1973);

Library Looking-Glass: A Personal Anthology (London: Constable, 1975; New York: Harper & Row, 1975);

A Portrait of Jane Austen (London: Constable, 1978; New York: Hill & Wang, 1979);

A Portrait of Charles Lamb (London: Constable, 1983; New York: Scribners, 1983);

Some Dorset Country Houses: A Personal Selection (Wimborne: Dovecote Press, 1985).

OTHER: Jane Austen, *Sense and Sensibility,* introduction by Cecil (London: Oxford University Press, 1931);

William Cowper, *Selections from Cowper: Poetry and Prose,* edited by Cecil (London: Methuen, 1933);

Sir Walter Scott, *Short Stories by Sir Walter Scott,* introduction by Cecil (London: Oxford University Press, 1934);

C. W. S. Williams: *The New Book of English Verse,* edited by Cecil, Ernest de Selincourt, and E. M. W. Tillyard (London: Gollancz, 1935);

An Anthology of Modern Biography, edited by Cecil (London: Nelson, 1936);

The Oxford Book of Christian Verse, compiled and edited by Cecil (Oxford: Oxford University Press, 1940);

"The R.A.F.: A Layman's Glimpse," in *Men of the R.A.F.,* by W. Rothenstein (London: Oxford University Press, 1942), pp. 63–84;

"The English Poets," in *Impressions of English Literature,* by W. J. Turner (London: Collins, 1944), pp. 61–100;

Desmond MacCarthy, *Humanities,* preface by Cecil (London: MacGibbon & Kee, 1953);

Augustus John: Fifty-Two Drawings, introduction by Cecil (London: George Rainbird, 1957);

Lord David Cecil (portrait circa 1943 by Augustus John)

Modern Verse in English, edited by Cecil and Allen Tate (London: Eyre & Spottiswoode, 1958; New York: Macmillan, 1958);

Joyce Cary, *The Captive and the Free,* introduction by Cecil (London: M. Joseph, 1959);

William S. Gilbert: The Savoy Operas, volume 1, introduction by Cecil (Oxford: Oxford University Press, 1962);

"Tribute to Aldous Huxley," in *Aldous Huxley 1894–1963: A Memorial Volume,* by Julian Huxley (London: Chatto & Windus, 1965), pp. 13–14;

Max Beerbohm, *Seven Men and Two Others,* introduction by Cecil (Oxford: Oxford University Press, 1966);

"Jane Austen's Lesser Works," in *Collected Reports of the Jane Austen Society, 1949–1965* (London: Dawson, 1967), pp. 273–281;

William Makepeace Thackeray, *Barry Lyndon,* introduction by Cecil (London: Cassell, 1967);

Arthur Russell, *Ruth Pitter: Homage to a Poet,* introduction by Cecil (London: Rapp & Whiting, 1969);

English Short Stories of My Time, edited by Cecil (Oxford: Oxford University Press, 1970);

The Bodley Head Max Beerbohm, edited by Cecil (London: Bodley Head, 1970);

A Choice of Tennyson's Verse, selected, with an introduction, by Cecil (London: Faber & Faber, 1971);

Walter de la Mare, edited by Cecil (London: Oxford University Press, 1973);

"The Hardy Mood," in *Thomas Hardy and the Modern World,* by F. B. Pinion (Dorchester: Thomas Hardy Society, 1974), pp. 106–112;

Graham Ovenden, *A Victorian Album: Julia Margaret Cameron and Her Circle,* introductory essay by Cecil (London: Secker & Warburg, 1975);

Carolyn G. Heilbrun, *Lady Ottoline's Album,* introduction by Cecil (London: M. Joseph, 1976);

"Hardy the Historian," in *The Genius of Thomas Hardy,* edited by Margaret Drabble (London: Weidenfeld, 1976), pp. 154–161;

"Jane Austen – A Summing Up," in *The Jane Austen Society: Report for the Year, 1979* (Alton: Jane Austen Society, 1980), pp. 19–24;

Austen, *Sir Charles Grandison,* edited by Brian Southam, foreword by Cecil (Oxford: Oxford University Press, 1980);

Austen, *Lady Susan,* edited by R. W. Chapman, foreword by Cecil (London: Athlone Press, 1984);

Desmond MacCarthy: The Man and his Writings, edited by Cecil (London: Constable, 1984);

Jane Austen: Volume the First, edited by Chapman, foreword by Cecil (London: Athlone Press, 1984);

Molly MacCarthy, *A Nineteenth Century Childhood,* foreword by Cecil (London: Constable, 1985);

A Choice of Bridge's Verse, edited by Cecil (London: Faber & Faber, 1987).

As a writer and biographer Lord David Cecil combined scholarly accuracy with elegance of style, and his work achieved a wide popular appeal. He had an instinctive grasp of narrative technique and an urbane style. By avoiding the complex and the abstract, he always kept the work close to the story line and in touch with the personalities involved. Even if his studies were not original, they were always fresh and readable. His most popular book was *A Portrait of Jane Austen,* published in 1978, when he was seventy-six years old.

Edward Christian David Gascoyne Cecil was born on 9 April 1902 at Hatfield House, one of England's finest and most famous stately homes, into the Cecil family, one of England's best-known aristocratic families. The family's fortunes were founded by Robert Cecil, First Earl of Salisbury, Elizabeth I's chief minister, who was one of the most remarkable personalities of his age. A small hunchback with a pale complexion and a remote manner, he outmaneuvered such grandiose rivals as the earl of Essex and Sir Walter Ralegh to maintain his position as the most powerful man in England. David Cecil's grandfather Robert Cecil was prime minister of Great Britain for most of the period between 1885 and 1902. Cecil was the youngest child of James Cecil, Fourth Marquess of Salisbury, and Lady Cicely Alice Gore, Fourth Marchioness. According to Cecil the "twentieth century Cecils were out of tune with their contemporaries. They were survivals: vigorous, confident, intelligent survivals from a hierarchic and religious period, living on into one growingly democratic and secular, in which people were accustomed more and more to question assumptions which the Cecils took for granted, and understood less and less of the assumptions on which the Cecils based their lives."

At birth Cecil was not expected to live, and he was in delicate health for the rest of his childhood. Frequently ill, particularly between the ages of nine and eleven, Cecil underwent an operation, performed on the nursery table, for the removal from his neck of a tubercular gland. He spent a great deal of time with his mother as she went about her duties on the Hatfield estates; at Cranborne Manor, the family's Dorset house; and in their London house. As a child he played with Lady Elizabeth Bowes-Lyon, later the Queen Mother, who was, he said, his first love. They remained firm friends, and he and his wife stayed with her each year at Sandringham for the Kings Lynn Festival. When not with his mother, he was with his uncles and aunts, who were intelligent, well informed, and socially involved. He was particularly fond of his uncle Lord Hugh, First Baron Quickswood, from whom, he said, he learned three important things: "I learnt always to think and not to talk sloppily, to use the best words you can and I think the most important, I learnt not to have package-deal opinions." He acknowledged the influence of his brother Robert in the dedication to *Library Looking-Glass: A Personal Anthology* (1975), where Robert is described as "*my dear brother* who, delightfully and when I was still a boy, introduced me to the writings of Keats and Shelley and Walter Pater and Max Beerbohm — and many others." His father, Lord Salisbury, because of his political work, spent little time with the family. Cecil was fond, though much in awe, of the deeply religious, melancholy man.

Cecil was sent to school as late as possible. He attended a neighboring preparatory school for a short time and entered Eton in 1915. Later he said

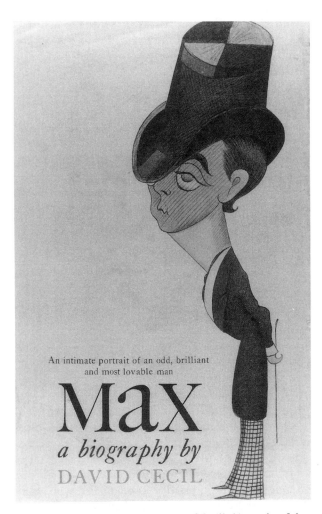

Dust jacket for the American edition of Cecil's biography of the British comic writer

rather revealingly that "Going away to school for the first time is as purely painful an experience as there is in most men's lives. It is like a rehearsal of one's execution." At Eton he was often in ill health, tired and overstrained, and was excused from games. It was said that he only survived Eton by spending a day a week in bed. He was taught by Aldous Huxley, who, he recalled, "just talked to one about literature. And he gave me books to read and all sorts of things like the Elizabethan dramatists that I hadn't read, the non-Shakespearean ones." He wrote a review of Lytton Strachey's *Eminent Victorians* (1918) for an Eton College magazine that demonstrated confidence, maturity, and wide reading. Strachey was so impressed with it that he invited him to lunch at the Café Royal. Strachey was impressed but surprised by Cecil: "I thought him really very nice," Strachey commented, "but so young . . . he made *me* feel positively in my *second* childhood!" Cecil went to Oxford in 1920 and was enrolled in Christ Church, where he read history. His health improved, though he always took great care of himself and never went anywhere without his thermometer. He made many influential friends and was invited by Lady Ottoline Morrell to Garsington Manor, where he met other literary figures. He became a member, albeit a fringe member, of the Bloomsbury group. He never shared their political or ethical views, being traditional both in his morality and personal relationships and a convinced though undemonstrative Christian, a faith that informed his life and his career.

He graduated with first-class honors in modern history. He applied for a fellowship at All Souls College but was not chosen. He was elected a Fellow of Wadham College in 1924. Henry Phelps Brown, an undergraduate tutored by him, commented that "He was interested above all in personality. When he spoke about the politics of the past century, it was as though the stiff figures in some faded photograph had suddenly come to life and begun to move and speak. When one came down into the quad after an hour with him, to meet Peel or Palmerston walking there would not have seemed remarkable." He spent his time writing, teaching, traveling, and developing friendships with, among others, Elizabeth Bowen. He traveled a great deal particularly in Portugal, France, Italy, and Germany. He often stayed in Venice with his lifelong friend L. P. Hartley, the novelist, who lived there. In 1926 he visited the United States.

Cecil's first book was a collaboration with Cynthia Asquith titled *Cans and Can'ts* (1927), which Asquith later described as "a game-book of literary questions and answers," which "is still my own favourite form of quiz." She adds that they made "but very few crumbs out of its publication." Cecil's book *The Stricken Deer, or The Life of Cowper,* a study of the poet William Cowper, was published in 1929 and had a wide popular and critical success. On 22 May 1930 he was awarded the Hawthornden Prize for its outstanding merit. The anonymous review in the *Times Literary Supplement* (19 December 1929) set the pattern for subsequent notices. The reviewer pointed out that for one page given to the poems or the letters – "that is to the only Cowper that matters" – he had given twenty to the victim of religious madness. The reviewer's more serious objection was that the work refers to no authorities and that "it is often difficult to distinguish in Lord David's narrative between what is known and can be related as fact and what is merely Lord David's conjectural construction of what the facts may have

been where little or no direct evidence exists." Nonetheless, the reviewer was sure that "As it is, he has written what is, no doubt, the best one-volume life of Cowper." Joan Haslip, in the *London Mercury* (April 1930), stressed that "it is the man, not the poet, in whom Lord David is primarily interested . . . unlike many biographers, he loves his hero; and he makes us love that rather neglected poet." She drew attention to the now-celebrated opening passage of the book, which "Beautifully and fastidiously written . . . conveys to us in a few pages the whole spirit of the age." She concluded that Cowper "has at last found a truly sympathetic biographer, one who possesses peculiar insight into the workings of the sensitive mind of a poet." Frederick E. Pierce, in the *Yale Review* (December 1930), made the most telling comment of all. He said that this biography "held me as few books have held me in a long time. It did not tell a great deal that was previously unknown: it had some obvious faults of detail; but it had a compelling power. Its characters lived with all the vividness of a first-class novel or drama . . . the very houses where the poet lived are given a character." The book was successful not as a study of Cowper's poetry but as a vivid re-creation of his life, which was quietly uneventful socially and politically and yet filled with the drama of inner torment. A later assessment, by Hartley in *William Cowper: The Continuing Revaluation* (1960), confirmed the book's achievement and continuing relevance: "Equipped with fine sensitivity, a confident knowledge of the eighteenth-century background, and an exceptionally attractive prose style, Lord David achieved a piece of literary portraiture that was a popular success and that is still regarded as a minor classic."

Following the success of his book and largely because of it, in 1930 Cecil resigned his fellowship at Wadham College in order to devote himself entirely to writing. On 13 October 1932 he married Rachel MacCarthy, the only daughter of Desmond MacCarthy, the well-known literary critic. Her novel, *Theresa's Choice* (1958), describes their courtship, though in a somewhat disguised form. Virginia Woolf attended the wedding, which she describes in her diary. They set up house in Rockbourne, a small village on the borders of Hampshire and Dorset. Rachel soon discovered her husband's inability to cope with the ordinary arrangements of day-to-day living and took control of all domestic and financial matters. By all accounts they enjoyed a happy, long, and devoted partnership. In 1963 Frances Partridge recorded in her diary that "Rachel and David are *happy,* I believe, and that's so rare that it's a great credit to them. They have worked hard to achieve it and, incidentally, give happiness to many others (such as me)." They had three children, Jonathan, Hugh, and Laura. Woolf describes Cecil in her diary of 4 February 1938 as "a thin slip of a man: like the stalk of a bluebell. Said he begins, at 36 [i.e. 1934], to feel stale. . . . A dried analytic mind. Not much room or verve in him. No juice: interesting as a type." She seems to have been wrong about his lack of "juice," and no one else seems to have thought he had an analytic mind. On the contrary, it was generally thought that his mind was creative and that, far from being dry, he was both warm and sympathetic.

After seven years as a writer, during which time he published several books of literary criticism and gave the Leslie Stephen Lecture at the University of Cambridge, he realized that he missed the social life of Oxford and the stimulation of teaching. When he was invited by H. A. L. Fisher to put his name forward as English Fellow of New College he was happy to do so. Fisher said that Cecil and philosopher Isaiah Berlin were imported to liven up the boredom of the Common Room.

Because of his delicate health there was no question of his joining the armed forces during the war, and he stayed at New College, Oxford, until his retirement in 1970. He was appointed as the first Goldsmiths Professor of English in 1949. He established an impressive circle of friends – which included Berlin, Maurice Bowra, Enid Starkie, Iris Murdoch, John Sparrow, Joyce Cary, Helen Gardner, Hugo Dyson, and many others – and was widely admired as a teacher and lecturer. One student later recalled that "his lectures were superb. People who had no right to attend them used to borrow gowns so as to look like undergraduates and get in." He entertained undergraduates and friends in his Oxford house every other Sunday lunchtime during term, and those who attended had abiding memories of these meetings of students and staff in an informal and friendly atmosphere. He was generally admired by his students and maintained warm relations with them long after they had left Oxford. Nonetheless, there were contrary views expressed, for instance, by novelist Kingsley Amis in his *Memoirs* (1991), who admitted that as a student he had a personal grudge against Cecil and remembered that "For much of male Oxford, especially undergraduate male Oxford, Lord David was a bit of a joke, one with a touch of lower middle-class resentment lurking in it. It was not so much the dramatic, Leslie Howard good looks, nor even the clothes, which were not particularly extravagant, but the mannerisms, the mobile head and floating hands, and

Cecil as a boy at Eton (photograph courtesy of Cecil)

above all the voice." Nonetheless, even Amis found much to admire, however condescendingly: "And yet, looking back, some of Cecil's writings, especially the early ones, are not negligible, the book on Melbourne has a good name with those interested in Melbourne, and *The Stricken Deer* really has something to say about Cowper." Later in Cecil's academic life, particularly in the 1960s, he felt that his lectures and writings had become less popular because of the ascendancy of F. R. Leavis, *Scrutiny,* and the Cambridge school of English. Certainly he seemed to stand for much that they most strongly opposed. As early as 1943 Q. D. Leavis, in "The Discipline of Letters" (*Scrutiny,* 1943), dismissed Cecil's views of modern poetry as "not judgments of literary criticism but gestures of social solidarity – the only kind of criticism that isn't Bad Form." She also attacked his book *Hardy, the Novelist: An Essay in Criticism* (1943) and concluded her review by stating, "I am registering a protest against his critical theory and practice." While pointing out that the *Times Lit-*

Dust jacket for the American edition of Cecil's pictorial biography of the Romantic novelist. The volume is the most popular of Cecil's books.

erary Supplement described Cecil's book as "criticism of the first rank" and "a wise and gracious book," she involved the literary establishment in her attack. It is hard to resist the feeling that her criticism is not only literary but seems to subsume a strong undercurrent of social resentment.

Cecil was a prolific writer throughout his life, and while he is best known as a biographer, particularly for his full-length biographies Cowper, Melbourne, and Beerbohm, he also produced an impressive amount of literary criticism, mainly on late-eighteenth-century and nineteenth-century literature, including a short book on the novels of Sir Walter Scott that reassesses Scott's achievements. He was also much in demand as a compiler and editor of anthologies and published, among others, *An Anthology of Modern Biography* (1936), *The Oxford Book of Christian Verse* (1940), and *English Short Stories of My Time* (1970), as well as selections from the poetry of Cowper, Alfred Tennyson, and Robert Bridges. He was never happy with the work of the modernists or, with one or two notable exceptions, that of his contemporaries, though nonetheless he was largely responsible for rediscovering the novels of

Barbara Pym and did much to further the reputations of Joyce Cary and Ruth Pitter. Moreover, his *Early Victorian Novelists: Essays in Revaluation* (1934) was one of the first attempts to place and evaluate those novelists who later became so central to English studies. His treatment of the work of Charles Dickens, William Makepeace Thackeray, Charlotte and Emily Brontë, Elizabeth Cleghorn Gaskell, Anthony Trollope, and George Eliot effectively laid down the agenda for subsequent discussions of their significance. Similarly, his *Hardy, the Novelist* was largely responsible for introducing Thomas Hardy into serious academic consideration. But his critical work was always directed toward appreciation rather than analysis, and he had little interest in critical theory. For him literature was "an integral part of life written by living men about life. It was to be seen against the background of their lives and their times." Often, however, his critical work adopted a predominantly biographical approach to its subject, a strategy he adopted deliberately when giving the Mellon Lectures in the United States. The lectures were published in 1969 as *Visionary & Dreamer: Two Poetic Painters, Samuel Palmer & Edward*

Burne-Jones, in which he presented the lives of Palmer and Burne-Jones in such a way as to relate them to their art while avoiding any direct, detailed examination of their painting.

His life of Cowper set the pattern for all his subsequent biographies. As the title of his short biographies of Dorothy Osborne and Thomas Gray suggests – *Two Quiet Lives* (1948) – he was interested in those who lived away from the mainstream and whose inner lives of sensitive contemplation were more important than their outward lives of day-to-day affairs. He was most strongly attracted to those who shared "some unusual fineness of nature; an eye for the truth, depth and delicacy of feeling, the presence to be detected in them of a strong and beautiful inner life." The exception to this perhaps was his life of Melbourne – a portrait of a public man – which because of the war he published in two parts. Woolf confirmed that he "divided Melbourne into 2vols: so that at least one should be printed" despite the outbreak of war. *The Young Melbourne and the Story of His Marriage with Caroline Lamb* in 1939 and *Lord M.: or the Later Life of Lord Melbourne* in 1954 give a brilliantly illuminating picture of the Regency period in England. This two-volume biography is exceptional among his books, as in them Cecil uses manuscript documents and includes original and previously unpublished materials. This more scholarly approach is used mainly because the biography is a work of filial piety devoted to a member of his mother's family. Despite the fact that he deals fully with his activities as a statesman, Cecil takes pains to draw Melbourne's portrait from the inside, so to speak, establishing his inner life of private loneliness and melancholy, which was not really reflected in his achievements as a politician. Melbourne's relationships with women – his wife, the unstable Caroline Lamb, the notorious Mrs. Norton, and Queen Victoria – carry the weight of the study with complete emotional conviction. It is a distinguished contribution to modern biography rather than to historical studies. First and foremost it is a study of Melbourne the man rather than Melbourne the politician. Other politicians recognized and applauded Cecil's emphasis, and he was delighted to learn that *Lord M.* was President John F. Kennedy's favorite bedside reading. *Lord M.* was praised for its "spun-glass lightness which is one of Lord David Cecil's characteristics as a biographer. . . . His biographical gift is one for painting a portrait not a panorama . . . a study at once polished, vivid and serene."

In *Essays and Poems Presented to Lord David Cecil,* which he edited in 1970, W. W. Robson summarizes Cecil's primary biographical aim as the desire "to bring out the unique individuality of human beings; to render the very essence of a Thomas Gray or a Max Beerbohm, a Caroline Lamb or a Dorothy Osborne. But he never neglects for long the larger social and spiritual context into which even the quietest of lives is interwoven. By choosing to write in a typical modern kind, the imaginative biography, he has acknowledged the stimulus of its inaugurator, Lytton Strachey. But Strachey may have sometimes sacrificed truth to literary effect: in contrast David Cecil is exact and scrupulous. And if his predecessor's tone tended to be one of mockery, his own astringency is mitigated with humor, and his irony with charity." The influence of Strachey is confirmed by Berlin, who says in *David Cecil. A Portrait by his Friends* (1990) that "Strachey did have a strong and lasting influence upon him – he believed that Strachey was the creator of biography as a conscious art form alongside the novel." Both Strachey and Cecil avoided notes and references and kept dates to a minimum in order to maintain the imaginative pressure at a level where, as with a novel, the work would generate its own intellectual and emotional reality.

In addition to Strachey, whose influence is clear, Cecil admired Woolf, particularly her ability to convey the individuality and distinction of the author she was discussing and the fact that she wrote so well. Of the writers of the past he especially envied William Hazlitt's gift of writing with the immediacy that brought people and situations so vividly alive, an effect he tried to emulate often with surprising success. He was fond of quoting Hazlitt's contention that a "genuine criticism should, as I take it, reflect the colours, the light and shade, the soul and body of a work . . . what the essence of the work is, what passion has been touched, or how skilfully, what tone and movement the author's mind imparts to his subject or receives from it." He tried to imbue his biographies as well as his literary criticism with this spirit and tended to use it as his touchstone against which to judge the work of others.

Cecil's own view of art is well summarized by Berlin in the memorial essays edited by Hannah Cranborne as being influenced by Pater (Cecil himself stressed the primacy of the aesthetic point of view in his Bede Lecture on Pater) when he says that "the aesthetic approach to life, which meant a very great deal to him, and which he defended in an unfavourable climate . . . [when] he declared that

Cecil, early 1970s

an unusually gifted and interesting man presented without undue partiality but with unusual sympathy and insight.

Evelyn Waugh, who knew the problems and difficulties of writing biographies, particularly of a life that was on the whole happy and uneventful, noted in the *Atlas* (January 1965) that "Lord David had been content to tell it in tactfully chosen, familiar extracts from his subject's own writing. The connecting passages present a problem. Beerbohm's own literary grace was so complete that the juxtaposition of another hand must inevitably make a crude contrast. Any attempt to emulate the master's own style would have been disastrous. But Lord David has an easy, Whiggish negligence of grammar which gives the happy illusion that he is reading aloud in the drawing room and occasionally pausing to comment colloquially on the entertainment." Waugh was always less than fair in his comments on Cecil's grammar; in a discussion of the prose style of his contemporaries he formulated the opinion that "Sir Maurice Bowra is learned and lucid, but dull: Lord David Cecil has grace but no grammar." Beerbohm's genius operated within narrow limits, and his life was largely uneventful and entirely without drama or sensation, but Cecil's biography is a compassionate study of the private inner life of the man and is full of light and shade and fascination. Many thought that Beerbohm was not significant enough to justify a full-length book, but Cecil, who came to feel a close affinity with his subject, proved them wrong. He demonstrates how a major biography can be written of a minor figure and fully justifies the eight years he spent writing it.

Cecil retired from Oxford in 1970 and went to live in the village of Cranborne, Dorset, in Red Lion House, which he had bought from his nephew in 1956. It was near Cranborne Manor, the house belonging to the Salisburys, where he had spent a good deal of his childhood. He continued to write and publish with undiminished enthusiasm. His outstanding works of this period are the pictorial biographies of Jane Austen (1978) and Charles Lamb (1983). Both are exemplars of the quiet life. *A Portrait of Jane Austen,* which is lavishly illustrated, is an attempt to reconstruct and depict her personality and to explore its relation to her art as well as to place her in the society of her time. It repeats much of what he said about her in his Leslie Stephen Lecture of 1935, often in the same words. Patricia Beer described it in the *Times Literary Supplement* (10 November 1978) as "a handsome book" and pointed out that Cecil "puts unusual stress on the fact that Jane Austen was 'a child of the gentry' and that her

the central purpose of art was to give delight, not to instruct, nor to disturb, nor to explain, nor to praise or condemn a movement, an idea, a regime, nor to help build a better world in the service of a church, a party, a nation, a class, but to irradiate the soul with a light which God had granted the artist the power to shed, and the reader or listener to absorb, understand, delight in, and thereby be drawn nearer its divine Creator." It was against these high standards that Cecil measured the achievements of others and wished his own work to be assessed.

In the autumn of 1956 Cecil was visited by Lady Beerbohm, Sir Max Beerbohm's widow, who told him that her husband had wished him to write his biography. Cecil, in the prefatory note to the book, said that this was "the finest compliment ever paid to me." *Max: A Biography* (1964) was his third full-length biography after writing the lives of Cowper and Melbourne and seemed at first sight to be the most risky insofar as the subject, however incomparable, was too slight and remote for such thorough treatment. Yet the book is a triumph of the biographer's art and a vindication of Cecil's methodology. He presents a brilliant synthesis of Beerbohm's writings and correspondence as well as memories, impressions, and anecdotes of those who knew him. The result of this mosaic is a portrait of

family would not have been on visiting terms with the families of George Eliot or Dickens." She welcomed it as a book for Janeites, a flourishing religion for which Cecil provides admirably. In fact, the book is popular biography at its best, direct and lucid without condescension. He achieves exactly the right approach for introducing her and her novels to nonspecialist readers. The commercial success of the book is a measure of his ability to reach such an audience without patronizing them or his subject. *A Portrait of Charles Lamb* is equally successful in this respect. Both books were obviously written with enthusiasm, and Cecil's admiration for his subjects is apparent on every page. To describe these books as "coffee-table biography" is to ignore the unobtrusive brilliance with which they have been written and compiled. Like the other Cecil biographies, there are no references, no bibliographies, and no suggestions for further reading, but they are, as Grevel Lindop wrote in the *Times Literary Supplement* of 10 June 1983, "a delight to the eye . . . engaging and readable."

Cecil was a gifted communicator and in his later years gained another kind of popularity by appearing on television and on the radio in programs such as *Any Questions* and *The Brain's Trust* as well as broadcasting on writers and literary topics. He received many honors: he was made a Companion of Honour in 1949 and a Companion of Literature in 1972; he was awarded honorary degrees from the Universities of Leeds, London, Liverpool, Saint Andrews, and Glasgow; among the many offices he held, he was president of the Poetry Society and of the Jane Austen Society. Above all he was loved and

honored as a man of modesty, integrity, and high ideals, a Christian and a gentleman of the kind that seemed to belong to a passing world. He was one of those he himself described as having a civilized heart; he valued the personal, the private, and the contemplative, and his work brought him fame and worldly success.

Rachel Cecil died after a long illness in March 1982. They had been married for more than fifty years. After his wife's death he determined to live as fully as he could and continued to write and work in a disciplined way, but he said that he "did not want to live long." His health deteriorated in late 1985, and he died from heart failure on New Year's Day 1986. A memorial service for him was held in Christ Church Cathedral, Oxford, on 1 May; his sons read excerpts from *The Fine Art of Reading* and the personal anthology of writing he compiled and published as *Library Looking-Glass*.

Cecil was born into a privileged, aristocratic family and social position but succeeded on his own merits. His biographies of Cowper, Melbourne, and Beerbohm remain as lasting monuments to his life and achievements; they have become classics of our literature.

References:

Hannah Cranborne, ed., *David Cecil. A Portrait by his Friends* (Wimborne: Dovecote Press, 1990);

Julian Fane, *Best Friends. Memoirs of Rachel and David Cecil, Cynthia Asquith, L. P. Hartley and Some Others* (London: Sinclair-Stevenson, 1990);

W. W. Robson, ed., *Essays and Poems Presented to Lord David Cecil* (London: Constable, 1970).

Edward Chitham

(16 May 1932 –   )

Margaret D. Sullivan
Hunter College of the City University of New York

BOOKS: *The Black Country* (London: Longman, 1972);

Ghost in the Water (Harmondsworth: Longman Young, 1973);

Brontë Facts and Brontë Problems, by Chitham and Tom Winnifrith (London: Macmillan, 1983);

The Brontës' Irish Background (London: Macmillan, 1986; New York: St. Martin's Press, 1986);

A Life of Emily Brontë (Oxford & New York: Blackwell, 1987);

Charlotte and Emily Brontë: A Literary Life, by Chitham and Winnifrith (London: Macmillan, 1989; New York: St. Martin's Press, 1989);

A Life of Anne Brontë (Oxford & New York: Blackwell, 1991).

OTHER: *The Poems of Anne Brontë,* edited, with an introduction, by Chitham (London: Macmillan, 1979; Totowa, N. J.: Roman & Littlefield, 1979);

Selected Brontë Poems, edited by Chitham and Tom Winnifrith, with a contribution by Chitham (Oxford & New York: Blackwell, 1985);

The Poems of Emily Brontë, edited by Chitham and Derek Roper (Oxford & New York: Oxford University Press, 1994).

Although he is perhaps best known as a Brontë scholar and editor of the poems of Anne and Emily Brontë, Edward Chitham has written a wide range of material, from children's fiction and local British historical accounts to literary criticism and biography. It is most likely his lucid prose style along with his facility in addressing his audience on scholarly topics without condescension or mystification that ensure his place as a preeminent biographer of the Brontës. His work is highly respected by academics as well as by general readers.

Born in Birmingham, England, on 16 May 1932, Chitham is the son of Norman E. and Elaine Chitham. Edward Chitham was educated at King Edward's School, Birmingham, and at Jesus College, Cambridge, where he was awarded a B.A. in 1955. He received a Certificate in Education in 1956 from the University of Birmingham and an M.A. from Cambridge in 1959. In 1956 he began his teaching career as master in charge of Latin at the Rowley Regis Grammar School in Old Hill, England, a post he held until 1961. He then became head of the Library Department in 1961, serving in that position until 1967. He married Mary Tilley on 29 December 1962 and is the father of three children. The family resides in Birmingham.

From 1967 to 1977 Chitham was lecturer and then senior lecturer in English at Dudley College of Education in Dudley. His book of local history, *The Black Country,* was published in 1972 and was followed in 1973 by *Ghost in the Water,* a children's book. In 1977 Chitham took the post of senior lecturer in English education at the Polytechnic in Wolverhampton, remaining until 1988. He earned a second master's degree at the University of Warwick in 1978 and a doctorate at the University of Sheffield in 1984.

In 1979 Chitham published *The Poems of Anne Brontë,* the first scholarly edited collection of the poetry from the manuscripts of the sister Chitham called, in an unpublished letter, "the least understood" of the Brontë family. He acknowledges his debt to "previous Brontë scholars, especially Miss Winifred Gerin . . . without whose labors I should never have encountered the work and personality of Anne Brontë." But he also notes that he, based on his painstaking examination of Brontë's work, does "occasionally disagree in these pages" with some of Gerin's conclusions in her biography, *Anne Brontë* (1959; revised and amended, 1976).

Chitham provides readers with a substantial introduction in which he carefully sifts and examines evidence, not, as he says, "to decry the Brontë 'myth,' " but to separate the available facts from legend in order "to begin to open the way for a new assessment of a slowly maturing writer whose art is as different from that of her sisters in some respects as it is like it in others."

The task of editing Anne's poems was not an easy one, primarily because, as Chitham notes in the introduction, "with the exception of the work of C. W. Hatfield, much Brontë editorship in the early part of the century was inefficient." Indeed, calling it inefficient is perhaps putting it too politely, since this was no accident nor was it a result of carelessness; it "stemmed from the involvement in the purchase and publication of Brontë material of T. J. Wise, who set up a virtual monopoly in Brontë manuscripts from the 1890s onward." After his death Wise was accused of forging manuscripts and of stealing material from the British Museum. In recent years it has come to light that he acquired many Brontë manuscripts by dishonest means, edited them poorly, often filling them with inaccuracies, and furthermore separated and scattered them, causing many to be now untraceable. Thus, Chitham's careful research and scrupulous editing, based on detective work he conducted both in Great Britain and in the United States, gives readers an accurately edited volume of Anne's poetry. Her poems are printed in chronological order with annotations, commentary, appendixes, and a bibliography.

Chitham then began work on *Brontë Facts and Brontë Problems* (1983) in collaboration with Tom Winnifrith, another highly respected Brontë scholar. The introduction states the purpose of the book as an attempt "to see the Brontës from many angles, considering poetry as well as prose, biography as well as criticism, Branwell and Anne as well as Emily and Charlotte." In addition to exploring the connections among the lives and the works, the volume addresses many of the problems confronting scholars and critics of the Brontës, including those questions of the accuracy of transmission of the manuscripts of all four writers. A glance at the chapter headings reveals the breadth of the problems discussed. The chapters written by Chitham are "Early Brontë Chronology," "The Inspiration for Emily's Poetry," "Gondal's Queen: Saga or Myth?," "Emily Brontë and Shelley," "Diverging Twins: Some Clues to Wildfell Hall," and "The Development of 'Vision' in Emily Brontë's Poems." Winnifrith contributed the following chapters: "Charlotte Brontë and Mr. Rochester," "Texts and Transmission," "Branwell Brontë and Ponden Hall," and "Wuthering Heights: One Volume or Two?"

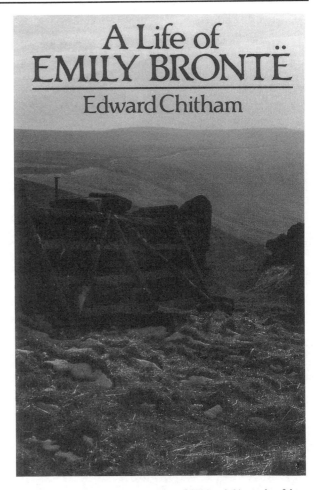

Front cover of the paperback edition of Chitham's biography of the author of Wuthering Heights

The second collaborative work of Chitham and Winnifrith, *Selected Brontë Poems*, was published in 1985. The two men compiled and edited this collection for a general, rather than a scholarly, audience. They acknowledge in their introduction that they are aware that "the complete editions we have produced, or are endeavouring to produce, are rather forbidding for the general reader." In this volume they hoped to avoid intimidating readers by limiting their selection to representative examples of Brontë poems and by omitting the "dense critical apparatus necessary to establish a correct text" which is required in more comprehensive collections. Indeed, it is because they were not attempting to be comprehensive in this endeavor that they were able to choose poems they considered the best of each writer's work and were not obliged to include "the large number of poems of indifferent quality which disfigure the poetry of all four Brontës, and especially that of Charlotte." The introductory material also includes a short section titled "The Poetic

A Life of ANNE BRONTË

Edward Chitham

Front cover of the paperback edition of Chitham's biography of the youngest of the Brontë sisters

Background and Achievement of the Brontës," further familiarizing the reader with the writers of the poems that follow.

Each man worked independently on the sections concerning the Brontës that he has studied most closely: Winnifrith collected and edited the poems of Charlotte and Branwell, and Chitham those of Emily and Anne. The chapters on the imaginary lands of Angria and Gondal were written by Winnifrith and Chitham, respectively.

In the final paragraph of the short biographical note, the editors warn that it is "dangerous to use fiction as an aid to biography, and even more dangerous to use poetry," and caution that "this is especially true of the Brontës who filled their drab lives with stories and poems about exciting fictional characters." Thus, the notes that follow the collected poems attempt to establish the amount of probable influence of events in the Brontës' lives on their work and aid readers in seeing any given poem in the most probable context.

This volume was followed by *The Brontës' Irish Background* (1986). Chitham was motivated to undertake this investigation because, as he points out in his introduction, earlier biographers have placed minor emphasis on the family's Irish heritage. "Some literary historians mention a Celtic temperament they discern in the work of Charlotte and Emily and the life of Branwell, but the majority of biographers begin their story in Liverpool or even at Cambridge." Chitham feels that the lack of attention to the family history is due to the belief of some scholars that "Mr. Brontë's past [is] too shadowy or remote to be able to establish any precise facts or even probabilities about it."

Chitham acknowledges that "a great deal of painstaking detective work" went into the book through his "searching out and carefully documenting everything that is known about the Irish milieu in which Patrick Brontë grew up and in which his father had in turn grown up." The purpose of the vigorous research is to trace "how far this background affected the life, thought patterns and literary expression" of Anne, Charlotte, Emily, and Branwell. He begins by reassessing the often disparaged work of William Wright, *The Brontës in Ireland* (1893), carefully sorting through inconsistencies and contradictions. A later chapter explores possible Irish influences in *Wuthering Heights* (1847) and in some of Emily's poems. A bibliography lists additional books on the Brontës' Irish ancestry along with the major biographies.

At first glance the volume seems only of interest to scholars, and, in the best traditions of excellence in scholarship the research is extremely thorough and fact is always scrupulously distinguished from speculation. But Chitham's clear, captivating prose makes his careful investigation fascinating reading for all Brontë devotees.

When Chitham's *A Life of Emily Brontë* was published in 1987, Stevie Davies began her review in the *Times Literary Supplement* of 15 January 1988 by asserting that "After nearly a century and a half, Emily Brontë has found her biographer." She further praises the book and its author, saying that "Through close attentive reading of the sources, ruthless discrimination between fact, hearsay and whimsy, the refusal to say 'definitely' when he means 'maybe,' and sensitive exercise of the creative imagination, Edward Chitham has breathed new life into the familiar Brontë material." Davies points out that, unlike much Brontë scholarship that has been guilty of rapturous, entranced, and intimate tones, Chitham's biography displays his "patient precision" in tracing the "structure of her life" as "an unfolding process in time." Winifred Gerin's 1971 biography, *Emily Brontë*, is, in Davies's opinion, "sensible" and "avoids excesses but softens and rationalizes." She also praises Chitham for his rigorous assessment of evidence: "Whenever practicable he reprints it in full, allowing the reader to check his evaluation; thus avoiding the Brontë biographers' tendency to produce double falsification by paraphrasing dubious sources."

As with Chitham's other publications, *A Life of Emily Brontë* is an example of excellence in scholarship, but never at the expense of readability. He begins his introduction by stating that "Emily Brontë's life and character are full of fascination," and the reader appreciates the fascination in the re-created life as well as the fascination Chitham feels in recounting it. His is an "investigative biography," and while he acknowledges that "a complete reconstruction is never going to be possible," he proceeds in the belief that "by patient delving and thought – especially about the neglected area of Emily's childhood – an approximation to a fair portrait of Emily Brontë can be slowly built up." Chitham ends his introduction by noting that "In life, she took few pains to be understood. I should like to think she might recognize herself in this portrait more easily than in most others." Readers of his biography will likely agree that she would.

A third collaborative work of Chitham with Winnifrith is *Charlotte and Emily Brontë* (1989), part of a series called Literary Lives. According to the general editor of the series, Richard Dutton, in a prefatory note to *Charlotte and Emily Brontë,* the purpose of the series is to provide the reader with "stimulating accounts of the literary careers of the most widely read British and Irish authors." The focus is "the writers' working lives, not in the spirit of traditional biography, but aiming to trace the professional, publishing and social contexts which shaped their writing." While he acknowledges that the "role and status of 'the author' as the creator of literary texts is a vexed issue in current critical theory," he nonetheless feels that this series aims at demonstrating "how an understanding of writers' careers can promote, for students and general readers alike, a more informed historical reading of their works."

Chitham and Winnifrith produced a volume rich in scholarship but which was aimed at a general audience. The organization of material is clear and the chapter headings give an indication of the struc-ture within which the two men trace the various influences on the Brontës' careers and the likely effects of their careers on their relationships. The first eight chapters are entitled "Life," "Origins," "Religion," "Schooling," "Reading," "Teaching," "Belgium," and "Poems"; the last two treat what is known of the atmosphere in which the novels were produced. One reviewer, G. B. Cross, noted in the December 1989 issue of *Choice* that the book helps to "focus attention on important matters. For those who believe that an author's life and experience are less important than the work itself this book may be salutary." He goes on to note that "Nobody wrote more out of experience than the Brontës, though as the book makes clear, they were profoundly imaginative from childhood."

In 1991, some twelve years after he first brought together a volume of her poetry, Chitham published *A Life of Anne Brontë*. He recalls in an unpublished letter that when he began his research for the earlier book, "one could not get a copy of her poems. I wanted to know about and understand her work and life. It's a very attractive quest to recreate the life of someone long dead, and to feel their emotions and thoughts near at hand." The youngest sister emerges as a rather different personality from her mild, gentle image in Brontë myth. Although shy, Anne was able to establish herself outside the home more successfully as a teacher than Charlotte or Emily. Probably thwarted as the baby of the family and subjected to Charlotte's often condescending and patronizing attitude toward her work, Anne nonetheless can be seen as a strong and independent thinker and a writer who is not afraid to portray violence convincingly in her novels. In writing *A Life of Anne Brontë*, Chitham achieved his aim, noted in an unpublished letter, "to communicate an *accurate* sense of the person and motivation of Anne Brontë . . . to the reader."

Chitham's most recent work, *The Poems of Emily Brontë*, which he edited with Derek Roper, was published in December 1994. This volume is an undertaking that more than rivals his earlier success in collecting and editing Anne's poetry.

Since 1988 Chitham has been part-time tutor at Newman College, Birmingham, and held that post at the University of Warwick from 1991 until 1992. He is also currently tutor and counselor at the Open University and an education consultant with the National Association for Gifted Children in Northampton.

Anthony Curtis

(12 March 1926 –   )

Robert Calder
University of Saskatchewan

BOOKS: *New Developments in the French Theatre: A Critical Introduction to the Plays of Jean-Paul Sartre, Simone de Beauvoir, Albert Camus, and Jean Anouilh* (London: Curtain, 1948);

The Pattern of Maugham: A Critical Portrait (London: Hamish Hamilton, 1974; New York: Taplinger, 1974);

Somerset Maugham (London: Weidenfeld & Nicolson, 1977; New York: Macmillan, 1977);

Spillington and the Whitewash Clowns, illustrated by Rosemary Bullens (Leeds: Papper Press, 1981);

Writers and Their Work: Somerset Maugham (Windsor: Profile, 1982).

OTHER: "W. S. Maugham's *Cakes and Ale*," in *Notes on Literature,* 12 (London: British Council, n.d.);

Ernest W. Hornung, *Raffles the Amateur Cracksman,* edited with an introduction by Curtis (London: Chatto & Windus, 1972);

The Rise and Fall of the Matinee Idol: Past Deities of Stage and Screen, Their Roles, Their Magic, and Their Worshippers, edited, with an introduction, by Curtis (London: Weidenfeld & Nicolson, 1974);

Terence Rattigan, *Collected Plays,* edited, with an introduction, by Curtis (London: Eyre Methuen, 1982);

Henry James, *The Aspern Papers and The Turn of the Screw,* edited, with an introduction, by Curtis (London: Penguin, 1984);

Rattigan, *Collected Plays II,* edited, with an introduction, by Curtis (London: Eyre Methuen, 1985);

W. Somerset Maugham: The Critical Heritage, edited, with an introduction, by Curtis and John Whitehead (London: Routledge & Kegan Paul, 1987);

"Larkin's Oxford," in *Larkin: The Man and His Work,* edited by Dale Salwak (London: Macmillan, 1989), pp. 7–17;

Anthony Curtis

"I Blame Lord Reith: Sex and Broadcasting," in *Ariel at Bay: Reflections on Broadcasting and the Arts,* edited by Robert Carver (Manchester: Carcanet, 1990);

W. Somerset Maugham, *The Razor's Edge,* edited, with an introduction, by Curtis (New York: Penguin, 1992);

Maugham, *Short Stories,* selected by Curtis (London: Minerva, 1994).

Anthony Curtis was born on 12 March 1926 in London to Eileen and Emanuel Curtis. Educated at The Hall School, Hampstead, and Midhurst

Grammar School in Sussex, he entered Merton College, Oxford, on a postmastership (scholarship) in 1944, where he did a six-month short course in history. In 1945 he joined the Royal Air Force, becoming a clerk at the Air Ministry before returning to Oxford in 1948 to read English. Awarded the Chancellor's Prize for an English essay on the subject of "Fancy," he earned a first-class honors degree from the School of English in 1950.

He spent the following year lecturing at the Institut Britannique de la Sorbonne in Paris, after which he became deputy editor of the *Times Literary Supplement* from 1952 to 1959. A Harkness Fellowship in journalism in 1959 enabled Curtis to study American literary criticism at Columbia University, Yale University, and the Huntington Library in California. In 1960 he helped found the *Sunday Telegraph* newspaper in London, serving as its first literary editor until 1970, when he became literary editor of the *Financial Times* for two decades. Retiring as editor in 1990, he remained with the *Financial Times* as one of its literary correspondents. In these positions, and through broadcasts on radio and television in Great Britain, he has established a reputation as one of Britain's best-known book reviewers and drama critics. Married to Sarah Myers in 1960, Curtis has three sons.

It was dramatic literature – the plays of Jean-Paul Sartre, Simone de Beauvoir, Albert Camus, and Jean Anouilh – that became the subject of Curtis's first book, a short pamphlet called *New Developments in the French Theatre* (1948). Examining representative works of these four existentialist playwrights, he argues that they dramatize man "achieving his liberty through making a free choice which becomes the assertion of a right" – *right* meaning the action that results from any choice that is made in absolute freedom. This drama, he says, is both relevant to a world in an age of violence and related to the great French classical drama of the seventeenth century.

In 1974 Curtis edited a book of popular culture, *The Rise and Fall of the Matinee Idol*. The same year, to celebrate the centenary of the birth of William Somerset Maugham, he published *The Pattern of Maugham: A Critical Portrait*. The subsequent addition of two further books on the prolific English writer, an edition of criticism and reviews, and introductions to two of his novels, have made Curtis one of the leading authorities on Maugham and his writing. While none of his works can be considered a full-scale biography, his approach has always been to place the writing within the context of its author's life and times, and in doing so he creates a

Dust jacket for the English edition of Curtis's critical work published in 1974 to mark the centenary of the birth of the British novelist, short-story writer, and playwright

useful and informative portrait of the man and the writer.

The Pattern of Maugham is a general survey, which, though articulate, balanced, and comprehensive, is of the sort that had already been done by Richard Cordell and Laurence Brander, but Curtis adds his own insights. Moving confidently through the literary and cultural history of late nineteenth- and early twentieth-century England, he is able to place his subject against the movements and atmosphere of his time more fruitfully than others have done. This is especially evident in the chapters dealing with Maugham's early career as a novelist and playwright, where interesting connections are made with George Gissing, William Makepeace Thackeray, Thomas Hardy, A. E. Housman, H. G. Wells, Arthur Wing Pinero, J. M. Barrie, and many other literary figures. Gissing in particular is identified as a formative influence, no-

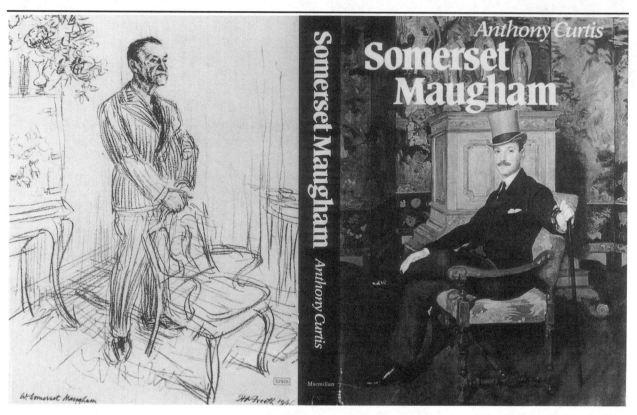

Dust jacket for the American edition of Curtis's biography of the British writer whose work he calls "the most perfect expression of the art of narrative in our literature"

tably in such early Maugham novels as *The Hero* (1901) and *The Merry-Go-Round* (1904).

The most original contribution of *The Pattern of Maugham* to an understanding of the man is its reading of the many Maugham plays constructed around female characters. Against the commonly held view of the author as a misogynist, Curtis argues that he actually had a remarkable empathy with women and understood them better than any other playwright in the early part of this century. In play after play, Curtis writes, female characters are represented as having only one profession open to them – marriage – and in most cases the marriage is examined from the woman's point of view. Actresses fought to play the "dissatisfied women, heartless women, self-sacrificing women, Anglo-American women, and one mercy-killing maternal woman," and his fiction dealt with many independent females, most notably the delightfully liberated Rosie in *Cakes and Ale* (1930).

The Pattern of Maugham is a book of literary criticism grounded on biographical detail; Curtis's next book, *Somerset Maugham* (1977), is a biography that leans heavily on Maugham's literary creations for its verification. Here, he explains in the fore-

word, the reader who has enjoyed Maugham's writing might discover "in general terms where the fact ends and the fiction begins," and that out of the confusing mass of published material – prefaces, introductions, autobiographical essays, books, and the memoirs of others – there might emerge "a broadbrush portrait of the writer and his world." Missing in all this are references to the several thousand Maugham letters held in various libraries and archives on both sides of the Atlantic, and to any significant material gained from interviews with those who knew him.

At the time of writing *Somerset Maugham,* Curtis was prevented by law from using unpublished Maugham materials and confronted by the silence of many of the author's friends and relatives. Maugham had always discouraged potential biographers, and his will instructed his literary executor, Spencer Curtis Brown, not to cooperate with anyone attempting to write his life. His daughter, Lady Glendevon, having had a horrible public battle with her father in his final, senile years, naturally did not wish to see their painful estrangement exposed in detail. Both Brown and Lady Glendevon later abandoned their objections to a biography in the face of

Ted Morgan's determination to publish one in 1980, but in 1977 Curtis could do little but honor the terms of Maugham's will.

Though forced to examine Maugham's life primarily from the outside, Curtis's judicious and informed reading of published materials provides a thoughtful and perceptive interpretation. He vividly evokes time and place: the privileged life of young "Willie" in Paris in the 1870s, the emotional bleakness of his orphan years in Whitstable, the bullied schoolboy experience of King's School in Canterbury, and the later ambience of his luxurious villa in the south of France. Curtis sets his subject in these and many other milieus and reconstructs the development of his temperament and personality. Maugham, he points out, was a late arrival in his family and went from a protective, loving family in France to the isolation of an austere vicarage in Kent, where he was humiliated by being under the will of a cold and parsimonious uncle. School failed to remove this isolation, and his stammer, translated fictionally into a clubfoot in *Of Human Bondage* (1915), sharpened his sense of separateness. Here, argues Curtis, the young Maugham developed his acute insight into human nature and his skill with language, as well as a weakness for being gripped by possessive and exclusive attachments.

Curtis analyzes Maugham's early attempts at writing not only as a product of his reading of the French naturalists and English realists, but of his medical training in London. He traces the source of one of Maugham's lifelong disappointments – his lack of acceptance as a writer of stature by the intelligentsia – to the period when he began to write for the popular theater rather than for the more avant-garde Stage Society. Behind *Of Human Bondage,* he says, lay the need of a man then professionally well established and financially secure "to go more deeply into the causes of his peculiar sense of alienation from life in the midst of so much prosperity, to follow his own emotional and intellectual progress throughout those early years with great but not absolute fidelity to fact."

Shortly after *Of Human Bondage* was published, Maugham married the socialite Syrie Barnardo Wellcome because, in Curtis's view, he wanted the appearance of social conformity, respectability, and normality of marriage. Never happy together, they were divorced in 1929, and Curtis shrewdly points out that Maugham's first literary work after the wedding, *The Moon and Sixpence* (1919), was about a man escaping a marriage by going to the South Seas. For Maugham, the period from 1918 to 1928 saw produced some of his finest work, though he

was personally torn between conventional life in London and travel to the Far East with his lover, Gerald Haxton. Frequently described in various memoirs in melodramatic terms, Haxton emerges in Curtis's book as an outgoing, extravagant, alcoholic rogue who appealed to a man himself restrained, private, and relatively orthodox. Curtis, moreover, dispels the myths that had grown up about Haxton's role in the author's professional life, demonstrating that Haxton could hardly have collected all the barroom tales that Maugham turned into his famous short stories.

Though Curtis writes at some length about the importance of Haxton in Maugham's life, some reviewers criticized the absence of any real explanation of the effect of Maugham's homosexuality on his life and his writing. Similarly, while the quarrel with his daughter is briefly summarized, it is not dealt with at any length or in any depth. On the other hand, Curtis correctly characterizes the final years as ones of introspection, of renewed interest in his roots in Whitstable and Canterbury, and of bitterness amidst the trappings of success.

In *The Pattern of Maugham,* Curtis had placed his subject in the second level of authors, below giants like Henry James, Marcel Proust, Leo Tolstoy, and Fyodor Dostoyevsky, but more comfortable to read because his work "seems to me to be the most perfect expression of the art of narrative in our literature." Despite being criticized by some reviewers for being too defensive about Maugham and by others for being too aggressive in his claims, he continued to offer this evaluation in *Somerset Maugham,* leading Richard Shone to observe in the *Spectator* that he would have been better to have kept to a simple account of the life and work rather than "pitting Maugham against the 'highbrows' thus doing himself and his subject a disservice."

In *Writers and Their Work: Somerset Maugham,* a pamphlet published in 1982, Curtis reformulates his judgment by suggesting that Maugham is a test case for measuring whether there can be a bridging of the gap between the popular and the serious reading publics. Maugham failed in the estimation of many serious modern readers, Curtis concludes, because, though he could describe surroundings, appearances, and material things, his prose lacked sensuousness. In his drama, this lack of richness in language was offset by a strong sense of dramatic form and timing. Curtis repeats his previous survey of early influences such as the realistic school, but he now stresses Maugham's recurring theme of the world well lost – a world, as in *The Moon and Sixpence,* thrown away not for love but for art, a vocation, or a commitment. Maugham's fiction, he concludes, presents parables "for people who no longer believe in God or in anything very much."

W. Somerset Maugham: The Critical Heritage (1987), coedited with John Whitehead, is constructed around a dialogue between critics alternately offering generous praise and caustic censure. In the process of selecting representative contemporary reactions to the author's work, Curtis and Whitehead reveal examples of the times that Maugham's treatment of sexual, religious, and class themes shocked audiences, readers, and reviewers. Moreover, this critical survey demonstrates that there was little relation between the themes of plays and novels being written at the same time, suggesting that Maugham saw his careers in fiction and drama as being almost entirely separate pursuits.

Curtis's introduction to the Penguin Twentieth-Century Classics edition of *The Razor's Edge* (1992) once again blends reworked material from his earlier studies with new critical and biographical com-

mentary. While demonstrating the genesis of the novel from the short story "The Fall of Edward Barnard" (1921) and the play "The Road Uphill" (1924), and arguing for the veracity of its portrayal of the interwar period of optimism and depression, he provides a biographical framework to both the writing of the work and to the creation of its characters. Wisely, he suggests that Maugham drew on traits from many people in shaping the protagonist, Larry Darrell, and the great triumph of the novel, Elliott Templeton.

Though not a biographer in the pure sense of one who pores over correspondence and unpublished manuscripts, and ferrets out endless small but significant details from obscure archives to produce a detailed, close-up picture, Curtis's contribution to an understanding of the complexity of Maugham is considerable. Moving easily and thoughtfully from the life to the writing and back again, he offers a portrait whose highlights tell us much about the man and his work.

Margaret Drabble

(4 June 1939 –   )

Valerie Grosvenor Myer
Cambridge University

See also the Drabble entry in *DLB 14: British Novelists Since 1960.*

BOOKS: *A Summer Bird-Cage* (London: Weidenfeld & Nicolson, 1963; New York: Morrow, 1963);

The Garrick Year (London: Weidenfeld & Nicolson, 1964; New York: Morrow, 1965);

The Millstone (London: Weidenfeld & Nicolson, 1964; New York: Morrow, 1966); published as *Thank You All Very Much* (New York: New American Library, 1969);

Wordsworth (London: Evans, 1966; New York: Arno, 1969);

Jerusalem the Golden (London: Weidenfeld & Nicolson, 1967; New York: Morrow, 1967);

The Waterfall (London: Weidenfeld & Nicolson, 1969; New York: Knopf, 1969);

The Needle's Eye (London: Weidenfeld & Nicolson, 1972; New York: Knopf, 1972);

Virginia Woolf: A Personal Debt (N.p.: Aloe Editions, 1973);

Arnold Bennett: A Biography (London: Weidenfeld & Nicolson, 1974; New York: Knopf, 1974);

The Realms of Gold (London: Weidenfeld & Nicolson, 1975; New York: Knopf, 1975);

The Ice Age (London: Weidenfeld & Nicolson, 1977; New York: Knopf, 1977);

For Queen and Country: Britain in the Victorian Age (London: Deutsch, 1978; New York: Seabury Press, 1979);

A Writer's Britain: Landscape in Literature (London: Thames & Hudson, 1979; New York: Knopf, 1979);

The Middle Ground (London: Weidenfeld & Nicolson, 1980; New York: Knopf, 1980);

The Tradition of Women's Fiction: Lectures in Japan (Tokyo: Oxford University Press, 1982);

The Radiant Way (London: Weidenfeld & Nicolson, 1987; New York: Knopf, 1987);

A Natural Curiosity (London: Viking, 1989; New York: Viking, 1989);

Margaret Drabble (photograph by Mark Gerson)

The Gates of Ivory (London: Viking, 1991; New York: Viking, 1992);

Angus Wilson: A Biography (London: Secker & Warburg, 1995).

PLAY PRODUCTION: *Bird of Paradise,* London, 1969.

MOTION PICTURE: *A Touch of Love* (adapted from *The Millstone*), screenplay by Drabble, Amicus Films, 1969.

TELEVISION: *Laura,* play, script by Drabble, BBC, 1964;

Isadora, script by Drabble, Melvyn Bragg, and Clive Exton, BBC, 1969.

OTHER: "Hassan's Tower," in *Winter's Tales 12,* edited by A. D. Maclean (London: Macmillan / New York: St. Martin's Press, 1966), pp. 41–59;

"The Reunion," in *Winter's Tales 14,* edited by Kevin Crossley-Holland (London: Macmillan / New York: St. Martin's Press, 1968), pp. 149–168; revised as "Faithful Lovers," *Saturday Evening Post* (6 April 1968): 62, 64–65;

"Crossing the Alps," in *Penguin Modern Stories 3* (Harmondsworth: Penguin, 1969), pp. 63–85;

"The Gifts of War," in *Winter's Tales 16,* edited by Maclean (London: Macmillan / New York: St. Martin's Press, 1970), pp. 20–36;

London Consequences, edited by Drabble and B. S. Johnson (London: Greater London Arts Association, 1972);

Jane Austen, Lady Susan/The Watsons/Sanditon, edited by Drabble (Harmondsworth: Penguin, 1974);

The Genius of Thomas Hardy, edited by Drabble (London: Weidenfeld & Nicolson, 1975; New York: Knopf, 1976);

New Stories 1, edited by Drabble and Charles Osborne (London: Arts Council, 1976);

Emily Brontë, Wuthering Heights, introduction by Drabble (London: Dent, 1978; New York: Dutton, 1979), pp. v–xxii;

Frieda Lawrence, *Not I, But the Wind,* introduction by Drabble (London: Granada, 1983), pp. vi–xii;

"Novelists as Inspired Gossips," in *People: Essays and Poems,* edited by Susan Hill (London: Hogarth Press, 1983), pp. 43–48;

The Oxford Companion to English Literature, edited by Drabble and Jenny Stringer (London: Oxford University Press, 1985);

The May Anthology: The Oxford and Cambridge Short Story Anthology, edited by Ian Critchley and Adrian Woolfson, introduction by Drabble (Cambridge: Varsity Publications, 1992).

SELECTED PERIODICAL PUBLICATIONS – UNCOLLECTED: "The Month," *Twentieth Century,* 168 (1960): 73–78;

"Out and About: The Stratford Season, 1960," *Twentieth Century* (November 1960): 468–472;

"The Feast of Margaret Drabble," *Punch* (February 1964): 202–204;

"*Les Liaisons Dangereuses,*" *Punch* (28 October 1964): 646–648;

"My Next Husband," *Punch* (1 September 1965): 310–312;

"Margaret Drabble Talking about Discipline," Manchester *Guardian,* 10 January 1966, p. 6;

"A Touch of the Boasts," *Punch* (9 February 1966): 188–189;

"The Name Droppers: Meeting the Right People," *Punch* (8 February 1967): 196–198;

"The Fearful Fame of Arnold Bennett," London *Observer,* 11 May 1967, pp. 12–14;

"The Sexual Revolution," Manchester *Guardian,* 12 October 1967, p. 9;

"A Voyage to Cythera," *Mademoiselle* (December 1967): 98–99, 148–150;

"Women," *Listener* (4 April 1968): 425–426;

"A Pyrrhic Victory," *Nova* (July 1968): 80, 84, 86;

"Baffled! Margaret Drabble Stalks Uncomprehendingly Round the Mystery of Masculinity," *Punch* (24 July 1968): 122–124;

"Slipping into Debt," Manchester *Guardian,* 12 August 1968, p. 7;

"Denying the Natural: Margaret Drabble on Fostering," *Listener* (5 December 1968): 750–751;

"Letter to the Editor," *Times Literary Supplement* (5 June 1969): 612;

"Money as a Subject for the Novelist," *Times Literary Supplement* (24 July 1969): 792–793;

"Doris Lessing: Cassandra in a World Under Siege," *Ramparts,* 10 (January 1972): 50–54;

"Margaret Drabble on Virginia Woolf," *Harper's Bazaar and Queen* (September 1972): 90–91, 128; revised and reprinted in *Ms.* (November 1972): 68–70, 72, 121;

"Margaret Drabble on Children," London *Sunday Times,* 8 July 1973, p. 33;

"A Day in the Life of a Smiling Woman," *Cosmopolitan* (October 1973): 224, 252–257;

"The Writer as Recluse: The Theme of Solitude in the Works of the Brontës," *Brontë Society Transactions,* 16 (1974): 259–269;

"Once Again in the Dark," *New York Times,* 6 January 1974, p. 15;

"Midway Through Motherhood," *Parents' Magazine* (April 1974): 44–46;

"A Success Story," *Ms.* (December 1974): 52–55, 94;

"Arnold Wesker," *New Review,* 1 (February 1975): 25–30;

"Homework," *Cosmopolitan* (England) (November 1975): 192, 194, 196, 198;

"Jane Fonda: Her Own Woman at Last?," *Ms.* (October 1977): 51–53, 88–89;

"Rape and Reason," London *Observer,* 10 December 1978, p. 9; revised as "Thinking about Rape," *New York Times,* 21 January 1979, p. 21;

"C. P. Snow, 1905–1980," London *Sunday Times,* 6
    July 1980, p. 42;

"Pamela Hansford Johnson," London *Sunday Times,*
    21 June 1981, p. 42;

"Wildlife Observed: Zambia, the Heart of Sun-
    light," *Observer Magazine* (20 December 1981):
    19, 21–22;

"Mimesis: The Representation of Reality in the
    Post-War Novel," *MOSAIC,* 20 (1987): 1–14;

"Child Abuse: When a Public Enquiry is Not
    Enough," London *Sunday Telegraph,* 2 August
    1987, pp. 14–16.

Margaret Drabble anticipated the feminist
movement by writing early in her career about educated women's experiences of marriage and motherhood in conflict with career ambition. Her range
has widened as she has been translated into sixteen
languages and received honorary doctorates and
the rank of Commander of the British Empire
(1980), but her preoccupations remain constant, reflecting her nonconformist background of conscientious striving and her socialist convictions. She was
born on 4 June 1939 in Sheffield, an industrial town
in the north of England. Her roots are provincial,
not cosmopolitan, though now she lives in Hampstead, a wealthy and fashionable part of London, inhabited by what its detractors ironically label
"champagne socialists," the British equivalent of
"radical chic." Drabble was the middle daughter of
the late John and Marie Bloor Drabble, both first-
generation Cambridge students from fairly humble
backgrounds. Her father's parents owned a small
candy factory, and John Drabble left school early to
work. Eventually, however, he found his way to
Cambridge University, after which he became a
lawyer and then a judge. Her mother's parents were
grimly religious Methodists who tended toward
Calvinism: such characters recur in Drabble's fiction. The eldest Drabble daughter is Antonia Susan
Byatt, the novelist and critic, winner of the 1990
Booker Prize. Both sisters, Drabble and Byatt, have
confessed to fierce sibling rivalry, which seems to
have lasted into adulthood. The third daughter is
Dr. Helen Langdon, an art historian. The only son,
Richard, is a barrister. Drabble has frequently observed that the family configuration resembles that
of the Brontës, who also lived in the county of
Yorkshire, remote geographically and socially from
the metropolis. All three girls were privately educated at the Mount School, York, a Quaker boarding establishment for girls, before reading English at
Newham College, Cambridge. The Quaker emphasis on self-examination, on conscience, and on

*Drabble at her Hampstead home, 6 July 1974 (Hulton
Deutsch Collection)*

moral seriousness was reinforced by the Cambridge
English school, then under the influence of F. R.
Leavis. His authority over that particular generation of creative writers was inhibiting, as many of
them, including Drabble, have testified. They developed a nervous fear of not meeting his exacting
standards, but eventually they found courage. Margaret Drabble started writing when traditional British morals were in flux, and her early work investigates woman's rights and what happens when those
rights are in conflict with her family duties. The
problem was her own, but women readers found
she echoed their own feelings.

Drabble, hoping to become an actress, married
at twenty-one the actor Clive Swift, whom she met
at Cambridge. Drabble followed her husband to the
Theatre Royal, Stratford-upon-Avon, where she understudied Vanessa Redgrave and Judi Dench but
did not succeed. This experience is the background
to her second novel, *The Garrick Year* (1964). Be-

coming pregnant, to her dismay, during the first months of marriage, she was astonished, on giving birth, to find a child a source of deep joy. She turned to writing, aware that she had material largely unexplored in literature, and became the novelist of motherhood. Drabble's son Adam, later a Fellow of Balliol College, Oxford, was followed by a sister, Rebecca, and a brother, Joseph.

Drabble's first novel, *A Summer Bird-Cage* (1963), attracted attention, despite editorial interference that excised a portrait of a marriage to concentrate on the girl with the Oxford first-class honors who did not know what to do with herself. Drabble gained not merely first-class honors herself but a "starred first," the highest possible result. Like her heroine Sarah in *A Summer Bird-Cage,* she decided not to take a further degree: Sarah asserts it is impossible to be a sexy don. *The Garrick Year,* about a former model married to an actor – a mother of two small children and bored and frustrated – is admittedly a reflection of her own experience: "It contained a lot of undigested unhappiness," Drabble remarked in a 1977 interview. Emma has an unsatisfactory affair, discovers her husband's infidelity, and they are reconciled.

In 1974 she published her biography of Arnold Bennett, a writer from her own part of the world whom she felt had been unfairly denigrated by Virginia Woolf's accusation that Bennett, H. G. Wells, and John Galsworthy, the Edwardian novelists, were materialists, concerned with the body and not the spirit, writing of unimportant things. Drabble wonders whether Woolf suspected "the physical tension" that Bennett suffered: "did she . . . connect it with her own physical manifestations of neurosis? Both of them were highly strung, but his was the sensitivity of a deprived working-class child, not of an upper-class aesthete." Drabble in her own practice rejects the subjective, internal novel of Virginia Woolf along with the dramatically tight structure enjoined by Henry James: it was her intention to write "a loose, baggy monster" of the kind James condemned. In her introduction she writes that Bennett's best books are "deeply moving, original and dealing with material that I had never before encountered in fiction, but only in life": indeed, Bennett's fictional picture is so compelling as to have become confused with reality. Drabble was drawn to the subject of Bennett because she admired him as a writer. Having been brought up to believe that even his best books were not very good, she was surprised to find how enjoyable she found even his lesser works. She confesses that she wrote the biography in "a partisan spirit, as an act of ap-

preciation." She was attracted, too, by the similarity between Bennett's origins and her own. Drabble's mother's family came from the industrial district of the Potteries that Bennett wrote about, and Drabble and Bennett were both reared in the distinctive Methodist-influenced culture of northern England, different in style and atmosphere from the blander south. She admires Bennett's passion for self-education. The biography was for Drabble "an act of self-exploration," and it throws light on Drabble's own inheritance: she concentrates on the Wesleyan emphasis on willpower, hard work, discipline, and self-help, and the belief that idleness was wicked. The book contains much valuable social history, interwoven with sympathetic treatment of Bennett's psychology. As she wrote, her admiration for Bennett not only as a writer but as a human being grew: "He was an exceptionally kind, good and generous man, who triumphed over considerable difficulties in his personal life; he was the kind of reliable, sensitive and tactful person who would make an ideal friend." She regretted that within the scope of the biography she could not deal with as much of Bennett's work as she would have liked. She found that the millions of words in journals and letters forced her to select rigorously.

Later Drabble admitted to feeling embarrassed because when she embarked on the Bennett biography she had neither the time nor the money to travel in connection with it. She charts the constant influence on Bennett of French literature and French culture: Bennett eventually lived in France, but all his life he "liked to sleep alone, could not let himself go, could not share his bed." Drabble records the breakdown of Bennett's marriage and his meeting with Dorothy Cheston, who lived with him at the end and took his surname. Drabble interviewed her. Drabble's final conclusion is that Bennett is one of "the most readable and versatile of major novelists, a writer much more honest and lasting than Galsworthy, and much more perceptive, in many areas, than Wells."

A Writer's Britain: Landscape in Literature (1979) offers some distinguished commentary on landscape in literary history. Drabble draws on her mental map of past and present, conscious of William Shakespeare's "great creating nature" (*natura naturata*) as well as *natura naturans;* on William Wordsworth's influential idea of nature as therapeutic; and on the impact made on the imaginations of novelists by the industrial revolution and its irreversible changes. The conflict between the pragmatic utilitarianism of Jeremy Bentham and the vitalist, dynamic visions of Samuel Taylor Coleridge and Thomas Carlyle re-

*Dust jacket for the American edition of Drabble's biography
of the British writer she calls "the most readable and
versatile of major novelists"*

verberate through the work of novelists such as Charles Dickens and are still resonating through Drabble's, as the nineteenth-century conflict between science and religion becomes a conflict between economic growth and moral decisions on a human scale, between industry and environment. Knowledge of the Bible and Shakespeare and John Milton and John Bunyan are no longer living popular culture, but products of the Cambridge English school in the 1950s are rooted in them. Drabble's works are essentially English in that they are informed by earlier literature, by history, Protestantism, empiricism, and eclecticism: as well as hostility to the influence of Leavis, she has expressed gratitude for it, and she exemplifies his ideal of culture: literate, liberal, humane. *A Writer's Britain* is the best gloss on her own works, original in form and distinguished in its own right. For foreigners studying English literature it is an invaluable tool, providing a learned and sensitive context. The sheer range of quotation is astonishing: all the quotations from writers are based securely on their lives and circumstances, providing original insights. She writes with

particular delicacy about poetry, suggesting that Wordsworth "painted place as it had never been painted before, and connected it in new ways with man's thought processes and moral being." She admires him for his "*faith* . . . that every flower enjoys the air it breathes." She suspects that he drew such a response because he was "drawing on deep sources of collective feeling, on a primitive animistic view of the world, certainly present in earlier times, but powerfully suppressed by the scientific seventeenth and eighteenth centuries." It is these unacknowledged "collective feelings" that form the structural principle of her later novels, *The Radiant Way* (1987) and *A Natural Curiosity* (1989).

Her novel *The Middle Ground* was published in 1980. During the next five years Drabble was re-editing *The Oxford Companion to English Literature* (1985), in which she acknowledges the help of her children for working as "research assistants, chauffeurs, photocopy operators, and telephone answering machines." In 1982 Drabble had married biographer Michael Holroyd. She also acknowledges the invaluable assistance of Holroyd and confesses to having made "merciless use of his scholarship, his library and his goodwill, all of which are remarkable."

In 1995 Drabble published *Angus Wilson: A Biography*. Drabble had compelling reasons for undertaking the biography of Sir Angus Wilson: early "addiction" to his work and later close personal friendship. Together with playwright Nell Dunn and poet Christopher Logue, Drabble and Wilson traveled together through Britain in 1969 on an Arts Council Writers' Tour. Drabble was interested in exploring the connections between life and work in a writer whose novels she knew well and who had greatly influenced her. "His was a brave life, which transformed pain, despair and disorder into art. He himself subscribed to a belief in the creative wound." He was the first contemporary writer she "discovered for myself." She was excited by the wit and authority with which he wrote about – high life and low life," redefining for Drabble, along with Simone de Beauvoir, the "post-war post-Freudian map," and demonstrating that it was "still possible to write a great novel," about the here and now. She writes with some bitterness that "the universities in the 1940s and 50s were intent on bringing literature to an end at the end of the nineteenth century."

The biography refrains from literary criticism and stylistic analysis, though it uses fiction to illumine the remarkable life and vice-versa, and draws on Wilson's own account of his imaginative wellsprings, *The Wild Garden* (1963). Drabble describes Wilson's insecure, shabby-genteel childhood, spent flitting from hotel to hotel and often in debt, a background reflected in his work, which deals with "society hostesses and rent boys, . . . civil servants and television personalities, . . . nightclub pianists and blackmailers and leftwing progressives and women on the edge of a nervous breakdown." Two of Wilson's brothers became male prostitutes.

An active member of the Labour Party, originally Wilson was an admirer of E. M. Forster, but Drabble records Wilson's increasing dissatisfaction with Forster's rentier world and its implicit snobbishness. Wilson openly acknowledged his companion, secretary, cook, and chauffeur, Tony Garrett, and blamed Forster for concealing a similar relationship, when he could have struck a blow for reform. (Homosexual relations did not become legal in Britain till 1967.)

Drabble describes in detail the breadth of Wilson's interests and his research methods (he read history at Oxford and worked on decoding enemy signals during the war). He corresponded with Fred Warburg about steroids, with Sir Solly

Zuckerman about pesticides and population, with Forrest Fulton about electron microscopes, Patrick Woodcock and neurologist Roger Gilliatt about cortisone, Kazu Serikawa (his Japanese translator) about Japanese revolutionary students and Yukio Mishima's followers, Nadine Gordimer about African legends, Patrick White about Australian homosexual novels, and studied protein plant breeding papers from Sweden, Hinduism, mesmerism, and St. Francis Xavier. "Each book was preceded by months of planning, and the passages of high-speed and quick-fire wit were the result of much thinking and rethinking."

Wilson's work had a high reputation among intellectuals but never sold well enough for him to be financially secure. Critical works have been written by J. L. Halio in America and Peter Faulkner in England. Wilson's later years were spent as professor at the new University of East Anglia and lecturing worldwide, especially in America, though he was gloomily convinced that other people were invited to the glamorous universities, while he and Garrett were stuck with the duller ones. After his retirement, when he became professor emeritus, he and Garrett moved to France, which was a mistake. Drabble charts sympathetically and with tact Wilson's failing physical and mental health, when he was a pensioner of the Royal Literary Fund.

Drabble's own research is exhaustive: as well as her own account of meetings and parties, she has provided a family tree going back to 1775, conducted numerous interviews with relatives and friends and examined letters and diaries. The book has full scholarly apparatus and includes an outline by Wilson of *No Laughing Matter,* which Drabble considers his most important novel. In the *Literary Review* (June 1995) A. N. Wilson calls Drabble's book a "magisterial biography" and "a labour of love for a writer whom she deeply appreciates and admires."

Phyllis Rose writes in *The New York Times Book Review* (7 September 1980) that Drabble is "the chronicler of contemporary Britain, the novelist people will turn to in a hundred years from now to find out what things were like, the person who will have done for late twentieth-century London what Dickens did for Victorian London, what Balzac did for Paris." Drabble has served on various important committees, including the literature panel of the Arts Council; toured schools to talk about literature; and traveled the world. She appears regularly on television and is a frequent contributor to newspapers as a reviewer and feature writer.

Interviews:

Nancy S. Hardin, "An Interview with Margaret Drabble," in *Contemporary Literature,* 14, no. 3 (1973): 273–295; reprinted in *Interviews with Contemporary Writers,* second series, 1972–1982, edited by L. S. Dembo (Madison: University of Wisconsin Press, 1983), pp. 89–111;

Nancy Poland, "Margaret Drabble: 'There must be a lot of people like me,' " *Midwest Quarterly,* 16 (Spring 1975): 255–267;

"Margaret Drabble in Conversation with Valerie Grosvenor Myer," Tape No. RI 2007 (London: British Council, 1977);

Mel Gussow, "Margaret Drabble: A Double Life," *New York Times Book Review,* 9 October 1977, pp. 7, 40–41;

Diana Cooper-Clark, "Margaret Drabble: Cautious Feminist," *Atlantic Monthly* (November 1980): 69–75; reprinted in *Critical Essays on Margaret Drabble,* edited by Ellen Cronan Rose (Boston: G. K. Hall, 1985), pp. 19–30;

Margaret Forster, "What Makes Margaret Drabble Run and Run," Manchester *Guardian,* 28 February 1981, p. 9;

Joanne V. Creighton, "An Interview with Margaret Drabble," in *Margaret Drabble: Golden Realms,* edited by Dorey Schmidt (Edinburg, Tex.: Pan American University, 1982), pp. 18–31;

Gillian Parker and Janet Todd, "Margaret Drabble," in *Women Writers Talking,* edited by Todd (New York: Holmes & Meier, 1983), pp. 160–178;

Olga Kenyon, *Women Writers Talk: Interviews with Women Writers* (Oxford: Lennard, 1989), pp. 25–52.

Bibliographies:

Joan S. Korenman, in *Critical Essays on Margaret Drabble,* edited by Ellen Cronan Rose (Boston: G. K. Hall, 1985), pp. 181–202;

Joan Garret Packer, *Margaret Drabble: An Annotated Bibliography* (New York: Garland, 1988).

References:

Joanne V. Creighton, *Margaret Drabble* (London & New York: Methuen, 1985);

Mary Hurley Moran, *Margaret Drabble: Existing Within Structures* (Carbondale: Southern Illinois University Press, 1983);

Valerie Grosvenor Myer, *Margaret Drabble: A Reader's Guide* (London: Vision, 1991; New York: St. Martin's Press, 1991).

Myer, *Margaret Drabble: Puritanism and Permissiveness* (London: Vision, 1974; Totowa, N. J.: Barnes & Noble, 1974);

Ellen Cronan Rose, *The Novels of Margaret Drabble: Equivocal Figures* (London: Macmillan, 1980);

Rose, ed., *Critical Essays on Margaret Drabble* (Boston: G. K. Hall, 1985);

Lynn Veach Sadler, *Margaret Drabble* (Boston: Twayne, 1986);

Dorey Schmidt, ed., *Margaret Drabble: Golden Realms,* Living Author Series 4 (Edinburg, Tex.: Pan American University School of Humanities, 1982).

Margaret Forster

(25 May 1938 –   )

David Bordelon
Queens College, City University of New York

BOOKS: *Dames Delight* (London: Cape, 1964);

Georgy Girl (London: Berkley, 1965);

The Bogeyman (London: Putnam, 1965; New York: Putnam, 1966);

The Travels of Maudie Tipstaff (London: Stein & Day, 1967);

The Park (London: Secker & Warburg, 1968);

Miss Owen-Owen Is at Home (London: Secker & Warburg, 1969); published as *Miss Owen-Owen* (New York: Simon & Schuster, 1969);

Fenella Phizackerley (London: Secker & Warburg, 1970; New York: Simon & Schuster, 1970);

Mr. Bone's Retreat (London: Secker & Warburg, 1971; New York: Simon & Schuster, 1971);

The Rash Adventurer: The Rise and Fall of Charles Edward Stuart (London: Stein & Day, 1973; New York: Stein & Day, 1974);

The Seduction of Mrs. Pendlebury (London: Secker & Warburg, 1974);

William Makepeace Thackeray: Memoirs of a Victorian Gentleman (London: Secker & Warburg, 1978); published as *Memoirs of a Victorian Gentleman: William Makepeace Thackeray* (New York: Morrow, 1978);

Mother Can You Hear Me? (London: Secker & Warburg, 1979);

The Bride of Lowther Fell: A Romance (London: Secker & Warburg, 1980; New York: Atheneum, 1980);

Marital Rites (London: Secker & Warburg, 1981; New York: Atheneum, 1982);

Significant Sisters: The Grassroots of Active Feminism 1839–1939 (London: Secker & Warburg, 1984; New York: Knopf, 1985);

Private Papers (London: Chatto & Windus, 1986);

Elizabeth Barrett Browning: A Biography (London: Chatto & Windus, 1988; New York: Doubleday, 1989);

Have the Men Had Enough? (London: Chatto & Windus, 1989);

Margaret Forster

Lady's Maid (London: Chatto & Windus, 1990); published as *Lady's Maid: A Novel of the Nineteenth Century* (New York: Doubleday, 1991);

The Battle for Christabel (London: Chatto & Windus, 1991);

Daphne du Maurier (London: Chatto & Windus, 1993); published as *Daphne du Maurier: The Secret Life of the Renowned Storyteller* (New York: Doubleday, 1993);

Mothers' Boys (London: Chatto & Windus, 1994);

Hidden Lives (London: Viking, 1995).

SCREENPLAY: *Georgy Girl,* by Forster and Peter Nichols, Columbia, 1966.

OTHER: *Drawn From Life: The Journalism of William Makepeace Thackeray,* selected, with an introductory essay, by Forster (London: Folio Society, 1984);

Selected Poems of Elizabeth Barrett Browning, selected, with an introductory essay, by Forster (London: Chatto & Windus, 1988); published as *Elizabeth Barrett Browning: Selected Poems* (Baltimore: Johns Hopkins University Press, 1988).

SELECTED PERIODICAL PUBLICATIONS – UNCOLLECTED: "Gossip," *Sunday Times,* 4 January 1976, p. 33;

"Margaret Forster is Now Forty . . . ," *Sunday Times,* 24 September 1978, p. 44;

"80 Memorable Years," *Sunday Times Magazine,* 3 August 1980, p. 12;

"This Is Sort of Your Life, Mary Wollstonecraft," review of *Vindication,* by Frances Sherwood, *New York Times Book Review,* 11 July 1993, p. 21.

Margaret Forster, who began her literary career writing fiction, brings to her biographies the dramatic sensibilities of a novelist as well as the analytic insight of a historian. Her biographies, including books on William Makepeace Thackeray, Elizabeth Barrett Browning, and Daphne du Maurier, are extensions of her fiction: Forster considers both realms of experimentation where techniques of narrative, characterization, and point of view are used, as she notes in a 1992 letter, to "catch the essence of the person and the spirit of their times." She employs these techniques whether the "person" is a character in a novel or the subject of a biography.

Forster was born in Carlisle, Cumberland, England, on 25 May 1938; her parents, Arthur Gordon, a mechanic, and Lilian Hind Forster, a housewife, provided Forster with a working-class upbringing. Though her parents seemed content and Forster cared for both of them, she nonetheless felt that her mother's ambitions had been thwarted by her domestic life; with her "intelligence and grace" Lilian provided a suitable home for her family but

in the process lost her sense of purpose and direction in life. Her mother's fate compelled Forster to pursue a different life. Looking back on her life at age forty, Forster noted that "from the cradle" she was "cautious, careful, conscientious, staid and self-righteous. I always saw the consequences and looked ahead and worried." While these attributes seem rather precocious in a child, they explain both her desire for a different life than her mother and her means of escape. For Forster this realization, in part, provided the initial stirring of feminism that would eventually find its most articulated response in the subjects of her later biographies.

Viewing education as a "gateway" leading her away from a similar life of domesticity, Forster developed an early interest in literature, especially the novels of Charles Dickens and the Brontë sisters. Although this feeling was not nurtured or shared by either her parents or siblings – the house was without books – Forster developed into a "voracious reader," which in turn led to an early desire to write. In a 1992 letter explaining her literary ambitions, she connects reading and writing: "What made me want [to write] was reading: reading truly inspired me to write, gave me the feeling that *I* could do this . . . one excitement of pleasure bred another."

Demonstrating an early proclivity for learning, Forster received a scholarship from Carlisle and County High School for girls in 1949 and then in 1957 a scholarship to Somerville College, Oxford. Although drawn to literature, Forster chose to read in history instead of English primarily because the English reading list ended in the nineteenth century. Though she describes herself as a desultory student, this early exposure to and focus on the analytic approach required for history might explain her predilection for detailed examination of character in her fiction and her later interest in biography. Additionally, the study of history, with its emphasis on research and cause-and-effect relationships, provided her with the necessary tools and strategies of a biographer.

After receiving a B.A. in 1960, Forster married Hunter Davies, a journalist she had known since they were both teenagers. Settling in London, they raised three children, Caitlan, Jake, and Flora. Interestingly, considering her view of her mother's life, Forster has often remarked that she enjoys a domestic role and takes pride and pleasure in never having employed a maid or nanny: as she noted in a 1993 interview, "I love being in charge of my own house." She attributes this to a "northern working-class feeling"; and this "feeling," or sympathy for working-class values, is apparent in her biographies as well.

Unlike many literary biographers, Forster has no affiliations with schools or universities. Although she taught from 1961 until 1963 at Barnsbury Girls' School in London, Forster has always concentrated on writing instead of teaching. Interested in not only informing but also entertaining the reader, her crisp prose style and strong sense of narrative make her biographies more engaging than works geared toward a strictly academic audience. While this approach has upset some critics, most have applauded her efforts to make literary biography more accessible and widen its audience.

Forster published her first novel, *Dames Delight,* in 1964. Her next novel, *Georgy Girl* (1965), was adapted with Peter Nichols into a screenplay and movie in 1966. A best-seller, *Georgy Girl* effectively launched her writing career and established her as a writer of popular fiction. A series of novels followed: *The Bogeyman* (1965), *The Travels of Maudie Tipstaff* (1967), *The Park* (1968), *Miss Owen-Owen Is at Home* (1969), *Fenella Phizackerley* (1970), and *Mr. Bone's Retreat* (1971) – all, as the nominal nature of the titles suggest, with a focus on character. Although she dismisses her early novels – referring to them in a 1967 interview as "third rate" – they exhibit many traits reflected in her biographies: a strong interest in character, a clear, unadorned prose style, and an interest in experimentation – particularly with point of view. Ascribing this penchant toward experimentation as a response to boredom, she told a 1967 interviewer that "Each [novel] I do has to be different or I get bored." But it also seems to reflect a deeper desire to push at the limits of a genre and challenge accepted doctrines, a desire she fulfilled in her biographies.

In an interview just prior to the publication of her first biography, *The Rash Adventurer: The Rise and Fall of Charles Edward Stuart* (1973), Forster suggests that the judgment by reviewers of her novels as "cold and analytical" led her to try a new field. But a 1976 article she wrote on gossip for the London *Sunday Times* offers an insight into her preoccupation with character and helps explain her shift in genre. Real gossip, she writes, "reveals traits of character or facets of [a person's] life that I would otherwise have no means of knowing." This curiosity, or "need" to learn the hidden tidbits of information that make up a person's life, is a more personal, and perhaps more honest, explanation of her interest in biography. The shift from fiction to nonfiction is a move toward a more heightened form of gossip: gossip based on fact, not rumor.

In *The Rash Adventurer* Forster aims "to fill the gap between a definitive history and a historical novel." She believes the two genres are interrelated and in fact feels that "the similarity [between the two] is more important" than the differences. For Forster the difference between a character in fiction and the subject of a biography is a shift from imagination governed by character, to imagination governed by fact. *The Rash Adventurer* departs from other works on the "Pretender" in its focus on Prince Charles's character as opposed to his political intrigues. Forster admits that "I wanted to write about Charles Edward, not Jacobite history. It is his dilemma as a man, not his place in history, that attracts me." For Forster, Stuart is not interesting because of his failure to regain the throne but for a much more personal and more emotional reason: "Here was a man groomed for stardom who performed in blazing limelight for two short years and then was yanked off the stage protesting all the way. What does this kind of rejection do to a man?" To answer this question Forster, while addressing the campaign to regain the throne, concentrates on "the forty-three years after 1745 [that] did not fit in with the legend" of the "Bonnie Prince." Forster revises the myth of a dashing, romantic, and ultimately tragic prince and replaces it with a portrait of a man lost in self-admiration and oblivious to the world around her. She ultimately concludes that "the years after 1745 show him disintegrating fast as an admirable person not because he was either weak or wicked but because failure was totally unacceptable to him. Failure soured him, failure panicked him, failure pushed him into actions which in his successful days he would have been bitterly ashamed of." Her critique is not based on his political aspirations, but on his moral character, and Forster, perhaps to the dismay of some critics, refuses to separate and judge the two independently.

Antonia Fraser, reviewing the book in the London *Sunday Times* (7 October 1973), praises its "accomplished mixture of skillful narrative and psychological insight" as well as Forster's concentration on Stuart's personality instead of the political ramifications of his actions. The elements to which Fraser objects, Forster's relaxed prose and judgmental tone, are elements that another reviewer, R. R. Rea, admires. Writing in the *Library Journal* (1 April 1974), Rea praises Forster's "light vernacular style" and notes that "the romantic tale of Bonny Prince Charlie has seldom been told [so] frankly and honestly." This concentration on the character and personality of her subjects combined with an accessible writing style are the two elements of her work that mark a dividing line for critics. She is either praised for her intellectual honesty and clear voice or criticized for her lack of objectivity and casual style.

After the publication of a novel, *The Seduction of Mrs. Pendlebury,* in 1974, Forster began research on a biography of William Makepeace Thackeray. Long an admirer of his work, she at first planned on writing a conventional biography similar to her book on Charles Stuart. But after delving into his letters and journals, Forster felt that she had to respect Thackeray's injunction against a biography of his life. Of course this posed a dilemma: how could she write about his life yet remain true to his request? Her answer lay in an approach that would combine Forster's talent as a novelist with her historical insight and would satisfy her desire for experimentation: a fictional autobiography. Through Forster, Thackeray becomes the writer of his posthumous "memoir," becoming, in *William Makepeace Thackeray: Memoirs of a Victorian Gentleman* (1978), a character in his own life.

This playful approach to biography, with its conflation of fictional/real and character/person, lends a distinctly postmodern flair to the book. Conscious of the futility of achieving objectivity, Forster abandons the attempt and instead concentrates on bringing her subject to life. By figuratively resuscitating Thackeray, Forster allows him to "write" a book after being dead for more than one hundred years. The "author" of this text is definitely dead – even at the time of composition – and Forster's text raises the same types of questions about objectivity and the status of the author posed by literary theorists such as Michel Foucault and Roland Barthes.

Forster realized that critics might object to the lack of objectivity inherent in her approach. She directly addresses this in an afterword to the book by acknowledging that "no [biography] written solely from Thackeray's point of view could be unprejudiced." But instead of seeing this as a liability, she uses it to achieve a more Thackerayan voice; it was only by shedding the biographer's cloak of objectivity that Forster felt that both Thackeray's injunction against biography and her desire to write a biography could be reconciled. In fact, she took the extreme position (for a biographer) of deciding that she "had no desire to know how far Thackeray was telling the truth about himself." However, this did not mean that she invented any details in the book. Forster takes pains to make it clear that though the "memoir" is indeed fictional, every incident, no matter how seemingly trivial, is based on material

Forster in 1974 (Hulton Deutsch)

she gleaned from his writings. She notes that "if Thackeray says in my book that he admired some dressing-gowns in Paris then he will have said somewhere in his letters or diaries that he did. If he had a picnic at Watford, then it is because he has mentioned one." Thus, her inventive impulse is continually reined in by the restrictions of fact: fiction is always bumping up against reality, and even in this, her most experimental biography, reality prevails.

In her afterword Forster argues that Thackeray himself would have approved of her unorthodox approach. She notes that he felt that "out of the fictitious book I get the expression of the life of the time; of the manner, of the movement, the dress, the pleasure, the laughter, the ridicules of society." Through her skills as a novelist Forster transforms the bare facts surrounding Thackeray into, as she labels it, an "expression of life."

As Forster anticipated, critical opinion of such a hybrid form of biography was mixed. Many reviewers objected to the narrow focus and subjectivity of the biography. In addition, the lack of notes or bibliography left some critics uncomfortable with the veracity of the text. Edgar Johnson, writing for

The New York Times (6 May 1979), objects to Forster's subjectivity and indifference toward Thackeray's literary works. But even with these objections, Johnson acknowledges that Forster accomplishes what he interprets as her primary goals, "conveying Thackeray's personality" and illustrating Thackeray's "long and unhappy" love affair with Jane Brookfield.

John Carey, reviewing the book in the *Sunday Times* (24 September 1978), peremptorily dismisses Forster's style, commenting that Thackeray now has "a whole autobiography to be dull in." Judging the book by its imitation of Thackeray's voice, he feels that it falls conspicuously short of the original. But J. I. M. Stewart takes a different view of Forster's voice. In contrast to Carey, he writes in the *Times Literary Supplement* (29 September 1978) that "the tone is undoubtedly Thackeray's" and praises her adaptation of Thackeray's style. Unlike other critics who were uncomfortable with the book's hybrid approach, Stewart does not judge Forster's method; instead, he judges the result. While noting that her approach seems "bizarre," he writes that "Miss Forster has provided Thackeray with a colorable and entertaining autobiography on a generous scale. It is a remarkable performance, and persuasive as soon as we have accepted the novelist as a kind of relaxed Ancient Mariner, holding us button-holed by the hour, but in an agreeably modest and self-deprecating way."

For Stewart and others the voice of Thackeray speaks from the pages of the biography – and that is crucial to its success. If the voice were not convincing, the project would, in effect, fall on its face. As Forster maintains in the afterword, her purpose was to make Thackeray "live"; by simulating the informal, colloquial style of his journals, diaries, and letters, and by subordinating her own style in a conscious effort to mimic Thackeray's, she accomplishes this difficult task. Although at times snippets of Thackeray's own writings appear, Forster weaves them into the fabric of the book, subverting her voice to create a cogent and believable Thackerayan narrator.

The story of Thackeray's life, illustrated throughout with his own sketches, unfolds in a series of vignettes. The incidents of his life are roughly grouped around what Forster presumes to be the major events of his life: early loss of wealth; marriage, children, and relationship with his wife; success of *Vanity Fair* (1848); his unrequited love for Jane Brookfield; life as lecturer; and, finally, life as respected literary lion and editor. In particular, Forster's decision to center Thackeray's life on

"happenings" rather than his works (the narrator comments, "I shan't let this become a catalogue of all my literary efforts – how weary you would grow if I did") fulfills her ambition to create a portrait of Thackeray the man rather than Thackeray the writer. Here, as in *The Rash Adventurer,* she is more interested in her subject's character than his deeds.

Through Forster's description of these events, Thackeray's character is fleshed out. His impulsive and obsessive nature, shown by his outbursts of anger and his behavior toward the Brookfields, is illustrated with more vigor and emotion than a standard biography. Since Thackeray is literally dramatized, Forster can let his "actions" subtly prove her point. Forster does not use explicit cause-and-effect relationships to prove her arguments; rather, her idiosyncratic approach lets readers interpret Thackeray's life for themselves. The structure of the book allows the narrator to reflect, "The truth is, I am sometimes governed by overwhelming impulses which I must follow or suffer appallingly from frustration." Since the conceit of Thackeray as a narrator is convincing, these revelations have the ring of truth and help create a fully realized character.

Based on a fictional, nonobjective approach, the biography did not affect scholarly opinion of Thackeray, yet its inventive approach and readability brought his life to a broad audience and helped widen the limits of biographical interpretations. It proved that biography can retain its veracity yet revel in the experimental qualities of fiction and address questions of objective authority posed by contemporary literary theory.

In 1984, after the novels *Mother Can You Hear Me?* (1979), *The Bride of Lowther Fell: A Romance* (1980), and *Marital Rites* (1981), a collection of Thackeray's journalism edited by Forster entitled *Drawn From Life: The Journalism of William Makepeace Thackeray* was published. Like *William Makepeace Thackeray,* the collection was aimed toward a general audience, and thus Forster's editorial goal was not (as might be expected given Thackeray's literary reputation) to complement his literary works or to offer a representation of his literary criticism, but an attempt to illustrate the range of his talents and sympathies. For Forster, the book represents a "highly personal selection," which purports to "demonstrate that Thackeray was the most *versatile* journalist there has ever been." The selections in the book range from social concerns ("Going to See a Man Hanged") to travel literature ("A Mississippi Bubble") and succeed in verifying Forster's claim of Thackeray's breadth of expertise.

As a companion to *William Makepeace Thackeray,* the collection allows readers to see the preoccupations of a writer who, as Forster carefully notes, "was a gentleman writing for other gentlemen." *Drawn From Life* also illustrates Forster's preoccupations with audience by demonstrating her commitment, even as a compiler, to general readers without, as she notes in a self-reflective comment on Thackeray, "compromising [her] principles." Forster's only editorial commentary is a succinct biographical introduction covering Thackeray's life from his boyhood in India to his death in 1863. This summary illustrates Forster's ability to compress the span of a person's life into a short, cogent essay – an ability she would employ in her next biographical project.

In 1981 Forster had begun work on a book inspired by her early questioning of the role of women in society. The result of this long and continuing examination, *Significant Sisters: The Grassroots of Active Feminism 1839–1939,* was published in 1984. Consisting of capsule biographies of women Forster considered pioneers of feminism, the book attempts to correct what Forster felt was a "lack of continuity and . . . development [in the] history of feminism."

Forster's initial stimulus to write the book came from her friends' reactions to the word *feminism.* She felt that many people, even women and men sympathetic to feminism, thought it entailed a belief in radical causes that denigrated men and family for the purpose of tearing down existing social structures. Forster wanted to change this opinion and believed a historical understanding of feminism would illuminate and clarify the discipline and thus change this stereotypical view.

But a deeper and more personal reason developed after the death of her mother in 1981. Forster's reappraisal of her mother's life, particularly her limited career options, raised painful questions about the status of women in the twentieth century. As a married, working-class woman, Lilian had felt that she could only raise children and keep house. This led Forster to consider, as she told Bell Mooney, "how it is I have been able to lead the sort of life I have led – born in 1938 – and how different it would have been had I been born in 1838. . . . How did we get to the stage we're at now? Was it all done by people, or by the tide of history?" These questions helped form the structure of her book and, in particular, its emphasis on the way individual women, the "significant sisters" of the title, influenced and directed the course of feminism. Divided into seven "spheres," the book matches a field with a representative subject: law, Caroline Norton;

the professions, Elizabeth Blackwell; employment, Florence Nightingale; sexual morality, Josephine Butler; politics, Elizabeth Cady Stanton; birth control, Margaret Sanger; and ideology, Emma Goldman. The book follows a set pattern throughout: after a brief sketch of their early lives, Forster concentrates on the way each of these women influenced events in their respective spheres, and at the end of each section Forster brings the debate surrounding that field into the present, relating its progress and current direction to its respective subject. This belief in biography as a chronicle of history reinforces her view of the power of the individual. For Forster one person can make a difference – a difference based on the force of her personality.

Moving away from the experimental style of *William Makepeace Thackeray, Significant Sisters* represents a more scholarly endeavor, complete with notes, index, and bibliographic appendix. This seems to be a conscious effort to enhance the seriousness of the project. Forster wanted this work, a legitimate history of the background of contemporary feminism, to be accepted as part of the academic discourse surrounding feminist studies. But *Significant Sisters* does retain one element from *William Makepeace Thackeray:* a reluctance to embrace the cold, objective stance of a conventional biographer-historian. Early in the book Forster declares her identification with feminism and, in fact, argues that "this sense [of identification] . . . is what the study of feminist history needs to bring to women." Forster believes a subjective approach increases solidarity among women and, in support of this claim, maintains that the individual efforts of her various subjects are all linked by a common desire to change society: "it is up to feminist history to prove that [women] are not [isolated]. There *is* a joint purpose, and this brings not just comfort but hope." Her biography can be interpreted as a call for unity amid the conflicting definitions, interpretations, and approaches to feminism, and her partisan approach is a reflection of this "joint purpose": by writing a history of the movement, Forster joins her voice with her subjects', becoming, like them, a "significant sister."

Since *feminism* carries different connotations for different people, Forster explicitly defines what she means by the term: "a kind of philosophy . . . a way of looking at and thinking of life for all women." She replaces what she feels is the commonly assumed connotation of a feminist as "a shrieking harridan obsessed with destruction" with "a man or woman who strives to secure a society in which neither sex finds gender alone a handicap to

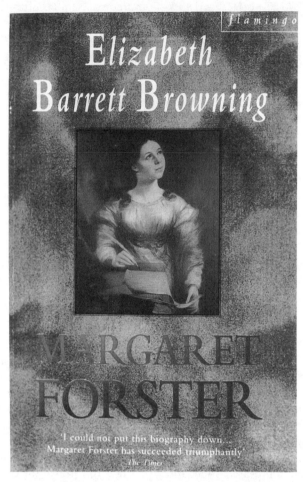

*Front cover for the paperback edition of Forster's biography
intended "to stimulate interest in Elizabeth Barrett
Browning's poetry"*

their progress." Sheila Rowbotham, while applauding Forster's attempt to codify the background of feminism, finds fault with this definition and thus with the book as a whole. Writing in the London *Times Literary Supplement* (28 September 1984), Rowbotham maintains that "the biggest problem in *Significant Sisters* is the use of the term 'feminism.'" Using this semantic difference as proof of a flaw in Forster's perspective, she concludes that "as an analysis of feminist dilemmas or as a historical perspective *Significant Sisters* is a disappointment. As a collection of lively character sketches of women who refused the common destiny of their sex and battled courageously through prejudice, heartache and conflict it is often inspiring."

Carole Klein, in *The New York Times Book Review* (17 February 1985), also voices objections to Forster's definition yet feels that overall the book is a success. She particularly praises both Forster's use of primary sources, "the diaries, private and pub-

lished papers and autobiographies," and her interpretation of controversial views, such as Blackwell's condemnation of feminism, from a historical perspective.

Combining historical background with her own opinions and definition of feminism, Forster creates a new reference work while offering an additional philosophical approach. As the arguments against her text prove, feminism is still a field in transition, and *Significant Sisters* marks Forster's attempt to offer a personal interpretation of the discipline while providing a historical context that traces both its nineteenth-century development and its modern adumbrations.

From approximately 1984 to 1988 Forster worked on a project closely allied to her feminist concerns. One of the major achievements of modern literary feminism is a reassessment of early women writers. After rereading Elizabeth Barrett Browning's poetry, which had languished in the shadows of Robert Browning's for most of the twentieth century, Forster became interested in the background of the poet. She felt that a contemporary reader needed to understand Browning's life and times to appreciate her work fully; she thus began working on the first new biography of Elizabeth Barrett Browning in thirty years. In *Significant Sisters* Forster discusses women who had made significant contributions in their fields. In *Elizabeth Barrett Browning* (1988) she makes it clear that Browning is also a "significant sister," striving for artistic respect on equal terms with men, and the aim of this biography respects this determination. Forster specifically notes that the main reason she wrote the biography was "to stimulate interest in Elizabeth Barrett Browning's poetry."

After reading the wealth of new material unearthed by contemporary scholars, including a trove of early letters, correspondence by and to other family members, diaries, and journals, Forster discovered that a major revision of Browning's life was needed. Instead of the prevailing view of a long-suffering poet imprisoned within the walls of Wimpole Street by a tyrannical and domineering father, Forster found a long-complaining, compliant captive and a father who, while intractable, was decidedly human. Though at times unflattering, this new perspective of Browning's life presents a more balanced portrait of the poet by dismissing some of the Victorian sentiment coloring and obscuring her life, which in turn allows contemporary scholars to reappraise and reinterpret her work more honestly. Unlike *William Makepeace Thackeray,* Forster's previous literary biography, *Elizabeth Barrett Browning* is a conventional biography, scrupulously footnoted and complete with a full bibliography and index. Forster's decision to create a more traditional biography rests in part on the need for a revised standard life and, as in *Significant Sisters,* a corresponding desire to enhance her subject's critical reputation.

In the course of the biography Forster strips away the myth surrounding Browning and replaces it with a factual rendering of her life. Forster divides Browning's life, as do most previous biographers, into two periods (before and after her marriage to Robert Browning); but unlike earlier biographies, each part is of equal length, resulting in a more balanced picture of her life. Forster contends that the accepted "myth" of Browning's life was due to an emphasis on the poet's later life and a neglect of her formative years. She shows how events in these early years, and more important, her responses to them, helped fashion the woman eventually "rescued" by Robert Browning from the castle keep of Wimpole Street. By delving more fully into Browning's life, Forster challenges the established interpretation of a life of agony and eventual ecstasy by placing her father's behaviors in a Victorian context and revealing the depth of her artistic convictions.

Forster's depiction of Browning's childhood paints a decidedly revisionist portrait of her father. Instead of the "Ogre of Wimpole Street," as many had mistakenly labeled him, Edward Mouton Barrett emerges as a man emotionally tormented by the loss of his wife and financially wrecked by his business failures. To regain the happiness of his earlier years, he tightens his grip on the family in a desperate bid to hold on to the happiness that remains. This "fierce pride in the importance of family" naturally led to tensions, especially when it became apparent that Edward Barrett's vision of "family" barred the marriage of any of his children. As Forster notes, "no child of his ever came to him with a chaste, respectable and irreproachably correct suitor." Instead of deriding this view, Forster softens its apparent harshness by putting it into historical perspective: "In fairness to him, it is true to say that few Victorian fathers would have approved the matches which his children proposed."

But the most important element in the reappraisal of Edward Barrett is Forster's discovery of Elizabeth's true feelings toward him. Previously, most scholars judged Edward Barrett by the way Elizabeth had described him in her letters to Robert Browning. But Forster shows that Elizabeth Barrett was in fact staving off the heated affections of Robert Browning by portraying her father as a man driven by passion and liable to fly into a rage at any moment. With this as an excuse, marriage between Robert Browning and Elizabeth Barrett could be indefinitely postponed – and, as Forster notes, Elizabeth's ennui could be difficult to overcome. Forster places much of the blame for the prevailing opinion of Edward on Elizabeth's lassitude and notes that "to a very great extent she created her own prison and it was one, moreover, in which she had wanted the warder on constant duty."

Forster's view of the second half of Elizabeth Barrett's life, the Browning years, is one of domestic bliss and burgeoning artistic talent. Her poetic vision coalesces in Italy, where she and Robert settled and where she worked on her most accomplished work, the prose poem *Aurora Leigh* (1857). But even when discussing her poetry, Forster concentrates on the work habits, reading, and philosophical and social concerns surrounding Browning's work instead of an in-depth analysis of the work itself. These "details" form the backbone of the second part of the book. As in *The Rash Adventurer* and *William Makepeace Thackeray,* Forster applies her novelist's eye for drama and setting, composing a series of vignettes (Browning working at her desk in Casa Guidi, her dejection over criticism of her work, Browning and son hailing Napoleon from a balcony) that illustrate the subject yet, as many reviewers noted, create a cogent and accessible narrative.

As in the previous biographies, *Elizabeth Barrett Browning* presents an honest, unflinching portrait of its subject. Forster points out the hypocrisies and unsavory aspects of Browning's life – her relationship with her father; her long and apparently self-induced illness; the capricious treatment of her maid, Elizabeth Wilson; her idolization of Napoleon – and judiciously attempts to explain them. Yet this honesty, set against Forster's depiction of a woman fully committed to her art and continually striving for (and ultimately achieving) aesthetic and personal fulfillment, gives the reader a more realistic portrait of Browning as an author and as a person.

The critical response to the biography was overwhelmingly positive. It won the award for biography from the Royal Society of Literature in 1989; the book's style, depth, and especially its bold revision of accepted views were praised by critics in both general and scholarly publications. Deirdre David, writing in *Victorian Studies* (Autumn 1990), states, "In sum, Forster's fair-minded, never sensational approach reveals an immensely intelligent and difficult woman – wife, mother, major Victorian poet – whose will to influence the world through poetry prevailed over uncontrollable and self-created obstacles." David also notes Forster's attention to detail, writing that "part of the pleasure of Forster's book resides in the sort of thing one always wants in biography: small telling details of a lived existence." This attention to detail comes from her experience as a novelist and from her corresponding desire, as in her earlier biographies, to make her subject "come alive" for the reader.

Concentrating on the biography's challenging of the accepted views of Browning, Robert Martin in the London *Times Literary Supplement* (19 August 1988) argues that "in its understated manner, this new biography is a daring book, for it shows us a far more complex woman than we have seen before. I am not sure that she is more lovable because of what we learn about her, but she is infinitely more interesting." The effect of the biography on Elizabeth Barrett Browning studies was twofold. First, it corrected many of the legends surrounding Browning; and, second, it offered a newfound awareness

of the background of Browning's early life and work. In particular, *Elizabeth Barrett Browning* presents a writer working on her craft from an early age, committed to artistic excellence and driven to succeed on her own terms.

In conjunction with the biography, Forster edited a volume of poetry, *Selected Poems of Elizabeth Barrett Browning,* published in 1988. Consisting of a chronological arrangement of shorter poems from all of her books, including her best known – *Sonnets from the Portuguese* (1850) – and several previously uncollected poems, the text offers a comprehensive view of Browning's work, exhibiting the range and especially the growth of her poetic talent. The book does not include any excerpts from *Aurora Leigh* because, as Forster notes, "Elizabeth Barrett Browning herself disliked extracts: a poem, to her, was an entity and she preferred the whole or nothing." As in *Drawn From Life* Forster offers a minimum of editorial intrusion beyond a biographical introduction and short prefatory notes at the beginning of each section. Ending the introduction with a brief appraisal of Browning's canonical status, Forster maintains that Browning is best read as a feminist writer and notes that some of the selections reflect this by illustrating "the oppression women suffer at the hands of men."

After publishing a novel, *Have the Men Had Enough?,* in 1989, Forster turned to a subject that had been on her mind since the Browning biography. Elizabeth Wilson, the Browning's maid, had intrigued Forster from the time she had first read about her. In fact, she said in a 1991 interview that "I wanted to write a biography of Elizabeth Wilson . . . but there's just not enough material." The resulting novel, *Lady's Maid* (1990), is an interesting exercise in point of view, marking a return to the experimental form of *William Makepeace Thackeray.* The book also offers an intriguing perspective on her definition of biography and a critique of Elizabeth Barrett Browning and her circle. A more subjective reflection on the Brownings, the book allows Forster to comment on the state of class relations in Victorian England.

Like *William Makepeace Thackeray, Lady's Maid* is a fictional work closely based on factual sources and events. Discussing the similarities between *Lady's Maid* and *Elizabeth Barrett Browning,* Forster commented in a 1992 letter that "both have to catch the essence of the person and the spirit of their times. The bio of Elizabeth Barrett Browning is distinct from *Lady's Maid* precisely because it never ventures beyond the proveable [*sic*]. That always leaves a gap and it is the gap that fiction fills – dan-

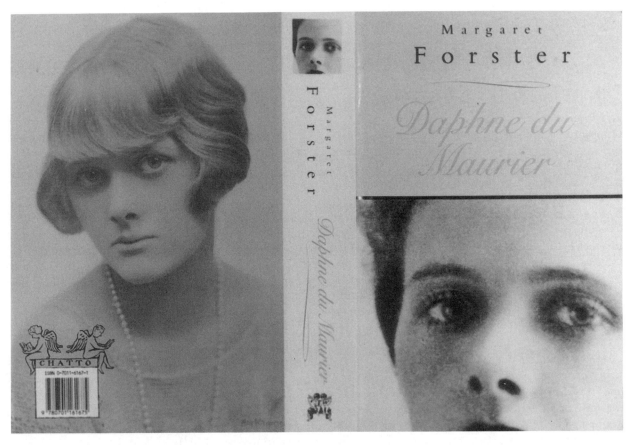

Dust jacket for Forster's biography of the British novelist. The biography has been widely acclaimed for its delicate handling of du Maurier's problems with her sexual identity.

gerously." Interestingly, instead of finding freedom in fiction, the imaginative impetus of the novel is still constrained by facts. In a 1990 interview Forster discussed the difficulty of writing a novel grounded so thoroughly in research: "I thought I would do something clever. Perhaps Wilson would reveal the secret of Elizabeth's true relationship with her father: she might see evidence of bullying or an incestuous moment. But I couldn't. I kept going back to the evidence." Forster's honesty extends to an afterword in *Lady's Maid* that separates the "fact and fiction" of the novel, explicitly stating where she takes artistic liberties, and, further, recounts the factual events of Wilson's life that extend beyond the time of the novel. In a 1993 review of Frances Sherwood's *Vindication,* a novel, like *Lady's Maid,* based on a real person (in this case the early feminist Mary Wollstonecraft), Forster offers a further gloss on her views of the relationships between fact and fiction and between fiction and biography. "Novels based on the lives of real people," she writes, "even long dead people, are always dangerous enterprises. Dangerous because they tamper

with received truth, dangerous because their avowed aim is to lie, all in the name of satisfying unsatisfied curiosity." For Forster, trained as a historian, imagination must never blur the line of truth; instead, it must complement it.

After completing her next novel, *The Battle for Christabel* (1991), Forster was free to complete a project that had resulted from an eerily serendipitous event. In April 1989 she was rearranging her bookshelf, when, as she told Valerie Grove in 1993, "out fell *Rebecca,* which I hadn't read since I was 13. Daphne du Maurier. . . . I wonder if anyone's doing a biography of her?" Just one day later, Forster received a call from a radio station: they wanted to know if she could write an obituary of Dame Daphne – who had died that morning. After the du Maurier children, who had read and admired *Elizabeth Barrett Browning,* agreed to make Forster the authorized biographer, she began her research in earnest. Her relationship with Daphne's children helped pave the way for interviews with surviving family members and friends, but it also illustrated the difficulty of writing an "official" biography. Due to pressure from the family, Forster had to maintain a certain reticence concerning the sensational revelations of Daphne's sexuality.

These revelations revolved around her relationship with the American actress Gertrude Lawrence. While *Daphne du Maurier* (1993) does not explicitly state that the two had an affair, Forster, in a later interview with Alison Roberts (prompted by a documentary on du Maurier that featured interviews by Forster), asserts that she did "think they loved each other" and had been sexually intimate. But Forster did not reveal du Maurier's relationship to titillate readers; instead she sees du Maurier's obsession with gender and sexuality as a formative force in her life and work. She believes that du Maurier's battle with her homosexual desires "fueled her creative powers," and, since "her whole life's work was an attempt to defy reality," the romantic resonance and atmosphere of works such as *Jamaica Inn* (1936) and *Rebecca* (1938) and the conflicts between their male and female characters are the spoils of her struggles with her masculinity.

Forster traces du Maurier's confusion over her gender to her father, Gerald du Maurier, the well-known British actor and theater manager. Desperate for a son, he did not hide his disappointment in du Maurier's gender, and, in a poem he wrote for his young daughter, he lamented, "And, if I'd had my way, / She would have been, a boy." Forster suggests that this, along with Gerald's philandering (and her mother Muriel's acquiescence) and overattachment to du Maurier, instilled in her a strong will for independence (bordering on egoism) that might have added to her sexual confusion and made her, if not the most affectionate wife and mother, a writer able to concentrate and work in both the torrid heat of Egypt and the damp cold of the English coast.

But the most important part of her childhood, at least as far as her writing is concerned, was the family's vivacity: "They were encouraged, even expected, to use their imaginations, to make their conversation as amusing and colorful as possible." Their love of creativity extended even to the confusion du Maurier felt over her sexual identity; the family was not concerned with du Maurier's gender confusion, because, as Forster notes, "In a family where flights of fancy, and fantasy, were positively encouraged, there was no objection to Daphne's passion of all things masculine." Thus, her adoption of a male alter ego, "Eric Avon," seemed perfectly natural, and Forster shows how "Eric" – or the "boy-in-the-box" – reappeared throughout her life,

coloring her fiction and relationships with men and especially with women.

In fact, Forster had finished *Daphne du Maurier* when a cache of letters from du Maurier to Ellen Doubleday, the wife of Nelson Doubleday (Forster's American publisher), was delivered. With this new material, Forster was able to illustrate the depth of Daphne's feelings for Ellen and her confusion over her sexual identity. Forster felt that "In her own mind, [du Maurier] had seen herself as something other – not a lesbian but 'a half-breed,' someone internally male and externally female."

This struggle with gender is evident in her fiction, which illustrates, according to Forster, a "total disillusionment with the relationship between men and women." This view is based, in part, on the two most important men in du Maurier's life: her husband, Maj. Tommy Browning, and her father. Forster depicts a marriage fraught with misunderstanding and, paradoxically, sustained by separation. Tracing this to du Maurier's overriding sense of alienation (a trait also resulting in the emotional neglect of her daughters), Forster links the influences of husband and father by noting emphatically that "she never, ever, wanted to find herself in the position she had found herself in with her father, with him desperate for support and demanding a complete devotion of body and soul, which she did not want to give." Similarly, throughout the book Forster describes du Maurier's fixation on the financial gains of writing and subtly relates it to du Maurier's strong sense of independence. The book illustrates a writer who, while devoted to her craft, is inspired by the marketplace as well as by the muses.

The book was greeted with critical acclaim on both sides of the Atlantic, with Carolyn G. Heilbrun proclaiming ecstatically in *The New York Times Book Review* (17 October 1993) that "We have here that rarest of marriages: the perfect subject and a gifted biographer." In particular, she praises Forster's delicate yet forthright handling of du Maurier's homosexuality and her insight into the complicated psyche of her views on gender. Victoria Glendinning, in the London *Times* (22 March 1993), writes that "As an ardent student of biography, I have hoped for this moment: when the biographer could sympathetically comprehend the inner life of a woman writer who was herself unable to disclose it." Like Heilbrun she singles out the skill with which Forster treats the sensationalist aspects of du Maurier's life. And Peter Kemp, writing in the London *Times Literary Supplement* (9 April 1993), calls the book "perceptive and revealing," noting its "sharp acuteness" and psychological insight.

In sum *Daphne du Maurier* presents a writer who, when beset by personal demons, transformed them into Gothic narratives infused with her emotional and sexual conflicts. As in her previous biographies, Forster's descriptive skills and psychological insight are used to create a detailed yet clear portrait of her subject as a person as well as a writer, and her matter-of-fact discussion of du Maurier's sexual ambiguity is a model for dealing with politically charged issues. Above all, the biography reflects its subject's individuality and her overriding sense of independence. This sense relates her to the feminist writers of Forster's earlier work, making du Maurier, like Elizabeth Barrett Browning before her, a "significant sister" and a logical addition to Forster's oeuvre. Since completing *Daphne du Maurier,* Forster has been working on an untitled novel.

From her early success as a writer of popular fiction, Forster has developed into a respected biographer by applying her talents in fiction to both experimental and conventional biographies. Combining elements of fiction and history into a coherent whole, she creates biographies that contain flights of literary imagination yet remain grounded in fact. Acknowledging contemporary criticism's questioning of authority, Forster plays with the idea of a biographer's supposed objectivity, and her experiments with point of view, voice, and narrative technique expand the genre while remaining firmly rooted in the commitment to fact and research that form the background of biography.

Interviews:
Tim Devlin, "Now Prince Charlie Looks a Little Less Bonnie," *Times* (London), 11 October 1973, p. 15;
Valerie Grove, "Virgin Birth: The View From the Kitchen," *Sunday Times,* 17 March 1991, pp. 2–3;
Celia Haddock, "Margaret Forster: 'I Write by the Clock,' " *Times* (London), 25 August 1967, p. 7a;
Angela Lambert, "From *Georgy Girl* to the Man in Daphne," *Independent,* 17 March 1993, p. 23;
Bel Mooney, "The Reluctant Feminist," *Times* (London), 14 September 1984, p. 11a;
Libby Purves, "Poetic Justice for the Maid," *Times* (London), 29 June 1990, p. 15.

References:
Valerie Grove, "Hot on the Scent of Daphne," *Times* (London), 15 March 1993, p. 12;
Alison Roberts, "Du Maurier Affair True, Says Writer," *Times* (London), 10 April 1993, p. 3.

P. N. Furbank

(23 May 1920 –)

Michael Herbert
University of Saint Andrews

BOOKS: *Samuel Butler (1836–1902)* (London: Cambridge University Press, 1948; Philadelphia: Folcroft Press, 1969);

Italo Svevo: The Man and the Writer (London: Secker & Warburg, 1966; Berkeley: University of California Press, 1967);

Reflections on the Word "Image" (London: Secker & Warburg, 1970);

W. B. Yeats (Milton Keynes: Open University Press, 1976);

E. M. Forster: A Life, 2 volumes (London: Secker & Warburg, 1977, 1978; New York: Harcourt Brace Jovanovich, 1978);

Unholy Pleasure: The Idea of Social Class (Oxford & New York: Oxford University Press, 1985);

Ezra Pound (Milton Keynes: Open University Press, 1985);

The Canonization of Daniel Defoe, by Furbank and W. R. Owens (New Haven: Yale University Press, 1988);

Diderot: A Critical Biography (London: Secker & Warburg, 1992; New York: Knopf, 1992).

OTHER: Henry Fielding, *Joseph Andrews,* edited by Furbank (Harmondsworth: Penguin, 1954);

"The Twentieth-Century Best-Seller," in *The Pelican Guide to English Literature,* volume 7, revised edition, edited by Boris Ford (Harmondsworth: Penguin, 1964), pp. 429–441;

Selected Poems of Thomas Hardy, edited by Furbank (London: Macmillan, 1964; New York: St. Martin's Press, 1966);

Charles Dickens, *Martin Chuzzlewit,* edited by Furbank (Harmondsworth: Penguin, 1968);

Thomas Hardy, *Tess of the d'Urbervilles,* edited by Furbank (London & New York: Macmillan, 1974);

"Chesterton the Edwardian," in *G. K. Chesterton: A Centenary Appraisal,* edited by John Sullivan (London: Elek, 1974), pp. 16–27;

P. N. Furbank

Twentieth Century Poetry: Critical Essays and Documents, edited by Furbank and Graham Martin (Milton Keynes: Open University Press, 1975);

"The Novel and Its 'Resemblance to Life,' " in *The Uses of Fiction: Essays on the Modern Novel in Honour of Arnold Kettle,* edited by Douglas Jefferson

and Graham Martin (Milton Keynes: Open
    University Press, 1982), pp. 31–40;
Leo Tolstoy, *The Raid and Other Stories,* edited by
    Furbank (Oxford: Oxford University Press,
    1982);
Selected Letters of E. M. Forster, 2 volumes, edited by
    Furbank and Mary Lago (Cambridge, Mass.:
    Harvard University Press / London: Collins,
    1983–1985);
The Notebooks of Samuel Butler, edited by Furbank
    (London: Hogarth Press, 1985);
E. M. Forster, *The New Collected Short Stories,* edited
    by Furbank (London: Sidgwick & Jackson,
    1985);
Rudyard Kipling, *Life's Handicap,* edited by Furbank
    (Harmondsworth: Penguin, 1987);
Harry Daley, *This Small Cloud,* edited by Furbank
    (London: Weidenfeld & Nicolson, 1988);
"The Philosophy of D. H. Lawrence," in *The Spirit
    of D. H. Lawrence: Centenary Studies,* edited by
    Gamini Salgado and G. K. Das (London: Mac-
    millan, 1988), pp. 144–153;
Livia Svevo, *Memoirs of Italo Svevo,* edited by
    Furbank (London: Libris, 1989);
"A Humanist Poet?," in *Life by Other Means: Essays on
    D. J. Enright,* edited by Jacqueline Simms (Ox-
    ford: Oxford University Press, 1990), pp. 97–
    104;
Daniel Defoe, *A Tour Through the Whole Island of
    Great Britain,* edited by Furbank, W. R.
    Owens, and A. J. Coulson (New Haven: Yale
    University Press, 1991);
Forster, *A Passage to India,* edited by Furbank (Lon-
    don: Everyman Library, 1991);
Denis Diderot, *This Is Not a Story; and Other Stories,*
    translated and edited by Furbank (Columbia:
    University of Missouri Press, 1991).

SELECTED PERIODICAL PUBLICATIONS –
UNCOLLECTED: "Domestic Portraiture,"
    Cornhill, 979 (Summer 1949): 37–52;
"Henry James: The Novelist as Actor," *Essays in
    Criticism,* 1 (1951): 404–420;
"Godwin's Novels," *Essays in Criticism,* 5 (1955):
    214–228;
"On the Idea of an Ideal Middle-Class Speech,"
    Twentieth Century (April 1957): 365–371;
"The Ideal," *Kenyon Review* (January 1967): 103–
    109;
"Northrop Frye: The Uses of Criticism," *Mosaic*
    (1970): 179–184;
"Mendacity in Mrs. Gaskell," *Encounter* (June
    1973): 51–55;

"The Shadows in the Cave: Some Thoughts on Cin-
    ema," *Encounter* (November 1978): 78–81.

P. N. Furbank has written three literary biographies: lives of Italo Svevo, E. M. Forster, and
Denis Diderot. The first has made a neglected Italian writer more widely known; the last has clarified
the myriad complexities of a famous French writer
of the Enlightenment. But it is his life of the
quintessentially English Forster that is Furbank's
chief claim to fame and one of the major literary biographies of the twentieth century.

Philip Nicholas "Nick" Furbank was born in
Cranleigh, Surrey, on 23 May 1920, the second son
of William Percival Furbank, a local bank manager,
and his wife Grace Furbank, of Brockham Green,
Surrey. He attended Reigate Grammar School in his
home county before entering Cambridge University
to read English, achieving a First in both parts of
the Tripos. His elder brother, who wrote short stories, was killed in a flying accident in 1941. At the
time of this tragedy, Furbank himself had already
joined the Royal Electrical and Mechanical Engi-
neers, staying in the army until the end of World
War II in 1945: he eventually ended up serving in
Italy, rising to the rank of corporal. From 1947 to
1953 he was a Fellow of Emmanuel College, Cambridge, then worked for some years in publishing
with Macmillan and as a freelance critic before returning to academic life as a Fellow of King's College, Cambridge, in 1970. In 1972 he joined the
Open University as lecturer in literature, retiring as
professor in 1985; he was appointed emeritus professor in 1992. He never married and lives in London, not far from Hampstead Heath.

Furbank's first book, a critical study of Samuel
Butler, was published when he was twenty-eight,
but it was another eighteen years before his next,
Italo Svevo: The Man and the Writer (1966). The first
part of this book is literary biography, the second
part (less than half as long) being a study of the
writings of this fascinating Triestine, whose real
name was Ettore Schmitz: Furbank explains his
pseudonym as "the Italian-Swabian," expressing his
sense of being a hybrid, with his mixed Jewish, Italian, Austrian, and German background. The book
sets out to show how a good writer could be unfairly neglected and languish in undeserved obscurity. For most of his life Svevo was known only as a
successful businessman, not as the author of the
lively but diffuse *A Life (Una vita,* 1893) or the remarkable study of a "senile" soul, *As a Man Grows
Older (Senelità,* 1898), taken to further psychological
depths and artistic heights in his masterpiece, *The*

Confessions of Zeno (*La coscienza di Zeno*, 1923), an indisputably major modernist novel. It was largely through the championship of James Joyce, who taught him English, that Svevo's genius became known internationally – and even then members of the Italian literary establishment, irritated that an Italian writer should first have been acclaimed abroad, tried to denigrate him by attacks on his deliberately antiliterary style, his use of Triestine dialect, even his grammar. Furbank traces the story of this disgraceful "Svevo affair" as clearly and effectively as he paints in the background of Trieste and of Svevo's connections. Much space is given, rightly, to the vital friendship with Joyce and to Svevo's visits to England, emphases that are understandable in an English biographer, who has nevertheless not hesitated to tackle the Italian aspects head-on, including providing his own translations.

In order to write his first biography, Furbank undertook a considerable amount of original research, spending some weeks in Trieste, where Svevo's daughter, Letizia Fonda Savio, not only talked to him at length but also let him examine her father's letters, which had not then been published, as well as other family papers. Furbank found Trieste, no longer a thriving port, a curious relic of the Austro-Hungarian Empire, frozen about the year 1914: it was fun roaming about in it, drinking at its Emperor Francis Joseph–style cafés and eating the favorite food (fried squid) of James Joyce, Svevo's teacher-cum-protégé (the Italian businessman gave the impoverished Irishman money far beyond what was owed for English lessons). He also remembered walking along the streets at night, blown about by the ferocious Triestine bora, a notoriously nasty Alpine wind, arm-in-arm with a minor Triestine writer, Anita Pittoni, who had edited the *Reminiscences* of Svevo's wife, Livia. From Pittoni, Furbank heard fascinating stories about Svevo and his relatives, supplemented by the anecdotes and recollections of others who had known him, and these helped to give the book flesh-and-blood characters and much humor. The humor is often combined with pathos, as in this representative example of Furbank's easy and natural style, with an eye for personal and social characterizations as sharp as Svevo's own, from chapter 4 ("The Business Man"):

> His first visit to England succeeded in making him thoroughly miserable. He had to wear his overcoat in June, he disliked the chilly English manner towards strangers, he found the coffee undrinkable (and they served it in pint mugs), and the barman in a public house demanded his money before you started to drink. Nobody could understand his English, and he misread the pronunciation code in his dictionary and had to start all over again. He was lonely and bored, though in the evenings he began writing a comedy, and the first time he began really enjoying a conversation – it was with the most adorable little English boy, whom he found perched on the back of his seat at the hotel, watching the smoke come out of his nostrils – an icy English voice called "Come along, Philip." The owner of the voice carefully managed not even to look at him.

> He found himself at a disadvantage in various ways. His collars weren't smart enough or his shaving good enough – in England you can wear a shabby coat but your collars have to be absolutely beyond reproach, and you had better be drunk than ill shaven.

All this research was useful training for Furbank's central biography. E. M. Forster had hundreds of friends and several surviving relatives, and Furbank diligently cut a great swath through them, but with consideration and tact. His tactfulness was evident from the start of the enterprise. It had long been thought that William Plomer would write Forster's biography, but near the end of his long life Forster thought Plomer's reticence about homosexuality, a sexual orientation they both happened to share, would be disabling and favored giving the task to Furbank. The situation was embarrassing, but Furbank handled it well and was amiably treated in return by Plomer, who even handed over the notes that he had started to make. Apart from his fiction and poetry, Plomer had written biographies of Cecil Rhodes and Ali Pasha and an interesting but discreet autobiography, in which the veil comes down with a thud at crucial moments. Therefore, although he may well have written an elegant and entertaining life of Forster, he could not and would not have wished to write anything remotely as revelatory as Forster himself had thought desirable, or at least allowable. With Furbank the aged Forster overcame his own Edwardian reserve and talked to his much younger friend freely on "everything," not making him feel any of his questions were tiresome or trivial.

Furbank showed a similar talent for eliciting what he wanted to know from Forster's friends and relations. It was for him an absorbing business, though sometimes he found it hard to keep the minds of his often elderly interviewees on the central topic. He would usually write down notes as soon as he got out of the door, not before, sometimes feeling guilty that he was practicing on people's innocence. Nothing too terrible in the way of private secrets was revealed, and Furbank remained in contact with several of Forster's circle.

Dust jacket for the one-volume British edition of Furbank's biography of the British novelist with whom he was friends from 1948 until Forster's death in 1970

His scrupulousness in worrying about using people is touching in an age when many biographers do not hesitate to use modern technology to record the actual conversations of their often unwitting interviewees. It shows a moral delicacy that compels respect and admiration.

There is much else to admire in the biography itself. One of its most notable strengths is the combination of the details of a long life with a magisterial sweep in both the tracing of themes and the strong narrative momentum, so that the details do not obscure the whole, leaving the reader unable to see the wood for the trees. The details are there, of course: Furbank compiled a set of loose-leaf ring-binders with a page for every month of Forster's life and, potentially, a line for every day, so that he could jot down any casual fact or event at the right chronological place. It is a handy method, presumably used by many other biographers, and certainly used again for Furbank's life of Diderot. It enables the biographer to draw on a great fund of the minutest specifics of the subject's life, once these facts have been accumulated, and is an obvious aid when evidence needs to be marshaled as to what the subject was doing or thinking at particular periods. But,

though exhaustive, Furbank is far from being one of those biographers – much more common in the twentieth century than in earlier times – who simply offload the contents of their filing cabinets onto the hapless reader, leaving the latter to sort and rank in significance and generally make sense of the indiscriminate piles of facts in these overstuffed but undershaped baggy monsters. At nearly six hundred pages, the life of Forster is hardly a slim volume, but nor is it loose, and, for what it does, it cannot be said to be too large. For, although it may not say "everything," it says an enormous amount about its subject within a superbly well-organized structure, thematically as well as chronologically. It is, for all its rich diversity of places and people, incidents, and insights, all of a piece: reviewing it in the *Times Literary Supplement* (24 March 1978), Lord Annan likened it to invisible mending, as "you cannot detect a stitch in the narrative."

Of the places and people that were important in Forster's life, India and Indians stand out prominently. Furbank went to India in the year of Forster's death, partly in search of local color, partly to stay with friends of Forster's such as the Mirza brothers in Hyderabad, distinguished judges (then retired) whom Forster first knew as law students in London in 1911. Although in those early days they had no clear idea that Forster was a novelist, the brothers had a lot to tell his biographer: "We thought him like an angel" was one comment of Abu Saeed Mirza. Forster's main Indian friend was Syed Ross Masood, with whom Forster fell in love: this was not reciprocated, but his long friendship with this larger-than-life character, as with the Maharajah of Dewas, is knowledgeably and sympathetically delineated by Furbank.

Friendship was the basis of Forster's beliefs, or what Furbank calls his "central preoccupation," and the varieties of friendship are a vivid thread in the unfolding tapestry of *E. M. Forster: A Life,* published in two volumes in 1977 and 1978. Most touching is Forster's loving friendship with Bob Buckingham, a policeman, and his wife May, depicted as frankly and delicately as anything in the book. But perhaps the most brilliant feature stems from the fact that here, as was not the case with his other two subjects, Furbank was himself a friend of the man whose life he was writing, and he could even include Boswell-like extracts from his own diary about meetings with the great man. Furbank knew Forster for a long time: from 1948 until his death more than two decades later. In the summer of 1953 the two spent a holiday together in Portugal, where the older man proved a remorseless sightseer but not a good map reader, so he frequently got the two of them lost. He was very moved by the beautiful Belem monastery in Lisbon, with its late-Gothic motifs of ropes and ships' anchors, and told his younger companion that it gave him a whiff of India. This sort of thing was not lost on Furbank, and his close personal knowledge bears fruit in many wise and witty observations throughout the biography, coming to a grand climax in its penultimate chapter, "E. M. Forster Described," a most distinguished piece of writing, pulling all the threads together, with the preceding accounts of Forster put into proportion. Here the reader learns what it was actually like to know Forster, to be in the same room with him, as in the following splendid passages:

> Straggling hair, broad brow, a long reddish nose, and under it a wispy moustache; fine eyes, in steel-rimmed glasses, and a most expressive and sensitive mouth, by turns tremulous, amused, morally reproving or full of scorn. It was the mouth, one felt, of a man defending the right to be sensitive. Physically he was awkward, limp and stiff at the same time. He would stand rather askew, as it were holding himself together by gripping his left hand in his right. By contrast his gestures were most graceful; he had a beautiful blessing gesture of the hand, and a curious and charming habit, when drinking tea, of describing a little circling motion with the cup. . . .

> A good way of visualizing Forster, I have found, is to imagine him being introduced to a dog or a cat. I never witnessed this, but can picture it. He would put himself on a level with the animal, approaching it tolerantly but non-committally. It *might* be a nice animal, but then again it might not; it was a mistake to have preconceptions on such matters: and at all events it didn't matter *much* what character an animal had – but it mattered a little. That would be his tone, I think; and he would shoot glances at the animal in the intervals of conversation, examining it from various angles till he had made up his mind about it. His mind was a vast breeding-ground for judgements and discriminations. He endlessly picked and chose and could distinguish one blade of grass from another. Similarly, no one ever made such *restrictive* remarks, giving and then drawing a limit to what was to be given. "X – , with an intelligent face, fairly," he might say; or "I am devoted to Y – 's son, slightly."

That passage is as delightful, charming, and disarming as Forster was himself, and with more than a little that is Forsterian in the style and the acuteness of perception, so empathetic has Furbank's identification with his subject become.

Whereas the biography of Svevo was not widely noticed, the biography of Forster received full and virtually universal praise for its prose style, devoid of mannerisms, its frankness, its sympathy combined with objectivity, and its masterly handling. The only negative comments tended to focus on what critics felt was omitted from the book rather than its undeniable achievements. For instance, it was noticed that Furbank avoided both literary criticism of Forster's books and also speculation about the sources of his creativity. Furbank did not like to interrupt the flow of the narrative with chunks of critical comment on a given work: he was scathing about the awkwardness of such a form, though changed his mind when he turned to Diderot. On the other point of criticism, Furbank remains unrepentant. He belongs to the school of literary biographers which holds that one should not think of the life as explaining the works, which, if successful as works of art, are not in need of this often reductive kind of explanation. The life of a writer seems to him a legitimate object of interest in its own right; and sometimes the works help to explain something in the life, as when the works explain the ethical theory that lay behind some gesture on the writer's part that puzzled the people around him, and that he may not have understood fully himself until he came to write about it. This is

*Dust jacket for the British edition of Furbank's biography of the
French writer, philosopher, and editor*

fair enough; but Furbank is too modest if he really believes that his lives have not also illuminated the works. In the life of Forster, particularly, much light is shed on the novels and their place in Forster's literary and personal development, their evolution, their use of real life acquaintances in the creation of characters, and their transmutation of actual experiences – and responses to those experiences – into fictional ones. For example, Furbank gives the reader, through his vivid portrayal of Masood, many insights into the character based upon him, Aziz in *A Passage to India* (1922–1924), and his relationships with characters such as Ralph Moore, whom Furbank shows to be a portrait of Forster when young.

Some critics complained that there should have been more coverage of Forster's delight in comedy, though it is in fact well covered. Another complaint was in the misjudgment of omitting discussion of music, which was important to Forster and plays a significant part in his writing. In Furbank's defense, focusing on such a nonnarrative

topic as music is perhaps less necessary in a biography than in a critical monograph. It was not a mistake (if mistake it was) that Furbank repeated in his life of Diderot: music and musicians and musicologists get their due attention there.

Diderot: A Critical Biography (1992) is both like and unlike *E. M. Forster: A Life*. The origins of the later book were very different. *Rameau's Nephew* (1821), Diderot's extraordinary dialogue-novel, was always one of Furbank's favorite books; and when he had to chair a course on the Enlightenment at the Open University, where courses are produced by a team working closely together over several years – the critical studies *W. B. Yeats* (1976) and *Ezra Pound* (1985) were products of this process – he tried to work the novel into the course as a set text but was argued down. This put him on his mettle, and when his publishers asked on what he would like to write, he opted for Diderot, polymath editor of the great *Encyclopédie,* leading philosopher of "enlightenment" in the face of superstition and despotism, virtual inventor of modern art criticism, and a genius who anticipated both Charles Darwin and Sigmund Freud, the typewriter and the cinema, modern stage production and modern avant-garde novels. Unraveling all this, and much more, took Furbank some five years, with many hours spent sweating over the photocopier, reproducing all of Diderot's brilliant and fascinating letters, often hugely long, especially those to his mistress, "Sophie" Volland.

Another difference from the Forster biography is that, whereas the earlier work is preeminent in its field, Furbank's book on Diderot is, as he modestly admits, in the shadow of Arthur M. Wilson's monumental two-volume biography (1957, 1972) and can add little to our knowledge of the man, just as anyone writing a biography of Forster now would be inevitably overshadowed by Furbank's achievement. But Furbank's aims are different from Wilson's, involving not only writing a guided tour of the mind of his subject, just as he had done with Forster, but also writing a critical biography, which he had not done with Forster. He did not follow the method of his book on Svevo either, with its two separate parts, biographical and critical, but interspersed the narrative chapters with chapters of literary criticism, a form he had previously disdained but now found inescapable. Partly this is because what interests Furbank about Diderot are the works by which his name continues to live: not his feeble plays; not his rational philosophy; not even the *Encyclopédie,* which means little to the English-speaking reader at whom Furbank's book is aimed; but the few short fictions, which Furbank has made much more accessible and attractive by his enthusiastic championship and interpretation.

Here Furbank's remarkable ability to make coherent sense of the bewildering diversity of Diderot's many-sided genius is added to his ability to make that polymath's variety of ideas sparkle with new and exciting life. As did Forster, Diderot also set great store by friendship as the basis for the establishment of moral values, and in the case of both men Furbank is thorough in exploring a range of relationships with many friends. Another unifying theme is provided by Diderot's lifelong attempts to distinguish appearance and reality, which manifests itself in various ways. Furbank shows how "reputation-making" is a fundamental theme of all of Diderot's work as a fictionist. As author of *Reflections on the Word "Image"* (1970), Furbank seems especially well placed to make a case for Diderot, with his obsession with statues and their function, as the originator of the image and his belief that people invent "statues" or images of themselves and then try to live up to them. As someone who has spent much of his life in teaching literature, Furbank is concerned with teaching the reader how to read the literary works he so much admires. He even provides new ways of apprehending and classifying the fictions, proposing a distinction between the novel of what he calls "accepted illusion" (the predominant genre) and the novel of "deception" (or "undeception"), which is what Diderot wrote and which works not by pretending to be real but by never allowing the reader the certainty of knowing whether it is real or not, never totally severing its ties with real life. Diderot produced a masterpiece in two separate veins of this second genre: his first novel, *The Nun* (1796), is a masterpiece of the fraudulent "true confession" type, banned because its sexual confessions were regarded as pornographic; his last, *Jacques the Fatalist* (1796), is a masterpiece of the kind of novel that disrupts narrator-reader relations, an "anti-novel" about determinism that refers to and subverts itself — a form that, as Furbank explains, has come to be seen as avant-garde on being rediscovered in the twentieth century. The theme of (un)deception, of appearance and reality, is taken further in stories like "This Is Not a Story," which Furbank uses to express Diderot's theory of fiction with breathtaking concision ("Fiction, for him, signified not a story, but the spectacle of somebody telling a story"), and the two famous dialogues, *Rameau's Nephew,* which Furbank illuminates as a meditation on the nature of genius and foolishness, and *D'Alembert's Dream* (1830), a philosophical fantasy on materialism, an unpromising subject that Furbank shows to be absorbing and entertaining, of psychological as well as intellectual interest, particularly as a study of the problem of personal identity.

Other work by Furbank contributed to incidental aspects of *Diderot.* For example, just as Furbank's personal knowledge of Forster's Cambridge milieu helped immeasurably in conveying its exact flavor, so did his lively *Unholy Pleasure: The Idea of Social Class* (1985) feed its sharp insights into the later biography, as in its teasing out of the implications of the master-servant relationship in *Jacques the Fatalist,* with its treatment of the "valet" as a social problem. As ever, though, Furbank's wide learning is never used to draw attention to his own cleverness, although his wise and witty asides and generalizations agreeably pepper all his work. Instead, all his massive scholarship is subordinated to the task in hand, which is always the same: to let the reader get to know and understand the subject — Svevo, Forster, Diderot — without any emphatic drawing of attention to the important points, a guide only by implication and one who leads us quietly, modestly, unassumingly, and, above all, effortlessly to that knowledge and understanding. As Norman Hampson wrote in the *London Review of Books* (20 August 1992): "Like Diderot himself, Furbank is more concerned to open up new perceptions than to bludgeon his readers with 'definitive' judgments about this and that. Perhaps no one could hope to do justice to Diderot, but Furbank has certainly done him proud."

On the whole, *Diderot* was well received, despite some carping from professional teachers of French literature who seemed to think their patch should not be intruded upon by strangers from "Eng. Lit." – even one who shows as much proficiency in translating from French (in the stories published separately as well as the biography itself) as he had done earlier in translating from Svevo's Italian. More representative were Lloyd Grossman in the (London) *Sunday Times* (19 April 1992), who prized this "sparkling" book as "a vivid and exciting portrait," and David Coward in the *Times Literary Supplement* (1 May 1992), who welcomed it as succeeding admirably as an introduction to the mercurial mind of "the performing flea of the Enlightenment." Supporting quotation from the book itself is difficult to make representative, as it undertakes so many different kinds of things in its various parts, but perhaps the account of Diderot's death is as characteristic as any: "All next morning, 31 July 1784, Diderot chatted cheerfully with friends and with his doctor, and then he sat down to dinner, saying he felt hungrier than he had done for weeks. He ate some soup and boiled mutton, and then seized an apricot, exclaiming blithely to Nanette, when she tried to stop him, 'Good God, what harm do you think it can do me?' Having eaten it, he stretched over the table for some cherries in syrup and gave a cough. Nanette asked him a question and, receiving no answer, she looked up and saw that he was dead. It was a cheerful and becoming death, very unlike the tortured scene that religious zealots liked to imagine for an atheist." This is cheerful and becoming in itself, and it is typical that it should come from the antepenultimate chapter, before one on the last novel and one on his subject's posthumous career.

Furbank produced one literary biography in his forties, another in his fifties, and a third that is mostly the product of his late sixties. Now that he is in his seventies, there is no telling what further work may lie ahead. But on the strength of these three his reputation as a biographer is assured; and had he written nothing but *E. M. Forster: A Life,* he would be remembered as one of the finest, for, as John Bayley observed in the *Listener* (28 July 1977), "It is impossible to overpraise Furbank's style and sympathy as a biographer."

Winifred Gérin

(7 October 1901 – 27 June 1981)

Barbara Mitchell
University of Leeds

BOOKS: *The Invitation to Parnassus and other Poems,* as W. E. Bourne (N.p.: Erskine Macdonald, 1930);

A Guide to Haworth: The Brontës Moorland Home, by Gérin and John Lock (Haworth: Petty, 1956);

Anne Brontë (London & New York: Thomas Nelson, 1959); revised and amended edition (London: Allen Lane, Penguin Books, 1976);

Branwell Brontë (London & New York: Thomas Nelson, 1961);

The Young Fanny Burney (London & New York: Thomas Nelson, 1961);

Charlotte Brontë: The Evolution of Genius (Oxford & New York: Clarendon Press, 1967);

Horatia Nelson (Oxford & New York: Oxford University Press, 1970);

Emily Brontë: A Biography (Oxford & New York: Clarendon Press, 1971; revised, 1972);

Writers and Their Work: The Brontës, 2 volumes (Bristol: Bristol Council, 1973);

Elizabeth Gaskell: A Biography (Oxford & New York: Clarendon Press, 1976);

Anne Thackeray Ritchie: A Biography (Oxford & New York: Oxford University Press, 1981).

PLAY PRODUCTION: *My Dear Master,* Amersham, Playhouse Theatre, May 1955; and Leeds, Art Theatre, October 1955.

TELEVISION: *Juniper Hall,* BBC, 1956.

RADIO: *Juniper Hall,* Australia and Canada, 1956.

OTHER: Charlotte Brontë, *Five Novelettes,* transcribed from original manuscripts and edited, with an introduction, by Gérin (London: Folio Press, 1971; Totowa, N.J.: Rowman & Littlefield, 1972);

Elizabeth Gaskell, *The Life of Charlotte Brontë,* edited, with an introduction, by Gérin (London: Folio Society, 1971);

Anne Brontë, *The Tenant of Wildfell Hall,* introduction by Gérin (London & New York: Penguin, 1979).

SELECTED PERIODICAL PUBLICATIONS – UNCOLLECTED: "The Montpensier Miniature of Shelley," *Keats-Shelley Memorial Bulletin,* 17 (1965): 1–11;

"The Effects of the Environment on the Brontë Writings," in *Essays by Divers Hands,* 36 (1970): 67–83;

"Byron's Influence on the Brontës," in *Essays by Divers Hands,* 37 (1972): 47–62.

Winifred Gérin is known as the biographer of the Brontës. In 1955 when she moved to Haworth, the home of the Brontës, she set out to write the biographies of all the Brontë children. In 1972 she completed that task, having written what are still considered standard biographies of Anne, Branwell, Charlotte, and Emily. Her husband, John Lock, along with W. T. Dixon, added to the project when he published the biography of the Reverend Patrick Brontë in 1965. Gérin also wrote two biographies on figures whose lives had touched Charlotte Brontë: Elizabeth Gaskell, who was Charlotte's first biographer, and Anne Thackeray Ritchie, who, at the age of thirteen, had met Charlotte at one of her father's dinner parties. Gérin has contributed much to Brontë research, and her biographies are marked by extensive research and an evocative and sympathetic narrative style. For her contributions to Brontë research and to the field of biography Gérin received two notable distinctions: she was made a Fellow of the Royal Society of Literature (FRSL) in 1968 and in 1975 an officer of the Order of the British Empire (OBE).

Winifred Eveleen Bourne was born on 7 October 1901 in Hamburg, Germany, where her father, Frederick Charles Bourne, was director of Nobel's Chemical Industries and her mother, Katharine, studied German and music. The youngest of a family of four, Winifred was closest to her only sister, Nell, who became a painter. Her parents were interested in all the arts – theater, painting, music, literature – and the girls showed talent in all these areas. Winifred played the piano well, read and wrote poetry from an early age, and later in her life sang with the London Philharmonic Choir.

She was brought up in Norwood in South London and attended Sydenham High School for Girls at Croydon. She entered Cambridge at the age of nineteen and was graduated from Newnham College in 1923 with a degree in English and Languages. She was fluent in French, German, and Spanish and after World War I was able to pick up odd jobs as a tour guide directing foreign students around London.

The love of literature, particularly of the Romantics and the Brontës, was instilled in her early. One of her earliest recollections is of her mother reading *Jane Eyre* (1847) to her. This interest in writing and poetry took her to Paris, the center of creative and experimental writing during the 1920s and 1930s, and it was there she began writing her own poetry. In 1930 she published her first volume of poetry, *The Invitation to Parnassus and other Poems*. Reviewed in 1931 in the *Times Literary Supplement*, the poems were described as having "musical force" and "elemental expressiveness," qualities Gérin was to bring to her biographical writing.

In Paris she met Eugène Gérin, a Belgian who was a professional cellist with the Monte Carlo Symphony. They shared a love of poetry and music. In September 1932 they were married in Croydon. The exciting atmosphere of the Paris scene and her marriage prompted numerous romantic poems.

When in 1940 the Germans invaded Belgium, she and her husband escaped from Brussels into France. Gérin had begun working for the British Foreign Office, where she showed courage and tenacity in her job. She later recalled "burning the Embassy's confidential papers as the German Invasion began." In France she and her husband helped refugees attempting to escape across the Pyrenees. It took them two years to return to England through Portugal. In England they worked together for the remainder of the war in the Political Intelligence Department for the Foreign Office. Eugène transmitted bulletins daily to Belgium for the Resistance. He died in 1945 at the age of forty-eight.

From 1945 until 1955 Winifred lived with her sister, Nell, in Kensington. During this time she was searching for her life's vocation; she sang with the London Philharmonic and Goldsmith's Choir and

Dust jacket for Gérin's biography of the British novelist and woman of letters

began writing plays. Her first play was *Juniper Hall*, a three-act drama about the romance between Fanny Burney and Gen. Alexandre d'Arblay. It first played in repertory theatre, then in 1956 was performed on BBC television, and subsequently on radio in Canada and Australia. Always interested in the Brontës, she visited Haworth in 1954 and was inspired to write her second play. *My Dear Master* concerns the last ten days of Charlotte's stay at the Pensionnat Heger in Brussels in December 1843. During her two years in Brussels Charlotte had formed a strong attachment to her tutor, M. Heger. Heger's wife, seeing the danger of such an unacceptable affection, engineered Charlotte's return to England. The play centers on the conflict between these two women. It was first performed in the Amersham Playhouse Theatre in May 1955 and then by the Leeds Art Theatre in October 1955. The reviewer for the *Yorkshire Post* (5 October 1955) called the Leeds production "a well-made play . . . [which] gains truth of period through the sustained excellence of the dialogue."

The year 1955 was momentous for Gérin. On a return visit to Haworth in 1954, to absorb the Yorkshire atmosphere for her play, she met John Lock, who had also developed an interest in the Brontës. In September 1955 they were engaged and in October of the same year were married in London. They bought a house on the edge of the Haworth moor within sight of the Brontë Parsonage and commenced their lifelong study of the Brontës. Ironically, Nell, Gérin's sister, thought Gérin would be wasting her talents up on the north moors and encouraged her to stay in London and pursue her playwriting career. But it was this momentous decision to turn from playwriting to biography and from London to Haworth that resulted in her fame.

Gérin and John Lock settled into their home named Gimmerton, after the fictional name for Haworth in Emily Brontë's *Wuthering Heights* (1847), and surrounded themselves with emotional reminders of the Brontës, such as a Yorkshire dresser built in 1801 (the date that begins *Wuthering Heights*). Their first work was a coproduction, a guide to Haworth, which was published in 1956. Although now out-of-date, it sold very well, going into a second printing of ten thousand copies in 1961. This was a significant beginning, for Gérin maintained that it was impossible to write of the Brontës without experiencing their landscape. To her it was of utmost importance to know and feel the locale in order to understand her subjects. Gérin's constant biographical aesthetic throughout her twenty-five years as a biographer was that the bare facts of a life must be imbued with the atmosphere of place and the feel of sympathetic liaison with her subjects. What she said in the preface to her first biography about living in Haworth and surrounding herself with Brontë relics stands as her biographical credo: "By such close contacts has something of the spirit of that family and of this place been able, I like to think, to enter into the composition of this book."

All her biographies exhibit evidence of strenuous research. She had near at hand, in the Brontë Parsonage Museum at Haworth, the original diaries, letters, and manuscripts of her subjects. She visited all the locations associated with them and traced official documents to their originals. She read the books and newspapers that they had read. In this aspect she was following the biographical trend of the 1960s, which put much emphasis on meticulous fact-gathering, but she refused to endorse the complementary deemphasis of narrative style and distrust of emotional attachment to the subject. Her original training in drama had made her sensitive to her audience. Three concerns – dedication to research, an evocation of landscape, and an expressivist style – characterize her biographical approach.

Gérin's first full-length biography, *Anne Brontë,* was published in 1959. According to Lock in a personal interview discussing his wife's work, *Anne Brontë* gave her the most pleasure to write. She chose to write about Anne first because Anne had been the silent, unacknowledged sister and because there had been to that date no full-length biography on her. Unlike her more famous sisters, Anne appeared conventional, moralistic, and dull. "Gentle" Anne, as she is often described, is redefined by Gérin as courageous, spiritual, and "greatly daring as a writer," in fact, "the bravest of the Brontës." The final chapter of the biography, "The Last Word," ends with Anne's dying word to Charlotte, "Courage," and encapsulates therein Gérin's view of Anne's unselfish, spiritual, and brave personality.

Gérin does much to dispel such myths as the view that the parsonage was a "prison-house," that the children did not have a happy childhood, and that Anne's writing was second-rate. But one myth of which she makes too much is the love between William Weightman and Anne. Because Anne writes about love, Gérin insists that she must have had a lover and concludes that the only possibility is Weightman. Gérin recognizes the questions raised by such autobiographical readings and does at one point acknowledge that the lover might be imaginary but feels that the strength of Anne's poetry belies such an explanation. Gérin speculates, for example, that Anne returned to Scarborough to die because her own heroine and hero in *Agnes Grey* (1847) declared their love in Scarborough. This implicit equation of Anne and the fictional character Agnes creates a highly poignant moment in the biography, but Gérin sacrifices credibility. Such a blend of factual detail, emotional rhetoric, and quotations from the fiction is illustrative of a tension nearly always present in Gérin's approach, that is, the tension between an objective rendering of emotional moments and a personal, interpretative one. Because the Brontës wrote autobiographically, the issue of paralleling their lives and their art is a troublesome one for their biographers.

Accompanying this paralleling of life and art, Gérin, at high dramatic moments, employs an imitative Brontë rhetoric: "The Gondals – oh! wild and happy rallies of their childhood, when they had ranged the moors! As fleet of foot, as free of mind, as light of heart as now mind and body were crushed under the intolerable burden!" She was to defend, a few years later, such rhetoric in her biographies on the grounds that it preserved sympathy with her subject and "convey[ed] the person and the period so much better than modern terms can do." Although never relenting on the necessity for warmth, as she called it, Gérin curbed some of the excesses of language in her later biographies.

Gérin has a talent not only for observing and recording detail but for drawing it to the reader's attention in a memorable way. For example, Anne and Emily's first diary paper is quoted at some length, and then Gérin adds: "There it lies, the much-blotted, disgracefully written scrap of paper scribbled on the corner of the kitchen table over a hundred and twenty years ago – Emily and Anne's uninhibited avowal of how they spent a Monday morning in their teens." So presented, the paper seems historic but immediate, venerable but ordinary.

This biography was well received, with special note being made of Gérin's "sense of intimacy with the Brontë home." For evocation of atmosphere another reviewer called it "a model of its kind." But reviewers did point out Gérin's "over-enthusiastic acceptance of Anne's novels as autobiographical."

Gérin's next project was the biography of Branwell Brontë, who, while he never gained fame through his own writing or painting, influenced his sisters in many ways. Gérin attempts to show that, while Branwell never had the depth or steadfastness of his three sisters, he contributed to their success and had an artistic energy and goodness most often overlooked by other biographers. He was the first, as early as 1837, to turn from the "artificial settings and 'intellectualised' action" of the Angrian writing to realistic writing; he was the impetus behind their early juvenilia; and he was a model, in part, for characters like Rochester, Heathcliff, and Lord Lowborough. In presenting him more completely and more complexly, Gérin suggests reasons for his failures. She believes that Branwell's infatuation with, and subsequent rejection by, Mrs. Robinson (his employer's wife) caused him to turn to opium, to alcohol, and to despairing idleness that arose from "the better side of his nature" and not from "an ignoble sorrow." Gérin writes sympathetically but temperately as she explores his relationship with his sisters and untangles, as much as anyone can, the stories about his relationship with Mrs. Robinson.

Although Gérin accumulates a convincing array of details she occasionally undermines her scholarly approach with a simplified chapter summary or, worse, a high-pitched conclusion. The ending of *Charlotte Brontë: The Evolution of Genius* (1967) was much criticized, and this tendency to oversimplify is evident early in *Branwell Brontë* (1961). To maintain a balance between climactic, memorable statements and truthful complexity is a challenge for the biographer, especially for a biographer like Gérin, who consciously wants from her audience an emotional response, not just an intellectual one. For example, Gérin writes in her epilogue that Mrs. Robinson "played a sufficient part in initiating a domestic tragedy that would sweep a whole family into its grave" and then ends her biography on this note: "It must remain a moot point whether the Brontës might not have lived into middle age if grief had not stood so early at their door. And it was Branwell's final misfortune that he it was who let the enemy in." The high rhetoric of tragedy, couched in such emotionally charged language, undermines the more complex analysis that has preceded this ending.

Extensive research into history and location are the strong points of this biography. Gérin's research into the early railway history of the locations where Branwell worked are of vital interest in creating a picture of her subject and his era. In discussing Branwell's employment as a clerk for the railway she includes details of salary, location, accommodation, and work routine that not only provide a backdrop for the socioeconomic picture but allow readers to interpret Branwell in a new light – to see how his creative energies were stimulated by his new role as clerk-in-charge of a small station, but also how he was unsuited to the responsibilities and solitariness of his employment.

In similar detail Gérin describes the landscape, using it not only to provide a sense of place but to suggest her subject's inner thoughts. Thus, Luddenden Foot, where Branwell was ignominiously fired for carelessness with the railway accounts, is described in detail with regard to its sinister landscape, its solitude, and its ghostly settings, all of which establish Branwell's despairing mental state.

Branwell Brontë was chosen as the nonfiction selection by the Book Society and a book of the month by John o'Londons. As a result of this success, the first edition was sold out before the publication date. Once again reviewers noted the tremendous research undertaken by Gérin, who read all of Branwell's manuscripts and read twenty years of *Blackwood's* to search out influences on his work. Some reviewers considered together Gérin's book and Daphne du Maurier's *Infernal World of Branwell*

Brontë (1960) and pointed out Gérin's more factual, solid, and less psychological approach.

The Young Fanny Burney (1961), a slim novelistic biography, appeared soon after *Branwell Brontë*. Gérin had produced in 1956 a stage drama based on Fanny Burney's marriage to General d'Arblay, but in this biographical study she concentrates on an earlier period between 1775 and 1778 when Burney wrote and published anonymously her first novel, *Evelina* (1778). Gérin had been inspired to take up this subject again by the appearance in 1958 of Joyce Hemlow's *The History of Fanny Burney,* which printed many of Fanny's letters. Writing for "the girl in her late teens," Gérin uses many fictional techniques – she employs dialogue, visualizes locations and weather conditions, creates climactic crises and suspense, and ascribes emotional states to her characters. She stretches the facts for dramatic purpose. For example, differing from Hemlow's more historical view, Gérin exaggerates the hostility between the daughter and the stepmother, creating a Cinderella-like ugly-stepmother figure. In this book Gérin was able to indulge her particular talent for dramatic biography, and she produced a lively and highly readable narrative.

Branwell Brontë and *Anne Brontë* were essential steps toward the larger project, *Charlotte Brontë: The Evolution of Genius.* The earlier biographies exhibited similar strengths (research and enthusiasm) and similar weaknesses (autobiographical readings and overdramatized rhetoric). Charlotte, of course, was a more central literary figure, and there was much more material with which to deal and more locations to visit. Furthermore, the editing process took much longer (three years) than with her first two biographies, and Gérin, forced to think about and defend many biographical presuppositions, matured a great deal during this time. While there is some harsh criticism for certain aspects of *Charlotte Brontë,* all in all the critics mark it as her best work. She, too, thought it her best, most rounded biography.

In June 1964 Gérin had a completed manuscript of her biography on Charlotte Brontë, but she had no publisher. The publisher of her last three books, Thomas Nelson and Sons, had changed hands, and they were no longer interested in publishing her type of book. She appealed to Oxford University Press, who agreed to look at her manuscript, and thus began her association with that press. Acceptance by Oxford meant a move into more-scholarly publication. During the lengthy editing process Gérin conducted an amicable dialogue with the editors regarding her expressive style and her copious use of detail. What the editors and

some critics called emotional rhetoric ("a sensational approach") Gérin and other critics defended as "warmth," necessary sympathy for the subject, and "persuasive force." Although this tension between an objective and a subjective approach had been apparent in her previous biographies, it was this move to a more scholarly press that brought it to a head.

A more scholarly style and approach is noticeable in the biography's footnoting style, the longer paragraphs, the clearer syntax, the extended literary analysis (still, however, not a priority with Gérin), and the attempt to be more cautious about equating life and fiction. Scholars, however, criticized her emotional ending with its dramatic description of the March gales and the sentimentalizing of Charlotte's death with references to how her spirit "leapt" to escape the real world and enter the "Celestial City." On the other hand, general readers liked this emotional engagement, and Gérin argued strongly that subjective description and passages of feeling must remain. She compromised over some passages, but not this final one, and it remains controversial today.

Gérin had been in Haworth for nearly ten years at this point and had spent the last five years exhaustively researching the Charlotte Brontë material. She visited as many descendants of Charlotte's friends as was possible – the Hegers' granddaughter, Elizabeth Gaskell's and Mary Taylor's families, and George Smith's granddaughter. Gérin's research, her investigation of all of Charlotte's juvenile manuscripts, her attempt to depict vividly and significantly the Haworth environment (and other locations), her discussion of influences on Charlotte's work, and her fair-minded unraveling of Charlotte's attachment to Heger extended the scope and depth of knowledge about Charlotte Brontë. While there is nothing vitally new in her findings, they add complexity and wholeness and substantiate many theories.

Gérin states in her introduction that her thesis is "the growth of Charlotte's moral and artistic stature." Building upon the metaphor of the education of the soul, Gérin points to Charlotte's "First Lessons" at the hands of Carus Wilson at Cowan Bridge School and then to the "lesson of her greatest experience in life" which occurred in 1852 in Brussels under the tutelage of Heger. Although this interpretation of the importance of the Brussels period is not in itself unique, for previous biographers have called it the turning point in her life, Gérin's attempt to construct an organic and complex wholeness out of these experiences is innovative.

This approach leads Gérin to look at Charlotte's relationship with Heger from all sides. She suggests that the rupture in the relationship with Madame Heger and Charlotte's recognition that her attachment to Heger was not entirely disinterested occurred after Charlotte had left Brussels and during the two years in which she attempted to correspond with Heger. Attempting to see the situation in all its complexity, Gérin points out that Madame Heger's actions were reasonable and that she was more charitable than the character Madame Beck, of whom she is usually considered to be the model. Perhaps this section, which shows an ability to question and probe with an even-handed and an unbiased sympathy, is Gérin's greatest contribution to Charlotte's story.

Throughout the biography Gérin plots the course of "the conflict of the two elements [the imagination and the conscience] warring within her [Charlotte] to tear her soul." In Gérin's view these warring elements are eventually resolved, Charlotte's personality is unified, and her greatest work, *Villette* (1853), is written. With this final novel Gérin believes that Charlotte was at last able to fuse her imaginary world (the Angrian world she had created in her juvenilia with its romantic visions of love, rejection, and despair) with her experiences of the real world, particularly those of Brussels.

Charlotte Brontë was distinguished by three major awards: the James Tait Black Memorial for the best biography of the year; the Royal Society of Literature Heinemann Prize for English literature; and the Rose Mary Crawshay Prize for English Literature. Critics called it "definitive" and the "standard biography," and it retains that status in the 1990s. There were criticisms, however, concerning Gérin's overexuberant prose style, her lack of literary analysis, and her tendency to ignore psychological issues. More recently, Tom Winnifrith, a Brontë scholar and author of *A New Life of Charlotte Brontë* (1988), has criticized Gérin for some factual errors and for reading the fiction autobiographically. Even Winnifrith acknowledges that "all students of the Brontës are greatly in her debt."

For the next seven to eight years Gérin was exceedingly busy, not simply with two more biographies but with lecturing, editing, and with writing a survey-type book on the Brontës for the Writers and Their Work series. This small two-volume book came out in 1973. Before that she transcribed and edited, from the unpublished manuscripts of Charlotte Brontë, five novelettes, an important addition to Brontë resources. Gérin also delivered two

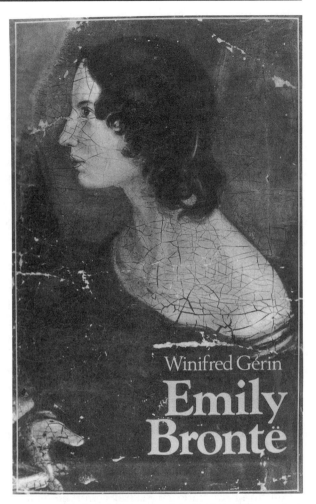

Dust jacket for Gérin's biography of the British novelist, praised by Phyllis Bentley for its "meticulous, scrupulous and comprehensive research"

lectures to the Royal Society of Literature, one on the influence of the environment on the Brontës (27 February 1969) and the second on the influence of Byron (22 October 1970). These were later published in *Essays by Divers Hands* in 1970 and 1972, respectively. In 1971 she wrote a lengthy introduction for the Folio Society for their publication of Gaskell's *The Life of Charlotte Brontë* (1971). These activities were, in a sense, peripheral, less satisfactory, and less interesting than her real vocation, writing biographies.

In 1968 Gérin was at work on her fifth biography. *Horatia Nelson* (1970) was a deliberate attempt to break the mold of being known as the Brontë biographer. Because this biography took a different direction, being historical rather than literary, Gérin was nervous about its reception at her publishers. Gérin cut the book's size by about forty thousand words, which gives some idea of the extensiveness of her material but also of her uncertainty about scope in a historical biography. As it stands there are perhaps still too many details about the extended Nelson family, with the result that the biography sometimes loses focus.

In selecting Horatia Nelson as her next subject, Gérin again shows sympathy for minor figures. She was the first to bring Anne Brontë out of the shadow of her two famous sisters, and with *Horatia Nelson* she was the first to devote a full-length biography to Lord Nelson's daughter. Certainly Lord Nelson figures prominently in the book, but he is seen more as a father than as a naval hero. As Gérin notes in her preface, Nelson "is, surprisingly, seen to greater advantage in his role of father than ever before."

Although generally accepted now that Horatia was the daughter of Lord Nelson and his mistress, Emma Hamilton, for many years the facts surrounding her parentage were cloaked in secrecy. Indeed, Gérin's biography is preoccupied with unraveling the subterfuge established by Lady Hamilton in concealing the truth about herself as the mother. The biography opens dramatically with Hamilton's nighttime ride to Mrs. Gibson's, where she left in her care the week-old baby Horatia. Gérin's interest is in domestic, not in political or naval, history: she follows Nelson's love for his only child, his passionate affection for Lady Hamilton, the machinations of the Nelson family after the death of Lord Nelson, Lady Hamilton's unmaternal feelings and her sordid death, and finally Horatia's life as a vicar's wife and mother of a large family. Nelson is not depicted in all his glory as the most famous of British naval leaders but as the devoted family man.

Gérin's research was again exhaustive, but she gives the biography a literary feel. As she describes it, the work is "a plain biography . . . about a *pursuit of identity.*" Thus, she divides the book into three parts, each dealing with one aspect of Horatia's developing identity. Part 1 is called "Horatia Nelson Thompson," Thompson referring to the pseudonym given her by her parents to conceal her true parentage. The second part, titled "Horatia Nelson Nelson," deals with Lady Hamilton's attempts to have Horatia recognized and honored as the legitimate heir of Nelson. The third part, "Horatia Nelson Ward," follows Horatia's life as wife of Philip Ward and mother of nine children.

Typically, Gérin put much store in visiting all the places associated with her subject and in contacting the descendants of the Nelsons. Thus she brings to light much new material from family records. It is understandable why this, of all her biog-

raphies, receives so much interest from readers — the story itself is fascinating and dramatic. The last section flags somewhat, not simply because the subject has moved out of the Nelson aura and into her own life but because the multitude of relatives, both on the Nelson side and her husband's side, crowd the picture and, indeed, take over.

Generally well received, the critics described Gérin's debut into historical biography as "exact, sympathetic and realistic," although some reviewers noted that the subject herself was "intrinsically uninteresting" or that Horatia seemed lost within the larger stories of her courageous father and intriguing mother. While not consciously challenging the notion of historical and literary canonization, Gérin shows with her choice of subjects — Branwell Brontë, Horatia Nelson, Fanny Burney, and Anne Thackeray Ritchie — a belief in and sympathy for peripheral shapers of history and culture. Despite the view of some critics that *Horatia Nelson* "does not succeed as a biography [because] Horatia did not lead a particularly exciting or unusual life," it sold well (four thousand copies of a five-thousand-copy printing), was reprinted as a paperback, and, according to John Lock, receives the most fan mail. In 1974 Gérin was invited, along with other writers on Lord Nelson, to a dinner with the Trafalgar Society aboard the *Victory*.

As usual Gérin had launched herself on a new subject even while editing her previous one. Before *Horatia Nelson* was accepted she was well into *Emily Brontë: A Biography* (1971). In April 1970 *Horatia Nelson* was published, and three weeks later *Emily Brontë* was accepted for publication. Although sixty-nine years old at the time, Gérin seemed tireless in her research and ideas for new projects.

Emily Brontë was published in February 1971. Emily was Gérin's favorite of all the Brontës, and it is her picture which hangs over the fireplace in Gérin's old home. That personal affinity, coupled with the scarcity of substantial material about Emily (only three personal letters exist) and her mysterious nature, made her a challenge to write about, and for those reasons she was left to the last. Although Gérin still tends at times to read the life backward from the works (and this is an even greater temptation with Emily, about whom there is little factual evidence), in many respects this biography is more scholarly in its presentation of documentation, more rigorous in its attempts to explain — not just delineate — personality, and more controlled stylistically than Gérin's other biographies.

Gérin is very good in documenting the importance of Emily's tenure at Law Hill to *Wuthering*

Heights (1847). She struggles convincingly with the concept of mysticism as it applies to Emily's philosophical and aesthetic beliefs, and she curbs her own emotional rhetoric, allowing the subject's own work to express the passion that Gérin, in her earlier books, had often taken upon herself to express. Thus, Emily's death is underplayed, and the biography, rather than closing down with a simplistic ending, opens up all that "is too transcendental to express" through the medium of Emily's own words from one of her poems.

Gérin's preoccupation with delineating growth in her subjects is especially significant in following the life of Emily who, as Gérin points out in her introduction, has so often been categorized as an inscrutable mystic. Gérin shows that this view is one-sided and that it focuses too much on the last three years of Emily's life. Gérin sets out to "show the degrees of her growth both as woman and visionary" and offsets Emily's mystical nature with examples of her practical, robust, reserved, and loving nature. Although Gérin devotes much time to sorting out the sibling relationships, there are times when Emily is admired at the expense of Charlotte and at the expense of solid documentation. This is especially obvious in Gérin's belief that Emily was much more sympathetic to Branwell than was Charlotte and that Emily's last few years of silence and withdrawal were largely due to Charlotte's authoritarian control of the sisters' artistic endeavors. Gérin stresses the rupture between Charlotte and Emily and sees Emily's last few months as "a direct opposition to Charlotte's dearest wishes." This oversimplification stretches the evidence, and Gérin, too romantically, concludes that Emily "willed" her own death.

In terms of literary analysis Gérin does a more complete job in this biography of pointing out influences and themes in the works, particularly in *Wuthering Heights*. Gérin is very good at locating real events, locations, and models that have served as inspiration for *Wuthering Heights*. She illustrates convincingly that Branwell, while not the only model for Heathcliff, provided "the emotional climate" for many scenes, and she argues that the background history of Law Hill, where Emily worked, with its story of family disinheritance and revenge, must have served as an impetus for *Wuthering Heights*. Alongside the real models, Gérin outlines such literary influences as Sir Walter Scott's depiction of rural types; Mary Shelley's and James Hogg's use of the Gothic horror story and the doppelgänger figure; and George Gordon, Lord Byron's, attitude to fate. What Gérin admires most about Emily Brontë is her ability to transform all the passion, the influences, the themes into something, not only original, not only Yorkshire, but "through and through English."

Emily Brontë sold well and is today the most popular of the Brontë biographies, probably because Emily's popularity, at present, has eclipsed Charlotte's. Because of Gérin's prolonged study of the family, this work has "an authority which few scholars can match," wrote one reviewer, and Mary Ellman in the *American Scholar* (Winter 1972–1973) likewise commented that it has "the authority of immersion." Although praising the biography for its "meticulous, scrupulous and comprehensive research," Phyllis Bentley, herself a Brontë biographer, disagreed with a number of Gérin's interpretations. For example, she was unconvinced that Emily was more sympathetic to Branwell than were the other sisters. Robert Bernard Martin in *Victorian Studies* (September 1972) is perhaps Gérin's harshest critic, calling this biography "a partial disappointment." He criticizes her lack of literary criticism, her equation of life and fiction (and thus her addiction to "invented attitudes and thoughts"), and her unscholarly handling of quotations (which were largely corrected in the 1972 reprinting). Martin's remarks point out one of the great difficulties for biographers, especially Brontë biographers, who either work from little evidence as in the case of Emily or are tempted by the Brontë autobiographical fiction to equate life and art. There is a difference between invention and speculation, and Gérin does, at times, fail to signpost the route to her conclusions, adopting a direct route from a poem to the life rather than indicating her own speculation. As well she occasionally turns a theory into a fact and from there asserts an interpretation. For example, she takes it as a fact that Charlotte confided to Emily all her heartbreak about Heger, but there is no certain evidence for this. From that point she argues that Emily agreed to the publication of the volume of poems in order to console Charlotte for her great sorrow. However, with the exception of the sibling rivalry theory she posits, Gérin is more careful to employ signs of uncertainty than in her other biographies, and she uses such phrases as "one cannot rule out the possibility" or "we can only guess" to indicate her speculation. Given Emily's passionate nature, the scarcity of documented evidence, and the autobiographical nature of the poetry in particular, Gérin succeeded in writing a most reasonable biography.

Each of Gérin's Brontë biographies is written from a special angle, and, while some material is necessarily repeated from one biography to the other, most scenes are keyed to the subject involved. Each biography commences in a fashion that illustrates Gérin's different approach to each personality. It is extraordinary that Gérin could so differentiate the four Brontë writers. Charlotte, who more than the others benefited from her worldly experiences, is first seen in the schoolroom, not in Haworth. The first lines of this biography introduce Charlotte as a little girl who "reads tolerably – Writes indifferently . . . "; Anne, on the other hand, is shown in the context of a happy family and a christening, which mark her as a more traditional and god-fearing personality; Branwell is introduced as "the only boy," indicative of the familial indulgence that led to his many failures. Emily is described as the "darling child" who managed to escape, through a mask of aloofness or a shield of silence, many of the religious and morbid scars of the common Brontë experience.

As her biography on Emily was going through the final publication stages, Gérin was thinking of possibilities for her next project. There were several false starts until, in May 1972, she started work on another historical biography, this one on Amy Robsart, the wife of Sir Robert Dudley, Earl of Leicester, who was a favorite with Queen Elizabeth I. This historical tale had all the ingredients of high drama: political intrigue, romance, scandal, jealousy, and finally the murder of Amy by her husband's envoy. Gérin spent two years writing this historical biography, only to find it turned down for publication. The disappointment about these wasted years persuaded her that literary biography was more her forte.

By December 1974 she was at work on a biography of Elizabeth Gaskell, the friend and the first biographer of Charlotte Brontë. *Elizabeth Gaskell: A Biography* was published in 1976 and won the Whitbread Award that year for the best biography. It is frequently cited as the standard biography of Gaskell. Gérin depicts a charming, maternal, humanitarian woman whose writing reflects her personality and personal experience. As the standard biography of Gaskell, Gérin's work has only recently been superseded by Jenny Uglow's *Elizabeth Gaskell: A Habit of Stories* (1993).

During her lifetime and until recently, Gaskell was best known for her *Life of Charlotte Brontë* (1857). Gérin calls it "one of the masterpieces of the century." But Gaskell was also a well-known writer of social-purpose novels such as *Mary Barton* (1848), *Ruth* (1853), and *North and South* (1855) and of novels of character growth such as *Sylvia's Lovers* (1863)

and her final novel, *Wives and Daughters* (1866), which Gérin considers her best. Gaskell was "a woman of her time"; she associated with the working classes through her church work, with religious leaders, and with literary figures such as Thomas Carlyle, Charles Dickens, William Makepeace Thackeray, and Charlotte Brontë. Gaskell was very popular and controversial among her contemporaries, not just because her *Life of Charlotte Brontë* resulted in a threatened libel suit and numerous public complaints but because her sympathetic depiction of prostitutes, unwed mothers, and her support for the working class in their fight against mill owners provoked much comment from the Victorian middle and upper classes. Interestingly, Gérin comments that in writing *Ruth* (and this can be extended to her other works) Gaskell "was no theorist and never thought or wrote in generalizations; she was intensely personal in her response to situations, and identified herself completely with the people whose tragedies came to her knowledge." In some degree this describes Gérin's own writing aesthetic, certainly one evident in this biography where her empathy with her subject makes this a very human and absorbing study. While no moralist like Gaskell, Gérin identifies strongly with her subjects and writes from a sympathetic distance.

Gérin, as a biographer of Charlotte Brontë, was in an excellent position to discuss Gaskell's *Life of Charlotte Brontë*. She gives it great importance, devoting more space to the biography than she does to the novels. A consequence of this kind of concentration, though, is that Gérin at other points in her discussion becomes too preoccupied with Charlotte Brontë. An occupational danger in knowing the field so thoroughly is to boost one subject at the expense of another. Occasionally this sort of competitiveness and bias slips into her biographies, as it does in this one when she comments that the "unpromising love-affair" between Margaret Hale and John Thornton in *North and South* "would have been better done by a Brontë."

Gérin makes her case for the need for a new biography of Elizabeth Gaskell on the grounds that *The Letters of Mrs. Gaskell,* published in 1966, contained personal letters which had not previously been incorporated into a biographical treatment. While she says these do not constitute "sensational revelations," they do show "a very complete human being." In her biography Gérin sets out to weave together the public and the private selves in a way not attempted before. She describes in more detail than do previous biographers Gaskell's domestic situation and how this affected her writing career, which, Gérin says, was always secondary to motherhood. In her objective to show the "special quality of radiance" of Elizabeth Gaskell and to show the "intensely personal character of her work," Gérin succeeds very well. It is possible to see in these statements a design that pervades all Gérin's work: a desire to see her subjects "whole" and "complete," to see them "growing," and to pinpoint this growth as a resolution of warring opposites: the tension between the real world of familial duties and the world of the creative imagination for Charlotte and Emily; and, for Gaskell, the dual pull of motherhood and authorship.

Certainly order is an attribute of Gérin's approach, and in this sense she is following conventional biographical practice. Signposting significant events in a writer's life is a part of the biographer's role, and a mark of Gérin's approach is to locate turning points in the lives of subjects as they move from innocence to experience. Thus, she sees Gaskell in terms of beginnings, ends, turning points, "Chrysalis Years" (the title of chapter 5), "new life" (the birth of her book to replace the death of her son), and finally, death, "the perfect consummation of her life."

Although not her best all-around biography, *Elizabeth Gaskell* could be described as her most balanced. Gérin shows both the happy and the black moments in Gaskell's life; she is fair in her assessment of Gaskell's literary status; she moderates her own prose style; and her literary analysis, although not extensive, is "balanced and reasonable," according to Arthur Pollard, the coeditor of *The Letters of Mrs. Gaskell* (1966).

The critical reception of *Elizabeth Gaskell* was mixed and perhaps somewhat unfair. The *Spectator* and the *Listener* criticized the biography for being, "like its subject," too "tiresome, worthy, dutiful and dull." The notion that a charming or nice person does not deserve a biography, or, alternatively, that a biographer's duty is to enhance the ordinary, raises questions about the purpose and integrity of biography. Although critics called it "orderly" and "readable," it was considered inferior in comparison to *Charlotte Brontë* and not critical enough of Gaskell's fiction.

By the autumn of 1976 Gérin had begun her biography of Lady Ritchie, and even ill health did not daunt her. At the age of seventy-five and suffering from the effects of a minor stroke, Gérin showed enthusiasm for her new project even from her hospital bed. Although she experienced some paralysis, she recovered and by January 1978 was back on track going through the numerous unpub-

Dust jacket for Gérin's biography of the British novelist and biographer who was the daughter of novelist William Makepeace Thackeray

lished family letters she had received from Ritchie's granddaughter. As her editor said, she had the "knack . . . to be on the spot to gather first-hand material," a research skill she had honed after years on the Brontë trail.

No doubt many factors drew Gérin to Anne Thackeray Ritchie. There had as yet been no full-length biography on Ritchie, motivation enough for her to take on the project. But there were more-personal reasons as well. Gérin had been a fan of William Makepeace Thackeray for years; she had read *The Rose and the Ring* (1855) when she was eight. Thus, in writing about the daughter she was also writing about the father but seeing him in a new light, not as the "cynic and snob" but as the kind father, the steadfast husband to a mentally handicapped wife, and a friend to many of the pre-eminent Victorian writers of the day such as

Charles Dickens, Alfred Tennyson, Thomas Carlyle, and John Ruskin. A second affinity for her subject had been formed much earlier when Gérin had quoted at length in *Charlotte Brontë* Anne's recall of the dinner party her father had given in honor of Brontë. Also, Anne Thackeray Ritchie's character and style were much like Gaskell's, and so there was a natural progression from *Elizabeth Gaskell;* as Gérin noted in her preface, "In the lambent quality of her [Anne Thackeray Ritchie's] wit, her closest affinity among the Victorians was with Mrs. Gaskell." Mrs. Ritchie's interest in "nature in all its moods" must have hit a sympathetic chord in Gérin's own spirit, and, finally, one senses that Gérin was at an age and point in her career where Ritchie's sympathetic look at the past and her reminiscential works such as *Chapters from Some Memoirs* (1894) and *From the Porch* (1913) would have special appeal for her. There is a sense in which Anne Thackeray Ritchie, in the words of her niece Virginia Woolf, "will be the un-acknowledged source of much that remains in men's minds about the Victorian age." *Anne Thackeray Ritchie: A Biography* (1981) was a fitting biography with which to end a career devoted to studying that era.

And yet, this was a brave project for Gérin to take on, for Anne Thackeray Ritchie was neither a well-known celebrity nor a first-rate novelist. Her charm is that she recalled in lively and feeling prose many of the great figures of her father's and her own era. She drew vivid pictures, for example, of Tennyson walking with his children in his garden and of Elizabeth Barrett Browning sitting in front of her fire. Through a fine selection of quotations Gérin conveys the style and personality of "Anny." Just as Anne was at her best describing atmosphere and emotion, so too Gérin is at her best describing the places associated with the Thackerays and the emotional value of a scene such as Thackeray's feelings at his first lecture series. There is a pervasively benevolent aura around Anne that suggests Gérin has colored the picture slightly. Anne's burdens — dealing with a mentally disturbed mother, a very authoritarian and religious grandmother, and her own marital crisis — seem very light in Gérin's treatment, and there is the sense that they are being seen with older, less judgmental eyes, more within the context of the past rather than the present.

Anne Thackeray Ritchie was to be her memorial; it was published three days before she died. The reviews came out after Gérin's death, and many commented on the appropriateness of this loving and gentle biography as a finale. Rebecca West opened her review with the lines, "How sad it is that Winifred Gérin has just died. But how satisfactory that the setting of her sun was so grand." The almost universal comment on the "scholarly, entertaining and benevolent" qualities of this biography take us full circle to those skills which so mark all the Gérin biographies — scholarly research, a keen observer's eye for detail, an empathy with her subjects, a courage of conviction about her choice of subject, and an expressivist style.

Winifred Gérin died on 27 June 1981. A year before her death she had started writing her autobiography. As usual she was looking forward and backward simultaneously but this time with her own life. Her memoir was to be called *The Years that Count,* and, as she wrote to her editor, it was to be "purely selective and relating only to vivid memories." If this volume is published, it will provide a sense of the making of the sensibility of an extraordinary biographer.

References:

Katherine Frank, "The Brontë Biographies: Romance, Reality, and Revision," *Biography,* 2 (Spring 1979): 141–156;

Elizabeth Jenkins, "Winifred Gérin: The Brontë Biographies," *Newnham College Roll* (1983): 34–37;

Margo Peters, "Biographies of Women," *Biography,* 2 (Summer 1979): 201–217;

Peters, "Charlotte Brontë: A Critico-Bibliographic Survey: Part I," *British Studies Monitor,* 6 (Summer 1976): 10–36;

Alan Shelston, "Biography and the Brontës," *Critical Quarterly,* 18 (Autumn 1976): 67–72.

Papers:

Gérin's unpublished correspondence is held in the archives of the Oxford University Press and can be consulted by permission of the secretary to the delegates of the press.

Victoria Glendinning

(23 April 1937 –)

David Hopkinson

BOOKS: *A Suppressed Cry: Life and Death of a Quaker Daughter* (London: Routledge, 1969);

Elizabeth Bowen: Portrait of a Writer (London: Weidenfeld & Nicolson, 1977; New York: Knopf, 1978);

Edith Sitwell: A Unicorn Among Lions (London: Weidenfeld & Nicolson, 1981; New York: Knopf, 1981);

Vita: The Life of Vita Sackville-West (London: Weidenfeld & Nicolson, 1983; New York: Knopf, 1983);

Rebecca West: A Life (London: Weidenfeld & Nicolson, 1987; New York: Knopf, 1987);

The Grown-ups (London: Weidenfeld & Nicolson, 1989; New York: Knopf, 1990);

Victoria Glendinning's Hertfordshire (London: Weidenfeld & Nicolson, 1989);

The Grown-Ups (London: Hutchinson, 1989; New York: Knopf, 1990);

Trollope (London: Hutchinson, 1992; New York: Knopf, 1993);

The New Woman (London: Collins & Brown, 1993);

Electricity (London: Hutchinson, 1995; Boston: Little, Brown, 1995).

OTHER: *Three Nineteenth Century Novels: Pride and Prejudice, Wuthering Heights, Silas Marner,* introduction by Glendinning (New York: New American Library, 1979);

"Speranza," in *Genius in the Drawing Room: The Literary Salon in the Nineteenth and Twentieth Centuries* (London: Weidenfeld & Nicolson, 1980);

Rebecca West, *The Return of the Soldier,* introduction by Glendinning (London: Virago, 1980; New York: Dial, 1982);

West, *Harriet Hume,* introduction by Glendinning (London: Virago, 1980);

Edith Wharton, *"Ethan Frome" and "Summer,"* introduction by Glendinning (Oxford: Oxford University Press, 1982);

Vita Sackville-West, *The Edwardians,* introduction by Glendinning (London: Virago, 1983);

Sackville-West, *All Passion Spent,* introduction by Glendinning (London: Virago, 1983);

Victoria Glendinning (photograph by Caroline Forbes)

West, *The Fountain Overflows,* introduction by Glendinning (London: Virago, 1984);

West, *The Thinking Reed,* introduction by Glendinning (London: Virago, 1984);

Sackville-West, *No Signposts in the Sea,* introduction by Glendinning (London: Virago, 1985);

West, *Cousin Rosamund,* afterword by Glendinning (London: Macmillan, 1985);

Violet Trefusis, *Broderie Anglaise,* introduction by Glendinning (New York: Harcourt Brace Jovanovich, 1985);

H. G. Wells, *The Wife of Sir Isaac Harman,* introduction by Glendinning (London: Hogarth Press, 1986);

Wells, *The Passionate Friends,* introduction by Glendinning (London: Hogarth Press, 1986);

West, *Sunflower,* afterword by Glendinning (London: Virago, 1986; New York: Viking, 1987);

Sackville-West, *Family History,* introduction by Glendinning (London: Virago, 1986);

"Lies and Silences," in *The Troubled Face of Biography,* edited by Eric Homberger and John Charmley (New York: St. Martin's Press, 1988), pp. 49–62;

Anthony Trollope, *Barchester Towers,* introduction by Glendinning (New York: Knopf, 1992).

Between 1969 and 1992 Victoria Glendinning wrote six biographies; five relate the story of a woman's life, and five provide examples of copious and outstanding literary achievement. Her books are notable for painstaking attention to detail, fine critical judgment, and candid but sympathetic perception of character. The quality of her writing is to be found in its lucidity and because fresh creative insights are expressed in direct terms without recourse to pretentious phraseology.

Victoria Seebohm was born on 23 April 1937, the second child of Frederic Seebohm, a banker, and Evangeline Seebohm, whose father was Sir Gerald Hurst, a scholar and a barrister who was for many years a Conservative member of Parliament and subsequently a judge. The Seebohms were Quakers of German origin who settled in the north of England, but Victoria's great-grandfather Frederic came south and married the daughter of a prosperous banker, thus becoming a partner in a business that continued to thrive. Of equal importance to him, it allowed him the leisure to engage in historical research. With no recognized academic background, he became a recognized authority with a national reputation and a wide circle of scholarly friends. His grandson Frederic was Victoria's father. He too was a banker – a distinguished one – and also an inheritor of the Quaker tradition. In addition to a strong social conscience, he possessed unsentimental coolness and confidence, and he added to his leading role in the counsels of Barclay's Bank a prominent part in national planning for the reform of social welfare services. He passed on to Victoria his energy and the confidence with which he accepted responsibility.

The Seebohm children received their early education in the Anglican rather than the Quaker tradition. The parents were ambitious for their three children, and at sixteen Victoria was sent, as one of its first female pupils, to what was then an innovative independent school. There she received intensive teaching which helped her to secure a place at Somerville College, Oxford. More important perhaps was a growing confidence in her own abilities, social as well as intellectual. She began to enjoy the society of clever, unpredictable contemporaries, male as well as female. She was a fast reader and

quick to acquire authority over language, her own as well as the French and Spanish she studied at Oxford. She married her tutor, Nigel Glendinning, at the end of her second year and was pregnant when she sat for her final examinations. Within the next six and a half years Glendinning had four sons. Thus, she slotted herself at an early age into a position where responsibilities had to be accepted and discharged. Her obligations were various, but she found herself able to contract a heavy workload and discharge it enthusiastically without diminishing the quality of her life. She had assumed a political stance well to the left of her parents, though her father, when given a seat in the House of Lords, became an active, independent, nonparty legislator. Glendinning had no leanings toward institutionalized religion. Her infatuation was with the created world, the people and places within reach and the feelings they could inspire, some closed to her but always with the chance that they might yield to intelligence and hard work.

In 1963 her husband was appointed to the Chair of Spanish at Southampton University, and there the family lived for the next seven years. During this period Glendinning trained as a psychiatric social worker, thus opening up a field of work which she was later to find useful in research for her biographies, especially those for which friends as well as documents were to be consulted. Her first book was published in 1969 when her youngest son was four years old. The family then moved to Dublin upon her husband's appointment to a professorship at Trinity College. There Glendinning worked at a child guidance clinic, but she also began reviewing for the *Times Literary Supplement* and for the *Irish Times.* When the family returned to England in 1974, it was to a home in north London, as Nigel was now professor of Spanish at Queen Mary College. Glendinning was by then launching into a new career as a journalist and author. Her first literary biography, that of the novelist Elizabeth Bowen, was in hand. She had a job on the *Times Literary Supplement,* and its editor, John Gross, had put forward her name for the Bowen project to its eventual publisher. Glendinning described Bowen as someone to be spoken of in the same breath as Virginia Woolf. She saw her work as providing a link between the absolute originality of Woolf and the less decorative, more incisive style of modern novelists such as Iris Murdoch and Muriel Spark. In writing her biography of Bowen something was owed to the fact that Glendinning had lived in Ireland, but more helpful was her friendship with the Irish writer Terence de Vere White. Their friendship and his book on the Anglo-Irish helped her to compose a portrait of Bowen which placed her in the tradition and legacy of Richard Brinsley Sheridan, Maria Edgeworth, George Moore, and Oscar Wilde.

The four Glendinning boys attended the same London comprehensive school and lived at home. Domestically this was a demanding period of Glendinning's life. During it she divorced Glendinning and later married Terence de Vere White. As a critic, reviewing novels and other books in daily and weekly papers, she brought a liberal, sympathetic, unbiased mind to the work. Her writing was clean of ideological adulteration and without academic pomposity. She produced a great deal of work while always seeming to retain a youthful wit and freshness of manner. During the 1980s she responded to demands from radio and television producers for appearances in serious and lighthearted programs. She involved herself in liberal and humanitarian causes and lived a socially active life. For some years she and de Vere White made an attractive home and garden in a Hertfordshire village. She wrote a guidebook, *Victoria Glendinning's Hertfordshire,* to that county where the Seebohms had been great figures in the past, and a novel, *The Grown-Ups,* both of which appeared in 1989. Her regular reviews, mainly for the London *Times,* continued, and in 1992 she was chosen as the first woman chair of the panel of judges for the Booker Prize.

A Suppressed Cry: Life and Death of a Quaker Daughter (1969) is a short book derived from Seebohm family papers. It was not widely reviewed, but on percipient readers it made a considerable impact. The telling of a tragic story is sentient but not sentimental. Any insensitive or unhistorical treatment of the characters and their background would have been unbearable, but there is none. The book is characterized by delicacy and detachment. The suppressed cry is that of Winnie, born into a wealthy Quaker family in 1863 and "left stranded on the shores of the nineteenth century." She died at the age of twenty-two, having spent one month of her brief life as a student at Newnham College, Cambridge, which had been founded a few years earlier. The story of Winnie touched its author's sympathy at several points, not merely for its family connection but as a study of Quaker aspirations and moral values. The story raises in an especially poignant way a young woman's passionate struggle for education and a place in the world where self-directed action in the interest of society might be made possible. In Winnie's case there was well-meaning family opposition to be overcome. This centered on the danger of college education to her health (she suffered from asthma) but also to her place in the right kind of social milieu and her future marriage prospects. Even when it was only an expressed wish, her longing for Cambridge provoked sarcastic comments from young men of her acquaintance. In the end the desired goal was attained, partly, it seemed, because some measure of family protection could be provided by her brother in his first year at King's College. At Newnham Winnie was carefully tended, perhaps too carefully, but letters home expressed her happiness in spite of increasing ill health. She fought bravely and suffered an honorable defeat. The family insisted that she should come home, and a day before the fateful day she wrote to her sister that "I am so grateful to *all* of you for taking so much trouble about me here, and sending the things that have made my room so sweet and dear."

Glendinning skillfully organized the telling of this story, which reflects upper-middle-class Victorian family life vividly. She concludes her book with comment on the causes of the physical collapse that followed close on Winnie's return home. Winnie died, she concludes, because no one could help her "to loosen the deadlock between her desire to go into the world and her fear of it," and this had been produced by the overprotection of the family which demanded an answering submission. The tension which resulted closed in and broke her. For this personal story Glendinning sometimes directly addresses the reader in a conversational manner and sometimes puts the narrative into the present tense; she quotes extensively from letters and other family records. She faced the censorship often imposed where family papers relate to such matters as mental health and broken engagements. When she discovered that almost everything related to Winnie's life in the year 1882 had disappeared, Glendinning found a clue in one surviving but mutilated letter. Further investigation yielded up the shadowy figure of an unnamed man who fell in love with Winnie and was dismissed from the house by her father. In this crisis it appeared that Winnie turned to God, persuading herself that the separation was his will as well as her father's. Nevertheless it is with indulgent affection for the family, against which one deviant member struggled, that the book concludes. On the title page a remark of Djuna Barnes is quoted, a subtle and significant remark for the consideration of biographers: "No one will be much or little, except in someone else's mind, so be careful of the minds

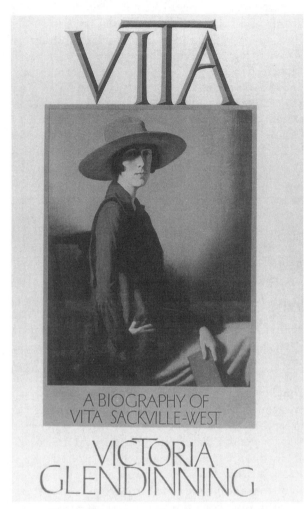

*Dust jacket for the American edition of Glendinning's biography
of the British novelist and biographer who was the close
friend of Virginia Woolf, wife of Harold Nicolson,
and mother of Nigel Nicolson*

writers who made their names in the 1920s and those who grouped themselves around the most influential literary editors of the 1930s and 1940s, John Lehmann and Cyril Connolly. But she wanted her books to distance themselves from their author and had always been averse to talking about their sources and her own life. This must have made difficulties for Bowen's biographer, but there were many friends with personal recollections to convey. The technique of acquiring and using oral evidence came easily to someone alert and yet composed, but Glendinning also acknowledged the helpfulness in this work of her psychiatric training and experience.

Only one of Elizabeth Bowen's early novels, *The Death of the Heart* (1938), achieved great success, and this was probably more than it deserved. Glendinning praises the atmospheric lyricism of her writing, but without strong threads of action this is hardly sufficient to sustain a lengthy novel. She was at her best in short stories and especially those in which the war is a central element. Bowen and her husband, who had fought in World War I, lived in central London during World War II and took part in its defense. A life of action, incurring physical risk, and a love affair with someone seven years younger than herself helped to produce her best work in the shape of some haunting short stories and one novel, *The Heat of the Day* (1949). In them ravished London becomes a new world of bombs and fires that break down not only buildings but barriers between people and so intensify the reality of love. Glendinning seems to hold back a little as she goes to meet a complex personality and an elusive writer. Her approach is generous and humane, but this book showed that she was not easily taken in. It is without the note of personal sympathy found in her first and some of her subsequent books.

The book which followed, *Edith Sitwell: A Unicorn Among Lions* (1981), is a biography of a woman whose name and fame seem certain to endure partly because her exotic personality made her a controversial public figure. Her poetry, sometimes mocking, sometimes exulting, sometimes deeply depressing, is of outstanding originality. She scarcely wrote a line that might be mistaken for that of another poet. Sitwell was certainly the most publicized woman poet in English literary history. She was a pioneer and a dissident but seemed to live under the shadow of a cruel self-consciousness and was preyed upon by mysterious fears. She was probably more caricatured than any other woman of her time. And yet she sometimes appeared as tireless

you get into." On the evidence of her first book, Glendinning's mind appears penetrating but humane, judicious but affectionate.

Elizabeth Bowen: Portrait of a Writer (1977) covers the life of a gifted novelist and short-story writer who lived through anxious periods of Irish and British history culminating in a terrible war to which her friend Virginia Woolf fell victim at the height of her productive life. Like Virginia Woolf, Bowen was a dedicated professional writer, but she was a tougher, high-handed character, stopping at nothing in pursuit of the experiences that might aid her writing. She fought her battles to clear space in which her work could flourish but at the same time was sociable and dependent on the affection of others. The biography brings out her notable gifts and her winning personality. She had many friends, including

and resolute as a figure by sculptor Henry Moore. Contradictions abound; she was childlike in her feuds and furies, but, as Glendinning points out, "less well documented have been her childlike lovingness and great generosity."

Glendinning's book accumulates such an intimacy with its subject that its success brought no surprise. It was a rounded achievement, movingly composed, and rightly rewarded with the Duff Cooper and the James Tait Black Memorial prizes for biography. Her collection and evaluation of evidence from many writers required patience and imperturbable confidence. The narrative achieves pace by making extensive use of short quotations as if they were the direct speeches of characters in a novel. The book often reads like a novel, although the emphasis is directed to Sitwell's poetry, which is emphatically presented as the central element in her life. From childhood onward she existed without the usual props which support a normal, balanced life. The landmarks usually identified by a biographer – a home of her own, husbands, lovers, children, "linchpins of most women's history," as Glendinning puts it – were all missing. The poetry brought her outward fame and inwardly a sense of glory, but neither set at rest her neurotic fear of hostile criticism. A biographer seeking to untangle the roots of such a plant as Edith Sitwell, and to lay them out for the readers' enlightenment, must face a laborious task. Many of Sitwell's friends and confidants were as volatile as she was herself. The poetry presented another problem. Fashions in literary criticism, received opinions, and political correctness come and go and in the case of an important poet's life must be charted. Cautiously, but convincingly, Glendinning presents the case for respecting the whole range of an extraordinary output, from its innocent, decorative beginnings, which are here especially valued, to the tremendous, emotionally charged work of the 1940s. She is restrained in her comments on these poems, which deeply affected good critics and a wide range of readers on their first appearance.

Vita: The Life of Vita Sackville-West (1983) was Glendinning's next book and, in terms of sales, her most successful to that date. Sackville-West's origins were bizarre in every possible respect. Her father was the third Lord Sackville and her mother the illegitimate daughter of the second Lord Sackville. She was brought up in one of the greatest of Britain's great houses, where a small army of servants was employed. She was an only child, but in a sense two fathers provided for her, the second being an enormously wealthy bachelor entranced by her

mother and eager to improve the family fortunes. Glendinning advises the reader to see Sackville-West's life as an adventure story, and the adventures that follow are indeed sensational. Her preface strikes a slightly dismissive note: "The Great House (of the Sackvilles) by an accident of gender could never be hers. As a poet she came to feel that she had failed." As the book unfolds its author is not moved to empathize with her heroine, as was the case with the Quaker girl and with Edith Sitwell. Sackville-West was as wildly passionate about her writing as about all the many activities into which she chose to throw herself. Virginia Woolf, though temporarily intoxicated by Sackville-West's romantic bearing, could see that there was something muted about her work. "The true art of expression and feeling was always just out of her reach. . . . She had a literal mind." The biography allots space to her many volumes of poetry, fiction, travel, and biography but makes no great claims for them. Her long poem *The Land* (1926) and her novel *The Edwardians* (1930) achieved remarkable popularity, and another novel, *All Passion Spent* (1931), is praised for its poignancy. She published nine books on gardens and gardening, some of which were collections of the weekly articles she contributed for many years to the *Observer,* but the main creative energy eventually found its finest outlet in the creation of a garden. With her husband, Harold Nicolson, another compulsive writer who was at the same time a politician and a journalist, she produced at Sissinghurst in Kent, where they had made their home, a garden which became one of the wonders of southern England.

Glendinning does not regard the Nicolson marriage as in itself so extraordinary, though it has become one about which an extraordinary number of words have been written for publication. In her view the fascination lies in the psychological complexity of a very unusual woman, gifted and at times dazzling, at other times full of dread and disappointment. She admires Sackville-West's fiercely guarded independence, her refusal to knuckle under, even if it meant behaving on many occasions like a spoiled child. She displayed an aristocratic disdain for politics and for domesticity of any kind. She would have liked to serve the best interests of her sons but seemed incapable of understanding the first thing about them. The compulsion to live life on her own terms drove her into acts of cruelty and contrariness. Glendinning treats even her wildest love affairs coolly and clinically. Apart from her garden, it seems likely that Vita Sackville-West will be remembered less for her own writings than for the portrait of her drawn in Virginia Woolf's *Orlando* (1928), which was the literary outcome of Woolf's passionate love, perhaps experienced for the first time. It is described on the title page as a biography but is in fact fantasy set on a moving stage of English history with a leading character whose sex is never permanently determined. It is described in Glendinning's biography of Sackville-West as "a phantasmagoria of images and incidents," reflecting the attributes and qualities in Vita which had captured Virginia's admiration and love. A candid and convincing study, organized with great skill, *Vita* was joint winner of the Whitbread Prize for Biography.

In *Rebecca West: A Life,* published in 1987, Glendinning was able to profit from her friendship with West, a friendship that extended over the last ten years of West's life. West's preoccupations as a writer were similar to Glendinning's, and the affinity was an aid to the biography. Both were concerned with the difficulties and conflicts raised by the twentieth-century emancipation of women in the West. They both worked to find a language resonant enough to convey ideas as well as to describe events. In this respect West was the unmistakable possessor of rare literary genius, although it was only with two novels published in her seventies that this was firmly established. Throughout her life she fought against the prejudices of a male-dominated society, the obfuscation of truth as she saw it, and, finally, as *Rebecca West: A Life* points out, against herself much of the time. That the iron of belligerency should have entered her soul is not surprising, but it is tragic that it should have caused her so much pain. In her life joy and suffering followed on the advances and retreats of women in general; she becomes an emblem of their triumphs and a monument to their failures. But her intelligence and emotional tension directed her into wider social and political battlegrounds where she sometimes lost her way. "She lived her life operatically and tinkered endlessly with the storyline, the score and the libretto. The plot remains unresolved."

Glendinning reverts to an earlier practice by opening up with a scene from 1975 in which West, her elder sister, and Glendinning talk together over lunch in West's apartment. Thereafter the book is divided into parts, each bearing the name by which West was known at different stages of her life. Glendinning not only masters her material, "the sheer brute evidence," as West called it in discussing biography as an art but employs it to climb further and further into West's mind. For the first time Glendinning in this biography confronts a woman with a burning interest in politics, ready to express violent political convictions. Her politics were never static, and her mind never grew stale. In youth she naturally gravitated toward the Left, but her close attachments were always to political activists rather than to factions or parties. She made heroes out of some unlikely human material, but at least they were live humans and not abstractions. H. G. Wells, her great love, had ruled himself out of an active part in politics before she met him. West built her reputation more on journalism than on her early novels. She wrote on literature, on art, and on current events with something more than a febrile fluency. Her success, at first that of an arresting critic and commentator, eventually evolved into that of a political thinker. By the time she was forty her reputation stood high in Britain and in the United States. By then her chaotic private life had erupted, with its bouts of ill health, its endless domestic problems, and its pathetically ill-judged attentions to her son, Anthony West. Anthony was not known to be H. G. Wells's son until West announced his identity on the boy's entry to a new, slightly offbeat English public school. This created a fresh battlefront in the war between the two parents. Rebecca West came to terms at last with what Carl Jung would have called "the meaning of her femininity," which repeatedly called for a partner in life; she married a learned, cosmopolitan banker and businessman who remains, even under the biographer's spotlight, a rather obscure figure. The war between mother and son, however, continued with a brutal violence of which the history of publicized lives reveals few, if any, parallels. The private disaster was almost equaled by the damage it did to the esteem in which West had been held and the real contribution she had made to the feminist cause. Women thought of her as one who had achieved a life of her own, on her own terms, sustained by her own talent and indomitable attack. Soon after she fell in with a husband, she fell in with the subject of a major work; in the end both were to become disappointments.

The project to which West devoted her powers for several years of peace and war was a blockbuster which Glendinning describes as the central book of her life; it is a pageant of history, archaeology, and modern Yugoslav politics, in which the author "formulated her views on religion, ethics, art, myth and gender." *Black Lamb and Grey Falcon* (1941) comprises two large volumes best treated, in her biographer's opinion, as "a work of art and of self-revelation." The extraordinary gifts with which Rebecca West had been endowed did not include those required in a historian. The result is an over-written, self-indulgent work in which some passages sound like self-parody. In contrast, her next book, *The Meaning of Treason* (1947 in the United States and 1949 in Britain), remains a contemporary document of great interest to historians and to psychologists. It deals with wartime traitors and in a later updated version with scientific and diplomatic espionage. Her writing here has even more of its customary bite, a stinging sharpness which shocked many readers at its first appearance and had a serious influence on public opinion. Her last novel, *The Birds Fall Down* (1966), deals with these same questions but in a different setting. It is the story of a Russian nobleman, a servant of the last czar, now in exile and near the end of his life. He and his young granddaughter are trapped together in a web of treachery, spying, and murder. Glendinning gives outspoken praise to this book, treating it as an important text for students of twentieth-century traumas.

Glendinning's *Trollope* (1992), on which she worked for four years, was a larger undertaking than any of her previous books. No writer had done more to convey a sense of English life and institutions in the middle of the nineteenth century, and no writer of like quality was more prolific. His novels, popular in their own day and then neglected, have attracted a large public and, in the last fifty years, much critical commentary. Trollope was obsessively interested in the way women conducted their lives. His mind was constantly occupied by questions of how women treat men and how men should treat women. Consequently a fresh view of the man was to be expected from his first woman biographer, especially one who had already shown a special sensitivity to human feelings and relationships. The women in his life were written into his novels, and Glendinning throws light on his attitudes and opinions based on what is revealed in his novels, short stories, and travel writing. As Trollope's fictional women were many and the women in his life few, it is surprising that, apart from his mother, they should have been so neglected by previous biographers. Attention to the partner in his unsensational marriage is essential, for she was, together with his home and the approval of his friends, the foundation of a successful and happy existence, attained after disastrous early years.

Next in importance came Trollope's working life, divided between his writing and various administrative assignments for the Post Office. His writings reflect his keen interest in politics. His close at-

Dust jacket for the American edition of Glendinning's biography of the Victorian novelist she calls a "worthwhile and lovable man"

tention to the lives of women was matched by his studied observation of social and political institutions, not only with the government at Westminster but with the politics of the private estate, the Cathedral Chapter, the parish, and the school. The law, the press, and eventually the financial world attracted his abiding interest. His masterpiece, in Glendinning's opinion, *The Way We Live Now* (1875), "grew out of the compost of a lifetime's observation, anger, amusement and writing experience." It dealt with the commercial profligacy of the age and constituted "a great shout in the long conversation that Anthony Trollope sustained, and sustains, with his readers about the betrayal of all that is honest and true." She holds that Trollope is of one mind, that "his discourse is unitary," whether he writes on personal morality, social, sexual, or commercial, or on the public morality of political, legal, and financial institutions. He has his values and does not shrink from expressing them.

Drawing on his published writing more than on his letters, Glendinning explores a man and a writer rather as one might explore an attractive landscape, steadily building up familiarity with its every detail. She does not disguise his limitations or gloss over his faults, but the book unfolds a deep respect and affection for this "worthwhile and lovable man." Trollope denied in his autobiography the intention of giving any record of his inner life, something which modern biographers would see as their first priority. Glendinning gets so close to Trollope that she seems to be producing a second autobiography but with a wider scope and total impartiality. Her method is to treat his published writings as her landmarks and to find a way into his inner life through reference to the great cast of characters he created. Her main concern as a biographer is to keep the reader alert and pleasantly surprised, following her lead through a long, carefully con-

structed life story. There is no labored artistry in her style, no grandiloquent philosophizing, no impressive rhetoric. Instead she employs finely tuned craftsmanship to open up a personal channel of communication with the reader, like that of a dinner guest or a good holiday companion. This sense of three-way companionship – author, subject, and reader – is one of the hallmarks of a fine biography. With her it is conspicuously present; Glendinning brings out the best in Trollope and he her highest skills as a biographer.

In 1995 Glendinning published *Electricity,* a novel set in the 1880s. Told by a young woman beset by deaths, desertions, and other catastrophes, the novel recounts her liberation through her experiences. She emerges with her intelligence sharpened and her energy preserved, consciously prepared for the post-Victorian world. The novel of ideas and high intelligence shows Glendinning's skills as a writer of fiction, skills she utilizes as a biographer.

Lyndall Gordon

(4 November 1941 –)

Lisa Tolhurst
New York University

BOOKS: *Eliot's Early Years* (London: Oxford University Press, 1977; New York: Farrar, Straus & Giroux, 1988);

Virginia Woolf: A Writer's Life (London: Oxford University Press, 1984; New York: Norton, 1984);

Eliot's New Life (London: Oxford University Press, 1988; New York: Farrar, Straus & Giroux, 1988);

Shared Lives (London: Bloomsbury, 1992; New York: Norton, 1992);

Charlotte Brontë: A Passionate Life (London: Chatto & Windus, 1994; New York: Norton, 1995).

OTHER: "Our Silent Life: Virginia Woolf and T. S. Eliot," in *Virginia Woolf: New Critical Essays,* edited by Patricia Clements and Isobel Grundy (London: Vision Press, 1983; Totowa, N.J.: Barnes & Noble, 1983), pp. 77–95;

"T. S. Eliot," in *The Craft of Literary Biography,* edited by Jeffrey Meyers (New York: Schocken, 1983), pp. 173–185;

"A Writer's Life," in *Virginia Woolf: A Centenary Perspective,* edited by Eric Warner (New York: St. Martin's Press, 1984), pp. 56–68;

"Eliot and Women," in *T. S. Eliot: The Modernist in History,* edited by Ronald Bush (Cambridge: Cambridge University Press, 1991), pp. 9–22.

SELECTED PERIODICAL PUBLICATIONS –
UNCOLLECTED: *"The Wasteland* Manuscript," *American Literature* (January 1974): 557–570;

"Love with Its Trousers Rolled," *New York Times Book Review,* 21 August 1988, pp. 28–29.

Lyndall Gordon (photograph by Mary S. Pitts)

Lyndall Gordon's unconventional approach to biography and her search for authenticity within that genre lead her to places in the writer's life that often transcend what can simply be observed. Her intellectual enlightenment consistently pays homage to unbiased and thoroughly documented research. Gordon is brutally honest when she asserts what is necessary of the biographer: "There will be no easy truth. It will be an imaginary meeting of divided halves: the biographer and the subject, the living and the dead." Her intent, as biographer, to expose a life that unfolds a simultaneity of truths, is accomplished in her biographies of T. S. Eliot, Virginia Woolf, and Charlotte Brontë and in her autobiographical work, *Shared Lives* (1992).

Growing up in the 1940s and 1950s in Cape Town, South Africa, Lyndall Gordon was enmeshed in a culture that acted unabashedly as subjugator of people of color and less explicitly as repressor toward the enfranchisement of women. In spite of this climate, and quite possibly because of it, her biographies of Eliot, Woolf, and Brontë show her to be a writer who seeks to reveal and illuminate the lives of her biographical subjects by refusing to segregate their personal histories from the fictional works that they created.

Gordon's first biography, *Eliot's Early Years* (1977), traverses his younger years as poet and creator of *The Wasteland* and infuses her interpretation of his poetry with lucid insights into the religious and cultural aspects of Eliot's life. Her sequel to this biography, *Eliot's New Life* (1988), continues in this vein, focusing on the works he produced in his "new life" after his conversion to Anglicanism. In *Virginia Woolf: A Writer's Life* (1984) Gordon renders a detailed portrayal of Woolf and her family; at the same time, she applies an analysis of these familial portraits to the characters and circumstances in Woolf's fiction in a way that encourages readers to understand better and make connections between Woolf and her authorial persona.

Gordon's insistence upon unveiling the secret lives of her subjects is brilliantly achieved in her most recent biography, *Charlotte Brontë: A Passionate Life* (1994). This biography is a testament to Gordon's great performance as a biographer who is at once an exacting researcher and an incisively perceptive and sensitive analyst of "autobiographical" fiction. In this work Gordon gives to her readers the quintessential portrait of Charlotte Brontë, whose passionate and truthful literary voice had the power to subvert the silencing of women in the Victorian era of hypocrisy and inequity. As Gordon states, "This, then, is a writer's life which will trace the rising spark, secret 'books,' and bold words which did not fear to speak about the experience of those alone and silent, unregarded and socially obscure: a new voice of passionate communion."

Born Lyndall Getz on 4 November 1941 in Cape Town, South Africa, the only daughter of Harry and Rhoda Getz, Gordon's childhood was spent in the coastal town of Sea Point, a thriving Jewish community comprised mainly of immigrants from eastern Europe. Her family spans three generations in South Africa. Her grandmother Annie Hoffman, born in 1892 in Johannesburg, was the eldest child of Jacob and Rebecca Hoffman, both of whom had emigrated from the town of Shillel in Lithuania to escape the pogroms of 1881. Jacob had come to Johannesburg in 1889, by way of Wisconsin, looking for gold and had shortly thereafter "sent for a bride from the Old Country." After her grandmother was widowed she came to live with her daughter's family and shared the "top room" of the house with Lyndall. Annie used to lock up "her copy of *Katherine* by Anya Seton, containing scenes which she judged unsuitable for a girl of twelve"; but Lyndall got hold of a duplicate key and shared her grandmother's taste in literature.

Annie played an influential role in Gordon's upbringing, as did her Aunt Berjulie, who had married Annie's son Hubert. Both of these women were "dutiful" matriarchs of the family: strong willed and extroverted, they "knew exactly what they wished to be – which was what all women should be." Gordon's father was much more akin to the outgoing Annie and Berjulie than to her literary and reflective mother, Rhoda. Harry was a sports commentator who was strong in verve but lacking in imagination. These pragmatic and conventional influences in Gordon's life were paralleled by her unorthodox mother, who was a philosophical and spiritual woman. Rhoda, an invalid because of epilepsy, was physically confined to bed for most of Lyndall's adolescence but gave to her daughter a spiritual awakening fueled by a renewal of religion during her time of illness. Before she took to bed, she was a politically active liberal who advanced the "prospect of black majority rule."

Gordon's initial awakening to the genre of biography (and later as a biographer), her choice of subjects, and her approach to them came from her mother's literary and spiritual influences, as well as her "biographic" reading of the Bible. "The Bible," her mother said, "is not one book. It is a whole library of books. The story of Abraham is the first great biography." By the time her mother was restricted to bed, Lyndall and Flora Gevint, her intimate childhood and adult friend, had come to appreciate deeply Rhoda's insights on life and the veld and her love for such poets as Emily Brontë as well as South African writers such as Nadine Gordimer and Anna M. Louw. Those writers, Gordon writes, convey "perfectly that sense that came to me, through my mother, of the pressure of the unknown, of unanswerable questions, and the strenuous ordeals of the soul on this earth – this bare exposed veld that brought you close to the testing landscapes of the Bible."

While her mother provided the literary and spiritual foundation from which Gordon's interests bloomed, Flora connected her, through their friendship and by example of the way in which she chose to live, to the liberation of self-expression. In *Shared Lives* Gordon compares Flora's impassioned approach to life with Joseph Conrad's philosophy: "There remains nothing but surrender to one's impulses, the fidelity to passing emotions which is perhaps a nearer approach to truth than any other philosophy of life."

Another profound influence in Gordon's life came from Siamon Gordon, whom she would later marry. She was seventeen when they first met in

1958, as participants in the socialist youth movement Habonim. Siamon Gordon's credo was that all people should occupy their lives with meaningful work, and early in their relationship he suggested that she "try biography," believing that her interests in literature and history would be consolidated in that genre. While Gordon had been exposed to her mother's poetic sensibility, she had also learned that a woman need not publicly display her creativity, a belief made explicit by her mother's act of secreting her own poetry "tied in a drawer." With his practical insistence that she combine her creative talent with a livelihood, Siamon Gordon acted as the catalyst for Gordon to break the tradition of creative secrecy that had restrained her mother.

Gordon's approach to biography, and subsequently to her teaching, was shaped by a desire to disengage from the unethical and rigid system of apartheid in South Africa and the stifling atmosphere of Good Hope Seminary, the women's high school which she entered in 1954. It was there that she met Flora as well as a small circle of young women, all of whom joined together to establish a process of education that fostered the sharing of knowledge. Their approach to learning, however, was not shared by the institutionalized, rigid procedures of Good Hope, which brought segregation into the classroom by the exclusion of blacks and through its competitive system. The staff at Good Hope said that, by sharing, these students were "cheating," but Gordon believed that "Our cheating made us a community of women bound by vital feelings of reciprocity."

From 1960 to 1963 Gordon attended the University of Cape Town where she majored in English and history, graduating with four firsts and a medal in history. Her understanding of South Africa grew as she learned more about its black majority from the School of African Studies. Following the Sharpeville massacre of 1960, there followed an even more rigorous system of apartheid that "allowed the police to imprison any person for ninety days without trial." These laws would, immediately after Gordon's graduation, impel her to leave South Africa, a country that she had come to love and to hate.

In her last year of study at the University of Cape Town, her mother, who had recently regained her health, came to join her there to begin a degree in English. Gordon says that she learned "more from discussions with her [mother], particularly about moralists and religious writers – Donne, Herbert, Vaughan, Jane Austen, Hopkins, and T. S. Eliot – than from lectures, which were filled with odd bits and pieces of preliminary 'background,'

but somehow never quite engaged with texts." During this time Gordon found and developed an inclination toward Eliot that would later, as a graduate student at Columbia University in New York City, induce her to explore his work more fully.

On 7 April 1963 Lyndall Getz married Siamon Gordon, and in 1964 they left South Africa to work in London. In April 1965 they moved to New York, where Siamon, a biologist, accepted a research position at Rockefeller University. Soon after their arrival, Gordon gave birth to their first child, Anna, and also began a graduate degree program in American literature at Columbia University.

Although she had expected deliverance from the narrow-minded regime of South Africa, she was now confronted by a university policy, even in the rebellious 1960s, that decreed that women with children did not merit assistance of any kind, including loans. Dismayed by this policy in a vast educational system that was largely unresponsive to women scholars, and far away from friends and family, Gordon battled with postpartum depression, eventually checking herself into Saint Luke's Hospital and undergoing electroconvulsive treatments. During this difficult time she fought against the urge to give herself over to depression. However, Gordon admits that it was not the therapists or their "supposed" treatments which retrieved her from the abyss during this period; it was a poem of Virgil's that she had been translating for a class in Latin: "It happened then that certain somber lines stirred some dulled response: the resolve of Aeneas, and his plea to comrades, to press on in the face of hopelessness." Gordon "pressed on," and by 1967 she had finished her thesis on "the development of religious ideas in T. S. Eliot, with a long chapter on *Four Quartets*," a work she would further explore in *Eliot's New Life*. Gordon also became involved with the *Little Magazine*, a poetry journal founded by a group of Columbia students. In 1971 she was editor of a women's issue that included works by Joyce Carol Oates, Marge Piercy, Susan Fromberg, Joanna Russ, and Mary Gordon.

In 1973 Gordon received her Ph.D. with distinctions for her dissertation on "Eliot's Early Years." Jacques Barzun suggested that she submit it for publication. It was rejected by Princeton University Press with a reader's report that concerned Gordon's deviations from standard Eliot criticism. Nevertheless, A. Walton Litz, then chairman of the English Department at Princeton, who had just written *Eliot in His Time* (1973), was impressed with Gordon's "dating of the fragments of *The Wasteland* manuscript, which had made it possible to attempt an account of the evolution of the poem over seven and a half years." Litz's interest soon linked Gordon to renowned Eliot scholars, and she began a correspondence with Dame Helen Gardner and Hugh Kenner, all "advancing their own theories about the evolution of the poem." Then in 1973 Gordon applied for a Rhodes fellowship at Saint Hilda's College, Oxford, unaware of Gardner's involvement with that school. She soon received a letter from Gardner notifying her that she would "viva" her; after a series of interviews Gordon was awarded this prestigious fellowship, and from 1973 through 1975 she tutored extensively for the college.

Eliot's Early Years was published in 1977 and won the 1978 British Academy's Rose Mary Crawshay Prize. In the book Gordon exposes Eliot's influences and motivations as poet of *The Wasteland*. The genesis of *The Wasteland* is traced through a vivid depiction of his childhood in Saint Louis, Missouri; his relationship with his mother, Charlotte Champe Eliot, a devoutly religious and spiritual woman who was herself a poet and whose "strength is essentially that of a preacher"; his frustrating first marriage to the Englishwoman Vivien Haigh-Wood, whom he met at the age of twenty-six in 1915 and who shortly thereafter became chronically ill; and, finally, his own spiritual and emotional inner life during this period. As Gordon states, "One motive for writing on Eliot was the discovery of a lot of his early unpublished work in the Berg Collection in the New York Public Library, which suggested that he was interested in the religious life very early on – this transformed the traditional view of his career which had separated his earlier, supposedly atheistical phase from his later religious phase."

Virginia Woolf and Ezra Pound were friends and supporters of Eliot's work throughout his life: Woolf published many of his poems, and Pound played a significant advisory role during the writing of *The Wasteland*. Pound had received a copy of *The Love Song of J. Alfred Prufrock* on 22 September 1914 and at that point declared that Eliot was the most talented of American poets. Gordon makes note that it was in the later drafts of *The Wasteland* during 1921 – with the influence of Pound – that he "shifted the emphasis of his poem from personal case history to cultural disease."

After *The Wasteland* was published Eliot became disheartened about its interpretation as being symbolic of a generation's "disillusion," since that only served to undermine a reading of his work as "religious vision." He also felt remorse about having edited, at Pound's encouragement, certain parts of *The Wasteland*. Gordon argues that the "new representativeness" which eventually took shape in the poem diminished his "visionary element" and that it became "depersonalized and even disguised. In place of the man with extraordinary powers there is now a 'form' and, in a later draft, merely a bat. And instead of a voice saying plainly 'I am the Resurrection,' the thunder now rumbles obscure Sanskrit words."

Gordon's analysis of Eliot's life and work expands to include his interpersonal relationships and his own psychological state, and in this way a reading of *The Wasteland* comes not only to represent the universal person but also to reflect Eliot the individual. In an article Gordon wrote for *American Literature* in January 1974 titled *The Wasteland Manuscript*, she puts forth the assertion that "for the most part, *The Wasteland* seems to have been originally a dirge for aspects of Eliot's identity that he had lost. Stripped of marital love in *Elegy* and *The Death of the Duchess*, stripped of divine love in *The Death of St. Narcissus*, stripped of flesh in *Dirge* and *Death by Water*, stripped of the right kind of fame in *Exequy*, he feels fatally reduced." In subsequent fragments of the poem Eliot showed a bitterness toward women that in part came from what he considered to be his own unhappy marriage; Gordon traces some of this anger to both his own "sexual failure" and to his wife's illness.

Piece by piece Gordon pursues the fragments of this epic poem, reuniting each segment to its particular place and history in Eliot's life over a "seven and a half year" period that began with earlier fragments in 1914 and that was "published in the *Criterion* and *Dial* in mid-October 1922." Beginning with his own religious "upheaval" in *The Death of St. Narcissus*, which predates *The Wasteland*, Gordon looks at Eliot's growing disillusionment toward a promise of salvation that had been nurtured at an early age by his devoutly religious mother. "It is crucial, I think, to see 'The Wasteland,' indeed all of Eliot's subsequent work, in the context of this martyr's tale, the story of an unsuccessful saint."

Eliot's Early Years was received enthusiastically by reviewers and scholars. Craig Raine in the *New Statesman* (10 June 1977) praised Gordon's work: "Sorely needed has been an adequate study of Eliot's early years, one which accounts for his later development as man, poet and thinker." And in *The New York Times Book Review* (17 July 1977) Doris Grumbach stated that Gordon has "interpreted the poet's early years and his early writings so that the life reflects the work, and vice versa. She shows that despite Eliot's insistence on the impersonality of art his poetry was rooted in his experience and had aspects of spiritual autobiography." However, some reviewers were resistant to Gordon's style; Thomas Stearns wrote, "If it is generally dangerous to interpret literary works in light of an author's biography, it is probably foolhardy to attempt its antithesis: the extrapolation of biography from an author's literary output" (*Best Sellers,* July 1977). But any negative criticism was far outweighed by positive opinion, as seen in the *Saturday Review* (11 June 1977): "Lyndall Gordon sets the work of this elusive, and in a sense intensely autobiographical poet in almost incandescent perspective."

In August 1975 Gordon returned to New York to teach English and comparative literature at Columbia University. In February 1976 Gordon's friend and confident, Flora – by now known as Romy – died unexpectedly from pneumonia. At this time Gordon began to think about writing the story of Romy's life, which would later appear in her book *Shared Lives* (1992), but her loss was too recent: "It was safer to study writers' lives, with their public achievements and tangible records." Instead she returned to the Berg Collection where she had uncovered so much on Eliot, this time to begin work on Virginia Woolf. Gordon had begun reading "Woolf's diaries – still, then, in manuscript only – for wonderful portraits of Eliot in his early years in London. The diaries were so enthralling that I'd read on, forgetting Eliot! That led me naturally into a biography of Woolf."

Gordon returned to London with her husband in September 1976, at which time he accepted a position as reader at the Sir William Dunn School of Pathology in Oxford. From 1977 through 1984 Gordon tutored in various colleges at Oxford, specializing in American literature. During this time she had her second child, Olivia, and wrote and finished her biography of Virginia Woolf. Published in 1984, *Virginia Woolf: A Writer's Life* received the James Tait Black Prize for biography in 1985.

Gordon's portrait of Woolf is more inclusive of her fiction than is Quentin Bell's 1972 biography, which does not intentionally evaluate Woolf's writing. Drawing on a vast pool of resources – which include the Berg Collection, Woolf's diaries, her published and unpublished letters, Leonard Woolf's *Autobiography* (1960–1969) and private papers, and Quentin Bell's allowance to use his unpublished papers – Gordon's biography is "a complementary effort to link the writing with the life."

Weaving in and out of Woolf's writing and her life, Gordon renders insightful analyses of both

the work and the author, pointing to how Woolf's early years influenced her fiction and her creativity in general: "This biography will follow her creative response to such memories. . . . Filled out in memory, the dead could take a final form; the living were unformed, like herself still in the making, though this did not deter her from shaping them, too, in her imagination. She transformed people whom she loved – parents, brother, sister, friends, husband – into fixed attitudes that could outlive their time."

These incisive portraits of Woolf and her family allow Gordon to extend personal themes from Woolf's history into her novels – or as she astutely calls Woolf's work, "fictional biography." Gordon is, however, quick to document the biographical readings of Woolf's fiction with quotes from Woolf and her family that testify to their authenticity. Mr. and Mrs. Ramsay in *To the Lighthouse* (1927) take on the biographical equivalent of Woolf's father, Leslie Stephen, and her mother, Julia, so effectively that her sister Vanessa Bell "confirmed the portrait's accuracy when the book was published in May 1927." This recognition surprised Woolf, who was hesitant to accept that she had truly captured the quintessence of their parents.

Virginia Woolf was a fantastically talented writer, a social commentator of her day, a principal personage of the literary time, a friend to many, a loving sister to Vanessa and wife to Leonard Woolf, and an exceptional person who in many ways shaped the voice of literature both by her style and by her person. Woolf was also an individual who had to overcome much emotional trauma in her life. When she was six years old her half brother Gerald – from her mother's first marriage to Herbert Duckworth – who was fifteen years her senior, began to molest her sexually; and after her mother's death in 1897 when she was fifteen, her half brother George began to violate her sexually as well, while her father, stricken with grief, cut her off emotionally.

These "twenty dark years," as Gordon terms them, would serve to ebb away Woolf's emotional strength. Gordon points out that the death of Stella (Woolf's elder half sister, born from her mother's first marriage to Herbert Duckworth, who died in 1870) two years after her mother's death "was to have two effects on the course of her life: it set off her hunger for women's love and it set off a pattern of mental breakdowns." Drawing from Woolf's final memoir, Gordon relates that although Woolf had originally been able to gather the emotional strength needed to cope with her mother's death, Stella's death tore through her layers of defense and exposed Woolf's immense suffering and vulnerability – and "her emotions were 'forced' into being."

Woolf's acumen into the depths of the psyche was handed over to her characters as they shared her experience and gave voice to it; through them she was able to "expose what lay in the recess of her mind." But Gordon is adamant to point out that this incredible woman was anything but mentally ill. "Madness or sanity, like all such defining terms, are absurd simplifications. . . . The most subversive element in Virginia Woolf's work – more so than her challenge of notions of madness and sanity – is her challenge of the category 'per se.' " Gordon does not glorify, in any way, Woolf's pained existence, which was also derived from a "fear of ridicule" in a world that was inimical to women writers, particularly to women who had strayed from what was to be considered the norm. Gordon concentrates on the inner turmoil present throughout Woolf's life and how Woolf thought it important for an artist to be able to abandon herself to truths that were often painful: "Submergence was her [Woolf's] image for the hidden act of imaginative daring."

Gordon states that in *A Room of One's Own* (1929) Woolf "points out that the indifference of the world which Keats and Flaubert and other men of genius found so difficult to bear was, in the woman's case, not indifference but hostility." Woolf was to experience this "hostility" in myriad ways, which included her mistreatment by doctors, particularly by Sir George Savage, who repeatedly sent her to Twickenham, a sanatorium that was, with its "phoney religious atmosphere," to drive Woolf toward suicide rather than away from it.

In *Mrs. Dalloway* (1925) Woolf displays this antagonism toward the medical establishment, who in their oversimplified, narrow-minded, and prejudiced vision of the world were blinded to the reality of what and who were actually before them. Gordon draws on Woolf's "fictional case study" of Septimus Warren Smith in *Mrs. Dalloway,* in which "sufferer and society share responsibility, though doctors blame him alone, particularly his resistance to their definitions of normality." And in *The Waves* (1931) the character Rhoda, like Septimus, commits suicide due to her overwhelming sense of alienation: Woolf "demonstrates through these characters the most terrifying experience she herself knew, which is to lose communication with the world outside one's mind."

To read Gordon's biography of Woolf is to see into her fiction and her life and to arrive at a position which allows for a fully realized portrait which depicts the struggles of a writer and of a woman. In Woolf's first novel, *The Voyage Out* (1912), the protagonist Rachel Vinrace "cannot take a novelistic place in English society," and Gordon argues that "there is no knowing what Rachel could be because she evolves in a way that is perhaps incompatible with the facts of existence." Gordon also states that Woolf desired, even in her first book, not just to write but to "transform the novel in ways that now seem quite consistent with contemporary experiments in modern art but which were for her, in 1908, solitary ambitions." Gordon makes careful correlations between Woolf and her character Rachel, particularly in the similarity of their backgrounds and positions and in their "voyage" to become writers. But where in reality Woolf was able to continue bravely on her path, becoming one of the most respected and prolific writers of the twentieth century, her fictional character Rachel is doomed.

Like Rachel, Orlando is a character who voyages out, but this time, through the passage of time and the transcendence of gender. Gordon asserts that *Orlando* (1928) is "a fictional biography of her aristocratic new friend, Victoria Sackville-West." Gordon includes part of a letter from Sackville-West to Woolf in which her friend tells her (when referring to *Orlando*), "I feel like one of those wax figures in a shop window, on which you have hung a robe stitched with jewels." In this work and others Gordon praises Woolf for her exacting and illuminating representation of England. "Her interest in the shape of English history, particularly the shift from one age to another and the unobserved part played by women, was to find its way into many of her writings, 'The Journal of Mistress Joan Martyn,' *To The Lighthouse, Orlando, The Years, Between the Acts,* and *Anon.*"

It is difficult not to note the authority with which Gordon writes about Woolf. Gordon's biography of Woolf received much praise from reviewers, as noted by Hermoine Lee in the *Times Literary Supplement* (21 December 1984), who acknowledged Gordon's insistence on "rocking between the life and the work." In *The New York Times Book Review* (10 February 1985) Carolyn Heilbrun wrote that "Mrs. Gordon's views on biography are radical in their refusal to find in the usual documentation the major events of a writer's life – she understands that profound events take place beyond record and are only later reflected in the creative act of fiction." Still, in the same review, it is pointed out that Gordon's attitude toward Vita Sackville-West is too harsh and that Woolf's love of women does not receive, from Gordon, the salience it deserves, especially in light of the important role it played throughout her life.

At the time *Virginia Woolf: A Writer's Life* was published, Gordon returned to Saint Hilda's as fellow and tutor in English and lecturer for the university; in 1987 she became senior English tutor. During that same year she began two major works: her memoir of Romy and her sequel to *Eliot's Early Years*, titled *Eliot's New Life*. Still, she was not emotionally prepared to face the task of writing Romy's story, and for the next three years she focused her work on Eliot. *Eliot's New Life* was published in 1988 and won the Southern Arts Prize in 1989.

Just as intensely as in *Eliot's Early Years*, the friendships, loves, and circumstances of Eliot's life are revealed, this time through papers that had previously been unpublished and unavailable. In *Eliot's New Life* Gordon continues to illuminate his inspirational sources, which, from approximately 1925 until his death in 1965, revolved around his ill-fated and deteriorating relationship with his first wife, Vivien; his revitalized love, in 1927, for Emily Hale (from whom he had been separated since 1914); his long friendship with Mary Trevelyan; and his conversion to Anglicanism.

Eliot's agonizing relationship with Vivien continued to drag him down, and, ironically, she provided him with inspiration as "his dark muse." Through documented sources and literary introspection, Gordon links Vivien's mental anguish to important characters and themes in *The Wasteland* (to which Vivien felt a strong connection), as well as several of his plays. She writes, "The early years of Eliot's marriage were the background to the macabre, unfinished play, *Sweeney Agonistes* (1926), and the later years of separation the background to the introspective nightmare of *The Family Reunion* (1939). These plays are complementary, for both expose a man's horror, almost possession, at the discovery of his capacity for violence." Tragically, Vivien was to end her days alone in an asylum, which she entered in 1936 and where she stayed until the age of fifty-eight when she died of heart problems. Where Eliot's marriage to Vivien drove him to expose his angrier, disillusioned, and darker self, his relationship with the American Emily Hale brought out a different quality in his writing and was, itself, of a different nature. "She became the model for silent, ethereal women in Eliot's poetry, La Figlia, the hyacinth girl, the Lady, who all elevate the poet's spirit." Gordon asserts that it was Hale, after all, who played the most influential role in his writing during their twenty-year relationship; and yet Gordon concludes that Theresa Eliot (his

brother Henry's wife) "put it neatly when she said that 'Vivien ruined Tom as a man, but made him as a poet.'"

During this same period, between the 1930s and 1950s, there was still another woman who played a significant role in his life. Mary Trevelyan, an outgoing and honest Englishwoman, became a large part of Eliot's public persona. Whereas Emily Hale reigned in his life and his work as a moral and spiritual ideal, and Vivien Haigh-Wood came to be his darker inspiration, Trevelyan was "his escort at parties, the theater, and, most often, church."

Gordon offers detailed and introspective analyses of Eliot's writing, pointing out that he was an artist whose "work forecasts the life, even determines it." She proposes that Eliot was a man who sought to realize the higher truths and ideals that are mostly unrecognizable in mundane existence. Using his art as a means of expression and attainment, he searched into universal truths of both atrocity and salvation and toward a spiritual ideal of life. Paying particular attention to *The Four Quartets* (1943), which, like *The Wasteland*, is considered to be a major work and which Eliot himself deemed, even in his more doubtful moments toward the end of his life, as "worthwhile," Gordon asserts that "*Four Quartets* follows emotions beyond those we ordinarily know as human, though we may have hints and guesses." She makes the important assertion that they need to be seen as a whole body of work: "To read *Four Quartets* accurately is not to dwell on its separate parts, but to experience a cumulative effect, like a great piece of music. As in music, there is a set form: each *Quartet* begins with an actual experience in Eliot's life; at the center of each is some action, say, a journey; at the end of each some struggle with language that parallels the effort at the perfect life."

As Eliot advanced to different stages in his life, he was often to leave behind the people closest to him; this would happen with Vivien, Emily, Mary, and his close friend John Hayward, but not in his more professional friendships with, for example, Virginia Woolf and Ezra Pound. When, in the winter of 1947, Vivien, who had been living in an asylum for many years, died, so too, metaphorically, did his relationship with Emily Hale. At that time Eliot had made his conversion to Anglicanism; and along with that had come a new outlook that had released him from his moral and spiritual bond with Emily Hale. But as Gordon relates, Eliot's relationship with Hale lingered for many years and, in fact, was not completely severed until 1957 when he married his secretary, Valerie Fletcher.

Gordon offers significant insight into Eliot and Hale's relationship from the inclusion of Hale's letters during their long period of separation. Hale's correspondence reveals not only a deep love for and understanding of Eliot but also an acute anguish due to her alienation from him. As Gordon asserts, the letters tell of a "real" woman and not just a "spiritual ideal" as Eliot had come to see her; but they also tell of a woman who had been waiting patiently for Eliot to be freed from his marital vows, so that they, in turn, could be married. But this was not to happen. Gordon writes, "Eliot saw her also as the material of religious poetry. And when his poetic searching of the soul came to an end, so too did his interest in her. In the last *Quartet,* as Eliot spelt out the end of the search in a new commitment to a Christian community, he spelt out too a new 'detachment' from individual ties." When he married Valerie in 1957, Mary Trevelyan and John Hayward expressed their surprise at the news, and directly after his marriage he intentionally lost touch with them but flourished in his relationship with his new wife. On the other hand, Emily Hale never fully recovered from their separation, and for years she underwent psychological trauma.

Eliot's correspondence with Ezra Pound continued into his last years. In these letters, as Gordon points out, Eliot "was taking retrospective views of his career," and "he speaks harshly of his sense of failure, of doubt, disgust, and despair." In his last public lecture – "To Criticize the Critic" – at the University of Leeds in July 1961, Eliot embraced a new "subjective" construct of criticism that was quite a different "position to the doctrinal impersonality of his earlier criticism."

As with Gordon's other biographies, *Eliot's New Life* received positive reviews. James W. Tuttleton in *National Review* (November 1988) wrote that "Miss Gordon has given us an inner life of the poet, for her a resolutely American poet of Puritan origins and sensibility, whose spiritual odyssey would be unintelligible without an understanding of the symbolic uses to which he put the real women in his life." The reviewer in the *New York Review of Books* (November 1988) stated that "Using Dante's La Vita Nuova as a metaphor for the spiritual life, Gordon successfully analyzes Eliot's life as a process of spiritual growth evident chiefly in such works as *The Four Quartets* and *The Family Reunion.* . . . Well written, amply illustrated and clearly developed, this work is strongly recommended."

In 1990 Gordon became a Dame Helen Gardner Fellow; and, along with her continued work at Saint Hilda's, she has given external lectures throughout the Oxford colleges and the university on a variety of subjects, including Woolf, Emily Brontë, and Henry James. Since 1987 she has lectured extensively in England, the United States, and Spain, as well as contributing to many educational programs featuring Woolf, Eliot, Emily Brontë, and Jane Austen.

In 1988, while Gordon was at the Trudeau Institute in the Adirondacks, she returned to her unfinished memoir of Romy (Flora Gevint) and the friendships that she had shared in her adolescence and adulthood in South Africa. The result of this endeavor became her fourth book, titled *Shared Lives,* which was published in 1992. Gordon states that in this book she "wished to see whether it would be possible to apply methods of biography to ordinary lives, assuming that ordinary lives could be as interesting as famous ones." She prefaces *Shared Lives* with a quote from Virginia Woolf: "Is not anyone who has lived a life, and left a record of that life, worthy of biography – the failures as well as the successes, the humble as well as the illustrious?" Her biography bares an affirmative answer to Woolf's question, as it draws readers into the life stories of the "not famous," rendering a veracious portrait of Romy, with whom she shared her private moments until her death.

Gordon's aspiration to capture Romy as truthfully as possible leads her to the exposition of their mutual experiences; and so this memoir of Flora also becomes an autobiography of Gordon, which is supplemented by the diaries and letters of their mutual friends. In her search to express the inexpressible about the life of a human being who meant so much to those she loved and who loved her, Gordon states, "Could we find her in that elusive 'between' in which women of our generation lived? How do we divine the language of the sigh or the scream or that state of pure happiness that we called, delightedly, 'hysteria?'" But Gordon does "find her" in these pages as she narrates the times of their youth in Sea Point, their school days, their families, their friends, their loves, their desires, and their accomplishments.

Judith Chettle, who also grew up in South Africa, wrote in her review in the *Washington Post* (18 October 1992) that "Moving back and forth from the first days they met to Gordon's later life in America and England, Gordon wants to 'record the end of a way of life, and, more elusive, the truncated lives of women' like Flora and two members of the group who also died young. This is a moving tribute to friendship, and an evocative memoir of a time and place, that, however bourgeois and racist in conduct and spirit, were and always will be home." *Publishers Weekly* (29 April 1992) noted that Gordon's book is "reminiscent of Simone de Beauvoir's *Memoirs of a Dutiful Daughter*," and *Library Journal* (1 May 1992) spoke of her "elegant, strong voice," and of her "vivid characterizations."

Gordon's intention is always to dive deeply into the silence of a life that, ironically, like almost all silence once exposed, is in fact not a silence at all but a deafening roar. It is not surprising that two of her subjects – Virginia Woolf and, most recently, Charlotte Brontë – are artists for whom the novel served as a means of expression for themselves as individuals and, in a larger context, for the condition of all women. Their collective works stand as powerful and transforming vehicles of their time, which continue to inform today.

Gordon, in *Charlotte Brontë: A Passionate Life*, gives voice to an artist of the nineteenth century who through her novels portrayed the struggle between the inner needs of women and the demands of the prevailing Victorian society. The social tenet which equated passion and individuality in a woman with depravity and a failure to duty would impel the three Brontë sisters, Charlotte, Emily, and Anne, to protect themselves by adopting male pseudonyms for their novels: Currer Bell, Ellis Bell, and Acton Bell, respectively.

In this biography Gordon immediately informs readers of her intention to revise the typical view of Charlotte Brontë as "a figure of pathos in the shadow of tombstones." Gordon accomplishes this by bringing to light Charlotte's inner existence that blossomed in her fiction, as well as in her relationships with her sisters Anne and Emily, her close confidants Ellen Nussey and feminist Mary Taylor, her frustrated love for mentor M. Heger, and her close friendship with her publisher, George Smith. As Gordon states, "The time has come to bring out the strength that turned loss to gain." Through Gordon's unfolding of Charlotte's life, readers see "a stranger creature: a survivor who mocked her brother's graveyard postures of doomed genius; a determinedly professional writer who was impatient, sarcastic, strong in spirit, with an unquenchable fire."

Gordon asserts that the landscape in which the Brontës lived, with its barren beauty, silence, and space, greatly informed Charlotte's, Emily's and Anne's creative works. "In this sense, the moor may have been the visible counterpart of their searching minds: space as counterpoise to strict training, quiet considerateness, and constant proximity to the facts of pain and death. Jane Eyre has a notion, in the last extremity, she will cast herself on the breast of nature as on the body of a mother." In Emily's *Wuthering Heights* (1847) Catherine Earnshaw "speaks of 'exile' from a landscape that was more to her than home." Gordon further states that "to leave the moor was to be exiled from the self."

While Branwell, as son, received private tutorship from his father, the sisters' education was overlooked, as was their talent. It would not be until 1847, after the publication of *Jane Eyre*, that Charlotte's father would be informed that she was a writer, and he only begrudgingly, upon her insistence, read her book. This blatant neglect on the part of their father would not prevent these young women from fulfilling their literary endeavors, and "from 1846 until 1853 the Brontë sisters published their combined *Poems, Agnes Grey, Jane Eyre, Wuthering Heights, The Tenant of Wildfell Hall, Shirley,* and *Villette*."

As a young girl Charlotte was absorbed into her brother's creative world of Angrian pirate war games with powerful male figures, aspects of which would someday resurface in the character of Rochester in *Jane Eyre*. As Gordon states, "her part in the Angrian saga was to develop love interest and to try to make sense of Branwell's wars by granting character to the actors." The Brontë sisters had accepted that, as a male, Branwell had the right to assert himself publicly, creatively or otherwise; and, they "prepared themselves to live through him." However, Charlotte, in her youth, "assumed equality through the male voice of her narrators . . . precursors to the famous 'Currer Bell' who published *Jane Eyre*."

This Angrian fantasy together with the "secret plays" the sisters made up in the evenings in their beds and Charlotte's self-education through the works of such writers as Sir Walter Scott; George Gordon, Lord Byron; William Shakespeare; John Milton; John Bunyan; Samuel Johnson; and William Wordsworth would become an integral part of her creative life. "The great verbal power that was to emerge in Charlotte Brontë ten years later came from an extraordinary liberty to transgress the frontiers of feeling . . . and it is obvious that this liberty was the fruit of the Romantic movement. But where the speakers for Romanticism were almost invariably men, her books claimed this range for women."

In 1831, at the age of fourteen, Charlotte was sent away to Roe Head School, where she would excel in her studies in spite of the conventional and restraining teaching methods of the Wooler sisters, who ran this girls' school. Roe Head was sur-

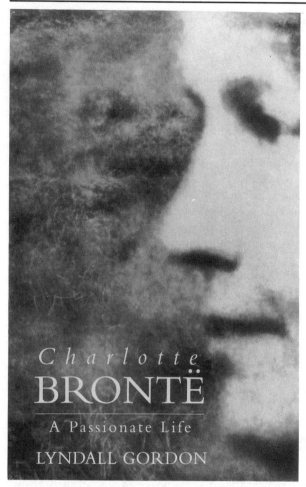

*Dust jacket for the British edition of Gordon's biography of the
British novelist who portrayed the struggle between the inner
needs of women and the demands of Victorian society*

rounded by industrial towns and had, as Gordon
stipulates, a more rigid, hierarchical social structure
than that of Haworth. Charlotte's years at Roe
Head would shape her as a person and a writer. It
was there that she befriended Ellen Nussey and
Mary Taylor, both of whom gave her love and support throughout her life. "Mary's independence and
Ellen's insight shaped Charlotte from the age of fifteen, an alternative group to sisters and a channel
for social and economic attitudes beyond the scope
of the Parsonage."

Ellen Nussey was a girl of great empathy and
sensitivity, while Mary Taylor, who later emerged
as an important feminist and writer, was forthright
and provocative and demanded veracity. In fact,
from Mary Taylor and Mary's father Charlotte
learned a great deal about the social injustices of
their time, and it was Mr. Taylor who "lent her the
novels of George Sand." Mr. Taylor would later
provide the portrait for "the ambiguous figure of

Mr. Hunsden in *The Professor*," and the whole Taylor family would appear as "the Yorkes in *Shirley*" —
a family portrait that Mary believed accurate and
true. However, it was Ellen who would provide the
setting for *Jane Eyre*, which was re-created from the
estate where her family had lived for many generations: "with its large rookery and fine chestnut
trees, one split by storms, The Rydings was to be a
source for Thornfield."

Throughout Charlotte's life she corresponded
with Mary and Ellen; but Mary, with whom Charlotte shared a more political and social dialogue,
confiscated most of Charlotte's letters, believing
them destructive "to Charlotte's reputation." And
Gordon questions: "Did she meet Mary's daring
with a strong voice of her own, as, in a sense, their
feminist novels still speak to each other?"

In 1835 Charlotte returned to Roe Head to
earn a living as a teacher, which would allow her
to finance Emily's education there. But Emily,
whose free spirit required a nonrestrictive environment, could not acclimate herself to this "disciplined routine," and a few months later "a pale,
wasted Emily was back at Haworth." Soon after,
Anne replaced Emily at Roe Head, but Charlotte's relationship with Anne was strained because they had both "competed for Emily." Charlotte kept her distance from Anne during the two
years Anne lived at Roe Head; it was only when
Anne became sick, in 1837, that Charlotte came
to her aid and made sure, against the benign neglect of Miss Wooler, that Anne was sent back to
Haworth to recover.

Although Charlotte was frustrated and unhappy at Roe Head, she spent three years there as
teacher, during which time she "invented the central character and exercised the voice of the novels
to come." Nevertheless, she was entrapped inside
Roe Head in both her alienation from her family
and the moor and in the lack of time she had to give
to her writing. As Gordon asserts, Charlotte's passionate yearning to write and her desire for a solitude that would allow her this creative expression
were the central motifs in her autobiographical writings of this period: "It was in these autobiographical
fragments that we first hear the vehement voice of
Jane Eyre. . . . Only when Jane is alone can she
open her inward ear to a tale that never ends."

Charlotte's private feelings of alienation in po-
larity with her public role as a teacher at Roe Head
created an anguish in her that was exposed in her
writings. As Gordon tells, the "striking fragments
are when struggle persists and becomes her subject:
it is here the crucial voice breaks through, not the

imitative sentiments of Angrian romance, but the restless fury that seems to take Charlotte to that psychic edge of the woman apart and alone, forcing the young writer to confront that condition which, later, her novels would explore with such boldness." Gordon correlates the fragments of Charlotte's writings from this period to the scenes and characters which later emerged in her novels, including "Miss Hall in 'Ashworth' (1839–1841) and the heroine of Charlotte Brontë's last, unfinished work, 'Emma' (1853)," whose conflict it was to be caught between the deceptive world of appearances and the inner truth of existence.

Christmas of 1836 saw Charlotte home at Haworth at which time she wrote to the poet laureate, Robert Southey, sending him her poetry, while her brother "wrote to Wordsworth," whose response was one of "contemptuous silence." Anne and Emily were writing as well, although Emily did not begin *Wuthering Heights* (1847) until 1846, a year before it would be "maligned for its savagery," while Anne was not to publish *The Tenant of Wildfell Hall* until 1848, after she had written *Agnes Grey*, "which tells the hard truths of such employment" as a governess, and is a "triumph of the inward spirit over deadening conditions."

When Charlotte eventually heard back from Southey, his response was that writing was not to be the work of a woman whose "duties" of home and family should keep her busy enough. Gordon perceives Charlotte's response to Southey's blatant disregard of creativity in the woman as twofold: one part of her did accept the "role of slave to duty" while the other saw through his misleading directive. This contention between the liberation of the woman and the restrainment placed on her by society was not resolved in Charlotte, and her own confusion about it was present in her written reply to Southey which "reverberates with veiled sarcasm . . . hiding undaunted creative fire under the public mask of perfect docility," while in public she "gave out that Southey had done her good in showing her that what she wished could not be."

On 8 February 1842 Charlotte and Emily traveled to Brussels to study at the Rue d'Isabelle under the tutelage of M. Heger, who became Charlotte's mentor. "M. Heger transformed Charlotte's ideas of manhood. Unlike Papa, Southey or Hartley Coleridge, here was a man who wished her to write." Heger was a dynamic professor who engaged Charlotte in a passionate embrace of knowledge and a shared devotion to writing. Gordon exposes the complexity of Charlotte's relationship with Heger which was "central to Charlotte's writing" and

which "had to be suppressed in Mrs. Gaskell's biography, and began to emerge only after Heger's death in 1896." Charlotte became enamored with Heger, who, although married, elicited her devotion through, as he stated in a letter to Charlotte, his "spiritual magnetic." As her feelings grew stronger, and she withered in her need for him, so too did her feelings of alienation, which were emphasized by his painlessly easy withdrawal from her.

Charlotte's attachment to M. Heger did not end when she left Brussels. She corresponded with him while living back at Haworth, "and the words they exchanged, fuelled her writing." By 1844 Emily was back at Haworth, and both sisters were busy writing but not participating in each other's work. Gordon explains that during the years 1843 to 1845 the Brontë sisters needed "to separate, each to find her individual voice." Emily was writing "Gondal Poems," Charlotte was writing poetry and would begin *Jane Eyre* in 1846, and Anne in 1845 "returned to the Parsonage after over four years as governess at Thorp Green, bringing two-thirds of *Agnes Grey*," which would be published in December 1847, along with Emily's *Wuthering Heights*. Branwell was already ensconced in a pattern of self-destruction, losing successive posts as tutor due to his drinking and opium taking.

This creative secrecy among the sisters soon ended, as Charlotte realized that it was time for all three of them to participate in each other's work and to look toward their eventual publication. This change of heart began when Charlotte chanced to come upon Emily's poems, read them in private, and then "convinced Emily of an audience, starting with her sisters." Charlotte believed that Emily had a "genius" in her poetry that was beyond her own poetic ability and that Emily's work "was unlike the poetry that women generally write." Gordon states that Branwell was excluded from the sisters' plans for publishing their works, most probably because of his "mental state" and his loquaciousness, "in view of his sisters' insistence on secrecy," rather than his ability to write poetry, which was, in fact, superior to Charlotte's and Anne's.

After their decision to publish was agreed upon and they had spent considerable time reading each other's work – bringing them to share creatively as they had in their childhoods – Charlotte defied the "current icon of fragile womanhood unsullied by contact with the sordid dealings of public life" and ventured into the world to act as "businesswoman." Wanting to avoid being pigeonholed into the category of "feminine" writers, which often, as the Brontë sisters stated, brought false praise or condemnation, they adopted the pseudonymous

Currer, Ellis, and Acton Bell. Gordon grounds the Brontës' decision to veil their true identities as women in a history of women writers such as Mary Wollstonecraft, whose private life was attacked in order to discredit her work; but Gordon also looks to Virginia Woolf and Sylvia Plath, who almost a century later "suffered the same attack."

Currer, Ellis, and Acton Bell published their poems in 1846, but Charlotte's novel *The Professor* (1857) "was rejected six times." Refusing to collapse under this rejection, Charlotte wrote *Jane Eyre,* which was published in 1847 by George Smith, who became the first editor of the *Dictionary of National Biography* and who would become Charlotte's close friend, to be represented in *Villette* as an "attractive champion." Unlike Emily's *Wuthering Heights,* which was also published in 1847, *Jane Eyre* was met with immediate acclaim. "Where *Jane Eyre* explores the danger of erotic oblivion, *Wuthering Heights* explores a stranger passion warped by social plots." Gordon explains that Emily "took a more extreme position than Charlotte: she saw the impossibility of spiritual wholeness in a shallow world which she despised and utterly shunned."

Gordon's holistic approach to the writer and her text incorporates the political and social significance of *Jane Eyre,* a penetrating examination of Charlotte's personal world as it related to her fictional one, and insightful character analysis. Tying these three critical aspects together, Gordon states that "As orphan she [Jane] stands for all who are dependent and alone, who are vulnerable to abuse, both crass abuse of child, class, or woman, and also that more subtle abuse explored in all Charlotte Brontë's work: denial of feeling."

Important to Gordon's analysis is her discussion of Bertha Mason Rochester, who embodies, for Charlotte, "a warning of mindless passion and madness" that is destructive and "vicious." Gordon explicitly states that Bertha should not be represented as that part of woman that is wrongly shunned. According to Gordon, Bertha is not part of a feminist rhetoric, and to confuse her as being so is an injustice to "what is there on the page as an emanation of its time and place." Gordon posits that Bertha is all things negative, because all reason has left her. The struggle between reason and passion was prominent in Charlotte's life, and she depicted this psychic conflict in her character Jane, whose "experience is to know the extremes of a seething, chaotic life and one of disciplined order." Gordon notes that Virginia Woolf "perceived in Currer Bell" this "inner strife" that "gave form and meaning to the private extrava-

gance of her own life tugged between the claims of the self and the claims of society."

Immediately after Anne's *The Tenant of Wildfell Hall* was published in June 1848, Charlotte and Anne set out to meet George Smith, in order to expose their true identities and set straight the "deception" of Mr. Newby, Ellis and Acton Bell's publisher, that Acton and Currer Bell were one and the same; a lie he constructed "to sell the *Tenant of Wildfell Hall* as Currer Bell's new novel to the American firm of Harper Brothers." Emily (Ellis Bell) remained at home. While the sisters revealed themselves privately to George Smith, they requested that their public persona, as the Bells, remain intact, although by now it was commonly known that the Bells were women; and as Charlotte had originally suspected, the critics used femininity as a means of maligning their creative works.

Like Charlotte, who eschewed public recognition but boldly put forth her ideologies about society and people in the privacy of her novels, her protagonist Shirley, in her 1849 novel by the same name, "speaks out, and she speaks most freely when she and her new friend, Caroline, are alone." In *Shirley* Charlotte "furthered the form of the polemical novel which explores the position of women" and "questions men's power over women and workers." While Charlotte moved into the more public arena as a writer, private tragedy was soon to come: in 1848 Branwell died suddenly; Emily contracted tuberculosis and died in December; and Anne became ill, dying in May 1849. Charlotte's "real salvation was work: the challenge of the final volume of *Shirley,*" which, as Gordon points out, greatly reflected the issues of her own life, both in the private dimension of tragic loss and in the social dimension of women's emancipation.

Between the years of 1851 and 1855 (the year of her death at age thirty-nine), Charlotte fell dangerously ill and recovered to undergo periods of depression, married Arthur Bell Nicholls (in 1854), and wrote *Villette* (1853) and her last, unfinished work, *Emma.* Gordon states that in *Villette* "events and interior dramas in Charlotte's life were transmuted into her most searching revelation of hidden character." For Charlotte, Lucy became a figure that inwardly transcended "the Victorian male judgement internalized by women in that way that enslaved them more profoundly than legal restrictions." Lucy's struggle to emancipate her "voice" through language is juxtaposed by her passive "role of womanly waiting" in her correspondence with Graham Bretton. Gordon asserts that this "waiting for the post" role was present in Charlotte's life in much the same way: first with M. Heger and later with George Smith, the separation from whom caused her to become severely depressed. Gordon perceives Lucy's eventual satisfaction as "derived not from wedding bells but from economic independence and letters." In *Villette,* Charlotte created a woman who "rising from the shadows . . . looks to the future" empowered by her self-liberated voice as a writer.

In 1853 Charlotte wrote "The Story of Willie Ellin," which was incorporated shortly after into her unfinished novel *Emma.* In these two works Charlotte "renewed her fictional attention to abused and abandoned children." Matilda, in *Emma,* is a young girl whose doll-like appearance belies her internal anguish, referred to as "a mystery of nature." Gordon states that Matilda functioned as a figure of allegory: "a visual image that conveys an automatic meaning (petted doll) which must be exploded and reconceived through the empirical methods of the novel, until we, as readers, penetrate a true image of the age." Less explicit than Lucy in *Villette,* Matilda emerges in the text as the internal triumphs over the external only through "Ellin, as investigator . . . and the reciprocal effort of the reader." Gordon asserts, "If Charlotte Brontë had lived to complete this work, the unidentified girl may have become an emblem of her sex, more than a decade before Mill set out his theory of an artifice so sealed that it would be virtually impossible to uncover women's nature."

In 1854 Charlotte married her longtime suitor, Nicholls, during what was to be her last year of life. It was at this time that Charlotte looked toward happiness through her marriage, rather than from her art. Gordon points out that this choice was by no means "predictable." Charlotte was a very successful writer by this time, and Gordon believes that in her marriage was a "daring to remake herself." But her union to Nicholls lacked the passion of the "Angrian romance," and she was "sober, unexcited, deliberate." She had witnessed what Victorian marriage did to wives – "wiping out independent character – and with full consciousness she allowed herself to vanish in this way"; yet she died with "human love on her lips." Her father outlived all his children, dying in 1861. Charlotte died at the age of thirty-nine, possibly, as Gordon states, from "digestive tract infection."

The medium of biography has been an enlightening vehicle for Gordon, who has extended it to seek a deeper understanding of art through the artist and of life through the human being. Since her insistence is on inclusion rather than exclusion, Gordon is able to create a viable dialogue among reader, subject, and biographer that is sustained by her willingness to see many perspectives and voices. This conviction is equally present in her approach to teaching, in which a system of mutual cooperation where people can "work out of shared interest instead of hugging to themselves their private achievements" can be fully realized. Gordon's professorship at Saint Hillary's College at Oxford and her performance in the genre of biography take her to places in the lives of human beings which defy boundaries and broaden our perspectives.

Ian Hamilton

(24 March 1938 –   )

Richard Greene
University of Toronto

See also the Hamilton entry in *DLB 40: Poets of Great Britain and Ireland Since 1960.*

BOOKS: *A Poetry Chronicle: Essays and Reviews* (London: Faber & Faber, 1963; New York: Barnes & Noble, 1973);

Pretending Not to Sleep (London: The Review, 1964);

The Visit: Poems (London: Faber & Faber, 1970);

Anniversary and Vigil (London: Poem-of-the-Month Club, 1971);

The Little Magazines: A Study of Six Editors (London: Weidenfeld & Nicolson, 1976);

Returning: Poems (N.p., 1976);

Robert Lowell: A Biography (New York: Random House, 1982; London: Faber & Faber, 1983);

Fifty Poems (London: Faber & Faber, 1988);

In Search of J. D. Salinger (New York: Random House, 1988);

Writers in Hollywood (London: Heinemann, 1990);

Keepers of the Flame: Literary Estates and the Rise of Biography (London: Hutchison, 1992; Winchester, Mass.: Faber & Faber, 1993);

Walking Possession: Essays and Reviews, 1962–93 (London: Bloomsbury, 1994).

OTHER: *The Poetry of War, 1939–45,* edited by Hamilton (London: Alan Ross, 1965);

Alun Lewis, *Selected Poetry and Prose,* edited by Hamilton (London: Allen & Unwin, 1966);

The Modern Poet: Essays from The Review, edited by Hamilton (London: Macdonald, 1968);

Eight Poets, edited by Hamilton (London: Poetry Book Society, 1968);

Robert Frost, *The Poetry of Robert Frost,* edited, with an introduction, by Hamilton (London: Cape, 1971); published as *Selected Poems* (Harmondsworth: Penguin, 1973);

Ian Hamilton (photograph by Nancy Crampton)

Poems Since 1900, edited by Hamilton and Colin Falck (London: Macdonald & Jane's, 1974; New York: Beekman, 1975);

Yorkshire: in Verse, edited by Hamilton (London: Secker & Warburg, 1984);

The New Review Anthology, edited by Hamilton (London: Heinemann, 1985);

Soho Square, edited by Hamilton (London: Bloomsbury, 1989);

The Faber Book of Soccer, edited by Hamilton (London: Faber & Faber, 1992);

The Oxford Companion to Twentieth-Century Poetry in English, edited by Hamilton (Oxford & New York: Oxford University Press, 1994).

RECORDING: Poetry Reading, The Poet Speaks Series, British Council Recording 1779 (London: British Council, 1972).

Ian Hamilton is perhaps best known for a literary biography that cannot legally be bought in the version in which it was first written. Having achieved a substantial reputation as a poet, editor, book reviewer, literary historian, and broadcaster, he published in 1982 a well-received biography of Robert Lowell. However, his unsuccessful attempt to publish a biography of J. D. Salinger in 1988 resulted in his becoming the most controversial biographer in recent times.

Robert Ian Hamilton was born on 24 March 1938, the son of Robert Tough Hamilton and Daisy McKay Hamilton, in King's Lynn, Norfolk. He has been married twice, first to Gisela Dietzel in 1963, and then to Ahdat Soueif in 1981. He has one son by his first marriage and two by his second.

He was educated at Darlington Grammar School and, later, at Keble College, Oxford, where he took his B.A. in 1962. While at Oxford he founded and edited the periodical *Tomorrow* from 1959 to 1960. In 1962 he founded *Review,* which he edited until 1972. The journal was relaunched as *New Review* in 1974, and he continued to edit it until 1979. From 1965 to 1973 he served as poetry and fiction editor of the *Times Literary Supplement.* He has also contributed numerous reviews to the *Observer* and the *London Magazine.* In 1972 and 1973 he worked as a lecturer in poetry at the University of Hull.

Although he has in three decades produced a small body of verse for which some critics have expressed warm regard, early in his career he was most noticeable as a reviewer and was particularly influential in the 1960s and 1970s as a promoter of poetry that was minimalist and highly controlled. In his assaults on various poets he did not admire — for example, William Carlos Williams — he has often adopted a tone of literary partisanship. Bernard Bergonzi, in *MLR* (1979), sees in Hamilton's criticism a tendency toward simple denunciation reminiscent of Geoffrey Grigson, the influential and often intemperate editor of the 1930s journal *New Verse.* Douglas Dunn, an admirer of Hamilton, speaks of his "gift for fastidious disparagement" (*Encounter,* September–October 1983); Dunn goes on to observe that he is "the sort of critic who pro-

ceeds from skepticism until convinced by testimony and evidence." His willingness to express strong opinions is certainly a vitalizing quality in his printed reviews, though it has been somewhat damaging to his work as a broadcaster. In his discussions of new books on the BBC program "Bookmark" (1984–1987), Hamilton was inclined to be harshly dismissive of some works and was often contentious in exchanges with other reviewers.

Hamilton's first substantial scholarly work was *The Little Magazines: A Study of Six Editors* (1976). This work examines the histories of six periodicals from the first half of the twentieth century: *Little Review, Poetry, Criterion, New Verse, Partisan Review,* and *Horizon.* The book's approach is largely narrative, but its cumulative effect is to provide an analysis of aesthetic and cultural concerns connected with the founding and operation of these literary journals.

Hamilton's first biography was *Robert Lowell: A Biography* (1982). He had become friends with Lowell during the poet's sojourn in England during the early 1970s, and a conversation between the two, published in *Review* in 1971 and since reprinted elsewhere, has become an important primary document for Lowell scholarship. Hamilton remained friends with Lowell and was selected to read a tribute to the poet by Christopher Ricks at a memorial gathering in New York on 25 October 1977.

The biography places Lowell in the context of a family history that became one of the central concerns of his poetry. Hamilton describes Lowell's mother, Charlotte Winslow, as a dominant, sharp-tongued young woman who worshiped her father, Arthur Winslow, and desired a husband who would worship her. Her choice settled on Robert Trail Spence Lowell III: "For both father and daughter, Bob's combination of weak character and strong lineage was indeed perfectly correct." Their child, Robert Trail Spence Lowell IV, came, in time, to regard his mother as an enthralling "adversary," and "from his father he learned that decency and good intentions can be abject." Hamilton does not advance a psychoanalytic interpretation of the poet's childhood, but his account of a powerful mother and a withdrawn, ineffectual father at least suggests that early experiences contributed to Lowell's subsequent mental illnesses.

Hamilton's treatment of Lowell's childhood, however, is brief: his first eighteen years are covered in only twenty-three pages. As he approaches adulthood, Lowell is seen surrounding himself at Saint Mark's, an Episcopalian boarding school, with disciples over whom he exercises remarkable dominance. He is also seen as disruptive and aggressive, in one case beating up a friend for falling under the influence of the poet Richard Eberhart, who was a master at the school. Lowell is also seen as intensely ambitious, undertaking by force of will in his late teens a transformation from "lout to man of sensibility."

Hamilton's coverage of Lowell's adult life begins with an unhappy year at Harvard followed by his studies at Kenyon College and Louisiana State University. In April 1940 he married Jean Stafford, and by the mid 1940s he had achieved public stature as one of America's leading poets.

The core of Hamilton's biography is the narrative of Lowell's mental breakdowns and hospitalizations, commencing in the late 1940s. Lowell, a manic-depressive, rarely passed a year without at least one breakdown. The phase of elation that would precede his hospitalizations was characterized typically by a new love affair, a fascination with political tyrants, and, occasionally, violence. Hamilton provides a detailed record of Lowell's illnesses and of their effects on him and on those around him. This aspect of the work, however, has drawn some sharp criticism. Bernard McCabe, in his review in the *Nation* (26 February 1983), maintains that Hamilton fails to illuminate the complex relationship between Lowell's life and his autobiographical poetry: "In *Life Studies* Lowell uses his life to contemplate history, faith and violence ('Beyond the Alps'), to discuss manners, death and war ('My Last Afternoon with Uncle Devereux Winslow'), to look at a dissolving, corrupted world ('Skunk Hour'), to see mania as a diagnostic instrument for confronting that world ('A Mad Negro Soldier Confined at Munich').... A true critical biography surely must work at assessing these strange exercises and Lowell's profoundly original use of a doppelgänger effect." In McCabe's view Hamilton falls well short of this objective: "The book exudes an odd Bedlam atmosphere, with the reader invited to peek at the mad poet in the straw, and with the poems becoming 'just symptoms' of this madness."

No biography of Lowell could fail to devote a great deal of attention to his mental illnesses. Hamilton's approach to Lowell's mind seems so pathological that he tends to underplay aspects of his thought and experience that do not connect with the cycles of collapse and recuperation. McCabe complains that Hamilton fails to discuss Lowell's involvement with the Catholic Worker Movement in the late 1940s as anything other than an expression of religious mania and so overlooks what was, for the poet, a significant intellectual engagement. Albert Gelpi maintains in *American Literature* (1983)

that the biography fails to present the poet's "inner life"; apart from his relationship with his second wife, Elizabeth Hardwick, who authorized the biography, few of Lowell's close friendships are examined in great detail, and only the most important of his connections with other writers are discussed in depth: "Nor do we even get a sense of the religious and political ideas and ideals that underlie the whole tangle of his hope and disillusionment." Gelpi finds that because the "essential Lowell is largely out of reach in Hamilton's account, its anecdotes and reminiscences have a glossy sheen that operates at times all too close to the level of literary gossip." Helen Vendler in the *New York Review of Books* (2 December 1982) finds the book admirable in many respects, but she also notes that it does not provide an account of the "inner life" and calls for an "intellectual biography" that will reveal the "evolution of Lowell's mind."

Hamilton's research must, however, be seen as original and extensive. His interviews with Lowell's wives and his surviving friends bring forward a wealth of information about the poet's life. He quotes widely from unpublished correspondence and is arguably at his most interesting when he compares various revisions of the poem "Waking in the Blue," thus using the manuscripts to produce a narrative of Lowell's creative process. But the book does not provide a full analysis either of Lowell's intellectual context or of the political contexts of his "public" poetry. For example, Hamilton chooses to quote at length Norman Mailer's account of Lowell's protests against the Vietnam War in *Armies of the Night* (1968) rather than embark on an analysis of the issues underlying those protests and Lowell's position as a public poet in opposition to his government.

Some charge that Hamilton lacks genuine sympathy for his subject. McCabe speaks of a "latent hostility to Lowell." James Wolcott in *Harper's* (December 1982) describes the work as "a curiously dour, dogged, and conscientiously chill effort." Hamilton's repeatedly negative appraisals of much of Lowell's work lead Wolcott to ask, "if enthusiasm for Lowell's work runs so thinly in his blood, then why write the book at all?" Hamilton has, in fact, shown an extraordinary willingness to dismiss as worthless much of what Lowell wrote. In an interview published in 1993 he roundly observes that Lowell's works contain "acres of rubbish." If Hamilton's regard for his subject's poetry is so qualified, it is little wonder that his biography focuses on mental illness rather than literary achievement.

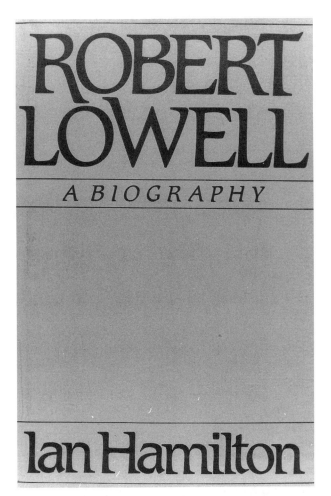

Dust jacket for the American edition of Hamilton's biography of the American poet whose decades of suffering from mental illness informed his autobiographical poetry

Hamilton's second biography, *In Search of J. D. Salinger* (1988), resulted in an extraordinary confrontation between author and subject. Salinger disappeared from public view in 1965. When Hamilton accepted his commission from Salinger to write a biography, he knew that Salinger would vigorously defend his privacy. In fact, he conceived of the book as a quest, "with Salinger as quarry." It was assumed that there would be an actual struggle between the two writers: "The idea – or one of the ideas – was to see what would happen if orthodox biographical procedures were to be applied to a subject who actively set himself to resist, and even to forestall, them." The role of biographer as quester became central to the work, as Salinger himself would never be overtaken: "It would be biography, yes, but it would also be a semispoof in which the biographer would play a leading, sometimes comic, role." In this sense, Hamilton foresaw a self-referential biography, not

so much the story of Salinger's life as the story of its own writing.

In 1983, as he was beginning his research, Hamilton wrote to all the Salingers in the Manhattan telephone directory hoping to find one of the novelist's relatives who would be willing to talk. It turned out that among the recipients of the form letter were the novelist's sister and son. At this point Hamilton received a letter from the novelist berating him for harassing his family and insisting that he could bear no more intrusions on his privacy – "not in a single lifetime." Hamilton's reaction perhaps indicates why he did not anticipate Salinger's ultimate resistance to his project: "The letter was touching in a way, but also just a shade repellant. It was as frigidly impersonal as it could be, and somewhat too composed, too pleased with its own polish for me to accept it as a direct cry from the heart." The passage shows that Hamilton as biographer was willing to adopt a surprisingly patronizing view of Salinger and to dismiss his unequivocal objections to the book as ironic posturing.

Hamilton responded to Salinger by telling him that he would be going ahead with the book, although he would not pursue his researches beyond 1965, when Salinger had left "the public domain," and he would not "bother his family and friends." Whether a writer's personal life, as opposed to his books, is ever in "the public domain" is an awkward question, but Hamilton adopted the view that the autobiographical element in Salinger's fiction had largely vitiated his claim to privacy. Hamilton proceeded with the book and was able to assemble a detailed picture of Salinger's childhood, his education at Valley Forge Academy, his military service, and his rise to literary fame.

One of his main sources was Salinger's letters, of which a substantial number are preserved at the University of Texas at Austin. The manuscript of "J. D. Salinger: A Writing Life" was delivered to Random House in July 1985. Legal objections were raised, however, to the amount of quotation from Salinger's letters. The book was rewritten by September 1986, reducing sharply the number of direct quotations to ensure that it did not go beyond the "fair use" provisions of copyright law. A copy of the new book was delivered to Salinger's lawyers on 18 September. A week later Salinger filed suit asserting that the book still drastically infringed his copyright; he was granted a temporary restraining order by a New York District Court on 3 October. In an affidavit Salinger claimed that "the core" of the biography was "in my own words." On 10 October Salinger made his deposition and was formally interviewed by Hamilton's lawyers. On 5 November 1986 Judge Pierre N. Leval brought down a judgment allowing publication of the revised biography: "It is a serious, well-researched history of a man who through his own literary accomplishments has become a figure of enormous public interest." In Leval's view, Hamilton had remained within the bounds of the "fair use" provisions of copyright law.

On 3 December Salinger lodged an appeal to the United States Court of Appeal. On 29 January 1987 Leval's judgment was overturned by Judges Jon O. Newman and Roger Miner, and a preliminary injunction was granted. The judges concluded that unpublished materials were entitled to particular protection under copyright law and that Hamilton's book would diminish the potential market value of the letters themselves. Moreover, they maintained that Hamilton's paraphrasing of Salinger's words was in many instances so close to the originals as to constitute infringement of copyright:

To deny a biographer like Hamilton the opportunity to copy the expressive content of unpublished letters is not, as appellees contend, to interfere in any significant way with the process of enhancing public knowledge of history or contemporary events. The facts may be reported. Salinger's letters contain a number of facts that students of his life and writings will no doubt find of interest, and Hamilton is entirely free to fashion a biography that reports these facts. But Salinger has a right to protect the expressive content of his unpublished writings for the term of his copyright, and that right prevails over a claim of fair use.

Although Hamilton could report facts, he was not entitled to appropriate Salinger's voice, the "expressive content" of his writings. Hamilton's lawyers subsequently filed a further petition to the Supreme Court, which on 5 October 1987 was denied.

The book that Hamilton finally published in 1988, *In Search of J. D. Salinger,* is certainly stripped of quotations and paraphrases, but, perhaps more important, Salinger ceases to be the real subject of the work. The book is conducted, in part, as a dialogue between two Hamilton personae: one who is mannerly, reticent, and scrupulous; and the other, a professional biographer, who is assertive, efficient, and pragmatic. It is an account of literary, ethical, and legal dilemmas faced by Hamilton as he made certain discoveries about the life of Salinger. The concluding section records the events surrounding the failed publication of the earlier biography. In a press release describing the final version of his biography, Hamilton claimed that "It has a stronger plot and certainly a more riveting denouement, and at the same time it raises key questions about the whole business of 'biography' – what is it for, why do we write it, why do people want to read it and so on. Also, it tells you just as much about Salinger, in fact more, than the earlier banned version did."

Certainly the book presents factual information essential to a standard biography. However, if this were all, the book would be short. In many places it is clear that it was written partly to explain and justify Hamilton's conduct through the whole affair. For example, in several places he reminds the reader of his decision not to probe Salinger's failed marriage, and much is made of a confidential meeting between himself and Dorothy Olding, Salinger's agent, who did not discourage him from his research.

In the end we see a project undertaken with a sense of mischief ending in embarrassment and frustration for Hamilton. By the same token, victory was worth little to Salinger, who saw the letters he wished to defend become a part of the public record. Christopher Lehmann-Haupt commented in *The New York Times* (19 May 1988) that one of the lessons to be drawn from the Hamilton-Salinger affair was "that to love a writer's work does not entitle one to possess him personally. And alternatively: to turn against a writer for whatever personal cause does not by itself permit one to reject his work."

Perhaps the most lasting consequence of the affair is that it established a legal precedent according to which it will be much more difficult to publish unauthorized biographies of literary figures whose works remain in copyright. As Hamilton remarked, ruefully, "my name and J. D. Salinger's will be linked in perpetuity as those of litigants or foes, in law school textbooks, on the shelves of the Supreme Court, and in the minds of everyone who reads this, the 'legal' version of my book."

The experience of writing the Salinger biography was, doubtless, the starting point for *Keepers of the Flame: Literary Estates and the Rise of Biography* (1992), in which Hamilton examines how the posthumous reputations and the biographical records of major writers have often been manipulated by literary estates. In the book he examines case histories from John Donne to Sylvia Plath and Philip Larkin. His particular interest is to explore how widows and executors have suppressed or destroyed evidence pertaining to the lives of the writers, either to preserve decency or merely to ensure themselves of a place in history beside the dead writer.

Hamilton, in his foreword, remarks that, provided no evidence is destroyed, fifty years may not be too long to wait for the full truth about a writer to come out. He accepts that "this may sound fishy, coming as it does from the biographer of Robert Lowell and the near, would-be or failed biographer of J. D. Salinger, but there it is. We live and learn." One reviewer suggests that with respect to Hamilton's earlier refusal to take Salinger's no for an answer, his contriteness does indeed "sound fishy." David Lehmann in the *New York Review of Books* (27 March 1994) writes that "For Mr. Hamilton . . . the heroic biographer is the truth teller going up against the masters of deception and spin control out to protect the reputation of great authors whose works may have been in better taste than their private lives."

Hamilton's work, researched mainly from secondary sources, some of them clearly out-of-date, is, in a subtle way, more polemical than scholarly. The style of argument is anecdotal, recounting famous episodes in the history of scholarship in a manner reminiscent of Richard Altick's *The Scholar Adventur-*ers (1982). These episodes, such as the struggle between Bolingbroke and William Warburton over the memory of Alexander Pope; the destruction of George Gordon, Lord Byron's autobiography; and the furor over Ted Hughes's handling of Sylvia Plath's literary estate, are well-known to most students of literature. The book contains almost no new information about these events; however, Hamilton examines within them the emergence of the craft of literary biography and the increasing efforts of literary estates to influence its practitioners. It is an interesting irony that Hamilton treats with cautious regard the efforts, however unsuccessful, of Henry James to frustrate his future biographers by burning papers and publishing a sanitized record of his own childhood. Since the parallels between James's efforts to conceal aspects of his life from posterity and those of Salinger are clear, it is reasonable to see in this section of Hamilton's book a coded tribute to his former antagonist, Salinger, who, like James, strove to be "his own keeper of the flame." Even as the book appears to be Hamilton's gracious farewell to the Salinger controversy, it nonetheless portrays the craft of literary biography in terms of a conflict between those who would discover truth and those who would conceal it.

Hamilton's accomplishments as a biographer are substantial. His biographies of Lowell and Salinger are extensively researched and make a considerable contribution to scholarship surrounding two major figures in American literature. His career as critic and biographer has, however, been characterized by a penchant for conflict. The negativism of his life of Robert Lowell must be seen as limiting its ultimate worth. Only a writer willing to assume the role of adversary could have attempted a biography of Salinger. The unconventional and self-concerned biography that he produced is, however, difficult to judge. Indeed, given Hamilton's need to explain himself, his conduct, and his feelings, it is hard to escape the conclusion that, in a significant way, Salinger, the "quarry," may have escaped.

Interviews:

"A Conversation with Ian Hamilton," *Review,* 26 (Summer 1971): 10–29;

"Ian Hamilton in Conversation with Peter Dale," *Agenda,* 31 (Summer 1993): 7–21.

Papers:

The Harry Ransom Humanities Research Center of the University of Texas at Austin owns a small collection of Hamilton's letters.

Ronald Hayman
(4 May 1932 –   )

Jason Berner
Marymount College

BOOKS: *Harold Pinter* (London: Heinemann, 1968; New York: Ungar, 1973);

John Arden (London: Heinemann, 1968);

John Osborne (London: Heinemann, 1968; New York: Ungar, 1972);

Samuel Beckett (London: Heinemann, 1968; New York: Ungar, 1973);

John Whiting (London: Heinemann, 1969);

Robert Bolt (London: Heinemann, 1969);

Techniques of Acting (London: Methuen, 1969; New York: Holt, Rinehart & Winston, 1971);

Arnold Wesker (London: Heinemann, 1970; New York: Ungar, 1973);

Arthur Miller (London: Heinemann, 1970; New York: Ungar, 1972);

Tolstoy (London: Routledge & Kegan Paul, 1970; New York: Humanities Press, 1970);

John Gielgud (New York: Random House, 1971);

Arguing with Walt Whitman: An Essay on His Influence on Twentieth-Century American Verse (London: Covent Garden Press, 1971);

Edward Albee (London: Heinemann, 1971; New York: Ungar, 1971);

Eugene Ionesco (London: Heinemann, 1972; New York: Ungar, 1976);

Playback (New York: Horizon Press, 1973);

The Set-Up: An Anatomy of the English Theatre Today (London: Eyre Methuen, 1973);

Playback II (New York: Horizon Press, 1974);

The First Thrust: The Chichester Festival Theatre (London: Davis-Poynter, 1975);

The Novel Today, 1967–1975 (Harlow: Longman for the British Council, 1976);

Leavis (London: Heinemann, 1976; Totowa, N.J.: Rowman & Littlefield, 1976);

How to Read a Play (London: Eyre Methuen, 1977);

Artaud and After (New York & Oxford: Oxford University Press, 1977);

Tom Stoppard (London: Heinemann, 1977; Totowa, N.J.: Rowman & Littlefield, 1977);

De Sade: A Critical Biography (London: Constable, 1978; New York: Crowell, 1978);

Ronald Hayman (photograph by John Haynes)

British Theatre Since 1955: A Reassessment (New York & London: Oxford University Press, 1979);

Theatre and Anti-Theatre: New Movements Since Beckett (New York: Oxford University Press, 1979);

Nietzsche: A Critical Life (New York: Oxford University Press, 1980);

Kafka: A Biography (New York: Oxford University Press, 1982);

Brecht: A Biography (New York: Oxford University Press, 1983);

Bertolt Brecht: The Plays (London: Heinemann, 1984; Totowa, N.J.: Barnes & Noble, 1984);

Fassbinder Film Maker (New York: Simon & Schuster, 1984);

Gunter Grass (London & New York: Methuen, 1985);

Secrets: Boyhood in a Jewish Hotel, 1932–1954 (London: Owen, 1985);

Writing Against: A Biography of Sartre (London: Weidenfeld & Nicolson, 1986); published as *Sartre: A Life* (New York: Simon & Schuster, 1987);

Proust: A Biography (New York: HarperCollins, 1990);

The Death and Life of Sylvia Plath (London: Heinemann, 1991; Secaucus, N.J.: Carol, 1991);

Tennessee Williams: Everyone Else Is an Audience (New Haven: Yale University Press, 1993);

Thomas Mann: A Biography (New York: Scribners, 1995).

OTHER: John Robert Whiting, *The Collected Plays of John Whiting,* edited by Hayman (London: Heinemann, 1969);

John Robert Whiting, *The Art of the Dramatist,* edited, with an introduction, by Hayman (London: London Magazine Editorial, 1970);

The German Theatre: A Symposium, edited, with an introduction, by Hayman (London: Wolff, 1975; New York: Barnes & Noble, 1975);

My Oxford, My Cambridge: Memories of University Life by Twenty-Four Distinguished Graduates, edited by Hayman and Ann Thwaite (New York: Taplinger, 1977);

"Bertolt Brecht," in *The Craft of Literary Biography,* edited by Jeffrey Meyers (New York: Schocken, 1983), pp. 186–198.

SELECTED PERIODICAL PUBLICATIONS –
UNCOLLECTED: "In Search of Kafka: Berlin, Prague, Vienna, London, Tel-Aviv," *Encounter,* 56 (May 1981): 52–59;

"Kafka and the Mice," *Partisan Review,* 48 (1981): 355–365;

"Cleaning the Tools," *The Missouri Review,* 7 (Fall 1983): 269–272;

"Brecht's Duplicity," *Partisan Review,* 51, no. 3 (1984): 424–432;

"Sartre and the Mice: A Reputation Reconsidered," *Encounter,* 65 (December 1985): 48–54;

"Jean-Paul Sartre," *Partisan Review,* 53, no. 3 (1986): 449–463;

"Proust and His Mother," *Grand Street,* 9 (Autumn 1989): 123–146.

Ronald Hayman is one of the most prolific literary biographers of the late twentieth century. His body of critical writing, encompassing an almost overwhelming variety of subject matter, defies simple categorization. Hayman has produced full-length biographies on Antonin Artaud, the Marquis de Sade, Friedrich Nietzsche, Franz Kafka, Bertolt Brecht, Jean-Paul Sartre, Marcel Proust, Sylvia Plath, Tennessee Williams, and, most recently, Thomas Mann, as well as shorter works on contemporary dramatists and other literary figures and theoretical works on theater, acting, and literary criticism. Perhaps the best assessment of his work is that, over a career spanning more than twenty-five years, Hayman has established himself as one of the premier "professional" literary biographers of the late twentieth century.

Ronald Hayman was born in Bournemouth, Hampshire, England, on 4 May 1932, the son of John and Sadie Hayman. Following a one-year tour of duty in the Royal Air Force (1950–1951), Hayman received his B.A. from Cambridge University in 1954. Upon graduation Hayman devoted the early part of his career to the theater, working first as a stage and television actor (from 1957 to 1961) and then as a director. During the 1960s Hayman directed such plays as Jean Genet's *Death Watch,* Bertolt Brecht's *Jungle of the Cities,* and Robin Maugham's *The Servant* before writing his first full-length book, *Techniques of Acting,* in 1969.

Hayman's oeuvre can be divided fairly neatly into two overlapping periods. The first, roughly spanning the years 1968 through 1979, was devoted primarily to theoretical works on theater and acting; with the 1977 publication of *Artaud and After,* Hayman initiated the second phase of his career as a literary biographer. While this division is helpful in categorizing Hayman's work, it should by no means be regarded as absolute. During the first half of his literary career Hayman produced short biographies for the Heinemann Contemporary Playwrights series, including *John Osborne* (1968), *Harold Pinter* (1968), *Samuel Beckett* (1968), *John Arden* (1968), *John Whiting* (1969), *Robert Bolt* (1969), *Arthur Miller* (1970), *Arnold Wesker* (1970), *Edward Albee* (1971), *Eugene Ionesco* (1972), and *Tom Stoppard* (1977). In 1984 Hayman provided a twelfth book for the series: *Bertolt Brecht: The Plays.* These books, providing brief overviews of the playwrights' careers, are designed to provide critical (yet at the same time accessible) discussions of a dramatist's work; they are scant on biographical information. If biographies are provided, they are relegated to the introductory section of the book.

Hayman's work for this series is indicative of his later biographical writing: while not offering de-

Dust jacket for the American edition of Hayman's biography of the German playwright

finitive commentary on an author's life, these early studies are solid examples of clear, professional writing. Throughout his career Hayman has been identified as a nondefinitive biographer as opposed to a definitive biographer. Devoting years to the study of a subject in an attempt to provide conclusive critical commentary on the author's life, Hayman proceeds in a more professional, freelance manner: selecting subjects who are interesting to him and writing, to a great extent, for nonscholarly readers. In his profile of Beckett, for example, Hayman immediately provides a clear, coherent thesis of the dramatist's masterpiece: "The achievement of *Waiting for Godot* is that like no other play it crystallizes inaction into a dramatic action." While Beckett scholars might consider such a thesis reductive, Hayman nevertheless succeeds in his primary objective: to provide a brief, nonesoteric point of reference for a general audience. Critics, such as the reviewer for *Choice* (September 1974), who complained that this book provides "nothing new in the

way of critical understanding and interpretation," or T. E. Luddy in the *Library Journal* (1 December 1977), who criticized the biographical outline in Hayman's 1977 study of Tom Stoppard as "too brief and sketchy," seem to be missing the point. Far more accurate is the assessment that the Stoppard work "should prove of value to undergraduate students seeking a not-too-pedantic introduction to the playwright" (*Choice*, February 1978). This is Hayman's primary objective in the Contemporary Playwrights series, as well as in his later work.

Early in his career, Hayman also produced a full-length biography of John Gielgud (1971) and many works of general theory, including *Playback* (1973), *The Set-Up: An Anatomy of the English Theatre Today* (1973), *Playback II* (1974), *The Novel Today, 1967–1975* (1976), *How to Read a Play* (1977), *British Theatre Since 1955: A Reassessment* (1979), and *Theatre and Anti-Theatre: New Movements Since Beckett* (1979). For this last book Hayman was praised by Luddy for "a clarity and precision that has been sadly lacking in other critics" (*Library Journal*, 15 May 1979). During this period Hayman also completed editorial projects and produced books which stand out among the other titles in his bibliography: *Tolstoy* (1970), *Arguing with Walt Whitman: An Essay on His Influence on Twentieth-Century American Verse* (1971), and *Leavis* (1976). These studies, with their wide range of subjects, attest to the nature of Hayman's career as a professional literary biographer. Despite his obvious interest in theater and French and German literature, Hayman has shown a consistent ability to write successfully upon subjects outside his immediate area of expertise.

Artaud and After was something of a crossover work for Hayman. Longer than the Heinemann studies, this book provides an extended biography of the French author/poet/director; but the central strength of this book, as in the Heinemann series, is Hayman's extensive critical study of Artaud's influences and the influence of Artaud's Theater of Cruelty upon such major figures of modern drama as Peter Brook, Jerzy Grotowski, and Genet. Given the unrealized potential for fruitful, in-depth psychological analysis of his subject, however, Hayman's biographical work in this volume must be considered neither definitive nor even particularly satisfactory. While generating little critical attention, *Artaud and After* was praised as "a literate and useful biography" (*Choice*, September 1978). As his first full-length literary biography, this book was something of a watershed for Hayman: since its publication, the author has devoted himself almost exclusively to the writing of literary biographies, the majority of which focus on major figures of French and German literature.

In the first of these, *De Sade: A Critical Biography* (1978), Hayman introduces what is to become a major thematic concern in his biographical work. He suggests that the notorious eighteenth-century libertine wrote in order to exert power over the world around him – a world he often found unmanageable. Although largely powerless during his many years in prison, the Marquis could symbolically inflict torture upon his accusers and persecutors through the depredations of his fiction. "If his opinions counted for nothing in the world outside the cell," Hayman writes, "what he needed was an alternative reality, a literary space, where he would be omnipotent." This idea of literature as a means of exerting control over one's environment becomes an important theme throughout Hayman's later biographies.

In addition to his fascination with the Marquis de Sade's literary motivations, Hayman offers criticism of earlier books on de Sade in explaining his reasons for writing the biography. He chides previous biographers for their reliance upon de Sade's fiction as a source of information. Hayman's book, therefore, becomes something of a corrective biography; in the introduction he states that he seeks to address some shortcomings of Gilbert Lely's two-volume *Vie du Marquis de Sade* (1952, 1957): Hayman felt this book was constructed "like a vicarious diary" which does not provide readers a clear picture of de Sade's development. H. F. Babinski in *Library Journal* (15 June 1978) praised Hayman for writing a "solid and useful study about the events in de Sade's life and about the way his pornographic imagination may have worked." John Sturrock, however, complained in the *New Statesman* (9 June 1978) that "Hayman is a simple man and his literary judgments tend to the elementary."

While *De Sade: A Critical Biography* received mixed reviews, Hayman's next major biography began to earn him widespread critical approval. *Nietzsche: A Critical Life* (1980) was considered "impressive" by the reviewer for the *Economist* (29 March 1980), who said that the biography "provides a rich and satisfying explanation of the connections between the mental and physical deterioration of the man and his mental pursuit for truth in a world inhabited by disorder, irrationality and a dead God." Despite the fact that some critics disapproved of Hayman's book because of perceived interpretative inaccuracies – J. M. Cameron, for example, wrote in the *New York Review of Books* (9 Oc-

tober 1980) that "Hayman is mistaken in the parallel he wants to establish between Nietzsche and [Ludwig] Wittgenstein" – and others felt Hayman did not do justice to the importance and impact of Nietzsche's philosophical work, most reviewers praised Hayman for his scholarship and "unpretentious, intelligent, and balanced" (*New Statesman,* 26 July 1980) view of Nietzsche's life.

Hayman continued to focus on German literature in his next book, *Kafka: A Biography* (1982). Franz Kafka is arguably the most influential writer in twentieth-century German and Austrian literature. His philosophical concerns and innovative use of symbolism fairly revolutionized modern literature. His life, however, poses many challenges to the biographer. Although Kafka has come to be hailed as a literary genius, his life was for the most part uneventful, which necessarily has an adverse impact upon any attempt at biography. Hayman's book does in fact suffer from the lack of noteworthy events in its subject's life. John Simon alluded to this when he wrote in *The New Republic* (10 March 1982) that Hayman's biography "is certainly most exhausting to read, though, given the subject, this must be taken not as derogation but as a compliment." James Atlas in *The New York Times Book Review* (17 January 1982) was less sympathetic, accusing Hayman of being "precise to the point of tedium" in describing the minutiae of Kafka's ordinary life.

The strength of Hayman's life of Kafka, however, lies in its attempt to explain the author's literature through a study of his life experiences. Kafka's writing is motivated almost completely by autobiographical concerns; his unprecedented symbolism therefore demands critical and biographical explication. As in his biography of de Sade, Hayman employs psychoanalysis to describe the life of Kafka: he focuses on the influence on the writing of Kafka's relationship with his father, his fascination with death, and his feelings of personal guilt. Using language reflective of Freudian theory, Hayman explains that, for Kafka "literature was to provide a permanent escape route to a temporary death" and also that writing was "a weapon that could be used against" his father. The overall theme of this biography is, once again, the idea of writing as a means of gaining control over the uncontrollable: Hayman explains that Kafka found "consolation . . . [in] writing masterfully controlled sentences about uncontrollable situations."

In general Hayman's biography received critical praise and furthered his growing reputation. G. R. Muller in the *Library Journal* (15 March 1982) lauded Hayman for writing "elegantly and lucidly." Another statement made by John Simon, however,

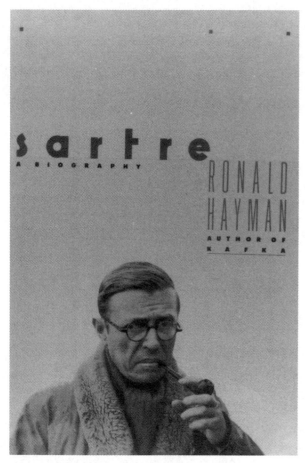

Dust jacket for the American edition of Hayman's biography of the French writer and philosopher

is more indicative of the critical perception of Ronald Hayman. *Kafka,* he wrote, "is a full-length portrait worth hanging alongside the writings: it is not, however, a key to hidden locks or an epiphany of genius. For that, we have to go to greater writers and critics" (*New Republic,* 10 March 1982). Hayman's prestige as a professional and graceful writer of literary biography was growing, yet at the same time it was becoming abundantly clear that he was not to be considered a definitive biographer.

Hayman's next biography focused on another major figure of twentieth-century German literature. *Brecht: A Biography* (1983), like *De Sade,* was described by the author as something of a corrective biography. In an essay for *The Craft of Literary Biography* (1983), Hayman states that, after reading Klaus Volker's *Brecht: A Biography* (1978), he "felt that Brecht's biography had not yet been written." The choice of Bertolt Brecht as a biographical subject seems natural for Hayman, given his interests in German literature and the theater. Brecht was largely responsible for developing the "alienation

techniques" that were later to have such a major impact on world theater. Brecht was also a noted poet, and Hayman describes him as a figure of major historical importance as well: "The choices he had to make involve issues and polarities that are crucial to twentieth-century history."

In this biography, as in *Kafka,* Hayman attempts to explain Brecht's work in close connection with his life. Once again, Hayman's central thesis is that Brecht's artistic creations were manifestations of a desire to assert power over his environment. Brecht, Hayman writes, "was . . . excited by the prospect of increasing his power over adults and contemporaries, and he was not held back by any notion of duty to tell the truth." The tone here, and throughout the book, is one of admiring accusation; Hayman freely admits the moral shortcomings of his subject, yet he feels no need to apologize for them. This is consistent with Hayman's own statements in *The Craft of Literary Biography* that he admired Brecht for his self-discipline and vitality, despite whatever reservations he might have felt about the author's character. Hayman's thesis of Brecht as power seeker helps explain a great portion of the latter's oeuvre. Much of Brecht's work involves games with language, and his theatrical career can be attributed to what Hayman describes as a desire "to build a counter-world, an alternative reality." Brecht was encouraged "to think of traditional literature as a superstructure created to protect the interests of the oppressors," and his nontraditional experiments with alienation can be read as attempts to seize power for himself.

Hayman received praise for a generally well-crafted biography but once again was not recognized as a definitive biographer. Timothy Garton Ash wrote in the *Times Literary Supplement* (9 December 1983) that Hayman provides "the facts of Brecht's life more fully and fairly than any previous biographer," but he went on to criticize Hayman for his comparative lack of attention to Brecht's poetry. This was a common criticism of the biography, as Peter Gay also commented in *The New York Times Book Review* (27 November 1983) that "with all its virtues, Mr. Hayman's life of Brecht is not definitive. . . . Brecht was a great poet, and his verse, I suspect, will outlive his plays and his prose – a conjectural eventuality for which Mr. Hayman's biography offers no house room."

The life of Brecht was followed by *Fassbinder Film Maker* (1984), a critically unsuccessful biography of German filmmaker Rainer Werner Fassbinder. In the *Library Journal* (January 1985) Thomas Wiener condemned the book as a "disorganized, superficial monograph masquerading as a biography," and the reviewer for the *Economist* (6 October 1984) concluded that "Hayman is not merely out of sympathy with Fassbinder; he plainly detests him." Whether or not the critical response was a factor in his decision, after the Fassbinder biography Hayman turned his attention away from German literature; his next two major books focus on twentieth-century French authors, Jean-Paul Sartre and Marcel Proust.

Writing Against: A Biography of Sartre (1986) was at the time Hayman's most ambitious project, inasmuch as the history of Jean-Paul Sartre is, to an extent, the history of twentieth-century France. Born in 1905, Sartre lived through two world wars and observed firsthand the sweeping changes these conflicts wrought upon nations and individuals. By the time of his death in 1980, Sartre had come to symbolize the intellectual life of the French nation. Hayman's primary objective in the biography (as in the biography of Nietzsche) was to document the development of an intellectual giant. Published almost simultaneously with two other Sartre biographies – Kenneth A. and Margaret Thompson's chronological *Sartre: Life and Works* (1984) and Annie Cohen-Solal's *Sartre: A Life* (1986) – the greatest achievement of Hayman's biography is perhaps its accessibility. Even when dealing with the most sophisticated arguments of existentialism, Hayman writes in clear, readable prose, portraying Sartre as a didactic, dominating, extremely self-confident – yet at the same time sympathetic – man.

In addition to his philosophical works, Sartre was himself a literary biographer, which might account somewhat for Hayman's interest in the subject. Sartre wrote lives of Jean Genet and Bernard Mallarmé, as well as an unfinished magnum opus: a biography of Gustave Flaubert. Sartre's primary biographical concern was to answer the question "How does a man make himself into a writer?" Not surprisingly, this is the very question Hayman attempts to answer in his own biography of Sartre. "The question of how Sartre made himself into a world historical figure cannot be answered briefly," Hayman writes in his introduction. "I would say that more courageously, more stubbornly, more cleverly, and more passionately than anyone else in this century he used his life to test ways of facing up to the evils of contemporary history." This passage also exemplifies one of Hayman's stylistic trademarks: a willingness to place himself and his own subjective reactions to his subjects within his biographies. Through this device Hayman allows himself

to be identified as an avid student of his subjects and their writings and consequently as someone who is very much affected by their work: "Particles of Sartre are in the blood that flows through our brains," Hayman writes; "his ideas, his categories, his formulations, his style of thinking are still affecting us." This identification allows Hayman's readers to feel something of the excitement originally generated for the biographer by the subjects themselves – to perceive the biographer as an enthusiastic reader rather than as a stuffy academician – and this in turn makes for a lively biography.

Hayman received deserved critical acclaim for this book, at the time his most ambitious and engaging biography. The reviewer for *Choice* (November 1987) described the biography as "a rich, detailed, carefully wrought in-depth look at the life and times of the best-known philosopher of the twentieth century," and Francisca Goldsmith of the *Library Journal* (15 June 1987) proclaimed Hayman's book "the first 'definitive' work on Sartre's life." Given what has been said of Hayman's "limitations," this last comment is particularly significant, as it marks the first time Hayman's work has been declared "definitive." Another, perhaps more typical, evaluation was, however, offered by Eamonn McArdle of the *New Statesman* (14 November 1986): "Together with the recently published life of Sartre by Cohen-Solal . . . Hayman's study will doubtless provide a starting point for any future evaluation of Sartre's work."

In his next book, *Proust: A Biography* (1990), Hayman faced many of the same difficulties presented by his earlier life of Kafka. As was the case with Kafka, the life of Marcel Proust poses two major challenges for the biographer. First, Proust's fiction is highly autobiographical. As Jean-Paul Sartre, originally a "disciple" of Proust, once remarked, Proust's "genius lies in the totality of his work considered as the totality of the manifestation of the person." The writer François Mauriac also remarked that "There was no real dichotomy between Proust's social life and his literary activity." Proust therefore provides a challenge to the biographer, who must meticulously sort through the subject's works in order to definitively separate fact from fiction.

The second major difficulty in preparing a life of Proust is that Proust led a relatively uneventful life. Like Kafka, Proust was extremely dependent upon his parents; as Hayman says, he lived in their home for "far too long," denying himself the physical and psychological space he needed to develop his own personality. Upon reaching adulthood Proust lived a sheltered (if not reclusive), rather

Dust jacket for the American edition of Hayman's biography of Plath. Hayman did not quote Plath's work in the book to avoid requesting permission to publish from Ted Hughes and the Plath estate.

work, many reviewers questioned the need for a new biography: "Hayman does present new evidence of Proust's transformation of details of his own life into the fabric of his novel and attributes a more positive role than Painter to Proust's mother in the development of his use of memory," wrote C. G. Hill in a review for *Choice* (April 1991), but "on the whole this is not a useful addition to the vast amount of material available on Proust."

The main strength of Hayman's biography is once again its accessibility to the lay reader; Hayman's style is "less painterly and more direct," wrote David Coward of the *Times Literary Supplement* (26 October 1990). He continued, "what makes his biography so absorbing is the sympathetic, nuanced portrait which he has teased with such industry out of the vast secondary literature." Furthermore, Hayman continues to engage his readers by presenting his subjects as sympathetic victims of life, employing literature as a means to gain control over oppressive situations. Hayman presents Proust's masterpiece, *Remembrance of Things Past* (1922–1932), as the product of an active mind in a deficient body; it is a novel Proust wrote in order to exercise control over the elements of his life. "Like his re-creation of his childhood, the process of transforming Alfred [his lover] into Albertine [a character in *Remembrance*] and their relationship into a heterosexual one helped [Proust] to gain control over experiences which had been uncontrollable at the time he was having them."

On the whole the Proust biography marked a major triumph for Hayman. When compared with the Kafka biography, the life of Proust displays an observable growth of Hayman's literary talent. Despite the fact that the Proust biography is almost twice as long as the earlier book — and subject to many of the same pitfalls (notably the excessive interpretation of minute details of the subject's life and the lack of eventful occurrences) — the later book is eminently readable and factually satisfactory, especially to a nonscholarly reader.

Hayman's next biography was something of a departure for him. *The Death and Life of Sylvia Plath* (1991) is a life of the American poet who committed suicide in 1963 at a time when her literary career was on the rise. Hayman voluntarily faced an unusual challenge in the preparation of this book. As Plath's estate is controlled by her husband, British poet Ted Hughes, and any use of her work must be approved by the estate before publication, much of the biographical work done on Sylvia Plath has been subject to Hughes's editorial intervention. In order to sidestep this proscription, Hayman chose

dilletantish life, seldom traveling and dying at a fairly young age after a prolonged period of invalidity. Hayman justifies his subject's lifestyle by proclaiming that "All literary activity involves the writer in shutting himself off from contact with other people at the moment of writing; the life Proust had evolved for himself was relentlessly pushing him towards literature." Whatever the accuracy of this noble sentiment, Proust's relative inactivity nevertheless leads to the distinct possibility of an uninteresting biography.

As an additional difficulty, Hayman was working under a tremendous literary shadow. Before Hayman even began his research, what many critics acknowledge as the definitive biography of Proust had already been written: George D. Painter's two-volume *Marcel Proust: A Biography* (1960, 1965). Given the existence of this master-

not to quote the poet directly, and thus he enabled himself to present Plath's story the way he saw fit. Admittedly, this avoidance of direct reference to his subject's work does lead to a somewhat forced structure and a certain lack of depth; as the critic Vincent D. Balitas pointed out, "simplistic paraphrase" must necessarily substitute for "analyses" (*Library Journal,* 1 September 1991). But once again Hayman produced what the *Economist* (10 August 1991) called a "balanced and concise" life of a celebrated literary figure – notably, another writer who felt overwhelmed by external forces. This biography can also be said to provide a supplement to the more complete biography of Sylvia Plath, Anne Stevenson's *Bitter Fame* (1990).

Hayman's *Tennessee Williams: Everyone Else Is an Audience* (1993) was written on commission from Yale University Press and, considered in connection with the life of Plath, indicates a new area of interest for Hayman: twentieth-century American literary figures. Critical response to the Williams biography was generally negative. However, as no definitive life of the playwright has yet been produced – Mel Gussow wrote in *The New York Times Book Review* (27 February 1994) that "The art [of Williams] endures; the life is still to be written" – only time will tell where Hayman's book belongs in the library of Williams criticism.

Turning from American authors, Hayman renewed his interest in German literature in his latest work, *Thomas Mann: A Biography* (1995), a life of the renowned novelist. In this work Hayman continues to explore the idea of the writer who seeks empowerment and control over his environment through the written word. Hayman quotes Mann, who once wrote that he sought to create "*novelistic* forms and

masks which can be displayed in public as a means of relaying my love, my hatred, my sympathy, my contempt, my pride, my scorn and the accusations I want to make." Like many of Hayman's other subjects, Mann felt the need to hide feelings of powerlessness behind the self-made "mask" of his own writing. With this ambitious work – considered in conjunction with his lives of Kafka, Brecht, Nietzsche, and his brief study of Gunter Grass (1985) – Hayman has provided a valuable overview of twentieth-century German literature.

There is no one subject area to which Ronald Hayman confines himself. He is a biographer in the tradition of professional biographers, who, in choosing his subjects, follows his own inclinations – as well as prevailing public interests – rather than adhering to any single scholarly preoccupation. Hayman's own career as an actor gives an indication of his motivations: in *The Craft of Literary Biography* Hayman writes that "Working at a biography, I always feel a bit like an actor who needs to steep himself so deeply in his character's habits of thinking that he can say [his subject's] words as if they were being spoken for the first time." Like a method actor Hayman is fascinated with truthful and engaging re-creations of memorable personages, be they on the stage or in the pages of a book. Perhaps because they represent the most sympathetic characters, Hayman has chosen as his subjects those authors who used writing as a weapon in a somewhat futile struggle against a despotic reality. Whatever his motivation, however, Hayman has consistently provided his readers with effective and informative profiles of some of the world's most significant authors. As such Hayman is undoubtedly a major voice within modern biographical literature.

Ronald Hingley

(26 April 1920 –   )

William Over
Saint John's University

BOOKS: *Chekhov: A Biographical and Critical Study* (London: Allen & Unwin, 1950; revised edition, London & New York: Barnes & Noble, 1966);

Up Jenkins! (Toronto: Longmans, Green, 1956);

Under Soviet Skins: An Untourist Approach (London: Hamilton, 1961);

The Undiscovered Dostoyevsky (London: Hamilton, 1962; Westport, Conn.: Greenwood Press, 1975);

Chekhov and the Art of Translating (Cambridge, Mass.: Russian Research Center, Harvard University, 1965);

Nihilists: Russian Radicals and Revolutionaries in the Reign of Alexander II, 1855–1881 (London: Weidenfeld & Nicolson, 1967; New York: Delacorte/Seymour Lawrence, 1969);

Russian Writers and Society, 1825–1904 (London: Weidenfeld & Nicolson, 1967; New York: McGraw-Hill, 1967);

The Tsars: Russian Autocrats: 1533–1917 (London: Weidenfeld & Nicolson, 1968; New York: Macmillan, 1968);

The Russian Secret Police: Muscovite, Imperial Russia and Soviet Political Security Operations (London: Hutchinson, 1970; New York: Simon & Schuster, 1971);

A Concise History of Russia (London: Thames & Hudson, 1972; New York: Viking, 1972);

Joseph Stalin: Man and Legend (London: Hutchinson, 1974; New York: McGraw-Hill, 1974);

A New Life of Anton Chekhov (London: Oxford University Press, 1976; New York: Knopf, 1976); published as *A Life of Anton Chekhov* (New York: Oxford University Press, 1989);

The Russian Mind (New York: Scribners, 1977; revised edition, London: Bodley Head, 1978);

Dostoyevsky: His Life and Work (London: Elek, 1978; New York: Scribners, 1978);

Russian Writers and Soviet Society, 1917–1978 (London: Weidenfeld & Nicolson, 1979; New York: Random House, 1979);

Ronald Hingley (photograph by Ivor Fields Ltd.)

Nightingale Fever: Russian Poets in Revolution (New York: Knopf, 1981; London: Weidenfeld & Nicolson, 1982);

Pasternak: A Biography (London: Weidenfeld & Nicolson, 1983; New York: Knopf, 1983);

Russia: A Concise History (London and New York: Thames & Hudson, 1991).

OTHER: *Soviet Prose,* edited by Hingley (London: Allen & Unwin, 1959; New York: Pitman, 1959);

Abram Tertz, *Fantastic Stories,* translated, with an introduction, by Hingley (New York: Pantheon, 1963);

Alexander Solzhenitsyn, *One Day in the Life of Ivan Denisovich,* translated by Hingley (New York: Praeger, 1963);

Anton Chekhov, *The Oxford Chekhov,* nine volumes, translated and edited, with an introduction, by Hingley (London & New York: Oxford University Press, 1964–1980);

Chekhov, *Five Major Plays by Anton Chekhov,* translated, with an introduction, by Hingley (New York: Bantam, 1982);

Chekhov, *Ward Number Six and Other Stories,* translated, with an introduction, by Hingley (Oxford: Oxford University Press, 1988);

Chekhov, *A Woman's Kingdom and Other Stories,* translated, with an introduction, by Hingley (Oxford: Oxford University Press, 1989);

Chekhov, *The Princess and Other Stories,* translated, with an introduction and notes, by Hingley (Oxford: Oxford University Press, 1990);

Chekhov, *Twelve Plays,* translated, with an introduction, by Hingley (London: Oxford University Press, 1992).

SELECTED PERIODICAL PUBLICATIONS – UNCOLLECTED: "Two Anton Chekhovs," *Times Literary Supplement,* 3869 (7 May 1976): 556;

"Max Hayward: A Memoir," *American Scholar,* 49 (Winter 1979–1980): 53–65;

"Pasternak's Shakespeare," *Encounter,* 55 (October 1980): 21–24;

"Stalin's Dead. Can Lenin Be Next?" *New York Times Book Review* (4 June 1989): 11;

"Everything Is Lost in Translation," *Spectator,* 264 (3 February 1990): 33;

"Multiple Musings," *Times Literary Supplement,* 4544 (4 May 1990): 479;

"Seventy Years on the Road to Nowhere," *New York Times Book Review* (7 October 1990): 7;

"Scribes at the Trough – Inside the Soviet Writers," *Times Literary Supplement,* 4599 (24 May 1991): 7–8;

"He Was Afraid of Flying," *New York Times Book Review* (29 September 1991): 9.

Inspired in his boyhood to learn Russian after reading the Catherine Garnett translation of Fyodor Dostoyevsky's *The Brothers Karamazov,* Ronald Hingley later devoted his life to the study of Russian literature and political history. In 1975 Hingley described himself as "a teacher by trade and an academic (not a professional) author." Although his scholarly activity has embraced literary criticism, translation, political analysis, and the examination of broad literary trends, Hingley's biographical

work is perhaps most worthy of note. His major effort in biography, and certainly his best-known work, is *A New Life of Anton Chekhov* (1976), a major revision of *Chekhov: A Biographical and Critical Study* (1950; revised 1966). Both works received critical praise for their prodigious use of primary and secondary sources, many of which had been made newly available for release by the Soviet government. Moreover, Hingley's perceptive analyses in both the original and revised biographies were enhanced by use of his own translations for direct quotation, which rendered his judgments with more clarity and authority. Somewhat shorter works on Dostoyevsky and Boris Pasternak appeared subsequent to his Chekhov study. In addition, Hingley has written broader-based books on groups of Russian poets and novelists who have been influenced by the Russian Revolution and the Stalinist era.

As a translator Hingley has chiefly distinguished himself for readable versions of Chekhov's short stories and for quite speakable and stage-worthy editions of Chekhov's plays. As a scholar Hingley's prose has been both praised as well as blamed for a certain engaging and informal style, at times wry but usually concise and clear. His second Chekhov biography won the James Tait Black Prize in 1976. Hingley has become a recognized authority on recent Russian history and Soviet communist affairs, his analyses having appeared in the *Times Literary Supplement* and other periodicals in both Britain and the United States.

Born on 26 April 1920 to Robert Henry Hingley and Ruth Esther Dye Hingley in Edinburgh, Scotland, Ronald Francis Hingley attended Kingswood School in Bath, England, and then Corpus Christi College, Oxford University. His undergraduate education was interrupted by World War II, in which Hingley served in the British Army from 1940 to 1945, leaving as a captain. After receiving his B.A. and M.A. in 1946 from Corpus Christi, he became assistant lecturer at the School of Slavonic and East European Studies, University of London, in 1947 and served as lecturer from 1950 to 1955. In 1951 he completed his Ph.D. at the University of London, while finishing his first Chekhov biography.

Hingley's academic career then moved quickly. After being director of studies for the Joint Services Language Course from 1951 to 1955, he was appointed University Lecturer in Russian at Oxford University in 1955. Appointed Research Fellow of St. Antony's College, Oxford, from 1961 to 1965, then Fellow in 1965, Hingley became Emeritas Fellow at St. Antony's. Concurrent with his scholarly activities, Hingley developed several introductory Russian language scripts for the British Broadcasting Corporation from 1959 to 1961.

The reception of his first publication, *Chekhov: A Biographical and Critical Study,* was generally laudatory. The *Times Literary Supplement* (2 February 1951) noted Hingley's conscientious handling of a particularly broad range of sources but felt his basic approach was "altogether too formal and too mechanical to enable him to bring out with any liveliness or force of persuasion the fascination of Chekhov's personality." V. S. Pritchett in the *New Statesman & Nation* (17 March 1951) also found this Chekhov biography lacking a certain sensitivity of treatment, especially regarding its subject's genius as a writer. Overall, however, Pritchett felt the biography solidly informative, recognizing in it all that was new to the English reader. G. L. Arnold in the Manchester *Guardian* (29 December 1951) found the biography both scholarly and readable, while other reviewers praised its meticulousness. Simon Karlinsky, in the *Times Literary Supplement* (23 January 1981), judged it the best biography of Chekhov available in English, remarking that Hingley offered "discerning, often subtle critical readings of Chekhov's work and able discussions of the myths and misconceptions . . . of Chekhov in the West."

The author's next full-length work to incorporate biographical analysis, *The Undiscovered Dostoyevsky* (1962), was primarily a critical endeavor for which the biographical detail served as descriptive background. Although Hingley was particularly concerned with exploring Dostoyevsky's humor and writing techniques, the attention to broad historical context evident in his first Chekhov biography reappeared in this study.

In 1967 Hingley published *Russian Writers and Society, 1825–1904,* a critical response to the conventional views of nineteenth-century Russian realism. Hingley's approach, however, is largely biographical, considering, for example, how the social positions of the major writers influenced their attitudes toward making a living from writing. The biographer's considerable historical knowledge presents vivid and comprehensive descriptions of the writers in context: the psychological demands upon the writers from the serializations of their works in periodicals, their commitments to social and political causes, and the particular material conditions of their lives – demographics, transportation, and the educational and cultural development of Russia. Often Hingley's extended examples are deftly handled, such as his description of the participation of Chekhov and Leo Tolstoy in the famine and chol-

era relief efforts of 1891–1892 and the mass panic and stampede at an assembly that killed one thousand people because of official negligence, an incident that eventually appeared in Tolstoy's *Khodynka* in 1912. Perhaps most impressive is Hingley's ability to weave political and sociological details into his biographical narrative. This is especially evident in his consideration of czarist censorship practices as they affected writers.

The much-acclaimed major revision of the Chekhov biography, *A New Life of Anton Chekhov,* reprinted simply as *A Life of Anton Chekhov* in 1989, involved a conscious effort to rethink the original 1950 study. During the twenty-six-year interim separating both works, a substantial body of primary sources had become available to the world, most especially the eight volumes of Chekhov's letters published in the Soviet Union. In addition, the letters of Olga Knipper, Chekhov's wife and the noted actress of his plays, were published in Russian in 1972; other collections containing previously unpublished documents were also released. Moreover, recently released secondary sources in Russian, including an important eight-hundred-page daily account of Chekhov's life, were consulted. From another direction, Virginia Llewellyn Smith, a doctoral student under Hingley's supervision, had become his acknowledged authority on Chekhov's love life through her book, *Anton Chekhov and the Lady with the Dog* (1973). Her expertise allowed Hingley to update the earlier biography by reconsidering Chekhov's personal relationships, notably his romantic involvements and his relations with women in general. Moreover, Hingley's experience as a translator, which at that time included seven volumes of his subject's fiction and drama, allowed him to "get inside his skin" in a way that demanded a second major analysis of Chekhov's life. Hingley admitted in the preface that his own experience with creative writing – the novel *Up Jenkins!* (1956) – enabled him to understand more fully Chekhov's attitudes and goals as a writer. Finally, the experience gained from writing full-length political, social, and historical works enabled the biographer to offer a more authentic context for his subject's life.

A New Life of Anton Chekhov uses an engaging prose style throughout, yet Hingley carefully qualifies his judgments of facts and quoted material. For example, quoting a friend of Chekhov, who enthused over the writer's lack of pretense – "He positively exuded secretions of sincerity" – Hingley concludes that "The tender smile, the sincerity . . . the secretions: we meet these again and again in Chekhovian hagiography. But the picture is not

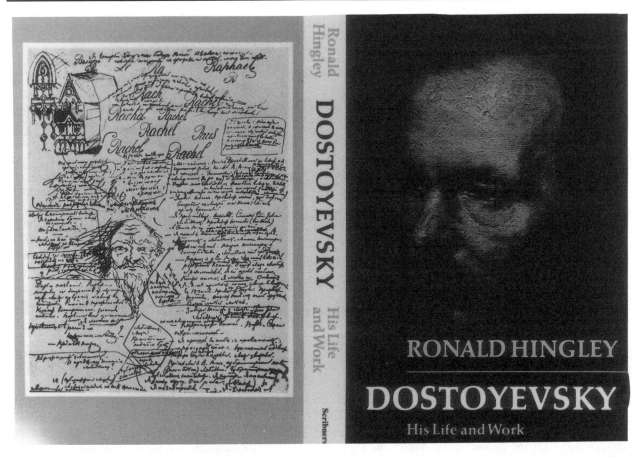

Dust jacket for the American edition of Hingley's biography of the nineteenth-century Russian novelist. Hingley made extensive use of the commentaries published with the first complete Soviet edition of Dostoyevsky's works (1972).

wholly misleading if we can ignore its unfortunate tone." At other times Hingley strives with great insight to suggest possible motivations for Chekhov's literary creativity: "We are also struck by his early, seemingly perverse, avoidance of themes on which his Moscow experiences best qualified him to write: the academic and medical worlds. This was the serious background of his life. Is that why he barely invoked it at all in facetious sketches, but left it for such a mature masterpiece as A Dreary Story?" At still other times Hingley does not avoid exploring the negative side of Chekhov's character. The latter's subtlety as a social manipulator, for example, can be teased out by a close reading of his letters, which Hingley illustrates thoughtfully and with balanced commentary: "Chekhov was apt to take one line when dealing with an individual directly, but a very different line when speaking of that same person to a third party. . . . it is worth noting as a corrective to the stereotype of Chekhov as too noble."

Hingley uses an organizational method for this biography that allows him to deal with chrono-

logical sequence and theme at the same time. Thus, while his chapters are arranged chronologically, by period, the titled divisions within chapters are arranged by theme – "Peasant Benefactor and Chronicler," for example – but also within short time periods, which might cover only from two to ten months each. This organizational scheme serves to codify the life progress of his subject, since the intervals are thematic as well as chronologic.

A prominent analytic technique used in *A New Life of Anton Chekhov* is to end a paragraph of close observations with a penetrating or challenging query. Thus, after quoting complaints by Chekhov of his disorganized living conditions, Hingley asks, "Did contemplation of so much domestic squalor help to confirm the bachelor Anton in his celibate status during most of his adult life?"

As promised in the preface, Hingley explores a new focus on the women of Chekhov's life, often with critical appraisal, such as Chekhov's condescending attitude toward women writers. Hingley's commentary on this theme reveals his very close scrutiny of primary sources: Anna Ivanovna "earned Chekhov's two highest expressions of appreciation: 'not boring' and 'doesn't think like a woman.' Indeed, of all the women he knew, Anna was 'the only one who has her own independent view of things.' " Observations on the real women in Chekhov's life are generally insightful, such as Hingley's perception that the writer's fondness for 'outgoing, active' women was in contrast to the heroines of his short stories, whom he generally idealized as youthful, naive, pure, "defenseless and physically weak." With this observation Hingley draws the thoughtful implication that Chekhov created fictional women possessing "standards more aesthetic" than those he knew in real life.

Arguing along with Chekhov that the brilliant short story, "A Dreary Story" (1889), did not give Chekhov's self-portrait, Hingley remarks cogently that "These sentiments are a warning to critics and biographers who unjustifiably quarry Chekhov's imaginative work, not for illustrations of his views (which is legitimate), but for direct evidence on those views." Hingley does, however, discern some resemblance between the story's elderly embittered hero and Chekhov – their skepticism, their refusal as writers to become ideologues, and their attitudes toward the theater of their day. Indeed, Hingley's demonstration of Chekhov's "lack of any unifying philosophy of life" is supported by ample references to his edition of Chekhov's correspondence.

Hingley is perhaps most controversial when explicating the complex motivations of his subject, which he usually considers piecemeal, but systematically. In chapter 7 the analysis of Chekhov's motivations for his sudden decision to move to Sakhalin, the penal colony in eastern Siberia, is thorough in its factual descriptions and balanced in its criticism. Hingley presents the complicated, seemingly contradictory motivations clearly and considers as well the four motives – literary, scientific, humanitarian, and personal – that Chekhov himself offers for such a drastic change of location. Similarly, in chapter 9, Hingley offers several reasons that led to Chekhov's decision to purchase the country house at Melikhovo in 1892, then considers each possibility, both from a broad social context and a narrower psychological perspective. Hingley accurately gauges Chekhov's contradictory needs for living in the country, with its promise of solitude but its threat of boredom and rural isolation.

Supporting materials for *A New Life of Anton Chekhov* are gathered from a wide variety of significant sources. Hingley's efforts include his own investigative work through firsthand information. For his section on Chekhov as peasant benefactor, for example, he interviewed aging collective farmers, often under the watchful eye of Soviet "guides." He also draws upon a spectrum of secondary sources in both Russian and English for biographical judgments and perspectives. Hingley's talent for succinctness appears at those moments, for example, when he considers the testimony of memoirists and earlier biographers, then offers his own, often pithy, remark: "Behind the lenses of his pince-nez, behind his jokes, could be sensed sadness and alienation. He could survey the scene distantly with the 'beautiful, wise eyes' invoked by so many memoirists. But he was not really enjoying himself."

Chekhov's relationship with Tolstoy is well documented in the sixteen pages Hingley devotes to it. What seems to intrigue Hingley most about their relationship is the great chasm which separates their personalities and opinions. Of Chekhov's social conscience Hingley has much to say and document, but he admits overstressing in the earlier biography Chekhov's phase of social protest evident in his stories of the 1890s, such as "Ward Number Six" (1892). For Hingley the new element of "implied protest" in Chekhov's writing is clearly apparent but needs to be placed in perspective: "to make this factor a dividing line in Chekhov's literary evolution, as I unfortunately did in my previous biography, is to exaggerate a secondary characteristic."

Hingley's description of the conditions of censorship in czarist Russia is often full of insight, particularly when these conditions influenced the writer's creativity and selection of subject matter. The biographer's wide knowledge of the governmental policies affecting cultural events inform his explanations of the banalities of czarist ineptitude and sloth; Hingley, however, also describes the government's often adroit handling of particular publications judged to criticize the monarchy or the church.

An ability to condense great amounts of material allows Hingley to present, for example, the relationship between Chekhov and Maxim Gorky in a concise one-page account, which includes Chekhov's advice to Gorky as a writer, the development of their relationship, and their regard for one another. Similarly, Hingley's presentation of the correspondence between Chekhov and Knipper is expertly condensed into short passages revealing their intimate concerns and frustrations, quarrels, accusations, and confessions.

Throughout *The New Life of Anton Chekhov* Hingley draws heavily upon his immense reserve of research material in order to explicate apparent tendencies in his subject's writings. For example,

Hingley attributes the often stereotypical portrayal in Chekhov's short stories of the Russian urban proletariat in the booming 1890s to the fact, apparent from the correspondence, that the writer possessed a limited knowledge of that group. Hingley assesses the official Soviet interpretation of Chekhov's short story, "A Marriageable Girl" (1903), with astuteness and savvy, carefully situating the Soviet penchant for finding revolutionary sentiment in czarist literature, while conceding certain implicit revolutionary themes in the story of a young woman's flight to the city for a job.

In the last chapter Hingley takes on the problematic task of interpreting *The Cherry Orchard* (1903) for the stage. Drawing heavily upon correspondence among Chekhov; Konstantine Stanislavsky, the father of modern acting; and V. I. Nemirovich-Danchenko, the head of the Moscow Art Theatre, Hingley concludes that Chekhov's insistence that the play was a comedy really only meant that it should be acted with restraint and irony, and not with the customary bombast of the Russian theater. "What [Chekhov] was really appealing for . . . was a lightness of touch, a throw-away casual style, an abandonment of the traditional over-theatricality of the . . . theatre." Also in the last chapter, Hingley carefully articulates Chekhov's critical views of czarist Russia, his underlying progressive attitudes, and his alternative notions; Hingley's agenda seems to include a response to the tendentious positions of those he terms the "blasing-eyed" memoirists, the contemporaries of Chekhov, later officially sanctioned by the Soviet government, who regarded him as an early advocate of Marxist ideology. Hingley concludes that his subject was more disillusioned with the czarist regime than an advocate of new systems, "Here . . . is the voice of the real Chekhov: one who indeed did believe in progress, but not at all in Progress."

Contemporary critics generally had high praise for the biography. The *Economist* (22 May 1976) felt Hingley's groundwork was particularly impressive, "meticulously analyzing the complex of interactions between particular stories, their place of first publication, their author's circumstances and needs, and the literary climate of the time." E. C. Haber, though observing that the book balanced the good and bad qualities of its subject, nevertheless concluded that it did not offer "a profound psychological analysis of its subject" (*Library Journal*, 15 April 1976). Other reviewers admired Hingley's exhaustive analyses but were less impressed by his critical judgments of Chekhov's writings. Howard Moss in *The New York Times Book Review* (20 June

1976) thought Hingley's new version achieved a coherent structure from a vast amount of biographical material that previously lacked continuity. Moss's chief reservation, however, regarded Hingley's attempt to deal with Chekhov's love life.

Dostoyevsky, Hingley's second subject for full-length literary biography, had his *Complete Works* published by the Soviet press only as late as 1972. *Dostoyevsky: His Life and Work* (1978) makes careful use of this expansive new edition's commentaries, as well as other new material previously unavailable in any language, such as Dostoyevsky's second wife's diary. Hingley directly confronts the Freudian interpretations of the murder of his subject's father by peasants; the allegations against his subject of debauchery and racism; and Dostoyevsky's long-lasting struggle with Ivan Turgenev. The reviewer Joy O'Rourke in *Best Sellers* (March 1979) found these attempts impressive, "Hingley eschews hindsight psychology and novelistic reconstruction," and noted his careful efforts to qualify his statements when sufficient evidence was missing. A reviewer for *Choice* (July/August 1979) considered the biography "the most concise and probably most accurate general biography of Dostoyevsky in English."

Although Hingley includes certain novelistic devices for his narrative method in *Dostoyevsky: His Life and Work,* his scholarship retains a consistently objective and balanced perspective. His reliance on secondary sources from Russian publications is considerable, yet Hingley endeavors to form his own critical judgment on the important controversies and ambiguities in the life study of Dostoyevsky. For example, Hingley remains skeptical about the long-standing claim that Dostoyevsky's father was murdered by his own peasants on a highway. He speculates, however, on the incident's significance as biographical fact upon the writing of *The Brothers Karamazov* (1880), wherein all three sons unconsciously wish their father's death. Remaining skeptically detached, Hingley adumbrates both Freudian and anti-Freudian interpretations of the incident.

Often skillfully weaving biographical observation into his overview of Dostoyevsky's major literary works, Hingley concludes that Prince Myshkin, hero of *The Idiot* (1868), was never conceived by the author as a humorous figure; similarly, Hingley notes, Dostoyevsky was never aware of his own social awkwardness, which bordered on the humorous at times.

Hingley's balanced approach toward his subject's character is also evident in his description of Dostoyevsky's calculating attempts to extract

Dust jacket for the American edition of Hingley's biography of the twentieth-century Soviet novelist. Joyce S. Toomre praised Hingley for asking "some awkward questions about the man and his work."

can only end with a platitude: "his supreme unpredictability is . . . a part of his charm."

Dostoyevsky's *Diary of a Writer* (1949) is analyzed from the perspective of the intense nationalism of the writer, his anti-European stance, and the never-specified New Word to come forth from Russia that would transform humankind into a fraternal order: while admitting its brilliance Hingley observes the suspicion and hatred suffusing the work. Dostoyevsky's anti-Semitism; his glorification of the war with Turkey in 1877; and his mystic regard for the Russian peasant, who remained conscious he was doing wrong even while sinning, are all presented as evidence of the writer's rash thinking. Hingley's comment on Dostoyevsky's regard for the self-consciousness of the Russian peasant is perceptive: "But at least this premiss is consistent with the view implied in much of his fiction: a person's acts do not matter, his state of mind is everything." Moreover, Hingley suggests that the vitriol prevalent in *Diary of a Writer* might have functioned as a necessary "purge" of the prejudice and hateful bombast within the writer before he was able to attempt the supremely reconcilable *Brothers Karamazov*.

Hingley does not elaborate on the implications of Dostoyevsky's assumption that he had been under police surveillance since 1875 – whether this misconception might have influenced his increasingly conservative political stance. Instead, Hingley merely suggests that perhaps there was a "submerged atheist" under his cloak of Loyalist. Hingley perceives *The Brothers Karamazov* as "an arena in which evil (intellectualism) clashes with good (instinctualism)." Unlike Dostoyevsky's previous novels, however, there was a more balanced struggle between these two psychic forces. In this way Hingley articulates a developmental view of the writer's vision.

The narrative style of the biography includes an occasional dramatic flourish characteristic of Hingley's previous biographical works. In chapter 12, for example, he offers a histrionic description of the writer's moments of nervous jealousy concerning his second wife. Hingley draws upon a wide spectrum of both primary and secondary sources for *Dostoyevsky,* and his illustrations are ample and selective.

Russian Writers and Soviet Society, 1917–1978 (1979) examines the influence of social context upon Russian literary figures in the post-revolutionary period. Hingley attempts a comprehensive survey of the various cultures among the Soviet peoples, including their complex power structures and class systems. Within this context he offers an ac-

more advances from his publishers: while admitting the moral limitations of his behavior, Hingley nevertheless concludes that Dostoyevsky "was temperamentally incapable of submitting material that fell below his best potential, as witness his practice of destroying extensive drafts and rewriting them until they satisfied his severest critic, himself."

After a careful reading of his subject's letters and the relevant passages in *The Devils* (1872), Hingley concludes that the nihilist characters of that novel, unlike Raskolnikov in *Crime and Punishment* (1866), were not guilty of an "excess of logic," as some critics have argued. Less impressive are Hingley's handling of the charges that Dostoyevsky showed a long-term interest in pederasty: although he offers for consideration evidence from both inside and outside the writer's works, in the end Hingley falls back upon his own conventional judgment of what would seem appropriate for so "civilized, sensitive, decent and kindly a man." In this he

count of how the literary profession functioned under Soviet influence. Jewish writers receive particular attention, and Hingley assesses Stalin's alleged anti-Semitic policies. Isaac Babel, Osip Mandelstam, Valentin Katayev, Aleksandr Fadeyev, Mikhail Skolokhov, Boris Pasternak, and Vasily Azhayev are among the many writers featured. Critics admired Hingley's even-handed assessment, and John Bayley for *The New York Times Book Review* (9 September 1979) particularly admired Hingley's style, which he says is written "fluently, sensibly and with an elegant and prickish play of humor."

Hingley returned to a broader perspective in *Nightingale Fever: Russian Poets in Revolution* (1981), an overview of Russian poets and poetry from the October Revolution to the outbreak of World War II. Using a continuous narrative of four poets, Mandelstam, Anna Akhmatova, Pasternak, and Marina Tsvetayeva, Hingley incorporates their verse selections to enhance his analyses, always from the perspective of social and political influences. His analysis reveals the complex relationship between the poets and the Russian state authorities.

Hingley's third full-length subject for literary biography, Pasternak, is given at times a highly critical treatment. Writing for the *Times Literary Supplement* (26 August 1983), Angela Livingstone considers *Pasternak: A Biography* (1983) "wholly unhampered by reverence," attempting a "sweepingly bold integration of the poet's life, work and age." Joyce S. Toomre in *Library Journal* (1 October 1983) admires the biographer's critical stance toward Pasternak, "Uncowed by his subject, Hingley asks some awkward questions about the man and his work." Noticing the biography's critical perspective, Bayley feels that Hingley's assessment of Pasternak's great reputation for meekness, which the biographer described as indistinguishable from "profound immodesty," was insightful. A reviewer for the *Economist* (13 August 1983) called *Pasternak: A Biography* "authoritative."

Hingley was able to interview his subject's family members and to locate a quite recent spectrum of opinion. Hingley traces the unfolding of Pasternak's poetic vision from his early symbolist period, which he left with the recognition of the movement's bankruptcy, to a more independent stance. Paralleling this change is a turn from a negative to a more positive tone. Hingley is particularly astute at lifting up the "muffled autobiographical echoes" from Pasternak's verse, and his explanation for Pasternak's important decision to leave the symbolist literary group Lirika in 1914 shows his com-

prehensive understanding of the intellectual life of late czarist Russia.

Hingley is particularly interested in exploring the contradictory nature of Pasternak, insofar as he possessed a lifelong desire for publicity but cultivated a reputation for shyness, humility, and withdrawal from the public eye. Hingley observes that "it would be naive to assume that his persistent claim to avoid publicity was not, in however slight a degree, a highly successful device for seeking publicity." Hingley endeavors to present a clear picture of his subject's paradoxical orientation through a selective examination of correspondence, an analysis of his collegial and personal relationships, and an investigation of his reputation among his contemporaries. Complicating the picture is Pasternak's complex relationship with Soviet censorship. Here Hingley once more proves his particular strength as a biographer – his ability to clarify the writer's relationship with the public, especially with respect to censorship and publishing practices. Hingley's assessment is cogent: "The trouble with . . . Pasternak, from the point of view of his would-be manipulators, is that he rarely has the faintest idea what he is going to say next, and that his expressions of revolutionary enthusiasm are always liable to veer off into paradox, irony, or sheer incomprehensibility."

Pasternak's movements in and out of literary organizations during the decade of World War I, explained by his uneasiness with political associations, are documented with specificity by Hingley. The poet's complicated relationship with Vladimir Mayakovsky, their political and artistic differences, and their regard for each other are considered in detail. Hingley's perception of Pasternak's passive political nature leads to a consideration of certain of Pasternak's author-protagonists as alter egos. Their temperamental passivity (Spektorsky, Yuri Zhivago) "accords with aspects of Pasternak's own nature, and also with his conception of the poet as a medium or sponge through which nature and art express themselves." Apparent in Hingley's evaluation, however, is his refusal to fix only one explanation for the writer's behavior. The biographer seeks throughout to describe the complexity of his subject's psychological life.

Hingley feels Pasternak was better at verse than prose and suggests that his temperament was better suited for the intensity of poetry, with its "effervescence." Special focus on Pasternak's private life is intended to present a fuller picture of the man than previous biographies had attempted. Thus, the account of Pasternak's idealization of women, beginning in his childhood and continuing throughout his life, appearing also in the women characters of his novels, is scrutinized with insight. *Doctor Zhivago* (1957), for example, projects "the passionate idealization of woman in the abstract to which the author had been prone since childhood." Hingley associates the presence of women figures in Pasternak's novels, and the juxtaposition of love and domesticity, with the writer's interpretation of Christianity. Missing in the analysis, however, is a discussion of the implied sexism evident in the novel's close association of women as domestic servants for men.

For the most part Hingley's critical analysis of *Doctor Zhivago* is trenchant. He takes note of Pasternak's tendency to ignore or dismiss social evils and the political scene in general and profitably compares the writer's hero Yuri with Prince Myshkin of Dostoyevsky's *The Idiot.* Hingley also suggests that both Yuri and Pasternak, his creator, may resemble the long-standing Russian image of the saintly buffoon; Hingley makes a similar correlation between Prince Myshkin and his creator in the Dostoyevsky biography. Although the parallel between the two authors is striking, Hingley leaves his comparison largely unexplored.

Hingley had a series of personal interviews and conversations with Pasternak in the summer of 1958, just before the Nobel Prize announcement. The circumstances surrounding the writer's rejection of the prize are rendered with much detail in the biography, including the intrigue, the anguish, and the drama of events. Pasternak's deal with the Soviet Central Committee, his subsequent near-suicide, and his eventual eclipse by Alexander Solzhenitsyn in the eyes of the West are carefully presented. Hingley's wide knowledge of Russian domestic political action serves him well throughout this section. He, however, relies heavily upon the recently published memoirs of Pasternak's mistress, Olga Ivinskaya, for much of the facts surrounding the prize. On the question of the reliability of her memoirs, Hingley devotes much attention. He concludes that the readiness for self-criticism exhibited in her memoirs, together with her expressions of regret for much of her behavior in the relationship, prove the objectivity of her recollections. Hingley's final comment is characteristic of his tendency for succinctness: Ivinskaya's memoirs "offend less, it may be suggested, in terms of accuracy than in matters of taste and tone."

Ronald Hingley has established a wide reputation through his ability to integrate the quite distinct fields of political history and literary biography. As much an authority on the inner workings of the Soviet government as on the inner lives of his literary subjects, he draws upon both areas of knowledge as a literary biographer. Most distinctive is Hingley's ability to establish a historical context, situating his writer within broad social and political movements, which he defines with abundant specificity and unusual clarity. He takes special care to reveal both the subtle and more-obvious changes in the personalities of his subjects, attending also to the development of their bodies of writing, always within well-articulated social and political parameters. Hingley's keen awareness of the strong forces of cultural as well as official censorship upon the writer and his works are manifest in all three literary studies: his additional interest in Russian social history articulated the backgrounds through which to view Chekhov, Dostoyevsky, and Pasternak.

Evident throughout the three major biographical studies is the large body of research materials at hand. Hingley allows his general reading audiences the opportunity to browse his prodigious documentation by supplying lists of relatively lengthy references, indexes, and appendices, sometimes at the cost of critical comment on their unnecessary length. Hingley's major revision of his Chekhov biography reveals his concern to bring forward more contemporary issues for scrutiny, particularly regarding Chekhov's relationships with women. Finally, Hingley's thoughtful, at times poignant, reflections on the motivations of his subjects demonstrate a wise humor but also an affection and affinity.

Richard Holmes

(5 November 1945 –)

Dennis Paoli
Hunter College of the City University of New York

BOOKS: *One for Sorrow, Two for Joy* (London: Cafe
Books, 1970);

Thomas Chatterton: The Case Reopened (London: John
Murray, 1970);

Shelley: The Pursuit (London: Weidenfield & Nicolson, 1974; New York: Dutton, 1975; revised
edition, London: HarperCollins, 1994);

Coleridge (Oxford: Oxford University Press, 1982);

Footsteps: Adventures of a Romantic Biographer (London:
Hodder & Stoughton, 1985; New York: Vik-
ing, 1985);

Coleridge: Early Visions (London: Hodder & Stoughton, 1989; New York: Viking, 1990);

Dr. Johnson & Mr. Savage (London: Hodder &
Stoughton, 1993; New York: Pantheon, 1993).

RADIO: *Inside the Tower,* play, British Broadcasting
Corporation-Radio 3, 1977.

OTHER: Theophile Gautier, *My Fantoms,* translated, with an afterword, by Holmes (London:
Quartet, 1976);

Percy Bysshe Shelley, *Shelley on Love,* edited, with
preface and introductions, by Holmes (Berkeley: University of California Press, 1980);

Gerard de Nerval, *Chimeras,* translated by Peter Jay,
with essays by Jay and Holmes (Redding
Ridge, Conn.: Black Swan, 1984);

Mary Wollstonecraft, *A Short Residence in Sweden,
Norway, and Denmark,* and William Godwin,
Memoirs of the Author of "The Rights of Woman,"
edited by Holmes (Harmondsworth: Penguin,
1987).

"And then I saw it, quite clearly against the
western sky, the old bridge of Langogne. It was
about fifty yards downstream, and it was broken,
crumbling, and covered with ivy." This is the first,
crucial epiphany in Richard Holmes's autobio-

graphical confessions, *Footsteps: Adventures of a Romantic Biographer* (1985), the origin tales of his biographical career. It has been, to this, its apparent
heart, a brilliant and controversial career, quite as
concerned with biography as its subject as it has
been with its subjects' biographies. Holmes was
eighteen, following, or trying to follow, the path of
Robert Louis Stevenson as described in his *Travels
with a Donkey in the Cevennes* (1879), when he saw the
ruin of the old bridge across the Allier from where
he stood on the modern, operative bridge to
Langogne. And it hit him: "So Stevenson had
crossed *there,* not on this modern bridge. There was
no way of following him, no way of meeting him.
His bridge was down. It was beyond my reach over
time, and this was the true sad sign." Holmes recognizes the ruin as a marker signifying the inevitable
breach in the empirical trail of biographical evidence, the limits of the biographical imagination,
the romantic fate of the biographer.

Holmes was born in London on 5 November
1945 to a lawyer and a poet, his father Dennis and
his mother Pamela. He went to Catholic boarding
schools and Churchill College, Cambridge. After attaining a B.A. in 1967, he went to London and took
temporary employment compiling the Westminster
City Council political register. Along the way he
lost his religious faith, though he finds that his religious training has provided him with a "frame of
reference" crucial to the study of eighteenth- and
nineteenth-century subjects, his biographical company, for whom the most profound issues of culture
and identity were usually religious or expressed in
religious terms. He also discovered a love of travel
and gained a fine working knowledge of French as
well as a profound capacity to hear voices. "Powerless to act on the petty injustices and miseries I
saw," he writes of his experience canvassing south
London, "I learned at least how to listen to other

Richard Holmes (photograph by John Foley)

people, and observe some of the forces that shaped their lives." He had listened well before that and would again in his work and journeys, to colorful locals and fellow foreigners in his continental trekking, to the voices of long-dead men and women in their correspondence and journals, to poets and philosophers, the provers of language, in a variety of rhetorics and idioms and tongues. He translates and enjoys writing for the radio; he was, and is, a poet. His mother, whose early verse was anthologized in a collection of poetry from World War II, went on to write children's poetry, and Holmes remembers her reading to him from Stevenson's *A Child's Garden of Verses* (1885). By the age of twelve he had won a school prize for his own poetry, and he submitted a group of poems in partial fulfillment of the requirements for his degree at Cambridge. Though he has no plans to publish any verse in the foreseeable future, he writes it steadily still. "Poetry is always there," he declared in an interview in *Contemporary Authors* in 1989. "It's *the* linguistic discipline for any writer; you can never get away from it."

It was as a prospective poet that he set out on Stevenson's trail in the summer of 1964, but along the way he "first encountered – without then realising it" what he later came to consider "the essential process of biography." He describes the encounter as a "haunting," "the creation of a fictional or imaginary relationship between the biographer and his subject," "a continuous living dialogue between the two as they move over the same historical ground,

the same trail of events." For Holmes this act of the historical imagination defines the biographical process, in its essence, as a Romantic quest, and almost all his subjects are Romantics.

It is ironic, then, that he never studied Romantic literature at Cambridge; it is intriguing that he took his A-level exams in history and was accepted to read history at Churchill, which had only recently been founded as a college dedicated primarily to the study of the sciences. Early on he took a course with George Steiner and immediately changed his major field of study to English literature, yet he always felt "lucky to be reading literature in an up-to-the-minute science context," and he continued his interest in history over the course of his academic career. Holmes considers literature "a part of history," if not "indistinguishable" from it, while the opportunity to read novels and Greek drama and eighteenth-century poetry – his specializations – in an intellectual environment suffused with the scientific method made Churchill "a wonderful place to be." An appreciation of the scientific principles of logic, observation, and experiment of literature as history and vice versa made a near perfect preparation for the vocation he would discover in the Cevennes.

The fact that he followed, or rather, accumulated his inclinations, from history to literature, from poetry to science, from voice to individual, made him a willing scholar, an avid reader, a poet with a purpose. Holmes does all his own research;

he never uses assistants. This personal involvement in every discovery and the integration of those discoveries into a biography afford him insights and challenges that keep the process dynamic and lend life to the life he is writing. It makes for hard work and lots of it. His prodigious, relentless scholarship, "the gathering of factual materials, the assembling of the chronological order of a man's 'journey' through the world," is, in this light, the empirical root system of Romanticism, its founding virtue of observation as it excites the sensibility. Describing the "physical presence" of the past "in landscapes, buildings, photographs, and above all the actual trace of handwriting on original letters or journals," Holmes sounds like a late–eighteenth century antiquarian (except, of course, for the photographs). Holmes, though, claims not to be a collector, unless it is in the imagination, where he can collect subjects. The "first element" of the process – the appreciation, in every sense, of objective evidence – makes the "second element," "a more or less conscious identification with the subject," "a type of hero- or heroine-worship," "a kind of love affair," possible.

These elements are necessary but not sufficient for the production of biography: "the true biographic process begins precisely at the moment, at the places, where this naive form of love and identification breaks down," like the old bridge to Langogne. The lives of literary subjects, unlike their works, come down to us through history in ruins, and the biographer, like the Romantics touring the Continent, must not be seduced by the merely picturesque but must enter into the existential nature of life writing, its lacks and gaps, its correlative sense of loss and nonexistence. When he writes that the "moment of personal disillusion is the moment of impersonal, objective re-creation," Holmes sounds like a nineteenth-century French poet anticipating a twentieth-century French philosopher.

Not only is there insufficient material available to do the job of biography, there is too much. The psychological penetration of the subject by the author, besides demonstrating the obvious – that the biographer has a profound interest in her or his subject – suggests, with the efficacy of a symbol, the interpenetration of the subject's life with the lives of other subjects numerous often beyond knowledge. The mental life of Samuel Taylor Coleridge is incomprehensible without an understanding of the mental life of William Wordsworth; the mental and love lives of Percy Bysshe Shelley cannot bear comment without reference to the thought and feeling of

Mary Shelley, responsively and independently; the love life of Stevenson did not exist without the love of Fanny Osborne, whom he followed across continents and whose influence on him became more and more apparent to Holmes as he climbed mountains and crossed fields she never graced, except as she lived in Stevenson's heart. Multiply these influences/presences by the number of parents and siblings and favorite teachers and school chums and lovers and rivals and disciples and servants and sycophants of note or interest in the subject's life – among dozens or hundreds of acquaintances and influences, fleeting, profound or unfathomable – and the task seems all but futile. Scholarly dedication is one thing, but the chaos, applying the term scientifically, of the "enormously intricate emotional web of other people's lives" must defeat the most monumental and subtle psychological effort of which a biographer is capable.

So Holmes does what all biographers do: he compromises, prioritizes, and makes the effort of deepest understanding in relation to the figures from whom he will reap the largest, surest, or most critical return. He just does it differently, attending most closely and analyzing most carefully not the highest profile among the figures surrounding the subject or the richest source among the subject's works, necessarily, but the most fascinating problem in the life. The "psychological complication" that comes to dominate his awareness of Stevenson as he hiked the Gevaudan was not the growth of the young writer but what the writer suppressed and why, what appears in the published text of *Travels* only as modified by a reading of the corresponding journals and correspondence and as deconstructed by desire. One episode "really brought out in him, I think, his intense sexual loneliness and longing for Fanny Osborne"; another passage is "in effect, a proposal of marriage to Fanny Osborne." It is a young man contemplating marriage to a mature woman, divorced with two children, his love for whom "challenged his identity," whose footsteps Holmes follows. And the reader appreciates the growth of the writer – be he Stevenson or Holmes – better for the "love affair" – be it between man and woman or biographer and subject.

Subjects' love lives are major themes in biographies, of course, but only in certain of their aspects. They provide piles of evidence, filling billets-doux and diary pages, and exert an unmistakable pull on the subject's literary efforts. The milestones – marriages, children, affairs, divorces – are easily tracked, with structural potential. But Holmes's next biographical discovery, occasioned by a trip to

Paris to observe, if not participate in, the "revolution" of 1968, was that an experience central to most love relationships – a period of domestic happiness – rarely ever appears in biography. It is not as dramatic as courtship or break-up and generates less "evidence"; it does not make as good a "read," as Holmes reminds us that Leo Tolstoy reports in the opening sentence of *Anna Karenina* (1873–1876). Yet domesticity can sustain, amplify, and complicate intimacy, often defining its nature for that particular relationship. When rifts occur they are as likely to tear the worn fabric of domesticity as they are to rip apart romance; when writers mature it is often in the bosom of domestic bliss, or at least stability. This is viable, if often ulterior, biographical material.

How does Holmes get to this insight from the experience of being assaulted by a uniformed trooper during a sweep of potential demonstrators on "the boul' Mich"? The epiphany this time is in the voice of the trooper, demanding of the writer, with typographically rendered rhetorical immediacy, why, as a foreigner, he does not mind his own business and go home. It is a better question than the trooper realizes, opening a rich vein of inquiry for a student of Romanticism, bearing as it does upon one of the central themes of English Romantic sensibility, the impression made and left by the French Revolution. Characteristically, Holmes first asks himself the question by asking historical figures in similar situations. Why did Wordsworth travel to France to see firsthand the revolution of 1789, the radical paradigm for the poor copy of 1968? What happened to the "White's Hotel group" of exiles, writers, and "Friends of the Rights of Man?" It was not until "many months later," however, that Holmes found "among a mass of minor papers" in the Central Library at Liverpool a letter written in a "voice" that "broke in on me like a new sound, a new dimension," a voice that could answer the trooper. He found his interlocutor, his alter ego, his subject – Mary Wollstonecraft. And following her through Paris – she arrived "almost the exact day that Wordsworth was leaving" – he pressed through the broad strokes of regicide politics and Mary's overarching ambition to write a history of the revolution to the fine work of her modest "Lessons for Children," "a dozen fragmentary pages" in which the careful critic finds "secret memories of the time of family happiness . . . a precious glimpse into that lost world of intimacy" shared by Mary, her daughter Fanny, and her husband, at least by "French law," Gilbert Imlay.

Holmes disagrees with Wollstonecraft's biographers, "mostly feminist writers," who have denigrated Imlay as a bad match and ultimately a bad man. He assembles evidence, and lack of it – Imlay's letters are lost – for his case, but his most telling exhibit is "the evident and extraordinary change that he produced in Mary as a writer." Holmes lives with the novelist Rose Tremain, and future critics may someday look in the works of each for the effect of the other, but they would be well advised to adopt Holmes's method and look and listen – for evidence, not controversy; he does not peddle his biographies over the bodies of predecessors, proclaiming his versions "new and improved." But when he hears a different drummer, he marches. And he seems always to find the "gaps." He works hard to fill the "gap between rational expectation and imaginative impact, or, to put it in its classical form, between Reason and Imagination" into which both French revolutions stepped and tripped, one into terror, the other into triviality, with "the wholly new emphasis [Wollstonecraft] gave to human affections and the faculty of the imagination in forming them." He has more luck with the "biographical gap," the "ordinariness, and . . . family intimacy" that "is the very thing that the biographer – as opposed to the novelist – cannot share or re-create." Because the effect is impossible, the reader grants authority to the effort and credit the meager evidence he musters as consequential. But since it is probable that only Holmes could have found this evidence, and this argument, in the first place, he earns the biographer's most potent lever of persuasion – trust.

His great work so far is his biography of Shelley, published when he was twenty-nine. Sleeping and studying days, writing nights, Holmes pursued Shelley with a passion. *Shelley: The Pursuit* (1974) is several books in one, not categorically or conceptually, but cognitively, in impression. On the one hand, it is sweeping and fluent; its prose propels; events advance, expand, and transcend description; and the reader achieves understanding – no mean feat when the subject is Shelley. Shelley is greatly complicated psychologically. On the other hand, the book is dense and partial, leaving the depths and shadows of many of the popular figures who parade through Shelley's life and the intricacies of many popular anthology pieces among his poetry to other biographers and critics, while focusing hard on what Holmes perceives to be understudied and underappreciated segments of Shelley's career and experience, especially his political thinking – and therefore his prose – and his relationship with Claire Clairmont.

It is not just the redistribution of weighty materials, though, that gives the biography such power, but the subtle accumulation of character in the dynamics of difficult relationships and the force of imagery revealing itself. A biographer could easily brighten and lighten a life so full of colorful eccentrics such as George Gordon, Lord Byron, and Leigh Hunt, major influences on Shelley, but that would be antic byplay. Observing Shelley's persistence, though, in hero-worshipping his father-in-law and father-in-effect, William Godwin, while dunning him for long-owed, much-needed funds is painful and enlightening in a character otherwise given to ditching bailiffs and belittling genius in contemporaries such as John Keats. Imagery from Shelley's poetry must spice his life, but when the young poet sells his solar microscope, "his most precious piece of 'philosophic' equipment," that he carried around England and Wales with him for years, to pay some debts, the object carries surprising symbolic freight: it signals a step in Shelley's unfinished forced march toward maturity. It would also affect his poetry without appearing in it, for when he stopped playing in the effects of science and applied its principles in his poetry, his work matured. His naturalist's eye proved essential to his inspiration: "This poem was conceived," he wrote of his "Ode to the West Wind," the only work Holmes quotes in its entirety, "on a day when that tempestuous wind, whose temperature is at once mild and animating, was collecting the vapours which pour down the autumnal rains. They began, as I foresaw, at sunset with a violent tempest of hail and rain, attended by that magnificent thunder and lightning peculiar to the Cisalpine regions." The poet had himself become a finely tuned scientific instrument, sensitive and responsive, observant and prescient. He was an empiricist less by practice than by nature, as he was a poet.

Holmes considers his own experience as a practicing poet "very important" to his comprehension of Shelley's work, the effort and craftsmanship. Poring over drafts of Shelley's poems in the Bodleian Library, he could "see Shelley working," his close correcting, revising through various versions; he could rediscover the "Ode to the West Wind" "coming into life," the arrival "in stages" of "the crucial moment in the Italian experience" of the poet, through the demonstration of "how a poem actually gets written." Holmes's firsthand knowledge of the composing process allows him to create pregnant, authentic images of the poet creating, to express the life of the writer at its most expressive.

In prose pictures of the poet picking up his pen, thrown angrily down in midresponse to a bad review, turning his notebook upside down, and dashing off the first draft of his famous ode, or composing *Prometheus Unbound* (1820) while sitting and strolling "upon the mountainous ruins of the Baths of Caracalla," or stripped to the waist in the sun-filled, glassed-in tower of the Villa Valsovano writing in a burst of incandescent imagination "the greatest poem of political protest ever written in English," *The Mask of Anarchy* (1832), the reader sees the physical conditions of his work and thrill at the labor. Empiricism empowers biographers, too, as Holmes knows and as his synthetic, dynamic images demonstrate.

Shelley has also been "under-appreciated," Holmes thinks, as a translator. Holmes's own translations are from the French, though he never formally studied the language. Shelley, expelled from Oxford, became a remarkable autodidact, "embarking on new literatures, new disciplines," often by embarking on a new language, be it Greek or Italian or German. The work left unfinished at his death was a translation of Johann Wolfgang von Goethe's *Faust* (1808, 1832). An extraordinary enthusiast of education, Shelley became, in Holmes's term, "a travelling university," suggesting again that his subject must "be reimagined," relative to Mary and Claire, his fellow travelers and pupils, and relative to himself, for with learning a new language comes "the possibility of a second identity," "a kind of displacement" by which a poet grows, matures, and reinvents himself.

Holmes is squarely in a mainstream – there are two – when he is understanding toward Shelley in considering his culpability in the case of Harriet Westbrook Shelley's suicide; no one could edit an anthology entitled *Shelley on Love* (1980), as Holmes did, if he or she thought or felt otherwise. The marriage to Mary Godwin Shelley, full of travel and sacrifice, nervous breakdowns and dangerous childbirth, frustration and *Frankenstein,* is appreciated as impressive but handled in standard fashion. The prominence and importance given to Claire Clairmont's journals and letters, on the other hand, is original and accurately reflects her dramatic stature in Shelley's story and is crucial in understanding Shelley's understanding of love, the core of his poetic credo, the end of his pursuit. The significance of the subtitle of *Shelley: The Pursuit* is the poet's spiritual struggle to unite with his demonic self and create, through the visionary powers of the Romantic imagination, a whole being. That is the biographer's quest, too, as Holmes sees it, to create and appreci-

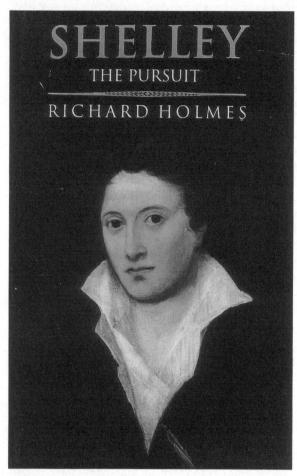

Dust jacket for Holmes's biography of the British Romantic poet that he calls "a young man's book"

ate the subject's whole being, or as near as possible. His success is apparent in the wide acceptance of the biography as the new standard life of the poet.

The dangers of pursuing a demon become more and more apparent as the reader passes on to the final two chapters of Holmes's next major work of and on biography, *Footsteps: Adventures of a Romantic Biographer*. The pivotal epiphany in the chapter on researching Shelley's last days at the Casa Magni on the shore at San Terenzo, Italy, "the final act in a biographical drama of immense complexity," has demonic overtones. Holmes makes a leap of perspective when, finding that Shelley's residence in Pisa is no longer standing, he takes a picture of what the view would have been *from* the house, what the Shelleys, looking out, would have seen; he fills a gap with a reflection. There is a sense that, walking in the "footsteps" of his subjects, Holmes is always a pace, at least, behind, pursuing doggedly, sometimes breathlessly, an ever-elusive source; but camera in hand, standing in the virtual footprints of the poet, he catches up and achieves a moment's

identification that, like Wallace Stevens's jar on a Tennessee hilltop, orients everything around it, not categorically as rational evidence, perhaps, but impressionistically as authentic experience. He gains perspective, another perspective, that grounds his knowledge and refreshes, relaunches "the true biographic process."

Later, though, looking at a photograph taken of the Casa Magni with his "thirty-year-old Ensign, with a bellows lens," which his father, an accomplished amateur photographer, had given him, Holmes spots a boy, the owners' child, who had wandered into the picture. For a moment he feels a "faint tingling sensation," as if he "was looking at a photograph of little William, Shelley's dead son." Though the double vision leads to a touching recognition of Shelley's love for "Willmouse," his favorite, and though a biographer's scalp may often tingle with excitement as her or his pursuit closes in or pays off, here Holmes is perilously close to acting as a medium in an extrasensory sense. Standing at the edge of the empirical grounds of biography, Holmes *loses* perspective and teeters vertiginously on the verge of the irrational, the documentary record shifting shape and source before his eyes.

Holmes is usually scrupulous about reality checking, about questioning his own speculations, often respeculating. In a 1989 personal interview, a decade and a half after the book's publication, he called *Shelley: The Pursuit* "a young man's book" and now believes that the scenario he creates in a unique appendix to one of the biography's chapters explaining the probable circumstances of birth and fosterage of Shelley's "Naples charge" is, upon further reflection, probably misguided and misleading. In the last episode of *Footsteps,* however, his method fails him. In Paris again in 1976, he is decompressing from his immersion in Shelley's life and planning to write a novel. But he is intrigued by the work of the nineteenth-century French photographer Felix Nadar, especially by a particular portrait of the poet and travel writer Gerard de Nerval. His biographer's nature rises to the bait, he is hooked, and soon he is researching Nerval, *poet maudite;* student of religions; believer in the Tarot; madman; and suicide. The life is fascinating, but the evidence is thin. What there is is highly suggestive, but the objective checks are inadequate to support or bring into focus a clear understanding of the central fact of Nerval's life and death – his madness. The chapter's central image, the labyrinth, is emblematic of the poet's plight, as well as the biographer's. Holmes investigates Nerval's complex relationships with his father and doctor; he visits the site of the suicide, reads the Tarot like a devotee, and haunts the shadows of century-old Parisian streets and stairways where the failed and insane poet would wander, lost to himself. Trapped in his identification with the mad Nerval, Holmes starts to fear for his own sanity. He could, after a double-take, identify the boy in the photograph of Casa Magni, but he cannot tell who the man in Nadar's portrait really is. He has enough information, and plenty of inspiration, to write a historical novel on Nerval but not enough real life for a biography. And that is not enough for Holmes. He left his life of Nerval unpublished, its title, "A Dream Biography," suggesting the reason. Dreams may be biographical, but a biography that is "dreamt" is rhetorical to the point of being metaphorical. Holmes had pursued Nerval across the line defining life writing and fiction, which is what he went to Paris to do in the first place, but which in the end left him in a literary cul de sac, staring off a broken bridge.

This psychological brinkmanship is part of Holmes's biographical process. First he does what he calls "deskwork," finding and reading and listening to the available texts, reading around in the period and the field, compiling the bibliography and living in libraries. Next is "fieldwork," "short, intense periods" of travel over the ground the subject walked, climbing the hills, looking out the windows, haunting the haunts still extant. A Londoner, Holmes is at home in the backstreets and cafe society of city life, but growing up he lived more and more in the country, in the still remote marshlands of Kent, and as a teenager he often lived rough on the west coast of Scotland, tenting and hiking. The further afield the fieldwork takes him, into labyrinthine alleyways or trackless wilderness, the closer Holmes comes, it seems, to his subject, sharing conditions in extremis and discovering images that yield insights into what had previously been virgin biographical territory, a perfect privacy. Last, and most perilous, is "dreamwork," when the writing has begun and the biographer is thinking about the subject's life "all the time," including in the subconscious mind during periods of apparent rest or distraction, a "speculation" so intense that Holmes admits to having "very vivid dreams about the work" at this stage. This is how mathematicians describe their problem-solving process, always working "at some level" toward a solution, "the bits being turned over" in the imagination until they find, as if for themselves, how they naturally fit. So, like theoretical scientists, biographers often speak in terms of discovery, not of new material evidence, but of the life of the subject itself.

The dream must be expressive, though; it must resolve itself in exposition. If it does not help the biographer write the biography, it is not "work," just "dream." He composes exclusively with pen and paper, in notebooks, and on "a family of Olivetti manual typewriters" – no computer. Working by hand he can, he says, "see a sentence better," and finally, the dream must help him see those sentences. His dream of Gerard de Nerval became a conundrum, an unresolvable problem, an idiom untranslatable yet central to understanding the language, and hence, the subject. A biographer must be intrepid, in nature and in intellect, and must expect sometimes to get lost, in thicket or in thought.

In the 1980s Holmes returned to familiar turf, the English Romantic poets, with his critical study *Coleridge* (1982), and to biography with *Coleridge: Early Visions* (1989), which evolved from the criticism. The former he refers to as "a pathfinder," written to reevaluate the works and to see if he could get a sense of whether or not he would be able to "get through a long and difficult life" like Samuel Taylor Coleridge's. He found that he could, but only in installments. The first volume of the life is a partial biography covering Coleridge's first thirty-one and a half years and displaying all Holmes's signature strengths. "I have tried," he writes in his preface, "from the very start, to set Coleridge *talking*," primarily because the subject was famous for his talk, public and private, for his conversation poems and one-sided conversation. Holmes, with his pitch-perfect ear, has clearly heard Coleridge and wants his reader to gain the benefit of his experience: "For the first time one can really hear the voice of the frantic young poet & intellectual" in a letter written to his brother George after the young poet had run off from his studies, and his debts, at Cambridge and joined the army under the boyish pseudonym Silas Tomkyn Comberbache; "One can hear both the poet and the lay preacher" in the "skilful maritime analogy" that opens Coleridge's inaugural professional lecture, likening "the present agitations of the public mind" to foundering "in a Tempest on board a crazy Bark." "Coleridge's own voice now comes recognisably through the verse" in his first characteristic compositions in "the Conversational mode"; a critical letter to Robert Southey betrays "something of the overtone of a lovers' quarrel"; William Hazlitt recalls Coleridge's "sonorous" reading of Wordsworth's "Betty Foy" and the "*chaunt*" in his recitation style, "full, animated, and varied," "more *dramatic*" than Wordsworth's own. The text is practically acoustic, resonant with echoes of pomposity, laughter, and velar fricatives illustrating the subject's self-deflating "sense of fun and farce," his execrable German accent, "the very worst . . . imaginable," and what passes in his prose for being struck speechless:

> Travelling along the ridge I came to the other side of those precipices and down below me on my left – no – no! no words can convey any idea of this prodigious wilderness. That precipice fine on this side was but its ridge, sharp as a jagged knife, level so long, and then ascending so boldly – what a frightful bulgy precipice I stand on and to my right how the Crag which corresponds to the other, how it plunges down, like a waterfall, reaches a level steepness, and again plunges!

And on, and on, the voice, its tone and overtones, adds layers of character and pierces veneers of myth and misconception. Pantisocracy, dismissed by many critics as a youthful enthusiasm that an older, apostate Coleridge himself dismissed, is reclaimed in all its "brilliant coherence" as "a permanent feature of his imagination," an aborted social experiment that begat an enduring " 'Susquehanna' of the mind." As with Shelley, Holmes finds the poet's prose, especially the notebooks and a series of autobiographic letters to Thomas Poole (and, he promises, the *Biographia Literaria* and the periodical journalism of *The Friend* in the next volume of the life) to be as vital and valuable as the verse, not just as biographical source material but as literature. Coleridge's West Country, rather than Wordsworth's Lake District, turns out to be the geographic cradle of Romanticism, where *Lyrical Ballads* (1798) was conceived and, for the most part, written. Holmes reorients opinion on Charles Lamb's, versus Wordsworth's, effect on Coleridge's poetic style, his role in the ascension of spontaneity and simplicity of diction as central tenets of Romantic sensibility, commending Lamb's critical penetration, his "natural taste and perception," his sensitive ear and unassuming talent, accumulating evidence for a reappraisal of the man and his work, and in the process making a case for Coleridge's attaining poetic maturity "well before he came under the personal influence of Wordsworth."

This was Holmes's first "experiment" in the biography, to let the subject, in part, tell the tale of his own life in his own voice; his second experiment was the use of extended glosslike footnotes throughout the text, forty-one in all, not so much like the conscious glosses the poet added to his Mariner's rhyme but more like the philosopher's marginalia,

his talking back to the texts he read. There are notes that expound on Coleridge's relations with friends, such as Sir Humphry Davy, William Hazlitt, "Citizen" John Thelwall, and Perdita Robinson (most of whom fell out with him eventually, and all of whom appear in an annotated list of figures rounding out "Coleridge's Circle" at the end of the text); that expand on the sources and technical features of his poetry, his plain style, and his plagiarism; and that probe unfamiliar, even uncanny, aspects of his intimacy with Wordsworth, like their peculiar humor and unconscious quoting of each other. The notes add another, detached, "downstage voice" used to both scholarly and Brechtian effect. The first one, for example, quotes substantially from a Henry James notebook entry on the dramatic potential of a biographical sketch of Coleridge, points to the quote as an illustration of the challenging prospect facing Holmes in writing the text the reader already has in hand, and floats the clever conceit that James leaves him little language to describe the subject. This is close to showing off, but the light touch leavens the respectful deference to the weight of James's musings and is finally winning.

In that it is a book, a biography begs coherence, shape, themes, climactic moments, and generalizations. In that it is a life, it defies all form except the organic and sprawls, sprouts, splits, spills, and splatters according to laws of chaos generally inapplicable to textual conventions and publishable concerns. Holmes's experiments – the footnotes and appended "Circle" of acquaintances in *Coleridge,* the midtext appendix in *Shelley* – evince his willing struggle with these two fundamental principles of biography and his ingenuity and integrity in the effort. He needs a method, a literary appliance, both plastic and plausible, mutable and monumental, and finds an obvious one ready to hand: "One of the great formal instruments of the biographer is the act of storytelling." However, though it might seem a "simple, almost primitive fact" that biography is "the *story* told of someone's life," the connotations and consequences of applying such a powerful instrument to biography quickly complicate matters. First, the writer must be careful "not to imply that it's a fiction, but . . . the narration, the unfolding of events" of a life. Then the biographer must get the story right; if it is, "two things happen." One, it is interesting, "almost like overhearing a conversation." Two, "when biography really works, you find there's a rhythm of moving between . . . a scene or a person or a group of people held in close-up, maybe in a room or a travel snapshot, and . . . setting that person or group in a much wider historical perspective." These are "filmic terms," implying a modern eye and sensibility that seeks to achieve in a text "a physical sense of (the subject's) immediate presence" and a sense of the subject "as part of a whole movement." Holmes's sense of "story," then, is diachronic, reaching from the "primitive" to the contemporary, open to techniques across media as well as across genres.

It takes a pliant and synthetic intelligence — that is, imagination — to effect a sense of being in the historical moment in the context of an overview of the historical culture, a functional double focus of presence and perspective. This revivification of the past while it remains distinctly "the past" gives biography its uncanny quality, the simultaneous sense of a "continuity of history" and its "separateness." To "reconstruct the culture" requires, according to Holmes, a "historical gap" of "fifty to ninety years" at a minimum. He needs to see the historical period whole, like the life. The definitive frustration for the biographer of discovering gaps in the recoverable evidence does not diminish for Holmes the "satisfaction" he feels at re-creating the social, political, intellectual, physical, and ultimately personal environment of literary movements and their major figures, at filling in, adequately to the biographical task, the history. When he succeeds, it restores a sense of cultural continuity and makes a mirror for modern readers in which they find their own interests addressed. He admires historian Barbara Tuchman's *A Distant Mirror* (1978), her pageant portrait and "hard facts" history of the second half of the fourteenth century, the "fifty years that follow the Black Death of 1348–1350." She chose "a coherent historical period" that she found "compelling" because it reflected her experience of "a period of similar disarray," another era of "collapsing assumptions," her own time, the midpoint of the second half of the twentieth century. That is the same time that Holmes was making similar choices in service of a variant vision of the contemporary experience as it related to a quite different analogue, Shelley and the Romantic age. Biographies are so popular and histories, like Tuchman's, become bestsellers because there is a desire in modern readers to reconnect to a sense of history that is "slipping," if not "slipped," away, a reintegration best achieved, according to Holmes, without explicit prompting, "not consciously," by a mind in the present imagining a sensibility — of an individual, of a movement — in the past.

In the case of each of his major biographies, Holmes confronts the challenge of being the latest in a line of the subject's biographers. There are ad-

vantages, too, of course, and not only the windfall of accumulated research but a critical perspective on the previous "stories." Necessarily trimmed-to-fit lives of the poets, shaped by ideologies, exigencies, and expedients, they leave room for "new" life, loose ends trailed to discoveries, new evidence and perspectives that make Holmes's biographies themselves experiments — in seeing Shelley in greater (not only closer) relation to Claire Clairmont, for instance; Coleridge in the context of continuous political thinking despite claims and confessions of a break with his republican past; and both poets against a background, pulled frequently into the foreground, of their prose. Biographies subsequent to a first effort are by nature corrective, contrary; even when they are repetitive, the familar material is renewed, refreshed with perspective and reappreciation as inherent to a novel whole. The best approach to the life, besides primary research, is to read at least several of the lives. Like interviews with a selection of people who knew the subject well, studies by selected biographers, who know the subject best, render a rounded, complex portrait of the artist as a mass of contradictions, like a real, or, increasingly realistic, life. Our understanding of Coleridge as a philosopher-poet conforms with the received impression of him as a dominator of conversation, procrastinator and depressive – as a Hamlet figure without the tragic dimension. A poor horseman in his youth and a corpulent sage in later years, metaphysician and mystic, poet in the Gothic and oriental modes, opium dreamer and solitary — one of his seminal conversation poems, "This Lime Tree Bower My Prison," is about his *not* joining his wife and friends for a pleasant walk in the countryside – the characterizations accumulate in a representation of a thinker, a man lost in thought, his head in books or the clouds, a man the reader sees in one of the abiding images of the boy, sneaking alone out a window onto the flat roof of Christ's Hospital to watch the stars come out. Holmes makes sure, though, that that image is contrasted with Charles Lamb's recollections of the gregarious adolescent, the center of his clique's attention. But the more vital contrast is with a "surprising" scene of the seven-year-old Samuel, the spoiled youngest of the family, attacking his nine-year-old brother with a kitchen knife in a quarrel over some cheese. If this suggests a nascent Hamlet, it is Hamlet the impulsive killer of Polonius, the thoughtless action hero, and prepares the reader for a more vigorous, physical figure, "an adventurous, daring Coleridge." When Holmes notes analogies between the young scholar's appetite for food and books and re-

Dust jacket for Holmes's autobiographical work on his career as a biographer

counts the adult poet's "passion for climbing hills and scaling mountain peaks," his "pounding" over the countryside in "epic walks" with parties of fellow pantisocrats or poets or solo, "clambering up the side of a torrent" and "chafing the skin of his chest with friction burns" in a dangerous descent, he corrects the cliché of Coleridge as all talk, cerebral and verbal, or doped up. "His impact was physical as much as intellectual," Holmes is anxious for us to recognize, so we can see more of the man and see the man more.

The Coleridge that Holmes admires is the poet, for whom verse is thought in action, for whom a stroll through an orchard or a struggle over a fell is a dialogue with nature, who had the rare capability of synthesizing thought and sweat in poetry. The similarities to Shelley – that Coleridge was a fine translator and a European among English Romantics – are similarities to Holmes, and the biographer is rather more sympathetic than most critics on the issue of the poet's plagiarism. Coleridge's inability to finish *Christabel* (1816), which he himself seemed to count a Sisyphean failure, is explained by Holmes as a kind of poet's passage "towards self-

consciousness," a case of having "outgrown" the poem and its technique. Holmes highlights the irony of his subject's self-criticism and self-doubt by supposing the possibilities, not only that Coleridge had missed but that he had achieved without appreciating: "he mourned the loss of one kind of creative power (his loss of inspiration in the ballad form) when he should have been celebrating the gain of another." Holmes enlarges Coleridge's life with the sense of possibility, even if it is also a sense of futility – "his fatal genius for being all things to all men" – or possibility dismissed. The question of Coleridge's sexuality, whether he was a repressed or active homosexual – a common psychoanalytic amplification in biographies of Romantics – is considered and rejected on the evidence as a simplification, but the rhetoric of the posing is characteristically measured and rich at the same time. Holmes does not, like many of the first Freudians in the field or current scholars of gay studies, "out" poets based on potential readings of their poetry or correspondence, though neither does he deny the romance in the relationships of Coleridge and Wordsworth and Coleridge and Southey (as in his handling in *Shelley* of the relationships of Shelley and Byron and Shelley and Hunt), accepting their strong feelings as genuine, even sexual. He is, after all, a biographer who espouses "love" for his subjects; but he is also a biographer who lets the facts speak for themselves, and the bald record of marriages, children, affairs, and undeconstructed love poetry retains the ballast of authority. Then a note on the Age of Sensibility creates a context of intellectual history, broadening our understanding of the tears and kisses men shared openly, often ostentatiously, in the late eighteenth century, the profound affection and physical contact that offered not a sexual or temperamental alternative to heterosexuality but an additional source of sentiment, an expression of shared values, the spirit of the age.

When, in the volume's postscript, Holmes suspends his subject in anticipation of the next half of his life, it is not with an echoing fall of voice, but "frozen in historical silhouette," reminding us that the book is full of pictures, too, of landscapes and famous faces and vivid opium dreams. Holmes presents Coleridge as a Coleridgean symbol, which we apprehend as that which it organically is and as a translucent, transcendant impression of an enlarged understanding. The reader is propelled by the abrupt stasis of the frozen image, as if we stepped off Coleridge's ship in full sail onto our own solid ground; we stumble, disoriented, our "knowledge" of Coleridge and of biography unsettled. Holmes, then, reorients us: the symbol, as powerful as it is, must fail, for "biography cannot stop, because it must conform to the complication, strength, and strangeness of life. (That is its power over fiction, the authority of truth.)"

The dialectic of form and "strangeness," of authority and authenticity, goes to the heart of the biographical process, to the first principles of biographical "truth," to Samuel Johnson. Holmes's 1993 *Dr. Johnson & Mr. Savage* is a "biography of a biography," the story of Samuel Johnson telling the story of his friend Richard Savage — poet, pardoned murderer, "Volunteer Laureate," Grub Street denizen. Universally agreed to be the protagonist of the first modern British literary biography, Johnson is in fact its creator. As both author of the *Life of Savage* (1744) and subject of James Boswell's *The Life of Samuel Johnson, LL.D.* (1791), the Great Cham is the first poser of and the quintessential answer to "the largest, imaginative questions," the ones biography asks: "how well can we know our fellow human beings; how far can we learn from someone else's struggles about the conditions of our own; what do the inti-

mate circumstances of one particular life tell us about human nature in general?"

Footsteps: Adventures of a Romantic Biographer uses personal history to introduce, investigate, and contemplate issues of literary biography and the psychological origins of life writing; *Dr. Johnson & Mr. Savage* uses the historical origin of literary biography as a prominent perch from which to survey and consider those issues in the longer view of literary history. Still, at the heart of each of Holmes' pursuits is the presence of the subject, as palpable and empirical as biographical evidence allows. "I have tried," he concludes, "to see Johnson and Savage almost as our contemporaries, living before our eyes." But this vision of historical synchronicity of event and record, of presence at the creation *and* the re-creation, keeps refracting and redoubling as we look through "layerings of time," through "stratified truth" for the "human truth, poised between fact and fiction, which a biographer can obtain as he tells the story of another's life, and thereby makes it his own (like a friendship) and the public's (like a betrayal)." When Johnson "invents a 'text'" for Judge Page's famous summary at Savage's trial for murder, he in all probability "mimics Savage mimicking Page," a case of "double ventriloquism" worthy of the most paranoid or playful postmodernism.

We receive Johnson through Boswell, Savage through Johnson — a tangled web, for deception is at the heart of biography, from its inception. Given Boswell's "great portrait" of "the great Dr. Johnson," Holmes proceeds from his modern perspective to read the charges: "Johnson did not attempt to unearth" evidence to the contrary of his friend Savage's claim that he was the unacknowledged bastard son of the Fourth Earl Rivers and his mistress, Lady Macclesfield; in fact, Johnson was "not interested in what a modern biographer would call 'research.'" The biographer's treatment of an apparent case of Savage extorting money from the former Lady Macclesfield is "close to a whitewashing." In presenting "the crisis and then the turning point of Savage's entire career," his trial for killing a man in a whorehouse swordfight, Johnson "appears anxious to avoid the evidence that is most damaging to Savage" and indeed, "under the appearance of magisterial impartiality," is "acting throughout as if he is counsel for the defence." By manipulating dates, giving a "quite false impression of the real sequence of events," Johnson "once again . . . obscured the record," misrepresenting "his friend's opportunism and malice" in another blackmail attempt on the woman he called "mother" as a "lonely act of poetic revenge" against an aristocratic conspiracy against talent. Johnson also lacked the necessary biographer's courage to "pursue these darker possibilities" and that his *Life of Savage* is an exercise in "masculine complicity" to exonerate and exalt a literary crony. Boswell is just about beyond utility, for to know Johnson the modern critic must "deconstruct almost entirely that powerful, domineering, confident, late-eighteenth-century figure whom Boswell created."

So there were two Savages, the poor but proud "Outcast Poet" in the tattered cloak who lived by the wit in his words and the dandified self-promoter who appointed himself "Volunteer Laureate" and stalked his chosen mother figure in the streets and in verse. There were also two Johnsons, Boswell's literary monument and the emotionally immature, sexually frustrated, self-conscious young Johnson who suffered from a " 'princess' syndrome" of idealizing love objects at the expense of his own self-image, creating a "pattern of longing, frustration and self-laceration." In addition there were two Boswells, the published moralist and the sex-driven diarist, the recorder of Johnson's life for public consumption and edification and the keeper of the *Tacenda* file, the hidden stash of Johnsoniana unfit for publication. So, too, there are two Holmses, the modern biographer whose exhaustive and meticulous research can distinguish which facts of Savage's life were available to Johnson at what times, whose commitment is to the accurate account of the life of the subject and the times in all their complexity, and the poet whose ear hears echoing ironies, whose eye finds representative images, and whose imagination is central to his biographical method. His "imaginary obituary" of Savage in the book's first chapter argues forcibly for Johnson's version of the life in that it fills, and therefore defines, a lack in the record, for Savage's death went unnoticed in print. Though he was a popular author, friend of Alexander Pope and James Thomson, and patron of Lord Tyrconnel, Savage died in obscurity, in cultural exile, a "genius" humiliated and defeated by the "infernal city." In that same first chapter Holmes appropriates a stratagem from the postscript of his previous work: his partial biography of Coleridge is recast as a fictional obituary of Johnson – filled with fact but fictional in its premise that Johnson died in 1749, at forty years old, five years after his *Life of Savage* but long before he became a "Doctor" or met Boswell. The point, of course, is to defamiliarize Johnson the monolithic late-Augustan archetype so readers may conceive of and

consider a more complex possibility of the man and the period. Holmes is ever aware, as he makes his readers aware, of his fictive play and its purpose, the value of imagination in attaining and maintaining the "poise" between fact and fiction essential to create and appreciate the "human truth" of biography, despite – indeed, dependent upon – the genre's duplicitous nature.

Holmes, therefore, does not advocate one biography over another, or two biographies, but a generous, pluralistic genre that reflects its genesis, "the new, hybrid nonfiction form" imagined and managed by Johnson, that "drew essentially on popular and indigenous English forms, of varying degrees of respectability": "scandal romance, the sensational Newgate confession, the sentimental ballad of folk archetypes, . . . the journalistic investigation and profile, the theatrical comedy of manners and the revelations of the courtroom drama." Johnson also introduced quoted poetry as biographical testimony. Today Holmes has the advantage of modern academic perspective; research and close reading techniques; and psychological and critical theory. This says nothing of the useful forms of popular fiction, the social-science-fiction novel of an alternative universe – in which Johnson might die at age forty, and Coleridge settle in "the Wild West" – and the crime thriller – in which Holmes, aptly named, solves the mystery of Savage's role in the murder through painstaking perusal of the trial transcripts, determining that in all likelihood he acted to defend a friend, though nowhere in the record does Savage or any of his party make this defense.

In rifling genres high and low for effective methods, in experimenting to expand upon traditional means, Holmes is in the tradition of the first biographers, including the "biographists" of the late seventeenth century, the antiquarian collectors of lives. He must not compromise truth, but he must have freedom to discover it; unlike Hamlet, he must know "seems" – to document inspiration: textual errors "suggest some fascinating combination of fact and fiction" in answer to the question of whether Savage "inspired" Eliza Haywood's novel *Memoirs of a Certain Island Adjaceant to Utopia* (1725) – to follow the loose threads of a life and "have a glimpse of a whole network of romantic intrigue surrounding Savage" – or to nudge a grand historical portrait into passion. "It seems strange to imagine Johnson in such romantic throes" as Holmes asks of his reader, and "it seems impossible to imagine Johnson in love," but "Johnson's private inspiration still seems" to be a Romantic ideal. What Holmes discovers in his historical pursuit of the founding of

English literary biography, and what might have drawn him in the first place, is "that against all expectation" Johnson's *Life of Savage* "heralds the coming of the Romantic generation," and beyond that, "biography itself, with its central tenet of empathy, is essentially a Romantic form; and that Johnson's friendship with Savage first crystallized its perils and its possibilities."

Holmes's central image of the friendship is an all-night walk-about through the streets of London, the outcast poet in the unfashionable coat and the young, spasmodic, near manic-depressive prospective journalist just in from the country, too poor to afford lodgings, wandering through neighborhoods and social strata, arguing over and ultimately agreeing about literature and politics. Holmes is adopting, he admits, an "anecdote," a "vivid, popular legend . . . a romantic, quixotic, heroic or mock-heroic picture, depending on one's point of view." "We can instantly imagine the scene," and Holmes does, in detail, but then characteristically asks, "how true is it?" So begins the dialectic of "story" and criticism, of creativity and hermeneutics that dissects the "composite memory" of anecdotal evidence but ultimately "reanimates" the author of the "Wanderer" and the author of "London," two of the important poems of the period, as they wandered London.

The point and final destination of any biographical pursuit is the presence of the subject, the presentation, persuasive to the reader, of the subject's essential "human truth." This principle is evident in Holmes's choice of quotes from Johnson on biography: "nobody can write the life of a man, but those who have eat and drunk and lived in social intercourse with him"; "[m]ore knowledge may be gained of a man's real character by a short conversation with one of his servants, than from a formal and studied narrative, begun with his pedigree and ended with his funeral"; "[m]ost accounts of particular persons are barren and useless. If a life be delayed till interest and envy are at an end, we may hope for impartiality, but we must expect little intelligence; for the incidents that give excellence to biography are of a volatile and evanescent kind, such as soon escape the memory, and are rarely transmitted by tradition." These principles might seem at odds with "modern biography" and Holmes's need for a "historical gap"; Holmes, however, recognizes a common objective, the "immediacy" of portraiture necessary to present the subjects "as our contemporaries, living before our eyes," and as embodiments of history, casting contrasting shadows across centuries: "Certainly it seems true that Johnson first discovered in

their night-walks the new form of intimate life-writing. It was to be like an extended conversation in the dark, taking ordinary facts and anecdotes, and pursuing them towards the shadowy and mysterious regions of a life, at the edge of the unknown or unknowable."

The stress on the empirical foundation of biography caused by its object might seem ironic, but it is fundamental. Johnson recognized the "danger" when "the biographer writes from personal knowledge," that "his interest, his fear, his gratitude, or his tenderness, overpowers his fidelity," but he knew, too, that these elements of empathy were crucial to capturing and communicating the "volatile and evanescent" life of Savage, that they were powers without which the attempt was impossible, and so, from author's instinct or youthful enthusiasm, he allowed himself to be "caught up in the romantic drama."

Reading the well-written story of a life, as Holmes says, is "almost like overhearing a conversation." When the writer is Holmes, often the conversation is with the reader. He ends the first paragraph of the last chapter of *Dr. Johnson & Mr. Savage* by exercising the biographer's prerogative "to speak *in propria persona* of what he experienced in Johnson and Savage's company, and how he tried to give an account of it." Johnson was only "rhetorically present" in his biography of his friend, but Holmes, especially in his metabiographies, is a public presence, autobiographically apparent, caught up in the romantic drama of his profession. He has called *Footsteps* "a one-off," "a very deliberate experiment and a deliberate cross of those apparent borderlines between biography and autobiography, which should be very sharp." But his biographies are so vital because of his personal engagement, his proclivity for experiment, and his wandering across the "borderlines": he revels in the process of life writing, which is essentially the story of his life, and reveals his methods and himself at work in the text. He is openly intrigued by "the single most inexplicable fact" in a life and self-consciously applies every resource of his craft — his fine ear and eye, intelligence and imagination — to explain that fact and in the process reanimate the subject in our imaginations, before our eyes and in our ears. He suggests parenthetically that one account of Johnson's story of his night walk with Savage "be read, perhaps, in a light Dublin brogue," to restore the voice of the teller, the "genial Irish playwright" Arthur Murphy. This is triple, perhaps quadruple, ventriloquism, the reader mimicking Murphy mimicking Johnson, who probably mimicked Savage; but the voice we hear most clearly, most deliberately, is Holmes's.

"Historical certainty is impossible" in many cases; still literary biography is privileged. Writers leave large records, generating generations of documentation. Yet they remain obscure, hidden behind their works, or opaque, viewed as a lens through which to scrutinize the writing. Watching a writer write is among the most boring activities in life or art, but rendering the struggle of literary creation is a harrowing and vast adventure. This is Holmes's contribution; he does not romanticize the lives he writes, but in the process of imagining them they are recognized as Romantic. "All I can say," he says at the end of the text, "is that I have given the evidence as I have found it, and allowed the story to create its own emotional and artistic logic." This describes organic form, which argues, in Romantic terms, for authenticity.

Even an honest effort, though, may find what it was looking for in the first place. Holmes suggests, without admitting, as much in the last paragraph of the last chapter when he calls the reader's attention to the "curious chord" of recognition his title may strike in some: "The echo you hear, of course, is of *Dr. Jekyll and Mr. Hyde.*" So we come round again to Holmes's first subject, Robert Louis Stevenson. Is he walking, then, in his own *Footsteps?* Is the biographer's "pursuit" of the subject necessarily circular, leading back to the biographer's own obsessions? "Whenever modern biographers set out on the long journey of research and writing," are they doomed to end up back where they started, recapitulating an unconscious premise or revisiting the dilemmas, compromises, and failures that Johnson and Boswell explored and that Holmes confronted on the bridge at Langogne? When Holmes declares that he has "tried to see Johnson and Savage almost as our contemporaries" he owns up to the limits of his craft, but he does not give up his pursuit of his subject, his vision of biography. Is biography, then, Holmes's demon?

On the evidence of Holmes's career, every honest return to a life previously written, every recognition of the central issues of life writing is made with greater understanding – of the subject, of history, of the process and potential of biography. The struggle through the temporal strata of history, through the "layered contents" of even one person's story, through the "labyrinth" of evidence, possibility, "double ventriloquisms" and dark London streets perforce yields discovery, of the "extraordinary fact" that "[n]o one has considered," and progress toward understanding. If Johnson passed "the

sacred baton of friendship" to Boswell, that was no small part of "the sacred duty of the biographer to tell the truth as candidly as possible." For "Johnson's powers as a biographer" are demonstrated finally not only by his daring, in the end, to "challenge the whole basis of (his) intimacy" with his subject by admitting "Savage's vanity, delusions and opportunism" but also by the fact that he "still extends sympathy and insight" in this compromised context, that "at this moment of crisis" at the birth of modern literary biography, "Johnson's extraordinary moral intelligence, and his own largeness of heart, become preeminent." Savage's "friendship," his friend admits, "was . . . of little value," except inasmuch as his friend was his biographer, who could see beyond offense to the whole being, for "none who candidly consider his fortune will think an apology either necessary or difficult." If Johnson's consideration of Savage is less than "candid," he does predicate the form's founding principles, that biographers are their subject's best and closest friends and that best friends tell the truth, out of trust that truth is beauty, beauty truth.

Biography is, in conception and practice, at root and in flower, Romantic because the biographer acts out of love, and Holmes pursues the biography of biography out of love for the subject. It has brought him honors – the James Tait Black Award for *Dr. Johnson & Mr. Savage,* and an Order of the British Empire conferred upon him in 1992, among others – but his own life leaves the impression that biography is a calling, a psychological imperative, a living in the broadest and deepest sense. Examine his avocations and the terms in which he talks about the "other things that go on during the time I'm writing" that provide a "balance to writing." Holmes, the amateur sailor who navigated the North Sea, or the "mad motorcyclist" who "absolutely adored" the pastime that "nearly killed him" when he was writing *Shelley,* replays in his "nonliterary life" the adventures of his literary "pursuits." "You can pursue it anywhere," he says of another "love," long-distance walking, and we hear in his voice, in the unconscious comparison, his passion for his literary life, his romance with his subjects, including biography itself. "I love gardening," he says, and when he describes "the independent rhythm of plants," he sounds much like himself observing "that when biography really works, you find there's a rhythm." You must find it, discover it, because, by nature or by an act of the imagination, it has grown to be freestanding, "independent," like a "particular geranium or standard rose quietly growing away," assuming its own organic form.

Holmes denies having any models among biographers, but he identifies Robert Gittings as an "inspiration": "When I read his book on (John) Keats . . . I thought, 'That's what it can be. *It can come to life like that.*' " "It can" if you catch it, volatile and evanescent, always a few steps ahead, "growing away."

For Holmes, "the act of writing is crucial in discovery" of insight, of what evidence turned over in the desk- and fieldwork works in the biography, and how. He points to the opening of the twelfth chapter of *Coleridge,* on the subject as "Lover," which begins at a low point, the new year 1801, describing the poet's "first bad winter of opium addiction." It starts with lists, of the philosphers he was reading, of the views "out through his panoramic windows" at Greta Hall, of his "spectacularly varied and unpleasant" symptoms of physical illness, of the equally grotesque "variety of nostrums" with which he was treated, of the elements of his imagination, mostly Gothic, that the metaphysics, weather, pains, and painkillers called forth from him. And then Holmes finds the curious fact, the "psychological complication," that calls forth *his* imagination: "It is significant, in this first period of really serious opium addiction, that though he thought much about poetry, he did not actually write it." Then the evidence falls into place, like a path of moonlight across a body of water just as the moon emerges from cloud cover: the "characteristic" passage from a February letter to Poole, the echoes of his childhood before and the great "Dejection: An Ode" (1802) to come by chapter's end, and looming larger still, "the growing religious orthodoxy – the need for a merciful, fatherly divinity to bless and release his powers" that "seemed to arise directly in response to the growing guilt he felt about his opium-taking, his prostration and procrastination." This last list, of failings familiar from the most superficial study of Coleridge, is suddenly understood in a context of its true cost, as no longer proverbial but primal and painful, preparing the reader for one of Holmes's sharpest, deepest insights into Coleridge's character and poetry, the paradox, achieved supremely in the "Dejection: An Ode" that he created much of his greatest verse, not about failure, but out of failure – that in many of his mature works it is not the subject, but the stuff, of his genius, which certainly complicates any idea of the poetry as triumph and affords an exquisite, existential sense of how hard Coleridge worked to write it. Another example Holmes gives of finding the idea in the act of finding the sentences is the opening trope of the eighth chapter – "Friendship" – of *Dr. Johnson & Mr. Savage,* in which the text returns to the

Dust jacket for the book about the relationship of the author of Lives of the Poets *(1779–1781) and the controversial eighteenth-century poet and dramatist*

friends' nocturnal odyssey after telling both their stories, where "the narrative doubles back on itself." Reconsidering the scene suggests almost immediately to Holmes that "in recounting Savage's career" Johnson "has . . . revealed much of himself that is new," that contradicts Boswell's standard model "Tory Clubman," and that suggests the larger process, "the peculiar mystery – or alchemy – of the form," that the "biographer has unconsciously written something of his own autobiography." Holmes, conscious that biography doubles back on the biographer, that it takes all a writer's resources, including the unconscious, to bring a life to life, responds imaginatively to the Johnson he has discovered, Johnson the biographer, who "loves Savage" but is also "poised" to "duel" with him, who defines the genre at its origin by his behavior, at the extremes of the largest imaginative responses to the largest imaginative questions. If biography is autobiographical, here we see Holmes rising to the challenge that asks the most and brings out the best in a writer, and the reader understands another way in which biography is Romantic, for the reader experiences the biographer as hero.

By the time he began his *Dr. Johnson & Mr. Savage,* Johnson could complain that "volumes have been written only to enumerate the miseries of the learned, and relate their unhappy lives and untimely deaths." Others before him had told stories of the "heroes of literary as well as civil history," but his biography, like his dictionary and much of his journalism, was a watershed. Literary biography was enriched, enlarged by Johnson's vision of what it could be. Keats, looking into George Chapman's Homer, imagined himself Balboa — whom he mistakenly identified as Cortez — staring astonished at a new sea; Holmes, following Johnson and his friend through the London night, overhears the genesis of a modern genre. In Holmes's imagination Johnson is a visionary and biography is an open sea, continually rediscovered. Its traditions of inclusion and experiment and all Holmes's intelligence, research, empathy, and talent convince him that "biography is still a very youthful, experimental form," and he knows from experience that "you never know quite what's going to happen" when you set out in pursuit of a subject's "human story," her or his "living footsteps through the world," because every step on the journey opens anew "the enormous range of possibilities in the way you can live, and what you can make of your one life."

Interview:

Jean W. Ross, *Contemporary Authors,* volume 133 (Detroit: Gale Research, 1991): 179–182.

Michael Holroyd

(27 August 1935 –)

A. R. Jones
University of Wales

BOOKS: *Hugh Kingsmill: A Critical Biography,* introduction by Malcolm Muggeridge (London: Unicorn Press, 1964; revised edition, London: Heinemann, 1971);

Lytton Strachey: A Critical Biography, 2 volumes (London: Heinemann, 1967–1968; New York: Holt, Rinehart & Winston, 1968); revised edition, 1 volume (London: Heinemann, 1973; New York: Penguin, 1979);

A Dog's Life (New York: Holt, Rinehart & Winston, 1969);

Unreceived Opinions (London: Heinemann, 1973; New York: Holt, Rinehart & Winston, 1973);

Augustus John: A Biography, 2 volumes – *Volume I: The Years of Innocence; Volume II: The Years of Experience* (London: Heinemann, 1974–1975; revised, 1976; New York: Holt, Rinehart & Winston, 1975);

Bernard Shaw, 6 volumes – *Volume I: 1856–1898 The Search for Love* [1988]; *Volume II: 1898–1918 The Pursuit of Power* [1989]; *Volume III: 1918–1950 The Lure of Fantasy* [1991]; *Volume IV: 1950–1991 The Last Laugh* [1992]; *Volumes V & VI: The Shaw Companion* [1992] (London: Chatto & Windus, 1988–1992; New York: Random House, 1988–1992);

Lytton Strachey: The New Biography (London: Chatto & Windus, 1994; New York: Farrar, Straus & Giroux, 1995).

OTHER: Lytton Strachey, *Ermyntude and Esmeralda: An Entertainment,* introduction by Holroyd (London: Anthony Blond, 1969);

Hugh Kingsmill Lunn, *The Best of Hugh Kingsmill,* introduction by Holroyd (London: Gollancz, 1970);

William Gerhardie, *The Revised Definitive Edition of the Works of William Gerhardie,* 10 volumes, edited, with prefaces, by Holroyd (London: Macdonald, 1970–1974);

Michael Holroyd

Lytton Strachey by Himself: A Self-Portrait, edited by Holroyd (London: Heinemann, 1971; New York: Holt, Rinehart & Winston, 1971);

The Art of Augustus John, edited by Holroyd and Malcolm Easton (London: Secker & Warburg, 1974);

"Damn and 'BLAST!': The Friendship of Wyndham Lewis and Augustus John," in *Essays by Divers Hands, Being the Transactions of the Royal Society of Literature,* new series 38 (Suffolk: Boydell Press, 1975), pp. 48–57;

Introduction and "Women and the Body Politic," in *The Genius of Shaw: A Symposium* (London: Hodder & Stoughton, 1979), pp. 9–11, 167–183;

Strachey, *The Shorter Strachey,* edited by Holroyd and Paul Levy (Oxford & New York: Oxford University Press, 1980; revised, 1989);

Gerhardie, *God's Fifth Column: A Biography of the Age: 1890–1981,* edited by Holroyd and Robert Skidelsky (London: Hodder & Stoughton, 1981; Woodstock, N.Y.: Overlook Press, 1991);

Virginia Woolf, *Moments of Being* [sound recording], edited by Holroyd (London: BBC Cassettes, 1981);

Essays by Divers Hands, Being the Transactions of the Royal Society of Literature, new series 42, introduction by Holroyd (Suffolk: Boydell Press, 1982), pp. ix–xi;

Gwen John, 1876–1939, edited by Holroyd (London: Anthony d'Offay, 1982);

Abuses of Literacy?, edited by Holroyd and Melvyn Bragg (London: Folio Society, 1985);

Richard Pennington, *Peterley Harvest: The Private Diary of David Peterley* [1960], preface by Holroyd (London: Secker & Warburg, 1985);

George Bernard Shaw, *Major Critical Essays,* edited, with an introduction, by Holroyd (Harmondsworth: Penguin, 1986);

"How I Fell into Biography," in *The Troubled Face of Biography,* edited by Eric Homberger and John Charmley (London: Macmillan, 1988), pp. 94–103.

SELECTED PERIODICAL PUBLICATIONS –
UNCOLLECTED: "The Big Advance: Burden or Blessing," *Author,* 76 (Winter 1965): 11–12;

"Involvement: Writers Reply," *London Magazine,* 8 (August 1968): 14–15;

"Why Is There No Shouting?," *Times* (London), 16 November 1968, pp. 19, 22;

"Authors and Their Publishers," *Author,* 80 (Spring 1969): 7–11;

"The Paradox of Public Lending Right," *Books,* 18–19 (Spring–Summer 1975): 37–42;

"Virginia Woolf and Her World," *Horizon,* 17 (Summer 1975): 49–56;

"Bernard Shaw's Secret Childhood," *Observer* (26 October 1975): 25;

"GBS: Sex and Second Childhood," *Observer* (2 November 1975): 25;

"G. B. S. and Ireland," *Sewanee Review,* 84 (Winter 1976): 35–55;

"Paradox of Shaw," *Books and Bookmen,* 21 (May 1976): 14–15;

"The Author as Victim," *New Statesman* (20 August 1976): 229–230;

"Po-Faced Shaw," *Books and Bookmen,* 23 (March 1977): 57–58;

"Unreal Estate: The Wrongs of Copyright," *Encounter,* 49 (August 1977): 34–35;

"My God, What Women!," *Books and Bookmen,* 23 (December 1977): 28–29;

"George Bernard Shaw: Women and the Body Politic," *Critical Inquiry,* 6 (1979): 17–32;

"Death, the Idol," *Spectator* (1 September 1979): 12–13;

"Reviewing at the Double," *Author,* 90 (Autumn 1979): 103–106;

"Devotions of a Dramatist," *Times Literary Supplement* (1 March 1981): 481–482;

"About Books? A Writer's View," *Bookseller* (21 March 1981): 1044–1047;

"Shaw and Biography," *Times Literary Supplement* (22 April 1983): 413–414;

"William Gerhardie," *Spectator* (28 May 1983): 29–30;

"Shaw and Society," *Author,* 95 (Summer 1984): 53–56;

"The State versus Literature," *Times Literary Supplement* (8 March 1985): 257–258;

"Yours Prodigally," *Times Literary Supplement* (31 May 1985): 595–596;

"Bernard Shaw," *Sunday Times Magazine* (London), 28 August 1988, pp. 46–47, 49;

"Life Studies," *Listener* (8 September 1988): 4–6;

"Loneliness of the Long Distance Biographer," *Times* (London), 10 September 1988, p. 37;

"Confessions of a Late Victorian Libertine," *Observer* (17 November 1991): 59;

"Shaw Shot," *Independent Magazine* (4 April 1992): 48–51;

"Abuse of Shaw's Literary Legacy," *Times Literary Supplement* (7 April 1992): 1.

Michael Holroyd is the author of three major biographies, all of which have been influential and widely acclaimed. His two-volume biography of Lytton Strachey not only initiated a revived interest in the Bloomsbury Group but also renewed interest in the art of biography by the way in which he combined careful scholarship, imaginative and psychological insight, and narrative skills. His lives of Augustus John and Bernard Shaw which followed clearly confirmed his stature as one of the leading biographers of our time.

Michael de Courcy Fraser Holroyd, the only son of Basil and Ulla Holroyd, was born in London on 27 August 1935 and lived in Drayton Gardens, South Kensington, until he was three years old. His parents had met on a North Sea ferry when

Holroyd's Anglo-Irish father was returning to England having been trying to sell Lalique glass in Sweden and his Swedish mother was coming to England to take up a post as an au pair. After they married they could not agree about anything. His father served as a squadron leader in the Royal Air Force during World War II, which finally disrupted the marriage, and at the end of the war they divorced. His father married a French publisher and lived in Paris while his mother married a Hungarian and remained in London (both parents were married three times).

Holroyd was sent to Maidenhead to be brought up by his paternal grandparents. He remembers the house as gloomy with dark oak paneling. "Birds hopped into the dining room to share our meals. That was the most exciting thing that happened." He felt that his life was very boring and also "extremely insecure, frightening." "I was brought up by my grandparents," he said, "and I lived in the regime of 70- and 80-year olds when I was seven or eight. So I filled my head with book adventures in order to have a more exciting life. What I really did, I think, was step from my own life — and there wasn't very much going on in it — into other people's lives which seemed much more exciting. I was able to live two lives simultaneously."

Because of the remarriages of his parents, he says that he often had to travel abroad to meet new stepparents. "Every holiday I seemed to have a new one." He turned to books early on and became addicted to Arthur Conan Doyle adventure stories, saying that "In books, unlike life, one could travel without apprehension." He developed a precocious interest in "other people's lives, mainly because there was more going on in them." "I always thought reading biography was a sign of being very grown up, because I was aware, quite early on, that I was taking novels from the library and adult people were taking out biographies. . . . I do think that in reading a novel you learn about one person. Basically you learn about the person who's written the novel, you learn their world, whereas in reading a biography you come across two worlds: the world of the author and of the author's subject."

In the entry he wrote for inclusion in *Who's Who,* Holroyd describes himself as having "read English literature at Maidenhead Public Library," which, while it pays an appropriate tribute to the time he spent there reading, also, perhaps, ill-conceals his regret that he did not at that point in his life read English in the more systematic and rigorous way imposed by a university degree course.

At the public library he says he "commanded there a magnificent range of books, from ancient classics to the latest publications, and was provided with excellent lighting, heating, the service of trained librarians, the most up-to-date magazines."

His subsequent attitude toward universities has been consistently hostile in the sense that he tends to divide the literary world between them and us, the academic mandarins, remote and imperious, on the one side and the professionals — like himself — who live in the real world and do the real literary work on the other. This often leads to a sense of being overlooked and undervalued, for instance, when he asserts that "literary biographers have felt themselves to be outside the family of literature. The family now lives in academe. There are departments of history but no departments of biography at our universities; there are departments of English, but biography is not on the curriculum. . . . I feel myself in some respects to be an amateur . . . it does, however, avoid the arid professionalism that has little raison d'être other than the lengthening of an academic curriculum vitae and the securing of tenure." Although this opinion is taken from a paper he read at a colloquium on biography organized by the University of East Anglia and published in *The Troubled Face of Biography* (1988), he demonstrates little understanding of universities. He confuses British and American universities in his reference to tenure (which is not an issue in British universities since academics have tenure on appointment). His suggestion that if there are departments of history there should also be departments of biography cannot be meant seriously. Moreover, his point about the neglect of biography in English departments is a more vexed topic than he seems to realize, and one which has been given a great deal of attention particularly in the last decades. He also chooses to ignore the fact that at least six of the eleven biographers who read papers at this colloquium, and the two conveners, are members of benighted academe. However, had he read English at a more conventional center, perhaps he would not have felt so excluded or been so ready to assume that universities represented a consensus of opinion regarding the canon of literature.

From a social point of view his upbringing was privileged upper middle class. He attended a local preparatory school after which he entered Eton, where he became captain of cricket, the pinnacle of many schoolboys' ambition. Nonetheless, he insists that at school he succeeded in making himself invisible, an unresolved contradiction. He did not distinguish himself academically, as his father insisted that he specialize in science rather than in arts subjects. When he left Eton he continued to live with his paternal grandparents and, as his father did not wish him to go to university, began work as an articled clerk with a view to becoming a solicitor: "So, on leaving school, instead of starting my National Service at an age when others were doing so, I was articled to a firm of solicitors at Windsor. . . . As with science, it took about two years to demonstrate my unfitness for any branch of the law, after which there was no further escape from National Service." He therefore did his National Service in the army between 1956 and 1958 and was commissioned in the Royal Fusiliers.

However much he may have resented his time in the army, it was during his time there that he made his most important literary contact: W. A. Gerhardie. Holroyd came across Gerhardie's books by chance and read most of them; his mother knew Gerhardie's niece Christina. "I thought William Gerhardie must be dead," Holroyd later remarked. "In fact I discovered he was merely buried alive." After meeting Gerhardie, and with his encouragement, Holroyd produced the first critical biography of Hugh Kingsmill. In 1956 W. A. Gerhardie was sixty-one years old; Holroyd was twenty-one. Looking back, Holroyd says that he cannot really explain what made him a biographer: "I was fortunate to find biography, because I was very much adrift in my twenties." Nonetheless, he took this step further into other people's lives, "like an actor assuming a part."

As he was Gerhardie's protégé, Gerhardie did everything he could to ensure Holroyd's advancement. Soon, however, it was Holroyd who was writing articles on Gerhardie and editing his works in an attempt to revive interest in him. Gerhardie had enjoyed widespread literary and social acclaim in the 1920s and 1930s, but by 1956 he had become a reclusive and rather neglected figure. Nevertheless, Holroyd's friendship with Gerhardie led to friendships with Gerhardie's friends. Gerhardie was thus Holroyd's introduction into the literary world of London, though Gerhardie's corner of that world was of an older generation and somewhat detached from the center. One of Gerhardie's closest friends for many years had been Hugh Kingsmill, who had died in 1949. Kingsmill was a prolific author and served as literary editor of *Punch* (1939–1945) and of *New English Review* (1945–1949). He collaborated with both Gerhardie and Hesketh Pearson in writing books, in addition to being the main character in Gerhardie's novel *Pending Heaven* (1930). His friends, Hesketh Pearson and Malcolm Muggeridge

in particular, still talked about him with love and admiration and published a series of letters between them as a celebration of his life and their friendship with him. Muggeridge provided an introduction for Holroyd's biography, and by the time of Pearson's death Holroyd had become trusted enough to be appointed Pearson's literary executor. Moreover, Pearson's autobiography, *Hesketh Pearson by Himself* (1965), is dedicated to "my friend Michael Holroyd." The first volume of Holroyd's biography of Lytton Strachey is dedicated to the memory of Pearson and his wife, Joyce Pearson.

Yet Holroyd had been familiar with Kingsmill's work before he met Gerhardie and his friends. The reading of biographies written by Kingsmill is described by Holroyd as a central part of his education at Maidenhead Public Library: "It was in this library that I had come by chance across the books of Hugh Kingsmill. Kingsmill gave me exactly what I wanted in my late teens and early twenties. No professor had chosen him for me: I had found him for myself. What he gave me was not part of the schoolroom but what goes on outside it – what is enjoyed rather than endured. What was it that appealed to me about Kingsmill? First of all, I think, he made literature real to me – that is to say, he made the connection factually and imaginatively between what we read and how we live." Kingsmill's attraction for Holroyd was both literary and personal, and it was, Holroyd said, under Kingsmill's influence that "I first became a biographer."

Holroyd recalls that "The winter of 1963–4 was for me a crucial one. After two years' work, and a further two years of waiting, I had had my first book published: a critical biography of Hugh Kingsmill. . . . But only two weeks after publication [of *Hugh Kingsmill*] I was being threatened with an action for libel. . . . My chief witness, Hesketh Pearson, who first encouraged me to write, suddenly died. I could muster other supporters . . . Malcolm Muggeridge . . . who had also attacked the Queen . . . John Davenport, the critic, who at that time had chosen to wear a prejudicial black beard . . . William Gerhardie, the distinguished novelist, who had not actually published a novel for the last quarter of a century . . . my publisher, Martin Secker, who was nearing eighty, appeared to find the predicament invigorating."

Hugh Kingsmill: A Critical Biography (1964) was respectfully, though not widely, reviewed. The exception was the review written by Gerhardie, to whom the book is dedicated and who reviewed the book in the *Spectator* (31 January 1964) under the

Dust jacket for the American edition of Holroyd's biography of the British painter

heading "Forgotten Immortal" with rather breathless enthusiasm. He referred to "Mr. Holroyd's entrancing and singularly profound . . . authoritative critical biographical study" that "draws us irresistibly into the whole complex of England's intellectual battle royal. What an amazing story, this, and how dexterously told! . . . there is no true exhilaration save when it is given to us to commune with an immortal. Hugh Kingsmill, dead at fifty-nine, was one. Michael Holroyd, extant in his twenties, is another." Presumably, his friendship with Kingsmill and Holroyd conferred immortality on them both. The more sober, anonymous reviewer in the *Times Literary Supplement* (20 February 1964), having noticed that "some chapters are slightly disjointed as a result of cutting required by the publisher," described it "in its total effect" as "an admirable study of an original, complex and enigmatic personality."

In fact the biography is an interesting, straightforward account of Kingsmill, his life and his works. There are no references, footnotes, or bibliography though Holroyd has been scrupulous in assembling his materials. He clarifies both the eccentricities of Kingsmill's personality and the oddity of his views without, however, inquiring too deeply into either. Yet, judging by the confidence and maturity which he brought to his life of Strachey, Holroyd learned the craft of the biographer in writing this book.

In revising the biography for a second edition, published in 1971, Holroyd recast entirely the portrait of Dorothy, Kingsmill's second wife, and gave a quite different impression of the marriage. In the first edition Dorothy is described in some detail and emerges as a pretentious, domineering, and unhappy woman who alienated Kingsmill from his friends. In the second edition Kingsmill is made responsible for the unsatisfactory nature of the marriage, and his wife virtually disappears from the biography. In the first edition Holroyd seems to have been directly influenced by Gerhardie, Muggeridge, Pearson, and other friends of Kingsmill who felt that Dorothy had done her best to blight their friendship with her husband; in the second edition he was perhaps influenced more by Dorothy and the threat of a libel action.

Though the biography was highly regarded, it was, as he recognized, the biography of a little-known writer by an unknown biographer. Nonetheless, it led to his writing the life of Lytton Strachey: "The first of the sixteen publishers to whom I had submitted my Kingsmill manuscript was Heinemann. Fortunately it had fallen into the hands of James Michie, the poet and translator of the odes of Horace." Michie encouraged Holroyd to choose a less obscure subject for his next biography. "Kingsmill, along with Philip Guedalla, Emil Ludwig, André Maurois, Harold Nicholson and others, had been categorised as one of those imitators of Lytton Strachey whose literary reputation he had helped to bring into disrepute. In order to demonstrate the injustice of this charge I had to examine Strachey's books in some detail. To my surprise I found there was no biography of him, and no wholly satisfactory critical study of his work. Here, it seemed to me, was the real need for a book. James Michie agreed, and a contract was drawn up in which I undertook to make a revaluation of Strachey's place as a serious historian. It would be about seventy thousand words long and take me, I estimated, at least a year."

In fact Holroyd had already made rather rough and ready distinction between the art of Kingsmill and Strachey by deciding that "On reading Kingsmill one is implicated oneself; on reading Strachey one is part of an audience." He discussed at some length the charge that Kingsmill had followed where Strachey led and had concluded that this was not the case. He expressed indignation that Kingsmill should be considered an imitator of anyone.

It soon became clear to Holroyd that Strachey's friends would only cooperate with him in the writing of a biography if he had the agreement of James Strachey, his brother and literary executor. In the preface to the 1971 revised edition of the first volume of *Lytton Strachey: A Critical Biography* (1967), Holroyd describes his meeting with James Strachey and the problems he encountered in writing the biography. However, after lunch with James and Alix Strachey he was allowed access to Lytton's materials – "So began what, for the next five years, was to prove not simply the composition of a larger book, but a way of life and an education."

Holroyd is explicit as to his objectives in writing the life of Strachey:

I intended to try and accomplish four things – to provide a selection of the best of Lytton's letters; to attempt a completely original reappraisement of his work; to present a panorama of the social and intellectual environment of a remarkable generation; and to write a definitive biography. These four ingredients I would endeavour to shape into the polychromatic design of a huge conversation piece around the figure of Lytton Strachey. "Discretion," Lytton himself had once said, "is not the better part of biography." I should not be discreet. My purpose was to fuse an imaginatively kindled re-creation of the inner life of my characters with the rigorous documentation and exactitude of strict biographical method.... I was setting out to do something entirely new in biography, to give Lytton's love-life the same prominence in my book as it had had in his career, to trace its effect on his work, and to treat the whole subject of homosexuality without any artificial veils of decorum – in exactly the same way as I would have treated heterosexuality. To have done otherwise would have been to admit tacitly a qualitative distinction, and tended to perpetuate prejudice rather than erode it.

He was also fully aware of the irony that "the life and work of Lytton Strachey should finally be commemorated by two fat volumes – that standard treatment of the illustrious dead that he was so effective in stamping out."

He finished the first volume in 1964. "In return for what he [James Strachey] called 'a bribe' of five hundred pounds, I agreed not to publish this first volume until I had finished the whole work. Both volumes could then be brought out together.... I felt like a marathon runner who, on completing the course, is asked whether he wouldn't mind immediately running round it all over again." James Strachey went through the manuscript with detailed and meticulous care making objections and suggestions at every point. In April 1967, shortly before the book was published, Strachey died suddenly of a heart attack.

Holroyd incorporated James Strachey's comments both in the text itself and in footnotes to the text when there was a disagreement in interpretation. James Strachey was very protective of his brother's reputation and at one point accused Holroyd of "an unceasing desire to run Lytton down – in this case to make people think he was impotent – which, believe me, he wasn't." On another occasion, apparently provoked by Holroyd's suggestion that Lytton Strachey's moustache was wispy, he attacked Holroyd for what he considered to be his prudery in the way he dealt with Strachey's obscene verse: "I've been positively staggered by some of your ethical judgements on the subject of sex and religion. Your remarks about Lytton's poems astound me ... the impression you give of holding up your hands in shocked horror at their fearful obscenity makes me wonder . . . why on earth you ever set out to write this book – and I feel inclined to want the whole thing thrown out of the window. The whole of Lytton's life was entirely directed to stopping critical attitudes of the sort that you seem to be expressing."

Such comments tend to undermine severely Holroyd's professed ambition to treat Lytton Strachey's homosexuality in the same way as he would have treated heterosexual activity. Nevertheless, Frances Partridge in her diaries, *Other People: Diaries 1963–1966* (1993), makes it clear that some of those involved with Strachey, including Duncan Grant and Roger Senhouse, were outraged by the way their lives had been exposed to public gaze and considered taking legal action against him. Nonetheless, Holroyd must have placated their distress between their reading the manuscript and the publication of the book since he congratulates them in the book on their determination to see the truth of their relationships fairly presented. Holroyd was fully aware that his intention to deal with Strachey's homosexuality "without any artificial veils of decorum . . . depended for its practicality on the cooperation of a band of mercurial octogenarians. It was for all of us a daunting prospect. 'Shall I be arrested?' one of them asked after reading through my typescript. And another, with deep pathos, exclaimed: 'When this comes out, they will never again allow me into Lord's.' In particular, it says much for the courage, candour and integrity of Duncan Grant and Roger Senhouse that, despite the shock of its unexpectedness, they did not object to what I had written." Despite James Strachey's defense of openness on sexual matters, when biography is dealing with those still alive or those who have relatives still alive, tact, diplomacy, and decorum are also necessary attributes in a biographer.

Nonetheless, Patrick Cruttwell in the *Hudson Review* (Winter 1968/1969) criticized Holroyd for his lack of courage in being "ridiculously reticent" and "totally inexplicit in describing this side of Strachey's life – [especially the mechanics of his physical sexuality and his dealings with working class boys – 'if I may put it with a plainness which would upset Mr. Holroyd's old Etonian sensibilities, we are never allowed to know what Strachey really did and with whom'] – as he is also in describing the pornographic and scatological stories and verses" of which Strachey wrote a good deal. With some justification, he cited James Strachey's remarks as supporting evidence. However, whereas Holroyd says that his intention was to treat homo-

sexuality no differently than he would heterosexuality, Cruttwell criticized him for not making homosexuality a separate issue. Noel Annan in the *New York Review of Books* (6 June 1968) isolated the whole problem when he wrote that "the cult of homosexuality at the beginning of this century was a European phenomenon whether in Berlin or Vienna, in the Paris of Proust or Gide, in Oscar Wilde's London, the same upper-class fashion in homosexuality could be observed, the same predilection for choirboys or footmen, or for the rougher stuff of guardsmen, sailors, and low-life characters . . . in England, the cult of homosexuality was specially reinforced in the upper-classes by their education." It is this aspect of Strachey's significance that Cruttwell criticized Holroyd for not exploring, though had he done so, it would have been a different kind of biography entirely.

Annan, in his review, summarized what he thought to be the work's merits: "Certainly Michael Holroyd's two-volume twelve-hundred-page biography is a remarkable achievement. He is the first to begin to make a map of Bloomsbury and to establish the identity of the minor as well as the major characters. Not for him the security of a university post: he worked in the most straitened circumstances. . . . He has not written a literary masterpiece and his style is at times overblown. . . . He needed to construct a work out of a mountain of material. . . . This he has done with skill and integrity. . . . And yet, time and again, one wishes that he had stepped back from the documents and analysed his subject. . . . Holroyd calls his work a critical biography, but it is only critical in a limited sense. He does not sufficiently criticize his sources and takes letters at their face value. . . . Holroyd is excellent when he tackles the vexed question about how accurate Strachey was in the use of his sources in his historical works. . . . But he does not assess the purpose and impact of Strachey's work as a whole." While Annan was sensitive to the virtues of Holroyd's work, both he and Cruttwell were quick, nonetheless, to notice the absence of analytical intelligence, though neither seemed to recognize that while that quality might well be an essential prerequisite in critics such as themselves, biography calls primarily for other virtues. Cyril Connolly's praise was not without qualification: "I rate Mr. Holroyd very highly as a biographer, almost in the Painter class." Nonetheless, he recognized in Holroyd "an inveterate gossip" who "has recorded everything he has found out," thus identifying Holroyd's insatiable curiosity about his subject, perhaps a more necessary ingredient in a biographer than intellectual analysis.

Michael Thorpe in retrospect seems to have made a more balanced assessment of Holroyd's achievement by comparing him with Strachey as a biographer. "This is a great biography of one who was not, in any sense great himself," he judged. "Its greatness [derives], ironically, from the many ways in which Mr. Holroyd has excelled his subject in the art of biography: he is copious and thorough, yet always stylish and economical, whereas Strachey was arbitrarily cursory and concise. His sympathies – except towards Leavisiate moral critics – are broad and deep: Strachey's were straitened in the extreme – in his writings that is. This last qualification saves Mr. Holroyd's re-created Strachey the man so that, ultimately he wins our sympathy and regard: despite his 'ugly thoughtlessness,' his self-pity and snobbery – the warts are all there, fully exposed – his patience and good humour in sickness, his tolerance and generosity toward the difficult people who gravitated toward him and his tenacious clinging to his artistic principles prove that he fought an honourable draw with weak flesh and a febrile spirit."

Holroyd's life of Lytton Strachey was outstandingly successful and firmly established his reputation as a biographer. It was also a great success commercially and was quickly published in paperback. He had shown a remarkable ability to master a wealth of heterogeneous material and to deal with events in detail without in any way losing touch with the narrative framework or with the interest of his readers.

The character of Strachey in all its contradictions and perversities emerges fully and convincingly as the biography progresses, while the minor characters surrounding Strachey are authentic in their own right while also authenticating the character of Strachey. At the end of the biography with the death of the subject followed by the suicide of Carrington, Holroyd achieves a rare pathos without seeming to manipulate either the reader's feelings or the actuality of the events. The biography carries conviction not only because of Holroyd's mastery in marshaling the multiplicity of facts but also because the narrative sweep of Strachey's life is brought to a satisfactory conclusion, a dignified death followed by a coda that seems to confirm its significance. We are as moved by Strachey's humanity, that which he shares with us all, just as strongly as we are impressed by his individual achievements.

In this respect Holroyd fully justifies his contention that biography and fiction are intimately related. He "set out," he says, "to escape into my subjects' lives rather than identify myself with them," and as "he pursues his research and finds out about his subject" he "makes discoveries about himself." In all this he functions like a novelist and "learned something of narrative, structure and plot. . . . Though the biographer may not invent dialogue – that is breaking the rules of the game – he may use quotations from letters and diaries to perform a function similar to dialogue in the narrative. I structure my story." He expresses his hope that "literary biography will increasingly be seen as a specialised branch of fiction" though he does not hide his conviction that literary biography, at least in Britain, is commonly seen as a branch of journalism.

Holroyd is a very self-conscious craftsman who does not "just plod through chronologically" but who aims to give his books a "symphonic sort of structure. There are motifs and themes that are brought back, with variation. And a long book needs to have different movements, variations of pace. At times one must change gear and speed along. The reader may need an outdoor scene at this point or a spin in the car." He cites as his model Samuel Johnson and his insistence that the first business of a biographer was not necessarily to dwell on "those performances and incidents which produce vulgar greatness," but to "lead the thoughts into domestic privacies, and to display the minute details of daily life." Holroyd is particularly successful in portraying the inner lives of his characters, whatever the performances and incidents of their public personae. His perception is both sharp and sensitive, and he has an instinct for the telling detail, the significant phrase, and the memorable vignette. Moreover, despite Cyril Connolly's remarks, Holroyd's style is lucid, economical, and flexible. While his attitude remains detached, his prose achieves that comfortable, middle style that encompasses the trivial and the significant, the idiomatic and the formal, without strain and that moves from the amusing to the pathetic with natural ease. Though he also has a gift for the illuminating image, he successfully maintains that conversational tone and idiom that establish a warm and friendly relationship with his reader. He has an easy and familiar charm and is careful never to patronize either his reader or his subject. He aims to engage the attentions of the general reader and includes neither references nor footnotes in order not to interrupt the narrative flow. He does, however, indicate in a short "Author's Note" his source materials and where they are to be found.

Holroyd's only novel, *A Dog's Life,* was published in the United States in 1969 but has never been published in Britain because, he said, his father threatened to sue him for libel. In 1973 Holroyd republished a selection of assorted articles and reviews under the title *Unreceived Opinions,* some of which have been heavily reworked and rewritten. Some of the reprinted articles are autobiographical, but most have a biographical slant. Most of them are on literary figures – Gerhardie, Strachey, Charlotte Mew, A. E. Housman, J. M. Barrie, Virginia Woolf – but there are also pieces on Bertrand Russell and Roger Fry and, learning from his work on Augustus John, on Delacroix, William Rothenstein, and Wilson Steer, and a description of the strange friendship between Wyndham Lewis and Augustus John. There is also a sensitive appreciation of Dorelia John, who died in her eighties in 1969. He also republished some of his contributions to the campaign for Public Lending Rights, in which he took an leading role. For the most part, however, these articles and reviews are slight though urbane, elegant and amusing, and adequately testify to the width of his reading, the liveliness of his mind, and the quality of his journalism.

Establishing the pattern that a minor character in his previous biography becomes the subject of the next, Holroyd followed his biography of Lytton Strachey with his biography of the artist Augustus John. *Augustus John: A Biography* (1974–1975) is also a two-volume biography and was widely criticized for its length: "The book has only one fault: it is too long," wrote Kenneth Clark in the *Times Literary Supplement* (18 October 1974). "His book might have gained in quality if he had used the blue pencil" (Denys Sutton, *Apollo,* December 1974) – though Diana Holman-Hunt in *Connoisseur* (November 1974) expressed the sentiments of most readers when she said that she "found it too long but could not put it down."

Yet Holroyd's mastery of his material is remarkable and his attention to detail – despite the minor errors noted by Sutton – scrupulous. The organization of the biography is equally impressive. Clark said that Holroyd "applies to near-contemporary life the industry of a Maurist; he tracks down every birth certificate, discovers and transcribes every letter, reads every related memoir." Sutton praised him for his stamina as a "patient chronicler" who "has talent for creating a mosaic of details." Moreover, although he says in his preface that it is not an "art book," as Holman-Hunt testified, "it includes many pages of sensitive and mature art criticism." Mainly, however, it concentrates attention on John's extraordinary and protean personality, which is also expressed through his art. Holroyd establishes in the first chapter of his biography the

multiple character that was Augustus John: "To know Augustus John was to know not a single man, but to know a crowd of people, all different, none of them quite convincing . . . and he did not know who he was." Holroyd undoubtedly "combines dedicated scholarship with an absorbing story, both passionate and violent." He enjoys describing John's many love affairs and the women with whom he was involved. But central to the whole design of John's life are his wife Dorelia John, who is vividly presented as both beautiful and enigmatic, and his sister Gwen, perhaps the more gifted artist, a rather remote though sad and haunting presence.

In view of his later attitude, it is interesting to notice that at one time he believed that a moderate advance from a publisher was to be preferred to a large one. However, his literary agent, Hilary Rubinstein, sold Holroyd's biography of George Bernard Shaw to Chatto and Windus for a record £625,000. Rubinstein described in the *Bookseller* (20 November 1987) how he invited sealed bids from nine publishers for the "finest biography of our time," and while one firm actually outbid Chatto and Windus, the fact that Random House had already bought the rights in the United States meant that the book would be published under the one umbrella throughout the English-speaking world. Rubinstein pointed out that while huge advances are often paid to the authors of commercial fiction, nonfiction had not previously commanded advances of that order: "There is often a heavy cost to be paid for the revelation that a work of a living author has fetched a stupendous price . . . while £625,000 would be an astronomic price for a single volume, it is much less aberrant as a reward for five or five-and-a-half books and for what will be, by the time the great work is finally finished, almost 25 years of Michael Holroyd's working life. . . . The publishing community should welcome such eloquent money being given for once to a work that all who have been privileged to read it consider a literary masterpiece. . . . My hope and belief is that the success – the very public success – of Michael Holroyd's *Bernard Shaw* will give a similar fillip to literary nonfiction." "The advance," said Holroyd in the London *Times* (10 September 1988), "will be paid to me over the years, like a middle-age pension."

Clearly, in view of the commercial success of Holroyd's biographies of Strachey and John, his new work seemed to offer publishers the opportunity of burnishing the literary image of their houses with the surety of long-term profits. Holroyd had achieved the enviable feat of maintaining the re-

Dust jacket for volume three of Holroyd's biography of the British playwright and social critic

spect and admiration of an intellectual audience while at the same time attracting a large readership for his work.

In the early 1970s the residuary legatees of the Shaw estate – the British Museum, the National Gallery of Ireland, and the Royal Academy of Dramatic Art – at the suggestion of Max Reinhardt, Shaw's publisher, invited Holroyd to write the authorized biography. They agreed that it was time for an assessment of Shaw for a new generation of readers and by a biographer who had not known Shaw personally. Nonetheless, the choice of Holroyd was controversial, since, as he later admitted, he "had no experience of politics or theatre, no academic qualifications, and no record of having worked on Shaw." "I was thirty-four. . . . I was writing a life of a flamboyant heterosexual, having previously published books about a notorious homosexual and an unknown impoverished writer who, following the appearance of my book, stubbornly remained unknown. People usually implored me not to write biographies of their friends and members of their family. Now I was gaining respectability, albeit controversial respectability." Also, he was aware of the vast amount of material he would have

to master: "I had heard that Shaw wrote ten letters a day, every day, all his adult life, and that people kept his letters. I knew that he had composed more than fifty plays, that there was a collected edition of almost forty volumes, and many library yards of books about him, as well as huge deposits of unpublished papers around the world. I began to suspect that . . . G. B. S. could actually write in a day more words than I could read in a day. Since he lived into his mid-nineties working vigorously to the end, this was a daunting prospect." Holroyd said it was "a moment of great terror" when he finally decided to accept the invitation. He realized, "It would be a long voyage and I didn't know the route, nor did I have confidence that I would reach the end. I thought it would take 10 years, possibly more – I didn't know then that it would take 15. I wondered whether the relationship between Shaw and myself would work. I wasn't a Shavian. Would I be stimulated and enthusiastic enough to do not just an inventory of his life but a worthwhile book? I was seriously worried that I might not be able to give anything new to it."

It is interesting to see just how quickly Holroyd established a close relationship with his subject: in the first volume of his biography, *The Search for Love* (1988), he demonstrates how Shaw had done his best to doctor the public version of his loveless and neglected childhood in which he was known by the nickname "Sonny" and that Sonny had been a vulnerable little boy with anarchic leanings – much like Holroyd, in fact. He admits a soft spot for Sonny: "To some extent," he says, "I shared his experience. I had a dull and rather fearful childhood." In other words he soon found himself identifying with his subject, or at least with a seminal part of his subject's experience. "I always keep Sonny in mind," he said, "and the subversive [effects] he had. I would like this book to give heart to those who feel they were dealt a bad hand in life." Holroyd's characterization of Sonny continues to play a significant role in his biography leading him, inevitably, to the conclusion that largely because of his childhood experience Shaw became "a kind of patron saint of the lonely and the misfits, who can give such people courage." Thus he turns his own experience to advantage, though he does so without apparently losing his detachment or falsifying the materials of the biography. Yet it is interesting to notice that Sonny – the unloved, vulnerable, lonely, anarchic boy – becomes something of a leitmotiv throughout the three volumes of Holroyd's biography. Holroyd's contention that "in his relationships with women Shaw was seeking a second childhood in which he could receive all the attention and happiness he had been denied by his mother" is fully illustrated in the second volume of his biography, particularly in his *mariage blanc* – the "sentiment of affectionate benevolence which has nothing to do with sexual passion." "Sonny, Holroyd believes," Peter Lewis commented in the (London) *Times* (10 September 1988), "always remained locked up inside G. B. S., slipping out, for instance, in the short-hand diaries which record such un-Supermanlike activities as lying in bed till 11, idling at the piano instead of working and being a hopeless duffer with his typewriter or bicycle. . . . He really did feel he was unloveable, so he replaced love with attention." Richard Holmes, reviewing the first volume of the biography in the (London) *Times* (15 September 1988), noticed "Shaw's frantic efforts to recreate [*sic*] himself out of a bereft Dublin childhood." Because of his continuing need for the solaces of childhood, he "shifted his desires into his literary life. Sexual excitement produced in him an ejaculation of words from which letters were conceived, novels and plays born." Moreover, in the third volume Holroyd quotes Shaw himself in old age harking back to Sonny – he would have pre-

ferred to be remembered "as Sonny than as the ghastly old skeleton of a celebrity I now am." Thus Holroyd maintains an important psychological link, however tenuous, between himself and his subject, and in classic Freudian mode the child is seen to become father of the man.

Holroyd deliberately gave neither references nor sources but kept the footnotes for inclusion in a separate volume, volume five. "I wanted to present," he said, "a 'pure' narrative that was neither interrupted by 'sequences of numbers nor undermined by a series of footnotes." He wished to capture the interest of the general reader by presenting Shaw as immediately as possible, and the reviews agreed that he had succeeded: "The first volume of his biography is highly readable" but is "for the 'general reader' rather than for academics. He is detached, but not without sympathy with and insight into his characters. The treatment of Shaw's life up to 1888 is, in the best sense, novelistic. Narrative flow is constant; the style limpid, enlivened by a gift for the luminous generalization." Yet whatever the reservations of "academics," the *Times Literary Supplement* (8–14 September 1989), in reviewing the second volume, did not hesitate to describe the biography as "monumental." John Sutherland, the reviewer, noticed that Holroyd "allocates this middle act of the Shavian drama twice the space per year on the grounds, presumably, that these years are the most eventful." He admires the way that so many strands are kept running in this volume; all the major works are described and discussed, the relations with the Webbs, H. G. Wells, Harley Granville-Barker, and others are fleshed out – "what seems like hundreds of other characters wander in and out of the narrative" – and all against the background of two wars, a revolution, the Irish uprising, the rise of the Labour party, votes for women and so on. He congratulates Holroyd for the way in which he controls Shaw and prevents his taking over the narrative. On the publication of the third volume, reviewers were generally impressed by the sheer scope of Holroyd's accomplishment and by his energy and powers of synopsis in mastering his materials. "Shaw's vastness has met its match in the biographer's energy" according to Sutherland in the *Times Literary Supplement* (6 September 1991), who drew attention to the way in which Holroyd had concentrated attention on the narrative: "Holroyd is not interested in the inner lives of his supporting cast and on occasions even seems to resent their calls on his time. . . . Nor does Holroyd waste words on commentary or authorial opinion. Chapters (sections is the better term) are not thematized, even to

LYTTON STRACHEY

THE NEW BIOGRAPHY

MICHAEL HOLROYD

Dust jacket for the American edition of the reworked biography of the innovative British biographer

"suited G. B. S. He hadn't appeared so well for a long time." This is a novelist's rather than a biographer's intervention in the narrative, a moment in which writer and reader share a humorous diversion from the painful memory of Shaw's "I tell you I am in hell. I want to die and I can't." Holroyd said that he had been educated by writing his biographies: "Strachey introduced me to Bloomsbury and the Bohemian world of personal relations. John sharpened my visual awareness and Shaw is making me far more politically aware." But if he has been affected by his subjects, his biographies, notwithstanding the reading and scholarship on which they are based, are all powered by his individual vision. Having completed his biography, Holroyd concluded that Shaw "covered up his vulnerability with dazzling panache: I have tried to uncover it and, without losing the sparkle of this panache, show the need he had for such brilliant covering." Holroyd's version of Shaw is a consistent and convincing recreation, though the hidden vulnerability that he says he has tried to uncover would seem to belong to the biographer as well as, perhaps, to his subject. "Subject and author," said Angela Lambert, "had in common unhappy childhoods. The funny stories Holroyd tells about his own are, on reflection, terribly sad" (*Independent Weekend*, 7 September 1991). The reviewers were generally agreed that the biography is, first and foremost, compellingly readable: "it sails along," as Richard Holmes put it in the (London) *Times* (15 September 1988), "with the swift, complex life of a major novel of manners.... If he does not make us like Shaw, he makes us understand him." G. J. Watson in the *Independent* (6 September 1991) agreed with him and pronounced, "This is one of the great biographies, and that Shaw now seems one of the burnt-out meteors of the century is not Mr. Holroyd's fault."

Reviewing Robert Gittings's *The Nature of Biography* (1978), Holroyd endorses his saying that the last "fifty years have been a golden age of biography" and that biography is "one of the most satisfying and established achievements of our present age.... The man who brought back to biography what it had lost since Boswell was, Mr. Gittings regrets, Lytton Strachey.... After Strachey, no good biographer has dared to be less than an artist." Holroyd served his apprenticeship as a biographer with Hugh Kingsmill before turning to Lytton Strachey and brought his artistry, fully developed, to the portrayal of Bernard Shaw. Biography may well be as he supposes, an "illegitimate child of biography and the novel," but Holroyd's work is an object lesson in how to achieve a seamless marriage

the extent of giving them titles.... The tale is all." Sutherland thought "the main curve of Holroyd's design is now clear. Shaw searched for love, and never found it ... pursues power and never possesses it," and the "lures of fantasy" similarly disappoint. The absence of commentary and authorial opinion and the loss of clear thematic resonance demonstrate Holroyd's reliance on his structural and narrative powers to hold the work together while at the same time fully engaging the attention of the general reader. Any lack of analytical intelligence — with which he was charged by Cruttwell and Annan in his biography of Lytton Strachey — is confidently compensated for by his ability to control his narrative. Rightly Sutherland concluded that "Holroyd's biography is a masterpiece of narrative efficiency." He draws attention to the fact that in describing the dying Shaw "Holroyd relaxes his customary austerity and relates these last scenes with great poignancy." Nonetheless, Holroyd does not resist the chance of lightening the pathos of Shaw's death with sardonic humor: "Death" he says

between the demands of fact and documentation on the one hand and the creative imagination on the other while keeping in close touch with actual life. Holroyd reiterated his dedication to his art, perhaps a trifle pretentiously, in the following terms: "My deepest involvement is with biography itself and its never-ending love-affair with humanity, and my aim has been to come a little nearer a biographical ideal described by Hugh Kingsmill as 'the complete sympathy of complete detachment.'"

In 1992 Holroyd published a fourth volume of his Shaw biography outlining Shaw's "posthumous" life. E. S. Turner in the (London) *Times Literary Supplement* (8 May 1992) well described it as a "lively and witty, if a shade emaciated, postscript to his three-volume biography. It offers an engaging run-down on those who, in the past forty years, defied or defended the playwright's wishes, or who used him to give lift-off or fulfilment to their careers."

The promised references for all four volumes were published in a fifth volume, entitled *The Shaw Companion* (1992) (it contains source notes, acknowledgments, and cumulative index), which was bound in with a further printing of volume four, *The Last Laugh* (1992). Some buyers who hoped to have the references in a separate volume expressed their displeasure at this way of publishing them.

Holroyd followed up all his biographies by editing selections from his subjects' work. The results were *The Best of Hugh Kingsmill* (1970); *Lytton Strachey by Himself: A Self-Portrait* (1971); *The Shorter Strachey* (1980), with Paul Levy; *The Art of Augustus John* (1974), with Malcolm Easton; and Shaw's *Major Critical Essays* (1986).

In 1982 Holroyd married Margaret Drabble, who had herself written two literary biographies – of William Wordsworth and Arnold Bennett – and some dozen novels and was at that time preparing the revised fifth edition of *The Oxford Companion to English Literature* in which she gives him, though not herself, an entry. Angela Lambert wrote: "Their domestic set-up is well known. They keep separate establishments, meeting on social occasions and at weekends [in their country house on the Somerset coast]. She has the house in Hampstead in which she brought up her three children (by her first husband); he keeps the large, bachelorish, book-lined flat in Ladbroke Grove."

He and his wife have become prominent public figures. They attend and speak at literary conferences and support writers' pressure groups. He has traveled widely in Britain and the United States and has given a good deal of his time and energies to working on behalf of writers; he was chairman of the National Book League from 1976 to 1978, president of P.E.N. from 1985 to 1988, and has been chairman of the Strachey Trust since 1990. He has written television scripts for Aquarius, Arena, and the South Bank Show and was a member of the BBC Archives Committee from 1976 to 1979. In spite of the fact that both he and his wife are members of the informal 20 June Group of Hampstead intellectuals founded by Harold Pinter and his wife Lady Antonia Fraser to oppose Thatcherism in all its guises, he was awarded the Commander of the British Empire in 1989 for his services to literature by the Thatcher government.

Elizabeth Jenkins

(31 October 1905 –   )

Charles Calder
University of Aberdeen

BOOKS: *Virginia Water* (London: Gollancz, 1930; New York: Smith, 1930);

The Winters (London: Gollancz, 1931);

Lady Caroline Lamb (London: Gollancz, 1932; Boston: Little, Brown, 1932; revised edition, London: Sphere Books, 1972);

Portrait of an Actor (London: Gollancz, 1933);

Harriet (London: Gollancz, 1934; New York: Doubleday, Doran, 1934); published as *Murder by Neglect* (London: Four Square Books, 1960);

Doubtful Joy (London: Gollancz, 1935; New York: Doubleday, Doran, 1935);

The Phoenix Nest (London: Gollancz, 1936);

Jane Austen: A Biography (London: Gollancz, 1938; New York: Farrar, Straus & Cudahy, 1949; New York: Grosset & Dunlap, 1949);

Robert and Helen (London: Gollancz, 1944);

Young Enthusiasts (London: Gollancz, 1947);

Henry Fielding (London: Home & Van Thal, 1947; Denver: Swallows, 1948);

Six Criminal Women (London: Sampson Low, 1949; New York: Duell, Sloan & Pearce, 1949);

The Tortoise and the Hare (London: Gollancz, 1954; New York: Coward-McCann, 1954);

Ten Fascinating Women (London: Odhams, 1955);

Elizabeth the Great (London: Gollancz, 1958; New York: Coward-McCann, 1958);

Joseph Lister (Edinburgh: Nelson, 1960);

Elizabeth and Leicester (London: Gollancz, 1961);

Brightness (London: Gollancz, 1963; New York: Coward-McCann, 1964);

Honey (London: Gollancz, 1968);

Dr. Gully (London: Joseph, 1972); published as *Dr. Gully's Story* (New York: Coward, McCann & Geoghegan, 1972);

The Mystery of King Arthur (London: Joseph, 1975; New York: Coward, McCann & Geoghegan, 1975);

The Princes in the Tower (London: Hamish Hamilton, 1978; New York: Coward, McCann & Geoghegan, 1978);

The Shadow and the Light (London: Hamish Hamilton, 1982).

OTHER: "Tennyson and Dr. Gully," *Tennyson Society Occasional Papers No. 3* (Lincoln: Tennyson Society, 1974);

Collected Reports of the Jane Austen Society, 1949–1965, introduction by Jenkins (London: Dawson, 1967);

Collected Reports of the Jane Austen Society, 1966–1975, introduction by Jenkins (London: Dawson, 1977).

Elizabeth Jenkins is a novelist and biographer who has followed her own path in disregard of fashion. As a biographer she has written on diverse subjects, but her reputation rests securely on three large-scale works: *Jane Austen: A Biography* (1938), *Elizabeth the Great* (1958), and *Elizabeth and Leicester* (1961). She sums up her creed in the introduction to *Jane Austen:* "This work can offer hardly any of the attractions that make fashionable biography so stimulating; on the subject of Jane Austen I myself have not felt able to be either patronizing or clinical; but I thought that some of her admirers who had not the leisure to make out a chronological account of her for themselves, might like to find it done for them." We notice that she offers, modestly, a "chronological account," not an "interpretation"; and we detect also a healthily anti-Stracheyan note in her disowning of biographical superciliousness. Jenkins is a lucid and sympathetic biographer. She is attracted to her subjects and believes that the careful retelling of their lives exerts sufficient appeal without the imposition of amateur psychological analysis. She writes a direct and unaffected prose that is well suited to the task in hand.

Margaret Elizabeth Heald Jenkins was born on 31 October 1905 at Hitchin, Hertfordshire, to James Heald Jenkins, a preparatory school headmaster, and Theodora Caldicott Ingram Jenkins. She read English and history at Cambridge, graduating in 1927. She earned her living as a teacher of English from 1929 to 1939, becoming a temporary civil servant during World War II. Since 1945 she has been a full-time writer.

While working as a teacher Jenkins produced a substantial amount of work in fiction and in biography. Following the novels *Virginia Water* (1930) and *The Winters* (1931), she produced *Lady Caroline Lamb* (1932), an enterprising choice of subject. A revised edition appeared in 1972. This first biographical project was succeeded six years later by *Jane Austen*. Jenkins's affection and knowledge inform this book. She is writing the story of a life, not literary criticism: but she interweaves apt comments on the novels at suitable points in the narrative. There is no doubting the author's grasp of her material (juvenilia, letters, novels); she rightly pays tribute to the work of R. W. Chapman as editor of Austen's *Letters* (1932).

There is a good deal to be said in favor of the approach Jenkins describes in her introduction. She notes that "studies of Jane Austen abound, but so far as known, none of them presents a full-length story of her life in strictly chronological order.... A life with little external incident may seem scarcely to justify so long a book, but Jane Austen's family were so important to her, that I hope other people besides myself may feel that the placing of them in the fullest and clearest light available has merited the space." This modest hope is, in the event, surpassed. *Jane Austen* is marked not just by careful recording of biographical detail but also by critical insight and common sense (if indeed these last two qualities are separable). The author's liking for Jane Austen informs every page; and she accommodates her discussion of the novels with no awkward changes of gear. She writes sensibly of the relationship between life and art. In discussing *Mansfield Park* (1814), for instance, she notes that "we have the authority of the Austen family for believing that the character of Mary Crawford, in some respects, is modelled on that of Eliza de Feuillide. The idea is a delightful one, but even with such sanction, one must take care not to build too much upon it." Jenkins observes that Eliza died in 1813 and that the next year Austen read *Mansfield Park* aloud to the widower, her brother Henry, during their coach journey to London. "Now when one considers that the judgment on Mary Crawford is on the whole markedly unfavourable, and that the best that even her lover can say for her is that she might have been very different had she not been ruined by bad training, one cannot imagine that Jane Austen would have read all this aloud to her favourite brother

within a year of his wife's death, if he had supposed, or if she had conceived the possibility of his supposing, that Mary Crawford was intended for a picture of that wife." This is a salutary caution that reminds us that Austen was not a copyist but a creator.

Jane Austen shows Jenkins's gift for evoking the texture of life, "a house in its park, a tea-cup, the type and binding of a book." She does not ignore the underside of eighteenth-century life; but her main business in chapter 1 is the depiction of Steventon Rectory and its occupants. We feel that Jenkins herself approves of the rationality and order that are the distinguishing traits of the Reverend George Austen. "He lived the life of a scholar, devoting the greater portion of his time that was left over from his parish duties to his books, and at the same time he preserved a simplicity complete enough for perfect freedom yet compatible with every reasonable comfort ... though he kept his carriage, the interior of the Rectory had in some respects the plainness of a cottage; the walls and ceiling were joined without any cornice, and some of the walls were white-washed; the sunlight ... brought out nothing rich, merely the essentials of a living-room in an age that made nothing crude or mean; chairs and a table, a pier glass, a glass-fronted cupboard with a gilt china tea service behind its panes." As for Cassandra Leigh Austen, "she had no idea of giving in to fine lady-ism, and people were welcome to call provided they did not expect her to put away the mending." This living biography; Jenkins uses these quotidian details to establish the salient features of her characters. The early chapters bring before us the high spirits, good nature, and intelligence that marked the Austen household. Who can say, inquires the author, how much of the Austen lucidity and strength derives from the circumstance that "she was daughter and sister of the Rev. George Austen's family"?

Jenkins is thoroughly at home in the literature of the time, and this inwardness gives the reader confidence in the judgments she makes on Austen's use of allusion and incorporation of diverse literary ingredients such as Thomas Gilpin's *Observations on Picturesque Beauty* (1804). But, as usual, Jenkins is interested not in the act of borrowing but in the fresh use that Austen makes of what she appropriates.

The personality Jenkins depicts is credible and attractive: lively, unpretentious, humorous, and independent in mind. Of her literary accomplishments Jenkins has this to say: "she possessed, through a happy combination of art and chance, a style composed of those elements of language which do not date." Austen's characters are not cabined

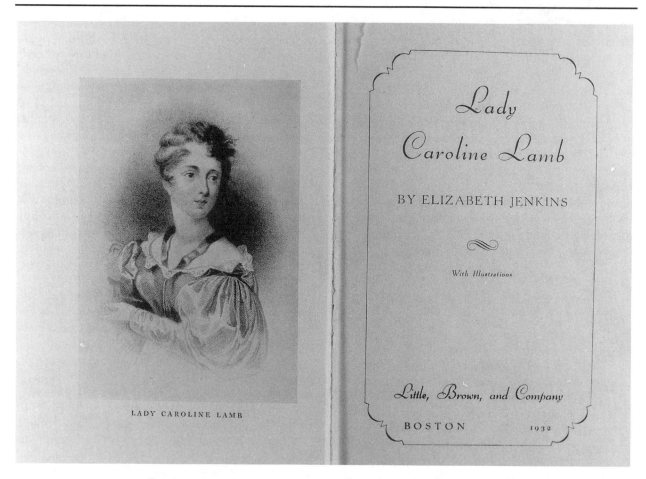

LADY CAROLINE LAMB

Lady Caroline Lamb

BY ELIZABETH JENKINS

With Illustrations

Little, Brown, and Company

BOSTON   1932

Frontispiece and title page for the American edition of Jenkins's first biography

and cribbed by chronology: they call each other Mister and Miss and ride in carriages, but "actually they seem to meet, not in time, but space." That is as succinct as one could wish. Jenkins appends to this assessment a heartfelt paragraph: "This is not an age favourable to the development of aesthetic genius; it may be that for a time all forms of art will pass into the domination of those who think that a good picture can be painted only if the artist's political views accord with theirs, and that it is only possible to write a good novel provided the author follows the rules they have laid down." A necessary warning, surely, in the cultural climate of the late 1930s.

Jenkins returned to the eighteenth century with her *Henry Fielding* (1947). Her next large-scale project was the biography *Elizabeth the Great*. This involved three years of research, but one imagines that the personality of the queen had been of interest to the author for much longer. Jenkins is not a delver into archives, and *Elizabeth the Great* relies upon published sources, but she creates a convincing portrait of Elizabeth and her times. A. L. Rowse wrote in the *Chicago Sunday Tribune* (1 March 1959)

that this was "quite the most perceptive book about Elizabeth I that I have ever read" — no small tribute to receive from the most learned of Elizabethan historians. Jenkins, in his opinion, had produced "a portrait that is unforgettable and very touching." Most readers would agree.

Her aim, wrote Jenkins, was to "collect interesting personal information about Queen Elizabeth I." Since the concentration is upon Elizabeth herself, "the shape of the book is very irregular; sometimes events of great importance are briefly mentioned or omitted while minor ones are dwelt on in detail." There is good reason for this procedure; as Jenkins notes, there is nothing in her book that had not previously been published; but some of the material she deploys is little known. "Historians have not room in their books for such matters and popular writers have not made use of them."

Jenkins maintains a strong narrative propulsion throughout this long book. Twenty-five out of its twenty-nine chapters are devoted to the reign. The author keeps her eye on the dominating personality of the queen; but she has a striking cast of supporting actors who surround the principal: Robert Dudley, Sir Walter Ralegh, Essex, Christopher Hatton (the assessment of Hatton is particularly welcome). And, always at the queen's side, is the sorely tried but resolutely faithful William Cecil, Lord Burleigh. Burleigh is shown as the necessary complement to the queen – indeed, he is perhaps the real hero of the reign. Jenkins depicts both the trials and the satisfactions that Burleigh's proximity to Elizabeth involved. "The Queen, though an indefatigable, an inspiring colleague, was not an easy one; but his life's work was his life's passion." Jenkins shows us a man who was speaking the simple truth when he claimed that "my service hath been but a piece of my duty, and my vocation hath been too great a reward." It is a characteristic of Jenkins to maintain a sense of proportion in depicting relationships. Thus she does not ignore "the mistrusts, the outbursts of nervous exasperation or flaming anger" that Burleigh had to endure, but she points out that the strength of the bond between sovereign and minister was such as to survive all strains. In Burleigh's own words, "her blasts be not as the storms of other Princes, though they be shrewd sometimes to those she loveth best." Elizabeth, for her part, felt deep gratitude to her first minister: "Her Majesty spoke . . . of his sound and deep judgment . . . using these words, that no Prince in Europe had such a counsellor as she had of him."

Jenkins varies the pace of her narrative for the sake of maintaining interest. She presents the set pieces of the reign in elaborated episodes that provide notable points of expansion or development: the recognition-procession through London, the stages of the Alençon courtship, the deathbed scenes. There are appealing touches of humor in the account of the Alençon wooing; the most vivid set piece is the royal progress to Kenilworth in 1575. Here the author has an opportunity for making the most of her descriptive skill. The "historic house-party," as Jenkins calls it, was "an exhibition, on epic scale, of Leicester's importance, his taste, his wealth, his adoration." She traces the sequence of events that filled those eighteen days in July 1575, showing us the odd combination of luxury, sophistication, homeliness, and barbarity that characterized the proceedings. As usual, Jenkins is sensitive to color. She records that Leicester "had hangings of scarlet leather stamped with gilt, and a Turkey carpet of a light-blue ground, fifty feet long. The four-poster beds were most of them hung with scarlet or crimson . . . but there was one of which the blue curtains were trimmed with gold and silver lace, one covered and furnished with peach-colour fringed

with ash-coloured silk . . . [and] one with white tinsel curtains embroidered with purple velvet and copper-gold." Jenkins gives us a strangely touching glimpse of one of the entertainments offered to Elizabeth during her visit. "On Tuesday evening the Queen, attended, went on foot over the bridge and into the tree-sprinkled meadows called the Chase. When she came back a barge was on the pool, filled with musicians playing and singing, and she stood on the bridge, listening in the evening light." But contemplative pleasures were varied by the authentically Elizabethan barbarity of bearbaiting. Jenkins does not gloss over the "hideous savagery" of such aspects of Tudor life.

Rereading *Elizabeth the Great* allows the appreciation of the solidity of the author's technique. She has a capacity for opening chapters in a brisk and arresting manner, for accommodating the elaborated incident or set piece, and for interleaving passages of analysis or summary. The incorporating of these ingredients within a firm and clear narrative ensures that there is no risk of monotony or tedium.

Jenkins portrays Queen Elizabeth as a woman who combines brilliant intellect and emotional instability. "When Elizabeth addressed a deputation from the Houses of Parliament she spoke with a pointed decision; on public occasions she was completely in command of herself . . . but to the men who worked in close association with her she seemed at times on the verge of nervous breakdown." Jenkins is no armchair psychologist; her concern is as always to assemble a coherent narrative. But no biographer of Elizabeth can avoid recording instances of irrational behavior or ignore altogether the tangled roots of the queen's sexuality. Jenkins remarks that "in a creature of such intensity and power, the emotions connected with a vital instinct were, inevitably, of tremendous force. Held up in the arms of her imploring mother to her terrible father as he frowned down upon them: hearing that a sword had cut off her mother's head: that her young stepmother had been dragged shrieking down the gallery when she tried to reach the King to entreat his mercy – these experiences, it would appear, had built up a resistance that nothing, no passion, no entreaty, no tenderness could conquer. In the fatally vulnerable years she had learned to connect the idea of sexual intercourse with terror and death." Jenkins depicts a woman who enjoyed, with an abnormal avidity, the process of courtship but never allowed the suitor to transform himself from adorer to possessor. The queen's true partnership was with her "dear lover England."

Elizabeth the Great won the author new admirers. The commendations of Rowse were complemented by praises from Richard Church and Margaret Lane. Church wrote in the *Bookman* that the biography was "uncommonly beautiful, both in expression and evocation. . . . She *feels* her way into the Renaissance period, and presents it in all its colourful, savage, fastidious, filthy, exquisite and wholly paradoxical distinction." Margaret Lane, writing in the London *Daily Telegraph,* applauded the book's "integrity of feeling and elegance of expression. . . . The impression of personality is clear and rounded, against a background so terrifying that one is left with a shuddering conviction of the unappeasable ferocity of man." Lane's assessment gets to the heart of the matter. Like Hester Chapman, Jenkins depicts a Tudor world that operates according to the *lex talionis*.

By 1961 *Elizabeth the Great* had reached its seventh impression. The author could well have rested on her laurels. But in that year she published *Elizabeth and Leicester,* a work that has claims to be even more satisfying than its precursor. *Elizabeth and Leicester* is not a comprehensive life of Robert Dudley but a study that illuminates his relations with the queen. The most interesting aspect of the man, in Jenkins's view, is "the hold which he maintained over the affections of Queen Elizabeth." Leicester's trading activities are omitted since they do not relate to the author's theme; "on the same principle I have reduced to a minimum the account of his military operations in the Netherlands." Even so, there is a large field to explore. Writing what is in effect a dual biography brings its own challenges – particularly when the interests of both parties are so various. If the scheme of the book prevents Jenkins from describing at length the military and commercial activities of Leicester, she still does justice to the favorite, courtier, and patron of letters.

The organization is sound. The opening chapter provides a sketch of the troubled association of the Dudleys and the Tudors. We begin to understand the degree to which Leicester was his father's son. The duke of Northumberland nearly succeeded in his plot to foist his daughter-in-law Lady Jane Grey onto the English people as queen regnant and thus gain the crown for the Dudleys. His son Robert made several attempts to marry Queen Elizabeth; one can see these as an expression of the vaulting ambition that characterized Northumberland. Just as John Dudley overcame the calamity that befell his father Edmund (executed by order of Henry VIII), so Robert Dudley overcame the disaster that befell his house when the nine-day reign col-

lapsed. Jenkins shows that Edmund, John, and Robert all possessed "a degree of ruthless self-interest rare even for the times in which they lived." She draws a picture of the enclave within which Robert Dudley grew up: "a self-contained world . . . inside which all the domestic virtues were cherished, while the world outside it was treated as the haunt of a savage beast foraging for its young."

Jenkins applies fairness and common sense to her judgments. She is careful in handling evidence. She is unconvinced of Leicester's complicity in the death of Amy Robsart, and she suggests the death may have been of natural causes. Jenkins's analysis of the sequence of events set out in De Quadra's dispatch of 11 September 1560 shows her usual concern for the sifting of detail. But if she exonerates the queen from the charge of guilty foreknowledge, she observes that Elizabeth was culpable in the sense that she encouraged Leicester in his desertion of a loyal wife.

The book gives a more expansive view of Elizabethan England than *Elizabeth the Great*. The life of the court is set in the context of Elizabethan civilization. Much of the book's appeal derives from the lavishness with which Jenkins depicts the material circumstances of the world inhabited by Leicester and his caste. The account of Leicester House in chapter 21 is of interest in itself; but the main purpose of the chapter is to suggest that "the extraordinary beauty and strangeness of the great houses built in the second half of Elizabeth's reign show that Spenser's fairy vision was much closer to visual experience than would be supposed by the present age; the epitome may be seen in Hardwick Hall in Derbyshire, where the enormous windows are filled with small diamond shaped panes of greenish glass, that outside show a scattered twinkling like dew on the grass and inside bestow a greenish acqueous light." Observation such as this enlivens *Elizabeth and Leicester* and makes the book much more than a routine biography. Jenkins writes well on all aspects of aristocratic life; her evocation of "the spectacle of the tilt yard" is excellent.

Indefatigable courtier though he was, Leicester never lost his taste for literature and learning. Jenkins notes examples of his encouragement of what Arthur Golding called the "painful exercise" of literary composition. It was fitting, Jenkins shows, that Leicester should be appointed chancellor of Oxford University: "he was worthy [of the honor] for his genuine interest in literature." Jenkins persuades us that, however inconstant Leicester may have been in other respects, he remained a staunch friend of the scholars and writers who were, like Golding, enriching the English language "with things not heretofore published in the same."

Jenkins incorporates testimony from the period in the form of extracts from conversations, letters, and dispatches. This gives immediacy to the narration. The letters of the principals are a rich source – here are the words of the chief actors in the drama. The strength of the tie that linked them is repeatedly demonstrated. Jenkins points out that the true and expressive memorial to Leicester is not the "soaring and resplendent monument" erected in the Beauchamp Chapel but the superscription written by Elizabeth on his letter of 29 August 1588: *His last letter*. Ambassadorial dispatches give shrewd and unillusioned comment on the court and its inhabitants.

Another source of information (or misinformation) is *Leicester's Commonwealth* (1584). This "entertaining and libelous work," as Jenkins calls it, is "a mine of contemporary gossip, so vivid and immediate that it conveys the effect of clair-audience." She notes that its influence has been such that "despite the lip-service paid to its unsoundness, statements about Leicester about which this book is the only source continue to be printed as matters of fact without reference to their origin." It is essential, therefore, that a responsible biographer should tackle the issue head-on. Jenkins examines the charges laid at Leicester's door by the anonymous author, while admitting that to assess the reliability of every detail "would require almost more knowledge than could now be available." *Leicester's Commonwealth* inspired Philip Sidney to write an indignant defense of his uncle; the extraordinary feature of the defense is Sidney's attitude to his grandfather Northumberland. Jenkins indicates that here is further testimony to the remarkable cohesiveness of the Dudley clan, the "enclosed family affection and admiration in which Northumberland's children and grandchildren had been reared."

Jenkins's sense of fair play is impressive. She does not disguise Leicester's unappealing Dudleyan traits: the rapacity and expediency that he showed in pursuing his self-interest. But she notes also instances of unforced charitableness. She assembles the evidence and assesses it scrupulously; she maintains our interest throughout this long biography.

Jenkins has also written *Six Criminal Women* (1949) and *Ten Fascinating Women* (1955). The first of these deals, among other subjects, with Alice Perrers, Frances Howard, Countess of Somerset, and Jane Webb. The second presents short studies of such personalities as Sarah, Duchess of Marlborough, Lady Blessington, Mary Fitton, and Elizabeth Tudor. In *Dr. Gully* (1972) she experimented with a blend of fiction and biography.

Jenkins, like Hester Chapman, combines the occupations of biographer and novelist. Chapman is another outstanding recorder of Tudor history. The same virtues are apparent in both writers: lucidity, judgment, and modesty. Both writers assemble material for the exhibition of personality and refrain from imposing interpretative theses. They show a pleasing readiness to let their characters speak for themselves. It is a tribute to the craftsmanship of Jenkins that she impresses, first and foremost, by the abundant vitality of her characters, not by the authorial skill that has been deployed in their presentation.

Jenkins was appointed OBE (Officer of the Order of the British Empire) in 1981 – a gratifying public recognition of her long and distinguished career. Her first historical essay appeared in 1932; she was still tackling historical subjects in the 1970s with *The Mystery of King Arthur* (1975) and *The Princes in the Tower* (1978). She has made a substantial contribution to English biography in this century. She is a popular biographer in the sense that her books have a wide appeal; she displays the virtues – but not, happily, the vices – of scholarly writing.

Elizabeth Longford

(30 August 1906 –)

Elizabeth Haddrell
Graduate Center of the City University of New York

BOOKS: *Points for Parents,* as Elizabeth Pakenham (London: Weidenfeld & Nicolson, 1954; revised edition, London: Universal-Tandem, 1970);

Jameson's Raid, as Pakenham (London: Weidenfeld & Nicolson, 1960);

The Pakenham Party Book, as Pakenham (London: Newnes, 1960);

Victoria R.I., as Countess of Longford (London: Weidenfeld & Nicolson, 1964); published as *Queen Victoria: Born to Succeed* (New York: Harper & Row, 1965); revised edition (London: Pan, 1983);

Wellington: The Years of the Sword (London: Weidenfeld & Nicolson, 1969; New York: Harper & Row, 1970);

Wellington: Pillar of State (London: Weidenfeld & Nicolson, 1973; New York: Harper & Row, 1974);

Piety in Queen Victoria's Reign (London: Dr. Williams's Trust, 1973);

The Royal House of Windsor (London: Weidenfeld & Nicolson, 1974; New York: Knopf, 1974);

Winston Churchill (London: Sidgwick & Jackson, 1974; Chicago: Rand McNally, 1974);

Byron's Greece (London: Weidenfeld & Nicolson, 1975; New York: Harper & Row, 1975);

Byron (London: Weidenfeld & Nicolson, 1976); published as *The Life of Byron* (Boston: Little, Brown, 1976);

A Pilgrimage of Passion: The Life of Wilfrid Scawen Blunt (London: Weidenfeld & Nicolson, 1979; New York: Knopf, 1980);

Images of Chelsea (Richmond-upon-Thames: Saint Helena Press, 1980);

Eminent Victorian Women (London: Weidenfeld & Nicolson, 1981; New York: Knopf, 1981);

The Queen Mother: A Biography (London: Weidenfeld & Nicolson, 1981; Chicago: Academy Chicago, 1986);

Elizabeth Longford

Elizabeth R: A Biography (London: Weidenfeld & Nicolson, 1983); published as *The Queen: The Life of Elizabeth II* (New York: Knopf, 1983);

The Pebbled Shore: The Memoirs of Elizabeth Longford (London: Weidenfeld & Nicolson, 1986; New York: Knopf, 1986).

OTHER: *Catholic Approaches to Modern Dilemmas and Eternal Truths,* edited by Longford as Pakenham (London: Weidenfeld & Nicolson, 1955; New York: Farrar, Straus, 1955);

Juliet M. Soskice, *Chapters From Childhood: Reminiscences of an Artist's Granddaughter,* introduction by Longford (Wilmington: Scholarly Resources, 1972);

Frank Pakenham, Earl of Longford, *Abraham Lincoln,* introduction by Longford (London: Weidenfeld & Nicolson, 1974; New York: Putnam, 1975);

Georgina Battiscombe, *Shaftesbury: The Great Reformer,* introduction by Longford (Boston: Houghton Mifflin, 1975);

Peter Brent, *T. E. Lawrence,* introduction by Longford (New York: Putnam, 1975);

Michael Grant, *Caesar,* introduction by Longford (Chicago: Follet, 1975);

Richard Humble, *Marco Polo,* introduction by Longford (New York: Putnam, 1975);

Louisa: Lady in Waiting, edited by Longford (London: Cape, 1979; New York: Mayflower, 1979);

Susan Raven, *Women of Achievement,* foreword by Longford (New York: Harmony Books, 1981);

Maud: The Illustrated Diary of a Victorian Woman, adapted by Flora Fraser, introduction by Longford (San Francisco: Chronicle, 1985);

"Wilfrid Scawen Blunt," in *The Craft of Literary Biography,* edited by Jeffrey Meyers (New York: Schocken Books, 1985), pp. 55–68;

The Oxford Book of Royal Anecdotes, edited by Longford (Oxford & New York: Oxford University Press, 1989);

Darling Loosy: Letters to Princess Louise, 1856–1939, edited by Longford (London: Weidenfeld & Nicolson, 1991);

Poet's Corner: An Anthology of Prose and Poetry by Those Commemorated at Westminster Abbey, edited by Longford (London: Weidenfeld & Nicolson, 1993).

Longford in 1925 (photograph by Dorothy Wilding)

Although some of her poetic and dramatic works were printed in student publications in the 1920s, the public writing career of Elizabeth Longford did not commence until the 1950s. Involved in the political process throughout her life and best known for her biographies of political figures, most notably the duke of Wellington and Queen Victoria, Longford's biographical subjects also include the poets George Gordon, Lord Byron and Wilfrid Scawen Blunt and offer a unique perspective into the lives of her subjects.

She was born Elizabeth Harman on 30 August 1906 in her family's home at 108 Harley Street in London. Both of Longford's parents, Nathaniel Bishop Harman and Katherine Chamberlain Harman, had qualified as doctors, although only her fa-

ther practiced. In her memoirs *The Pebbled Shore* (1986), Longford describes her mother as a woman endowed with "intelligence, exceptional memory and unsleeping sympathies" whose marriage to her father "suppressed the assertive side of her character." She remembers her father as a brilliant ophthalmic surgeon, inventor, and poet who was "inventive with design as well as ideas," but "not at his best with children." Although both sides of the family were Dissenters (the Chamberlains were Unitarians and the Harmans were Baptists), Longford's mother came from a family in which "culture rather than religion dominated." Furthermore, many members of the Chamberlain family were involved in politics, and Katherine Harman's first cousin Neville Chamberlain was to become the prime minister of England.

Longford's school years were spent first as a day student at the Francis Holland Church of England School for Girls and were "enlivened by the zeppelin raids" on London during World War I. The diary she began at the suggestion of a friend "flourished" during school vacations at the small cottage the family rented at Detling in Kent. The house was called "Lynchfield," and Longford attributed the "happiness of my childhood" to the time

*Longford at a house party with (from left) Alastair Graham
and Evelyn Waugh; John Betjeman, out of frame, is holding
the tennis racket (Collection of Elizabeth Longford)*

spent there engaging in amateur theatrics, bicycle trips, and family picnics.

In 1920 Longford began studies at the Headington School for Girls, a relatively new boarding school outside Oxford, and it was there that both her taste in reading materials and her own writing style began to mature. She won numerous school awards including one for history for which she chose the prize of Lytton Strachey's *Queen Victoria,* a "subtle and entertaining book" that had been published the year before and "was to have a profound effect on my ideas of biography."

Despite her great interest in history, Longford's abiding love was poetry. She filled notebooks with favorite lines and phrases and began to compose her own poems, one of which was printed in a 1925 *Spectator* magazine competition. She determined to study poetry at Oxford, but her university plans were put on hold when the results of her sixth-form English literature examination failed to win her even an interview at the college. Although the next eighteen months saw Longford traveling abroad and attending a round of parties, she eventually returned to her studies with a six-month university course in Grenoble, France, in 1924. This course earned her three separate certificates and served the

secondary purpose of encouraging her to try again for an entrance to Oxford. After intensive private tuition, she was awarded a scholarship in English literature to Lady Margaret Hall, Oxford.

Longford and her close friend Audrey Townsend spent their first year at Oxford surrounded by relatives. Longford's first cousin, Michael Hope, was studying classics at Christ Church, while Audrey's cousin Hugh Gaitskell, the future Labour Party politician, was reading modern greats at New College. Gaitskell introduced Longford to the "circle of Oxford aesthetes," which in those years included Evelyn Waugh and John Betjeman, and to Maurice Bowra, the dean of Wadham College, whose influence encouraged Longford to change her studies to classics from the "less typically feminine" English.

Although Longford's future was to be intrinsically bound with politics, she assiduously avoided all involvement with political organizations while at Oxford. Neither was she to be touched by religion, despite its importance to her mentor Bowra, until many years later. Instead, she spent her university years devoting equal time to social engagements (often with Hugh Gaitskell, or his cousin Arthur), theatrical productions (writing plays and performing for the Oxford University Dramatic Society), and a concentration "on the classics, poetry and my 'aesthete' friends for whom Maurice [Bowra's] rooms in Wadham were the unchallenged focal point." Her diary had been temporarily abandoned, but a record of those years remain in the letters she sent her parents each week. The care with which she dated these letters left her later convinced of "the beginnings of historical aptitude."

The years following Oxford were to be marked by two closely related developments. The first was the entrance of politics into her "closed world," and the second was her relationship with Frank Pakenham, whom Longford had met occasionally during her early Oxford days. Pakenham asked her to volunteer her services for a week and give a young woman private instruction in political science at the Worker's Educational Association (WEA) summer school in 1930. The work she undertook at the WEA school offered Longford a glimpse into a different world. Previously, she had known "the working class well only as domestic servants." The WEA was a "non-political, non-sectarian and non-vocational . . . education body for bringing the finest university learning to those who had left school probably at ten or twelve." Frank Pakenham, although a political conservative, was encouraging Longford's involvement in a venture that was ultimately to be partly responsible for shaping her Labour sympathies. Later that same summer Pakenham brought their friendship to a more personal level by inviting her to visit his family's home in Ireland.

The home, Pakenham Hall, was "presided over" by Frank's older brother, Edward, Earl of Longford, and his wife, Christine. The Pakenham family had settled in Ireland in the seventeenth century, and by the eighteenth century had been given an Irish peerage. The second earl of Longford had been brother-in-law to Wellington, which prompted Longford's interest in the "Iron Duke" as a subject for one of her earliest biographies.

Longford and Pakenham grew closer at this late-summer house party at which Alastair Graham, John Betjeman, and Evelyn Waugh were also in attendance. Upon their return to England Longford and Pakenham continued to lecture for the WEA in the outlying counties, returning to London at the end of each weekend. Longford developed a left-leaning political sensibility that she considered primarily emotional, in contrast to the more serious focus of Pakenham who had been "brought into the political arena" under the wing of Lady Astor, the first woman to enter Parliament.

Although their political leanings were in opposite directions, Longford and Pakenham's affections toward each other were deepening, yet he was uncomfortable with expressing his feelings. Alternatively drawing back and pressing his suit, Pakenham finally put aside his reservations as to whether he would ultimately prove to be a good husband, and the two were married on 3 November 1931.

In the midst of preparations for the wedding, politics continued to be one of the major focuses of Longford and Pakenham's lives. Their wedding date had even been postponed because a general election had been called for the same day. Longford had been asked to stand as a Labour candidate for Parliament, and although she turned this request down, she actively supported the candidacies of Hugh Gaitskell, Even Durbin, and Dick Mitchison. Pakenham, meanwhile, was working for the Conservative Party candidates, although due to his close association with Longford, Winston Churchill was reported to have commented that "I hear that young Pakenham is likely to turn Socialist soon."

The young couple settled into their first home, "Stairways," near Aylesbury in Buckinghamshire, and on 27 August 1932 they had their first child, Antonia. They had thought to name her after the heroine of Willa Cather's *My Antonia,* but the accent over the 'í' was forgotten over time. Shortly after the birth of their second child, Thomas, Pakenham was offered a fellowship in politics at Christ Church College, and the family moved to Oxford.

After World War II Longford began what was to be a two-year commitment to writing weekly articles on family subjects for the *Daily Express,* "an incomparable platform for what [she] regarded as progressive views on the upbringing of children." She credited Anthony Hern, then features editor of the paper, with training her in the art of journalism. Longford's articles constituted the basis for her first book, *Points for Parents* (1954), which was published by George Weidenfeld, who had been Pakenham's friend for many years and for whom Antonia was then working as an editor.

After *Points for Parents* was published, Weidenfeld proposed that Longford edit a collection of essays by influential Catholics on subjects "ranging from Sex to the End of the World." The book, *Catholic Approaches to Modern Dilemma and Eternal Truths* (1955), appeared to less than universal enthusiasm.

When a newspaper strike in 1955 kept further *Express* articles from being published, Longford took a Hellenic cruise with many of her old friends on board as lecturers. These included Bowra, whom the trip had sent back " 'to the old boys and their books' – to the histories of Herodotus and Thucydides." It also served to send Longford back to England with a desire to write history herself.

She decided to write a complete biography about her great-uncle Joseph Chamberlain. Chamberlain's "Nonconformist reforming zeal" and "personal impact on Parliament" seemed at odds with what Longford believed to be the "pushful characteristics that had propelled him . . . into the pitfalls of imperialism." Although she believed that Chamberlain would never have let Hitler push him around as he did Chamberlain's son Neville, she still possessed ambivalent feelings toward him and to settle them started to look more carefully into his life.

Longford began by visiting her older relatives to hear their recollections about Chamberlain, but after five months of interviews and extensive reading she discovered that the official Chamberlain papers would not be available until Birmingham University was able to accept them. Instead of completely abandoning the project, Longford opted to concentrate on one episode in his life "for which there seemed to be abundant original sources." The episode she selected to launch her biographical career became *Jameson's Raid* (1960), which looked at Chamberlain's days as British Colonial Secretary and his possible complicity in "a buccaneering at-

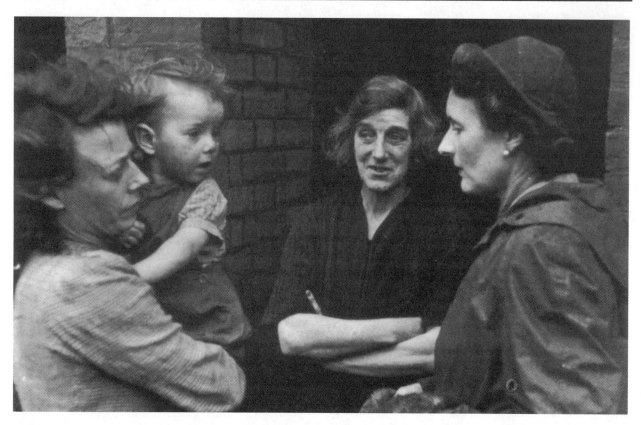

Longford, right, campaigning as a Labour Party candidate in the 1950 General Election (Hulton Deutsch)

tempt by Cecil Rhodes to seize Johannesburg and so the whole of South Africa for the British Empire." Torn between a belief in Chamberlain's lack of intent, yet not fully accepting the "not guilty" verdict that had been handed down by the Committee of Inquiry, Longford investigated the part he played against the "African background of the Raid [which] had started a sinister chain of disasters that led in the end to ... apartheid." Longford's research experience taught her several invaluable lessons for her future biographical endeavors, including how to "look for the cover-up in history."

During the late 1950s, while she was working on *Jameson's Raid,* Longford was also involved in committee work, television and radio panel discussions, and in writing a series of articles for the tabloid publication *News of the World.* She noted that she "often referred to the *News of the World* as the *Observer,* Frank said because [she] was secretly ashamed of writing for the former." When *Jameson's Raid* was published on 29 January 1960, the "generous reviewers more than made up for the cautious purchasers; Alan Taylor chose it as his 'book of the year', and Robert Blake described the 'chapter on the Colonial Secretary's character as the best pen portrait of Chamberlain he knew.' "

After the publication of her first biography, Longford returned to journalism temporarily. She began a series of family articles for the *Sunday Times* for which she not only wrote but commissioned others to write. Two years of this venture came to an end when she placed a piece by the comedian Harry Secombe in the *Times* on the same Sunday that the *Observer* began a similar series with their inaugural article written by Dr. Benjamin Spock. Evidently, "to put up Secombe against Spock ... was an affront to the 'gravitas' of our newspaper," and Longford soon had unexpected time to become immersed in a new enterprise: the life of Queen Victoria.

While *Jameson's Raid* was nearing publication Longford had been searching for another subject. This time, she wanted to write about a woman of the nineteenth century, one who was not bound by the conventions of the Victorian age yet was also not a "suffragette" whom she considered "too extreme for the subtle contrasts [she] envisaged." Her agent, Graham Watson, was the one who finally suggested Queen Victoria herself. Apart from Lytton Strachey's *Queen Victoria* (1921) that she had read as a girl, Longford saw that the popular conception of the queen was of an "abysmally solemn, unqualified Victorian" and she wanted to present the "other Victoria" with neither the "early sentimental adulation which she herself would have been the first to deride nor with the impatience which succeeded it."

To do this, however, necessitated "getting inside the Royal Archives." The archives at Windsor were not available to students, journalists, or indeed to any writer but an author who had written at least one book which won official approval. Longford sent *Jameson's Raid* to her friend Martin Charteris, then the queen's assistant private secretary, and he forwarded it to the relevant committee. The committee found it satisfactory and gave Longford permission to do her research in the archives; this had the secondary effect of blocking any other author from using the Royal Archives to research the same subject.

Since the archives were located in the Round Tower at Windsor Castle, Longford was given the added advantage of being surrounded by the sights and sounds of her subject. Longford noted that to "enter into another human life I have to follow as far as possible in his or her footsteps, look at the houses, gardens, scenery they knew." Closeted away and separated for long periods of time from her family, Longford began to identify with Queen Victoria's "contrary pulls . . . between her family and her public life." Able to draw not only on official state documents but also on Queen Victoria's private journals, which had been copied by hand by her daughter, the princess Beatrice, Longford's portrait showed a fully rounded woman. The queen's troubled youth, passion for her husband, public and private friendships, love of country, and final grasp of politics, which "after Prince Albert's spoon-feeding, had seemed incomprehensible," all combined in a vivid narration of a monarch who refused to be a "mere puppet." When finally published in 1964, *Victoria R.I.* enjoyed popular success and also won the James Tait Black Prize for biography.

In 1961 Pakenham's older brother, Edward, died suddenly, and Pakenham became the seventh Earl of Longford, making Elizabeth a countess. Pakenham had considered renouncing his peerages to support Hugh Gaitskell's candidacy for Labour Prime Minister, but Gaitskell's untimely death in 1963 brought an end to this plan; in her memoir Longford indicated that the names "Frank and Elizabeth Pakenham were never to reappear." Although all her previous works had been released under the name Pakenham, *Victoria R.I.* was the first book Longford published under her new name.

Longford's agent suggested her next biography should be about Mary, Queen of Scots. However, Longford considered Mary to be "outside her period," and when she mentioned the possibility to her eldest daughter Antonia Fraser, then married to Member of Parliament Hugh Fraser, it was clear that Fraser had already claimed Mary as "her" subject. Longford's publisher, Weidenfeld, agreed that Longford should find a different subject and decided that she "*must* do Wellington." This was an interesting prospect from a number of vantage points. Not only had Wellington figured prominently in the research Longford had just undertaken for the Victoria biography but his wife had been "Catherine (Kitty) Pakenham, a shadowy figure, but Frank's great-great-aunt."

The Wellington papers were in the possession of Gerald, Seventh Duke of Wellington, who was himself a historian. When his initial choice for biographer, Philip Magnus, turned down the project, Gerald contacted Longford and released into her hands all the Wellington family papers. Longford worked for two years at Apsley House in Piccadilly and at the family's country seat, Stratfield Saye in Hampshire, studying documents, letters, and journals. She also flew to the Continent to visit the sites of Wellington's famous battles, including the battle of Waterloo.

The Longford family's pursuits by this time had spread far afield. Longford's own political participation at this time was confined to electioneering, but Pakenham was a cabinet minister as Leader of the House of Lords. In 1965 he was also given the Colonial Secretaryship. The children were all grown and leading lives of their own in England and overseas. The years 1968 and 1969 saw six members of the Longford family publishing books, including the first of Longford's own two-volume Wellington biography, *Wellington: The Years of the Sword* (1969), and Antonia's *Mary, Queen of Scots,* for which she won the James Tait Black Prize. In addition, Longford's son Kevin had founded a magazine at Oxford called *Cover,* and her daughter Catherine was working for the *Sunday Telegraph* magazine. The good fortunes of the Longford family were to be abruptly interrupted in August of 1969 when Catherine, returning with friends from a stay in East Anglia, was killed in an automobile accident.

Longford subsequently returned to the life of Wellington and published the second volume of the biography, *Wellington: Pillar of State* in 1973. Both volumes contained far more historical background than had been seen in the earlier Victoria biography and were as much about the age as about the man.

Longford, right, with T.S. Eliot, Valerie Eliot, and Anne-Pauline Hall at the Garden Party, Buckingham Palace, 1957 (Collection of Elizabeth Longford)

Longford found some differences in writing about male and female subjects because the "male characters . . . tend, conveniently for the biographer, to compartmentalize their lives. Women, even public women, are more 'open plan.' " Still, when her next biographies appeared, both on poets, it was less easy to separate their public and personal lives.

Byron (1976) appeared as a volume of the Library of World Biography series. J. H. Plumb, the general editor, states that this series of biographies was created to "explain the greatness of men and women, not only how they managed to secure their niche in the great pantheon of Time, but also why they have continued to fascinate subsequent generations." He goes on to write that as Longford "subtly portrays, there is far more in Byron than the extravagant romantic, far more than Childe Harold on a tragic pilgrimage."

The biography is relatively brief (only 230 pages) yet touches on all the pivotal events in Byron's brief life. In both her treatment of Byron and the later work on Blunt, Longford distinguishes between works of literary criticism and literary biography. She opts against loading either book with quotations from the poetry itself but rather quotes from "the largest possible number of contemporary opinions," yet Claire Tomalin, in her *New Statesman*

review (22 October 1976), notes that Longford's "knowledge and enthusiasm for even [Byron's] minor verse is one of the excellences of her biography." Longford focuses her attentions on Byron's family and his love interests (both of which had met in the person of his half-sister Augusta) and their influence on his romantic vision, which left at least one reviewer with the impression that Longford is "too consciously striving to be racy." The question of "whether Byron was more affected by his ancestry or his [lame foot]," Longford leaves open to debate yet suggests his lameness was perhaps the reason he was so keen to develop his "compensatory talents for boxing, swimming, riding, target shooting and lovemaking," to say nothing of his wish to prove himself as a revolutionary leader of men.

As Mary Wollstonecraft Shelley writes, "no action of Lord Byron's life – scarce a line he has written – but was influenced by his personal defect." Both his writings and his very public private life earned him the reputation of being "mad – bad – and dangerous to know" in the oft-quoted words of Lady Caroline Lamb. Certainly, Byron's wife, Annabella, could not understand her husband's actions, finding no logical reason for his "excesses." Longford recognizes Byron's belief that "poets have an uneasy mind in an uneasy body," as he had written in a letter to Leigh Hunt. "Collins, Chatterton and Cowper mad, Pope crooked, Milton blind. Byron was capable of exalting any humiliation whether of debt or deformity into an excessive horror. Then the troubled waters would clear, if left to themselves. But Annabella knew only how to stir them." Certainly what blame was deserved for Byron's behavior could not be laid at Annabella's doorstep. But Byron's oft-mentioned need to be "managed" and "governed" by a "gentle guide" could not be fulfilled by Annabella, who could only alternate between "her exhortations or her self-abasement."

Longford's biography stresses the "inseparability of [Byron's] life and poetry." Easing into the Byronic hero mold of the "soldier-poet," Byron could only "love . . . romantically and lose . . . tragically" and showed no patience for any "intermediate sensibilities" in love. Even his manner of dying after a final illness brought on by storms in Missolonghi only demonstrates the romantic hero he might have continued to be had he lived. Although Byron's wish was to let his body "not be sent to England," it was, and Longford even includes a peculiar appendix to this biography with A. E. Houldsworth's notes on the "Opening of Lord Byron's Vault" from June 1938.

The influence of the Byronic vision on both his contemporaries and future generations of poets is discussed at length and is continued in Longford's next full-length biography, that of Wilfrid Scawen Blunt. Longford writes that "if it is asked why relatively few writers have concerned themselves biographically with a diarist so much quoted, a poet so much anthologized and a personality so colourful, there can be only one answer: the half-century ban on the material concerning his private life." In 1972 Blunt's "secret diaries," which were at the Fitzwilliam Museum in Cambridge, were opened. Shortly thereafter Professor Michael Jaffe, one of the trustees of the collection, asked Longford if she would write the official biography of Blunt.

Poet, diarist, politician, horse breeder, and amorist, Blunt, whose ambition was "to act my own part of hero in the world, not merely to be the bard of heroes," proved to be a particular challenge for Longford as she wrote *A Pilgrimage of Passion: The Life of Wilfred Scawen Blunt* (1979). He was a "man of genius without being 'great' or indeed known at all to . . . the majority of potential readers," and Frances Taliaferro's review in *Harper's* (April 1980) suggests that Blunt was a "colorful enough person and one whose life touched the lives of other colorful characters — but a figure too frail to support the weight of such a laborious edifice as *A Pilgrimage of Passion*." In any case his manner of living was such that Longford had her only experience with feeling her "empathy oozing away while in the midst of writing a biography." Blunt's secret diaries are a chronicle of Byronic womanizing and contain mentions of no fewer than thirty-eight separate women with whom Blunt made love, most of whom were members of the aristocracy and whose attentions Blunt sought while married. Longford believes the main problem in writing Blunt's story is "to prevent the beauty of Blunt's best poetry, the virility of his prose, and the courage and effectiveness of his political career from being damaged by the monotony of his lusts." It was only Blunt's own recognition that he was "prostituting his poetry to an unworthy mode of life" that allows Longford's sympathy for her subject to return.

Having access to all papers concerning Blunt, Longford had the added bonus of a previous familiarity with his life through her research into the life of Byron. Not only did Blunt pattern much of his poetry on Byron's romanticism but he was also married to Byron's only granddaughter, Annabella. This marriage eventually ended in divorce. In discussing Blunt's wife (more often referred to as

Anne), Longford writes that "the unforgiving spirit of her grandmother Annabella had by no means entered into Anne; no more was her great charm of a Byronic kind. According to her contemporaries she was 'quaint,' 'original,' 'a trump,' 'a brick,' 'a good sort' . . . certainly it required a very good sort indeed to put up with the conditions of her marriage for thirty-six years." Anne was all too aware of Blunt's extramarital liaisons.

Blunt's sexual passions were not his only point of common ground with Anne's grandfather; his political interests were similarly influenced by Byron's desire to battle against tyranny, and Blunt spent years in championing fights for nationalistic freedom, first in Egypt and later in India and Ireland. Although he had been brought into the Catholic Church at a young age, Blunt had developed a fascination with the religions of the East which he retained through most of his life, and he only returned to the Catholic faith in his last year. In the end Longford believes that it was not any of his pursuits but "the strength of his personality that left the greatest impression" on those around him.

After finishing *A Pilgrimage of Passion* Longford returned to historical and political subjects. Much of her later work focused on the royal family, as seen with the publication of *The Royal House of Windsor* (1974), *The Queen Mother: A Biography* (1981), and *Elizabeth R: A Biography* (1983). She also wrote a life of Winston Churchill, published in 1974. Now almost ninety, Longford continues to be active in literary pursuits and in 1993 published *Poet's Corner,* an anthology edited by Longford containing selections from the works of those poets whose remains lie in Westminster Abbey. Toward the end of *The Pebbled Shore,* Longford notes the development in the 1960s of the "need to add to [her] duties as biographer 'the roles of interpreter, mediator between other writers' views, and analyst.' " Benjamin Disraeli once said that reading biography was preferable to reading history because the former was "life without theory." Longford only feared that the "analytic game [might] become . . . too seductive"; she is determined that her biographies will not become theory without life.

References:

Frank Pakenham, *Born to Believe: An Autobiography* (London: Cape, 1953);

Pakenham, *The Grain of Wheat* (London: Collins, 1974).

Michael Meyer

(11 June 1921 –   )

William Over
Saint John's University

BOOKS: *The End of the Corridor* (London: Collins, 1951);

Henrik Ibsen, 3 volumes: volume 1, *The Making of a Dramatist* (London: Hart-Davis, 1967); volume 2, *The Farewell to Poetry* (London: Hart-Davis, 1971); volume 3, *The Top of a Cold Mountain* (London: Hart-Davis, 1971); republished in one volume as *Ibsen: A Biography* (Garden City, N.Y.: Doubleday, 1971);

The Ortolan (London: Hart-Davis, 1967);

Lunatic and Lover (London: Methuen, 1981);

Strindberg (New York: Random House, 1985; London: Secker & Warburg, 1985);

Not Prince Hamlet (London: Secker & Warburg, 1989); published as *Words Through a Window-pane: A Life in Literary and Theatrical London* (New York: Grove Weidenfeld, 1989);

The Odd Women, A Play by Michael Meyer; After the Novel by George Gissing (London: French, 1993).

PLAY PRODUCTIONS: *The Ortolan,* Oxford, Oxford University, 1953;

Rogues and Vagabonds, London, Old Vic, 1975;

He and She, Edinburgh Festival, 1977;

Lunatic and Lover, Edinburgh Fringe, 1978;

Fun and Games, Edinburgh Festival, 1978;

The Odd Women, Manchester, England, Royal Exchange Theatre, 19 November 1992.

TELEVISION PRODUCTIONS: Ibsen and Strindberg programs, *All the World's a Stage,* 1989;

Ibsen program, *Ten Great Writers,* 1989.

RADIO PRODUCTION: *A Meeting in Rome,* BBC 3 Radio, 29 October 1991.

OTHER: *Eight Oxford Poets,* edited by Meyer and Sidney Keyes (London: Routledge & Kegan Paul, 1941);

Michael Meyer (photograph by Jerry Bauer)

The Collected Poems of Sidney Keyes, edited, with memoir and notes, by Meyer (London: Routledge & Kegan Paul, 1945; New York: Holt, 1947);

Keith Foottit and Andrew Tod, *The End of the Day,* edited, with an introduction, by Meyer (London: Routledge, 1948);

Sidney Keyes, *Minos of Crete: Plays and Stories,* edited, with a preface, by Meyer (London: Routledge, 1948);

Frans G. Bengtsson, *The Long Ships,* translated by Meyer (New York: Knopf, 1954);

Henrik Ibsen, *When We Dead Awaken,* translated by Meyer (London: Hart-Davis, 1960);

Ibsen, *When We Dead Awaken and Three Other Plays,* translated by Meyer (Garden City, N.Y.: Anchor, 1960);

Ibsen, *Brand,* translated by Meyer (Garden City, N.Y.: Anchor, 1960);

Ibsen, *The Lady from the Sea,* translated by Meyer (London: Hart-Davis, 1960);

Ibsen, *John Gabriel Borkman,* translated by Meyer (London: Hart-Davis, 1960);

Ibsen, *Little Eyolf,* translated by Meyer (London: Hart-Davis, 1960);

Ibsen, *The Pillars of Society, The Wild Duck, Hedda Gabler, Little Eyolf,* translated by Meyer (Garden City, N.Y.: Anchor, 1961);

Ibsen, *Ghosts,* translated by Meyer (London: Hart-Davis, 1962);

Ibsen, *Peer Gynt,* translated by Meyer (Garden City, N.Y.: Anchor, 1963);

Ibsen, *An Enemy of the People,* translated by Meyer (Garden City, N.Y.: Anchor, 1963);

Ibsen, *The Pretenders,* translated by Meyer (London: Hart-Davis, 1964);

August Strindberg, *The Plays of Strindberg,* 2 volumes, translated, with an introduction, by Meyer (New York: Vintage, 1964, 1976);

Ibsen, *A Doll's House,* translated by Meyer (London: Hart-Davis, 1965);

Ibsen, *Rosmersholm,* translated by Meyer (London: Hart-Davis, 1966);

Hedi Fried, *Fragments of a Life,* translated by Meyer (London: Hale, 1990).

SELECTED PERIODICAL PUBLICATIONS –
UNCOLLECTED: "A Playwright's Crusade," *Maclean's,* 98 (1 September 1985): 6;

"A Long Game of Scrabble: A Memoir of Graham Greene," *Paris Review,* 31 (Fall 1989): 229–250;

"On Translating the Sub-Text," *Christian Science Monitor* (25 January 1990): 13;

"On the Way to Being Famous," *Times Literary Supplement,* 4522 (29 January 1990): 703;

"Ascending the Mountain," *Times Literary Supplement,* 4535 (2 March 1990): 224;

"Signalling a Wide," *Times Literary Supplement,* 4615 (13 September 1991): 18;

"The Horn of Death," *Times Literary Supplement,* 4671 (9 October 1992): 19.

Coming of age in the cultural renaissance of postwar Britain, Michael Meyer became close friends with many of the literary and theatrical figures of the period. Discouraged from playwriting early in his career, his knowledge of Swedish and Norwegian led Meyer into translating, where he produced stage-worthy editions of works by August Strindberg and Henrik Ibsen. His translations of Strindberg earned for Meyer the recognition of being the first Englishman to receive the Gold Medal of the Swedish Academy in 1964 and have been sought after by stage directors and actors. Of equal importance, however, has been Meyer's contribution to biography. His three-volume biography of Ibsen (1967–1971) received wide praise and won the Whitbread Biography Prize in 1971. Finished seven years behind schedule, Meyer's biographical approach involved prodigious background research and extensive translation by the author. His tendency to include rather than exclude letters and other primary sources in the text followed from the biographer's conscious method to, in his own words, "state the facts and comment only sparingly, leaving the reader to draw his or her own conclusions." Meyer's second major biography, *Strindberg* (1985), published after his successfully produced drama about Strindberg, *Lunatic and Lover* (1981), was finished three years behind schedule and won the George Freedley Memorial Award in 1985.

As a biographer Meyer presents his subjects critically and without flattery. Both biographies are characterized by a strong sense of their subjects' personalities within carefully presented historical contexts. Meyer's comprehensive understanding of his subjects' contemporary audiences reveals the connectedness of the individual and his culture.

Born on 11 June 1921, the youngest of three sons of Percy Barrington Meyer, a timber importer, and Nora Benjamin Meyer, Michael Leverson Meyer spent his childhood in London. By his own account he became "self-educated" at Wellington College, Berkshire, from 1935 to 1939, and again at Christ Church, Oxford, from 1939 to 1942 and 1946 to 1947, where his tutor in English was the critic Edmund Blunden. He received his M.A. from Oxford University in 1947. Meyer's undergraduate career was interrupted by his service in World War II as a public relations writer in the Operational Research Section of Bomber Command, 1942–1945. At Oxford in 1940 Meyer became editor of the university literary magazine, *Cherwell,* which, since its founding in 1920, had as editors and contributors many distinguished writers and critics. While editor, Meyer met several of the new generation of

Dust jacket for the American edition of Meyer's biography of the Norwegian poet and playwright

writers entering Oxford in the 1940s. His contributors included the poets Sidney Keyes, Philip Larkin, John Mortimer, and Keith Douglas. Meyer came to feel that "next to [Keyes] I was not poet at all," just as his later friendships with Graham Greene and George Orwell would "cool my ambition to become a novelist." Meyer was contributor and coeditor with Keyes of *Eight Oxford Poets* (1941), an anthology which received critical praise. In 1947 he edited and wrote a memoir for a selection of Keyes's works, *The Collected Poems of Sidney Keyes* (1945), and he later edited a collection of Keyes's plays, stories, and letters, *Minos of Crete* (1948).

Meyer's career took a sharp turn in direction with the acceptance of a lectureship in English literature at the University of Uppsala, Sweden, a position held during 1947 and 1950. During this period he learned Swedish and began his career as a translator. While lecturing at Stockholm University, Meyer attended the Royal Dramatic Theatre, *Dramaten,* then in its golden period, an activity that spurred his interest in the theater and film. Meyer's first translation, date unknown, was an unproduced play by Ingmar Bergman, *Rachel and the Cinema Usher.* While at Uppsala Meyer wrote *The End of the Corridor* (1951), a novel that he later described as "thinly dis-

guised autobiography . . . myself in my worst moments." John Betjeman, however, praised it in the *Daily Telegraph* (13 March 1951) and named it one of his books of the year.

The acceptance of his novel in England and his father's decision to present him with a large financial settlement allowed Meyer to leave teaching and focus completely on writing; "It enabled me to spend twenty-five years translating and writing biographies . . . which I otherwise would not have done." In 1953 Meyer began his twenty-year appointment as chief inspector for *The Good Food Guide,* edited by Raymond Postgate, for which he was required to write nearly a third of the entries on tested restaurants in the style of Postgate's own critical writing. Meyer credited this considerable writing experience for the development of his scholarly style, for Postgate "was the perfect model (and editor) for a young writer, demanding maximum concision and clarity, and severe on any hint of pretentiousness or floridity."

When the theater director Casper Wrede produced Meyer's play *The Ortolan* in 1953 at Oxford University, Meyer began a more direct involvement with the theater. According to Meyer, Wrede "taught me about playwriting and the theatre in general, he taught the difference between translating plays and novels, and he turned me from a dilettante to a professional." Meyer wrote articles for the Swedish newspaper *Svenska Dagbladet* while touring several Asian countries during 1957–1958. In 1958, however, Wrede asked Meyer to begin a series of translations of Ibsen's plays, beginning with *Lady from the Sea* (1888), intended for BBC television production. The following year Meyer was contracted by Doubleday to translate all of Ibsen's plays and write a biography of Ibsen as well. Between 1962 and 1964 Meyer published his translations of all the plays of Strindberg, which have been praised for their tautness of dialogue and their sensitivity to the spoken word. The foreword and introduction to each drama in *The Plays of Strindberg* show Meyer's acute understanding of the theatrical exigencies and stagecraft of these pieces. However, they also reveal a knowledge of Strindberg's readings of Sigmund Freud's predecessors in psychology. Meyer depends heavily upon Strindberg's own observations in his correspondence about the composition of these plays, especially during the so-called "inferno years." Also evident is Meyer's full understanding of the directorial history of each play's performance in and outside Sweden.

Meyer had his one-act plays produced in the West End in London and at the Edinburgh Festival. These included *Rogues and Vagabonds,* produced in 1975; *He and She,* produced in 1977; and *Fun and Games,* produced in 1978. Martin Esslin, as head of BBC radio drama, asked Meyer to write a radio drama for the BBC about Strindberg. This became *Lunatic and Lover,* not published until 1981, runner-up for the best radio documentary drama that year and produced for the stage at the Edinburgh Fringe in 1978. Meyer has been associated with many Royal Shakespeare Company productions of Ibsen's and Strindberg's plays between 1971 and 1989, and from 1989 and 1991 he wrote BBC radio programs and a radio play titled *A Meeting in Rome,* about an imaginary meeting between Ibsen and Strindberg. He has been visiting professor at Dartmouth College (1978), the University of Colorado (1986), Colorado College (1988), Hofstra University (1989), and the University of California, Los Angeles (1991). In 1992 Meyer's play *The Odd Women* was performed at the Royal Exchange Theatre in Manchester, England.

Meyer's earliest attempt at biography, the memoir included in his edition of *The Collected Poems of Sidney Keyes,* was written during wartime at the Royal Air Force Station in High Wycombe, England. It is based on a close reading of his subject's autobiographical poems and various correspondence. A close friend and literary colleague, Keyes died fighting in North Africa the previous year, 1944. Meyer's concluding remarks eulogize a fellow soldier: "The fulfillment of his promise rests with the survivors of his generation." His poetic assessment of Keyes is mainly laudatory, though descriptive: "with his exceptional sensibility to the face of Nature, his detailed knowledge of legend, and his intuitive assessment of the conjuring power of words, he fashioned symbolism into a precision instrument."

The Ibsen biography presented Meyer with certain problems from the beginning. Observing that Ibsen was essentially a loner, Meyer comments, "The main difficulty in writing a life of Ibsen lay in concealing from the reader that, outwardly, nothing much happened to him after he had fathered an illegitimate child at the age of eighteen." Accordingly, Meyer devotes considerable attention to the various cultural environments of his subject, attends to the social and political currents of the time, and carefully plots the development of Ibsen's drama and of its influence throughout the world. However, the publication of the completed *Ibsen: A Biography* in 1971 brought near universal critical praise. Halvdan Koht's esteemed biography of Ibsen, published in 1928 for the Ibsen centenary and translated into English in 1931, was quickly regarded as superseded by Meyer's work. Comparing both biographies, many critics identified the greater emphasis Meyer placed on his subject's personal life, but they also recognized Meyer's special interest in Ibsen's innovative stagecraft and in Ibsen's interactions with contemporary authors. Victor Howes of the *Christian Science Monitor* (19 August 1971) called Meyer's work "leisurely and massive," while Anthony Storr for *Book World* (8 August 1971) regarded it as "clearly the definitive life of Ibsen in our generation." J. A. Avant in the *Library Journal* (15 September 1971) admired Meyer's writing style and comprehensive knowledge of drama but felt that he includes too many sources and facts. Similarly, in *Saturday Review* (14 August 1971) Eva LeGallienne opined that the general reader might find Meyer's frequent quotations "redundant, even tedious." Carla Waal also felt that Meyer could have used more selectivity in his inclusion of material. At least one reviewer, Avant, questioned Meyer's judgment as a drama critic, finding his responses to Ibsen's major plays often banal. In fact, Meyer, using his understanding of Norwegian and Swedish, had undertaken an immense investigation for the biography. He consulted Koht's biography,

Dust jacket for the American edition of Meyer's biography of the Swedish playwright

numerous contemporary newspapers, many earlier treatments such as the Henrik Jaeger biography of 1888, Ibsen's correspondence with Bjørnstjerne Bjørnson and Georg Brandes, memoirs of Ibsen's friends such as Kristofer Janson and John Paulsen, and much more. Meyer's enormous investigative efforts included traveling to several library collections in Norway and Sweden as well as Britain. Equally impressive is the use of his own translations for his subject's letters, speeches, articles, and important passages from Scandinavian scholars.

Meyer attempts to fill significant gaps in earlier Ibsen biographies. The five-year period of Ibsen's directorship of the failed Norwegian Theatre in Christiania, his life in Rome while writing *Brand* (1866) and *Peer Gynt* (1867), and his so-called unproductive years in Dresden are all chronological gaps Meyer strives to fill. In addition, he probes more deeply into the relationship between Ibsen and Suzannah, and between Ibsen and the young women he attracted in old age. Meyer also treats for

the first time the effects of Ibsen's dramatic work on his famous contemporaries Strindberg, Freud, Leo Tolstoy, Anton Chekhov, James Joyce, and others. Finally, Meyer seeks to look more closely at the development of Ibsen's stagecraft and the changing theatrical world he inspired. Above all, Meyer considers Ibsen a writer for the theater rather than for the printed page and writes his biography from that perspective.

Meyer's tendency to quote long passages from primary sources is instanced in his treatment of the early childhood period, which draws heavily upon Ibsen's own written reminiscences. For the early life record, Meyer also relies upon Norwegian scholars of the nineteenth and twentieth centuries, whose letters and testimonies of acquaintances are for the most part translated by the author. Meyer traveled to Grimstad and other cities of Ibsen's youth for firsthand impressions of the physical locale. Chapter 1 details the Ibsen family's financial disgrace and explains the charge of illegitimacy against Ibsen, two negative influences that would haunt the playwright in later decades of his life. The problem of early intellectual influences Meyer approaches with caution, doubting, for instance, Ibsen's knowledge of Søren Kierkegaard and G. W. F. Hegel, which former biographers had assumed. However, he accepts the influence on Ibsen of the Danish poet Johan Ludvig Heiberg. Meyer also includes two early poems of Ibsen in their entirety, "The Miner" (1851) and "The Bird and the Trapper" (1851), as foreshadowings of future literary concerns.

Descriptions of the historic background of nineteenth-century Norway are extensive, including, for instance, even detailed descriptions of the Christiania daily newspapers of the time, which Meyer observes averaged only four pages in length. Beginning with Ibsen's career as stage director of the Bergen Theatre in Norway, Meyer relies upon his own theatrical background for a revealing analysis of the state of the drama, the stage conditions, and performance style of the period. For this, Meyer examines Ibsen's sketches from his promptbooks for notions of how Ibsen attempted a more realistic blocking of actors on the stage.

Meyer's approach in his first biography builds upon a careful combination of astute scholarship and comprehensive detail, but also upon occasional informality, as when commenting on Ibsen's failed love affair with Rikke Holst: "Most of us have loved and lost in our early twenties; it is an essential part of any artist's education; and at least his love had been reciprocated." Characteristically,

Meyer follows this assessment by quoting a lyric poem written by Ibsen while grieving his love loss.

The tendency to include mundane background documentation is also characteristic of Meyer's style. For example, the biography includes in its entirety an elaborate menu of a typical dinner in Alexandria, Egypt, intended to demonstrate Ibsen's luxurious lifestyle during his travels. Meyer further offers samples of Ibsen's club speeches and itemized accounts of his income for certain periods. Although criticized by some reviewers, Meyer's penchant for lengthy quotations in *Ibsen* generally serves him well, as when he devotes six pages of the biography to reproduce revealing passages from Ibsen's travel diary of Egypt, offering as reason that it "is especially interesting for the rare evidence it provides of Ibsen's sharp eye as an observer of landscape." Meyer allows his readers to judge with minimum commentary from the biographer, which is his stated intention. Of Ibsen's travel writing, Meyer observes that Ibsen was capable of writing sharp and sensitive narrative prose; however, "one can only surmise that it bored him, and that . . . he disliked writing in the first person, except under the mask of prose."

Meyer draws a remarkably clear line of chronology for his subject, always aware of gaps that would appear in the documentation. For instance, although the two weeks Ibsen spent in Paris in 1869 were undocumented, Meyer takes care to suggest possible places he might have visited, such as early Impressionist exhibitions and well-known cafés and watering holes. The selection of photographs for the biography is impressive and includes reproductions of a page from Ibsen's promptbook as stage director and the famous portrait of Strindberg that Ibsen kept in his study.

Meyer's treatment of the writing and production histories of *A Doll's House* (1869) include quotations from Ibsen's preliminary notes on the characters, early plot outlines, and themes. Particularly illuminating are selections from the original reviewers, translated by Meyer. For example, Erik Vullum's comment on the absence of images in the play was cogent: "Ibsen no longer needed them. He has so worked out what he wants to portray that he no longer needs to resort to any graphic aid to natural dialogue." Another reviewer of the play's first production, Erik Bogh, noted its extreme simplicity of dramatic structure and economy of language. Meyer deepens the insight by commenting succinctly that the play "achieved the most powerful and moving effect by the highly untraditional

methods of extreme simplicity and economy of language – a kind of literary Cubism."

With the publication of the last volume of the Ibsen biography, Meyer put off for seven years offers to write a biography of Strindberg, feeling that the latter's prolific writing career (seventy-five collected volumes) made the task too formidable. Strindberg's tendency to ignore the difference between truth and reality in his writings further discouraged Meyer, who felt that every biographical detail would need confirmation from other sources. Finally, Meyer disliked certain petty and malicious character traits exhibited by Strindberg over the years and hence felt that he would lose interest in his subject. However, "In the end I felt it was time that someone who recognized both his genius and the qualities in him that inspired affection and love . . . tried to paint him, warts and all."

The long-awaited Strindberg biography met with general critical acceptance in 1985, especially for its wealth of detail and avoidance of irrelevant and trivial material. The sizable documentation; the comprehensive bibliography, which included selected Swedish sources; and the excellent photographic accompaniment were all mentioned by reviewers. A. H. Silverman found that Meyer emphasizes Strindberg the playwright much more than does the Olof Lagercrantz biography, which virtually ignores the dramas. However, Silverman considered Meyer's analyses of the plays "more often judgment than criticism," preferring instead Evert Sprinchorn's *Strindberg as Dramatist* (1982) in that area. Starr E. Smith, reviewing for *Library Journal* (1 September 1988), admired the full biographical presentation and close chronology of events in Meyer's work, but also lauded the biographer's ability to digest the large amount of difficult material. "He makes apt use of primary sources to enlarge his commentary, particularly regarding Strindberg's marriages and children." Smith further remarked on Meyer's cogent analyses and his ability to set forth useful information. Eric Bentley in *The New York Times Book Review* (1 September 1985) offered the most critical praise, calling the book "the most shocking portrait of a major artist . . . since Robert W. Futman's magisterial *Richard Wagner*." However, Bentley joined other reviewers in regarding Meyer's literary and dramatic criticism inadequate. Inga-Stina Ewbank in the *Times Literary Supplement* (25 October 1985) faulted Meyer for an overemphasis on the love and hate duality in the marriages at the cost of other themes in Strindberg's life; she found that Meyer at times tends to ignore the subtle interactions of these other themes in Strindberg's literary works.

In the preface Meyer demonstrates his wide understanding of the Scandinavian scholarship attending Strindberg's life. He explains the especially difficult task he faced separating reality from projection in the primary sources. Observing that his subject made enemies throughout his life and that many of these friends and acquaintances wrote with "the same hatred and malice of which he himself was so often guilty," Meyer nevertheless concludes perceptively that "the evidence of enemies is as important to a biography as that of friends. Love can distort the truth as much as hostility."

The translations Meyer uses in the book are generally his own. He displays the same thorough background research evident in the Ibsen biography, painting once again a broad cultural picture in preference to a more interior, psychological approach toward his subject. Details on the cost of living at Uppsala in the 1870s when Strindberg was a student and the nature of his living accommodations there are balanced by the occasional succinct psychological query, such as the effects of his mother's death upon the young Strindberg: "Did Strindberg exaggerate his love of his mother? Was it perhaps an abstraction and an ideal that haunted him rather than the woman herself and his memories of her?" Such reasonable hypotheses for motivations are sparing but incisive. Meyer often attempts a close integration of dramatic criticism and biographical interpretation, together with a close analysis of his subject's theater audiences. The broad biographical approach allows for a particularly large number of well-chosen observations by Strindberg's colleagues and personal friends, but Strindberg's prodigious autobiographical material helps Meyer as well. Meyer at times generalizes about Strindberg's behavior, but he tends more often to offer instead a wide spectrum of opinion, as he does, for example, when considering the critical reaction to *The Red Room* (1879). But Meyer possesses an ability to summarize events and incorporate them smoothly into the larger narrative.

Meyer handles the anti-Semitism rife in Strindberg's letters and literary works through a developmental approach, explaining with specificity Strindberg's dependence on Jews for publication and play production. The careful attention given Strindberg's maturing voice as a writer includes revealing comparisons with Ibsen and astute comments on Strindberg's lack of focus at the beginning of his writing career. The young Strindberg "wanted to bash around at everything and everyone, and this was perhaps the chief reason why he shrank from the theatre and took so long to develop as a playwright."

The censorship scandal surrounding *Getting Married* (1882) is well documented, as is the background of Strindberg's legendary chauvinism, which according to Meyer had its roots in his first wife, Siri's, success as an actress coupled with Strindberg's initial failure as a playwright. Strindberg's struggle for recognition in Europe is also particularly well documented, with ample quotes and descriptive evaluations. The particularly comprehensive scope of this biography emulates Meyer's biography of Ibsen in the thoroughness of its investigation. His well-researched approach is evident in the wealth of relevant detail offered the reader, such as which people at the office of Strindberg's publisher, Albert Bonnier, could speak foreign languages.

Meyer sustains an insightful comparison between Ibsen and Strindberg, contrasting their brands of liberalism and advanced views. Furthermore, Meyer is generally successful in applying his own theater experience to the analysis of Strindberg's revolutionary stagecraft. Meyer thoroughly researched each play's reception, included casting recommendations for such plays as *Easter* (1898) and *The Dance of Death* (1901), and offers the reader succinct plot summaries.

The publication of *August Strindbergs Brev* (1948–1976) presented Meyer with copious notes for particularly fine background detail, as for instance the comments of two actors in Strindberg's company whom he had accused of sleeping with Siri. Also helpful, however, was the open nature of Strindberg's writing, which presented Meyer with self-disclosing material otherwise undocumented, such as his taking money from his servant Eva's savings book to pay debts. In the well-told account of the breakup with Siri and Strindberg's campaign against her female friends, Meyer shows a talent for building narrative suspense and foreshadowing future reversals.

The publication of Meyer's memoirs, *Not Prince Hamlet,* in 1989, received wide acclamation for its charm, wit, and ribald stories of the famous, but also for offering a discerning glimpse into the postwar British theater and into his own craft as translator of drama. The title of the American edition of Meyer's autobiography, *Words Through a Windowpane,* is a metaphor for the process of translation. A good translator will not draw attention to the translation but will render it invisible, like a clear windowpane. As Meyer notes, the failure to have his drama performed in 1958 propelled him into translation, "to regard myself as a window-pane," and from there into the biographies of Ibsen and Strindberg. The subtitle, *A Life in Literary and Theatrical London,* is somewhat misleading, since Meyer devotes the first three chapters to his childhood and life at Oxford and chapter 7 to his crucial experience in Sweden. Although avowing that he found "it difficult to turn the spotlight on to that self," nevertheless, Meyer's judgment of his own character in the epilogue reveals an exceptional capacity for emotional disclosure. Also, the straightforward account of his family scandals and the assessment of his youthful turmoil in chapter 1 indicate serious efforts at truthful depiction.

Meyer's acquaintances in the British literary and theatrical world span five decades and include many of the major novelists, poets, and playwrights as well as most of the best-known actors and directors. His portrait in his autobiography of Ingmar Bergman and other Scandinavian theater figures is memorable and perceptive. Meyer's sense of humor and probing wit create deeply etched profiles of such major figures as Graham Greene, George Orwell, W. H. Auden, Edith Sitwell, Wyndham Lewis, Terence Rattigan, H. G. Wells, Max Beerbohm, and George Bernard Shaw. Anecdotes handed down by these and other writers extend his inside knowledge to include revealing accounts of Walt Whitman and other nineteenth-century writers. Moreover, the author's longtime friendships with several Oxford poets supplied wonderful portraits of the generation of the 1940s and 1950s. Minor literary figures abound, including such novelists as the enigmatic Mervyn Peake and Elias Canetti, the latter an early discovery of Meyer's. Many personalities range beyond the strictly literary, such as the influential food adviser Postgate, whom Meyer regards as a "father-figure."

Most expansive about his close friendships with Orwell and Greene, Meyer devotes separate chapters to each. The author's account of the publishing history of Orwell's *Animal Farm* (1945) proves especially illuminating, as is Orwell's advice to Meyer on writing fiction. Greene reappears throughout these memoirs, but Meyer focuses more upon the personality than upon the craft of the novelist by presenting gracious and ribald narratives of their times together. Meyer's experience as a dramatist is apparent in his ability to select entertaining and perceptive moments of character revelation for the Greene sections.

Profiles of other major figures are presented briefly but generally with insight and humor, as is Meyer's visit with Shaw at his home in Ayot Saint Lawrence. A glimpse of the older Shaw's everyday manner and relationship with his wife unfolds as Shaw kindly allows the young Meyer to dominate the conversation, a fact that surprises Meyer: "I had expected to find him hard and brilliant, and prepared myself to listen to an entertaining monologue, but he . . . kept asking me questions so as to make conversation ('What do young people today feel about . . . ?'). Perhaps this was a habit of his generation, for later I was to find it in Max Beerbohm, and Beerbohm told me it was characteristic of Oscar Wilde." In addition, Meyer carefully renders those observations of Shaw that have critical and scholarly significance.

In his major biographies and memoir Meyer demonstrates the novelist's gift for the thumbnail sketch of personality, the dramatic setting of mood, and the inclusion of the telling incident. These narrative qualities make his full-length works readable in spite of their heavy use of background material and lengthy quotations. Although his books are solidly researched and rife with descriptive background detail, Meyer nevertheless has an instinct for material essentials that clarify the historical picture. The selection of biographical facts reveals his great skill for discovering significances amid the banalities of historical particularities. Moreover, Meyer possesses the ability to highlight specific events and incorporate them smoothly in the broader narrative.

Meyer's success as a biographer derives from his possession of a rare combination of artistic sensibility and scholarly love of research, qualities that define his writing style. His biographies sustain the reader's interest no matter how wide-ranging and prodigious the presentation of material. Finally, Meyer's practical knowledge of theater production, derived from years of experience as a translator of drama and as a playwright, brings a unique quality of authenticity to his explanations of the professional challenges confronting both Ibsen and Strindberg. Meyer's prose style is rich in metaphor but concise, disciplined, and exact. His personal charm and intelligence are brought forth in his easy command of the language, qualities of personality that make his works popular but also informative.

Reference:
"Michael Meyer," *Drama,* 168 (Spring 1988): 5–8.

Mary C. Moorman

(19 February 1905 – 21 January 1994)

Gillian E. Boughton
St. John's College, University of Durham

BOOKS: *William the Third and the Defence of Holland, 1672–1674,* as Mary Caroline Trevelyan (London & New York: Longmans, Green, 1930);

Anna Maria Philips: A Memoir, by Moorman and W. R. Price (Arbroath, U.K.: Privately printed, 1948?);

William Wordsworth: A Biography, 2 volumes (Oxford: Clarendon Press, 1957, 1965; New York: Oxford University Press, 1957, 1966);

Poets and Historians: A Family Inheritance (Lincoln, U.K.: Tennyson Society, Tennyson Research Centre, 1974);

George Macaulay Trevelyan: A Memoir by His Daughter (London: Hamilton, 1980; New York: Hamish Hamilton in association with David & Charles, 1980).

OTHER: *The Letters of William and Dorothy Wordsworth,* 6 volumes, edited by Ernest de Selincourt, revised by Moorman, Alan G. Hill, and Chester L. Shaver (Oxford: Clarendon Press, 1967–1982);

Journals of Dorothy Wordsworth, edited by Moorman (London & New York: Oxford University Press, 1971);

"Wordsworth at Cockermouth and Allan Bank," in *Writers at Home,* edited by Jonathan Marsden (London: Trefoil Books, 1985), pp. 35–47.

Mary C. Moorman (pastel portrait by Enaid Yones; photograph by Mike Hamand)

Mary C. Moorman's biography of William Wordsworth (1957, 1965) has been a standard life of the Romantic poet since the appearance of the second volume. Although she wrote several other books, edited Dorothy Wordsworth's journal (1971), and made a significant contribution to the editing of William and Dorothy Wordsworth's letters (1967–1982), the biography, which reflects thirty years of research, reflection, and writing, is her greatest achievement and has a scholarly authority matched by few literary biographies in English.

Mary Caroline Trevelyan was born in London on 19 February 1905, the eldest of three children of George Macaulay Trevelyan and Janet Ward Trevelyan; her brothers' names were Theo and Humphry. The family had many literary connections. George Trevelyan was an eminent historian, and both parents were published authors. Their only daughter was named Mary after her maternal grandmother, the novelist Mrs. Humphry Ward, who had been born Mary Augusta Arnold and whose father was poet Matthew Arnold's younger brother; Mrs. Ward's sister Julia was the mother of Julian and Aldous Huxley. Mary Trevelyan's maternal grandfather, T. Humphry Ward, had been an editorial writer and art critic for the *Times* of London and had edited the four-volume anthology *The English Poets* (1880). Mary's middle name came from that of her paternal grandmother, Lady Caroline Trevelyan, the wife of the politician, biographer, and historian Sir George Otto Trevelyan, a nephew of Thomas Babington Macaulay. Her father's wide circle of friends included the philosopher Bertrand Russell and the novelist E. M. Forster, whose conversations with her parents she absorbed.

The Trevelyan family spent the summer months at their Northumberland country seat at Wallington, dividing the rest of their time between their London home in Grosvenor Crescent and their mansion, Welcombe, at Stratford-upon-Avon. They took holidays at the cottage Robin Ghyll, in Langdale in the Lake District, a landscape that was little altered since Wordsworth's time.

Moorman's parents enjoyed reading aloud from the works of William Shakespeare and also from the Bible, though orthodox religion found no place in family life: Mrs. Humphry Ward had written a wedding service that excluded any reference to the divinity of Christ for George and Janet Trevelyan's marriage in Oxford, and none of the conventional rites of Christianity, such as infant baptism, were performed for the children. The parents' love of nature and poetry might have derived its intensity as compensation for this rigorous exclusion of conventional spiritual experience, and they passed on to the children a voracious appetite for poetry of all kinds. Mary and Theo could recite their granduncle Thomas Macaulay's "Horatius" from *Lays of Ancient Rome* (1842) before the age of five; they often did so on trains to confound fellow travelers.

At the age of six Mary Trevelyan recited Wordsworth's "Poor Susan" to her grandaunt Fan, the youngest sister of Matthew Arnold, at the Arnold family home, Fox Howe, Ambleside, in the Lake District. Matthew and Fan Arnold's father, Dr. Thomas Arnold, headmaster of Rugby School, had built the house so that he and his family could spend holidays near his friend Wordsworth, who had designed the chimneys for the house; Fox Howe is within half a mile of Rydal Mount, where Wordsworth lived during the later part of his life. His grandson Gordon Wordsworth, an old friend of the Arnold and Ward families, was studying Wordsworth's manuscripts in a nearby cottage during Trevelyan's childhood, and she got to know him well.

On Easter 1911, while the family was on a seaside holiday at Swanage with the family of George

Moorman, left, as a child with her father, the historian G. M. Trevelyan, and her brother Theo in Langdale, the English Lake District, in 1910 (photograph courtesy of the estate of Mary Moorman)

Trevelyan's brother Charles, Theo died of a ruptured appendix at the age of four and a half. Theo had been Mary's closest companion – Humphry was only two at that time – and his death isolated Mary within the family. Her parents' grief was never assuaged; Janet Trevelyan began to write a book about Theo and remained absorbed in her memories of him for many years.

In London, Mary Trevelyan attended small preparatory schools in Kensington, with extra classes in French and music and attendance at a gymnasium. She was fully aware, from its great contrast with the enthusiastic and informed discussion of history at home, how feeble her school history lessons were. Her literary gifts became apparent when her father went to Italy in 1915, during World War I, to serve with the Red Cross First Ambulance Unit. She, her mother, and Humphry wrote to him as often as possible, enclosing poetry and small presents to be shared with his friends. Mary's letters and poems gained a discriminating and appreciative

Moorman with her husband, John R. H. Moorman, bishop of Ripon, England (photograph courtesy of G. E. Boughton)

audience among the men, and her father praised her writing in his letters to her.

At the time of the first air raids on London, Mrs. Humphry Ward invited her daughter Janet Trevelyan and the children to move to the country near her mansion, Stocks, in Hertfordshire. Mary impressed the lord chamberlain, Lord Sandhurst, with her knowledge of plants and birds in a chance meeting on a walk in her grandmother's woods and maintained a correspondence with the naturalist W. H. Hudson from the age of twelve. George Trevelyan eventually purchased a home, Pen Rose, in the nearby town of Berkhamsted, which had good schools for Mary and Humphry. Mary's writing was published in the Berkhamsted Girls' School magazine.

She was unsure whether she wanted to attend a university, but her father, who was convinced that she would not be happy without the companionship of men and women of equal intellectual ability, persuaded her to enroll in 1923 at Somerville College, Oxford, which Mrs. Humphry Ward had helped to found in the 1880s. By the time she gained an upper second class honors degree in history in the summer of 1926, she had found a subject that was to occupy her in the years immediately after her graduation. Reading the novels of Marjorie Bowen, Trevelyan

and a friend at Somerville College, Nesca Robb, conceived a passionate interest in William III of England. They set themselves to learn Dutch – Trevelyan had a few initial lessons in the language from her aunt Bessie Trevelyan (the wife of her father's elder brother Robert, a classical scholar and minor poet), who was Dutch by birth – and spent the autumn of 1926 in Leiden, examining source documents in the original language, traveling to the places that had proved decisive in William's defense of his country against the invading Louis XIV of France, mapping the course of the old Rhine, and mastering the technical difficulties involved in the Dutch defensive strategy of flooding the polders. Trevelyan returned to Holland on later visits, once with her father, whose methods of historical research and writing greatly influenced her approach in her first book.

William the Third and the Defence of Holland, 1672–1674 (1930) concentrates on two critically significant years in Dutch history but covers, as background, the childhood of William of Orange, later to become William III of England, whose mother was the only daughter of Charles I of England. William saw little of her as she devoted her life to pressing the interests of her brother, Charles II, in Europe after the beheading of their father. William was orphaned while still young, and his education was taken in hand by Dutch statesman Johan de Witt. His childhood and early adulthood were spent in dependence on men of high principles who ruthlessly pursued the interests of the Dutch Republic at the expense of the child's affections and friendships. When Louis XIV invaded the Netherlands, William's dedication to the country and to Protestantism, and his hatred of the arrogant despotism that Louis seemed to him to embody, caused him to set about resisting Louis's armies with great determination; throughout Europe, William alone managed to organize and sustain an effective military resistance. The consequent rise in his popularity and the disillusionment of the Dutch with the earlier regime resulted in the murder of de Witt and his brother Cornelis by a mob.

Trevelyan sets out the background material clearly and depicts William's character vividly. Dutch historians criticized her for absolving him of any responsibility for the de Witt murders; she does not allow him, in fact, to appear in any but a favorable light. This lack of objectivity would be overcome in her work on Wordsworth, though William III and Wordsworth, as she depicts them, share a proud independence of spirit and the capacity to pursue their calling with great integrity and in spite of slender support.

Longmans, Green, which had published her grandfather George Otto Trevelyan's *The Life and Letters of Lord Macaulay* (1876) and *The American Revolution* (1880–1914) and her father's *Garibaldi's Defence of the Roman Republic* (1907) and *History of England* (1926), accepted the book. It had a modest degree of success and received serious responses from Dutch and British historians. In a private letter Sir John Fortescue, historian of the British army, gave her advice on controlling narrative but also noted that she possessed an almost instinctive ability to subordinate minor to major detail. In the letter to the author he wrote: "Let me say, as a fellow student, that I have derived from your book the rare satisfaction that can be given only by a really good piece of work. It is, if I may say so, astonishingly mature. You are mistress of your material and have not allowed it to master you." In another letter the historian F. S. Oliver offered advice: "I want to talk to you a) about your characters b) about your story. I am desirous that you should become a high [underlined three times] priestess of Clio. But you have been very wise . . . in making your first work so hard a piece of collar work. You may be often grateful in years to come to the discipline you have voluntarily submitted to. But I shouldn't like you to be-

come smothered in self-discipline. I want to hear the beating of your wings."

At this time the Trevelyans were living in Cambridge, where George Trevelyan was master of Trinity College. At a singing group that met at the home of the poet Frances Cornford, Mary Trevelyan had met John Richard Humpidge Moorman, who was studying for holy orders in the Church of England. He was the son of a poet and professor of English literature at the University of Leeds. They were married in Trinity College Chapel on 29 September 1930 and began their life together in Moorman's native city of Leeds, where his first curacy was at the Church of Saint Matthew, Holbeck. The marriage required Mary Moorman to adjust to life in a series of Anglican parishes, and it was five years before she began to think seriously about writing again. John's second curacy was in Leighton Buzzard, in Bedfordshire, and after that he became the rector of Fallowfield, in Manchester. By the time Mary Moorman began her research on Wordsworth, a large number of source documents were available in Grasmere, in the Lake District — not impossibly far from the Moormans' home in Manchester — thanks to the work of the Dove Cottage Trust, of which her father had been a trustee as early as 1917.

During World War II the Moormans, who had no children of their own, organized and ran a school for children who had not been evacuated to the countryside to avoid the air raids; she also took on voluntary work as a prison visitor. Toward the end of the war, when her husband became a farmer for a time, she taught history at a Manchester boys' school during the week and joined him in the country on weekends. John Moorman was also a distinguished writer, producing many books on the history of the Church of England, on Saint Francis of Assisi, and on the history of the Franciscan order.

Mary Moorman did not find life in Manchester entirely congenial; intellectually and socially it was redeemed for her in part by the near presence of her grandaunt Anna Maria Philips, her grandmother Caroline Trevelyan's sister, who lived at The Park, Prestwich. After Philips's death in 1946 Moorman and her cousin Robin Price wrote and privately published *Anna Maria Philips: A Memoir* (1948?).

After the war John Moorman became principal of Chichester Theological College in Sussex. There the Moormans met the poet and biographer of John Keats, Robert Gittings, and his wife, Jo Manton. A deep friendship ensued, and Moorman would dedi-

Moorman with Jonathan Wordsworth, left, and a librarian at Cornell University (photograph by Sol Goldberg)

cate the second volume of her Wordsworth biography to them.

The first volume of Moorman's 632-page *William Wordsworth: A Biography,* covering the years 1770 to 1803, was published in February 1957 by the Clarendon Press of Oxford University. Twenty years of intermittent research had gone into the work while the Moormans were living in Manchester and Chichester; they had also kept a vacation home close to the Lake District.

Moorman opens the book with a poetic image of her own: "To share, however imperfectly, in his life, has seemed to me indeed like treading a high mountain range where precipices often block the path entirely, although we find, as he himself said, that someone has planted many of the crevices with flowers. Any poet's life must take us into high and dangerous places. . . . His poetry is itself the chief justification for a biography: it is of the mind and soul of the author of *Lyrical Ballads* and *Poems in Two Volumes* and *The Prelude* and *The Excursion* that his biographer must write and that those who care for him will wish to read." She explains that she is not inter-

ested in overtly psychological, or "psycho-analytical," investigation; her method is historical, and her emotional sensitivity to William and his sister Dorothy Wordsworth and their responses to events is one of a highly tuned sensibility and imaginative sympathy steeped in a climate of late Victorian liberal taste. Moorman later said that the book was "old-fashioned," but this characteristic gives it a unique authority: she is able to interpret Wordsworth for the twentieth century because she understands the literary, intellectual, and moral climate that Wordsworth's poetry helped to create. In evaluating Wordsworth's poetic achievement she identifies, perhaps, more with the sensibility of her father's generation than with that of her own. Nevertheless, the book sets out with impeccable scholarship and argument the facts of the poet's life and develops a sense of his character. She honors her subject without exonerating him from faults and without adulation.

Perhaps the most striking evidence of her historical and poetic imagination is found in her treatment of Wordsworth's childhood, which sets the foundation for his adult character and provides the background to his unique contribution to English Romantic poetry. Her attentiveness to documentary evidence, including letters, journals, and bills, as well as her intimate knowledge of the landscape of the Lake District give her writing authority. Moorman traces Wordsworth's self-sufficiency and hatred of dependence to the circumstances that followed his father's sudden death, when Wordsworth was placed in the care of relations whom he did not like, and to the financial problems created by Sir James Lowther's failure to remunerate his father for years of political activity – a debt that took the Lowther family many years to settle. Her insight into Dorothy's character is also profound, and she makes it apparent that without Dorothy's responsive, subtle, and imaginative understanding, Wordsworth might not have survived as a poet. She ends the volume with Wordsworth and Dorothy in their new home, Dove Cottage, Grasmere, shortly before Wordsworth's marriage.

Moorman's lifelong love of Wordsworth's poetry is disciplined by a detached and detailed scholarly comparison of the variant readings that Wordsworth's habit of revision provides. This approach is of particular value in her discussion of *The Prelude* (1850), which Wordsworth explicitly intended to reflect the growth of his own mind. Moorman shows that he reorganized events, places, and visionary experiences for poetic and aesthetic purposes.

To late-twentieth-century readers, Moorman's account of Wordsworth's love affair with Annette Vallon is too sparse, though she gives a profound sense of the passion of their relationship. Perhaps in reaction to some French accounts, she plays down the significance of Wordsworth's sense of having betrayed Vallon for the interpretation of the extremely dark poetry that appeared after his return to England. For example, Moorman interprets "The Female Vagrant," published in his and Samuel Taylor Coleridge's *Lyrical Ballads* (1798) and one of the first poems to emerge after his period of depression, purely in Godwinian terms: "It is the bitterest, most unsparing indictment of social injustice that he ever wrote; its tragedy is quite unrelieved." The female vagrant in the poem dies; the sailor gives himself up to be "hanged as the only escape from the torments of conscience." A modern analysis of this poem would almost certainly deal with Wordsworth's projection of his own sense of guilt and self-condemnation over his relationship with Vallon.

The book was reviewed in the *Times Literary Supplement* on 15 March 1957. The review praised her critical balance and control of narrative; it also drew attention to gaps in Moorman's handling of Wordsworth's relationship with Vallon yet agrees with her sense that political and philosophical disillusionment also contributed to Wordsworth's depression after his return to England.

It was clear that the first volume of the biography had great merit, but the hardest part of Moorman's work had not yet begun. The later years of Wordsworth's life, popularly supposed to be poetically sterile and politically complacent, had to be explored. She had to sort through and arrange into explicable order what her father had described as "the mass of rubbish with which [Wordsworth] surrounded his throne."

During the 1960s John Moorman, who was then bishop of Ripon, was often in Rome as Anglican observer at the Second Vatican Ecumenical Council. Mary joined him there at intervals, but it was not always possible for her to do so. At these times of enforced separation she completed the second volume of her life of Wordsworth, which established her reputation as a biographer. She was awarded the James Tait Black Memorial Prize for the work in 1965 and honorary degrees from the University of Leeds in 1967 and the University of Durham in 1968. (The latter institution had been the first to offer Wordsworth an honorary degree in 1842.)

Unlike the younger generation of English Romantic poets, including John Keats, Percy Bysshe Shelley, and George Gordon, Lord Byron, Wordsworth had lived a long life; in his later years he became part of the establishment, involving himself in conservative politics that seemed worlds away from his youthful passionate sympathy for the early French Revolution and accepting the laureateship at a time when he had long since ceased to produce memorable poetry. He was popularly regarded as a pompous, self-important, and dull figure, and it is against this background that Moorman's second volume achieved a large measure of rehabilitation for the poet's later years. As the presentation address that accompanied her honorary doctor of letters degree from the University of Leeds says: "Mrs. Moorman was able to show by means of the same sympathy and scholarship which had taken her successfully through the early years that the later ones had also their interest and achievement. She matched the first volume with the second and completed a noble addition to the great treasure of English biography."

Moorman begins the second volume where the first had left off: with William and Dorothy

*Moorman in 1991 at the age of eighty-six (photograph by
G. E. Boughton)*

Wordsworth established at Dove Cottage just before his marriage to Mary Hutchinson. The 631-page volume deals with the death at sea of John Wordsworth, William and Dorothy's favorite brother; Wordworth's marriage to Hutchinson and the births of their children; his estrangement from Samuel Taylor Coleridge; his rise to fame as a poet; his political activities; his increasing melancholy; Dorothy's mental illness; and the deaths of Coleridge, Robert Southey, others of Wordsworth's friends, and three of his children. At the end Moorman writes of Wordsworth's own death with a gentle lyricism that elicited a response in a letter from a fellow biographer, Veronica Wedgwood: "Your last paragraph of all is quite beautiful, just right and had me in floods of tears." The poet Norman Nicholson also wrote her: "I read it slowly – perhaps averaging 20 pages a day – since there was other reading more immediately pressing. Yet I was held by every word. I should have thought it impossible to have made the second half of Wordsworth's life as interesting as the first, yet you have thoroughly succeeded, and indeed – though it is difficult to com-

pare one's reactions at a space of over ten years – I think the second volume may even be the more enjoyable of the two. Certainly it is a triumph of craftsmanship, as you order and select the enormous amount of material you had to hand. And the way you have managed to preserve a continuous line of narrative or thought is just marvellous. . . . Anyway, this is a memorable, enjoyable, rewarding and immensely valuable book – so is the whole work. Thousands of readers must be greatly in your debt."

The *Times Literary Supplement* placed its review of the book on the front page of the 20 January 1966 issue. The review said that in Moorman's account "the essential unity of Wordsworth's life and character reveals itself again and again in those later, less poetically fruitful years. The total effect is not so much of a blaze of genius followed by a prolonged sad decline, but of a satisfying completeness." The review by F. W. Bateson in the *New York Review of Books* for 29 December 1966 said: "Both of Mrs. Moorman's volumes are . . . indispensable, if only as extraordinarily comprehensive and reliable works of reference. Here are more facts about Wordsworth the man – who was also, though the coincidence sometimes strains our credulity, Wordsworth the poet – than have ever been packed before into a biography of him. And, since Wordsworth was the most autobiographical of English poets, facts about his daily life are what we need most of all to respond properly to what Keats, embellishing a phrase of Hazlitt's, called his 'egotistical sublime.' "

After the deaths in 1961 of the Oxford scholar Helen Darbishire and her pupil, Beatrix Hogan, who had been preparing for publication the many letters of William and Dorothy Wordsworth that had come to light since Ernest de Selincourt's edition (1935–1939), Moorman was asked by the Oxford University Press to take over the work. Moorman had already consulted all the extant letters at Dove Cottage while doing the research for her biography; this editorial task, therefore, flowed naturally from her earlier work. It soon became apparent, however, that the material was so extensive that a division of labor would be desirable. Moorman found a collaborator in Alan G. Hill, who took responsibility for the correspondence after 1820. The revision and enlargement of the de Selincourt edition was published in six volumes as *The Letters of William and Dorothy Wordsworth* (1967–1982).

Typical of the reviews of the two volumes that Moorman edited was one by W. J. B. Owen in the *Modern Languages Review* of April 1971: "On the score of new material, this is the most important volume of the revised series yet to be issued. There are 140-odd new letters, including, most importantly, more than forty to Lord Lonsdale and Lord Lowther concerned mainly with the Westmorland election of 1818, and throwing considerable light on this significant if not very pleasing episode in Wordsworth's career in politics. . . . The annotation is fuller than de Selincourt's and generally most useful."

The same rigorous and creative approach is evident in Moorman's edition of the *Journals of Dorothy Wordsworth* for Oxford Paperbacks, which was published in 1971 and was still in print and selling well in the 1990s. The book is faithful to Dorothy's original punctuation and capitalization, so that the modern reader is as close as possible to Dorothy's own expression of her thoughts.

Moorman's *Poets and Historians: A Family Inheritance* (1974), which began as a lecture to the Tennyson Society on 13 April 1973, traces the influence of ancestors on both sides of her family who contributed through their writing to national life:

Macaulay, Dr. Thomas Arnold, and Matthew Arnold. Moorman draws attention to Macaulay's view of the importance for historical research of the study of contemporary documents and topography. She points out that Dr. Arnold, in addition to being headmaster of Rugby School, was also Regius Professor of Modern History at Oxford and drove to Oxford each term to give his periodic lectures. He was also a friend of Wordsworth's. Moorman records Matthew Arnold's response to Wordsworth's poetry: "joy offered to us in nature, and the joy offered to us in the simple primary affections and duties." She concludes with a summary of the life and work of these distinguished forebears: "They all loved with passion and conviction the literary work to which they gave their lives, and believed, with varying degrees of hope, according to their temperaments, that it would be a help to men." Her final book, which is devoted to her father's life and writing, elaborates this theme.

In *George Macaulay Trevelyan: A Memoir by His Daughter* (1980) Moorman barely mentions herself, but her account of her father's calling throws oblique light on her own approach to writing biography. She quotes from a letter George Trevelyan wrote as an undergraduate at Trinity College, Cambridge, to his brother Charles concerning his fellow students of history: "intellectual people are as much pleasure-seekers as the rest of the non-working aristocracy, except that their pleasure is intellectual instead of consisting of betting and drinking." He desires, he goes on, something less self-indulgent: a relationship to past events disciplined not only by scholarly research but by the exercise of creative imagination, so that the result will be communicable and enjoyable to the ordinary reader. As he puts it in the letter: "If one could make alive again for other people some cobwebbed skein of old dead intrigues, and breathe breath and character into dead names and stiff portraits. That is history to me! Even as it was to [Thomas] Carlyle." In the autumn of 1895, when he was nineteen, he said: "I have definitely, and I believe finally, chosen the amelioration and enlightenment of others as the first object, instead of the pursuit of truth as truth." Moorman comments that this assertion seems both overly dogmatic and patronizing, but that it was reflected in his writing and actions for the rest of his life. Moorman, too, chose to write history in such a way as to make it attractive to the nonspecialist; reviews of her Wordsworth biography pointed out that its length might prove daunting to ordinary readers, but that once they had begun it they would stick with it.

As acknowledgments in many books and articles attest, Moorman treated students and writers who came to her in her later years in search of materials relating to Matthew Arnold, Dr. Thomas Arnold, Mrs. Humphry Ward, or her father with great consideration, allowing them free access to manuscripts and photographs. Since 24 September 1960 she had been a trustee of Dove Cottage, the repository of a priceless collection of manuscripts and documents relating to Wordsworth and other poets and writers associated with the English Romantic movement. She was made chairman of the trustees in 1974, resigning when she and her husband moved from Ripon to Durham at the time of his retirement in 1977.

Moorman's memoir of her father was her last full-length book. In 1985 she wrote an engaging essay for the National Trust on two properties associated with Wordsworth, but the piece was not intended to add to her earlier work in any substantial way. Her husband died in 1989; she died at her home in Durham on 21 January 1994.

In her later years Moorman judged her biography of Wordsworth, which she jokingly referred to as "The Good Book," to be "old-fashioned." This characterization is accurate in the sense that the work is literary in style and uninfluenced by academic psychological theories. From the standpoint of common sense and humane insight, however, it is utterly psychologically convincing. Her depiction of a coherent, human character, spanning seventy years of poetic and ordinary life, written and researched over a period of thirty years, remains a major contribution to twentieth-century literary biography. Reviews of more recent works on Wordsworth into the 1990s have almost invariably held up her biography as a standard of comparison. Unless new documents relating to obscure periods in Wordsworth's life come to light, its completeness will remain unchallenged; even new discoveries could not detract from the artistic harmony of the work or from the clarity and the poetic luminosity that give Moorman's work the quality of literature in its own right.

Nigel Nicolson

(19 January 1917 –)

Charles Calder
University of Aberdeen

BOOKS: *The Grenadier Guards in the War of 1939–1945: The Mediterranean Campaigns* (Aldershot, U.K.: Gale & Polden, 1949);

People and Parliament (London: Weidenfeld & Nicolson, 1958; Westport, Conn.: Greenwood Press, 1974);

Lord of the Isles: Lord Leverhulme in the Hebrides (London: Weidenfeld & Nicolson, 1960);

Great Houses of Britain (London: Weidenfeld & Nicolson, 1965; New York: Putnam, 1965);

Great Houses (London: Weidenfeld & Nicolson, 1968); republished as *Great Houses of the Western World* (London & New York: Spring, 1972);

Alex: The Life of Field Marshal Earl Alexander of Tunis (London: Weidenfeld & Nicolson, 1973; New York: Atheneum, 1973);

Portrait of a Marriage (London: Weidenfeld & Nicolson, 1973; New York: Atheneum, 1973; illustrated edition, London: Weidenfeld & Nicolson, 1990);

The Himalayas (Amsterdam: Time-Life Books, 1975);

Mary Curzon (London: Weidenfeld & Nicolson, 1977);

Napoleon, 1812 (London: Weidenfeld & Nicolson, 1985);

Two Roads to Dodge City, by Nigel Nicolson and Adam Nicolson (London: Weidenfeld & Nicolson, 1986; New York: Harper & Row, 1987);

Kent (London: Weidenfeld & Nicolson, 1988; New York: Harmony, 1988);

The World of Jane Austen (London: Weidenfeld & Nicolson, 1991).

OTHER: *The United Nations: A Reply to Its Critics,* edited by Nicolson (London: United Nations Association, 1963);

Sissinghurst Castle: An Illustrated Guide, edited by Nicolson (Bedford: Sidney Press, 1966);

Harold Nicolson: Diaries and Letters, 1930–1962, edited by Nicolson, 3 volumes (London: Collins,

Nigel Nicolson (courtesy of Nigel Nicolson)

1966–1968; New York: Atheneum, 1966–1968);

The Letters of Virginia Woolf, edited by Nicolson and Joanne Trautmann, 6 volumes (London: Hogarth Press, 1975–1980; New York: Harcourt Brace Jovanovich, 1975–1982);

Vita and Harold: The Letters of Vita Sackville-West and Harold Nicolson, 1910–1962, edited by Nicolson (London: Weidenfeld & Nicolson, 1991; New York: Putnam, 1992).

Nigel Nicolson is both biographer and editor. Indeed, *Harold Nicolson: Diaries and Letters, 1930–1962* (1966–1968) shows a felicitous combination of those two skills. In reducing his father's diaries from three million words to approximately 150,000, Nicolson performed a demanding feat of selection and compression. The annotations, connecting passages, and correspondence that he inserted between diary extracts ensure that the narrative flows smoothly and effortlessly and that the reader is given sufficient information to follow events. The story told in *Diaries and Letters* is completed by Nicolson's *Portrait of a Marriage* (1973). Nicolson had used this title phrase in the introduction to volume one of the diaries, but it was not possible to reveal the full "portrait" while Harold Nicolson and Violet Trefusis still lived. The other literary enterprise with which one associates Nicolson is his coediting with Joanne Trautmann of *The Letters of Virginia Woolf,* published in six volumes from 1975 to 1980. The publication of the *The Letters* and the *Diary of Virginia Woolf,* edited by Anne Olivier Bell, provides readers full access to the range of Woolf's writings.

Nigel Nicolson was born on 19 January 1917, the second son of Harold Nicolson and Vita Sackville-West. His elder brother, Benedict (Ben), became a celebrated art historian. His paternal grandfather was the distinguished diplomat Arthur Nicolson, First Lord Carnock. His mother's family, the Sackvilles, had been prominent in English life since the reign of Elizabeth I; had Vita Sackville-West been born a boy, she would have inherited Knole, the family house. The Nicolson ancestry left its mark on both Harold and Nigel. In his diary entry for 9 August 1938 Harold Nicolson reflected that "nothing is so ridiculous as the Sassenach who pretends to be a Highlander. Yet deep in me is a dislike of the English . . . and my joy at knowing that by origin I belong to these solemn proud hills [of Skye] is certainly not anything but deeply sincere."

Nicolson was educated at Eton and Balliol (his father's old college); he graduated with a third class in history in 1938. In 1936 he had received a legacy from his grandmother, Lady Sackville; this allowed him independence. He used part of his inheritance to buy the Shiant Islands in the Outer Hebrides; his father recorded the exhilaration of a visit to the islands in his diary entries for August 1938. During World War II Nicolson served with the Grenadier Guards in Tunisia and Italy. He published his history of the wartime regiment, *The Grenadier Guards in the War of 1939–1945: The Mediterranean Campaigns,* in 1949. He began his connection with the publisher George Weidenfeld when he joined *Contact Magazine* in 1946.

Nicolson, who was, unlike his father, a Conservative, contested the parliamentary seat of North West Leicester in the 1950 general election; he stood again (for Falmouth and Camborne) in the following year. In 1952 he entered the House of Commons as member of Parliament for Bournemouth East and Christchurch. The next year he

married Philippa Tennyson-d'Eyncourt. His criticism of the government's handling of the Suez crisis put an end to his political career. He comments in the *Spectator* (7 November 1992) that "not many people can isolate a single moment which they call central to their lives, but I can. It was at 10 p.m. on 8 November 1956, when I sat silent in the library of the House of Commons while all but seven of my Conservative colleagues filed into the lobby in support of Anthony Eden's handling of the Suez crisis. I knew that my abstention could lead to the loss of my seat, as it did, but nothing that I have ever done gives me greater pleasure now." Nicolson's failure to support the government opened up a dispute with his constituency association, which declined by ninety-one votes to readopt him as candidate at the 1959 general election. "I reflected (but that was some time afterwards) that if I had won by 91 it would have been much worse." It is desirable for a parliamentary rebel to have, in Nicolson's words, "a second profession in reserve." Since 1959 he has concentrated on two professions: publishing and writing. He inherited the family home, Sissinghurst, on his mother's death in 1962.

Harold Nicolson died in 1968. His melancholy last years have been recorded by James Lees-Milne in the final chapter of *Harold Nicolson: A Biography* (1980, 1981). He had never recovered from the death of his wife: "with Vita's departure the light of his life went out." There were financial difficulties; it was impossible to sustain a prewar mode of life in the 1960s on the seven thousand pounds bequeathed by his wife. Retrenchment was necessary, and the Albany flat was given up. Lees-Milne relates that serialization rights to Harold's diaries were sold for three thousand pounds; volume rights brought in five thousand pounds. "He [Nigel] thought it might amuse Harold to prepare them for the press. But the idea did not work out. The references to Vita made his father so sad he could not bear to read them. So Nicolson undertook the editorship of the first volume himself on the understanding that his father should approve the typescript. By the time it was ready Harold was incapable of taking it in. He twice read the typescript without recollecting a single entry."

The diaries reflect the breadth of mind and variety of interests that characterize their author. They provide a picture of "literary, political and social London. . . . But they also form the portrait of a marriage." One day in October 1964 Nicolson and his brother Ben asked their father why he had kept his diary for so many years. He had not written for publication; he had not shown it to anyone else; he

Nicolson, in hat, with his brother, Ben, his father, Harold Nicolson, and his mother, Vita Sackville-West, in 1927

had only rarely consulted it himself. All they could glean from their father was that he thought the diary might some day amuse them. "Six months later, lunching alone with him at Sissinghurst, I repeated my question. He replied that the diary became a habit. 'Like brushing your teeth?' 'Exactly.'"

In 1919, while serving at the Paris Peace Conference, Harold Nicolson had maintained a diary, which he later published under the title *Peacemaking, 1919* (1933). On 1 January 1930 he began anew. At this time Harold Nicolson was forty-three; he had resigned from the Foreign Office and embraced a new profession as a journalist for the *Evening Standard*. He kept up his resumed diary without interruption until 4 October 1964. Nicolson has described his father's routine: "He typed it every morning after breakfast on both sides of loose sheets of quarto paper, slipping one completed page after another into a folder which at the end of the year was filed in a steel cabinet at Sissinghurst. . . . On an average day he would type half a page, on

occasion extending it to two or three pages or reducing it to a few lines. The diary for the year 1938, for example, covers 95 double-sided sheets and contains about 105,000 words."

Nicolson makes the reader's task enjoyable. His father wrote (as he spoke) with ease and elegant precision. The diarist sums up his nature using characteristic imagery. "I am still very promising [he was fifty] and shall continue to be so until the day of my death. . . . I suppose I am too volatile and fluid. But few people can have extracted such happiness from fluidity, and when I look back upon my life, it is as gay as an Alpine meadow patinated with the stars of varied flowers. Would I feel happier if I had stuck to a single crop of lucerne or clover? NO." This passage (21 December 1936) exemplifies the charm and felicity of the diarist's style – or, more properly, it illustrates one aspect of his style; for this writer varies his manner in accordance with the requirements of his matter, so preserving literary decorum.

The material at Nicolson's disposal was of great intrinsic interest; but those millions of words had to be trimmed to manageable proportions; and the whole story had to be made comprehensible through the use of connecting narrative supplied by the editor. Each year is prefaced by a summary of events. In addition, Nicolson intervenes at significant moments (for example, the general elections of 1931 and 1945) to set his father's history in a national context. These interventions are helpful in enabling the reader to follow, in particular, the tangled threads of parliamentary politics in the 1930s. There are other interventions of a more personal and intimate kind. It is rare to find an editor who can amplify the material he is presenting through his own testimony. The entries in the first volume dealing with the purchase and restoration of Sissinghurst Castle are enriched by Nicolson's first-hand evidence. He describes how his parents went about the task of restoring the garden at Sissinghurst. "They had cleared the soil of the accumulated rubbish of centuries and formed the two main courtyards. Now was the time to extend the garden into the cabbage patches and open fields around the house, and in the evenings Harold Nicolson would sit down with squared paper, rulers and india-rubber, and sometimes send his sons out after dark to check a measurement by torchlight. The White Garden . . . was laid out first, then the avenues of poplars to the front entrance and down to the lake, next the lime-avenue with the spring-border and the circular yew-hedges to the present rose-garden, and finally the vista from the tower-steps through the orchard to the moat." The intimacy and knowledge of such recording raises Nicolson's contributions above mere annotation and converts the editor effectively into a collaborator or literary coadjutor.

The full title of the publication indicates that Nicolson has enriched the volumes by incorporating correspondence. His parents, frequently separated by Harold's public duties, bridged the gap by letters. Selections from these letters add considerably to the interest of the diaries. We can glimpse the depth and security of the relationship through reading these extracts. There is occasional turbulence and tempest; but what shines through is the enduring strength of the link that bound these two apparently incompatible spirits together.

The first volume covers the years 1930 to 1939. This is the decade in which Harold Nicolson flirted with Oswald Mosley's neofascist New Party; wrote such books as *Curzon: The Last Phase, 1919–1925* (1934) and *Diplomacy* (1939); produced a large quantity of journalism; and entered Parliament in 1935 as National Labour M.P. for West Leicester. He held the seat until 1945. His knowledge of foreign affairs and his fascination with parliamentary life give his recording of events authority and immediacy. He is especially good at evoking the notable parliamentary occasions of the decade: Stanley Baldwin's speech on the abdication (10 December 1936); Neville Chamberlain's speech of 28 September 1938 announcing his impending visit to Munich to confer with Hitler; and the eruption in the House on 2 September 1939 following the delay in the issue of an ultimatum to Germany. These and other great occasions are captured vividly. But the width of the diarist's interests makes this much more than a political chronicle; the keenly observed sketches of literary and academic life vary the texture and contribute a welcome leavening. A constant characteristic of the writer is his capacity to evoke a sense of place: London, Sissinghurst, the Shiants, the United States – wherever he finds himself. There is special eloquence in the allusions to Oxford (his allegiance to Balliol remained constant); and the diary testifies repeatedly to his love of France, its language, and its civilization.

The richest of the three volumes is the second. Nicolson devotes this to his father's wartime diaries. The result is a memorable record of the strains and triumphs of the period 1939–1945. Raymond Mortimer (an intimate friend) commented in the *Sunday Times* that the diaries are "so enjoyable that one may easily overlook their historical importance. This second volume is by far the most vivid account we have of life in London during the last war. But what gives the book its peculiar fascination is the author's curiosity about human nature. Mr. Nigel Nicolson again proves an exemplary editor." An amusing entry for 18 December 1943 indicates how little appeal the diary held for one contemporary. "Walk in the orchards with James [Pope-Hennessy]. He reads my diary. He finds it unbelievable that a man who in ordinary life is gay and amusing should become so pompous and dull when he comes to write his diary. 'But it's all about politics!' he says in indignation." Nicolson's editorial procedure ensures that pomposity and dullness are largely avoided and that (in spite of the predominance of public affairs) variety is maintained.

As parliamentary secretary to the Ministry of Information from May 1940 to July 1941, Harold Nicolson was able to observe the workings of government from the inside. His background, his training, and his inventiveness qualified him for the post; and he greatly enjoyed working in the ministry under Duff Cooper. He was dismissed by Win-

*Nicolson, center, with his son Adam and his father, Harold
Nicolson, a few days after the death of Vita Sackville-West in
1962 (photograph by Edwin Smith)*

ston Churchill on 18 July 1941, being appointed instead a governor of the British Broadcasting Corporation. His post was given to Ernest Thurtle, a Labour M.P., as part of the distribution of places in the coalition. He remained in the House until he lost his seat in the general election of 1945.

Harold Nicolson laid down the rule that "one should write one's diary for one's great-grandson. . . . The purely private diary becomes too self-centred and morbid. One should have a remote, but not too remote, audience" (28 December 1941). These wartime diaries – in their edited form – speak vividly to this "remote, but not too remote, audience." As Nicolson comments, "He tried to satisfy the curiosity of his great-grandchild by filling the gaps left by contemporary journalism and official records such as *Hansard*. Accounts of private conversations form the major part of the diary. At the same time, he would describe the look and feel, the sound and smell, of London under fire; the precise circumstances in which he came to

hear the most dramatic news; the gestures with which Churchill accompanied his greatest phrases, and how his manner changed when he left the Chamber for the smoking-room." And indeed Churchill is the star of this volume; he dominates the parliamentary scene, and his mastery of the House is superbly recorded. But one gains, too, a sense of the London that lies beyond the clubs and the Palace of Westminster. Moreover, Nicolson's technique of intercutting shows us glimpses of what is happening outside London. Vita's letters to Harold set the occurrences of official and parliamentary London in the larger context of England. A typical extract occurs on page eighty-five. "The young officer [in charge of searchlights] was obviously longing for German planes to choose Sissinghurst or Bettenham to land on. I wasn't so sure that I shared his longing. Nor was Ozzy [Beale, the tenant-farmer of Sissinghurst Castle farm]. 'My wheat. . . . ,' he remarked ruefully." (V S-W to HN, 24 May 1940).

Harold Nicolson's diary-letters to his sons provide another rich source of material regarding his personal and family life. Lees-Milne notes that he wrote "130 joint diary-letters of about 3,000 words each to his two sons. . . . This weekly task was additional to his daily letter to Vita when they were apart during the week, and his diary." They contain, as Lees-Milne observes, a store of information about what their writer was doing and thinking: "they are enchanting letters of a father to his sons. Whatever came into Harold's head was typed out by him, without forethought. And yet it was always interesting." These letters contribute vitally to *Diaries and Letters* and testify to the editor's skill in disposition. When Raymond Mortimer called Nicolson an "exemplary editor" he was not indulging in hyperbole; Nicolson always provides what the reader requires in the way of annotation and linking summary and does it with the minimum of fuss. His assembling of material from diverse sources and his skill in blending these materials harmoniously together are evidence of a creative presence, and his achievement is one that exceeds the ordinary bounds of editing.

The final volume shows Harold Nicolson removed from the center of affairs. He never returned to the House of Commons, though he stood as Labour candidate for North Croydon at a by-election in 1948 (his "North Croydon crucifixion"). He did not receive the peerage he might have expected. Illness and financial worries cloud the later portions of volume three. But the diarist remains as observant a recorder and as felicitous a stylist as ever. We come to the end of the third volume feeling that Harold Nicolson might not have been the most formidable politician of his day; but he must have been one of the most likable and gifted.

The year 1973 was marked for Nicolson by the appearance of two contrasting works: *Portrait of a Marriage* and *Alex: The Life of Field Marshal Earl Alexander of Tunis*. Alexander had agreed that Nicolson should write his biography and had promised cooperation. Following Alexander's death in June 1969, his widow accorded Nicolson every facility he required. The book is based on four categories of sources: Alexander's letters and private documents; the Alexander Papers in the Public Record Office (on military strategy in World War II); published books (including Alexander's dispatches); and taped recollections by friends and colleagues. Nicolson includes verbatim excerpts from these taped reminiscences; this allows him to "vary the pace and style of the narrative, and to preserve unparaphrased the recollections of people who knew

Alexander best at decisive moments of his life." The bulk of the work is devoted to World War II. Nicolson treats the postwar years with a fairly stringent economy; his emphasis is on Alexander's military achievements in Burma, Africa, and Italy.

In the introduction to the first volume of *Diaries and Letters,* Nicolson refers to "a crisis" in the relationship between his parents that had occurred in 1920. In *Portrait of a Marriage* he unravels the circumstances that created the crisis and records the aftermath. He relates the manner in which he discovered, in 1962, an autobiography written by his mother between 23 July and 26 October 1920 (there is a postscript dated 28 March 1921). As her executor, Nicolson examined his mother's personal papers. In the course of this, he found "a locked Gladstone bag . . . [which] contained something – a tiara in its case, for all I knew. Having no key, I cut the leather from around its lock to open it. Inside was a large notebook in a flexible cover, page after page filled by her neat pencilled manuscript. . . . I read it through to the end without stirring from her table. It was an autobiography written when she was aged twenty-eight, a confession, an attempt to purge her mind and heart of a love which had possessed her, a love for another woman, Violet Trefusis."

Nicolson's view was that the confession was not just written to gain emotional release; it "assumed an audience." Vita writes: "I am not writing this for fun, but for several reasons which I will explain: (1) As I started by saying, because I want to tell the 'entire' truth; (2) because I know of no truthful record of such a connection – one that is written, I mean, with no desire to appeal to a vicious taste in any possible readers; and (3) because I hold the conviction that as centuries go on, and the sexes become more nearly merged on account of their increasing resemblances, I hold the conviction that such connections will to a very large extent cease to be regarded as merely unnatural, and will be understood far better, at least in their 'intellectual' if not in their physical aspect" (27 September 1920). She imagines a time when a "spirit of candour" will permit recognition of the psychology "of people like myself" and will lead to openness of discussion. Vita testifies to her own case of dual personality, a personality in which "the feminine and the masculine elements alternately preponderate." She holds nothing back. Indeed, the autobiography is a remarkable work of self-revelation. Virginia Woolf observed, in a letter to Vita, that there was something "reserved, muted" in her writing. Many readers would assent. But in the autobiography she achieves that "central transparency," which in

Manuscript for an installment of Nicolson's weekly column, "Long Life," published in the Spectator *(courtesy of Nigel Nicolson)*

Woolf's opinion sometimes eluded her. There is no muting or reservation in the confession; here is absolute candor.

Portrait of a Marriage is in effect a collaboration between mother and son. Part 1 is by Vita (autobiography: 23 July to 1 August 1920); part 2 by Nicolson; part 3 by Vita (autobiography: 27 September 1920 to 28 March 1921); parts 4 and 5 by Nicolson. The contributions by Nicolson are essential; in parts 2 and 4 he provides a commentary on the autobiography; in part 5 he narrates, in summary form, the course of his parents' relationship up to Vita's death. He shows that their love "survived all further threats to it and made of a non-marriage a marriage which succeeded beyond their dreams." The London *Times* reviewer wrote that *Portrait of a Marriage* supplied "the perfect complement to the *Diaries and Letters*" and that Nicolson had shown an equal degree of "filial love and editorial skill" in his handling of both texts. The *Times Literary Supplement* (30 November 1973) noted the delicate tact and acute perceptions that Nicolson displayed. And it is this combination of delicacy and acuteness that is his distinguishing characteristic as editor and commentator.

Nicolson has always written vividly about Woolf. Part 5 of *Portrait* contains some attractive glimpses of Woolf as he remembered her from his childhood at Long Barn. "To us she was not Virginia who had been mad and could go mad again, nor Virginia Woolf who had uncovered a whole new seam of literary perception. She was Virginia. Virginia who was fun, Virginia who was easy, who asked us questions about school and holidays (gathering copy, though we did not know it), and who floated in and out of our lives like a godmother.... There would come a moment when she would pay no attention to my mother ('Vita, go away! Can't you see I'm talking to Ben and Nigel'), and then she spoke to us about our simple lives, handing back to us as diamonds what we had given her as lumps of coal." In volume one of *Diaries and Letters,* Nicolson recalls the technique practiced by Woolf (" 'What happened this morning?' 'Well, after breakfast ... ' 'No, no, no. Start at the beginning. What woke you up?' 'The sun.' 'What sort of sun?' "); an apparently inconsequential game was in fact a lesson. Particularly memorable were the visits that Woolf paid to Long Barn while writing *Orlando,* "the longest and most charming love letter in literature."

In 1972 Hogarth Press published Quentin Bell's two-volume biography, *Virginia Woolf.* A valuable feature of this work is the detailed chronology that was prepared by Bell's wife, Anne Olivier Bell.

This chronology was of great assistance to Nicolson and Trautmann in their editing of *The Letters.* The edition was undertaken at the invitation of the copyright holders, Quentin Bell and his sister Angelica Garnett. The first volume of *The Letters, The Flight of the Mind,* appeared in 1975; the sixth and final volume, *Leave the Letters Till We're Dead,* in 1980. In 1977 the Hogarth Press began publishing Anne Olivier Bell's edition of *The Diary of Virginia Woolf* as a companion series to *The Letters.* Thus readers have available not only the biography but also the documentary material on which the biography is built. *The Diary* is, in Quentin Bell's phrase, "a major work"; *The Letters* "are of supreme interest because [Woolf] became a writer of genius. The origins of her style and the newness of her vision are all to be found here."

Nicolson and Hogarth Press decided to publish all the letters that were available without abridgment (although a few letters of a purely social character were left out as having no intrinsic interest). This was a bold decision that entailed the printing of approximately four thousand letters. But the arguments in the introduction for full publication were compelling: "Future generations would rightly think that an opportunity had been lost if nothing more than [selections] were published now."

Nicolson and Trautmann retain Woolf's punctuation and spelling and interfere as little as possible with the presentation of what Woolf set down. It was not Woolf's custom to date letters; this was the main problem facing the editors. They supply identifications and explain obscurities; but the task of annotating the letters is much lighter (as one would expect) than that of annotating the diary, which is full of private allusions. Nicolson contributes a substantial introduction to each volume. These prefaces establish a context for the letters, but they are of more than merely practical help. Together, these introductory papers supply a first-rate assessment of Woolf and capture the characteristic qualities that informed her personality and its literary expression. Nicolson presents a woman who "warded off loneliness by maintaining conversations in writing.... Friendship must be fed in absence, and the only food (before the telephone replaced it) was the written word." But he reminds us that Woolf had a second (and equally strong) reason for corresponding so lavishly – to practice writing. "She described people as if they had no substance until their differences from other people had been analysed, and events as if none had really taken place until it had been recorded, and recorded in a manner unmistakably her own, imagining the smile, the frown, of the recipient, rarely repeating a phrase, so grateful for the wealth of the language that she scatters it wilfully, as lavish with words as a pianist is with notes, knowing that it is inexhaustible."

These six volumes, enriched by Nicolson's authoritative introductions, testify to the humor, vivacity, and brilliance of Woolf and contribute to our understanding of the world of Bloomsbury. Each volume has its fascinations: of particular interest is volume three, *A Change of Perspective,* which covers the years 1923 to 1928. As usual, Vanessa Bell occupies a special place – *the* special place. But these years were also marked by the flowering of the love between Virginia and Vita Sackville-West. Nicolson sketched out the course of the affair in part 5 of *Portrait of a Marriage,* and *A Change of Perspective* traces the development of the relationship through the unpremeditated words of one of the lovers. One could not ask for a more helpful guide

than Nicolson, who consistently finds the right mode of unforced intimacy. Like Quentin Bell he possesses easy literary tact and deftness of touch; his commentaries are worthy of the material that inspired them.

Nicolson's former wife, Philippa Tennyson-d'Eyncourt, died in 1987; the marriage had been dissolved in 1970. Nicolson continues to live at Sissinghurst Castle, which is now in the care of the National Trust. He is still publishing and writing; *Two Roads to Dodge City* (1986) was written in collaboration with his son Adam. In recent years Nicolson has written *The World of Jane Austen* (1991) and has returned to his parents' writings, editing *Vita and Harold: The Letters of Vita Sackville-West and Harold Nicolson, 1910–1962* (1991). In his late seventies, Nigel Nicolson remains as accomplished a literary practitioner as ever.

Iris Origo
(15 August 1902 – 28 June 1988)

Marika Brussel
Sarah Lawrence College

BOOKS: *Giani* (N.p., 1933);

Leopardi: A Biography (London: Humphrey Milford, 1935; New York: Oxford University Press, 1935); republished as *Leopardi: A Study in Solitude* (London: Hamish Hamilton, 1953);

Allegra (London: Hogarth Press, 1935);

Tribune of Rome: A Biography of Cola di Rienzo (London: Hogarth Press, 1938);

War in Val d'Orcia: A Diary (London: Cape, 1947); published as *War in Val d'Orcia: 1943–1944: A Diary* (Boston: Godine, 1984);

The Last Attachment: The Story of Byron and Teresa Guiccioli as Told in Their Unpublished Letters and Other Family Papers (London: Cape / John Murray, 1949; New York: Scribners, 1949); republished as *The Story of Byron and Teresa Guiccioli as Told in Their Unpublished Letters & Other Family Papers* (London & Glasgow: Collins, 1962; London: John Murray, 1971);

Giovanni and Jane (London: Cape, 1950);

A Measure of Love (London: Cape, 1957; New York: Pantheon, 1958);

The Merchant of Prato: Francesco di Marco Dantini, 1335–1410 (London: Cape, 1957; New York: Knopf, 1957; revised edition, Harmondsworth: Peregrine Books/Penguin, 1963);

The World of San Bernadino (New York: Harcourt, Brace & World, 1962; London: Cape, 1963);

Images and Shadows: Part of a Life (London: John Murray, 1970; New York: Harcourt Brace Jovanovich, 1971);

A Need to Testify: Portraits of Lauro de Bosis, Ruth Draper, Gaetano Salvemini, Ignazio Silone and an Essay on Biography (London: John Murray, 1983; San Diego: Harcourt Brace Jovanovich, 1984).

OTHER: Rainer Maria Rilke, "Autumn," translated by Origo, *Times Literary Supplement* (6 August 1954): 41;

Iris Origo and her son, Gianni, in 1930

Sunset and Twilight: From the Diaries of 1947–1958 by Bernard Berenson, introduction by Origo (London: Hamish Hamilton, 1964);

Giacomo Leopardi: Selected Prose and Poetry, translated by Origo and John Heath-Stubbs (Oxford: Oxford University Press, 1966; New York: New American Literature, 1966);

The Vagabond Path: An Anthology, edited by Origo (London: Chatto & Windus, 1972; New York: Scribners, 1972).

SELECTED PERIODICAL PUBLICATIONS –
UNCOLLECTED: "The Accademia Etrusca of Cortona," *Times Literary Supplement* (1 December 1950): 776;

"Notes on the Way: Italy, Straws in the Wind,"
  Time & Tide (3 March 1951): 183–184;

"The Homecoming," *New Statesman* (16 February
  1957): 199–200;

"The Death of Professor Salvemini: Impartiality Is
  a Dream and Honesty a Duty," *New Republic*
  (21 October 1957): 8–9;

"The Hospital of the Holy Spirit," *History Today*
  (April 1959): 252–261;

"Biography: True and False," *Atlantic* (Fall 1959):
  37–42;

"The Education of Renaissance Man," *Horizon* (January 1960): 57–68;

"The Long Pilgrimage: One Aspect of Bernard Berenson," *Cornhill* (Spring 1960): 139–155;

"The Insatiable Traveler: Bernard Berenson's
  Quest," *Atlantic* (April 1960): 56–62;

"Eve or Mary? The Tuscan Women of the Fifteenth
  Century, as Seen by San Bernadino of Siena,"
  Cornhill (Winter 1962/1963): 65–84;

"Bernard Berenson: A Summing Up," *Atlantic* (November 1963);

"Portrait of Marguerite," *Cornhill* (Winter 1964/
  1965): 223–240;

"The Pleasures of Bath in the Eighteenth Century,"
  Horizon (Winter 1965): 4–14;

"Marquerite Caetani," *Atlantic* (February 1965): 81–
  88;

"The Pursuit of Happiness in a Villa," *Horizon*
  (Spring 1969): 14–16;

"Letters: Isabelle de Charrière," *Times Literary Supplement* (7 June 1985): 637.

Known mainly for *The Last Attachment: The Story
of Byron and Teresa Guiccioli as Told in Their Unpublished
Letters and Other Family Papers* (1949), Iris Origo was a
biographer who was interested in the subjects of her
writing as individuals, fascinated by the small details
that make up a person's life. *The Last Attachment* casts
new light on the life of George Gordon, Lord Byron,
because of the vast amount of new material that Origo
uncovered and incorporated. Because she was English
but had spent the larger part of her life in Italy, she
brought a cultural familiarity to Byron's years in that
country. Her biographical subjects spanned from the
Italian poet Giacomo Leopardi; to Byron's illegitimate
daughter, Allegra Byron; to Francesco di Marco Dantini, a fourteenth-century merchant. Origo believed
that "it is not necessary that the subject of such Lives
be giants themselves."

Born Iris Margaret Cutting on 15 August 1902
in Birdlip, Gloucestershire, England, near where
her father, William Bayard Cutting, was convalescing from tuberculosis, Origo spent her first years
traveling with her parents as they looked for a cure
for Cutting's illness. He was an American diplomat
from an old New York family. Her mother, Lady
Sybil Marjorie Cuffe Cutting, was of Anglo-Irish descent. Much of Origo's childhood was spent living
at the estates of the two families in Long Island and
Ireland. When her father died in 1910, she and her
mother moved to an estate in Fiesole, Italy. Her father had wished for his daughter to be brought up
either in France or Italy – "somewhere she does not
belong" – so as to escape nationalism, which he felt
"makes people so unhappy."

The next six years were rather solitary for
Origo. In keeping with the privileged lifestyle of
her mother, Origo was brought up with a governess and kept apart from other children. In 1914, at
the age of twelve, she persuaded her mother to
dismiss the much-disliked governess. On the recommendation of Bernard Berenson, who was a
friend to the family, she began a classical education with Professor Solone Monti in his home.
Origo mentions in her autobiography, *Images and
Shadows: Part of a Life* (1970), that the years studying with Monti were some of the happiest of her
life. She learned Latin and Greek by reading the
classics; at night she taught herself the grammar.
Monti instilled in her a love for learning and for
poetry. "Say it in any language you like," he told
her, "only feel the poetry."

In 1917 Monti died, and with him died Origo's
excitement about formal learning. That same year her
mother married Geoffrey Scott, a writer and architect
who had designed their Italian home. Scott was more
importantly known for writing *The Portrait of Zélide*
(1925), a biography of Madame de Charrière, notable
for her friendship with James Boswell. Because of its
narrative style, *The Portrait of Zélide* changed the standard of writing biography; it became a model of the
portrait biography. This was Origo's first glimpse into
the literary world from a writer's point of view, and
she was enthralled. Scott frequently sought her opinions and, later, her advice. As she was later to say,
"While this book was taking shape, I too had a small
share in it – at least to the extent of listening eagerly
to each chapter as it was read aloud and to the discussions about its protagonists." One of the major criticisms of *The Portrait of Zélide* is its lack of factual material; to this, however, Origo brings some insight to the
issue: "Here and there – as in most biographies worth
reading – the biographer's intuition was called upon
to supplement the facts. . . . I had the pleasure of being
with Geoffrey several years later, when, as he was sorting and examining the fabulous treasures . . . in Malahide Castle, he came upon Zélide's letters and discov-

Origo and her father in California in 1904

ered that wherever he had only guessed, he had guessed right."

Throughout Origo's childhood her mother had a great many English visitors, including Berenson, the poet Herbert Trench, Edith Wharton (a good friend of William Bayard Cutting's), and Robert Trevelyan. Most of her childhood was spent in the shadows of her mother's parties, and Origo decided early on that she was not suited for such a lifestyle. "If I stayed on in Italy after I was grownup," she said, "it would only be to marry an Italian. I did not wish . . . to go on belonging to the 'English colony.' " When the family moved to Rome for a short while in 1918, Origo began studying privately with a new teacher, Professor Nicola Festa. Unfortunately, she found him uninterested in her studies and too scholarly for her taste. The experience increased her disdain for formal learning.

Between the ages of ten and seventeen Origo was beginning to discover an interest in writing: she wrote some fictional romances; attempted poetry; and translated Sappho, Leopardi, and Giovanni Pascoli. She also wrote a short biography of the Medici children, not surprising subjects considering that Origo was living near their estate. All of these attempts showed assiduousness and, she later thought, not much talent. Despite this judgment,

Origo was showing her first interest in what would become her craft.

In 1920, instead of being allowed to pursue her studies at Oxford as she wished, Origo began a period of "coming out." She was introduced to society in Italy, England, and the United States. During the year of her debut she met the Marchese Antonio Origo, who would become her husband. Two years later they met again in Florence where he was taking care of his dying father. When her mother saw their seriousness she insisted upon a six-month separation. Afterward they reunited, and within a short period of time Antonio Origo went to England to meet her maternal grandparents. He joined her at Westbrook (her paternal grandparents' home on Long Island), where they announced their engagement. Before their marriage on 4 March 1924, Origo and her future husband bought a run-down estate (La Foce) in southern Tuscany.

The first nine years of their marriage were, for the most part, devoted to learning about farming and enjoying the marriage itself. When the Origos first moved to La Foce, 80 percent of the population was illiterate. When they realized this, the Origos immediately organized classes for adults. The local government soon built three new schools, one at La Foce. The Origos themselves built three nursery schools, one also at La Foce. Later, during World War II, they turned the school into a home for orphaned and abandoned children. It was not until 1933, when their eldest child, Gianni, died of a childhood disease at the age of seven, that Origo began to write. Origo and her husband had two other children, Benedetta and Donata. Her first book was written as a private record of Gianni's life; there were only a few copies privately published for their close friends and family.

Origo's second book was *Leopardi: A Biography* (1935), which depicts the life of the fourteenth-century poet Giacomo Leopardi. She chose to write biography because she knew she "had neither the creative imagination nor the sharp ear for dialogue that produces good novels." Although she did not have a formal historian's background, she had always preferred the reading of memoirs and journals. Foremost at her disposal was an intense interest in other people. The "small change of daily life" was something she lacked, having had little contact with people on a daily basis while she was growing up, and this may have fueled her interest in biography as an art form.

Largely due to the influence of biographers Geoffrey Scott and Lytton Strachey and his "insistence on brevity, on careful selection of colourful details, on emancipation from reverence," the perspective on writing biography had been changing. Leopardi seemed the perfect subject for the times: "young, deformed, lonely, ambitious and embittered." Origo must have found some parallels with his life; he, like Origo, had belonged to a closed society; both were of a social class that was, by its nature, alienating – particularly for children. Growing up, they had both led sheltered, privileged lives. Origo's aptitude for research led her to Recanti, Leopardi's home. She felt it was vital to see the home of the person she would be describing. She began to understand what Leopardi's studies were like only after having spent time in his workroom. Origo visited Recanti in different seasons so as to understand his life more fully. "And even after seeing all this," she wrote in her autobiography, "and letting it sink into me, did I feel that I could even begin to write. For such journeys are more than a sentimental pilgrimage: they are more akin to the need felt by a man whose sight is dim, to pass his hands over a face."

Origo felt that even with research it was not possible to know a subject truly unless one was also familiar with the world in which the subject lived. "A lack of this kind of familiarity may produce unexpected pitfalls," she states in "Biography: True and False" (1959). She goes on to describe a translation problem in a Leopardi poem. A sentence in which a bundle of grass was described was apparently translated. The manner in which it was translated alluded to images of green hay fields. But that was not the reality of Leopardi's landscape: Recanti is not green; there are only "steep dun-coloured hills on which olive trees grow, with wheat beneath them and perhaps a few vines. . . . A single misleading sentence – written not because the translator did not know Italian, but because he did not know Leopardi's birthplace – conjured up a non-existent world." The biography was successful, in part, because of the fact that Leopardi was indeed an ideal subject for the times – when biographical studies were being redefined and broadened.

Origo was experimental in her use of the epistolary method in many of her biographies, beginning with *Leopardi*. She believed that this book did well because of the numerous quotations from Leopardi's own journals and letters. She leaned toward the use of such literature because she strongly felt that "the biographer's real business . . . is simply this: to bring the dead back to life," and that it would further her purpose if she were to put the text in the words of the subject as much as possible. One critic for the *Times Literary Supplement* (20 June 1935) said, "Her comments . . . are always wise and illuminating. She brings a wide culture and sound judgement to her task and is obviously well read in the literature that has gathered round the past." Basil de Selincourt, writing for the *Observer* (9 June 1935), called *Leopardi* "an achievement: a wholly delightful achievement." With the exception of an essay by James Thomson and an introduction to a translation of his work by G. L. Bickersteth, no study of Leopardi existed in English prior to Origo's biography.

After *Leopardi* Origo decided to write a book focusing on the children of some nineteenth-century writers. It was perhaps because of the recent death of her young son that Origo was drawn to such material. The first part was to be about the children of Leigh Hunt. Working on Leopardi's biography might have also reminded Origo of her own isolated childhood among famous writers and brought about a desire to explore the childhoods of children in similar circumstances. Although that book was never written, it brought about the writing of *Allegra* (1935), a biography of Allegra Byron, Lord Byron's illegitimate daughter. Though Origo preferred to have her characters "speak for themselves" as much as possible, this was difficult since Allegra had died at the age of five. Origo pieced her story together from letters of Byron, Claire Clairmont (Allegra's mother), Percy Bysshe Shelley, and Mary Shelley. She used Percy Bysshe Shelley's diary for much of the material as well. Because the book attempts to take the point of view of the child, and because the child's story is tragic, the views she gives of the adults (with the exception of Shelley) are not particularly flattering: "Shelley stands out from among all those who influenced the course of Allegra's little life as the most disinterested and most devoted and wise friend she had. Byron's vanity and egotism; Claire's passionate possessiveness, prejudice and jealousy; and Mary's care, perhaps natural to protect the security of her own little family – all these conflicting emotions alloyed any love she received from elsewhere."

Allegra differs from *Leopardi,* and from most of Origo's other biographies, in that the form is narrative, whereas the others are more epistolary in style. Origo pieces together the events that led to Allegra's untimely death and creates a story. Origo looks at the situation through Allegra's eyes: "Was Papa [Byron] glad to see her? It is hard to tell." It is the first of two biographies by Origo that takes a definite stance toward the subject and those surrounding her. It would seem that when the subject was close to Origo, she had no choice but to write subjectively. In the case of Allegra, the child bears resemblance to Origo's own son: mainly, early death due to disease. The subjectivity does not detract from the validity of the material or the authority with which the author writes.

Between 1933 and 1938 Origo traveled back and forth to England. She met supporters of the pacifist movement who seem to have influenced her social activism during World War II. It was during this period, in June 1935, that Origo met Leonard and Virginia Woolf at a party given by Lord David Cecil. Virginia Woolf took an immediate liking to her; indeed, in a letter to her sister, Vanessa Bell, Woolf wrote, "I've fallen in love with a charming Marchesa Origo. . . . But then Leo Myers is in love with her . . . so what chance have I?" Myers, a novelist, subsequently dedicated *The Root and the Flower* (1947), his major novel, "To Iris."

Origo was strongly influenced by Virginia Woolf; her ideas about biography were heightened and somewhat transformed by Woolf's opinions on the subject. She relates, both in her autobiography and in an essay about biography, an incident that occurred with Woolf when Origo brought her a manuscript. "Now tell me," Origo was asked, "what does it *feel* like to wake up in the morning on a Tuscan farm?" From this question Origo realized

that it "was only by discovering what life 'felt like,' to our subject – at least in fleeting moments – that we can become aware of him as a *person* at all." It was this idea, then, that Origo ascribed to – a more classical idea of the biography, rather than a medieval one: biography "with the admission that heros too, might be shown as naked and fallible." Origo and Woolf kept up a social and working relationship for many years.

Allegra was published by the Woolfs' Hogarth Press in 1935. During this time Origo was keeping a detailed diary of her experiences in World War II which was later published, in part, as *War in Val d'Orcia: A Diary* (1947). During the mid 1930s she worked with the Italian Red Cross and later with the American Red Cross. In 1938 Hogarth Press published *Tribune of Rome: A Biography of Cola di Rienzo.* During the latter part of World War II Origo began an effort that would realize her early interest in humanitarianism. When the war moved into her town in Italy, Val d'Orcia, Origo and her husband set up a shelter for refugee children. They converted one of the schools on La Foce into a home, the other into hospital facilities. Origo became very involved with the lives of the people she helped. Even after the war ended she kept in contact with the refugees. In her autobiography Origo discusses ten children, their histories as well as what happened to them following her time with them. The Origos also opened their home to Italian partisans and Allied prisoners of war. During this time much of La Foce was destroyed, but as soon as it was possible the Origos began rebuilding it and continued their work with homeless children.

In 1949 Origo published her biography of Lord Byron's years in Italy, *The Last Attachment.* The biography focuses primarily on Byron's tumultuous relationship with the married Teresa Guiccioli. Origo brought her own culturally diverse background and familiarity with Italy into the subject's biography. The reader is shown, as Clive Bell remarked in a review, "not a new Byron, but the old Byron from a new angle. We see the poet through Italian eyes" (*The Spectator,* 16 September 1949). Origo's angle is, however, more complex than that. It is precisely because Origo was brought up English in the Italian culture, and because she chose Italy as her home, that her slant on Byron is so unique.

Origo's research for Byron's biography began more than ten years earlier when she was compiling information for *Allegra.* She was the first author allowed access to Teresa Guiccioli's cache of letters, which was owned by Count Carlo Gamba, Guiccioli's nephew and heir. "My fear of meeting

Origo in her library in Rome

with a refusal was not unfounded," states Origo, "since Count Gamba . . . had already refused access to several people, including André Maurois." Although Origo was not entirely certain why it was she who was allowed to use the material, she suspected that it was because "his niece knew me, and he did not think that I looked too foreign or unreliable." Thus she began the painstaking process of sorting and editing the letters and journals. While originally looking through this material for information about Allegra Byron, Origo discovered information about Lord Byron himself, from which he began to appear to her in a new light.

In the introduction to the biography Origo says that "it is the papers themselves – the scribbled, passionate love-letters . . . the gossip of observant contemporaries – that must tell the story." Origo's philosophy of writing biography was stern: "Three insidious temptations assail a biographer: to suppress, to invent, and to sit in judgement." She was also adamant that the writer's voice not interfere with the subject's. Interwoven among the correspondence is Origo's own text, based on the information she found after reading the letters. Through

the careful choice of letters emerges an unbiased account of the story of Byron and Guiccioli – a complicated affair that lasted for five years.

Byron's letters trace his initial infatuation with Guiccioli in 1819 (when she was a newly married woman), through her separation from her husband (to whom she returned only after Byron's death), up until 1824, when in his last published letter to her, Byron writes in English to her for the first time. Guiccioli's letters are less abundant in the text than his (perhaps because they were difficult to unearth), but her notebooks are frequently quoted. Not all of the biography shows the pair in an attractive light. "It is not . . . a wholly pleasant story," Origo writes, "and it is one which is difficult to tell impartially. There is a temptation to take sides." It is interesting that Origo should find the latter sentiment to be true, for it is nearly impossible for the reader to discern which side it is that she is tempted to take. We are shown different aspects of Byron and Guiccioli: Byron the lover and tormentor; Guiccioli as caring and loving at times and at others as a spoiled, demanding, and selfish woman. Among Guiccioli's notebooks are various scattered notes.

One undated letter from Byron was found in three pieces. "Teresa appears first to have destroyed another page of the letter; then she cut several passages out of this page; and finally she put the remaining fragments into a folder titled: 'unjust letters – to be destroyed!'" Yet we also see Guiccioli caring for Byron's daughter Allegra, which would seem to go against the nature of the spoiled woman whom we met earlier; we also see her so obviously deeply infatuated with Byron that it becomes difficult to label her one way or the other. It is a similar case with Byron: from the information Origo gives us, which shows him in different dimensions of his character – besotted by Guiccioli, frustrated by an unfamiliar culture and customs, and finally fed up with the situation entirely – it becomes impossible to judge him as well.

Clive Bell called the biography "fascinating" and said, "I use the much abused word deliberately. Byron 'fans' will tumble over each other to buy or borrow it; and the common reader – anyone, that is, who cares for a first rate biography with a dash of mystery – may be well advised to follow suit." He continued in the same admiring tone about Origo herself. "She is not in the least sentimental; indeed, one surmises she is more of an intellectual than she cares to admit" (*The Spectator,* 16 September 1949). A critic for the *New York Herald Tribune* (6 November 1949) said that *The Last Attachment* was "no 'fictionalized' biography," and also remarked that it shed new light on Byron's life.

Perhaps because of the wealth of information afforded to her, Origo's involvement with Byron (via his daughter and friends) did not end with *The Last Attachment.* In 1957 *A Measure of Love* was published; it is comprised of five short biographies, including a reprint of *Allegra.* In all of the biographical essays Origo stays true to her subjects, who can be seen anew with each rereading. In "The Lady in the Gondola: Countess Marina Benzon" the reader is shown different aspects of a woman who was a peripheral character in both *The Last Attachment* and *Allegra.* In her own short biography she becomes more than a caretaker, benefactor, and patron. Here she is portrayed as the primary subject, as well as a woman who was involved with Byron. "He [Byron] was perhaps first attracted to her by the morbid fascination that any rumour of incest held for him, for Venetian gossip had it that Marina's half-brother . . . was also the father of her son Vittore." Looking at another of the essays, "The Carlyles and the Ashburtons," it becomes clear that Origo's interest does indeed lie within the confines of daily life. She writes of incidents at parties: what the relation-

ships of people were and how they were enacted, what they ate, or what they wore – in short, the small details that add up to a life.

During the 1950s Origo's publications consisted mainly of periodical articles. She was also reworking the Leopardi biography because she had found that with time she had learned more about his life and about Italy in general. Origo's interest in a subject often did not end with the publication of a book. In 1966 she translated a book of Leopardi's prose and poetry into English, which indicates the particular dedication she had to her subjects. In the mid 1950s, while researching an article about the importation of slaves into Florence after the Black Death in 1348 ("The Domestic Enemy: The Eastern Slaves in Tuscany in The Fourteenth and Fifteenth Centuries"), Origo found the deed to the sale of a ten-year-old girl to a merchant. The merchant was Francesco di Marco Dantini, and he became the subject of her next book, *The Merchant of Prato* (1957). She found the deed intriguing because the merchant's demands were so specific: "young and rustic, between eight and ten years old, of good health and temper, so that I may bring her up in my own way." Origo was curious to find what sort of a person this man could be. Her initial research led her further into the work. Among Dantini's papers she found almost 126,000 letters. Most of the letters were between the merchant and his wife, documenting their daily activities. Origo had the letters transcribed and found that they included what interested her most: those small details about daily occurrences. His wife often described her days to her husband: when she went to the market, what she bought, the prices and quality of such. From these letters Origo could piece together their lives. Tracing the information took up a vast amount of time. "Her books were enormous," said Origo's secretary in an article by Wallis Wilde-Menozzi. "Many took years. There were so many facts to check. . . . But she wanted to do everything herself. Dantini's notes, they were all transcribed and spread out everywhere."

What interested Origo about Dantini, and all her subjects, was not what they did, but the humanity of the subjects themselves. Her emphasis on the individual was part of the shifting focus in biography. "Through the individual peephole of the man whose life we are describing," Origo wrote, "we can see history in the course of being lived." *The Merchant of Prato* was not written because Origo was especially drawn to merchants, or to Dantini himself, "but largely to the accident of stumbling upon some irresistibly good material," all those letters that she had had transcribed. Although this biography is of interest mainly to scholars, it is one of the few books of Origo's that is still in print.

Origo's *The World of San Bernadino,* a biography of a thirteenth-century preacher, was published in 1962. Again, for this biography Origo relied on the subject's own words to tell the story. "For any Life of San Bernadino must be in his own words," she writes in the preface, "his Latin sermons, as he set them down for his own use and for that of his friars, but above all, his sermons in the vulgar." Although the words, for the most part, were his, the focus of the book is Origo's. "His interest was in men's hearts, and it was these that he sought to move . . . he considered every facet of human life to have some interest or importance." That said, it is not hard to see what drew Origo to San Bernadino, their interests being the same: simple humanity.

Origo's "partial" autobiography, *Images and Shadows,* was published in 1970. It is structured in an intriguing manner, one that seems indicative of her life. The subject of writing is contained in a single chapter. According to Wilde-Menozzi in the *Southwest Review* (Autumn 1990), "Writing did not contain the whole of her identity. It was central, obsessive, but never a matter of life and death." Origo was a private person, choosing to focus on a few close relationships with friends, and with her family. In the mid 1970s Origo's husband, Antonio, suffered a stroke which left him incapable of living his normal active life. Origo focused her attention on her husband, which prevented her from writing until his death in 1976.

Origo continued to write into her eighties. In 1983 *A Need to Testify,* her last biography, was published. This work is a portrait of four people whom Origo knew: Lauro de Bosis, Ruth Draper, Gaetano Salvemini, and Ignazio Silone, all of whom had been resisters of fascism during World War II. It seems that when Origo wrote of people she knew personally (including herself in *Images and Shadows*), her style changed. Letters and journals are used to a lesser degree, and narrative style pervades. Clearly

this is because Origo had less need to rely on these sources for information; she also, to a certain extent, disregarded her previous concern with objectivity. The subtitle of the section on Ignazio Silone, "A Study in Integrity," clearly shows Origo's personal opinion of her subject. However, this subjectivity does not take away from Origo's continued focus. She does not suddenly begin to discuss banalities or trivialities; her interest in how people form their lives around what they care about is still very much evident, even when she is closer to the biographical subject.

Origo's emphasis on the individual was an aspect of her own character, and it added a compassionate perspective to her writing and to the art of biography. Her significant contribution to the war resistance in Italy during the 1940s was further proof of her dedication to humanity. She believed "in the light and warmth of human affection, and in the disinterested acts of kindness and compassion of complete strangers." This belief comes through in her work; she focuses on what makes people, no matter what their professions, human beings. She developed a particular sensitivity to a continuity in the lives of all human beings: repetitions of action, continuity of emotion. Origo died in Rome on 28 June 1988.

Bibliography:

Cathe Giffuni, "Iris Origo: A Bibliography," *Bulletin of Bibliography,* 47 (September 1990): 169–176.

References:

James L. Clifford, ed., *Biography as an Art* (New York: Oxford University Press, 1962);

Wallis Wilde-Menozzi, "Iris Origo, 1902–1988, An Encomium," *Southwest Review,* 75 (Autumn 1990): 483–501;

Virginia Woolf, *The Diaries of Virginia Woolf, Volume 4 1931–1935, Volume 6 1936–1941* (New York: Harcourt Brace Jovanovich, 1977);

Woolf, *The Letters of Virginia Woolf, Volume 6 1936–1941* (New York: Harcourt Brace Jovanovich, 1975).

George D. Painter

(5 June 1914 –)

Douglas W. Alden
University of Virginia

BOOKS: *The Road to Sinodun: A Winter and Summer Monodrama* (London: Hart-Davis, 1951);

André Gide: A Critical and Biographical Study (London: Barker, 1951; New York: Roy, 1951); revised as *André Gide: A Critical Biography* (London: Weidenfeld & Nicolson, 1968; New York: Atheneum, 1968);

Marcel Proust: A Biography, 2 volumes (London: Chatto & Windus, 1959, 1965) – volume 1 published as *Proust: the Early Years* (Boston: Little, Brown, 1959); volume 2 published as *Proust: The Later Years* (Boston & Toronto: Little, Brown, 1965); revised edition, with a preface by Painter (London: Chatto & Windus, 1989; New York: Random House, 1989);

The Hypnerotomachia Poliphili of 1499: An Introduction on the Dream, the Dreamer, the Artist and the Printer (London: Eugrammia Press, 1963);

William Caxton: A Quincentenary Biography of England's First Printer (London: Chatto & Windus, 1976); published as *William Caxton: A Biography* (New York: Putnam, 1977);

Chateaubriand: A Biography, volume 1 (London: Chatto & Windus, 1977; New York: Knopf, 1978);

Studies in Fifteenth-Century Printing (London: Pindar Press, 1984).

OTHER: André Gide, *Marshlands and Prometheus Misbound: Two Satires,* translated by Painter (London & New York: Secker & Warburg, 1953);

Marcel Proust, Letters to His Mother, translated and edited by Painter (London: Rider, 1956; New York: Citadel, 1957);

The Vinland Map and the Tartar Relation, translated by Painter, R. A. Skelton, and Thomas E. Marston (New Haven: Yale University Press, 1965); revised edition, with an introduction by Painter (New Haven: Yale University Press, 1995);

George D. Painter (courtesy of George D. Painter)

André Maurois, *The Chelsea Way, or Marcel Proust in England,* translated, with an introduction and notes, by Painter (London: Weidenfeld & Nicolson, 1966; New York: Heinemann, 1967).

George Duncan Painter will always be best known as *the* biographer of Marcel Proust. Like so many contemporary authors who suddenly discover in their past a moment of illumination from which their lifelong inspiration springs, Painter

228

once claimed in an interview that reading *Swann's Way* in C. K. Scott-Moncrieff's translation was the greatest experience of his adolescence because it revealed to him what literature was about.

Painter was born on 5 June 1914 in Birmingham, England, to George Charles Painter, a musician, singer, and teacher of English, and Minnie Rosendale Taylor Painter, an artist. In school his emphasis was Latin and Greek, and he subsequently spent a brilliant five years at Trinity College, Cambridge, in the same fields, accumulating fellowships and honors (he earned three scholarships, including the Parson and the Waddington, and was Bell Exhibitioner, Craven Student, and a classical medalist). In his interview he said: "I went right through Latin and Greek literature. Instead of attending lectures or paying any attention to what my teachers tried to teach, I taught myself." These five years turned him into the scholar that he has always remained.

His first employment, in 1937, was as assistant lecturer in Latin at the University of Liverpool. He was enticed into a new job with more-lucrative prospects the following year. The British Museum badly needed someone with his knowledge of Latin and Greek to work on incunabula. He rose in rank to become, in 1954, assistant keeper in charge of fifteenth-century books. Although he once implied that this employment was only a way of earning a livelihood and that he might have preferred something else, he enjoyed this kind of detail and went on to a distinguished career as a librarian. He succeeded to the editorship of the *Catalogue of Books Printed in the XVth Century Now in the British Museum*, published *The Hypnerotomachia Poliphili of 1499: An Introduction on the Dream, the Dreamer, the Artist and the Printer* (1963), contributed a study for *The Vinland Map and the Tartar Relation* (1965), and finally, in 1984, brought together twenty-six of his scholarly articles in his *Studies in Fifteenth-Century Printing*.

His literary career began with what must be called his romantic period when he thought he would be a poet. Between September 1940 and October 1941, with bombs echoing now and then through his poetry, he wrote sixty-two short poems, some of which appeared later in the *Listener* and *New Statesman*. During World War II Painter served for five years as a private, doing manual labor in England and Scotland. He was forced to commute from the Chiltern Hills, which accounts for the title that he gave his poetry when he published it in 1951 as *The Road to Sinodun: A Winter and Summer Monodrama*. Lest Sinodun might be thought to be somewhere on the road to Xanadu, he explained in a note that it was a domed hill on the Thames opposite Dorchester. Conventional in the sense that they rhymed and scanned, the poems registered an amorous disposition with titles such as "In the Thames valley I lay with my love" or "Amy with her little head." In 1942 he married, but it was not Amy, rather his cousin Joan Britton, by whom he had two daughters.

Now and then doppelgängers appear in his poems. In his interview he said that he was haunted by this "wraith of myself, sometimes friendly, sometimes violently hostile." Whatever might be the real meaning of the poem "Farewell, my doppelgänger," he must have taken leave of this other half when he married since he wrote no more poems. Yet his life continued as though he had a split personality, for in the daytime he sorted things out for the British Museum, but in the evening or on weekends he led the existence of a literary scholar. In the mid 1940s he became a regular book reviewer for the *Listener* and the *New Statesman* but ceased this collaboration after a few years while continuing to produce an occasional review, especially on French topics, for the *Times Literary Supplement*.

In his interview he said that a bout with the flu in 1947 gave him the chance to read Proust's letters, and he decided that he would be a biographer; however, his first biographical effort was *André Gide: A Critical and Biographical Study* (1951). A modest little volume with uninspired typography, it does not seem to be a trial balloon for the later work of saturation on Proust. Its chief merit is not the collection of new information about Gide's life but the clear explication of Gide's numerous works one after the other as they chronicle the fluctuations of his innermost problems. In the volume Painter has already reached his mature stride as a stylist and is writing in the words and syntax of the finest English writers, without affectation and with the vocabulary range of someone who has been immersed all of his life in the great classics. Even today this is a useful book for a serious overview of Gide's work.

In his preface Painter asserts that "no one so far has attempted to describe the actual nature and content of his work, and to show its organic growth from the history of his mind and heart." He is quite right in claiming the title of pioneer since the leading works of Gidian scholarship, Jean Delay's two-volume *La Jeunesse d'André Gide* (1956–1957) and Justin O'Brien's *Portrait of André Gide* (1953), as well as a host of lesser works, although soon to appear, were not yet in print. Most of all, he wants to share his enthusiasm for Gide: "He has no modern equal as a giver of sheer pleasure, aesthetic, intellectual,

Painter, circa 1965

pages on this long novel, he even indulges in what will later become one of his favorite pastimes, the identification of the characters with their real-life models. His explication concludes on a Freudian note when he points to a passage in the *Journals* (1939–1950) in which Gide dreamed that, by pulling a string, he ruined Proust's copy of the *Memoirs of Saint-Simon*. This, says Painter, is an unconscious feeling of rivalry in producing *Les Faux-Monnayeurs* and of guilt for once having refused Proust's manuscript.

It is impossible to explain Gide's works without recourse to his biography, but biography seems to be on the back burner in this stage of Painter's career. In the first place, Gide's autobiographical *Si le grain ne meurt* (1920, 1921; translated as *If It Die . . .*, 1935), one of the great "confessions" of all times, simplifies the task of the biographer. All of the essential elements are right there: the dominant mother, the love for the distraught cousin Madeleine, the sexual revolt at Biskra. Painter tells the story simply but adds nothing new. He could have been more melodramatic but preferred now and then a little poetry, such as: "By the menhirs of the sea-cliff they watched the lighthouses beginning one by one to flash." A biographer has the right to romanticize now and then to keep his reader awake. For the remainder of Gide's life after his marriage to Madeleine, Painter no longer had a ready-made narrative to follow, but at least he had the extensive *Journals,* from which he was able to disengage the major elements of Gide's personal life as they paralleled his literary evolution from individualism to social concern (that is, to communism and then back). He defines Gide's unconsummated marriage as "incestuous" because Madeleine has become a mother figure. The reader understands that this relationship has its ups and downs, although, once again, Painter does not dramatize. The fugue with Marc Allégret; the nighttime prowlings with Ghéon; the resistance to Catholicism, which produces an estrangement from his wife (as well as its literary expression in *Numquid et tu, Le Retour de l'Enfant prodigue* and *La Symphonie pastorale*), are all noted in passing. Painter does not draw attention to the fact Gide fathers a child by a person (unnamed in this first edition of Painter's book) who was the inspiration for Laura in *Les Faux-Monnayeurs*. More than on the misunderstandings, Painter insists on the reconciliations that follow in Gide's unusual marriage. He concludes that "Their mutual love was the profoundest truth of his life and hers; it continued to exist, consciously for him, unconsciously in her and the estrangement caused by her symbolic act of

and sensory; but he is even more important as a source of spiritual joy, as a heroic guide in the acquisition of personal happiness, virtue, and liberty." Thus, Painter's interpretation always tends to be in Gide's favor. Of *Les Nourritures terrestres* (1897; translated as *The Fruits of the Earth,* 1933) he says: "Undoubtedly, one of the causes of Gide's explosive liberation was his discovery of sexual pleasure, but an equal cause was his discovery of travel. Sensual love is a powerful symbol; but so also is the ability to wander." Of the "gratuitous act" in *Paludes* (1895; translated as *Marshlands,* 1953), *Le Prométhée mal enchaîné* (1899; translated as *Prometheus Misbound,* 1953), and *Les Caves du Vatican* (1914; translated as *The Vatican Swindle,* 1925) he says: "He believed in it, if at all, not as a fact, but as a fabulous absolute, a moral and aesthetic concept not valid in itself, but showing the way to new discoveries." Painter considers *Les Faux-Monnayeurs* (1925; translated as *The Counterfeiters,* 1927), despite the occasional adverse criticism to which it has been subjected, to be "one of the world's greatest novels." Spending many

murder and suicide [the burning of her husband's letters] was the more tragic for being onesided and false."

Gide died in 1951, the same year, of course, that Painter published his book, and Painter was able to revise his text to include the death. But it was too late to include Gide's posthumous *Et nunc manet in te* (1947; translated as *The Secret Drama of My Life,* 1951), which came out the same year. In 1968, when Painter already had an international reputation as the biographer of Proust, he issued a revised edition of his Gide book with an altered title. *André Gide: A Critical Biography* was admirably printed on much larger pages and illustrated. The text covered only 134 pages this time, whereas the smaller first edition had 185 pages of text. Revisions were inevitable because of *Et nunc manet in te* and the later posthumous *Ainsi soit-il ou les jeux sont faits* (1952; translated as *So Be It; or, The Chips are Down,* 1959). Early in his book, during his protagonist's honeymoon, Painter inserts without comment a brief paragraph on photographing nude boys in Rome and, near the end of his book, adds an essentially new chapter, "The End of Marriage." Without alluding to the controversy that the publication of the posthumous texts and their subsequent discussion by Martin du Gard and Schlumberger had provoked, he discusses in much greater detail Gide's new revelations. He no longer believes that the estrangement of Gide and his wife should not be exaggerated; instead he concludes that "Their estrangement in the next few years was a weary and hopeless truce."

In the preface of his *Marcel Proust: A Biography* (1959, 1965), Painter says that he began dating the undated correspondence of Proust before Philip Kolb published *La Correspondance de Marcel Proust: chronologie et commentaire critique* (1949) on that very subject. That means that he was working on Proust before 1949, and at the same time he was researching Gide. After his *André Gide* of 1951, this parallel interest continued, and Painter published in 1953 his translation of *Marshlands and Prometheus Misbound: Two Satires* and then, in 1956, his translation of Proust's *Letters to His Mother,* based on Philip Kolb's French edition of 1953 but with his own biographical introduction and annotations.

In 1959 appeared *Marcel Proust: A Biography: Volume One,* called *Proust: The Early Years* in the simultaneous American edition. To understand its impact on the gradually increasing group of Proustian scholars and devotees, one must remember that in 1959 there was no satisfactory biography of Proust. The first biography, remarkable for its time, had been published by Léon Pierre-Quint in 1929

before *Le Temps retrouvé* (1927; translated as *The Past Recaptured,* 1932) had become available. Proust went into a popular decline at the time that Gide and André Malraux were courting communism. Meanwhile it was known to a chosen few that Suzy Mante-Proust, the niece of Proust, had a gold mine of Proust documents that she would not allow anyone to examine. In the late 1940s, however, she had relented and had given the master biographer, André Maurois, access to her papers. In 1949 he published his *A la recherche de Marcel Proust,* which he is said to have considered one of his best biographies. But Maurois's book was a failure; this became evident when his erstwhile research assistant, Bernard de Fallois, published Proust's *Le Balzac de Monsieur de Guermantes* (1950), *Jean Santeuil* (1952), and *Contre Sainte-Beuve* (1954), amazing manuscripts which Maurois had missed and the absence of which rendered his work obsolete. Painter, of course, had these at his disposal as well as the first Pléiade edition of *A la recherche du temps perdu* (1954), prepared with devotion and scholarship by Pierre Clarac and André Ferré.

Painter never mentions Maurois's biography of Proust, but his opinion is manifest when he says in his preface that "the subject has never yet been treated with anything approaching scholarly method." His purpose is now "to write a definitive biography of Proust." He continues: "There seems to be no good reason why an interesting subject should be made boring in the name of scholarship, or why the most scrupulous accuracy should not be achievable without draining the lifeblood from a living theme. . . . I have invented nothing whatever; and even when I give the words of a conversation, or describe the state of the weather or a facial expression at a particular moment, I do so from evidence that seems reliable." Perhaps to avoid appearing too scholarly, Painter held back all of his references until the second volume. This work of saturation, using every detail after a scholarly sorting out, differs radically from his *André Gide* in that it is not an exegesis of the literary works; the minor ones are explicated in detail but primarily for their relation to the major work, whereas the major work, which the reader is expected to know on his own, will be explicated only in its relation to reality.

Characteristically, Painter starts out, as though to startle the average Proustian, by insisting that a major event in the novel actually took place at a given time in Proust's biography. The dramatic episode of the good-night kiss, he says, occurred at Auteuil, not at Illiers, because Proust makes a vague allusion to it later in a letter to his mother and be-

Dust jacket for Painter's biography of the English printer and translator, written at the request of the librarian of Westminster Abbey

Painter speculates whether the episode in the bushes really took place, after which his imagination takes over and he describes a visit to the Benardaky house as though Proust really went there, even though the account of the Kossichef episode in *Jean Santeuil,* which Painter usually prefers as a biographical source at this stage, ends quite differently.

In succeeding chapters Painter covers Proust's schooling, military service, and gradual penetration into society as he tries to become a writer in defiance of his father. As Proust encounters on his way Madame de Caillavet, Anatole France, Robert de Montesquiou, Madame de Chevigné, and Madame Greffuhle, among many others, Painter interrupts the main narrative each time to indulge in a lengthy biography à la Balzac, complete with a very original physical description. When he arrives at Proust's participation in the Dreyfus affair, he brings a whole period of recent French history to life in a long digression. Surprisingly, given the example of his *André Gide,* Painter's exegesis of *Les Plaisirs et les jours* (1896; translated as *Pleasures and Regrets,* 1948), Proust's collection of short stories and sketches, is not concentrated in one spot or even particularly literary, but rather it is dispersed among other events of the period. In fact, Painter seems to dislike this early work when he speaks of "the sterile tone of a literary exercise."

Invoking Sigmund Freud occasionally, Painter also concentrates on Proust's character. As to be expected, since Proust uses the episode of the good-night kiss in the same manner in his novel, Painter considers it to be the central trauma of Proust's life. From it develops not only the occasional remorse that Proust also discovers in his narrator but also a strong love-hate relationship with his mother deriving from sibling rivalry. Proust's ever-increasing illness, his asthma, is seen as an attention-getting device. While it might be expected that Painter should use a Freudian explanation of Proust's homosexuality, he appears reluctant to do so because he is convinced that Proust remained partly heterosexual up to the very end of his life. He does not doubt that young Marcel was in love with Marie de Benardaky, even though he "wills" himself into breaking with her (Painter did not know that none of this willing was in the first set of Grasset proofs in 1913). This willing, according to Painter, changes into a subconscious procedure so that Proust is first enamored of Jeanne Pouquet because she is safe, being already engaged, and then his attentions, whatever they are, are directed toward married women such as Madame de Chevigné who are safe

cause the text of *A la recherche du temps perdu* states that the house where this happened was later destroyed, which is true, whereas the house at Illiers is still standing. This first chapter, "The Garden of Auteuil," has family antecedents as its main subject. The second chapter, "The Garden of Illiers," and the third, "The Two Ways," give more information on antecedents but are essentially a typical Painter digression, fascinating for the informed reader, on the geography of Illiers and its hinterland. Again, as is characteristic with Painter, the reader, following what must have been the biographer's own peregrinations, meets the real inhabitants of Illiers, who are promptly metamorphosed into the fictional inhabitants of Combray. Similarly, chapter 4, "The Garden of the Champs-Elysées," introduces Marie de Benardaky, the original of Gilberte Swann, and

because they are married. Nevertheless, he might have been in love with Marie Finaly for a short period. At this point in the biography Painter makes little of the fact that Jacques-Emile Blanche, the painter who made the famous portrait of Proust, hinted that young Proust had an affair with Laure Hayman, his uncle's mistress and one of the originals of Odette de Crécy. He returns to the subject of Proust's heterosexuality in volume two. But Proust's homosexuality also cannot be denied, although Painter did not know that it began much earlier than he suspected, as a newly discovered letter proves. Proust's sentimental involvement with Reynaldo Hahn – transformed into Jean Santeuil's friend in the novel Proust was then writing – and next with Lucien Daudet – an affair that led to Proust's duel with Jean Lorrain – were already well-known chapters in Proust's life, and Painter inevitably discusses these episodes in detail. He also discusses as well Proust's "unrequited" affection for the noble Bertrand de Fénelon, who becomes the fictional Saint-Loup. Volume one ends with the death of Proust's father, Dr. Adrien Proust; having abandoned *Jean Santeuil,* Proust is in the midst of his work on John Ruskin.

In his preface Painter had promised that his second volume would be out in "two year's time"; it was, however, six years later that *Marcel Proust: Volume Two* appeared. The second volume seems almost to have a greater density because there is less need for digressive background material whereas there is more evidence, especially from the correspondence, of Proust's daily activities. The narrative moves both downward and upward: downward as Proust degenerates physically and becomes a shabby individual who ends up in a male brothel; upward as this same person, using his asthma as a justification for withdrawing from society so as to devote all of his time and energy to his great work, forges ahead in his cork-lined room.

Everything Proust does Painter now interprets in terms of the love-hate relationship with his mother. He promises her to reform and to go to bed and rise at normal times; but in the end he does not change. When his mother dies, he is overwhelmed with grief and then, complying at last with her wishes, puts himself in a sanatorium to overcome his asthma. He then subconsciously avenges himself by not getting cured. His great work is composed in a feeling of remorse and vindication (in the novel the narrator's mother lives on forever, whereas Madame Proust's death is transferred to the narrator's grandmother), and yet it contains the profanation episode in which the lesbian Mademoiselle Vinteuil

spits on her father's portrait. In real life Proust is alleged to have done something similar at Le Cuziat's brothel.

Painter's views of Proust's sexuality differ radically from those of Maurois, who was doubtless inspired by his wife, the daughter of Jeanne Pouquet whom Proust "pretended" to love. Maurois maintained that Proust was always a homosexual who continuously put up smoke screens of this kind. On the contrary Painter insists now more than ever on Proust's heterosexual tendencies and that he actually had some kind of physical relations with Louisa de Mornand, the mistress of his friend Albufera. This time Painter lets his imagination go: "As he lay beside her Proust saw through the open door the crimson wallpaper of the drawing room." What happened next is as equivocal as it was when Albertine lay with the narrator. Proust's correspondence with Louisa suggests that all this might be true. But Painter goes even further; he discovers a "young girl" who was the object of Proust's attentions at Cabourg and Paris and who asked Prince Antoine Bibesco "not to print her name." Six times Painter refers to this mysterious person who was presumably the one Proust mentions in his correspondence as someone he might have married. On page 192 Painter even asserts that they might have had physical relations.

After vague allusions to a period when Proust probably had ancillary homosexual affairs, Painter comes to the well-known story of Agostinelli, who "escaped" and drowned in the Mediterranean. When Agostinelli was Proust's chauffeur at Cabourg, Painter calls him "this honest and amiable young man." A few years later, when Agostinelli was Proust's secretary in Paris, Painter does not believe that there was any physical relation between them but that Proust was jealous of his protégé's relations with other women. Painter records the presence of other secretaries and protégés, such as Henri Rochat, but does not see them as male Albertines, as Maurois had done. On the other hand, Maurois consciously avoided (the proof is that he read the book but says only that Le Cuziat was the model for Jupien) a much more painful subject, the revelations which Maurice Sachs had made in *Le Sabbat* as early as 1946. Painter plunges into the midst of these revelations, now confirmed, he says, by other sources which he enumerates carefully, contrary to his usual practice of avoiding such systematic argumentation. He insists that the story of the rats and of the profanation of the family pictures unquestionably happened, and he goes even further to suggest that Charlus's perverted acts at Jupien's brothel were really committed by Proust. For Painter this is another chapter in the love-hate relationship with the long-dead mother. Later Painter says that Proust recognized in his final illness the symptoms of his mother's illness and therefore refused to be cured by his brother, Dr. Robert Proust, and other physicians because he identified with his mother and wanted to die as she did. To counteract this portrait of a perverse Proust, Painter juxtaposed the portrait of the "noble and intelligent" Céleste Albaret, Proust's "governess" in his final years; describing Proust's relations with her, Painter is impelled to speak of "Proust's profound goodness." When Painter's biography appeared in French, Kolb and Alden called on Céleste at Montfort-l'Amaury and asked what she thought of Painter's book; she said then, as she said later in her *Monsieur Proust,* that Proust went to Le Cuziat's brothel only for documentation and that the story of the rats was malicious gossip. She said she would never read Painter.

Painter's purpose is not to denigrate Proust but rather to analyze the complexities of a genius. Was it not Proust who claimed that geniuses were not like other people? In a long digression which could logically have been an introduction to volume two (there was none), Painter responded to Proust's criticism of Sainte-Beuve for "using the external features of a writer's life and character to explain his work." A literary biographer, says Painter, "must discover, beneath the mask of the artist's every-day, objective life, the secret life from which he extracted his work; show how, in the apparently sterile persons and places of that external life, he found the hidden, universal meanings which are the themes of his book." Painter never pauses elsewhere to say, "See what I have done." In fact, he never really explicates *A la recherche du temps perdu;* always he looks at it intensely to see to what extent reality has crept into it. Volume two spends as much time on "keys" to the fictional characters as the preceding volume, but fewer digressions are needed, the only lengthy ones being the Eulenburg homosexual scandal in the German court and the lesbians gathered around Natalie Clifford Barney whom Proust "consulted." When *A la recherche du temps perdu* had appeared in several volumes, all the "keys," as revealed by the correspondence, revolted in real life when they recognized themselves in Proust's novel.

Volume two is flooded with the minute details of Proust's everyday life. In every letter he mentions his latest asthma attack, and one gets the impression that he seldom rises from his bed. Yet on every page of the biography, which necessarily con-

denses time, he is up and going, albeit late at night, in order to meet his new friend and admirer, Madame Scheikévitch, or even to attend a social function where he encounters Princess Marthe Bibesco. For many years still he goes back to Cabourg in the summer to work. A great deal happens in volume two, and the important part has to do with the writing, the marketing, and the publication of *A la recherche du temps perdu.* When volume two begins, he is still working on Ruskin, translating *Sesame and Lilies,* published in 1906 with the help of Reynaldo Hahn's English cousin, Marie Nordlinger. The chapter is titled "Visits from Albertine" because the unconventional English girl comes and goes freely in the Proust apartment just like Albertine. The next steps toward the *A la recherche du temps perdu* are the pastiches of famous authors, which Proust published in the *Figaro* and the unfinished *Contre Sainte-Beuve,* in which Proust begins to develop his aesthetic theories. In a very detailed analysis of this latter work Painter is relying on the unscientific version published by Bernard de Fallois in 1954, a text that differs radically from the Pléiade version published by Pierre Clarac and Yves Sandre in 1971. Proust scholars have not yet forgiven Painter for inventing the "lost novel of 1905–8." He asserts: "The new version of [this] novel, begun in February and abandoned in November 1908, survives in seventy-five unpublished loose leaves." Fallois makes no such claim, although he does mention "soixante-quinze feuillets." Since Proust was in the habit of using the same notebook at different times and for different purposes, Fallois failed to distinguish between the *Contre Sainte-Beuve* fragments and the passages that Proust was composing at the same time for a new novel which was to become *A la recherche du temps perdu.* There was never any abandonment, only continuation.

"It was on or about 1 January 1909 that Proust returned, late at night, along the snow-covered Boulevard Haussmann, to experience one of the most momentous events of his life." With this statement, as in the case of the good-night kiss, Painter assigns nearly a specific time to another event which might well have been outside time, as it is in the novel: the cup of tea and toast of *Contre Sainte-Beuve* (the toast becoming a madeleine cake in the *Recherche*). Obviously, after the banal incipit of *Jean Santeuil,* Proust was looking for a new beginning for his novel, and one might argue that he chose one in harmony with the Symbolist aesthetic which he had once disavowed in his youthful essay, "Contre l'obscurité." Involuntary memory was "in the air" at this time and was being discussed by psychologists and crit-

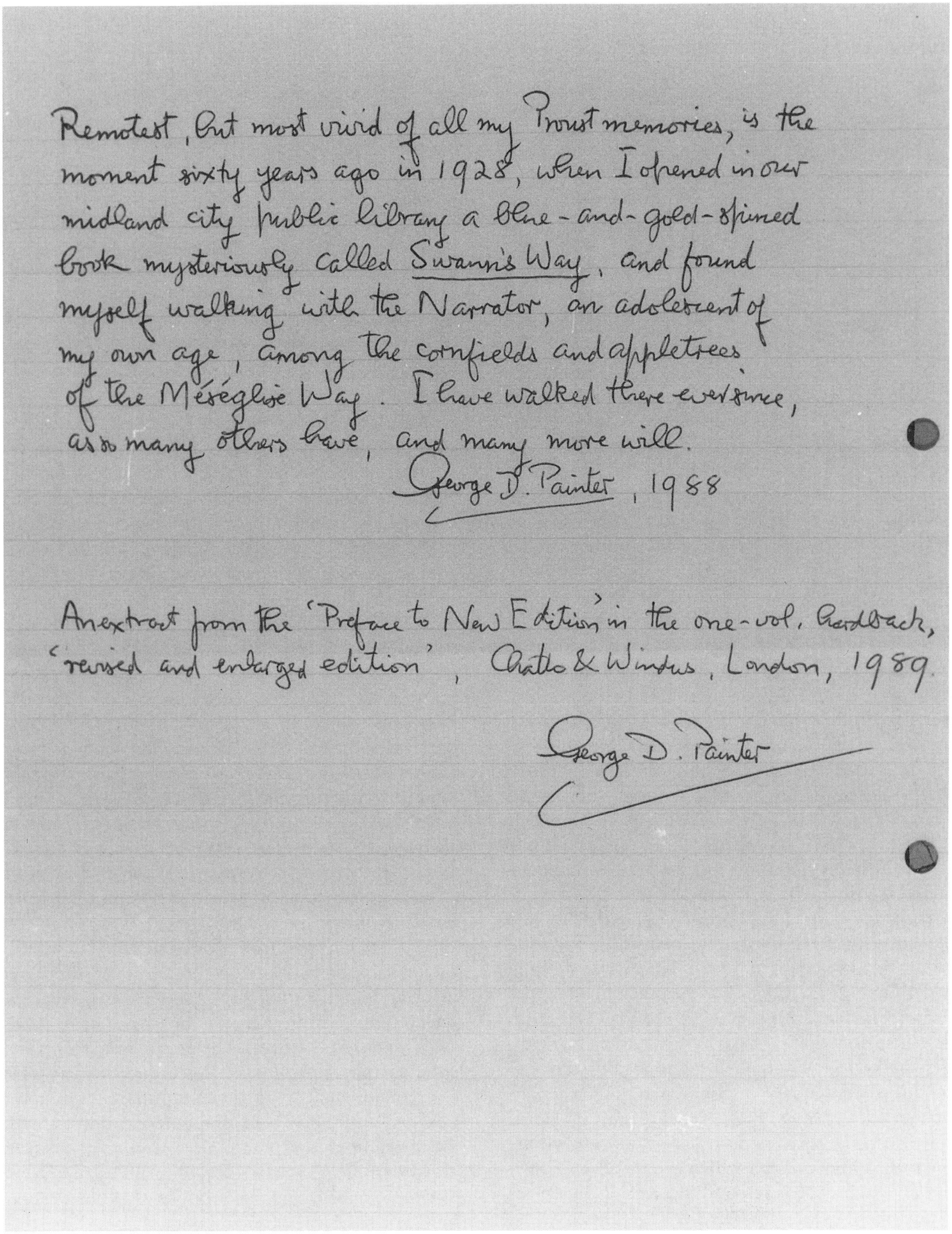

Remotest, but most vivid of all my Proust memories, is the moment sixty years ago in 1928, when I opened in our midland city public library a blue-and-gold-spined book mysteriously called <u>Swann's Way</u>, and found myself walking with the Narrator, an adolescent of my own age, among the cornfields and appletrees of the Méséglise Way. I have walked there ever since, as so many others have, and many more will.

George D. Painter, 1988

An extract from the 'Preface to New Edition' in the one-vol. hardback, 'revised and enlarged edition', Chatto & Windus, London, 1989.

George D. Painter

Manuscript for an extract from the "Preface to New Edition" in the 1989 revised edition of Marcel Proust: A Biography
(courtesy of George D. Painter)

ics. The episode might well have happened at this time, but it might have been a self-induced psychological experiment rather than an extraordinary revelation.

If Painter had begun his biography of Proust some thirty years later, he would have had available, beginning in 1971, Philip Kolb's monumental *Correspondance de Marcel Proust* and would have been able to study the elaboration of *A la recherche du temps perdu* from the inside because the manuscripts, once jealously guarded by Suzy Mante-Proust, in addition to manuscripts from other sources, have long been available (although less available now) at the Bibliothèque Nationale and have been the subject of intense study. However, Painter was not bereft of information concerning the writing and publication of the *A la recherche du temps perdu*. From Léon Pierre-Quint's *Comment parut "Du côté de chez Swann,"* (1930, which, curiously, he does not mention in his bibliography) and from the abundant if unedited correspondence, he knew the full details of Proust's efforts to interest various publishers, including the Nouvelle Revue Française (Gide was responsible for the refusal), and of how Proust finally published with Grasset at his own expense. From the earliest scholarly study on Proust, Albert Feuillerat's *Comment Marcel Proust a composé son roman* (1934), Painter knew that somewhere (Feuillerat carefully does not say where) there was a set of unused Grasset proofs going beyond *Du côté de chez Swann,* which appeared in late 1913. He knew, therefore, that Albertine did not exist in these proofs, although they were otherwise to serve for the postwar volume *A l'ombre des jeunes filles en fleurs* (1919; translated as *Within a Budding Grove,* 1924). Nevertheless, he rejects the prevailing theory that Albertine would not have existed if Agostinelli had not fallen into the Mediterranean, since he has all along contended that, as a character, Albertine has only feminine models. As Proust makes new friends who admire his work, especially writers and critics, as he gradually gains international fame after winning the Prix Goncourt for *A l'ombre des jeune filles en fleurs* and as he struggles simultaneously to publish and to continue writing the posthumously published parts of the *A la recherche du temps perdu,* Painter sketches an ascension that is Proust's redemption, for "the self we are born with and the self which we acquire, always join at last, for the rarest and the greatest in a work of art, in death for everyone."

Painter's biography is also a work of art, a classic among biographies. Philip Toynbee called it "One of the greatest English biographies of any time; it is not only eloquent and witty but infused by that unashamed love for its subject which, above all other qualities, made Boswell's *Life of Johnson* the masterpiece it is."

Painter did not forsake Proust immediately, since in 1966 he translated a Proustian pastiche by André Maurois as *The Chelsea Way, or Marcel Proust in England.* For the next ten or eleven years he published no more biographies, although he might well have been working on two at the same time. The first to appear was *William Caxton: A Quincentenary Biography of England's First Printer* (1976). Painter seems to have started work on it in 1974 at the request of the librarian of Westminster Abbey, intending it for the Caxton Commemoration of 1976. Certainly no one was more qualified than Painter to write this biography of the fifteenth-century printer, the first to print a book in English. But the subject was a challenge in the sense that little is known about Caxton. His name comes up now and then in the commercial records of trade with Flanders and in a few legal documents, but, otherwise, the only source of information is what he says about himself in the dedications to the noble lords and royal personages who subsidized his printing by buying his expensive books. Born sometime between 1415 and 1424, Caxton was apprenticed in his youth to a mercer and became a member of the Mercers' Company. His early career was as a merchant engaged in trade with Flanders, and soon he was established in Bruges, where he became, by royal appointment, "governor beyond the sea" of the English merchants operating there. At one point he headed the exodus of English merchants to Utrecht when relations between England and Flanders became strained. With the Lancastrian restoration of 1470–1471 he lost his governorship but remained in Bruges at the court of Duchess Margaret, wife of Charles the Bold of Burgundy and sister of Edward IV of England. As one of her royal prerogatives, the duchess engaged in the textile trade and therefore needed Caxton's expertise; a learned lady, she also encouraged him to continue his translation (from the French) of the *Recuyell of the Histories of Troy* and even corrected his English. In 1472 Caxton was at Cologne, probably on a mercantile or diplomatic mission, and there, becoming interested in the new art of printing, he bought a press and type which he set up in Bruges in order to print in 1474 his *Recuyell.* Some of his early books were in French, but most of his 107 known books were in English – notably *The Canterbury Tales* – and often they were his own translations from French, or, once, from Dutch (*Reynard the Fox*). Caxton never physically printed his own books; that was the task of his assistants. In 1476 he moved his publishing business to the precincts of Westminster Abbey, where, after a long and essentially successful career, he died "towards the close of the year 1491."

Almost every line of Painter's account of Caxton's life is peppered with adverbs such as "perhaps" or "probably." Even the documentary evidence he has to interpret with the same hesitation since the experts often do not agree. But Painter again makes reasonable conjectures that certain things did happen when he has no proof. Describing the marriage of Charles the Bold to Margaret of York on 3 July 1468, he says: "The English merchants, no doubt with Governor Caxton at their head, escorted the happy couple through the streets next day (it poured rain, of course) under the banner of St. George." No longer does he say that this did indeed happen, as he was wont to do speaking of Proust; this time he protects himself with "no doubt." If things did not necessarily happen that way, this book on Caxton is still overwhelming in its documentation. Not only does Painter inform us thoroughly on trade in the fifteenth century or digress at length in a description of Bruges at that time, but he uses historical allusions even in the technical process of dating Caxton's books. The history of this turbulent period runs through Painter's entire book and is analyzed in detail because it has a direct bearing on Caxton's life. Much of the time he is on the wrong side politically when Edward IV is in exile on the Continent and even more so later when his friend and literary collaborator Arnold Earl Rivers, the uncle and guardian of the princes executed in the Tower, is himself beheaded. In the precinct of Westminster Abbey he is the neighbor and friend of Edward's queen after she seeks sanctuary there. All of this history is somewhat complicated, at least for those who are not born British subjects, and this time Painter does not simplify, so that it is often difficult to be sure who is beheading whom in this War of the Roses. Much more complicated is the discussion of Caxton's books, which are taken up one after the other in this mesh of history. Summaries of the subject are enlightening, but the reader goes astray in this technical information on type and format, much of it necessary to establish dates and relationships. For example, Painter appears to be arguing against the specialists when he maintains that, because of technicalities in the type, Veldener taught Caxton in Cologne and that Mansion helped at Bruges. Since at least half of the text, if not more, is spent on Caxton's books that become events in the narrative, it is obvious that Painter is aiming at his fellow bibliophiles more than at the ca-

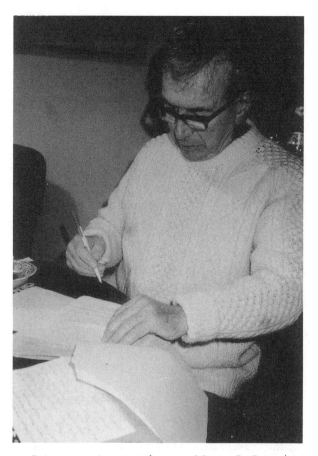

Painter at work in 1992 (courtesy of George D. Painter)

sual reader; yet this book is still of the highest Painter quality.

According to Dennis E. Rhode in his introduction to Painter's later *Studies in Fifteenth-Century Printing,* Painter retired from the British Museum in 1974 to devote himself to the study of François-René de Chateaubriand. In 1977 he published *Chateaubriand: A Biography,* subtitled *Volume One (1868–1893): The Longed-for Tempests.* There is no introduction to this volume to explain why, how, or when Painter began this work. In the 1983 interview he said that there would be two more volumes but that he had no idea how long the second volume would take. Twelve years later it still has not appeared. In the interview he said: "I had to lean over backwards to understand Proust, but Chateaubriand was a person I could live with more easily."

In volume one, covering the period up to Chateaubriand's exile in England, Painter had only an exciting life to relate and did not have to contend with the later Chateaubriand, who is hardly a popular writer these days and, in his lifestyle, was something of a poseur. The book is superbly written and reads almost like a novel for the first nine chapters, which recount François-René's capers and misdeeds as a neglected younger son in Saint Malo, then his brooding life in the haunted medieval castle of Combourg, as his austere father paces the half-lit room. As a young man he dreams of sylphides, nearly commits suicide, and might have had an incestuous relationship with his neglected sister Lucile. Except for the possible incest suggested by the later novelette *René* (1802), Painter has no need for adverbs of doubt or probability since all of the emotions which he ascribes freely to his protagonist are recorded in Chateaubriand's *Mémoires d'outre-tombe* (1848–1850). With his usual erudition he is able to go far beyond the memoirs in elucidating details concerning the genealogy and people encountered. As he follows the career of this frustrated young man from his failure to receive an appointment to the royal naval school at Brest to becoming a knight of Malta (in order to have a fixed income since, as a younger son, he was entitled to only a small portion of his father's estate), and ending up finally as a sublieutenant in the Navarre regiment that soon excluded him when reducing manpower, Painter vividly creates his settings and brings even minor characters to life. The narrative becomes amusing when the young chevalier appears at the court of Versailles and makes several blunders. But the really exciting part is not amusing, since it has to do with a revolution that is brewing and in which Chateaubriand, influenced particularly by his relative-in-law, the statesman Malesherbes, tries to be a liberal and then is overwhelmed by events. He witnesses the fall of the Bastille and sees severed heads on pikes parading through the streets. What is amazing in all this is that life goes on; people rent hotel rooms, attend literary dinners, go to the theater, and François-René sells a stock of stockings in order to pay his debts.

In occasional remarks, without seeming to press the point, Painter shows Chateaubriand evolving into a writer, frequenting the Parnys and the Ginguenés of the day, writing a poem or two for the *Almanach des muses,* and dreaming of writing about noble savages in America. Painter even thinks that the young man's trip to the United States was motivated more by the desire to write than to seek the Northwest Passage, the "official" mission which he set for himself. At any rate, François-René did go looking for the Northwest Passage (and might have read many books, which Painter thinks he read in preparation), and that has become, for Chateaubriand specialists, the controversial part of his memoirs. All of this is meat for an archivist such as Painter who makes himself into a specialist on American history and geography to refute the skeptics among Chateaubriandists. Abruptly the style changes from novelistic technique to demonstration. In his memoirs Chateaubriand relates with apparent accuracy (except his call on George Washington) his arrival in Maryland, his stops in Philadelphia and New York, his side trip to Lexington, and, finally, his life among the Indians in the Mohawk Valley, where he found a fiddling Frenchman teaching the Indians to dance European style. Did Chateaubriand, after breaking his arm in his foolhardy climb down the cliff to look at Niagara Falls, continue to Pittsburgh and finally to the mouth of the Ohio, before turning back and returning to Philadelphia by way of Nashville and the Shenandoah Valley of Virginia? In fact, Painter even supposes, without evidence from Chateaubriand, that the latter made a side trip to the Natural Bridge, where the owner, Thomas Jefferson, already maintained a cabin for tourists. Chateaubriand had become convinced that one man alone could not discover the Northwest Passage, even by fraternizing with the Indians. Painter contends that he really did follow the itinerary he describes, even though his memoirs are sketchy about it and even though the parallel *Voyage en Amérique* is laced with borrowings from Bartram (whom Chateaubriand names several times in his text), the author of a travel book of the period. In reconstructing the continuation of Chateaubriand's trip, Painter fills us in on the Indian wars (an American army had just lost the greatest battle in Indian war history, with eight hundred dead by the time Chateaubriand returned to Philadelphia) and on the complete geography of the region, inch by inch, together with a detailed description of the frontier towns which Chateaubriand never mentions in his memoirs, being intent on seeing around him only exotic nature, prehistoric Indian mounds, and noble savages (for he managed to travel during a lull in the wars and apparently never saw any but noble savages). By consulting every travel account of the period, Painter is able to state accurately how one traveled in frontier America and how long it took from one point to the next. This enables him, with a chart of statistics interrupting his narrative, to prove that Chateaubriand really could have made, with time to spare, the trip that he claims to have made. On the other hand, with evidence from Washington's bout with a carbuncle, Painter proves that Chateaubriand was wrong in saying that he called on Washington at the beginning of his sojourn in America; but he is convinced that he did see the president on his return to Philadelphia.

While in a farmhouse that Painter situates near Abingdon, Virginia, Chateaubriand reads in an old newspaper that Louis XVI has been captured at Varennes and brought back to Paris in custody. Chateaubriand returns to France. At this point, with a near shipwreck on the Breton coast, Painter returns to the novelistic tone. After a marriage of convenience, which produces no convenience since his own pittance of a fortune after his father's death and his wife's expected wealth add up to nothing in the turbulent times, François-René escapes to Brussels and joins the Royalist army, in which former officers now serve as privates. The French units are attached to various parts of the Prussian army invading France; dysentery, more than the French Republican army, defeats the invaders, and Chateaubriand is severely wounded near Thionville. He manages to drag himself across Belgium to Jersey, where his own relatives, who have taken refuge there, nurse him back to health. Here ends volume one. For this part Painter has not had to prove much since, once again, he had a complete account in the *Mémoires d'outre-tombe*.

In the *Times Literary Supplement* (21 October 1977) Anita Brookner called Painter's book "amazing, incredible, both as an achievement and as a narrative." The chapters on America, particularly, she says, are an "extraordinary piece of sustained research" and "so breathtaking . . . that it is almost possible to swallow the meeting with Washington."

However, she is disinclined to swallow since she mistrusts Chateaubriand more than Painter; in fact, she thinks that the dinner party with Washington re-created by Painter is "fantasized." What Brookner does not say is whether or not she is convinced that Chateaubriand went beyond the Mohawk Valley.

At present it is uncertain if Painter will produce a second volume of *Chateaubriand*. His revised biography of Proust, however, was republished in 1989 both in English and in French, with a new preface by him. In this preface he says with good reason that, in spite of numerous attempts by other biographers to outdistance him, his biography is still considered to be the best. Will there ever be another revised *Proust?* This time his answer by way of the preface is categorical: "The ultimate biography of Proust must await completion of the current publications of Proust's correspondence and manuscripts, and the long labours of a wiser and younger biographer than myself."

Painter received the Order of the British Empire in 1974 and an honorary D.Litt. from the University of Edinburgh in 1979. His *Proust* had received the Duff Cooper Memorial Prize, and his *Chateaubriand* the James Tait Black Memorial Prize.

Interview:
Phyllis Grosskurth, "Interviews with Literary Biographers," *Salmagundi*, 61 (Fall 1983): 22–50.

Sir Peter Quennell

(9 March 1905 – 27 October 1993)

A. R. Jones
University of Wales

BOOKS: *Masques and Poems* (Berkshire: Golden Cockerel Press, 1922);

Poems (London: Chatto & Windus, 1926);

Baudelaire and the Symbolists: Five Essays (London: Chatto & Windus, 1929; Port Washington, N.Y.: Kennikat Press, 1970);

Inscription on a Fountain-Head with Drawings by Albert Rutherston (London: Faber & Faber, 1929);

Poems (London: Chatto & Windus, 1930);

The Phoenix-Kind: A Novel (London: Chatto & Windus, 1931);

A Letter to Mrs. Virginia Woolf (London: Hogarth Press, 1932);

A Superficial Journey through Tokyo and Peking (London: Faber & Faber, 1932);

Sympathy, and Other Stories (London: Faber & Faber, 1933);

Byron (London: Duckworth, 1934);

Byron: The Years of Fame (London: Faber & Faber, 1935; New York: Viking, 1935);

Somerset: Shell Guide, by Quennell and C. H. B. Quennell (London: Architectural Press, 1936);

Caroline of England: An Augustan Portrait (London: Collins, 1939; New York: Viking, 1940);

Byron in Italy (London: Collins, 1941; New York: Viking, 1941);

Four Portraits: Studies of the Eighteenth Century (London: Collins, 1945);

John Ruskin: The Portrait of a Prophet (London: Collins, 1949; New York: Viking, 1949);

The Singular Preference: Portraits and Essays (London: Collins, 1952; New York: Viking, 1953);

Spring in Sicily (London: Weidenfeld & Nicolson, 1952);

Hogarth's Progress (London: Collins, 1955; New York: Viking, 1955);

John Ruskin (London: Longmans, Green, 1956);

The Sign of the Fish (London: Collins, 1960; New York: Viking, 1960);

Shakespeare: The Poet and His Background (London: Weidenfeld & Nicolson, 1963; Cleveland: World, 1963);

Alexander Pope: The Education of a Genius 1688–1728 (London: Weidenfeld & Nicolson, 1968; New York: Stein & Day, 1968);

Romantic England: Writing and Painting, 1717–1851 (London: Weidenfeld & Nicolson, 1970; New York: Macmillan, 1970);

Casanova in London, and Other Essays (London: Weidenfeld & Nicolson, 1971; New York: Stein & Day, 1971);

Samuel Johnson: His Friends and Enemies (London: Weidenfeld & Nicolson, 1972; New York: American Heritage, 1973);

The Marble Foot: An Autobiography, 1905–1938 (London: Collins, 1976; New York: Viking, 1977);

The Wanton Chase: An Autobiography from 1939 (London: Collins, 1980; New York: Atheneum, 1980);

Customs and Characters: Contemporary Portraits (London: Weidenfeld & Nicolson, 1982; Boston: Little, Brown, 1982);

The Pursuit of Happiness (London: Constable, 1988; Boston: Little, Brown, 1988).

OTHER: *Aspects of Seventeenth Century Verse,* edited by Quennell (London: Cape, 1933);

The Private Letters of Princess Lieven to Prince Metternich: 1820–1826, edited, with a biographical foreword, by Quennell (London: Murray, 1937; New York: Dutton, 1938);

Victorian Panorama: A Survey of Life & Fashion from Contemporary Photographs, edited by Quennell (London: Batsford, 1937; New York: Scribners, 1937);

"To Lord Byron": Feminine Profiles Based upon Unpublished Letters 1807–1824, edited by Quennell and Emily Morse Symonds (London: Murray, 1939; New York: Scribners, 1939);

Peter Quennell and his fifth wife, Marilyn, in 1967 (Hulton Deutsch)

Cecil Beaton, *Time Exposure,* edited by Quennell (London: Batsford, 1941; New York: Scribners, 1941);

Novels by the Brontë Sisters, edited by Quennell (London: Pilot, 1947);

Mayhew's London: Being Selections from "London Labour and the London Poor," edited by Quennell (London: Pilot, 1949);

The Pleasures of Pope, edited by Quennell (London: Hamish Hamilton, 1949; New York: Pantheon, 1950);

Byron: Selections from Poetry, Letters and Journals, edited by Quennell (London: Nonesuch Press, 1949);

My Heart Laid Bare and Other Prose Writings by Charles Baudelaire, edited by Quennell (London: Soho Books, 1950);

Henry Mayhew, *London's Underworld: Being Selections from "Those that will not Work,"* edited by Quennell (London: Kimber, 1950);

Byron: A Self-Portrait, Letters and Diaries, 1798–1824, 2 volumes, edited by Quennell (London: Murray, 1950; New York: Scribners, 1950);

Mayhew's Characters, edited by Quennell (London: Spring Books, 1951);

Selected Writings of John Ruskin, edited by Quennell (London: Falcon Press, 1952);

Jonathan Swift, *Gulliver's Travels,* edited by Quennell (London: Collins, 1952; New York: Norton, 1952);

Diversions of History, edited by Quennell (London: Wingate, 1954);

Byron: Selected Verse and Prose Works, including Letters and Extracts from Lord Byron's Journals and Diaries, edited by Quennell (London: Collins, 1959);

Byronic Thoughts: Maxims, Reflections, Portraits from the Prose and Verse of Lord Byron, edited by Quennell (London: Murray, 1960; New York: Harcourt, Brace, 1961);

The Past We Share: An Illustrated History of the British and American Peoples, edited by Quennell and Alan Hodge (London: Weidenfeld & Nicolson, 1960; New York: Prometheus, 1960);

Memoirs of William Hickey, edited by Quennell (London: Hutchinson, 1960);

English Life Series, 8 volumes, edited by Quennell (London: Batsford, 1960–1966);

Henri de Montherlant: Selected Essays, edited by Quennell (London: Weidenfeld & Nicolson, 1960);

Beaton, *Royal Portraits,* introduction by Quennell (Indianapolis: Bobbs-Merrill, 1963);

The Journal of Thomas Moore, 1818–1841, edited by Quennell (London: Batsford, 1964; New York: Macmillan, 1964);

Montherlant, *The Girls: A Tetralogy of Novels,* edited by Quennell (London: Weidenfeld & Nicolson, 1968);

Marcel Proust, 1871–1922: A Centenary Volume, edited by Quennell (London: Weidenfeld & Nicolson, 1971; New York: Simon & Schuster, 1971);

Quotations from Shakespeare, edited by Quennell (London: Michael Joseph, 1971: Boston: Plays, 1971);

A History of English Literature, edited by Quennell and Hamish Johnson (London: Weidenfeld & Nicolson, 1973; Springfield, Mass.: Merriam, 1973);

The Colosseum, edited by Quennell (New York: Newsweek, 1973);

Who's Who in Shakespeare, edited by Quennell and Johnson (London: Weidenfeld & Nicolson, 1973; New York: Morrow, 1973);

The Day Before Yesterday: A Photographic Album of Daily Life in Victorian and Edwardian Britain, edited by Quennell (London: Dent, 1978; New York: Scribners, 1978);

Vladimir Nabokov, A Tribute: His Life, His Work, His World, edited by Quennell (London: Weidenfeld & Nicolson, 1979; New York: Morrow, 1980);

Genius in the Drawing-Room: The Literary Salon in the Nineteenth and Twentieth Centuries, edited by Quennell (London: Weidenfeld & Nicolson, 1980);

A Lonely Business: A Self-Portrait of James Pope-Hennessy, edited by Quennell (London: Weidenfeld & Nicolson, 1981);

The Last Edwardians: An Illustrated History of Violet Trefusis & Alice Keppel, edited by Quennell (Boston: Athenaeum, 1985);

John Macdonald: Memoirs of an Eighteenth Century Footman, edited by Quennell (London: Century, 1985);

An Illustrated Companion to World Literature by Tore Ulf Axel Zetterholm, edited by Quennell (London: Orbis, 1986; New York: Excalibur, 1986).

Peter Courtney Quennell was described in the (London) *Times* (29 October 1993) obituary notice as "probably the last genuine example of the English man of letters. The type, which reached its apogee in the Edwardian era, is traditionally characterized by someone who adopts literature as his profession and spends his entire life in its service without any other form of paid work." Indeed, apart from his war work and a brief period when he worked for an advertising agency, he made his living as an author, a biographer, an essayist, a travel writer, a book reviewer, and an editor. He built up an impressive body of work on which his reputation now securely rests.

He was born in Bromley, Kent, on 9 March 1905, the eldest son of Charles Quennell, an architect, and Marjorie Quennell, the eldest daughter of Alan and Clara Courtney. Soon after he was born the family moved into a house at Bickley that was designed and built by his father. His sister, Gillian, was born in September 1909, and his brother, Paul, in June 1915. His father published his first book, *Modern Suburban Houses,* in 1906, and in 1916 his parents cooperated in the writing and compiling of a series of books titled *A History of Everyday Things* for which they are now chiefly remembered. He attended St. Alfred's School in Chistlehurst, and when the family moved to Berkhamsted in 1917 he attended Berkhamsted School as a day boy. Although Berkhamsted was a grammar school it had acquired the status of a public school. At that time the headmaster was Charles Greene, the father of Graham Greene, who became one of Quennell's closest school friends. Together they read revolutionary French novels among the tombstones of neighboring churchyards. Quennell's father persuaded the headmaster that Peter needed special treatment since he was high-strung, unduly sensitive, and, like his mother, had a weak heart. He was excused from games and from the Officers' Training Corps and spent his afternoons brass-rubbing.

While still at school he made a precocious reputation as a poet. His poems "Epilogue to the Three Beasts," a piece of free verse, and "A Man to a Sunflower" were published in *Public School Verse: An Anthology Volume II 1920–1921* (1922), and a further four poems, "An Invocation," "Rubbish," "Perception," and "Pursuit" in *Public School Verse: An Anthology Volume III 1921–1922* (1923). More important, four of these poems were printed by Edward Marsh in *Georgian Poetry 1920–1922* (1923), which also included poems by established poets such as Edmund Blunden, Walter de la Mare, Robert Graves, Richard Hughes, and D. H. Lawrence. In 1922 he published a slim volume of poems titled *Masques and Poems,* which was printed by the Golden Cockerel Press.

He was awarded the English scholarship at Balliol College, Oxford University, which he entered in October 1923. Edward Marsh had already introduced him into literary society, and he formed friendships with Richard Hughes, with whom he visited Italy and Sicily; the Sitwells, with whom he stayed at Renishaw; and Lady Ottoline Morrell, whom he visited at Garsington. Graham Greene was already in residence when he went up to Oxford, but he also developed friendships with Evelyn Waugh, Cyril Connolly, Anthony Powell, Henry Yorke, David Cecil, Edward Sackville-West, and others, including Harold Acton, who tended to dominate the aesthetic circles of Oxford life. Acton describes Quennell at Oxford in his book *Memoirs of an Aesthete* (1948): "Edith [Sitwell] had praised the poems of Peter Quennell who came up to Balliol that year. Edmund Gosse had been so impressed by this stripling that he declared he had not met so poetical a poet since Swinburne. And Marsh had not been so excited since the heyday of Rupert Brooke. Comparisons with the young Shelley were murmured. . . . At the age of eighteen or nineteen Peter's literary taste was completely formed. He was discriminating to a degree that killed appreciation: everything froze at his touch . . . he had evidently grown up in a pre-Raphaelite conservatory, skinny and narrow-chested with a piping voice, high shoulders and a dancing gait . . . he was pining for the *vie de Bohème,* the Café Royal. In Chelsea he would be fêted, whereas at Oxford. . . . It was sad to witness such discontent when I was enjoying myself. He detested our clubs . . . he shunned our publications and literary societies: whenever he could, he caught the train to London." He edited *Oxford Poetry 1924,* with Acton as his long-suffering coeditor, but otherwise lived a rather frantic social life and read widely. His academic career was not entirely satisfactory, and he was sent down in October 1925 for committing a "number of crimes." He had, he said, "fornicated, broken bounds and told the Vice-Chancellor outrageous lies. . . . I was condemned to rustication – sent down for a single term – and would then be gated, as soon as I reappeared, for the remainder of my Oxford life."

He went off to Italy where he stayed first with the Sitwell brothers at Amalfi and then with Francis Brett-Young and his wife. He visited Max Beerbohm and caught a brief glimpse of Lawrence at Ravenna. He did not return to the university but settled in London and began reviewing for Desmond MacCarthy in the *New Statesman.* He published a collection titled simply *Poems* in 1926, which deservedly earned him a reputation as a young poet of outstanding promise and gained him entry to the literary world where influential figures such as Marsh, Edith Sitwell, and Harold Munro, all of whom admired his work, held sway.

Indeed, he quickly became something of a man about town. His obituary in the London *Times* (29 October 1993) reports that "It soon became clear . . . that this tall, remarkably good-looking young man, with strong features that were as well proportioned as those of the Apollonian heroes he celebrated in his poetry, had uncommon social gifts. In society drawing-rooms where people of talent and wit were gathered together he was frequently in demand by fashionable hostesses. Quennell dressed with perfect taste and lack of ostentation, and he knew how to exert charm particularly toward those likely to further his career." Acton and his contemporaries admired his poetry greatly, but, more impressively, the poet F. T. Prince, writing forty years later, describes *Poems* as "one of the most unjustly neglected 'slim volumes' of its time." Prince adds, "The fact that Peter Quennell's poetry failed to develop further should not prevent us from admiring to the full the handful of vital and luminous pieces in which it came to a precocious perfection." Nonetheless, after the publication of *Poems,* Quennell found that his interest in writing poetry was fading, and he stopped writing verse. He recalls that the "need to write verse . . . became gradually less and less imperative, and I ceased to experience the moods of visionary excitement that I felt obliged to translate into a rhythmic and verbal pattern." One of his last acts as a poet – though he published "Inscription on a Fountain-head," a single poem, as a pamphlet in the Ariel series in 1929 – was to reply to Virginia Woolf's pamphlet *A Letter to a Young Poet,* which the Hogarth Press published in 1932. On behalf of contemporary poets, he describes the quandary in which they find themselves, poetic drama long since dead, narrative appropriated by the novel, and the language in a transitional crisis between science and the past. He characterizes the modern poet bleakly as a forlorn traveler trying to kindle fire with damp twigs and a morsel of broken glass. All he could advise was patience until times became more propitious.

At the same time his interest in writing prose was strengthening. His work as a whole is characterized by his fastidious care for the precision and clarity of his writing, and he acknowledged the early help of both Clive Bell and Arthur Waley in disciplining his prose style. "Largely at the suggestion of T. S. Eliot," he wrote *Baudelaire and the Symbolists: Five Essays* (1929), and thus, he said, "I became a biographer; and, despite one or two excursions into allied fields, a biographer I have ever since remained. Biography is a rewarding branch of literature, at least for those who practise it – One relives the past, moves through the crowded scenes of an unfamiliar social period, makes odd friends, is told fantastic stories and, above all else, plunges into the mysterious existence of a true creative artist, who very often creates upon one plane, but destroys himself upon another. In Baudelaire's life I was struck by the close connection between his weakness and his strength, between his failures and his triumphs." Although his book on Baudelaire was respectfully received by the reviewers, it did not sell well, though it was the product of patient and sensitive care devoted not only to the subject matter but also to the style and fashioning of the presentation. He remained a fastidious stylist and maintained his lifelong interest in France and French literature. Though he followed MacCarthy to *Life & Letters* as a reviewer when MacCarthy became the editor, he was making only a precarious living from his writing. When he was offered an appointment to a newly founded chair of English literature at the University of Tokyo Bunrika Daigaku, primarily a teachers' training college, he accepted happily. Yet it quickly became apparent that it was a post for which he had no training and, as he, his colleagues, and his students became aware, very little aptitude.

The marriage that he had contracted before going to Japan also began to suffer what he called a "slow process of conversational attrition," and he and his wife divorced in 1935. Although he was married five times, Quennell suppressed so far as possible all information about his marital history, omitting all details from his entry in *Who's Who* on the grounds that he did not think that it was any business of anyone but himself and his wives.

He turned his experiences in Japan and the Far East into a strange kind of a travel book that he published as *A Superficial Journey through Tokyo and Peking* (1932). The epithet *superficial* is well chosen since the book makes it quite clear that he did not enjoy Japan or the Japanese, whom he makes no pretense to like or to understand. His comments are tainted by prejudice, but despite this, or perhaps even because of this, he was judged, by a reviewer in the *Times Literary Supplement* (21 July 1932), to have presented "vivid pictures of what he saw and excellent, often amusing, sometimes witty descriptions of what he did. . . . He is especially good, even brilliant, in describing the varieties of Japanese theatre. . . . He was happier in China than in Japan," though he fully recognized that "the West has nothing to give to the East because it long ago attained its culmination and has ceased to grow." The form he adopted to create his travel book is a loose and baggy collection of observations and reminiscences in which he mixes history, aestheticism, and personal anecdote in an entertaining eclecticism. His obvious pleasure in writing the book is matched by the pleasure derived from its reading.

After his time in Japan and the publication of a novel and a book of short stories, Quennell channeled his gifts to discussing, reanimating, and appraising the work and genius of other writers. He disciplined himself and his creativity most successfully through the writing of biography. He says in *Customs and Characters: Contemporary Portraits* (1982) that the "relationship of a biographer and his subject is a very curious one, for no biography can be totally objective. We can only understand our hero or heroine through our personal experience of the world; and every portrait we draw contains some reflections, however slight and desultory, of the draughtsman's own features." In submitting himself to the portrayal of other lives in other historical periods, he found sufficient scope for self-expression. In 1935 he published what he later described as "my first genuinely adult book," the first part of his life of George Gordon, Lord Byron, titled *Byron: The Years of Fame.*

He had already contributed a book on Byron to the Great Lives Series, published by Duckworth in 1934. *Byron* is a limited treatment of the poet's life which, nonetheless, remains a good, brief critical introduction to its subject and his works. It shows Byron as both the author and the victim of his own legend and singles out *English Bards and Scotch Reviewers* (1809), *Childe Harold* (1816, 1817) and *Don Juan* (1819–1824) as his best poetry. However, it is best regarded as a trial run for the later and far more impressive work on the poet, for he followed *Byron: The Years of Fame* by its sequel, *Byron in Italy* (1941), and together the two volumes set entirely new standards in Byron criticism. They represented by far the most thorough accounts of the life of the poet, his background in England and Italy, and the period in which he lived. Quennell drew on some new material, notably John Cam Hobhouse's annotated copy of Thomas Moore's *Letters and Journals of Lord Byron, with notices of his life* (1830) and some letters from the John Murray archive, though he does not include anything really that was not already known except perhaps for the support he gives for suspicions of Byron's homosexuality. The biography's strength is in the way in which the material is handled and the narrative of the events of the life retold. The people surrounding Byron, his friends, enemies, and acquaintances are sketched in vivid lines and faithful colors, and the social, intellectual, and political landscapes that formed the backdrop to his life are given picturesque and wholly convincing reality. Moreover, he deals with the character of Byron himself with detachment and a rare sense of balanced judgment that carries both insight and conviction. He is much less successful when he tries to generalize about the nature of Romanticism, for instance, or when he discusses the poetry. Theorizing and abstractions were always beyond his scope. Nonetheless, these volumes remain as outstanding examples of the biographer's art. Though superseded, perhaps, so far as facts and opinions are concerned, they are still read for the fascination of the way in which the events of Byron's life are retold, for their excitement, lucidity, and the extraordinary quality of Quennell's prose style. Above all, they are still read because they are so wonderfully readable.

In 1939 he completed and published a volume begun by Emily Morse Symonds, most of which she had published already in articles in *Cornhill,* titled *"To Lord Byron": Feminine Profiles Based upon Unpublished Letters 1807–1824,* which includes unpublished letters written between 1807 and 1824 by thirteen women correspondents. Later, in 1949, Quennell published an anthology of Byron's poetry and prose writings in the Nonesuch library and followed that by an altogether more ambitious two-volume edition of his letters and diaries titled *Byron: A Self-Portrait,* a selection of letters spanning his entire career from the first letter he ever wrote to letters sent from Greece shortly before his death. Though each section is introduced by a biographical summary describing the particular phases of his life, Byron is otherwise allowed to speak for himself. It is an enterprising and entertaining work that set the pattern for others to follow. Nonetheless, as has been pointed out by C. T. Goode, "Quennell's work as editor is not as felicitous as his accomplishments as Byron's biographer: his introduction of

new material is only incidental, the restored portions of the letters are not indicated in the text, errors in transcription are frequent, numerous texts are taken from inferior printed sources instead of available manuscripts, and the annotations are quixotic rather than systematic and contain errors." But Quennell never pretended to be an academic or professional editor and could never withstand criticism of such a scrupulous and exacting kind. Yet in having Byron ghostwrite, so to speak, his own biography, Quennell conceived an idea the originality of which is surely well beyond the creative scope of those who would question the provenance and authority of his texts.

Quennell's father died in 1936, but he had the satisfaction of cooperating with him in writing and publishing, in 1936, a guide to Somerset in the Shell County Guide series, which was under the general editorship of his friend John Betjeman. Quennell had always been closer to his mother, whom he thought he resembled temperamentally, and, though his relations with his father had never been close, the writing of the book seems to have reconciled them as friends as well as father and son.

Also at about that time he joined an advertising agency as a junior copywriter, his first theme being to present a brand of corsets. For two years he crossed the Atlantic every five or six months to represent his agency at Elizabeth Arden's in New York. His salary helped him to support his lifestyle and to live more within his means, but "although it [the advertising work] amused me and had brought me moderate success, secretly I could not help despising."

In 1939, just before the outbreak of World War II, he published his biography of Caroline of Anspach, consort of George II and, he believed, "since Elizabeth I, certainly the shrewdest and most cultivated woman ever to occupy an English throne. I had a magnificent cast – the sovereign himself, an explosive martinet. . . . Sir Robert Walpole, that herculean cynic, who governed his master with the Queen's connivance; the brilliant, self-destructive Bolingbroke, and the fascinating, effeminate Lord Hervey; besides a long array of fine subsidiary personages, Pope and Swift and Lord Burlington, and Lord Burlington's aide, 'The Signior' William Kent. My book was not, nor did I mean that it should be, a lasting contribution to the study of the early eighteenth century; but I like to think that it reflected the period's ethos, which I believed I understood." The biography was extremely popular and sold well: "my study of Caroline" he recalled, "had had larger sales [than *Byron: The Years of Fame*] – books on royal personages invariably appeal to the English

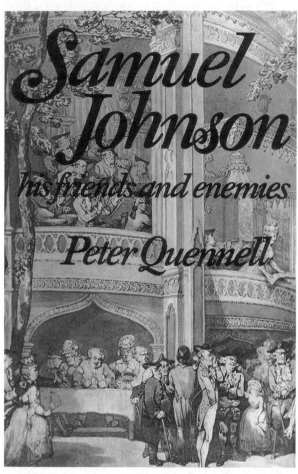

Dust jacket for the American edition of Quennell's book on the eighteenth-century writer and his times. H. G. Kahn described the book as "a lively social history."

taste." He succeeds brilliantly in bringing Caroline to life even if he does endow her with a more complex personality and a more unconventional attitude than history or human nature would seem to support, when he says she encouraged her husband's adulteries because she believed that an unfaithful husband was more likely to be a contented one. Nonetheless, he is probably right to believe that she had such a hold on her husband that for him "adultery was a duty, marriage a pleasure." Quennell did not undertake any new research in preparation for the writing of his book, nor does his book contain any new facts about his subject or her times. In the verdict of the reviewer for the *Times Literary Supplement* (11 November 1939), "he has relied on his own literary gifts to attract his readers and to set the Queen in a new light. He has succeeded extremely well . . . [his] style – at once amusing and mordant but never lapsing into mere denigration – is well fitted to his task." The Queen, the

background, and the early Hanoverian court "come amusingly and convincingly to life."

During the war he worked mainly in London as a press censor at the Ministry of Information. He was sacked for being lazy and unenthusiastic and sent to Belfast, where he spent three or four depressing weeks before using his influence to get himself posted back to the Ministry of Economic Warfare in London. He was a most reluctant conscript to the Fire Service, though it was late in the war and the only fire he attended blazed three months before peace was declared and raids were a thing of the past. His last wartime job, by far his most congenial one, was with Radio News Reel, a branch of the British Broadcasting Corporation. He lived a rootless, rather bohemian life, living in one flat after another, lodging with one person after another, throughout the London blitz, which he also recalls as a time of clubs and social enjoyments. His love life apparently became even more enjoyably complicated. The death of his younger brother, Paul, who was killed in Belgium in May 1940 by German artillery fire, was a source of grief and recurring regret for many years after.

His close friendship with Ann Rothermere, who later became the wife of Ian Fleming, led her to use her influence with her then-husband, Lord Rothermere, to have Quennell appointed as book critic on Rothermere's newspaper, the *Daily Mail*, a position he retained from 1943 to 1956. During the thirteen years he worked for the *Daily Mail*, he said, "I tried the patience of a series of editors and subeditors, who hesitated, I suppose, to sack me because I had a friend, or friends, behind the scenes. . . . I enjoyed the business of praising a praiseworthy book . . . and I was not averse from mounting a full-scale attack against a thoroughly bad novel or slipshod popular biography." Yet he began to resent the fact that it took up so much of his time. He spent half the week reading the books he was reviewing and writing his seven- or eight-hundred-word reviews. He was also, in January 1944, appointed editor of the *Cornhill Magazine*, where he remained until 1951. His editorial policy on the *Cornhill Magazine*, which had once been edited by William Makepeace Thackeray, was simple and straightforward: he printed what he considered to be most worth printing, irrespective of the author's age or ideological position. He published, among others, pieces by Louis Aragon, Max Beerbohm, Clive Bell, Isaiah Berlin, John Betjeman, Elizabeth Bowen, Maurice Bowra, Truman Capote, Kenneth Clark, André Gide, Harley Granville-Barker, Margaret Lane, Rose Macaulay, Somerset Maugham, Harold Nicolson, Anthony Powell, Steven Runciman, William Sansom, Freya Stark, Robert Trevelyan, Hugh Trevor Roper, Arthur Waley, Evelyn Waugh, and H. G. Wells.

In 1951 he became coeditor, with Alan Hodge, of *History Today*. For the next twenty-eight years he was largely responsible for maintaining civilized values in a nonspecialist "but elegant fashion to as broad a community of intelligent people as possible." He was outstandingly successful as an editor, and by the time he relinquished his editorial post *History Today* was firmly established as the leading journal of its kind.

Despite the demands made on him as a book reviewer and journal editor, he continued to publish a steady stream of books. His *Four Portraits: Studies of the Eighteenth Century,* published in 1945, is one of the best known of all his books. It consists of four biographical portraits – of James Boswell, Edward Gibbon, Laurence Sterne, and John Wilkes. He was clearly fascinated by those qualities that they shared despite their dissimilarities and the clashes of opinions and taste that frequently divided them. "I endeavoured," he explained, "to unite my four heroes in a single literary pattern, which would serve to illustrate the broader pattern of the age. I respected them all – Gibbon for the fidelity to his own genius; Sterne for his imaginative scope, his command of the language and his romantic sensibility; Wilkes, for his dash and courage and gusto and unconquerable love of life. But to Boswell I grew particularly attached. . . . Boswell's faults – his excitability, his childish impetuosity and his desperate vulnerability – were another aspect of his high creative virtues. . . . Boswell had a consuming appetite for truth, and hankered after knowledge as eagerly, and at times as indiscriminately, as he lusted after women." Quennell shows himself to be thoroughly at ease in the eighteenth century and writes about his chosen figures with great understanding. Certainly he makes the short study of each of his subjects an elegant and authoritative demonstration of the biographer's art. The book achieved both critical acclaim and popular success. Nevertheless, the book had what he describes as a rather modest sale. Between 1945 and 1949 the first edition earned nearly £2,760.

In 1949 Quennell published *John Ruskin: The Portrait of a Prophet.* He recalled his father's regard for Ruskin's *The Stones of Venice* (1851–1853) as "The far-off starting point of my long Ruskinian expedition," although he seemed to be even more impressed by Marcel Proust's regard for Ruskin and the similarities between them: "Proust and Ruskin . . . had shared many traits besides their genius and their love of art. Both had been weak children; both were brought up by anxiously devoted parents; both were attracted toward very young girls; and both carried the burden of an ill-adjusted sexual nature. Ruskin's nympholeptic passion for Rose La Touche – at their earliest meeting, in 1858, she was not yet ten years old . . . lasted until she died in 1875. This pathetic episode a biographer must somehow reconcile with the story of his intellectual progress." Though his book is titled *The Portrait of a Prophet,* it is a detailed and personal study of Ruskin's private life. He passes over the vexed question of the collapse of Ruskin's marriage to Effie Chalmers Gray because of his failure to consummate it, and her subsequent marriage to John Everett Millais. Instead, he concentrates his attention on Ruskin's long, drawn-out obsession with Rose La Touche. "Though his admiration for Ruskin may be qualified, he errs on the side of generosity," concluded a reviewer in the *Times Literary Supplement* (23 December 1949). "He directs the reader's eyes towards the kindly things which were said about him. . . . [T]his penetrating and splendidly written book . . . [distorts] his greatness." Bernard Shaw expressed his surprise at the picture of Ruskin that emerged: "I have little time for reading now; but I have somehow contrived lately to read Peter Quennell's life of Ruskin. . . . The revelation of Ruskin as a lifelong monster milksop is astounding, and hardly bearable. Millais alone ticketed him accurately, having the advantage of being married to the quondam Mrs. Ruskin, who divorced him for an entirely false impotence, the truth being that he was abnormally sexed."

Quennell returned to the subject of the eighteenth century in *Hogarth's Progress* (1955). Again, this volume was not the result of primary research. He had discovered no new facts about William Hogarth, nor did he give any new interpretation of the known and familiar facts. What he achieved, and achieved with great skill, was "to set the painter in his own picture, to put the dramatist on his own stage. He has written," a contemporary reviewer commented in the *Times Literary Supplement* (5 August 1955), "at one and the same time, a most readable biography and a rewardingly inquisitive guidebook to eighteenth-century London – for which latter, by ingenious posthumous collaboration, Hogarth has provided the illustrations." "I had," Quennell said, "many good reasons for becoming attached to Hogarth – the greatest social historian of a period that particularly interested me. . . . I was fascinated by the steady evolution of his genius." In fact, it is the life of Hogarth's age that is so vividly presented rather than the life of Hogarth himself.

Throughout the postwar years Quennell continued to live a rich and privileged social life. He was very much, as Kingsley Amis later described him in *Memoirs* (1991), "Somebody one ran into at parties." He cultivated friendships with the party-giving hostesses of the time, including Ann Rothermere and Emerald Cunard. He was also invited to stay at the British Embassy in Paris by Diana and Duff Cooper, much to the chagrin of Evelyn Waugh. He extended his knowledge of France and of French literature by his friendships with Colette, André Gide, and Henry de Montherlant as well as by frequent visits to France. He introduced the work of Montherlant to England by editing a volume of his essays and introducing translations of some of his novels. He also wrote *Shakespeare: The Poet and His Background* (1963), which was overshadowed by A. L. Rowse's *William Shakespeare: A Biography,* which also appeared in 1963. Quennell said that initially the book was called *In Search of Shakespeare,* and, although that title was later discarded, it more aptly described his purpose in writing the book. "I have attempted," he says in his preface, "to reach the poet at once through his work and through his times. My hero is the ambitious Stratford player." One reviewer in the *Times Literary Supplement* (2 January 1964) says "that the study was often interesting on the historical background to the dramatist's career; it is with the setting of his subject against this background that one must admit to a feeling of disappointment." The reviewer then lists some of the book's many factual errors and unproven assertions. Stanley Wells, however, writing in *Shakespeare Survey* (1965), was more generous in his assessment of the book's merits, which he describes as "sprightly but more temperate in tone" than Rowse's study, "notably well illustrated, and offering a sound historical background." Oddly, he believes Quennell's book is written "by a historian obliged by his subject to treat of literary matters," an assertion probably confused by the fact that Quennell was editor of *History Today.* He concludes that though the author "is a critic of some sophistication, he nevertheless shows survivals of generally outmoded attitudes: for him, for instances, *Love's Labour's Lost* is not an adult work," and Malvolio "deserves to rank among the dramatist's tragic characters."

Quennell's work is always beguiling, always stylish, and never dull. But he was always happiest writing about the eighteenth century – except perhaps when writing about his contemporaries – where he carried his learning lightly. While not a professional scholar, and certainly no pedant, he was often read and admired by scholars as well as by the general reader. *Alexander Pope: The Education of a Genius 1688–1728,* published in 1968, is a good example of his contributing something uniquely his own to a subject covered by an already crowded field of critical and biographical works. A review written by Rachel Trickett, a scholar on the eighteenth century, and published in *Review of English Studies* (1970) summarizes the book as throwing no new light on Pope but providing "a lively and vigourous picture of the poet in his setting. . . . It sets out to investigate the personality of one of the most autobiographical poets and the character of his age in an elegant, persuasive style, intended rather for the general reader than for the professional." The book, while intended for the general reader, also impressed the scholarly and professional reader.

In *Samuel Johnson: His Friends and Enemies,* published in 1972, Quennell goes over more familiar ground. His subject is Johnson the man – "The chapter on his works can hardly be taken seriously," pronounced the reviewer in the *Times Literary Supplement* (20 October 1972) – "in conversation and at his ease in Streatham with the Thrales or in the London drawing room. He has been outstandingly successful in his aim to produce a literary conversation-piece, in which [the] hero stands at the centre of the picture, surrounded by his friends and enemies, against the background of his period." The book is organized so that Johnson becomes the excuse for re-creating the celebrities of his age together with the social and domestic scenes they inhabited and the sensibilities they expressed and enjoyed. He offers the reader recognizable portraits of most of the leading figures in the intellectual life of the eighteenth century. "Anecdotes, illustrations and pronouncements from many firsthand sources make this work a lively social history . . . eminently readable," concludes H. G. Hahn in his notice published in the *Library Journal* (1 April 1973). The writer and critic V. S. Pritchett also praised the book, saying in the *New Statesman* (24 November 1972) that it "is made doubly interesting by a large number of well-chosen pictures of decorous London and the caricatures that tell the other side of the story. . . . The attraction of the [book] lies in its critical discursiveness and its pin-pointing of contrast. Fashionable Europe talked: surrounding portraits . . . are engagingly brought to life, not simply as persons, but as talents or temperaments astutely observed."

Looking back to his childhood, Quennell remembered his father receiving a letter that referred to the happiness that both he and his wife must have surely enjoyed because they wrote and illustrated their books working side by side. His father considered the matter for a moment and then suddenly remarked, much to his mother's hurt, "Well, we're not happy, are we?" It is precisely this question of being happy, unhappy, or not happy that Quennell addresses in his last book, *The Pursuit of Happiness,* published in 1988. After all, the question is one that, as he says, has "perplexed and fascinated imaginative artists for the last two thousand years." Quennell examines the experiences of the past and involves writers, painters, and public figures in his discussion. Roy Porter, writing in *History Today* (November 1988), describes the book as "ever wise, humane and a joy to read." He describes how Quennell "interweaves his unmatched familiarity with the personalities of the past with autobiographical vignettes. There is a delightful account of himself, under the influence of medically prescribed morphine after an accident, 'tripping' on a London bus; and a no less joyous jacket photograph of the author posing in an armchair as Horace's 'happy man,' surrounded with his cats and books." "Quennell rightly emphasizes how love and work have so often proved the keys to happiness. . . . Thanks to volumes like this, reading will always remain one of the royal roads to happiness." In other words, he has transmitted to the reader the happiness that his argument pursues. D. J. Enright, in the *Times Literary Supplement* (7 October 1988), makes a further observation when he describes the work as "a cultivated and relaxed conducted tour through history, plotting the pursuit of happiness as recorded by creative artists. . . . [A] commonly shared conclusion, Quennell remarks, has it that happiness is found in looking back or looking forward rather than looking around. The true paradises are paradises we have lost, regained only in memory." There is no disguising Quennell's own pleasure in ransacking the past in pursuit of his quarry, an activity undertaken for its own sake rather than for the sake of any answers he may find. His book ends as he watches his old friend John Betjeman in a wheelchair, happy nonetheless in the contemplation of a work of art. As an octogenarian, Quennell in this book renews his enjoyment of life by recounting the ways in which happiness has been captured, lost, and captured again. He looks back with evident pleasure and looks forward with an undimmed appetite to the happiness he is certain is still in store for him. It is a remarkably resilient, assured, and enjoyable performance.

Quennell published his autobiography in two volumes, *The Marble Foot* (1976) and *The Wanton Chase* (1980). Two other volumes, *The Sign of the Fish* (1960) and *Customs and Characters: Contemporary Portraits,* contain mainly reminiscences concerning his early friendships and acquaintances. *The Sign of the Fish* is a vivid, interesting, and amusing miscellany based largely on materials he had previously published in articles for a variety of journals. It is in effect a charming mixture of literary gossip, anecdotes, and personal memories of the Sitwells, Edward Marsh, Ottoline Morrell, Gide, and others who for the most part belonged firmly to the earlier years of the century. The whole book is structured only insofar as the author moves from memories of one to another in a rather loose, associative way, thus lending it the informality of good conversation between informed and civilized people. Quennell displays the art that so cleverly disguises art in the way he captures and charms his readers. *Customs and Characters: Contemporary Portraits* is a similar book that provides portraits and memories of, among others, Greta Garbo, Mrs. George Keppel and Violet Keppel, Augustus John, Elizabeth Bowen, Daisy Fellowes, and Randolph Churchill. Quennell's portraits of his friends and acquaintances are always enlivened and diversified by animated asides, anecdotes, and personal memories. He is never dull or boring company and likes the subjects he presents, whom he also wants us to like. Nevertheless, it is noticeable that the company he keeps is often more remarkable for its social graces than its intellectual rigor. He pays in full his debt to his dead friends by meeting their requirements, which he defined thus: "to be remembered, talked over, even perhaps sometimes laughed at, is surely the only tribute that the dead require."

The first volume of his autobiography, *The Marble Foot,* covers Quennell's life to 1938 and is by far the most informative of the two volumes, as it deals with his childhood, his early years, and his experiences in literary and social London. Yet it is a curiously reticent book all the same. Mark Amory, reviewing the second volume, *The Wanton Chase,* in the *Times Literary Supplement* (13 June 1980), makes the point in an amusing way when he says that "I have the impression that he got married quite a bit but the only reference to this activity comes in an exchange with Maugham whom he deems it tactful to tell that he is 'not *un*happy' with a new bride." Both volumes conceal quite as much as they reveal. He is careful to protect his privacy while writing his life story, which, as a difficult undertaking, confines him for the most part to a discussion of the public persona while leaving the private person out of account. His prose style is a finely tempered artifice, self-consciously balanced, elegant, and precise, though the substance is often less than sustaining. He is, however, an acute and witty observer of his contemporaries and a wonderful painter of the social scene. It seems a pity, perhaps, that modesty, good taste, and good breeding should not from time to time have given way to frankness and even vulgarity. The anguish and happiness of his love affairs and marriages are hinted at but not explained, and his work as book critic for the *Daily Mail,* his editorship of the *Cornhill Magazine* and of *History Today* are recorded, but he says little or nothing about what this work entailed. Yet despite such reticence, Michael Grant in *History Today* (December 1993), who said that the autobiographies were his favorites among his writings, is surely right when he comments that "autobiography is about the hardest of all literary *genres* to handle successfully. . . . Peter's books about himself . . . are not only vivid and exact and pungent, but extremely funny (often about himself, which more pompous autobiographers cannot achieve). 'Compulsive reading,' said the late Sir John Betjeman and he was perfectly right. This is just one more reason to regard Peter, as I do, as one of the best *writers* of our time, and all the more so because of his light touch."

Quennell was always a productive editor of other people's work. Some of his editorial work has the mark of high originality, as, for instance, his book *Victorian Panorama* (1937), the subtitle of which, *A Survey of Life & Fashion from Contemporary Photographs,* explains its contents. It is an important work of sociology in its own right and shows him to be the son of the parents who produced the history of everyday things. His edition of *The Private Letters of Princess Lieven to Prince Metternich: 1820–1826* (1937) has a unique historical importance as well as a good deal of human and personal interest. In some instances he was responsible for putting back into print important works that had long been neglected, such as Henry Mayhew's *London Labour and the London Poor,* of which he edited several selections in 1949, and *The Journal of Thomas Moore, 1818–1841* (1964). The memoirs of William Hickey and John Macdonald are minor but significant contributions to the social history of their times. Sometimes he edited the work of those he admired, such as Byron and Ruskin. Sometimes he edited a volume in order to express his admiration of the subject, as he did in

his tributes to Marcel Proust and to Vladimir Nabokov, both of whom he valued highly as creative artists and as stylists.

He was highly regarded by his fellow authors for his achievements and for his sociability. Near the beginning of his career, his friend Cyril Connolly dedicated his novel *The Rock Pool* (1936) to him, and Kingsley Amis, a writer of an altogether different generation, dedicated his novel *The Folks Who Lived On the Hill* (1990) to him. Indeed, Amis, who would seem to be something of an expert on such matters, nominated Quennell as "the best story-teller one is likely to meet, always funny or surprising and to the point." He was honored for his services to history and literature by being awarded a CBE in 1973 and a knighthood in 1992. On his eighty-fifth birthday he was acclaimed by Patrick Taylor-Martin in the 4 March 1990 *Sunday Times* as the "most active and accessible of the few surviving members of the so-called Brideshead Generation. . . . Talking to him is like leafing through a mischievously annotated copy of *Who Was Who.*" A similarly celebratory article had earlier appeared in the 9 March 1985 *Spectator* under the heading "Survivors." Despite his age he continued writing, and his interviewers remark on the youthfulness of his appearance. "His back is straight, his cheeks are rosy, his handsome face still bears that expression of mildly mandarin amusement which one suspects went down so well in the Far East." The American novelist Duncan Fallowell, who visited him when he was eighty-five, describes him in the *American Scholar* (Autumn 1992) as "altogether a most elegant, insouciant figure – even his handwriting and fine black socks are elegant – it is obvious why he has proven so attractive to women."

Quennell died at the University College Hospital in London on 27 October 1993, aged eighty-eight. The funeral was held at St. Mark's Church, Regent's Park, followed by a private cremation service. He had been married for the fifth time in 1967 to Marilyn, Lady Peek, and they had one son, Alexander. Both survived him, together with a daughter, Sarah, from his third marriage. A thanksgiving service for him was held at St. James's Church, Piccadilly, on 12 January 1994 when, among other addresses and appreciations, his daughter read from his work and Lucy Robinson read Matthew Arnold's "Dover Beach" and his own poem "Procne."

A. L. Rowse

(4 December 1903 –)

Vicki K. Janik
State University of New York at Farmingdale

BOOKS: *On History: A Study of Present Tendencies* (London: Kegan Paul, Trench, Trubner, 1927); published as *Science and History: A New View of History* (New York: Norton, 1928);

Politics and the Younger Generation (London: Faber & Faber, 1931);

The Question of the House of Lords (London: Hogarth Press, 1934);

Queen Elizabeth and Her Subjects, by Rowse and George B. Harrison (London: Allen & Unwin, 1935; Freeport, N.Y.: Books for Libraries Press, 1970);

Mr. Keynes and the Labour Movement (London: Macmillan, 1936);

Sir Richard Grenville of the Revenge: An Elizabethan Hero (Boston & New York: Houghton Mifflin, 1937; London: Cape, 1937);

Tudor Cornwall: Portrait of a Society (London: Cape, 1941; New York: Scribners, 1969);

Poems of a Decade: 1931–1941 (London: Faber, 1941);

A Cornish Childhood: Autobiography of a Cornishman (London: Cape, 1942; New York: Macmillan, 1947);

The Spirit of English History (London: Cape, 1943; London & New York: Published for the British Council by Longmans, Green, 1943);

Poems Chiefly Cornish (London: Faber & Faber, 1944);

The English Spirit: Essays in History and Literature (London: Macmillan, 1944; New York: Macmillan, 1945); revised as *The English Spirit: Essays in Literature and History* (London: Macmillan, 1966; New York: Funk & Wagnalls, 1967);

West-Country Stories (London: Macmillan, 1945; New York: Macmillan, 1947);

The Use of History (London: Published by Hodder & Stoughton for the English Universities Press, 1946; New York: Macmillan, 1948; revised edition, London: English Universities Press, 1963; New York: Collier, 1963);

Poems of Deliverance (London: Faber & Faber, 1946);

A. L. Rowse (courtesy of A. L. Rowse)

The End of an Epoch: Reflections on Contemporary History (London: Macmillan, 1947);

The Elizabethan Age, volume 1: *The England of Elizabeth: The Structure of Society* (London: Macmillan, 1950; New York: Macmillan, 1950); volume 2: *The Expansion of Elizabethan England* (London: Macmillan, 1955; New York: St. Martin's Press, 1955); volume 3: *The Elizabethan Renaissance,* part 1, *The Life of the Society* (London: Macmillan, 1971; New York: Scribners, 1972); part 2, *The Cultural Achieve-*

ment (London: Macmillan, 1972; New York: Scribners, 1972);

The English Past: Evocations of Places and Persons (London: Macmillan, 1951; New York: Macmillan, 1952); revised as *Times, Persons, Places: Essays in Literature* (London: Macmillan, 1965);

A New Elizabethan Age? (London: Oxford University Press, 1952);

Royal Homes Illustrated (London: Odhams, 1953);

An Elizabethan Garland (London: Macmillan / New York: St. Martin's Press, 1953);

The Early Churchills: An English Family (London: Macmillan, 1956; New York: Harper, 1956);

Sir Richard Grenville's Place in English History: Raleigh Lecture on History, from the Proceedings of the British Academy (London: Oxford University Press, 1957);

The Churchills: From the Death of Marlborough to the Present (New York: Harper, 1958); published as *The Later Churchills* (London: Macmillan, 1958);

Poems Partly American (London: Faber & Faber, 1959);

The Elizabethans and America (London: Macmillan, 1959; New York: Harper, 1959);

St. Austell: Church, Town, Parish (Saint Austell: Warne, 1960);

Appeasement: A Study in Political Decline, 1933–1939 (New York: Norton, 1961); published as *All Souls and Appeasement: A Contribution to Contemporary History* (London: Macmillan, 1961; New York: St. Martin's Press, 1961);

Ralegh and the Throckmortons (London: Macmillan, 1962; New York: St. Martin's Press, 1962); published as *Sir Walter Ralegh: His Family and Private Life* (New York: Harper, 1962);

William Shakespeare: A Biography (London: Macmillan, 1963; New York: Harper & Row, 1963; revised edition, London: New English Library, 1967);

Christopher Marlowe: A Biography (London: Macmillan, 1964; New York: Harper & Row, 1964); published as *Christopher Marlowe: His Life and Work* (London: Harper & Row, 1965);

A Cornishman at Oxford: The Education of a Cornishman (London: Cape, 1965);

Shakespeare's Southampton, Patron of Virginia (London: Macmillan, 1965; New York: Harper & Row, 1965);

Bosworth Field, from Medieval to Tudor England (Garden City, N. Y.: Doubleday, 1966); published as *Bosworth Field and the Wars of the Roses* (London: Macmillan, 1966);

Cornish Stories (London: Macmillan, 1967);

Poems of Cornwall and America (London: Faber, 1967);

The Contribution of Cornwall and Cornishmen to Britain (Newton Abbot, U.K.: Seale-Hayne Agricultural College, 1969);

The Cornish in America (London: Macmillan, 1969); published as *The Cousin Jacks: The Cornish in America* (New York: Scribners, 1969);

Strange Encounter (London: Cape, 1972);

The Tower of London in the History of the Nation (London: Weidenfeld & Nicolson, 1972); published as *The Tower of London in the History of England* (New York: Putnam, 1972);

Westminster Abbey in the History of the Nation (London: Weidenfeld & Nicolson, 1972; Radnor, Pa.: Annenberg School Press, 1972);

Shakespeare the Man (London: Macmillan, 1973; New York: Harper & Row, 1973; revised, Houndmills, Basingstoke, U.K.: Macmillan, 1988; New York: St. Martin's Press, 1988);

Peter, the White Cat of Trenarren (London: Joseph, 1974);

Simon Forman: Sex and Society in Shakespeare's Age (London: Weidenfeld & Nicolson, 1974); published as *Sex and Society in Shakespeare's Age: Simon Forman the Astrologer* (New York: Scribners, 1974);

Windsor Castle in the History of the Nation (London: Weidenfeld & Nicolson, 1974); published as *Windsor Castle in the History of England* (New York: Putnam, 1974);

Jonathan Swift: Major Prophet (London: Thames & Hudson, 1975); published as *Jonathan Swift* (New York: Scribners, 1975);

Oxford in the History of the Nation (London: Weidenfeld & Nicolson, 1975); published as *Oxford in the History of England* (New York: Putnam, 1975);

Discoveries and Reviews: From Renaissance to Restoration (London: Macmillan, 1975; New York: Barnes & Noble, 1975);

Matthew Arnold: Poet and Prophet (London: Thames & Hudson, 1976; Lanham, Md.: University Press of America, 1986);

Brown Buck: A Californian Fantasy (London: Joseph, 1976);

A Cornishman Abroad (London: Cape, 1976);

Homosexuals in History: A Study of Ambivalence in Society, Literature, and the Arts (London: Weidenfeld & Nicolson, 1977; New York: Macmillan, 1977);

Shakespeare the Elizabethan (London: Weidenfeld & Nicolson, 1977; New York: Putnam, 1977);

Rowse, with Agatha Christie, left, and Lady Camoys in 1971

Milton the Puritan: Portrait of a Mind (London: Macmillan, 1977; Lanham, Md.: University Press of America, 1985);

Heritage of Britain (London: Artus, 1977; New York: Putnam, 1977);

The Road to Oxford (London: Cape, 1978);

The Byrons and Trevanions (London: Weidenfeld & Nicolson, 1978; New York: St. Martin's Press, 1979);

Three Cornish Cats (London: Weidenfeld & Nicolson, 1978); enlarged as *A Quartet of Cornish Cats* (London: Weidenfeld & Nicolson, 1986);

A Man of the Thirties (London: Weidenfeld & Nicolson, 1979);

Portraits and Views: Literary and Historical (London: Macmillan, 1979; New York: Barnes & Noble, 1979);

The Story of Britain (London: Treasure, 1979; New York: British Heritage Press, 1979);

Memories of Men and Women (London: Eyre Methuen, 1980); published as *Memories of Men and Women: American and British* (Lanham, Md.: University Press of America, 1983);

Shakespeare's Globe, His Intellectual and Moral Outlook (London: Weidenfeld & Nicolson, 1981);

What Shakespeare Read — And Thought (New York: Coward-McCann, 1981);

A Life: Collected Poems (Edinburgh: Blackwood, 1981);

Eminent Elizabethans (London: Macmillan, 1983; Athens: University of Georgia Press, 1983);

Shakespeare's Characters, A Complete Guide (London: Methuen, 1984);

Night at the Carn, and Other Stories (London: Kimber, 1984);

Glimpses of the Great (London: Methuen, 1985; Lanham, Md.: University Press of America, 1985);

Stories from Trenarren (London: Kimber, 1986);

Reflections on the Puritan Revolution (London: Methuen, 1986);

The Little Land of Cornwall (Gloucester: Sutton, 1986);

In Shakespeare's Land: A Journey through the Landscape of Elizabethan England (London: Weidenfeld & Nicolson, 1986); published as *Shakespeare's Land: A Journey through the Landscape of Elizabethan England* (San Francisco: Chronicle Books, 1987);

Froude the Historian: Victorian Man of Letters (Gloucester, U.K.: Sutton, 1987);

Court and Country: Studies in Tudor Social History (Brighton, U.K.: Harvester, 1987; Athens: University of Georgia Press, 1987);

The Poet Auden: A Personal Memoir (London: Methuen, 1987; New York: Weidenfeld & Nicolson, 1988);

Quiller Couch: A Portrait of "Q" (London: Methuen, 1988);

A. L. Rowse's Cornwall: A Journey through Cornwall's Past and Present (London: Weidenfeld & Nicolson, 1988);

Friends and Contemporaries (London: Methuen, 1989);

Transatlantic: Later Poems (Padstow, U.K.: Tabb House, 1989);

The Controversial Colensos (Redruth, U.K.: Truran, 1989);

Discovering Shakespeare: A Chapter in Literary History (London: Weidenfeld & Nicolson, 1989);

Selected Poems (Penzance, U.K.: Hodge, 1990);

Prompting the Age: Poems Early and Late (Redruth, U.K.: Truran, 1990);

The Regicides and the Puritan Revolution (London: Duckworth, 1994).

OTHER: *Essays in Cornish History,* edited by Rowse and Charles G. Henderson (Oxford: Clarendon Press, 1935);

Alun Lewis, *Letters from India,* preface by Rowse (Cardiff, Wales: Penmark Press, 1946);

Men and Their Time Series, edited by Rowse (London: Hodder & Stoughton, 1947);

Lewis, *In the Green Tree,* preface by Rowse (London: Allen & Unwin, 1948);

The West in English History, edited by Rowse (London: Hodder & Stoughton, 1949);

Lucien Romier, *A History of France,* edited and translated by Rowse (New York: St. Martin's Press, 1953; London: Macmillan, 1962);

Martyn Skinner, *The Return of Arthur* (London: Chapman & Hall, 1955);

William Shakespeare, *Sonnets,* edited by Rowse (London: Macmillan, 1964; New York:

Harper, 1964); published as *Shakespeare's Sonnets: The Problems Solved* (London: Macmillan, 1973; New York: Harper, 1973);

The Generall Historie of Virginia, New-England, and the Summer Isles by John Smith, 1624, edited by Rowse (Cleveland: World, 1966);

The Discoverie of Guiana, by Sir Walter Ralegh, 1596, and The Discoveries of the World, by Antonio Galvo, 1601 (Cleveland: World, 1966);

A Cornish Anthology, edited by Rowse (London: Macmillan, 1968);

James Anthony Froude, *The Two Chiefs of Dunboy: A Story of Eighteenth-Century Ireland,* edited by Rowse (London: Chatto & Windus, 1969);

Michael J. Brown, *Itinerant Ambassador* (Lexington: University Press of Kentucky, 1970);

"The Scholar and Responsibility to the Public," in *The Professor and the Public: The Role of the Scholar in the Modern World,* compiled by Goldwin Smith (Detroit: Wayne State University Press, 1972);

Peter Pindar's Poems, edited by Rowse (Bath, U.K.: Adam & Dart, 1972);

Victorian and Edwardian Cornwall from Old Photographs, compiled by Rowse and Sir John Betjeman (London: Batsford, 1974);

Martin Andrews, *Canon's Folly,* edited by Rowse (London: M. Joseph, 1974);

The Case Books of Simon Forman, edited by Rowse (London: Pan, 1976);

Jonathan Swift, *Gulliver's Travels,* edited by Rowse (London: Pan, 1977);

Burke's Guide to the British Monarchy (London: Burke's Peerage Limited, in conjunction with New English Library, 1977);

Aemilia Lanyer, *The Poems of Shakespeare's Dark Lady,* edited by Rowse (London: Cape, 1978); published as *The Poems of Shakespeare's Dark Lady — Salve Deus Rex Judæorum* (New York: Potter, 1979);

The Annotated Shakespeare, 3 volumes, edited, with a biography and bibliography, by Rowse (New York: Potter, 1978);

A Man of Singular Virtue: Being a Life of Sir Thomas More by his Son-in-Law William Roper, and a Selection of More's Letters, edited by Rowse (London: Folio Society, 1980);

Shakespeare, *King Richard the Second,* edited by Rowse (Lanham, Md.: University Press of America, 1984);

Shakespeare, *King Lear,* edited by Rowse (Lanham, Md.: University Press of America, 1984);

Rowse's library and workroom at Trenarren House in Cornwall (courtesy of A. L. Rowse)

Shakespeare, *Twelfth Night,* edited by Rowse (Lanham, Md.: University Press of America, 1984);

Shakespeare, *The Tempest,* edited by Rowse (Lanham, Md.: University Press of America, 1984);

Shakespeare, *Hamlet,* edited by Rowse (Lanham, Md.: University Press of America, 1984);

Shakespeare, *A Midsummer Night's Dream,* edited by Rowse (Lanham, Md.: University Press of America, 1984);

Shakespeare, *Julius Caesar,* edited by Rowse (Lanham, Md.: University Press of America, 1984);

Shakespeare, *Romeo and Juliet,* edited by Rowse (Lanham, Md.: University Press of America, 1984);

Shakespeare, *The Merchant of Venice,* edited by Rowse (Lanham, Md.: University Press of America, 1984);

Shakespeare, *As You Like It,* edited by Rowse (Lanham, Md.: University Press of America, 1984);

Shakespeare, *Coriolanus,* edited by Rowse (Lanham, Md.: University Press of America, 1984);

Shakespeare, *The Winter's Tale,* edited by Rowse (Lanham, Md.: University Press of America, 1985);

Shakespeare, *King Henry the Fourth, Part I,* edited by Rowse (Lanham, Md.: University Press of America, 1985);

Shakespeare, *King Henry the Fourth, Part II,* edited by Rowse (Lanham, Md.: University Press of America, 1985);

Shakespeare, *Love's Labour's Lost,* edited by Rowse (Lanham, Md.: University Press of America, 1985);

Shakespeare, *Othello,* edited by Rowse (Lanham, Md.: University Press of America, 1985);

Shakespeare, *The Taming of the Shrew,* edited by Rowse (Lanham, Md.: University Press of America, 1985);

Shakespeare, *Henry V,* edited by Rowse (Lanham, Md.: University Press of America, 1985);

Shakespeare, *Macbeth,* edited by Rowse (Lanham, Md.: University Press of America, 1985);

Shakespeare, *All's Well That Ends Well,* edited by Rowse (Lanham, Md.: University Press of America, 1985);

Shakespeare, *King Richard the Third,* edited by Rowse (Lanham, Md.: University Press of America, 1985);

Shakespeare, *Troilus and Cressida,* edited by Rowse (Lanham, Md.: University Press of America, 1986);

Shakespeare, *Antony and Cleopatra,* edited by Rowse (Lanham, Md.: University Press of America, 1986);

Shakespeare, *The Two Gentlemen of Verona,* edited by Rowse (Lanham, Md.: University Press of America, 1986);

Shakespeare, *Measure for Measure,* edited by Rowse (Lanham, Md.: University Press of America, 1986);

Shakespeare, *Merry Wives of Windsor,* edited by Rowse (Lanham, Md.: University Press of America, 1986);

Richard Hakluyt, *Voyages to the Virginia Colonies,* edited by Rowse (London: Century, 1986);

Hakluyt, *The First Colonists: A Modern Version,* edited by Rowse (London: Folio Society, 1986);

Shakespeare, *Cymbeline,* edited by Rowse (Lanham, Md.: University Press of America, 1987);

Shakespeare, *Much Ado about Nothing,* edited by Rowse (Lanham, Md.: University Press of America, 1987);

Shakespeare, *The Comedy of Errors,* edited by Rowse (Lanham, Md.: University Press of America, 1987);

Shakespeare, *Titus Andronicus,* edited by Rowse (Lanham, Md.: University Press of America, 1987);

Shakespeare, *Pericles, Prince of Tyre,* edited by Rowse (Lanham, Md.: University Press of America, 1987);

Shakespeare, *King Henry the Sixth, Part One,* edited by Rowse (Lanham, Md.: University Press of America, 1987);

Shakespeare, *King Henry the Sixth, Part Two,* edited by Rowse (Lanham, Md.: University Press of America, 1987);

Shakespeare, *King Henry the Sixth, Part Three,* edited by Rowse (Lanham, Md.: University Press of America, 1987);

Shakespeare, *King John,* edited by Rowse (Lanham, Md.: University Press of America, 1987);

Shakespeare, *King Henry the Eighth,* edited by Rowse (Lanham, Md.: University Press of America, 1987);

Sir Anthony Richard Wagner, *John Anstis, Garter King of Arms,* edited by Rowse (London: H.M.S.O., 1992);

The Sayings of Shakespeare, edited by Rowse (London: Duckworth, 1993).

Known for his scholarship in history, his insight into literature, and his own literary creativity, A. L. Rowse is also respected as one of the foremost British biographers of the twentieth century. Focusing on but not limiting himself to the Elizabethan period, Rowse has written many volumes in history, biography, literary scholarship, poetry, and fiction with characteristically colorful style, extensive detail, strong historical scholarship, and assertively presented hypotheses. But over his long career, he has received dramatically varied responses to his works from readers. Among his more controversial qualities are his strong dependence on history as the basis of literary analysis, his paradoxically elitist and colloquial tone, his subjectivity, and his sometimes dogmatic pronouncements. Rowse is extremely prolific and over the years has developed a style that is not easily mistaken for that of any other scholar-writer.

Alfred Leslie Rowse was born on 4 December 1903 in Saint Austell, Cornwall, to Richard Rowse, a laborer in the local china-clay works, and Ann Rowse, née Vanson. He grew up in the nearby village of Tregonissey. He was educated at the Carglaze Elementary School and the Saint Austell secondary school, winning a scholarship to the latter. In October 1922 he entered Christ Church College, Oxford, as the Douglas Jerrold Scholar in English literature but soon switched to history. In his autobiographical *A Cornishman at Oxford: The Education of a Cornishman* (1965), Rowse describes the "whole process of education of a scholarship boy from the working class." Although he suffered during these years from appendicitis and ulcers, he found what he calls his "true nature" at Oxford: he would enjoy the academic lifestyle, at once free and ascetic, throughout his career. His only regret about his education is that he did not learn Greek. In 1925 he graduated with first-class honors in modern history and became the first member of the working class to be elected as a Fellow of All Souls College. He also made his first trip outside England, traveling to France, Germany, and Austria. He earned an M.A. in 1929, the same year that he made the first of three unsuccessful runs as a Labour Party candidate for Parliament from Cornwall; the others were in 1931 and 1935.

Rowse in 1988 at the church in Stratford-upon-Avon where William Shakespeare is buried (photograph by Simon Grosset, courtesy of A. L. Rowse)

His early publications include *On History: A Study of Present Tendencies* (1927), *Mr. Keynes and the Labour Movement* (1936), and his first autobiography, *A Cornish Childhood: Autobiography of a Cornishman* (1942). Finally he settled most consistently into publications about the English Renaissance. After producing several shorter works, in 1950 he published the first of three extensive volumes examining the sixteenth century in England: *The Elizabethan Age: The England of Elizabeth*. It was followed by *The Expansion of Elizabethan England* (1955) and *The Elizabethan Renaissance*, parts 1 and 2 (1971, 1972).

In 1952–1953 Rowse was the George A. Millar Visiting Professor at the University of Illinois. He received a Litt.D. from Oxford in 1953. After a year as Ralegh Lecturer at the British Academy in 1957 he was a visiting professor at the University of Wisconsin in 1957–1958. He ended 1958 as the Trevelyan Lecturer at Cambridge University. Intermittently from 1962 to 1969 he worked as a senior research fellow at the Henry E. Huntington Memorial Library in San Marino, California. In addition,

he was the Beatty Memorial Lecturer at McGill University in Montreal in 1963.

During these two decades he continued his studies in the Elizabethan Age, but he did not confine himself to that period. In 1956 and 1958, for example, appeared *The Early Churchills: An English Family* and *The Churchills: From the Death of Marlborough to the Present*. Rowse's point of view in the volumes is almost worshipful, but, as always, his attention to detail and provision of background information are masterful.

During his stay at the Huntington Library he completed some of his major biographies of sixteenth-century literary figures. Before *William Shakespeare: A Biography* was published in 1963, Rowse wrote four articles about the topic in the *Times* and gave a television interview in which he offered a taste of the book's contents; as a result of the publicity, the first printing sold out in England in one day. In the preface Rowse says that his investigation of the life and times of Shakespeare uses "proper historical method," which enables him "to solve, for the first time, and definitively, the problem of 'the Sonnets' ": Henry Wriothesley, Third Earl of Southampton, is the young man addressed in the early sonnets, and Christopher Marlowe is the "rival poet." He also claims that he has been able to set up "firm chronologies, even for such plays as *A Midsummer Night's Dream, Love's Labour's Lost, Troilus and Cressida,* and *Romeo and Juliet*," based on "knowledge of the circumstances and events of Shakespeare's time."

Critics take issue with Rowse's use of Shakespeare's works as biographical sources; for example, he writes: "We know so much more about Shakespeare's education, as the result of the detailed study in our time of the way in which the whole process is reflected in his plays." He also suggests that the many biblical echoes in the plays prove that Shakespeare attended church a great deal and that the references to hunting substantiate Shakespeare's personal involvement in the sport. Writing in *Book Week* (15 January 1964), the Shakespearean scholar George B. Harrison acknowledges that the book is the "liveliest and most elaborate account of Shakespeare in his age that has yet been written" but considers it "more impressive as a sensitive work of art and imagination than as definitive historical biography." Rowse, he says, makes "confident statements for which there is no verifiable evidence" and "suppresses inconvenient evidence." An anonymous review in the *Economist* (19 October 1963) notes Rowse's "formidable stock of knowledge about social and political life in Elizabethan England" but criticizes the "coarseness in writing." The reviewer characterizes Rowse's "assertions that plausible conjectures are true" as "arrogance" and concludes that the main defect of the book is its "authoritarian tone."

Rowse is also criticized for his failure to acknowledge the work of other scholars. In the *New York Review of Books* (5 January 1964), Edward Hubner stresses that "nothing that Mr. Rowse brings forth is both new and indisputably true," noting, for example, that in 1817 Nathan Drake had first suggested Southampton as the young man in the first section of the sonnets and that William Cartwright had named Marlowe as the rival poet in 1859. Further, Hubner claims that Rowse "possesses a complete absence of an esthetic" and "treats a poem like a legal document." On the other hand, Orville Prescott writes in *The New York Times* (6 January 1964) that of the five Shakespeare biographies he has reviewed, Rowse's is "much the most interesting, much the best-written, and much the longest." The book, he says, makes the Elizabethan world "vivid

and immediate" with a "wealth of historical information that is immensely interesting." He calls Rowse a "brilliant writer" whose conclusions are stated with "marvelous self-confidence." Similarly, Christopher Sykes says in the *Nation* (27 January 1964) that the book is "fascinating" and praises its "colloquial" style. He laments that if only Rowse did "not order us about so unnecessarily and sometimes so offensively, we should have all followed him like lambs."

Rowse's stated intention in *Christopher Marlowe: A Biography* (1964) is to use Marlowe's works and the works of his contemporaries not to develop what he calls "pure criticism" but rather to seek out "the reality of biography." He again identifies Marlowe as Shakespeare's "rival poet," using as evidence lines from Shakespeare's sonnets and *Venus and Adonis* (1593) and Marlowe's *Hero and Leander* (1598), along with historical facts about the period 1592 to 1595. Because the plague had closed the theaters in London during this time, both Shakespeare and Marlowe were rivals for the favor of the young Earl of Southampton, who, Rowse claims, is the model for Marlowe's Leander. The work often compares Marlowe to Shakespeare: Shakespeare is "the more pliable and suggestible"; whereas "Marlowe gave the law, he did not receive it, he laid it down for others, he did not accept anything from anyone." Marlowe's "mind was fired by ideas rather than" – as was the case with Shakespeare – "by his immediate contacts with life or by his close observation of his fellow human beings." Finally, Marlowe was "a scholar in the old traditional sense," whereas "Shakespeare was not."

Like the Shakespeare biography, the book is valuable for its detailed representation of Elizabethan times; but, also like the earlier biography, it uses literary works as if they were primary historical sources. Rowse writes, for example, on the basis of *Tamburlaine the Great* (1587–1588) that Marlowe "never had any of his countryman's . . . respect for hierarchy and degree." At the end of the book Rowse asks what might seem to be a rhetorical question: "What might not Marlowe have achieved if he had lived?" But he proceeds to answer it: more lyrics, more narrative poems (since Shakespeare wrote more), more historical plays, and, probably, satire and realistic drama like that of Ben Jonson. Marlowe's death at age twenty-nine was, he concludes, "the greatest individual loss our literature has ever suffered."

In the same year the Marlowe biography appeared, Rowse's edition of Shakespeare's sonnets was published. Each sonnet appears on a verso page

Rowse at work (courtesy of A. L. Rowse)

with a modernized prose version, accompanied by a literary-biographical analysis, on the facing recto page. The sonnets are treated as biography containing clues that identify Mr. W. H., the "rival poet," the dating of the cycle, and the nature of the two lovers. The review in the *Times Literary Supplement* (12 March 1964) says that "few think that a poem can be elucidated or illuminated by a prose version" and notes that the introduction merely repeats chapters 9 and 10 of the Shakespeare biography. Harrison in *Book Week* (26 April 1964) says that "the story is not a work of historical research but of the creative imagination," but the review in *Best Sellers* (1 May 1964) calls the book "delightful for the Shakespearean scholar" and claims that it "presents a tightly reasoned and documented theory which is reasonable and probable."

In 1974 Rowse became an emeritus fellow at All Souls and moved to Trenarren House in Saint Austell. His *Homosexuals in History: A Study of Ambivalence in Society, Literature, and the Arts* (1977) com-

prises short biographical sketches of homosexuals from various historical periods, such as Leonardo da Vinci, Desiderius Erasmus, Michelangelo, Francis Bacon, James I of England, Frederick the Great, Oscar Wilde, and Keynes. Rowse offers the standard Freudian explanation for homosexuality – the influence of a strong mother and a weak father – but neither this thesis nor Rowse's frustration with society's hypocritical responses to homosexuals is suggested as a reason for the recitation of the details of these particular lives; the basis for inclusion in the volume seems to be random. The biographies, most of which are five to ten pages long, describe the lives and works of the subjects. The reviewer in the *Economist* (18 June 1977) calls the book "an entertaining and erudite romp through history" but says that, because of its concentration on public events rather than private passion, it offers only a "flat perspective." Clayton Hudnall says in *Best Sellers* (July 1977) that Rowse, for no obvious reason, "tells of homosexuals up to and including his contemporaries and (one gradually understands) himself." Perhaps, Hudnall theorizes, Rowse believed "that a long relentless chronicle which makes routine and even tedious what has always made people uncomfortable will make them less so. As such it is a useful book." And while N. R. Shipley in the *Library Journal* (15 May 1977) finds no "general thesis or insight informing the book," he suggests that it can be read as "an extended gossip column" by a writer who is "annoyed with the world's hypocrisy and ill-treatment of homosexuals." Arthur Calder-Marshall in the *Times Literary Supplement* (13 May 1977) notes dryly that the book bears out Rowse's confession that he is not reliable on anything after 1603 but agrees with the general critical consensus: "what [Rowse] lacks in scholarship however he makes up in gusto, as he treads the well-worn paths, bellowing discoveries which when not well-known are for the most part unfounded."

Although in his biography of Shakespeare and his edition of the sonnets Rowse had expressed doubt that anyone would ever identify the "Dark Lady" of the sonnets, in 1978 he brought out an edition of Aemilia Lanyer's *Salve Deus Rex Judæorum* (1611) under the title *The Poems of Shakespeare's Dark Lady*. He establishes Lanyer as the Dark Lady by depending to a great extent on the diaries of Simon Forman, an astrologer and confidant of many prominent Elizabethans, and on Lanyer's poetry itself.

Rowse's Contemporary Shakespeare Series (1984–1987), published by the University Press of America, is intended to present Shakespeare to readers, especially younger ones, who have difficulty with "the language of 400 years ago." Rowse has edited the plays to remove what is "no longer good grammar" ("keep a few subjunctives, if you must, but reduce them to a minimum"); the "thou's, thee's, hath's, and doth's"; and archaic word forms (such as *reechy*) and expletives. The introductions discuss literary influences on the plays and the historical events referred to in them, but the texts offer no notes, glossary, dating, or critical analysis.

Rowse's *The Poet Auden: A Personal Memoir* (1987) is partially based on Rowse's acquaintance with W. H. Auden, dating from 1925 when Auden began his studies in English literature at Christ Church College. From the first, he says, he "had no doubt of his [Auden's] genius," and he notes Auden's own prediction to his teacher Neville Coghill that he (Auden) would become a "great poet." Rowse's volume is filled with offhanded references to some of the most brilliant people of the mid twentieth century: "the bullying figure of C. S. Lewis"; "the grand guru [T. S.] Eliot"; Philip Larkin, who "had a horror of the family"; and the "young ass," Christopher Isherwood, who had "hair parted down the middle, [and] prissy lips." Auden's political liberalism and his homosexuality are often referred to as part of what Rowse identifies as Auden's need to be loved, an "obsession all through his life." Rowse also mentions Auden's mediocre scholarship: he ranked in the Thirds at school. But Auden's genius as a poet compensates for this performance.

Rowse describes Auden's face in later life as "an extraordinary corrugated map of wrinkles – an off-putting lizard-like integument. Perhaps fifty cigarettes a day (ugh!) had something to do with it." He postulates that Auden's "secret wish" was "to have been an Adonis" in order to have been loved more deeply, but, Rowse says, "Love is central to life but it is not all of everything, and it is very far from occupying the whole area of anyone's life. Many people can do without it or have to do without it." Reflecting on the close relationships between the lives and works of writers who were his friends and acquaintances, Rowse was even more convinced of the autobiographical nature of literature.

Rowse has received many awards and honors. He is a Fellow in the British Academy and the Royal Society of Literature; he served as the president of the English Association in 1952–1953 and of the Shakespeare Club in 1970–1971; and he was granted the D. Litt. from the University of Exeter in 1960 and the D.C.L. from the University of New Brunswick in 1960. His obvious love for scholarship is ingenuous and contagious, and readers are easily seduced by his energetic fascination with his occupation.

Martin Seymour-Smith

(24 April 1928 –   )

Angus Somerville
Brock University

BOOKS: *Poems,* by Seymour-Smith, Rex Taylor, and Terence Hards (Dorchester: Longmans, Green, 1952);

[Poems by] *Martin Seymour-Smith,* The Fantasy Poets No. 10 (Oxford: Fantasy Press, 1953);

All Devils Fading (Palma, Mallorca: Divers Press, 1954);

Robert Graves (London: Longmans, Green, 1956; revised, 1965; revised again, 1970);

Tea with Miss Stockport: 24 Poems (London & New York: Abelard Schuman, 1963);

Bluff Your Way in Literature (London: Wolfe, 1966; New York: Cowles, 1968);

Fallen Women: A Sceptical Inquiry into the Treatment of Prostitutes, Their Clients, and Their Pimps in Literature (London: Nelson, 1969);

Poets Through Their Letters, Volume 1 (London: Constable, 1969; New York: Holt, Rinehart, 1969);

Inside Poetry, with James Reeves (London: Heinemann, 1970; New York: Barnes & Noble, 1970);

Reminiscences of Norma: Poems 1963–1970 (London: Constable, 1971);

Guide to Modern World Literature (London: Wolfe, 1973; revised edition, 4 volumes, London: Hodder & Stoughton, 1975; revised again, 1 volume, London: Macmillan, 1985); republished as *Funk and Wagnalls Guide to Modern World Literature* (New York: Funk & Wagnalls, 1973); revised and republished as *The New Guide to Modern World Literature* (New York: Bedrick, 1985);

Sex and Society (London: Hodder & Stoughton, 1975);

Who's Who in Twentieth-Century Literature (London: Weidenfeld & Nicolson, 1976; New York: McGraw-Hill, 1977);

An Introduction to Fifty European Novels (London: Pan, 1979); republished as *A Reader's Guide to Fifty European Novels* (London: Heinemann, 1980; New York: Barnes & Noble, 1980);

Martin Seymour-Smith

The New Astrologer (London: Sidgwick & Jackson, 1981; New York: Macmillan, 1982);

Robert Graves: His Life and Work (London: Hutchinson, 1982; New York: Holt, Rinehart, 1983);

How to Succeed in Poetry Without Really Reading or Writing (London: Anvil Press, 1986);

Rudyard Kipling: A Biography (London: Macdonald, 1989; New York: St. Martin's Press, 1989);

Wilderness: 36 Poems 1972–93 (London: Greenwich Exchange, 1994);

Hardy (London: Bloomsbury, 1994; New York: St. Martin's Press, 1994).

OTHER: *Poetry from Oxford,* edited by Seymour-Smith (London: Fortune Press, 1953);

Shakespeare's Sonnets, edited by Seymour-Smith (London: Heinemann, 1963; New York: Barnes & Noble, 1966);

A Cupful of Tears: Sixteen Victorian Novelettes, edited by Seymour-Smith (London: Wolfe, 1965);

Ben Jonson, *Every Man in His Humour,* edited by Seymour-Smith (London: Benn, 1966; New York: Hill & Wang, 1968);

A New Canon of English Poetry, edited by Seymour-Smith and James Reeves (London: Heinemann, 1967; New York: Barnes & Noble, 1967);

The Poems of Andrew Marvell, edited by Seymour-Smith and Reeves (London: Heinemann, 1969; New York: Barnes & Noble, 1969);

Cumulative Index to the Shakespeare Quarterly, Volumes 1–15, 1950–1964, compiled by Seymour-Smith (New York: AMS, 1969);

Longer Elizabethan Poems, edited by Seymour-Smith (London: Heinemann, 1972; New York: Barnes & Noble, 1972);

Robert Graves, *Collected Poems,* edited by Seymour-Smith (London: Cassell, 1975; revised, 1986);

Walt Whitman, *Selected Poems,* edited by Seymour-Smith and Reeves (London: Heinemann, 1976);

The English Sermon, Volume I: 1550–1650, edited by Seymour-Smith (Cheadle, U.K.: Carcanet, 1976);

Thomas Hardy, *The Mayor of Casterbridge,* edited by Seymour-Smith (London: Penguin, 1978);

Novels and Novelists: A Guide to the World of Fiction, edited by Seymour-Smith (London: Windward, 1980; New York: St. Martin's Press, 1980);

Joseph Conrad, *Nostromo,* edited by Seymour-Smith (London: Penguin, 1984);

Conrad, *The Secret Agent: A Simple Tale,* edited by Seymour-Smith (London: Penguin, 1984);

The Dent Dictionary of Fictional Characters, edited by Seymour-Smith (London: Dent, 1990);

From Bed to Verse, compiled by Seymour-Smith (London: Souvenir, 1991).

Martin Seymour-Smith defies easy classification as an author. He has written a considerable amount of toughly elegant lyric poetry that can be both tender and ironic. He produced the first monograph, as well as the earliest critical biography on his friend Robert Graves. His controversial 1989 biography of Rudyard Kipling is a necessary touchstone for all subsequent approaches to that writer. He has edited works by William Shakespeare, Ben Jonson, and other Renaissance poets. He collaborated with James Reeves on editions of Andrew Marvell and Walt Whitman. He has produced satire and extensive works of what may only be called social anthropology. He is equally remarkable for the encyclopedic erudition that informs his *Guide to Modern World Literature* (1973) and *Who's Who in Twentieth-Century Literature* (1976). This impressive output in books has been accompanied by a stream of reviews and articles in various periodicals.

In his *Bluff Your Way in Literature* (1966) Seymour-Smith describes biographical criticism as "explorative, intuitive and . . . speculative." Had he added *intelligent* and *uncompromisingly honest,* he might well have been describing his own way of writing and thinking whether in his lyrical poetry or in his critical and scholarly work. Whether attempting to make sense of himself or the world, the same qualities of intelligence, intuition, and integrity are evident in his writing. His writing stands as the record of a coherent endeavor to understand the human situation, chiefly through literature. Seymour-Smith's literary criticism has always been basically biographical and psychological in method, without being rigidly tied to any particular psychological or analytical theory. His later work shows an increasing use of anthropology and philosophy while remaining fundamentally psychological in its orientation. These qualities of mind and this steadily maintained approach to all aspects of literary criticism give coherence and continuity to his immensely varied literary output.

Martin Seymour-Smith was born in London on 24 April 1928 to Frank and Marjorie Harris Seymour-Smith. From 1939 to 1946 he attended Highgate School. While still a schoolboy he made his first contact with the poet Graves. In 1943 he sent some of his early poems to Graves, who responded warmly and encouragingly. The relationship was to continue for the rest of Graves's life. After military service in the Middle East (in the course of which he reached the rank of sergeant), Seymour-Smith continued his education from 1948 to 1951 at Saint Edmund Hall, Oxford, from which he took his B.A. In 1950–1951 he was poetry editor of *Isis.*

From 1951 to 1954 Seymour-Smith worked in Mallorca as tutor to one of Graves's sons. During that period he published his three earliest collections of poems, collections that are mainly love lyrics shot through with a disturbing and dark irony. In 1952 Seymour-Smith married Julia de Glanville in Mallorca; they have two daughters. His wife had read Greats at Oxford and assisted Graves with the preparatory work for his *The Greek Myths* (1955). In

*Dust jacket for the American edition of Seymour-Smith's
biography of the British poet, which sheds much light
on Graves's relationship with American poet
Laura Riding*

1953 Seymour-Smith edited *Poetry from Oxford,* an anthology of university poets.

From 1954 until 1960 Seymour-Smith worked as a schoolmaster; he regards this as the unhappiest period of his life. Since 1960 Seymour-Smith has supported himself by his writing. From 1955 to 1958 he was poetry editor for the weekly *Truth.* Seymour-Smith's first work on Graves, titled *Robert Graves,* appeared in 1956 as a British Council pamphlet. The pamphlet opens with a brief life and continues with an assessment of Graves's work; it is notable for its sensitive reading of Graves's poetry. The concluding passages of the brief life insist on the intimate relationship between the poet's biography and his poetry. Insistence on that relationship remains an important element in Seymour-Smith's critical approach. Clearly, this early work hints at the belief, to be stated explicitly and amplified later, that to know the man is to deepen one's understanding of his work.

In 1963 he produced his original-spelling edition of Shakespeare's sonnets and a collection of poetry, *Tea with Miss Stockport: 24 Poems.* The critical edition, *Shakespeare's Sonnets,* has been widely used in schools and universities. The introduction and commentary are both lucid and helpful, particularly in explaining the vexed textual and critical history of the sonnets. The appearance of this pioneering edition raised expectations that Seymour-Smith might fashion a career in Renaissance studies, as he was (and is) clearly competent to do. Although he has continued to edit texts of the period, he has not chosen to make it the major part of his work.

The poems collected in *Tea with Miss Stockport* are versatile and sinuous in their versification. Technically, the collection shows considerable assurance. The macabre "He Came to Visit Me" (reprinted from his earliest collection), the ironic "The Punishment," and the satiric "The Administrators"

263

are all particularly noteworthy. In the title poem an elderly spinster escapes from her role and murders all but one of her patronizing guests, whom she rapes.

Work as poetry editor of *The Scotsman* and literary adviser to the publishing firm of Hodder and Stoughton (both from 1963 until 1967) did not interrupt the steady flow of books from Seymour-Smith. In 1965 he published *A Cupful of Tears: Sixteen Victorian Novelettes,* which makes fascinating and sometimes hilarious reading. Unfortunately, Seymour-Smith confined his activities to selecting the novelettes. His commentary on the texts would have been illuminating. Also in 1965 Seymour-Smith began to review regularly for the *Spectator.*

An edition of Ben Jonson's *Every Man in His Humour* (1598) and the satiric *Bluff Your Way in Literature* followed in 1966. The edition of Jonson's play was published as part of the New Mermaids series. As with his later editions of Thomas Hardy and Joseph Conrad, Seymour-Smith provides an admirable and scholarly critical introduction. *Bluff Your Way in Literature* is not entirely satiric. Mixed with sardonic advice to the followers of literary fashion such as "You don't have to admire Kafka these days; but you must be 'aware' of him" are serious and devastating judgments like this of Ted Hughes: "He was overrated from the start. . . . His early poems were often about animals, and showed understanding of them. When he ran out of animals (as it was put at the time) he became pretentious, and the violence in his poetry became disturbingly gratuitous and self-indulgent." On T. S. Eliot he is equally provocative

> Eliot was basically a satirical poet, full of disdain for humanity, and reverence for culture, who tried to carve out a position for himself as a devotional poet. Like his friend Pound, although with much more cunning, he had a very strong nostalgia for the authoritarian past, and in his poetry he never managed to be objective about this. All his later poetry is a form of propaganda for this cause and for a milk-and-water type of mysticism: politically he ended up in predictable quarters.

Of course, the skilled bluffer will avoid such judgments. Such terse honesty is typical of Seymour-Smith's criticism.

His account of biographical criticism in *Bluff Your Way in Literature* is interesting and, in the light of his later work in that area, evocative of his method:

> Biographical criticism . . . is interpretative. An attempt is made to assess the personality of an author, and to un-

derstand it. Frequently the meaning of an author is interpreted in the light of his total intentions (both conscious and unconscious). Biographical criticism is explorative, intuitive and, of course, speculative in a way that historical criticism never is. At its worst, when for example it relies upon rigid psychoanalytical principles, biographical criticism can be both absurd and without value; at its best, when the critic's approach is cautious, eclectic and not too literal-minded, it can add immeasurably to our understanding of an author.

Not surprising, elsewhere in *Bluff Your Way in Literature* he expresses impatience with both the intentionalist and affective fallacies. Most important, the tacit assumption of *Robert Graves* is made explicit. The exploration of a writer's personality and the assessment of his intentions, properly conducted, will lead to a fuller understanding of his meaning. Further, the biographical critic is ideally to be "eclectic" and his criticism "explorative, intuitive . . . and speculative." This passage is perhaps the clearest account Seymour-Smith has given of his methods as a literary biographer.

Seymour-Smith collaborated with Reeves on his next book, *A New Canon of English Poetry* (1967). Reeves was a teacher and, despite being a graduate of Cambridge University, a member of Graves's circle in Mallorca. He and Seymour-Smith produced an anthology of "the unaccountably neglected – the poems which Oxgrave ought to have known about and admired." (Oxgrave is a portmanteau word for *The Oxford Book of English Verse* and *Palgrave's Golden Treasury.*) The title is misleading since *A New Canon of English Poetry* does not really set out to remake the canon so much as to produce an appendix to it. There are healthy doses of John Skelton, Fulke Greville, and Sir Walter Ralegh as well as a surprising amount of Trumbull Stickney. This is perhaps Seymour-Smith's least satisfactory work. He and Reeves print much interesting poetry but do not attempt to deliver on the promise of radical restructuring of the canon implied by the title. The two collaborated again in 1969 on *The Poems of Andrew Marvell.* The introduction makes brief but good sense of the "enigmatic" Marvell, to whom Seymour-Smith was shortly to return in *Poets Through Their Letters, Volume 1,* also published in 1969.

Poets Through Their Letters, intended as the first of two volumes, scrutinizes the letters of Sir Thomas Wyatt, Thomas Kyd, Sir Philip Sidney, Alexander Pope, Thomas Gray, William Wordsworth, Ralegh, Jonson, Marvell, and others. Seymour-Smith describes his aims in the preface: "I have considered my material less as correspondence than as a means of elucidating the poetry of those who wrote it. If we are interested in poetry, then we study the personalities of poets not in order to appreciate their epistolary skill but in order to understand their poems more fully." Once again understanding poetry is the object of biographical criticism; knowledge of the man leads to elucidation of the poetry.

The chapters dealing with Marvell, Swift, and Gray give a good sense of how the book works. Marvell's letters as a member of Parliament to his constituents seem unpromising material at first blush. However, Seymour-Smith shows them to be "self-revealing . . . in the subtle deliberation of their reticence." This illuminates Marvell's rhetorical posture in the political poetry that he wrote after deciding to enter the employ of the republicans. As Seymour-Smith concludes: "But this kind of presentation of bare facts, or non-emotive recording of events, does operate in Marvell, right from the time of the *Ode,* as a particular, perhaps unique, kind of irony; an irony he chose to exercise when, as a man, he was placed in the position of being unable to influence events."

Analysis of Swift's letters sheds light on his abandonment of his early attempts to write the "sublime" poetry in which he believed and his subsequent adoption of the satiric mode. Essentially, Swift "found his times and his own temperament incompatible with the kind of poetry he believed in." In an age when the Muse could find neither virtue nor innocence to celebrate, "Swift is one of the true poets of that prose-age, although he achieved it by adopting the role of an anti-poet: he scraped up the age's anti-lyrical resources, as no one else did, to tell the truth about it and himself."

Poets Through Their Letters deserves to be better known. The scholarship and analysis are both excellent and presented in such a way as to be accessible to the least specialist of readers. Despite favorable reviews, this very useful and sensitively written book has never enjoyed the popularity it deserves.

Fallen Women: A Sceptical Inquiry into the Treatment of Prostitutes, Their Clients, and Their Pimps in Literature also appeared in 1969. This work draws attention to another of Seymour-Smith's qualities as a writer: his willingness to undertake monumental tasks that transcend the comfortable specialist limits within which most contemporary scholars and critics are sheltered. The scale of the book is immense. Seymour-Smith begins with the book of Genesis and ends with a glance at modern pornography. Along the way he looks at writers from every major period in the Western tradition. Chapter 3 contains a per-

ceptive discussion of Catullus and Horace. Chapter 4 discusses the influence of Saint Paul on subsequent sexual attitudes. Chapter 7, which discusses the period from 1660 to 1800, is one of the most entertaining in a stimulating book. In it Seymour-Smith deals at some length with John Cleland and contrasts him in an illuminating way with Samuel Richardson. The same chapter also illustrates the wit and pungency with which Seymour-Smith points his arguments: "Eighteenth-century 'passion' was not unlike eighteenth-century beauty: its 'wildness' was severely and reassuringly limited." The same wit is shown in this remark about James Boswell: "the romantic James Boswell . . . can be considered as a prototype for the tough, no-nonsense client." He ends with the suggestion that a brothel should be attached to the House of Commons as a means of improving the quality of debate. The quality of the literary criticism in this book is, as usual, excellent. The integration of criticism with the perspectives of social anthropology is gracefully and unobtrusively achieved. Most remarkable is the energy and intelligence with which the whole is carried forward. The entire work is informed by a humane and skeptical liberalism and concludes that "while we insist on separating sexual pleasure from love, there will have to be 'fallen women.' "

In 1970 Seymour-Smith collaborated again with Reeves, this time on *Inside Poetry,* an illustrated introduction to the practical criticism of poetry that presents analyses of texts and a section containing texts for analysis by the reader. The introduction provides an outline of the critical principles employed by Reeves and Seymour-Smith. While they see the strengths of close, textual criticism, they argue that, "Where, however, this method requires the elimination of the subjective response and of knowledge extraneous to the text . . . we consider it harmful and limiting, and ultimately sterile. The more we know of our own minds and the minds and lives of the poets, the more we shall understand poetry. No relevant information — biographical, psychological, historical, linguistic or whatever — is without use." This eclectic and pragmatic strain is constant in Seymour-Smith's criticism.

In 1971–1972 Seymour-Smith was visiting professor of English and poet in residence at the Parkside campus of the University of Wisconsin. *Longer Elizabethan Poems,* an edition of poems by Christopher Marlowe, George Chapman, John Davies, Edmund Spenser, and Ralegh, was published in 1972. The texts are lucidly introduced and intelligently edited and annotated, as the following note on line 247 of Marlowe's *Hero and Leander* shows:

Dust jacket for the American edition of Seymour-Smith's biography of the British novelist and short-story writer, which was widely criticized for its speculations on Kipling's sexuality

"faire jem, sweet in the losse alone: virginity is sweet only in the losing of it (a male generalization not universally borne out by female reports on the subject)." This is an appropriate comment from the writer of *Fallen Women* and biographer of Graves.

While in Wisconsin he worked on his *Guide to Modern World Literature*. This book "extends to writers of all nationalities, who survived 31 December 1899." The work is organized in national sections, alphabetically ordered. His critical organization of the book is admirably lucid. He begins by defining the terminology in which he will discuss the major literary movements of the period (including realism, naturalism, and neoromanticism). He goes on to describe and justify his use of the terms *naive* and *sentimentive* (a translation of Friedrich Schiller's *sentimentalische*) as broad classifications in his discussion of individual writers. The result is an admira-

bly accessible treatment of what might have been overwhelmingly diverse material. A work such as this might easily have degenerated into a mere catalogue. However, Seymour-Smith's engagement with literature is not of a kind that will allow him to degenerate into a mere drudge. The forthright shrewdness that characterizes all of his criticism is present here also. Some reviewers objected to the sharpness and authoritativeness of his judgments. For example, he writes that Evelyn Waugh "uses his famous detached manner – much vaunted as 'objectivity' – to cover up his own incapacity for that psychological understanding which amounts to compassion." Clearly, Seymour-Smith sees no reason why an encyclopedist should be obliged to shut off his critical intelligence. No one should underestimate the nerve required to undertake a work of this extensiveness and complexity.

In 1973 Seymour-Smith began to review poetry and fiction for the *Financial Times*. *Sex and Society* appeared in 1975. This book is predominantly anthropological in its approach to the major writings on sexuality produced since the early nineteenth century. *Sex and Society* compares and analyzes these texts both as part of a chronological survey and as part of a topical analysis of the subject. As always with Seymour-Smith's work, the book is frequently provocative and pungent. It is a massive attempt to talk frankly about a divisive topic. Unfortunately, the work suffers from a lack of clarity in its outline and a want of orderliness in its structure. Seymour-Smith appears to have had an overpowering anxiety to include everything; despite its structural flaws the book is well worth reading.

In 1976 Seymour-Smith published three more books. He edited *Selected Poems* of Walt Whitman in collaboration with Reeves. The introduction is a perceptive discussion of Whitman as naive poet, and the editorial work is of the high standard that had come to be expected of Seymour-Smith and Reeves. *The English Sermon, Volume I: 1550–1650* testifies to Seymour-Smith's continuing engagement with the English Renaissance. As well as providing usable texts of little-read writers such as Edgeworth, Thomas Cranmer, Hugh Latimer, and many others who wrote in a period crucial to the development of English prose, Seymour-Smith gives brief introductory biographies of each writer. That of Archbishop Cranmer is more balanced and generous than the generally received view of him. *Who's Who in Twentieth-Century Literature* worked the encyclopedic vein first opened in *Guide to Modern World Literature*. There is the same erudition and the same refusal to avoid making judgments.

Seymour-Smith's first published work concerning Hardy was an edition of *The Mayor of Casterbridge* (1886) in 1978. The introduction does not dwell on Hardy's life, but it does give a remarkably detailed and sensitive reading of the novel. The notes are informative. It is a sad comment on contemporary literacy that Seymour-Smith should have found it desirable to gloss for his readers words such as "nimbus" and "furlough."

Novelists and the novel continued to occupy Seymour-Smith during the next two years. In 1979 *An Introduction to Fifty European Novels* was published; the book provides clear plot outlines and straightforward explanation of a good selection of novels by writers from François Rabelais to Aleksandr Solzhenitsyn. The bibliographical and biographical sections are useful. This was followed in 1980 by *Novels and Novelists: A Guide to the World of Fiction,* a popular and lavishly illustrated introduction to the history and variety of the novel. Seymour-Smith wrote the introduction, which is unusually and refreshingly judgmental for a work that is so clearly designed to be introductory and popular. He does not assume that those who are in need of an introduction to the novel are necessarily incapable of independent thought. The other sections, edited by Seymour-Smith, are by a variety of contributors and cover areas such as science fiction (Brian Aldiss), crime (H. R. F. Keating), and many others.

The New Astrologer (1981) is an introduction to astrology and an attempt to show what it can do. Few are competent to comment on such a work. However J. Bruce Brackenbridge, reviewing the book in the *Times Literary Supplement* (9 July 1982), drew attention to what he saw as many scientific and historical inaccuracies in Seymour-Smith's argument in defense of astrology. The reviewer concluded by saying that "Everything necessary for the self-made astrologer is there, offering, as the author suggests, 'the basis of an intelligent parlour-game, or a quest for self-knowledge.' The author clearly holds for the second option, but unless the reader already shares with him the conviction that astrology 'works,' it is unlikely that this book will convince anyone of its validity."

Robert Graves: His Life and Work was published in 1982. Seymour-Smith was in an unusually good position to write Graves's biography. His friendship with Graves had begun in 1943 and had continued and deepened over the years. He stayed with Graves in Mallorca in 1949; he and his wife worked with Graves in the early 1950s. Thereafter, Seymour-Smith continued to visit and correspond with Graves, with whom he spent much time while the biography was being prepared. The introduction acknowledges the help given by Graves as research for the book continued. Thus while the book does not claim to be the "authorized" biography, it does have a unique authority.

The following passage articulates the tension which Seymour-Smith finds running through Graves's life and work; it provides, too, an outline of the framework that organizes the biography in its careful integration of the life and work: "One of the keys to Graves's personality, and therefore to his poetry, lies in the fact that he is in a continual state of terror; he relieved this, challenged it, by an increasingly sophisticated romanticism – but a romanticism that is willfully designed to punish him for his pride, which prevents his loving wholly, and which in that special sense may be the 'ancestral sin' of the poem 'Reproach.' . . . Physical desire and the sexual act, the 'thing,' is what terrifies him." The elegance and clarity of the biography owe much to Seymour-Smith's ability to arrive at perceptions of this degree of simplicity. The thread of Graves's terror and his response to it runs through and, to a large extent, organizes the entire book.

Seymour-Smith passes lightly over Graves's boyhood, relying heavily on Graves's *Goodbye to All That* (1927; revised, 1957); Seymour-Smith interprets it in ways perhaps not possible for its writer. He notes that the war did not so much create the neurasthenia of men like Graves as it removed their ability to defend themselves against their psychic and sexual problems. Graves's terror and his horror of offending women helps to explain much in his terrible relationships with his first wife, Nancy, and with Laura Riding, the American poet. Seymour-Smith shows that Graves had come close to inventing Laura Riding before he actually met her. His need for a dominant and perhaps cruel muse had become clear in his poetry before he and Riding knew one another. Thus it is wrong to see the White Goddess as the deification of Riding as many do. Interestingly, Seymour-Smith also shows that Graves's critical theories had essentially formed themselves before his involvement with Riding. Seymour-Smith sheds much light on the Graves-Riding relationship. Not least fascinating is his account of its final days. Paradoxically, the wealth of detail serves to make these moments more bizarre and less comprehensible.

The entire book is shot through with quotation from and analysis of Graves's poetry. A constant reciprocity exists between the life and the work in Seymour-Smith's familiar biographical manner. Seymour-Smith admires Graves but does not indulge in hero worship. Graves's arrogance and the frequent ferocity of his literary judgments have their place in the book. So, too, does the insensitivity of Graves's refusal to do anything to help Ezra Pound in his difficulties after World War II. All in all, Seymour-Smith's is an excellent biography of his friend Robert Graves.

Editions of Conrad's *Nostromo* (1904) and *The Secret Agent: A Simple Tale* (1907) followed in 1984. In 1985 Seymour-Smith received a Society of Authors travel scholarship. His *How to Succeed in Poetry Without Really Reading or Writing* was published in 1986. However, the next major event in Seymour-Smith's career was the publication of his biography *Rudyard Kipling* in 1989.

Rudyard Kipling: A Biography attracted much negative and hostile criticism, of which Seymour-Smith complains in the preface to the first American edition (1989) of the book. As in *Robert Graves,* Seymour-Smith has found a terrible inner tension in his subject. In Kipling's case the tension arose from his guilty recognition of his homosexuality. Seymour-Smith finds the effects of this terrible strain both in Kipling's life and in his art. For example, Seymour-Smith argues persuasively that Kipling's "engagement" to Florence Garrard was largely a screen and his feelings for her "a cluster of self-protective devices."

Then there is the suggestiveness of Kipling's persistent re-creation of his own past. For example, the head master in *Stalky and Co.* (1899) is Kipling's fictionalized version of Cormell Price, head of United Services College when Kipling was a pupil there. The head in *Stalky and Co.* prepares future empire builders by means of a regimen of hard flogging and injustice. Price was, in fact, nothing like that. Indeed, as Seymour-Smith shows, he was a rather decent and pacific man who (with his friends Edward Burne-Jones and William Morris) protested against Prime Minister Benjamin Disraeli's bellicose and imperialist policies. Yet it was no secret that Kipling intended the head in *Stalky and Co.* to represent Price. Kipling was creating for himself the kind of past that was required of every manly imperialist.

Then, too, there is Kipling's often reiterated insistence that United Services College was remarkably "clean." Seymour-Smith cites evidence that strongly suggests that Kipling may at the least have been suspected of behavior that was less than "clean."

For Seymour-Smith, Kipling's adulation of the knowers and doers of empire, his attempt to create a manly past for himself, his intense secrecy, and his parade of affection for Garrard all suggest a man

in flight from homosexual guilt. His relationship with Wolcott Balestier is, for Seymour-Smith, conclusive. Seymour-Smith has no patience with the hesitation of critics such as Angus Wilson and Leon Edel in seeing the relationship for what, in all probability, it was. The two men loved one another. Whether or not their relationship was physical is, as Seymour-Smith argues, unimportant. After Wolcott's death Kipling married Wolcott's sister Carrie. Seymour-Smith's view that Carrie "was able to seize Kipling for life because of his vulnerability in the matter of her brother" is strained. However, such a theory might go some way toward explaining her inordinate protectiveness of Kipling's privacy.

Kipling's manly imperialism masked guilt and a real tenderness that he could rarely afford to show. In this way Seymour-Smith attempts to explain the paradox that a writer capable of so much coarse, jingoist rant was also capable of the tenderness of "Without Benefit of Clergy" or the complexities of "Mary Postgate." The objections of the reviewers were predictable: that Seymour-Smith fails to recognize that imperialism must be taken seriously as an idea; that many writers have re-created their pasts; and that Seymour-Smith is too boldly speculative. These are serious objections. However, Seymour-Smith's book is concerned with why the idea of imperialism appealed as it did to one very particular individual, Kipling. The objection that Kipling's fictionalization of self is more Victorian than Kiplingesque is a weighty one and deserves more attention than it receives in Seymour-Smith's book. The biography is undoubtedly boldly speculative and intuitive, and sometimes disquieting. However, the disquiet is perhaps mainly over matters of detail. Arguably there is a fit between the larger outlines of Seymour-Smith's speculation and the biographical and literary material with which he is working.

If for no other reason, the book is worth reading for the shrewdness with which Seymour-Smith reads and analyzes Kipling's prose and verse. As in *Robert Graves,* life and works are skillfully interwoven in this biography that is never less than stimulating. *Rudyard Kipling* was followed in 1990 by another encyclopedic work edited by Seymour-Smith, *The Dent Dictionary of Fictional Characters,* and in 1991 by *From Bed to Verse,* which he compiled.

In 1994 Seymour-Smith's biography of Thomas Hardy was published. *Hardy* provides a stimulating reading of its subject's work. The vigorous defence of Hardy's less popular novels is notable, even if not entirely persuasive. Seymour-Smith's approach to Hardy's autobiographical poetry, though sensitive and perceptive, fails to render those poems any less enigmatic than they have always been.

Hardy was less than kind to his future biographers. On the death of his first wife, he destroyed many documents. After his own death, his second wife destroyed even more on Hardy's instructions. His autobiography, completed by Florence Hardy and published in two volumes in 1928 and 1930, reveals little of the private man, providing mainly a record of work accomplished, awards and honours received, and the like.

On the surviving evidence, Seymour-Smith does manage to provide a few refreshingly new perspectives on the life. He is more sensible than other biographers on the supposed problem of Hardy's virility and sex life at various points in his life. Seymour-Smith shows that there is little reason to doubt Hardy's sexual performance. Similarly, Seymour-Smith's Hardy is intellectually much more solid than other versions; there is nothing of the intellectual country bumpkin about him.

That said, Seymour-Smith does not escape the problems presented by Hardy's secrecy. In the absence of solid material on Hardy's life, Seymour-Smith fills too much space with discussion of the fiction; the reader often loses sight of the biography. Where facts fail, Seymour-Smith is sometimes tempted into speculation, most notably on the "relationship" between Florence Hardy and Sir Thornley Stoker. Seymour-Smith has never been afraid of speculation, and sometimes his speculations ring true. However, on this occasion, the speculation appears more than mildly problematic. Finally, too much time is spent in taking pointless potshots at other biographers of Hardy, who, like Seymour-Smith, are very much at the mercy of Hardy's reticence in personal matters. Such carping adds a needless stridency to the book.

Martin Seymour-Smith has not yet produced a major work that is absolutely commensurate with his energy, industry, and abilities. His output is so varied that perhaps he has spread himself too thin. But he appears to have done what he wanted to do, and that is surely something. At the very least Seymour-Smith has made a living as an uncompromisingly honest and independent writer for upward of thirty years. He has never been less than interesting and usually succeeds in challenging his readers' assumptions.

Papers:

Martin Seymour-Smith's papers are at the Harry Ransom Humanities Research Center, University of Texas at Austin.

Norman Sherry

(6 July 1935 –   )

Ethan Casey

BOOKS: *Conrad's Eastern World* (Cambridge: Cambridge University Press, 1966);
Jane Austen (London: Evans, 1966; New York: Arco, 1969);
Charlotte and Emily Brontë (London: Evans, 1969; New York: Arco, 1970);
Conrad's Western World (Cambridge & New York: Cambridge University Press, 1971);
Conrad and His World (London: Thames & Hudson, 1972; New York: Scribners, 1977);
Conrad in Conference (London: Macmillan, 1976);
The Life of Graham Greene, Volume One: 1904–1939 (London: Cape, 1989; New York: Viking, 1989);
The Life of Graham Greene, Volume Two: 1939–1955 (London: Cape, 1994; New York: Viking, 1995).

OTHER: Joseph Conrad, *Lord Jim,* edited by Thomas Moser, with notes by Sherry (New York: Norton, 1968); with a new introduction and notes by Sherry (London: Dent, 1974);
Conrad: The Critical Heritage, edited, with an introduction, by Sherry (London & Boston: Routledge & Kegan Paul, 1973);
Conrad, *An Outpost of Progress and Heart of Darkness,* edited, with an introduction, by Sherry (London: Dent, 1973);
Conrad, *Nostromo,* edited, with an introduction and notes, by Sherry (London: Dent, 1974);
Conrad, *The Secret Agent: A Simple Tale,* edited, with an introduction and notes, by Sherry (London: Dent, 1974);
Conrad, *The Nigger of the "Narcissus," Typhoon, Falk and Other Stories,* edited, with an introduction and notes, by Sherry (London: Dent, 1975; New York: Dutton, 1979).

Norman Sherry's *The Life of Graham Greene, Volume One: 1904–1939* was a major event in literary biography and in publishing at large when it appeared in 1989. It was serialized in the London *Sunday Times* and elsewhere, and climbed to fourth place on the *Sunday Times* best-seller list. The *Sunday*

Norman Sherry (photograph by Claudette Victoria)

Express named it biography of the decade, and it won the 1990 Edgar Allan Poe Award for best critical/biographical study.

The dust jacket contains high praise from contemporary authors. Margaret Atwood calls it the "definitive biography of one of the twentieth century's most important writers," though it was the first biography of Greene and only the first of three planned volumes. Francis Steegmuller lauds it as "Probably the fullest and richest biography of a living novelist ever written – a heroic, thoughtful work, worthy of its extraordinary subject." Joyce Carol Oates writes that "Greene's prodigious energies and inspiration are well matched by Norman Sherry's intelligence, sympathy, and powers of analysis."

The Life of Graham Greene, Volume 1: 1904–1939 was a best-seller on both sides of the Atlantic and widely reviewed in the popular press. Reviewers generally were extremely respectful of the enormous amount of work, travel, and scholarship Sherry had put into the book. Stephen Becker in the *Chicago Sun-Times* (18 June 1989) gushes that "If you care about modern literature, and the prickly, committed writer . . . if you care about God or England or the political 20th century, you will need this biography." George Woodcock in the Ottawa *Citizen* (29 June 1989) calls the biography "near to a model of literary biography." Keith Brace in the Birmingham (England) *Post* (13 April 1989) predicts that "the completed work will rank with [Leon] Edel's *Henry James*." Philip French in *The Listener* (17 April 1989) calls it "probably the best biography ever written of a living author."

Some reviewers were taken aback, a few even offended, at the biographer's temerity in writing 725 pages (plus notes and index) covering only his subject's first thirty-five years. "Comprehensive, to say the least," sniffs Becker, despite his praise. "There is little doubt that if anybody wanted to know everything a human being can possibly learn about the life of Graham Greene this is the volume to turn to," writes Paul Hollander in the *Wall Street Journal* (23 June 1989). Holly Hildebrand in the *Houston Post* (23 July 1989) claims wearily that Sherry's book "contains everything you never needed to know about [Greene] and never cared to ask" and that Sherry "doesn't know how to say no to a 'fact.' " "The book makes its demands on the reader's arms as well as his time," writes Anthony Curtis in the *Financial Times* (15 April 1989), though he allows that "these are richly rewarded." Many reviewers assumed in error that surely a second volume would complete Sherry's task.

Volume one is an extremely bold offering; much of its great value lies in its throwing into relief several important issues in literary biography as a form. First, Sherry's methods as a self-proclaimed "literary detective," used first in his highly respected critical books *Conrad's Eastern World* (1966) and *Conrad's Western World* (1971), set new standards for scholarly doggedness and blazed new trails in discovery of and speculation on the real-life sources of an author's creative work. Second, his "architectural" method of building up huge mountains of sheer fact struck many critics and colleagues as an unfortunate substitute for analysis. Finally, Sherry's close friendship with Greene, developed between their first meeting in 1974 and Greene's death in 1991 (a relationship about which

Sherry is frank and unapologetic), raised the eternal question of the "proper" relationship between biographer and subject.

Sherry first made his mark in 1966 with *Conrad's Eastern World,* a book that painstakingly re-created, from thousands of contemporary newspapers and ships' registers, the sources of characters and episodes in Joseph Conrad's novels and stories set in Asia, including the original of the title character in *Lord Jim* (1900). He intended, he says in an interview, to emulate John Dosier Gordan, who had gone to Singapore to write *Joseph Conrad: The Making of a Novelist* (1940). Gordan, he says, "got stopped because of the Japanese invasion. I went out trying to do what he had done, but if I may say so, more than he had done. Because I had decided to live there, to get a job there." Sherry dedicated *Conrad's Eastern World* to the William Butler Yeats scholar Peter Ure, who had first suggested he find the sources of Conrad's fiction. "I had no idea what he was asking," remembers Sherry. "I asked him: How would I do it? He didn't know how I'd do it, but he thought it'd be wonderful if I could. So I did."

The first book was well received. "Norman Sherry . . . has done a job to delight those who enjoy the best sort of literary detective work," writes Anthony Powell in the London *Daily Telegraph*. Sherry followed *Conrad's Eastern World* with books on Jane Austen and Charlotte and Emily Brontë. *Conrad's Western World* focuses on the sources of *Heart of Darkness* (1902), *Nostromo* (1904), and *The Secret Agent* (1907). "No one can travel without leaving tracks," says Sherry. "Nothing in this world is purely of imagination. You must have some substructure of fact."

Michael Norman Sherry and his twin brother Alan were born on 6 July 1935 in Newcastle upon Tyne in northeast England. His Irish father, Michael Sherry, was in his fifties when Norman was born and died soon after of tuberculosis. His mother, Sarah (née Taylor), was forty-seven at Norman's birth. Michael Sherry, unemployable because of his illness, was, Sherry remembers, "an Irishman with a lovely voice, and a wonderful ability to tell stories. Quick-tempered. Catholic, but not while I knew him, as they say." Sherry "never knew him working," though he believes his father had been a truck driver. His father had "a very good mind" and was a habitual reader. "If there are books around, you read books too." Sarah Sherry was "a small, quiet lady" from an English Protestant family. The Sherrys were not well off, though "there was money for education." They were supported by Sarah's family, who owned a factory.

Sherry in 1989

As a child, Sherry was certain of what he wanted to be: "a traveler and a writer. I didn't see myself as a biographer; I saw myself as a novelist traveling the world, and dreaming a lot." Instead of achieving his original ambition, he has written the biography of the novelist he wanted to be, he says. He believes his obsessive curiosity arose from his family's response to his extreme sensitivity. "I remember very distinctly, it became the habit in the house: 'Shh! Don't tell Norman.' And this business of being excluded from grace – when really they were trying to protect me – I think so established the kind of nature I have. If you met me, you'd know very well I'd soon be asking you questions. I'd soon want to know about you: Who you are, what you are, why you are. Almost to the point of insult. Not meaning to be; but I want to know. Human life is a mystery. Human beings are a mystery, and I want to *know* the mystery."

Sherry received his B.A. from the University of Durham in 1958. In 1960 he married Sylvia Brunt, and in 1961 he began a five-year stint as a lecturer at the University of Singapore. He received

his Ph.D. from the University of Singapore in 1964. His dissertation was on the sources of Conrad's Eastern novels. Its publication by Cambridge University Press launched him as a noted Conrad scholar, which in turn led him to Greene. "I came from nowhere," he says, "which is the *best* way to do things."

Sociologist Edward Shils of the University of Chicago "came through Singapore just when I put the last full stop to the doctorate," he recalls. "This chap was crazy about Conrad, had a bust of Conrad's that had been done by a famous sculptor. He wanted to see the chap who had done some work on Conrad. Then he said, 'I'm going off to Cambridge now. I'll see Cambridge University Press while I'm there.' Six weeks later, the chief editor of Cambridge University Press flew out to Singapore to speak to me."

From 1963 to 1965 Sherry worked as Singapore correspondent for the British newspaper the *Guardian.* In 1966 Sherry became a lecturer at the University of Liverpool and published *Jane Austen,* a short critical and biographical book for the general reader; he published a similar book titled *Charlotte and Emily Brontë* in 1969. In 1970 he moved to the University of Lancaster, where he became head of the Department of English and remained until 1983. In 1971 Cambridge University Press published *Conrad's Western World,* called by Anthony Powell "another splendid job" and "remarkable detective work on sources." When *The Nigger of the "Narcissus," Typhoon, Falk and Other Stories,* one of several Conrad texts edited by Sherry, appeared in 1975, *British Book News* (June 1975) wrote, "With an artist as subtle and complex as Conrad we need all the help we can get and it is good that this welcome new edition of some of his finest shorter pieces has been entrusted to a scholar of Professor Sherry's distinction in the field of Conrad studies."

It was *Conrad's Western World* that brought Sherry to Greene's attention. *The Life of Graham Greene* "had its origins in a list which Graham Greene kept . . . of the books he reads," recounts Sherry in his preface to the first volume. "Against . . . *Conrad's Western World* he had put in July 1971 two ticks, indicating special approval. Three years later the journalist William Igoe told me, over lunch, 'There is a man who is a legend in his own time and who admires your work.' That man was Graham Greene. When he was next in London we were introduced."

Greene "loped into the morning room of the Saville Club, exactly on time," recalls Sherry in an obituary of Greene published in the *San Francisco Ex-*

aminer (2 April 1991). "His eyes were bright and nervously alive. He seemed very innocent, very human." Sherry found himself "fascinated by his singular smile and eyes so blue that they gave off a curious sense of blindness."

"He suddenly said, 'You wouldn't be able to write about me as you wrote about Conrad – you wouldn't be able to get into Saigon' (the setting of *The Quiet American*)," continues Sherry in the preface. "I told him that after a ten-year stint on Conrad I was looking for another subject and he immediately backed off: 'Oh I wouldn't like anyone looking into my life.' Then he added with what I am sure was the instinctive decision of a novelist, 'If I were to have my biography written, I would choose you,' and later, as we parted in Brook Street, he made up his mind. I was to be his biographer, and we shook hands on it."

Anthony Burgess, reviewing volume one in the London *Weekend Telegraph* (8 April 1989), writes that "there was an acceptance of discreet flattery in the handshake Greene offered to seal the assignment. But there was also a recognition that here was a biographer who would do his work the hard way." Greene "never wanted a biography," asserts Sherry. "But then ultimately he felt he had to have one. He loved Conrad. But he thought Conrad was a great traveler. And therefore he wanted a biographer who was a traveler."

Sherry believes the serendipity of the encounter and Greene's sudden, instinctive decision were crucial. "I'm quite certain that if I had sought him out and said, 'Here are my credentials and I'd like to write your biography,' he would have been appalled at the suggestion," he told Herbert Mitgang in *The New York Times* (10 September 1989).

Conrad and His World, a short, handsomely illustrated biography of Conrad published in 1972, displays well Sherry's style and concerns: a great enthusiasm for his subject; a zest for the adventure of following clues and speculating on origins and intentions; and an almost conversational tone intended to submit his methods and findings to the reader for judgment. All these qualities also characterize the Greene biography.

The "substructure of fact" beneath a writer's imaginative work is Sherry's quarry. "If it were possible to go back as far as Christ," he speculates, "and be, say, eighty years after him, as I was eighty years after Conrad, there are all sorts of facts about that area, and about the people who had then lived. Eighty years later some of them might still be alive. If not, their sons would be alive. If not their sons, their grandsons. I wanted to tap into oral history,

and to go to those strange, some of them lost, forgotten places that people would not have visited and that would not have changed. When I went up into the mountains in Mexico, to a little village there, there was no question that nothing had changed since Greene had been there forty years before." He says his task is "attempting to rescue, in the great rush of time, that which is gone and cannot be brought back. But it *can* be brought back. It's a kind of antidote to death."

Sherry calls himself "a very different kind of biographer." Fiction, he says, is "a selection" of a writer's "total experience." He wants to "bring back into existence" a "total experience of the man: What it was like for Conrad when he was in Singapore, what it was like for Greene when he was at the leper colony in the Congo – If you can go back, then you can learn so much more about the creative act."

Sherry claims to have found the original for the famous mestizo Judas figure in Greene's masterpiece set in Mexico, *The Power and the Glory* (1940). His account of meeting the mestizo shows his obsession with sources and his conception of biography as the biographer's own personal journey of discovery. "Of the mestizo I heard from many people. His name was Don Porfirio Masariegos, but he was known everywhere as Don Pelito, born on 5 February 1902. . . . In 1978 Father Loren, priest at Yajalon, and I met Don Pelito. We were walking towards the Plaza and the church. Dogs slept in the shade of lime trees; in the bell tower small boys leapt up on to the bell ropes; in the church peasants sat on marble seats, white shirts hanging over white trousers, sombreros in hand. Don Pelito was sitting on a wooden bench. He was only 4 ft 6 in. tall. His hair was dirty; everything about him was dirty; there was soft grit on his hand. (I realised afterwards that it was excrement.) . . . His ears stood out and he was toothless – no yellow fangs at each end of his mouth."

Not all reviewers have appreciated Sherry's approach. "Macho scholarship may satisfy a personal need," wrote R. Z. Sheppard in *Time* (12 June 1989), "but Sherry's tribulations do not yield much about Greene's nature." To which charge Sherry might well reply (as he writes in his preface to volume one): "The journeys Greene made, I made, for it was a promise I had given him on our first meeting. I had to experience, as far as possible, what my subject experienced."

That Sherry revels in his adventure is plain. A brochure his office makes available (titled "Norman Sherry: Author, Traveller, Speaker") reads in part: "In following in the footsteps of the great-

Sherry in his office at Trinity University in Texas

specialist Dr. Michel Lechat, to whom Greene dedicated *A Burnt-Out Case* (1961), "will be a danger to life and limb, but the discoveries made, about himself and his subject, will no doubt make a riveting biographical work." He proudly says his trip through Liberia, retracing Greene's for *Journey without Maps* (1936), was "hell on earth." Sherry wants it known to what lengths he has gone.

Mark Lawson in *Punch* (14 April 1989) chides "the biographer's trope of magnificent but wholly irrelevant knowingness." Echoing Brian Masters in the *Evening Standard* (6 April 1989), who in a generally positive review called Sherry's volume "not a critical biography," Lawson writes that "To the disadvantage of a work which is, after all, the life of a writer, Sherry is far more concerned with the provenances of the novels than with their quality."

Sherry approaches Greene's creative work through the writer's experiences and the factual, discoverable sources of his fiction. "It's easier to be a biographer who's not going to worry about truth," he says. Sherry gleans truth from mountains of facts. "You can never have too much material," he told Reuters in the *Sunday Star* (11 June 1989). "How many of us know ourselves? So how much more difficult to know another person, in particular as complex, shy and reserved a person as Greene was and is."

While marveling at Sherry's "doggedness," Lawson in *Punch* also objects to it. "Greene writes, in his autobiography, that the newspaper office in Nottingham in which the novelist worked as a subeditor had a front door overhung with the stone heads of Liberal statesmen so that 'on rainy days, the nose of Gladstone dripped on my head as I came in.' Now, in the biography, Sherry comes along to correct the cavalier grip of the author's memory. The biographer rebukes his subject: 'It could not have been Gladstone's, but Palmerston's nose which dripped water on Greene's head.' . . . [A]t such triumphant, Sherlockian moments, the reader can be permitted a few doubts about the biographer-policeman method. Knowledge about an author is not everything."

Sherry cherishes each factoid. Lawson in *Punch* notes with sympathy but, like many other reviewers, fails to share Sherry's joy in discovering Greene's mistake about Gladstone's versus Palmerston's nose. "It strikes you, like a sudden drip from a stone statesman's nose, that Sherry has taken the trouble to walk into the Nottingham office in the rain," writes Lawson incredulously. Because he is so deeply immersed in his subject, Sherry really does care about the date Greene cut his first tooth.

est writers, Sherry has found adventure in lost forgotten places and in the trouble spots of the world. His lectures are based on his experiences as a literary detective, revealing discoveries he has made in remote locations, sometimes at great risk to himself. In the rain forest of Tabasco and the mountains of Chiapas he had dysentery, but struggled through to see the ancient Indian graveyard, 9,000 feet up, where tall black crosses (some twenty feet high) stood against an empty sky; in Haiti, then the Nightmare republic, he was interrogated by the hated Ton Ton Macoute (known to torture and kill without compunction); in Asuncion, Paraguay, he caught a stomach virus which later developed into gangrene of the intestine. In Sierra Leone, he fought off fever and in Liberia tangled with corrupt police, meeting many of the officials who were shot the following week on the sands outside Monrovia in a revolt led by Sergeant Doe. That he has survived the dangers and disease of his travels, is due in part, no doubt to his half-Irish blood."

The brochure also claims Sherry's future trip to the leper colony in Zaire to meet famous leper

And such is the intensity of his passion and the quality of his writing that many if not most readers (to judge from reviews) come to care also. As Waugh concedes, "however much one sneers at the *usefulness* of such a biography, the fact remains that it makes compulsive reading."

Samuel Hynes writes in probably the most intelligently sympathetic review of Sherry's first volume (*Times Literary Supplement*, 26 May–1 June 1989) that "One comes to the end of Volume One a bit winded, but persuaded that Sherry's way is the right way, the only way to tell Greene's story." Greene's biographer, writes Hynes, "must lower the dramatic tone and moderate the lighting to get rid of the novelist shadows" in the subject's life and must "fill in the dark spaces in the narrative with verifiable facts. . . . One reads those accumulating particulars with a certain nervousness: is it *all* going to be like this? Well yes, it is. . . . Yet out of this vast accumulation comes the book's great virtue – its total convincingness."

One of several virtues of Hynes's excellent review is that his starting point is Greene's own writing on literary biography. The cliché that the British are notably interested in biography as a form is well supported by Greene's own selections for his *Collected Essays* (1969), many of which are reviews of literary biographies. Hynes juxtaposes Sherry's work to Greene's criticism, published in *Collected Essays*, of Maisie Ward's life of G. K. Chesterton: "Mrs. Ward is too fond of her subject and too close to it to reduce her material into a portrait for strangers. Her biography is . . . too long for its material, too cumbered with affectionate trivialities." Hynes concludes that all the adjectives apply to Sherry, but he discards the negative judgment. "Norman Sherry has recounted the first part of [Greene's] life in a fond, close, long, cumbered biography that is admirable and a bit awesome."

Sherry's "huge wager" on Greene's immortality was in large part a high-stakes bet on his own time and future reputation. Sherry was not sure at first if he wanted to take the risk. "My agent was amazed that I didn't want to close on the contract immediately," he told Alan Franks of the London *Times* (1 April 1989). "But I was seriously asking myself whether Greene was worth it, whether he was worth spending 10 years of my life studying in the closest possible depth; whether, in the end, I could muster the same passion that I had for Conrad for this tall, cool, aloof Englishman in his casual clothes." On rereading Greene's novel *The Power and the Glory*, Sherry's "passion declared itself unequivocally," reported Franks, who called Sherry's

work "a hairy exercise in what can only be described as method-writing, with Sherry virtually living the Life he is shadowing." The eventual completeness of identification between biographer and subject brings to mind Leon Edel's protectiveness of his professional turf against other Henry James scholars.

"The reason I'm writing a literary biography, rather than just a biography of a man," he says, "is that so often writers – and Greene was a good example – will tell the truth of things in their fictional work, and will religiously *not* tell the truth when you interview them. That man is so closed. So much like a Russian doll – you open one and find another, open another and find another." Sherry says, "the constant battle – but done in a gentlemanly way – was that he wanted to take his secrets down into the grave, and I wanted to prevent that." Greene, to whom he did not show the manuscript until just before it was published, "was utterly shocked when the first volume came out," Sherry claims proudly. "He said to his sister, 'Where did Sherry get this information? *I* never gave it to him.' I found it by simply building up fact upon fact upon fact, and trying to look at the core of a person."

Sherry bristles at the suggestion that his biography is the product not of his own tireless work but of calculation on Greene's part. He says Greene knew that "if he didn't choose, it would be chosen for him. Whether he liked it or not, people were going to write about his life. One, Greene never wanted me to write about private things. Two, he himself would never give me private letters. It is fortunate that those letters had been sold by his wife when his marriage broke up." Greene was ambitious, asserts Sherry, but "quite a modest man," not personally vain. "Fame was part of the spur, but only part. I think he was ambitious to write well."

Punch reviewer Lawson objected to Sherry's close personal relationship with Greene. Noting that Sherry dedicates his first volume to Greene's sister, Elisabeth Dennys, "with love," he calls Sherry's "cosy Grahaming of the subject" and his obsession with detail "serious setbacks to the success of the book." If Sherry's personal friendship with Greene perhaps softens his critical edge, to his credit he is completely honest about it. If he notes "with some pride" (as Lawson remarks) the moment he and Greene achieved a first-name basis, by the same token he never asks the reader to believe in him as a distanced, "objective" biographer. This is yet another sense in which he is like Boswell, who cherished his inclusion in Johnson's circle of eminent literary friends. And Sherry is at pains to point out that he did not know Greene at all until the meeting in 1974, arranged because Greene had admired *Conrad's Western World.* "I knew the man very well finally," he says with satisfaction.

Sherry speculates that his own father's Catholicism might be one source of his interest in Greene — though he claims to have been unaware of a close affinity until he began the biography. He says that though he began as a literary critic, "what I'm really interested in is to know how the world works." His method is to choose "a special person" and to "mine" the subject's depths. "No shallow surface stuff. . . . Ultimately you will know things that you could not have ever known. And soon there comes a sense in which you are living in that part of time."

Greene is important, says Sherry, because he is "a historical figure strolling into difficulties and dangers, deliberately. If he's doing that, then he's going to be reflecting the crisis of his age. He straddles the age." His biography is a work of history, he says, because Greene's life "touched on so many dangerous crises of this century." As he told Herbert Mitgang for *The New York Times Book Review* (18 June 1989): "When I started out, Greene gave me a map of the world with a great rash of crosses showing where he had been. . . . I believe the story of this remarkable man will tell a child born today what life was like for a large part of our century." Bryce Milligan in the 9 July 1989 *Dallas Morning News* agreed, calling Sherry's first volume "as insightful a history of pre–World War II England as has ever been written."

Volume two of Sherry's planned three-volume biography, covering the years 1939 through 1955, was published in England in 1994. Sherry writes in "Seeking Greene," a short preface to the volume, "As this work bears down quickly on the twentieth year, I am aware of the expense of spirit, and of the difficulties of transforming raw research into a life, but the compensation for this biographical endeavour lies in those serendipitous discoveries which, for one crazy moment, bring fate to heel." The excitement, adventure, and drudgery of placing Greene's life ahead of his own makes *The Life of Graham Greene* an ambivalent experience for many critics. Greene himself, according to David Lodge in the *New York Review of Books* (8 June 1995), "suffered frequent misgivings about the whole enterprise" and even predicted "that he would live to read Sherry's first volume, but not the second, and that Sherry would not live to read the third." To call Sherry obsessive may not be fair, but neither would it be an understatement. His research costs were paid mostly by himself through royalty advances. A *Publishers Weekly* article in 1995 (27 February) reports that Sherry is £78,000 in debt to his publishers.

After *The Life of Graham Greene,* Sherry says wistfully, he will "write my own stuff . . . my own plays, and poetry, and novels, and my own travel books. Do my own thing." He says "probably" his next book will be *In the Footsteps of Graham Greene.* And he plans to revise his early books on Jane Austen and the Brontë sisters, enhancing the biographical sections, employing his "literary detective" methods. These books will be republished by Macmillan.

He believes his methods have influenced other biographers, including Peter Ackroyd, author of the acclaimed *Dickens* (1990). "I don't want to make a fuss about it," he says. "Once it's been done, other people are heirs to it. I don't mind that. That's fine. You're not a writer in order to keep secrets; you're a writer in order to make secrets available."

Since 1983 Sherry has been O. R. Mitchell Distinguished Professor in the English Department at Trinity University in San Antonio, Texas. He came to Trinity to be close to Greene's letters, which the University of Texas at Austin had bought through Sotheby's. He also has been a visiting professor at the University of Texas at Austin (1977–1978) and at the University of Sierra Leone (1980). On 10 May 1989 the governor of Texas proclaimed him an Honorary Texas Citizen. Sherry likes Texas and the United States in general; "Unlike Greene, I'm pro-American," he says.

Frances Spalding

(16 July 1950 –   )

Tracy Seeley
University of San Francisco

BOOKS: *Magnificent Dreams: Burne-Jones and the Late Victorians* (Oxford: Phaidon, 1978; New York: Dutton, 1978);

Whistler (Oxford: Phaidon, 1979);

Roger Fry, Art and Life (London: Granada Publishing, 1980; Berkeley: University of California Press, 1980);

Vanessa Bell (London: Weidenfeld & Nicolson, 1983; New Haven: Ticknor & Fields, 1983);

British Art Since 1900 (London: Thames & Hudson, 1986; New York: Thames & Hudson, 1986);

Stevie Smith (London: Faber, 1988; New York: Norton, 1989);

20th Century Painters and Sculptors (Woodbridge: Antique Collectors Club, 1990);

Dance Till the Stars Come Down (London: Hodder & Stoughton, 1991).

OTHER: Virginia Woolf, *Paper Darts,* selected and introduced by Spalding (London: Collins & Brown, 1991).

SELECTED PERIODICAL PUBLICATIONS –
UNCOLLECTED: Reviews of *The Obstacle Race,* by Germaine Greer; and *Paula Modersohn-Becker,* by Gillian Perry, *Burlington Magazine,* 122 (July 1980): 513–517;

"Roger Fry and His Critics in a Post-Modernist Age," *Burlington Magazine,* 128 (July 1986): 489–492.

Frances Spalding

Frances Spalding is an art historian with a passion for artist's stories. Her books on Roger Fry and Vanessa Bell bring to the fore two instrumental figures in Bloomsbury's rise to artistic prominence. These books, together with her biographies of poet Stevie Smith and painter John Minton, make important contributions to the history of late–nineteenth and early–twentieth century British art and poetry.

Spalding was born Frances Crabtree on 16 July 1950 in Surrey, England, the daughter of Hedley Crabtree and Margaret Holiday Crabtree. When she was quite small, her father, an aeronautical engineer, installed a child's writing desk in his study, supplying hand-sewn blank books for her to fill. By the time her father left the family, when Spalding was only six, her love of books was already well established. She joined the village library at the earliest possible age, carried home her allotted three to five books, and sometimes returned for new books on the same day. When she outgrew the library, her mother took her to the bookshop in Caterham, where as an adolescent she discovered the works of Aldous Huxley and Jean-Paul Sartre.

From age nine Spalding attended Farringtons, a Methodist boarding school. Although she looked forward to school, she continued to develop an inner life "protected and hidden from all the vagaries of daily life" – a development she credits in part for her ability to write. While working on A-level art history in the sixth form, she began to find the subject for her writing. Spalding recalls that the art teacher would say, "Write an essay on Donatello – I *think* he was a sculptor" and leave the students to their own devices. Spalding loved ferreting out material in the library and "became fascinated by these stories about artists and their works." This fascination led her to read fine art and art history at the University of Nottingham, where she graduated with first-class honors in art history in 1972. In 1974 she married Julian Spalding, an art gallery director, and also began as a research assistant at Sheffield City Polytechnic. She became a part-time lecturer after three years and finally a full-time lecturer beginning in 1978, the year she finished her Ph.D. in art history. She became a noted specialist in late–nineteenth and twentieth-century British art and in 1988 left teaching to write full-time.

While researching her dissertation on Roger Fry, Spalding had several encounters which shaped her development as a biographer. In 1975 she went to interview Marjorie Rackstraw, who had known Fry and who began conversing about "the war." Spalding realized she meant World War I, and suddenly "our conversation . . . set vibrating a ribbon of time that went back to the trenches. . . . Ever since then I have been fascinated by the interweaving of the past with the present, the aliveness of the past in the present, the importance of salvaging it." Her commitment to salvaging the past received further encouragement two years later, when she was invited to lecture on Fry at the University of San Francisco. Buoyed by American enthusiasm and new confidence, Spalding returned to England and wrote *Magnificent Dreams: Burne-Jones and the Late Victorians* (1978).

Before beginning *Magnificent Dreams,* Spalding had become a frequent reviewer for *Arts Review* and other publications. Her review of a Sir Lawrence Alma-Tadema exhibition for *Burlington Magazine* impressed Keith Roberts, a commissioning editor for Phaidon Press, who then suggested that she write for a series by young art historians. Thus, *Magnificent Dreams* began. Peyton Skipwith, a reviewer in *Burlington Magazine* (November 1978), praised the book on Victorian classicism as "serious and erudite." Again at Phaidon's suggestion, Spalding fol-

lowed this auspicious beginning with *Whistler* (1979).

Her first two books received small notice; but with the publication of *Roger Fry, Art and Life* (1980) Spalding's reputation was made. Fry, who as a critic had introduced the Post-Impressionists to England and broken down barriers in making art more accessible to the public, had long been due a revaluation. Tackling Fry, Spalding faced formidable obstacles, first among them Virginia Woolf's biography of her subject. Because of Fry's position as a Bloomsbury insider, Woolf had known the man as a later biographer could not. Woolf's assessment of her own *Roger Fry* (1940), that she had successfully caught the man, is one to which Spalding accedes. But Woolf also lacked many details and felt the need to suppress others, all available in Spalding's account. Fry's affair with Vanessa Bell, Woolf's sister, for example, a central event in his life, was largely glossed over in Woolf's account. Even more important, Spalding the art historian and critic knew Fry's painting and place in modern art history as Woolf had not. Unlike his Bloomsbury contemporaries, Fry had thought himself a painter first and critic second. Accordingly, Spalding treats his paintings seriously and in detail. For Fry, "there was no separation between" life and work; Spalding's biography, far more than Woolf's could, traces the interconnections between Fry's personal life and his efforts in painting, criticism, and the Omega, a design workshop dedicated to formalism in the decorative arts.

Spalding argues in her introduction that Fry's creativity "embraced life as whole. He had . . . a kind of genius for living combining boundless energy with alert sensibility, impulsiveness, ruthlessness, irreverence and profound belief, an intoxicating sense of fun with an underlying seriousness." His fully integrated creative life made him a compelling subject for Spalding. And his antielitist approach to art gives him continuing relevance in the late twentieth century. For Spalding contemporary art criticism poses a threat to the accessibility of art, alienating those uninitiated into the scholarly languages of postmodern theory. In a *Burlington Magazine* essay (July 1986) Spalding underscores the value of Fry's approach and her affinity with it: "If he were still active today, he would, I think, have regretted the gap that exists between modern art and the general public, between art historians and a lay audience. . . . He remains a provocative exemplar in a more self-regarding, less generous and only outwardly more democratic age."

Almost universally critics recognize Spalding's important contribution to twentieth-century art criticism and to a better understanding of Fry. In the lead review for the *Times Literary Supplement* (21 March 1980), Quentin Bell begins with the inevitable comparison of Woolf and Spalding. Bell prefers Woolf's prose but finds Spalding far better at handling facts. Spalding "pursues them with admirable rapacity and, better still, she knows what to do with them when she has got them." Bell also praises her "care, knowledge and sympathy" in evaluating Fry's paintings and her recognition of Fry's role in expanding the public audience for art. Overall, Bell concludes, Spalding's revaluation leaves the "final impression . . . that Fry the artist was a more impressive and substantial figure than most of his friends supposed." Hilton Kramer, chief art critic for *The New York Times* (5 October 1980), faults Spalding's account of Fry's American endeavors (especially in making acquisitions for the Metropolitan Museum); nevertheless, he finds that Fry's ideas, "which underwent some rapid changes in his meteoric career, are traced here with exemplary lucidity." J. B. Bullen's assessment in the *Review of English Studies* (May 1982) argues that Spalding's biography is the kind "Fry himself would have approved." By interweaving Fry's ideas, painting, and personal life with the skill of a diligent researcher and knowledgeable art critic, Spalding created the "standard work for some time to come."

Digging amid abundant Bloomsbury documentation for the Fry biography led Spalding naturally enough to her next work, *Vanessa Bell* (1983). As a painter Bell was deeply influenced by Fry and Duncan Grant and herself deeply influenced the creative and social life of Bloomsbury. Renowned for her grace in making a home, her household was nevertheless far from conventional in both its personal and its artistic dimensions. Married to Clive Bell, she had affairs first with Fry and later with Duncan Grant – with whom she had a child and lifetime partnership. In all her relationships Bell's emotional life and commitment to art were inextricably intertwined. Spalding's biography restores Bell to her rightful place in Bloomsbury's history by focusing on both. Of the talents assembled around that place Spalding writes, "Vanessa Bell's personal achievement may appear the most extreme, the most monumental."

As a woman Bell faced the draining of energies entailed in domesticity and the threat of obscurity often posed by her gender. The minutiae of Bell's daily life as she cared for children and household make for interesting contention among critics. In the *London Review of Books* (15 March 1984) Peter Campbell laments the "phases of [Bell's] life which

Dust jacket for the American edition of Spalding's biography of the British poet and novelist. Hermione Lee called the book "careful, informative and worthwhile."

leave nothing to be recorded except externals," making her "an unwilling," even inappropriate, subject for biography. But the seemingly external is often the point in a biography sensitive to the tangle of the creative and everyday in a painter who is also a woman. Understanding this, John Russell, in the *Times Literary Supplement* (16 September 1983), finds that Spalding excels in "the texture of everyday life at Charleston and elsewhere and on the intuitive skill and subtlety with which Vanessa Bell dealt with" those around her. Generally, critics welcome this multidimensional portrait of Bell; Samuel Hynes, in his review in *The New York Times* (23 October 1983), praises Spalding's biography as a redress for Bell's historical obscurity. Hilary Spurling in the *Observer* (28 August 1983) finds Spalding "especially good on the courage and alacrity with which the Stephen sisters, led always by Vanessa, discarded the stifling social, moral, intellectual and aesthetic conventions" of their Victorian predecessors. Spurling also understands the importance of gender in Bell's life; "the way her life flourished at her art's expense is documented here with great subtlety and penetration."

While there is little critical agreement about Bell's artistic talent, reviewers grant that Spalding, as in her biography of Fry, treats the painting seriously. The book traces her artistic career from early lessons with Ebenezer Cooke through experiments after the Post-Impressionists, the decorative work for Omega Workshops and in her home at Charleston. Throughout, Bell's unwavering devotion to her art "runs like a rod of steel through her life."

In no small measure Spalding's biography of Bell begins a project she had called for in a 1980 review of Germaine Greer's *Obstacle Race* (*Burlington Magazine,* 22 July 1980). In that extended essay she declares the need for an investigation that would show "the challenge certain women artists presented to institutionalised practices in their radical contributions to the art of this century." Fittingly, her portrait of Bell is of a complex and multiply talented woman who was instrumental in the century's early social and artistic revolutions. Spalding's continuing interest in Bell and Bloomsbury led her to take on the editorship of *Charleston Magazine* in 1992. She is also on the Council of Charleston Trust.

After finishing *Vanessa Bell,* Spalding decided to have a child, who attended the book's publication party at the age of two weeks. In 1986 her massive reference work, *British Art Since 1900,* was published. By then Spalding had long been thinking about her next biography, a departure from art history into the literary world of Stevie Smith. Spalding's inspiration came in reading *Me Again* (1981), Smith's collected writings, during a train journey to Oxford. In several of the book's collected letters, Spalding found a voice so close to that of Smith's novels that she felt a biography could better illuminate the autobiographical in Smith's work. Smith's literary executor, James MacGibbon, welcomed Spalding's request to write Smith's life, even though he had put off previous researchers Jack Barbera and William McBrien. Eventually, with Spalding's agreement, he was persuaded to allow Barbera and McBrien to proceed as well; their biography appeared in 1985, Spalding's in 1988. Both articulate the difficulties of writing about the private, elusive poet of Palmer's Green.

Externally Smith's life was uneventful; she lived in the same house most of her life, worked as a secretary, had few close friends, never married, and enjoyed two major periods of popularity, with dispiriting obscurity in between. Her poetry is also sui generis; despite being able to find Smith's roots in the Romantics and others, Spalding concludes that "Stevie's power seems to lie in her ducking or subverting of traditional expectations," writing with "allusive, apparent simplicity." Both the paucity of biographical fact and complex simplicity of the writing intrigued Spalding. She found Smith's anonymous background a challenge after the abundance of Bloomsbury documentation; more especially, she loved Smith's mind and work. Threadlike motifs of death, cruelty, and, in Smith's words, the "ticklish comic element in human suffering" wind through both work and life, and Spalding assiduously explores the relationship between the two.

Novel on Yellow Paper (1936) brought Smith's first real notoriety and something of a cult following. Spalding carefully traces the thinly disguised biographical revelations in that novel and its sequel, *Over the Frontier* (1938). Smith's poetry is a bit more elusive, but Spalding focuses on Smith's recurring and contradictory images, where hilarity and suffering exist in tandem. The poet's tragicomic worldview comes through most lucidly in Spalding's reading of "Not Waving but Drowning," a poem inspired by misinterpreted signals for help. Descriptions of Smith at her many readings also capture the contradictory and often puzzling aspects of Spalding's subject.

Critics passionate about Stevie Smith have impassioned things to say about Spalding's book. All agree that Stevie necessarily remains elusive; she "evades total capture" and is a "mystery." Carol Kino, in *The New York Times Book Review* (13 August 1989), thinks Spalding too reticent on "the one central mystery of this life: what made Stevie Smith so afraid of it to begin with?" Equally elusive for some is the link between life and work; the *Village Voice* review by Walter Kendrick (July 1989) concludes that the paradoxical effect of Stevie's poetry "is her trademark, and I can't blame Spalding for failing to account for it." He finally concedes that "I can't either, and I know of no one who can." Patricia Beer criticizes Spalding's readings of the poetry and claims that after all the meticulous research the reader is left with only the facts (*Times Literary Supplement,* 4 November 1988). Hermione Lee, who has herself written about Smith's poetry, is more sympathetic. She finds Spalding's work "careful, informative and worthwhile" (*Observer,* 23 October 1988). The book's main virtue, in Lee's estimate, is its "thorough use of [Smith's] reading notebooks, review essays and manuscripts . . . to explore the really interesting story, that of Stevie Smith's intellectual life." Lee argues that, in contrast with Smith's other biographers, Spalding "has a better ear for Stevie's shifts of tone and discomforting disingenuities." Anthony Thwaite, who knew both Smith and her work, finds value in Spalding's corrective account of Smith's personality (*London Review of Books,* 27 October 1988). Rather than the popular image of helplessness, Smith appears in Spalding's book as a "powerful presence." Thwaite also argues that Spalding has "caught very seriously and sharply the identification between person and poem, together with the essential enigma: who, or what, was Stevie Smith?"

After the publication of *Stevie Smith* Spalding separated from her husband; the marriage was dissolved in 1991. Professionally, she returned to the world of painters, this time in Neo-Romantics of mid–twentieth century England. *Dance Till the Stars Come Down* (1991), the biography of John Minton, had already been a desired project for several years when Spalding was approached by the publisher John Curtis to do a book on Minton. Two images of Minton haunted Spalding and inform the biography. The first is Lucian Freud's portrait of Minton, showing his long, angular face, averted gaze, and anguished expression bespeaking the profound sadness that eventually led him to suïcide. The other image, of Minton dancing for hours by himself in a Soho club, conveys his characteristic duality, "his limbs expressing frenzied gaiety, his face utterly mournful." Exuberant, depressed, ecstatic, despairing, this image inspired the book's title and encapsulates the man.

Equally attentive to the art, Spalding carefully follows Minton's career from Saint John's Wood Art School through the heyday of the Neo-Romantics, to the devastation and artistic possibilities of the war, and finally to Minton's despair that in modern art there was nothing left to be done. She gives ample and balanced attention to Minton as illustrator, which some critics say was his only field of excellence. At the time, however, he enjoyed considerable fame. Together with his personal gifts and dramatic presence in the bohemian Soho of the 1940s and 1950s, Minton is "as conspicuous a symbol of his day as Aubrey Beardsley is of the 1890s."

Andrew Motion, in his *Observer* review (12 May 1991), takes issue with Spalding's perhaps overly generous appraisal of Minton's art: "[She] can't bring herself to say what is abundantly clear from the book's many illustrations: Minton is a distinctly second rate painter." Nevertheless, Motion praises her "loving and detailed" biography. She is "excellent on Minton's Soho – it's a subject which has often been tackled but never with such panache." The wild gaiety of the Soho era proves elusive, however, for Julian Bell (*Times Literary Supplement,* 31 May 1991). As the life of every party, Minton evades capture; "such persons inhabit the printed page in a morning-after fashion. The odd phrase resurfaces as you survey the empties . . . but the effervescence has effervesced: the point of the man is gone."

But the biographical subject is always elusive, and Spalding has proven her mettle repeatedly, first with a devotion to the task of recovering facts, or in Virginia Woolf's phrase, the "granite" whose counterpart is "rainbow." The acknowledgment pages of Spalding's books bespeak a generosity to sources and a thoroughness manifest on every page of her books. Equally clear is her conviction, despite current ideological critiques of the individual subject, that the personality behind and in the works, whether poetry or painting, matters. Her portrait of Minton is perhaps her most moving and eloquent biography, because she has so knowingly and sympathetically reconstructed not only his suffering but his ways of understanding. Her biography of Duncan Grant in progress promises to show the same adeptness and care.

One of Spalding's touchstones as a beginning writer was Rainer Maria Rilke's *Letters to a Young Poet* (1954). In that slim volume Rilke speaks about the value of everyday life, suggesting that for the writer there is "no poor, indifferent place." Further, he counsels having patience with life's unresolved questions. These seem Spalding's trademark talents: a sympathy for, and openness to, the value of her subjects' everyday lives and the patience to live with the biographer's difficult and elusive questions.

Martin Stannard

(25 October 1947 –   )

Fiona Stafford
Somerville College, Oxford

BOOKS: *Evelyn Waugh: The Early Years 1903–1939*
(London: Dent, 1986; New York: Norton,
1987);
Evelyn Waugh: No Abiding City 1939–1966 (London:
Dent, 1992); published as *Evelyn Waugh: The
Later Years 1939–1966* (New York: Norton,
1992).

OTHER: *Evelyn Waugh: The Critical Heritage,* edited
by Stannard (London & Boston: Routledge &
Kegan Paul, 1984);
Ford Madox Ford, *The Good Soldier,* edited by
Stannard (New York: Norton, 1995).

SELECTED PERIODICAL PUBLICATIONS –
UNCOLLECTED: "No Admittance on Business,"
Essays in Criticism, 26 (1976): 182–186;
"Davie's Lamp," *New Review,* 3 (1976): 52–54;
"Objecting to Correlatives," *New Review,* 4 (1977):
60;
"Misleading Cases," *Essays in Criticism,* 28 (1977):
60;
"*Work Suspended:* Waugh's Climacteric," *Essays in
Criticism,* 28 (1978): 302–320;
"Les Jeux Absurdes," *Novel: A Forum on Fiction,* 13
(1980): 240–242;
"Debunking the Jungle: The Context of Evelyn
Waugh's Travel Books, 1930–1939," *Prose
Studies,* 5 (May 1982): 105–126;
"Waugh at Work," *Essays in Criticism,* 32 (1982):
384–388;
"The Mystery of the Missing Manuscript," *Times
Higher Educational Supplement,* 1 June 1984;
"In Search of Himselves: An Essay on the Autobio-
graphical Writings of Graham Greene," *Prose
Studies,* 8 (September 1985): 139–155;
"The Men Running up to Bowl: Aspects of Stasis in
Larkin and Amis," *Ideas and Production,* 9–10
(1989): 45–46;
"Dickens on Fire: Burning Issues in *Bleak House,*"
*Proceedings of the English Language Association
North,* 5 (1990): 16–29.

Martin Stannard (photograph by Mark Gerson)

Martin Stannard's reputation as a literary biographer rests on his two-volume study of Evelyn
Waugh, *The Early Years 1903–1939* (1986), and *No
Abiding City 1939–1966* (1992). His success in re-
creating the complicated personality of his subject
has been widely acclaimed, and his work is already
one of the standard points of reference for anyone
interested in the life and writings of Evelyn Waugh.
Stannard's work as a biographer is part of his academic career, but his careful scholarship is combined with a strong sense of narrative and a fine
prose style, which have attracted a large general
readership as well as a specialist audience. He has
also reviewed many recent lives of twentieth-
century literary figures, thus developing his own
views on biography as a distinct form through his
assessments of fellow writers.

Martin Stannard was born on 25 October 1947, in Harrow, on the outskirts of London. He was educated in Sussex at Crowborough County Secondary School and Lewes County Grammar School before going to the University of Warwick in 1967 to read English and American literature. It was during this time as an undergraduate that he first became interested in Evelyn Waugh. Among his formative intellectual experiences was a lecture on *A Handful of Dust* (1934) given by one of his tutors, the distinguished critic Bernard Bergonzi. Coming to the novel for the first time, Stannard found it quite unlike anything he had ever read: "It hurt me in a way powerful literary works often do," he recalls. "It was not so much what was said as what was left out." Waugh's "art of elision" fascinated him and made him wonder about the sort of man who could write such a book.

But it was not until he embarked on a postgraduate degree course at the University of Sussex in 1970 that there was any real opportunity to develop his thoughts on Waugh. Although the master of arts course focused on nineteenth-century literature, students were required to write a dissertation on a subject of their own choice over the summer vacation. Stannard had always been interested in authors whom he regarded as being unfairly neglected and initially thought to write on Oscar Wilde, who was then seen as a literary lightweight. After a few weeks, however, he turned his attention to Waugh and proceeded to read the complete works. The dissertation was written in a mere two weeks and gained Stannard a special commendation from the examiners, David Lodge and W. W. Robson.

As a result of his outstanding performance, Stannard was subsequently awarded a Major State Studentship from the Department of Education and Science that would have enabled him to pursue his research for a D.Phil. The results of the M.A. were not published until November, however, and by that time he had already enrolled for a Postgraduate Certificate in Education at Sussex. During the course he was offered a post at the school where he did his teaching practice – Brighton, Hove and Sussex Grammar School for Boys – so he taught there for a year in order to complete his training. Although this was not a conscious part of his research on Waugh, he was in effect shadowing the early career of his future subject in reverse, for after a year at the boys' grammar school he began studies at Oxford.

Beginning in October 1973 Stannard spent three years at Lincoln College, Oxford, studying the early work of Evelyn Waugh under the supervision of Stephen Wall, Fellow of Keble College. The same interest in reclaiming literary reputation guided his approach, as he set about uncovering the serious aesthetic principles that lay behind even Waugh's apparently lighthearted early work. As he commented in the preface of his thesis, existing studies of Waugh such as Christopher Sykes's *Evelyn Waugh: A Biography* (1975) were not only "inaccurate in detail" but had also failed to make any sustained attempt to understand Waugh "as an artist." To redress these deficiencies, Stannard began to delve into a mass of unpublished letters, journals, and manuscripts, many of which had been acquired by the Harry Ransom Humanities Research Center at the University of Texas at Austin. He also interviewed and corresponded with many of Waugh's friends and relations and was thus laying extremely solid foundations for his subsequent biography.

Stannard's biographical approach is hinted at in the title of his dissertation: "The Development of Evelyn Waugh's Literary Career with Special Reference to his Aesthetic Principles, 1917–1939." The first chapter begins with a brief resume of Waugh's school career, extracted from the *Lancing College Magazine* for 1922, which is then analyzed to demonstrate the gulf between the public and private images of the man, even as a teenager. It is an unusually compelling start for a thesis and shows the same awareness of the reader that marks the later biography.

As Stannard analyzed Waugh's experiments with form and narratorial stance, he was developing his own methods of presenting material. The chapter on Waugh's *Rossetti: His Life and Works* (1928), for example, allows scope for a discussion of biography – post–Lytton Strachey's controversial *Eminent Victorians* (1918) – although it is characteristic of Stannard to convey ideas through direct quotation from Waugh: "No doubt ... with the years, we shall once more learn to assist with our fathers' decorum at the lying-in-state of our great men. ... Meanwhile we must keep our tongue in our cheek, must we not, for fear it should loll out and reveal the idiot? We have discovered a jollier way of honouring the dead. The corpse has become a marionette. With bells on its fingers and wires on its toes it is jigged about to a 'period dance' of our own piping." Throughout the thesis Stannard explicitly prefers to let Waugh "put his own case," but the careful selection of material and revealing commentary combine to produce a very persuasive account of a serious writer in the making.

Stannard is not merely a gifted narrator, however, but also a meticulous textual scholar, and much of the thesis is taken up with presenting evidence from manuscript sources. As a research student, he undertook the formal classes in bibliography and palaeography offered by the English faculty at Oxford. For those whose interests were modern, the emphasis on early handwriting and book production offered little practical help, but the awareness of bibliographical problems was to prove vitally important. Part of Stannard's reclamation of Waugh as a serious writer rather than as a talented dilettante has been his elucidation of the novelist's methods of composition. For although Waugh cultivated an image of himself as a careless genius capable of turning out a book in a matter of weeks, Stannard's study of the manuscripts revealed an extremely careful writer, revising the minutest details of his novels. It was the typescripts, however, that were of particular interest, since Waugh would send his handwritten drafts to be typed in sections and then use the first typed version as his working text. Unfortunately, most of the corrected typescripts have been lost, making the process of revision difficult to reconstruct, despite the considerable variations that often exist between the manuscripts and the first published editions of the novels.

When he visited the University of Texas at Austin in 1974, Stannard discovered that the manuscripts of prewar Waugh's novels were clean and beautifully bound, giving every impression that they had been written rapidly with little revision. The only missing manuscript was that of *Vile Bodies* (1930), but in its place was a typescript of the first half of the novel, and it was here that Waugh's careful changes to his text could be seen. There was a further complication, however, in that the first printed edition did not follow the revised version, with its generally lightened tone. Ten years later Stannard wrote an article for the *Times Higher Educational Supplement* (1 June 1984), describing his eventual recovery of the lost manuscript of *Vile Bodies* in Paris and explaining how he had initially solved the textual mystery in "an odd case in which bibliography and biography became mutually supportive." Using both types of evidence, he concluded that Waugh's first wife, Evelyn Gardner, had left him at the point when the revisions to the first typed draft of the novel had been completed. When Waugh returned to work on the novel in a state of considerable depression, he decided to retain the original text with its darker tone, rather than carry on from the revised version. Stannard was thus able to qualify Sykes's view that the somber atmosphere of *Vile Bodies* was no reflection of Waugh's separation from his wife by demonstrating that the process of composition was longer and more complicated than had been assumed.

Studies of the differences between the manuscripts and the printed texts also revealed much about the context in which Waugh wrote his early novels. In *Decline and Fall* (1929), for example, the satire was originally much more irreverent and scatological, but in order to find a publisher Waugh cut many sentences that might have offended readers of 1928. Instead of being thrown into "the lavatory," for example, the Matisse had to be deposited in "the water jug," while references to the Welsh mating "freely with the sheep" became "their sons and daughters rarely mate with humankind except their own blood relations." Stannard's detailed bibliographical work thus provided important insight not only into the novels themselves but also into the character of the author.

As the first scholar to engage in detailed work on the manuscripts, Stannard rapidly became a recognized authority on Waugh, and by 1976 he was being invited to review contemporary publications, such as Michael Davie's edition of the *Diaries of Evelyn Waugh* (1976). In the same year he became the first Leverhulme Fellow in English Literature at the University of Edinburgh. Although primarily a research fellowship, the post also offered Stannard valuable teaching and lecturing experience as a member of the Department of English. After a year in Scotland he completed his doctorate, and in 1979 he obtained a tenured position as an English lecturer at the University of Leicester. He has played an active role in the department ever since; in addition to administrative commitments and a wide range of teaching in the literature of the nineteenth and twentieth centuries, he has toured Italy with the University Theatre and given papers and lectures in Europe and the United States. He was promoted to a Readership in 1993 and in 1995 to a Personal Chair as the Professor of Modern Literature at Leicester.

Despite the heavy workload facing English academics in the 1980s, Stannard maintained his research interests and published the results of his prolonged study of Evelyn Waugh. In 1984 his reclamation of Waugh began to appear in book form, with an edition of critical comments and essays collected by Stannard for the Routledge Critical Heritage series. This was followed by *Evelyn Waugh: The Early Years 1903–1939* in 1986 and its companion, *Evelyn Waugh: No Abiding City 1939–1966* in 1992.

The most recent study drew on material Stannard had collected for the thesis but also benefited from a vast amount of new information, amassed from papers, letters, and interviews specially for the biography. Even when the same material is used in *The Early Years 1903–1939,* the treatment differs significantly because of the change in purpose. For although Stannard was still as keen to present Waugh as a serious artist in his biography as he had been as a doctoral student, the focus of the book is quite different. Where the thesis draws on diaries, letters, and autobiography in order to illuminate aesthetic principles, Waugh's life is the subject of the biography, and Stannard makes anecdotes and reminiscences central. Although Waugh's novels form an important part of the discussion, they are presented in terms of the author's development rather than in the miniessays that often interrupt the flow of literary biographies.

Stannard is also careful to avoid reducing the novels to biographical footnotes, despite the obvious parallels between the situations of many of Waugh's fictional characters and his own life. His insistence on Waugh's craftsmanship and icy detachment preclude the possibility of naive readings of the novels as disguised autobiography. Even in a work such as *The Ordeal of Gilbert Pinfold* (1957), in which the personal elements are pronounced, Stannard emphasizes Waugh's determination to create works that were completely external to himself. Waugh's skills as an illustrator and graphic designer are linked to his attitude to composition, which involved using language as "a precise and perfect instrument" in order to produce a beautiful work of art. Describing the composition of *Scoop* (1938), for example, Stannard observes that "Waugh worked on his manuscript like a cabinet-maker inserting inlay." Whatever the raw materials of Waugh's fiction, then, the final artifacts were independent pieces and should be seen as such, rather than being read merely as comments on the author's life.

At the same time, however, Waugh's use of his own experiences in the novels provides interesting insight into his own character and, as Stannard observes in his article on the *Vile Bodies* manuscript, "while the critic should refrain from using details of an author's life to explain his or her art, it is surely tenable for biographers to use a novel as another document in the file." This concern with the relationship between the work and the life reflects the critical debates of the 1980s. As an English lecturer, Stannard is fully conversant with Barthesian ideas on "The Death of the Author" and "the birth of the reader," while his interest in textual scholarship has brought with it an awareness of the problems of

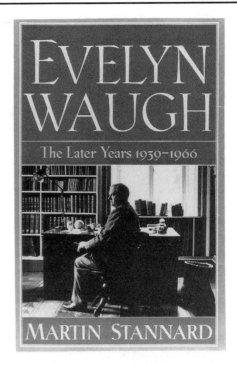

Dust jacket for the American edition of the volume of Stannard's biography of the British novelist covering the years following the publication of Scoop *(1938) to Waugh's death*

intentionalism and the difficulty of defining texts. Rather than finding such problems inhibiting, however, Stannard confronts the theoretical issues, and the biography contains several revealing comments on the hazards of "attempting to correlate an author's life with incidents in his fiction." What he is anxious to avoid is the impression that a literary biography provides the "correct" way to read the works of the subject, "but," he adds, "it is helpful to know the author's view insofar as that is possible. The reader can then use the information or not as he or she pleases."

This awareness of the reader guides Stannard at every stage of his work. He tends to avoid commentary, preferring to convey his facts as unobtrusively as possible, while sustaining the energy of the narration through the friction generated between the different sections of his text. At times he feels that comment is unavoidable – when correcting traditional misconceptions about his subject or when he wished to distance himself from some of Waugh's attitudes. To present an anti-Semitic statement, for example, without authorial comment might be interpreted as an endorsement of his view. In general, however, Stannard sees the responsibility of the biographer to be to present solid evidence about his subject and to provide a historical context against which to set the experiences and attitudes under discussion.

Stannard's notion of "historical context" is not restricted to a dry catalogue of important public events. The narrative impulse that emerges even in his dissertation can be seen throughout the biography, making it an imaginative as well as informative experience for the reader. At Oxford, for example, Waugh "found himself poked away up a stair in the oldest building overlooking New College Lane and above the Junior Common Room Buttery with its clattering plates and cooking smells," and it is details such as this that bring the account to life. Indeed, Stannard sees direct parallels between the work of the biographer and the novelist, not only in the creation of an impression of the period and the characters surrounding the main subject but also in terms of structure. Of all the reviews his biography has attracted, the most telling is that by Jonathan Raban, who stated in *The Independent on Sunday* (19 April 1992) that "*No Abiding City* has an enthralling narrative urgency: Stannard skillfully pits scene against scene, cutting and shuffling his raw material with the speed and ironic eye of a good novelist." But, despite the use of novelistic devices, the biographer's imaginative flights are always circumscribed by the facts of the case, and especially when the work is explicitly designed to correct earlier myths concerning the subject. Throughout the composition of the second volume, for instance, Stannard had in mind the extraordinary story of Waugh's death and the discovery of the body in the toilet. Further research rapidly proved that, despite Graham Greene's insistence that Waugh had drowned and that there was water in his lungs, this was not borne out by fact. Rather than forfeit such an ending entirely, however, Stannard included the more colorful account as a prelude to his own more prosaic version of Waugh's death (turning it into a story about Greene's relationship to Waugh) and thus maintaining his characteristic balance of entertainment and accuracy to the very end. The account of Waugh's death is another example of the "ironic eye," which Raban saw as the chief strength of Stannard's work and which has attracted readers from such a wide spectrum.

The same sense of irony is also seen in the brief epilogue, where Stannard reflects on the personality of the man he has spent so many years attempting to reconstruct. Despite Waugh's obvious idiosyncrasies and failings, he was loved by his friends for his spontaneous gaiety and sweet nature. But these are qualities that are rarely remembered other than as mere generalities, and Stannard's final comment on the art of biography suggests a sense of mild frustration: "The problem for the biographer is that 'disarming gentleness' is not the stuff of anecdotes. Those moments pass, if not unremarked, largely unrecorded." It is a comment and yet one that raises an important question about the nature and purpose of biography. It is also typical of Stannard's method to end with a conclusion in which nothing is concluded and to leave the reader to pursue the implications of his comment or not.

Since finishing *Evelyn Waugh* Stannard has published a new scholarly edition of Ford Madox Ford's *The Good Soldier* (1915), which has involved further travel to the United States and Germany in search of the manuscript and related documents. He has appeared on several radio programs and at literary festivals in connection with his biography of Evelyn Waugh and in 1988 completed a lecture tour in the United States. He is presently at work on a biography of novelist Muriel Spark. He lives in Leicester with his partner Sharon Ouditt and their daughter Zuleika, who was born in 1989.

Lionel Stevenson

(16 July 1902 – 23 December 1973)

Robert G. Blake
Elon College

BOOKS: *Appraisals of Canadian Literature* (Toronto: Macmillan, 1926);

Darwin Among the Poets (Chicago: University of Chicago Press, 1932);

The Wild Irish Girl: The Life of Lady Morgan (London: Chapman & Hall, 1936);

Doctor Quicksilver: The Life of Charles Lever (London: Chapman & Hall, 1939);

The Showman of Vanity Fair: The Life of W. M. Thackeray (New York: Scribners, 1947; London: Chapman & Hall, 1947);

English Literature of the Victorian Period, by Stevenson and John D. Cooke (New York: Appleton-Century-Crofts, 1949);

The Ordeal of George Meredith: A Biography (New York: Scribners, 1953; London: Peter Owen, 1954);

The English Novel: A Panorama (Boston: Houghton Mifflin, 1960; London: Constable, 1961);

The Pre-Raphaelite Poets (Chapel Hill: University of North Carolina Press, 1972).

OTHER: John Galsworthy, *The Man of Property,* introduction by Stevenson (New York: Scribners, 1949);

W. M. Thackeray, *The History of Henry Esmond,* introduction by Stevenson (New York: Harper, 1950);

George Meredith, *The Ordeal of Richard Feverel,* introduction by Stevenson (New York: Random House, 1950);

Meredith, *The Egoist,* introduction by Stevenson (Boston: Houghton Mifflin, 1958);

Thackeray, *Vanity Fair,* introduction by Stevenson (New York: Pocket Books, 1958);

Thackeray, *The History of Henry Esmond,* introduction by Stevenson (New York: Bantam Books, 1961);

George Moore, *Esther Waters,* introduction by Stevenson (Boston: Houghton Mifflin, 1963).

SELECTED PERIODICAL PUBLICATIONS –
UNCOLLECTED: "The Significance of Canadian Literature," *University of California Chronicle,* 27 (January 1925): 32–42;

"A French Text Book by Robert Browning," *Modern Language Notes,* 42 (May 1927): 299–305;

"A Source for Barrie's *Peter Pan,*" *Philological Quarterly,* 8 (April 1929): 210–214;

"Stepfathers of Victorianism," *Virginia Quarterly Review,* 6 (April 1930): 251–267;

"The Ideas in Kipling's Poetry," *University of Toronto Quarterly,* 1 (July 1932): 467–489;

"*Vanity Fair* and Lady Morgan," *PMLA,* 48 (June 1933): 547–551;

"Romanticism Run to Seed," *Virginia Quarterly Review,* 9 (October 1933): 510–525;

"Dickens's Dark Novels, 1851–1857," *Sewanee Review,* 51 (Summer 1943): 398–409;

"Tennyson, Browning, and a Romantic Fallacy," *University of Toronto Quarterly,* 8 (January 1944): 175–195;

"The 'High-born Maiden' Symbol in Tennyson," *PMLA,* 63 (March 1948): 234–243;

" 'The Ancient Mariner' as a Dramatic Monologue," *Personalist,* 30 (Winter 1949): 34–44;

"The Pertinacious Victorian Poets," *University of Toronto Quarterly,* 21 (April 1952): 232–245;

"Meredith and the Problem of Style in the Novel," *Zeitschrift für Angelistik und Amerikanistic,* 6 (Summer 1958): 181–189;

" 'My Last Duchess' and *Parisina,*" *Modern Language Notes,* 74 (June 1959): 489–492;

"Matthew Arnold's Poetry: A Modern Appraisal," *Tennessee Studies in Literature,* 4 (1959): 31–41;

"Darwin and the Novel," *Nineteenth-Century Fiction,* 15 (June 1960): 29–38;

"The Death of Love: A Touchstone of Poetic Realism," *Western Humanities Review,* 14 (Autumn 1960): 365–376;

Lionel Stevenson (Duke University Archives)

"The Modern Values of Victorian Fiction," *College Language Association Journal,* 4 (September 1960): 1–7;

"The Unfinished Gothic Cathedral: A Study of the Organic Unity of Wordsworth's Poetry," *University of Toronto Quarterly,* 32 (January 1963): 170–183;

"Joyce Cary and the Anglo-Irish Tradition," *Modern Fiction Studies,* 9 (Autumn 1963): 210–216.

Scholar, biographer, teacher, administrator, editor, and poet, Lionel Stevenson lived a life of rare dedication to the pursuit and sharing of knowledge. He was proud of his Scots-Irish heritage (he was related to Sir Walter Scott and Joyce Cary), and he was fascinated by genealogy. His biographies all begin generations before their subjects are born. Stevenson's large body of scholarship is fundamentally biographical in approach and orientation, from the early *Darwin Among the Poets* (1932) to the final, award-winning *The Pre-Raphaelite Poets*

(1972). Though his historical and social criticism is substantial and helpful, his basic interest as a critic is to locate those points where a writer's life and works intersect. He is skilled at uncovering real-life models for characters and events in the novels of his writers, and his analysis of George Meredith's *Modern Love* (1862) is a paradigm of biographical criticism.

The only child of Henry and Mabel Cary Stevenson, Arthur Henry Lionel Stevenson was born in Edinburgh, Scotland, on 16 July 1902. When he was five years old the family immigrated to Canada in an effort to improve his father's health. Shortly thereafter, his father died, and Stevenson was raised on his uncle's farm in Maple Bay, near Vancouver. He early displayed a sensitivity to the beauties of nature, which is reflected in his poetry and his life-long love of the English countryside. A precocious student, Stevenson won the Gold Medal at Duncan High School, graduated with a B.A. from the University of British Columbia when he was twenty, and was awarded an Open Fellowship to the University of Toronto, from which he received his M.A. the following year.

In 1923 Stevenson enrolled in the University of California, where he was a teaching fellow in English for two years and where he received his Ph.D. at the age of twenty-three. The following year saw the publication of his first book, *Appraisals of Canadian Literature* (1926). Stevenson remained at the University of California as an instructor in English until 1930, when he became professor and chair of the English Department at Arizona State College. During the seven years at Arizona State, Stevenson was naturalized as an American citizen; published *Darwin Among the Poets;* earned the B.Litt. from Oxford University; and wrote *The Wild Irish Girl: The Life of Lady Morgan* (1936), the first of his four biographies.

In the preface to *The Wild Irish Girl* Stevenson calls Lady Morgan "our first successful professional woman's author – the first to rise to social, intellectual and financial prestige entirely through her business-like exploitation of her literary talent." Sydney Owenson, Lady Morgan, was both a hugely prolific writer and a dominant social presence in Dublin and later in London. Stevenson interweaves Lady Morgan's career, from her employment as a governess to her position as "Dowager of Pimlico," and her writings, spanning a period of fifty-seven years, in fourteen fast-paced chapters of approximately twenty pages each, liberally interspersed with dialogue, extensive quotations from letters, and lively anecdotes to produce an overall effect like that of a novel.

In Stevenson's eminently readable pages Lady Morgan, now all but forgotten except by literary historians, takes on the warmth and complexity of a living presence. Not wanting to be a bluestocking but rather to be "every inch a woman," Lady Morgan was a writer with causes to champion. Her concern for the poor and bad social conditions predates Charles Dickens and Elizabeth Gaskell by thirty years. In *Woman, or Ida of Athens,* a four-volume novel of 1809, she sought to speak for the merits of womanhood and civil and religious liberty. Her novel *France* (1817) created a firestorm of controversy in England for its republican sentiments, and in France the royalist press censured the book. In *Italy* (1821) she attacked the economic rapacity and intellectual obscurantism of the Roman Catholic Church as well as the English government for its craven policy of handing Italy over to the tyranny of Austria. The book was banned by the Roman Catholic Church and prohibited throughout Germany and Italy. Her social conscience was no mere

literary pose, as Stevenson indicates in a fascinating account of her interceding with the authorities to save the life of one Barnaby Fitzpatrick, who had been sentenced to death for stealing a money order out of a letter. Fitzpatrick was transported and lived to become a respected citizen of New South Wales.

In this, as in Stevenson's other biographies, a major strength is the attention devoted to the world of nineteenth-century publishing, which was fraught with intricate intrigue, double-dealing, and personal invective. In haggling with Richard Phillips and Henry Colburn, shrewd, money-grubbing publishers, Lady Morgan displayed great business acumen, besting them at their own game. She also more than held her own against the many critical attacks made upon her in the course of her long career. The chapter titles "Putrescent Puddles of Billingsgate" and "The Audacious Worm" attest to their viciousness, the most savage coming from the dreaded John Wilson Crocker, whose relentless efforts to destroy her merely enhanced her reputation. She portrayed him as the detestable Counselor Conway Townshend Crawley in her immensely popular novel *Florence Macarthy* (1816).

Yet another strong feature of this biography is the large number of dramatic scenes, which vivify the characters and the milieu. Worthy of note are Sydney Owenson's first meeting at the estate of the marquis and marchioness of Abercorn with her future husband, the physician Charles Morgan, who tried to elude her by leaping from an open window to the garden below. Stevenson also presents her first London rout at the famous countess of Cork home where she saw George Gordon, Lord Byron, and met an inebriated John Philip Kemble who fixed his fingers in her wig and asked, "Little girl, where did you buy your wig?"; her sad visit late in life with a senile Samuel Rogers, who recognized her in a fleeting moment of lucidity; her practice during long sleepless nights in her old age, her loved ones all dead, of rehearsing in her memory the Irish songs that her father sang to her when she was a child; and her words to her maid in her last illness, "Put a touch of rouge on my cheeks; one might as well look one's best at the last."

In 1937 Stevenson took an appointment as an assistant professor of English at the University of Southern California, where he was to remain until 1955. A popular member of the faculty, he served as president of the men's faculty club in 1942–1943. Buttressed by prolific contributions to professional journals and the publication of *Doctor Quicksilver: The Life of Charles Lever* in 1939, his career progressed steadily. He became chair of the English Department in 1943, and the next year he was promoted to the rank of full professor. On 10 April 1954 Stevenson married Lillian Sprague Jones.

Enamored of all things Irish, Stevenson chose as the subject of his second biography another hugely popular nineteenth-century Irish novelist of prodigious output. Like Lady Morgan, Charles Lever was a cosmopolitan bon vivant who felt more at home on the Continent than in his native country. Also like her, he had a social conscience that colored many of his works. As fast paced as *The Wild Irish Girl, Doctor Quicksilver: The Life of Charles Lever* consists of sixteen chapters of fifteen to twenty pages, each limited to a time span of four or five years except for the first, "Perpetrator of Pranks, 1806–1827." Sample chapter titles give a sense of the organization: "Wandering Scholar, 1827–1830," "Onlooker in France, 1847–1850," and "Exile of the Adriatic, 1867–1872." Stevenson's ample use of quotations from contemporary records, reconstructed verbatim dialogue, and focus on dramatic episodes in Lever's life cause this biography to read much like a picaresque novel.

Lever was born in Dublin in 1806 and spent a happy childhood with his parents and older brother, John, in a cheerful home that was nicknamed "The Sunny Bank." As a child Lever enjoyed storytelling more than studying, a quality that made him popular with his classmates. He matriculated at Trinity College in Dublin when he was sixteen, but he did not apply himself academically, so that it took him five years to receive his B.A. degree. After graduation Lever traveled to Canada, where in the Tuscarora district he made friends with Indians from whom he was finally forced to escape. In 1828 he made his way to Germany, where he served as second in a duel in Göttingen and met Johann Wolfgang von Goethe at Weimar. Back in Ireland facing the need to prepare for a career, Lever studied medicine at Trinity College and in 1831 received his degree of Bachelor of Medicine, which officially entitled him to practice. He never took the simple steps to acquire the M.D.

Stevenson gives a colorful chronicle of Lever's years as a practicing physician. Memorable events include Lever working in County Claire during a terrible cholera epidemic for ten shillings a day and moving to Brussels in 1837 to practice medicine while passing himself off as "physician to the Embassy" and becoming part of the leading society of that city. As a young doctor Lever was popular with the country people, and because of his riding exploits they conferred on him the affectionate name of "Doctor Quicksilver."

Lever turned to writing to supplement his income. In 1836 his first story was published, a romantic tale titled "The Black Mask." The next year *The Confessions of Harry Lorrequer* (1837) began serialization in the *Dublin University Magazine* as a disjointed series of sketches. It was transformed into a monthly serial and took three years to complete. Though it proved to be extremely popular and established Lever as a writer, the final installments were written under protest. At this time Lever was more interested in his medical career than in writing, which for him early on was slow and laborious. The extra income proved irresistible, however, and for years he would doctor all day and write half the night while plagued with gout. After the publication of *Charles O'Malley, The Irish Dragoon* in 1841 he suddenly became one of the most prolific writers of the age, and by 1850 he was completely committed to writing two novels simultaneously, a practice he continued for the duration of his career.

In 1841 Lever became editor of the *Dublin University Magazine,* and although the handsome salary enabled him to live the extravagant lifestyle that he preferred, he was not entirely happy in his new position. He was disillusioned by the savage political and religious bickering that was poisoning the atmosphere of Dublin, and in 1843 he journeyed to England to challenge one Samuel Carter Hall to a duel because of a literary quarrel. After four years as editor, Lever and his family moved to the Continent and never lived in Ireland again.

A happier time in Lever's life was his tenure as vice consul at Spezia. Meeting the demands of the position with a minimum of exertion and solemnity and privately referring to himself as "Her Majesty's Sweep," he was rejuvenated by the sun and sea of Italy. He often boasted to visitors of being able to swim with his eldest daughters the three miles across the bay at Spezia, and he once wrote that if he could live at Spezia he might rival Methuselah. But shadows darkened his family life: his wife, Kate, began showing the symptoms of the illness that would claim her life within a decade; his brother John died in 1862; and the next year his only son, Charley, died suddenly after a high-spirited life like that of the fictional Charles O'Malley.

Lever spent his last five years as consul in Trieste, a place he loathed but from which he was unable to secure a transfer. Convivial to the end, Lever died in his sleep on 1 June 1872 after an evening of entertaining friends that included the publisher John Blackwood and his wife and daughter.

Stevenson believes that Lever's novels provide the best revelation to be had of the Anglo-Irish char-

Stevenson, circa 1959 (Duke University Archives)

acter, but their sheer number precludes all but a limited analysis of them. The focus of this biography is the man, not the works. Lever's struggles with his publishers and his constant financial straits are given prominent attention, and his last visit to Ireland is powerfully described. One wishes for more detail about Lever's relations with his contemporaries, particularly Charles Dickens and William Makepeace Thackeray, and a more intensive analysis of his feelings of inferiority and severe mood swings, which are touched upon only briefly. The near complete absence in the text of references to specific years makes for an unclear and sometimes bewildering chronology, which is a vexing problem with all of Stevenson's biographies. The bibliography of Lever's complete works with dates of serial and volume publication is especially helpful.

In 1947 Stevenson published *The Showman of Vanity Fair: The Life of W. M. Thackeray,* a deeply researched and extremely readable life that was a Book-of-the-Month Club alternate. Consisting of twenty-four chapters and profusely illustrated with Thackeray's drawings, this study recounts the novelist's life in vivid detail from his immigration to

England from India as a child to his death at age fifty-one as one of the foremost novelists of his time. This biography is more leisurely in pace and richer in detail than the previous ones. Thackeray emerges as a very human, complex, and sympathetic man who triumphed over personal tragedy to achieve literary acclaim, social prominence, and a considerable fortune.

As a child Thackeray was forced to live away from his mother among strangers, and he suffered real cruelty in school. He was rendered physically grotesque by a childhood bully who flattened his nose beyond repair, and for the rest of his life he was sensitive about his appearance. He was prematurely aged, and by his mid thirties his white hair and wrinkled face made him appear far older than he was. He remained pathetically grateful to anyone who gave no hint of thinking him peculiar. Thackeray was a leisurely student at Cambridge and left the university without a degree or qualification for a career. He toyed with being an artist, and he spent time in Weimar. He bought a sword that once belonged to Friedrich von Schiller and had a private audience with Goethe. As a young man he lost his inheritance of £20,000 through extravagant living and bad investments. Struggling to find himself, he read for the law at the Middle Temple but heartily disliked it and never practiced. Thackeray enjoyed only four years of happiness with Isabella Getkin Creagh Shawe, whom he married in 1836. Their second daughter died in infancy, and in 1840, after the birth of a third daughter, Isabella went insane. The insanity occurred just after Thackeray had signed a contract with Chapman and Hall for a book on Irish travels. Even more devastating than the loss of his wife was the rupture of his friendship years later with Jane Brookfield.

Thackeray was inwardly a troubled man, preoccupied in his thirties by thoughts of aging and death and suffering for many years from a painful but unnamed illness that eventually proved fatal. He was a heavy drinker of wine – in his words he had drunk "Enough to float a seventy-four gun ship." Outwardly he was convivial and a lover of his clubs. He was also a man of immense generosity, especially to children and fellow writers down on their luck. A loving father to his two daughters, he told them about God and the Bible and took them to church as children. Although he was a man of deep feelings that were often hidden under a veneer of cynicism, he was capable of genuinely ill-tempered attacks on others in his professional life. He was good-natured in his personal relations, but he could not patiently endure the prolonged intimacy even of people he loved and admired. Hence his frequent travels and numerous social contacts. After *Vanity Fair* (1847–1848) established his fame he was a welcomed figure in the best society on both sides of the Atlantic. He was a guest at the White House on his first American tour, and he dined with Louis Napoleon on a visit to France.

Thackeray's literary career began in 1834 when he became a contributor to *Fraser's Magazine*. Early on, he wrote book reviews for the *Morning Chronicle* and a monthly letter for the *Calcutta Star*. By 1839 he was regarded as the cleverest of the London periodical writers, his *Yellowplush* papers enjoying wide popularity in England and America. In 1843 Thackeray joined the staff of *Punch*. His series on *The Snobs of England* in 1846 helped give respectability to that publication and establish the word "snob" in the English language. By the time he came to write *Vanity Fair* he had spent ten years writing for every type of publication in a wide variety of forms that included travel articles, political reporting, short stories, burlesques, and criticism of books and art. Stevenson believes that Thackeray's adversities prepared him as a satirist.

His ability to sublimate personal experience into art may go a long way to explain the success of *Vanity Fair* and his other novels as well. He felt that he knew his characters as real people and at times he could identify so thoroughly with scenes he was describing that he could hardly believe he had not actually been there. His novels in progress were for him a troubling obsession, as he agonized over writing and put it off as much as possible. He was always conscious of what he considered his limited creative resources, especially when compared with Charles Dickens's imaginative fecundity. His literary career concluded with his appointment in 1859 as the first editor of the *Cornhill Magazine*.

In *The Showman of Vanity Fair*, as in the earlier biographies, Stevenson enriches his narrative with scenes of extraordinary clarity from his subject's life. He shows Thackeray as a child reading his first novel, *The Scottish Chiefs*, as he hears the church bells pealing for the coronation of George IV and becoming from that moment a slave to fiction. Stevenson makes the reader feel present on a visit to Bleinheim when Thackeray sees Arthur Hugh Clough sitting down in the inn yard to teach a ragged child to read off a page of *Punch* that had been lying on the ground. There is a memorable account of Thackeray's first meeting with Dickens after Robert Seymour's suicide. Thackeray sought to illustrate *The Posthumous Papers of the Pickwick Club* (1836–1837), but Dickens turned him down. Equally noteworthy are Thackeray's several meetings with Charlotte Brontë, the shy, intimidated author of *Jane Eyre* (1847) who adulated the author of *Vanity Fair*. Unforgettable, too, is Thackeray's meeting with the young Henry James during his first lecture tour of America. According to Stevenson, when Thackeray remarked about the child's many-buttoned jacket, little Henry received in a flash of intuition that Americans were "queer," a discovery that gave him material for "a life-long series of novels." Thackeray's two lecture tours of America are replete with memorable moments, of which the most humorous is his reply to the question "How do you feel?" after he had been treated to a serving of especially large oysters in Boston, "Profoundly grateful, and as if I had swallowed a little baby." Last scene of all, on Christmas Eve 1863 a servant discovered Thackeray's lifeless body stretched out in bed, his arms above his head and his hands clutching the bed rail in a final agony.

A major strength of *The Showman of Vanity Fair* is the large number of profiles of colorful personalities both well known and obscure. Henry Wadsworth Longfellow, William Cullen Bryant,

Washington Irving, George P. Putnam, Bayard Taylor, and John Pendleton Kennedy figure prominently in the pages on the American tours. William Bradford Reed, district attorney for Philadelphia and professor of American history at the University of Pennsylvania, was an admirer and host. Closer to home are people as strange as any characters from fiction: the quarrelsome Frank Mahony – "Father Prout" – a slovenly little Irish priest known equally well in London, Paris, and Rome as an erudite newspaper writer; Douglas Jerrold, a dwarf with a vicious temper and cutting tongue and a key figure at *Punch;* Frederick William Hamstede, a hunchback dwarf and retired clerk who wrote execrable poetry and managed the business affairs of Our Club; William Maginn, the language prodigy and editor of the leading Tory paper of the time; Antoine-Jean Gros, the French artist who killed himself when he was ridiculed by the Romantics; Richard Martin, M.P., the great Irish duelist and founder of the Society for the Prevention of Cruelty to Animals and owner of the largest estate in Ireland; Phineas T. Barnum, abroad to recoup his fortune, paying a call on Thackeray; and Ivan Turgenev, who made Thackeray shake with laughter with a Russian folk song.

The Showman of Vanity Fair was the definitive life of Thackeray until the publication in 1955 and 1958 of Gordon N. Ray's two-volume biography of the novelist. Stevenson's work remains valuable as the best single-volume introduction to Thackeray and one of the most sympathetic biographies of a major writer.

The Ordeal of George Meredith: A Biography was published in 1953. This most multifaceted of Stevenson's biographies makes extensive use of contemporary accounts of Meredith, providing as thorough an examination as one could hope for in one volume of Meredith's personality, social life, intellectual development, and literary works. Perhaps more than most other literary lives, Meredith's was characterized by struggle – hence Stevenson's title. As the "lonely child" growing up in Portsmouth, Meredith was estranged from his father, Augustus, whom he held in lifelong contempt for weakness of character. He antagonized his playmates by his pretty countenance and drawling intonation of speech, which gave point to the sarcasm and poetic images that filled his conversation. His early education at the Moravian School at Neuwied on the Rhine instilled in him a philosophy of stoicism by which he was to live for the rest of his life. Just before he turned eighteen Meredith was apprenticed to study law but did not take to it and resorted to

journalism. Meredith's penurious early years as a writer were made even more frustrating by his stormy marriage to Mary Ellen Nicolls, the widowed daughter of Thomas Love Peacock, which produced a son who proved to be a disappointment and ended with her elopement with the painter Henry Wallis. His second marriage was much happier but not without pain. Marie Vulliamy Meredith died on 17 September 1884, just when Meredith was finally achieving recognition as a great writer.

Stevenson chronicles in minute detail Meredith's involvement in the rough-and-tumble publishing world of the later nineteenth century. The old-boy network that characterized this world is exemplified in Meredith's various journalistic appointments, but it is through Meredith's position as a reader for Chapman and Hall that Stevenson provides some of the more interesting glimpses into Meredith's literary life. Meredith was a demanding and scornful reader, rejecting submissions by Samuel Butler and George Bernard Shaw. His rejection of Mrs. Henry Wood's *East Lynne* (1861), one of the phenomenal best-sellers of the century, was perhaps his greatest misjudgment. He discovered George Gissing and was a major influence on the young Thomas Hardy. Over the years Meredith did not mellow as a reader; in fact, as he grew older his rejections became more scornful, and his weekly reports were "read by the office staff with unholy glee."

In *The Ordeal of George Meredith* Stevenson examines all of Meredith's significant work – poetry and prose – within the context of his long and arduous struggle for success as a writer. At the outset of his literary career Meredith devoted himself sedulously to poetry, imitating various poetic forms including English and Scottish folk ballads and poems on Greek mythological themes in the manner of Richard Henry Horne, John Keats, and Alfred, Lord Tennyson. One of the longest of his early efforts was "Daphne," presenting the legend of Apollo and the laurel somewhat in the manner of Keats's *Endymion.* The advice of his friend Horne to write on modern topics resulted in "London by Lamplight," a grim poem of social protest, and "Picture of the Rhine," which reflected the poet's love of German scenery from his school days at Neuwied. In 1851 Meredith published his first volume of poems at his own expense, and despite the fact that the volume contained some beautiful nature poems, including the often-anthologized "Love in the Valley," it did not sell, and the hard-pressed Meredith was out of pocket fifty or sixty pounds. After this fiasco Meredith wrote poems in the manner of the long-forgotten Spasmodic poets for which he thought editors would be willing to pay a few shillings. Although Meredith's novels bulk far larger in his corpus than his poems, his first love was poetry, and in the twilight of his creative life he turned back to it. His late French odes receive high praise from Robert Louis Stevenson, who asserts that even "[Algernon Charles] Swinburne's eloquence sometimes sounds shrill beside Meredith's rugged grandeur." Meredith himself regarded "The Day of the Daughter of Hades" as his most important poem. It sets forth his doctrine of defying life's sorrow and brevity.

Meredith's career as a prose writer began in 1856 with *The Shaving of Shagpat: An Arabian Entertainment* and concluded forty years later with *The Amazing Marriage* (1895). For each of Meredith's novels Stevenson provides an extensive analysis in terms of biographical affinities, thematic interconnections, and historical importance followed by a survey of its critical reception. The surveys are extremely valuable in giving a sense both of the critical and cultural milieu in which Meredith worked and the difficulties he encountered in his quest for recognition. In *The Shaving of Shagpat* Stevenson uncovers thematic affinities with Thomas Carlyle's Calvanistic apotheosis of deity and Robert Browning's doctrine of heroic self-affirmation at crucial moments in life. *The Ordeal of Richard Feverel* (1859) is seen as "an extended personal essay in the guise of fiction," a promulgation of Meredith's ideas and opinions rather than an imitation of reality, and as a work that together with George Eliot's *Adam Bede* (1859) endowed "English fiction with artistic and intellectual self-respect."

The Egoist (1879) and *Diana of the Crossways* (1885) reflect Meredith's concern for women's rights not as an issue for political or social legislation but as a fundamental human need for psychological and spiritual growth and independence, and they established him as the novelist of choice for the emancipated women of the 1880s. Stevenson's analysis of the style of *The Egoist* is especially enlightening: its use of delayed reaction in dialogue comes closer to actual human speech than any previous English novel had managed to do, demonstrating that "the process of thinking was a confused sequence of images and almost formless concepts, rather than the organized reasoning that previous novelists had chronicled." The critical reception of this novel was the turning point of Meredith's fame. *The Adventures of Harry Richmond* (1871) is compared to Dickens's *Great Expectations* (1861) and Thackeray's *Pendennis* (1848–1850). In *Rhoda Fleming* (1865) Stevenson finds parallels with George Eliot's novels. An entire chapter is devoted to *Beauchamp's Career* (1876). *The Amazing Marriage* is called Meredith's tenderest, least worldly, and most poetic novel.

Despite his acerbic and overbearing personality Meredith had many friends, and they extended over a broad range of Victorian life. All apparently make their way into the pages of this book. Among them are Frederich Augustus Maxse, a naval officer and perhaps Meredith's best friend; George Virtue, publisher of art books; William Hardman, a London barrister; Leslie Stephen, critic; John Morley, editor of the *Fortnightly Review;* Grant Allen, popularizer of science; and Mrs. Benjamin Wood, a rich, eccentric old lady in Kent who paid Meredith handsomely to read to her weekly and to talk about religion and politics. There is a memorable account of Meredith's first meeting with Robert Louis Stevenson, who won favor by his vigorous retorts to Meredith's habitual banter. Meredith's relations with Swinburne and the Rossetti brothers are portrayed unforgettably in chapter 5, "The House in Chelsea."

When he was an old man Meredith became a national icon. Sir Arthur Conan Doyle lectured on Meredith as the foremost English novelist. Meredith succeeded Tennyson as president of the Society of Authors, and writers of the stature of George Bernard Shaw and G. K. Chesterton called on him at Flint Cottage, where his beautiful daughter, Mariette, served as his hostess. Fame was accompanied by the decline of his physical powers. In 1899 the once vigorous walker had to refuse an honorary degree from Oxford University because he could not travel to receive it. The occasion of Meredith's eightieth birthday was "a journalistic orgy" with a testimonial of 250 famous names from both sides of the Atlantic. To a group of reporters Meredith said "Life is a long and continuous struggle. It is necessarily combative. Otherwise, we cease. Let the struggle go on. Let us be combative; but let us also be kind." Early in the morning of 18 May 1909, "facing the dawn that glowed above the green slope of Box Hill," Meredith died. After forty years *The Ordeal of George Meredith* remains of first importance.

A prominent feature of Stevenson's biographies is the empathy he has for his subjects. It is clear that he likes and admires Sydney Owenson, Charles Lever, William Makepeace Thackeray, and George Meredith. A diverse group temperamentally, they share a prodigality of creative energy, an exuberant affirmation of life, and a dogged perseverance to overcome obstacles in their struggle for self-fulfillment. All achieved great fame in their time, even to the point of celebrity, but ironically their times of greatest success were marred by personal tragedy: loss of loved ones, health, or fortune. In recounting this archetypal irony of human experience in the lives of his subjects, Stevenson conveys a sense of understanding and compassion, and in his selection and use of detail he creates a sense of intimacy, so that the reader is inclined actually to care about these writers of a century ago as persons.

Stevenson joined the Duke University faculty in 1955 as James B. Duke Professor of English. He served as chair of the Department of English at Duke from 1964 to 1967. From 1967 to 1968 he was the Berg Visiting Professor of English at New York University. Upon retiring from Duke in 1971, Stevenson taught at the University of Houston for one year. In 1973 he was appointed the first Distinguished Visiting Professor of English at the University of British Columbia, his alma mater. In the course of a long career Stevenson was a visiting pro-

fessor at the University of Illinois at Urbana from 1952 to 1953 and a senior lecturer at Oxford University from 1960 to 1961. In 1951 he was elected a fellow of the Royal Society of Literature. Stevenson was an honorary member of Phi Beta Kappa and a Guggenheim fellow. His professional leadership roles included a term as chair of the Victorian Literature section of the Modern Language Association and membership on the boards of the *South Atlantic Quarterly, Nineteenth-Century Fiction, Victorian Studies,* and *College English,* to name but a few. Lionel Stevenson died suddenly in Vancouver on 23 December 1973, leaving his wife, Lillian, and adopted daughter, Marietta.

Papers:

Stevenson's personal papers, including the Lionel Stevenson Collection of Canadiana, are housed at the Perkins Library, Duke University, Durham, North Carolina.

Julian Symons

(30 May 1912 – 19 November 1994)

W. P. Kenney
Manhattan College

See also the Symons entries in *DLB 87: British Mystery and Thriller Writers Since 1940, First Series* and *DLB Yearbook: 1992.*

BOOKS: *Confusions about X* (London: Fortune, 1939);

The Second Man (London: Routledge, 1943);

The Immaterial Murder Case (London: Gollancz, 1945; New York, Macmillan, 1957);

A Man Called Jones (London: Gollancz, 1947);

Bland Beginning (London: Gollancz, 1949; New York: Harper, 1949);

A. J. A. Symons: His Life and Speculations (London: Eyre & Spottiswoode, 1950);

The Thirty-First of February (London: Gollancz, 1950; New York: Harper, 1951);

Charles Dickens (London: Barker, 1951; New York: Roy, 1951);

Thomas Carlyle: The Life and Ideas of a Prophet (London: Gollancz, 1952; New York: Oxford University Press, 1952);

The Broken Penny (London: Gollancz, 1953; New York: Harper, 1953);

The Narrowing Circle (London: Gollancz, 1954; New York: Harper, 1955);

Horatio Bottomley: A Biography (London: Cresset, 1955);

The Paper Chase (London: Collins, 1956); published as *Bogue's Fortune* (New York: Harper, 1957);

The Colour of Murder (London: Collins, 1957; New York: Harper, 1957);

The General Strike: A Historical Portrait (London: Cresset, 1957; Chester Springs, Pa.: Dufour, 1957);

The Gigantic Shadow ((London: Collins, 1958); published as *The Pipe Dream* (New York: Harper, 1959);

The Progress of a Crime (London: Collins, 1960; New York: Harper, 1960);

A Reasonable Doubt: Some Criminal Cases Reexamined (London: Cresset, 1960);

Julian Symons

The Thirties: A Dream Resolved (London: Cresset, 1960; Westport, Conn.: Greenwood, 1973; revised edition, London: Faber & Faber, 1975); republished in *The Thirties and the Nineties* (Manchester: Carcanet, 1991);

Murder! Murder! (London: Fontana, 1961);

The Detective Story in Britain (London: Longmans, Green, 1962; expanded, 1969);

The Killing of Francie Lake (London: Collins, 1962); published as *The Plain Man* (New York: Harper & Row, 1962);

Buller's Campaign (London: Cresset, 1963);

The End of Solomon Grundy (London: Collins, 1964; New York: Harper & Row, 1964);

The Belting Inheritance (London: Collins, 1965; New York: Harper & Row, 1965);

England's Pride: The Story of the Gordon Relief Expedition (London: Hamilton, 1965);

Francis Quarles Investigates (London: Panther, 1965);

The Man Who Killed Himself (London: Collins, 1965; New York: Harper & Row, 1965);

Critical Occasions (London: Hamilton, 1966);

Crime and Detection: An Illustrated History from 1840 (London: Studio Vista, 1966); published as *A Pictorial History of Crime* (New York: Crown, 1966);

The Man Whose Dreams Came True (London: Collins, 1968; New York: Harper & Row, 1968);

The Man Who Lost His Wife (London: Collins, 1970; New York: Harper & Row, 1970);

Bloody Murder: From the Detective Story to the Crime Novel (London: Faber & Faber, 1972); published as *Mortal Consequences: A History from the Detective Story to the Crime Novel* (New York: Harper & Row, 1972); revised as *Bloody Murder* (Harmondsworth: Penguin, 1974; revised again, 1985; New York: Mysterious Press, 1993);

Notes from Another Country (London: London Magazine Editions, 1972);

The Players and the Game (London: Collins, 1972; New York: Harper & Row, 1972);

The Plot Against Roger Rider (London: Collins, 1973; New York: Harper & Row, 1973);

The Object of an Affair, and Other Poems (Edinburgh: Tragara, 1974);

A Three Pipe Problem (London: Collins, 1975; New York: Harper & Row, 1975);

Ellery Queen Presents Julian Symons' How to Trap a Crook and 12 Other Mysteries, edited, with an introduction, by Ellery Queen (Frederic Dannay and Manfred B. Lee) (New York: Davis, 1977);

The Blackheath Poisonings: A Victorian Murder Mystery (London: Collins, 1978; New York: Harper & Row, 1978);

The Tell-Tale Heart: The Life and Works of Edgar Allan Poe (London: Faber & Faber, 1978; New York: Harper & Row, 1978);

Conan Doyle: Portrait of an Artist (London: Whizzard, 1979; New York: Mysterious Press, 1988);

The Modern Crime Story (Edinburgh: Tragara, 1980);

Sweet Adelaide: A Victorian Puzzle Solved (London: Collins, 1980; New York: Harper & Row, 1980);

Critical Observations (London & Boston: Faber & Faber, 1981; New Haven, Conn.: Ticknor & Fields, 1981);

The Great Detectives: Seven Original Investigations (London: Orbis, 1981; New York: Abrams, 1981);

A. J. A. Symons to Wyndham Lewis (Edinburgh: Tragara, 1982);

The Detling Murders (London: Macmillan, 1982); published as *The Detling Secret* (New York: Viking, 1983; Harmondsworth & New York: Penguin, 1984);

The Tigers of Subtopia, and Other Stories (London: Macmillan, 1982; New York: Viking, 1983);

The Name of Annabel Lee (London: Macmillan, 1983; New York: Viking, 1983);

1948 and 1984 (Edinburgh: Tragara, 1984);

The Criminal Comedy of the Contented Couple (London: Macmillan, 1985); published as *A Criminal Comedy* (New York: Viking, 1986);

Dashiell Hammett (San Diego: Harcourt Brace Jovanovich, 1985);

Two Brothers: Fragments of a Correspondence (Edinburgh: Tragara, 1985);

Makers of the New (London: Deutsch, 1987; New York: Random House, 1987);

The Kentish Manor Murders (London: Macmillan, 1988; New York: Viking, 1988);

Death's Darkest Face (London: Macmillan, 1990; New York: Viking, 1991);

The Thirties and the Nineties (Manchester: Carcanet, 1991);

Portraits of the Missing: Imaginary Biographies (London: Deutsch, 1991; Pomfret, Vt.: Trafalgar Square, 1991);

Something Like a Love Affair (London: Macmillan, 1992; New York: Mysterious Press, 1993);

Criminal Practices: Symons on Crime Writing: 60s to 90s (London: Macmillan, 1994);

Playing Happy Families (London: Macmillan, 1994; New York: Mysterious Press, 1995);

The Man Who Hated Television, and Other Stories (London: Macmillan, 1995).

Collections: *The Julian Symons Omnibus,* introduction by Symons (London: Collins, 1966);

The Julian Symons Omnibus (Harmondsworth: Penguin, 1984).

OTHER: *An Anthology of War Poetry* (Harmondsworth & New York: Penguin, 1942);

Essays and Biographies by A. J. A. Symons, edited, with an introduction, by Symons (London: Cassell, 1969);

Between the Wars: Britain in Photographs (London: Batsford, 1972);

"Progress of a Crime Writer," in *The Mystery and Detection Annual,* edited by Donald K. Adams (Beverly Hills, Cal.: Adams, 1974), pp. 238–243;

Verdict of Thirteen: A Detective Club Anthology, edited by Symons (New York: Harper & Row, 1979);

Tom Adams, *Agatha Christie: The Art of Her Crimes,* commentary by Symons (New York: Everest House, 1981);

George Orwell, *Animal Farm,* with an introduction by Symons (New York: Knopf, 1993).

Julian Symons cheerfully accepted being recognized primarily as a writer of crime fiction, indeed as one of a small group of writers who definitively established the claim of crime fiction to a place of respect within our literary culture. Yet his accomplishments in crime fiction represent only a part of the achievement of one of the most versatile men of letters of his generation. A recognized poet, even if in his own view a minor one, editor of an influential journal of poetry in the 1930s, respected critic and historian of literature, an informed and perceptive observer of modern society, and the author of seven biographies, Symons, who had no long-term academic affiliation, impressively lived the vocation of freelance writer.

The youngest of seven children, two of whom died in infancy, Julian Symons was born in London on 30 May 1912, the son of Morris Albert Symons, a Jewish immigrant whose country of origin his son never knew, and Minnie Louise (Bull) Symons. During the war years the elder Symons enjoyed a degree of business success that allowed the family to know briefly the satisfaction of a middle-class existence, but this prosperity was short-lived. When the elder Symons died in 1929, his estate was valued at four pounds.

Symons's formal education ended when he was fourteen years old. In his late teens, Julian embarked on an intensive course of self-education. He read the British writers of the 1890s, the Elizabethan and Jacobean dramatists, John Dryden, and Alexander Pope. He read more verse than prose, but among novelists he preferred Leo Tolstoy, Ivan Turgenev, and, above all, Fyodor Dostoyevsky. He generally avoided the major Romantic and Victorian writers preferred by his literary friends. This was in part, he would later perceive, a matter of cultural snobbery, but it also reflected a genuine preference for the harsh over the bland, for satire and realism over romance.

Symons's self-designed course of study yielded a kind of intellectual excitement that perhaps could not have been generated by the prescriptions of formal education and prepared him well for the immersion in modern literature that was the next major stage in his intellectual development. Of the great Moderns, Wyndham Lewis, whom Symons admired as a true maverick and honored as

the most remarkable English stylist of the twentieth century, would assume special importance for him. But Symons's position in relation to modern literature is not only that of a student. In addition to writing poetry, Symons founded in 1937 *Twentieth Century Verse,* a magazine he ran single-handedly until the war. *Twentieth Century Verse* provided a forum for poets outside the circle of W. H. Auden, at that time the dominant figure in English poetry.

Like many of his generation, Symons became involved during the 1930s in left-wing politics. What this meant for him was an adherence to theoretical Trotskyism for several years beginning in 1938. Although he would never entirely abandon the posture of nonaffiliated leftist, Symons would later reject Marxism as unacceptably optimistic in light of the concentration camps, which, for Symons, constitute the crucial reality of the twentieth century. At the beginning of World War II, however, Symons's convictions compelled him to refuse conscription. His plea rejected, Symons accepted induction in 1942. He spent nearly two years in the army, nine months of them in the hospital as the result of botched surgery. He returned to civilian life in January 1944.

Married to Kathleen Clark in 1941, Symons found work as a copywriter for an advertising agency. He maintained this position for four years, until he established himself as a weekly columnist for the *Manchester Evening News.* He took over the column that had been written by George Orwell, whom he had known since 1943, and was recommended for the position by Orwell himself. Symons's first child, Sarah, was born in 1948. A son, Maurice, was born in 1951. By then Symons had fully entered upon his career as a freelance writer.

The subject of Symons's first biography reflects the importance of family relationships in shaping his thought and character. That subject was in fact Julian's older brother Alphonse (1900–1941), who, in his teens, had elected to be called AJ and who, as A. J. A. Symons, established himself as a writer, especially a biographer, of some significance. AJ combined a gift for fantasy and self-dramatization with a head for business. As a young man of the period between the wars, he defined himself as a dandy and a good deal of a dilettante but with some claim to genuine connoisseurship. He was a founder of the First Editions Club and of the Wine and Food Society, as well as a dedicated collector of music boxes and Victoriana. Above all it seems he succeeded in creating himself as a personality of distinction and flair among the sophisticates of his era.

That era was brought brutally to an end by the out-break of World War II, but AJ, declaring that he had built his life for peace, may never have fully grasped how utterly all had been altered and seemed indeed unwilling to acknowledge that anything fundamental had changed. His death in 1941 meant that he never had to adapt to the postwar world.

A. J. A. Symons's reputation as a writer rests primarily on his second book, *The Quest for Corvo* (1934), the biography of Frederick William Rolfe (Baron Corvo), the author of *Hadrian VII* (1904). By no means a forgotten writer, Corvo nevertheless must be regarded as a marginal one. Yet Symons generates intense interest in a writer of fiction whose real life was a triumph of artifice. Corvo's success at self-creation no doubt struck a responsive chord in Symons; it is unlikely that any later biographer will surpass the vivacity of Symons's portrait of his subject.

To readers who turn today to Julian Symons's life of his brother, A. J. A. Symons may himself seem at best a marginal figure. Yet a personality at once so individual and so representative of an era certainly deserves the tribute of a biography, and Symons's testimony to his brother's character remains a minor triumph of the biographer's craft. Treating his subject with the affection of a brother, Julian also establishes a carefully maintained detachment. All that was excessive and ego-driven in A. J. A. Symons is presented judicially but not judgmentally. The qualities of his brother's personality that manifest themselves in his choice and treatment of subjects are so vividly presented that this book remains unique among Julian Symons's literary biographies for its illuminating delineation of the link between the life and the work. In his brother, one feels, A. J. A. Symons has found his ideal biographer; the book has precisely the weight its subject deserves.

The life of his brother, then, marked an auspicious debut for Julian Symons as a literary biographer. Whether he could effectively treat a subject with whom he had not enjoyed so resonant a personal relationship, of course, remained unsettled. But Symons's career as a writer was otherwise well under way. In the same year in which his biography of his brother appeared, Symons completed *The Thirty-First of February,* the fourth of his crime novels but the first he would later look back on with pleasure. In his own judgment at least, for the first time Symons realized to a significant degree the ambition of producing a crime novel that can stand comparison with the

Drawing of Symons by Wyndham Lewis, 1938

"straight" novel for character development and for the critical observation of society. The pursuit of this ambition would motivate Symons's long and distinguished career as a crime novelist.

Symons's second effort at biography was a commissioned work; he agreed to write *Charles Dickens* (1951). Dickens had not been one of Symons's early enthusiasms, but his course of self-education had eventually led him to the great Victorian novelist. Although written for a popular audience and not intended as a work of original scholarship, the project required a commitment to research, and Symons found here and elsewhere that his lack of formal education, and therefore of formal training in methods of research, meant that he was often uncertain and inefficient in searching for and organizing data.

Symons constructs the life of Dickens in three parts: the Life, the Work, and the Artist. The sharp division thus established between life and work, while no doubt a suitable expository device given the book's intent, has the effect of aborting any close examination of the relations between the two, the kind of examination that many would regard as the principal raison d'être of literary biography.

The third section of the book involves a general evaluation and a commentary on Dickens's critical reputation.

No account of Dickens's life, according to Symons, could afford to overlook the insights of psychology as that discipline had developed in the years since Dickens's death. This does not mean, however, that Symons aims at a Freudian study of his subject. He rather finds in the emotional peaks and valleys evident throughout Dickens's life a clear, explanatory pattern: Dickens was manic-depressive. Symons seems to have succumbed too readily to the temptation of the available category. Would a formal university education have taught him to look with an appropriate suspicion at such a sweeping and reductive interpretation of the life of a highly complex man?

In introducing his discussion of the work, Symons discerns three "strands" in Dickens: the radical, the comic-sentimental, and the horrific. Dickens's radicalism, according to Symons, based as it is on the moral perceptions and feelings of the individual, must seem insufficiently scientific and analytical to the twentieth-century reader, especially the reader whose standards, like Symons's, are those of the Left. That does not, of course, imply that this radicalism could not serve adequately as motivation for Dickens the artist. But Symons finds in the gradual darkening of the work evidence of Dickens's own consciousness of failure in what he had sentimentally perceived as a personal struggle against the forces of oppression.

In his examination of symbolism in Dickens, Symons assumes a stance that will remain constant in his literary biographies. While conceding that an artist's symbols may originate in the unconscious, Symons is most comfortable when satisfied that what he perceives as symbolism is a totally conscious literary device. He will often seem to insist on understanding other critics' readings of a text in symbolic terms as implying a claim, whether justified or not, that what the critic has found is what the author consciously intended. Some readers will hear in this the voice of common sense; others may regard it as a commitment to superficiality. There should be little controversy, however, about the fineness of perception Symons, a working novelist as well as a biographer and critic, brings to questions of craft in Dickens's fiction. An informed responsiveness to craftsmanship will continue to characterize Symons's mature criticism.

In Symons's summing-up, Dickens is the greatest literary genius of the Victorian Age in England, but his limitations become clear when compared to an artist of Dostoyevsky's stature. These limitations Symons traces to the Philistinism, prudery, and sentimentality of the age itself and to Dickens's failure to evolve a form adequate to his apprehension of the world. That an age may fail to meet the needs of the artist may be deemed a provocative and at least arguable notion; certainly it is a question a biographer may legitimately explore, although such an exploration would probably require at the very least more space than Symons had at his disposal. But the reader may wonder whether Dickens failed to evolve a form adequate to his own or to Symons's apprehension of the world. The difficulty, of course, lies in separating an author's apprehension of the world from the form in and through which that apprehension is displayed to the reader. In his evaluation Symons may have been insufficiently sensitive to that difficulty.

Reviews of *Charles Dickens* emphasized its value as an introductory or summarizing work for the nonspecialist. The most negative review focused on Symons's diagnosis of Dickens as manic-depressive. One reviewer dismissed Symons's reading as an irresponsible indulgence in the cliché that artists of genius are madmen underneath it all, a cliché that has already done sufficient harm.

Symons's next literary biography, *Thomas Carlyle: The Life and Ideas of a Prophet* (1952), represented a new level of ambition in Symons's biographical writing. There is no trace here of the sort of imposed format that created difficulties in *Charles Dickens*. The two great themes of the book are introduced with a craftsman's art in the first chapter. Symons departs from the chronological organization that dominates the book to bring directly before the reader a moment of triumph in the life of Carlyle: his election in 1865 to the post of rector of Edinburgh University. In spite of Carlyle's professed fear of speaking in public, the speech he delivered on that occasion was a triumph. But what Symons encourages us to see in the event is the tribute the aged rebel pays to respectability. An even more bitter irony resides in the content of the speech. Carlyle's academic triumph marks for Symons the culminating and defining moment of his moral failure. Carlyle the old radical has become the champion of authority and his age's most scathing critic of the democratic principle. The intellectual portrait of Carlyle that Symons offers is precisely that of the failed radical.

But Symons's interest in his subject is not limited to the intellectual portrait. Like Carlyle's other biographers, Symons devotes much of his attention to Carlyle's marriage. The first chapter of the book ends with the death of his wife Jane Welsh Carlyle, which occurred before Carlyle's return from Edinburgh. Their troubled relationship provides the second major theme of the book.

Symons brings a craftsman's appreciation to his discussion of Carlyle as a writer and says much that is perceptive about such matters as the development of Carlyle's prose style. His account of Carlyle as a thinker is more questionable. To see Carlyle's celebration of authority and of hero-worship as proto-Fascist may be justifiable and certainly could have seemed so to a man of the Left writing not so long after the end of World War II. Yet this reading may go too far toward judging Carlyle in terms of Symons's time, rather than trying to understand Carlyle in terms of his own. The challenge of Carlyle's counterstatement to the progressive pieties of much Victorian thought seems seriously underestimated by Symons. And this may in turn seriously compromise any attempt to estimate Carlyle's significance for later generations.

What may be involved here, of course, is simply that any attempt to evaluate Carlyle's thought must prove controversial. Yet it could be that discussions of Carlyle's marriage have given rise to more partisan fanaticism than have any of the more obviously ideological issues that confront his biographer. While more sympathetic than many writers to Carlyle, Symons is above all fair and temperate. He certainly conveys the attractive force of Jane's personality. But what most characterizes Symons's treatment of this subject is his emphasis on the unique importance each partner in the relationship had for the other. In Symons's hands the judgments of outsiders on the fierce intimacy of Thomas and Jane Carlyle come to seem merely irrelevant.

Symons's talents as a novelist are surely at work in the balance of tact and power evident in his treatment of this emotional material. The same talent also informs Symons's delineation of the often uneasy relationship of both Thomas and Jane to a social environment to which neither could ever have conformed. Symons is never more persuasive than in placing before us Carlyle's curious combination of intellectual power and social gaucherie as those who knew him may have seen it.

The critical response to *Thomas Carlyle,* while generally favorable in the popular press, was mixed on the whole. Most reviewers appreciated Symons's portrayal of the Carlyles' emotional life, and many were prepared to recommend the book as a popular biography for the general reader. But those reviewers who were primarily interested in the treatment of Carlyle's thought argued that Symons's apparent ideological biases prevented him from finding his

way to the authentic greatness of Carlyle as a thinker. On balance, however, most reviewers acknowledged that Symons's sympathy for Carlyle as a man survives his rejection of Carlyle as a thinker. And that sympathy, combined with Symons's intelligence, gives the book much of its genuine strength.

Symons's interest in Horatio Bottomley, the subject of his next biography, was aroused in part by his early perception of Bottomley, a notorious swindler, as another instance of a radical gone wrong. In fact, as Symons soon realized, Bottomley's articulation of radical sentiments had never been more than an instrument in his swindles. The finished book, then, deviates from Symons's original intention. Its success may suggest, however, that Bottomley's attraction for Symons involved sources other than those he acknowledged. Since Bottomley was not a writer, the book is not a literary biography, but Bottomley did create one impressive fictional character: himself. The coldness at the center of this manipulator of others emerges as a central theme of Symons's study. Bottomley is, of course, not the first of Symons's biographical subjects to create himself as a character, to engage in forms of manipulation, to deny to others access to his inner self. Seen in this light, Bottomley seems a malign variant on the figure of A. J. A. Symons, and it is perhaps this association, at least as much as a false perception of Bottomley as one more failed radical, that drew Symons to Bottomley as a subject.

Symons himself might dismiss this suggestion as idle speculation, yet he would certainly agree that there is more than a little that is mysterious about the relationships of biographers and their subjects. The view of biography that he has himself articulated emphasizes the artistic, even creative, function of the biographer. It is not, in this view, the business of the biographer to create facts or, for that matter, to delete from the biographical account the relevant and significant facts to be found in the record. But it is the biographer's business to choose, and the biographer's choices must arise in part from a personal approach to the subject, an individual point of view. Thus, the portrait of the subject finally offered by the biographer can never claim to be objectively true. In fact, according to Symons, one of the ways a biographer can be dishonest is in claiming to offer the final truth about the subject. A successful biography is never merely a record of social and historical fact. It is rather a creative interpretation of the facts that constitute the record.

Two decades later, by 1978, the year in which *The Tell-Tale Heart: The Life and Works of Edgar Allan*

*Dust jacket for the first American edition of Symons's brief
illustrated biography of Sir Arthur Conan Doyle*

Poe appeared, Symons was established as one of
the most respected writers of crime fiction in the
English-speaking world and beyond. That this respect was felt, not only by readers and critics but
by his peers, is reflected in such honors as his
election, succeeding Agatha Christie, to the presi-
dency of the Detection Club, a society of British
crime writers. Other honors would follow, including the Grand Master Award from the Mystery
Writers of America. In 1972 Symons had published his critical history of crime fiction, *Bloody
Murder: From the Detective Story to the Crime Novel*.
Twice revised, the book is recognized as the standard one-volume treatment of its subject. Given
his interests, as practitioner and scholar, in crime
fiction and his standing as a biographer, it seems
all but inevitable that Symons would eventually
undertake a biography of Poe, who was, among
other things, the inventor and first master of the
detective story.

Toward a subject who might prove irresistibly
tempting to the biographer's bent for fanciful speculation, Symons, characteristically, assumes a stance
of hardheaded common sense. He resolutely resists
the many opportunities for melodrama, perhaps to
the point at which such resistance becomes itself a
kind of excess. Whatever motivated Poe's marriage
to his sickly and adolescent cousin Virginia Clemm,
Symons shows us a devoted husband and, what is
more, a loving son-in-law to Virginia's mother.
Poe's drinking is accounted for as a response to un-
endurable stress. And Symons remains unconvinced that Poe was addicted to opium. In general,
Symons seems determined to provide a corrective
to the lurid picture of Poe, now part of our literary
folklore and ultimately derived from the libelous accounts of Poe's unscrupulous literary executor and
first biographer, Rufus Griswold. A regrettable consequence is that Symons seems at times motivated
not so much by an individual point of view toward
his subject, called for by his view of the biographer's art, as by an individual point of view toward other people's treatments of his subject.

In organizing his material, Symons makes an
odd and questionable choice. Although presumably
free to devise his own format, as he might not have
been in a commissioned work, Symons reverts to a
pattern not unlike the one that organized his study
of Dickens. The first and longest section is concerned with the Life; an epilogue gives some account of the posthumous reputation of Poe the man.
A second section, about one-third as long as the
first, is devoted to the Work. A third section offers
a highly selective survey of Poe criticism and a brief
summing-up.

Symons's rationale for thus separating life and
work is that he wants to show the life as it was actually lived. But is the life of any great writer – of Poe
above all – actually lived as something so separate
from the work? Even Symons, however inconsis-
tently, insists in his summing-up that Poe's personality is everywhere present in his work. At any rate,
readers for whom literary biography justifies itself
precisely insofar as it illuminates the connection between the life and the work must recognize that *The
Tell-Tale Heart* is not, is determined not to be, what
they are looking for.

Symons's discussion of the work is organized
around the claim that there are two Poes: the Visionary Poe and the Logical Poe. Much of the critical commentary itself is devoted to declaring which
Poe does what. Thus, the Logical Poe produces the
criticism, the Visionary Poe produces the horror
stories; the Visionary Poe determines the purpose

of "Ulalume," while the Logical Poe devises the way of carrying it out. The sort of two-valued distinction Symons employs here has much to recommend it as a point of departure, but it proves finally restrictive as an overall organizing principle. Was there anything in Poe's art that was neither Logical nor Visionary? Does Poe ever achieve a complete fusion of the Logical and Visionary? Symons provides no answers to such questions.

In his survey of Poe criticism, Symons tends to be sweepingly dismissive of any critical approach that deviates to any significant degree from his own, which is mostly concerned with the work of art as the more or less successful fulfillment of the artist's conscious intention. One must note with regret that in his discussion of other critics Symons often adopts a tone of undisguised and unrestrained hostility, at times approaching contempt; these chapters are sometimes unpleasant reading. Symons is predictably harsh on the Freudian approach to Poe, but he seems unaware that the specific approach he attacks would have been considered outmoded by Freudians by the time his book was published. He is in general impatient with symbolic readings of Poe, from the Freudian to the Formalist, but his inability, noted as early as his study of Dickens more than a quarter century before, to entertain the idea of symbolism as other than a conscious literary device renders him unable to debate the issues in terms his antagonists could accept.

As in his earlier biographies, Symons's talents as a novelist contribute to much that is most attractive. Whether or not one finally accepts Symons's portrayal of Poe, it is vividly rendered, as are Poe's relationships with others. Again, as in his life of Carlyle, Symons conveys with particular force the comedy and pathos that arise out of the inability of a man of genius and imagination to function in the ordinary circumstances of social intercourse.

Critics, while noting that Symons's book could make no claim to original scholarship, recommended it to general readers, although a few found it less satisfactory than Wolf Mankowitz's *The Extraordinary Mr. Poe,* published in the same year. Daniel Hoffman, one of the critics Symons had attacked (for writing "gobbledygook"), wrote a generous appreciation in *The New York Times Book Review* (9 July 1978), praising the book as a dependable account of the life, heightened by a novelist's insights into character and social situations. But Hoffman, like others, found the book's critical passages perfunctory and regretted that, on the whole, Symons seemed to prefer his Poe unexamined.

The Tell-Tale Heart was followed by two commissioned biographies. Yet the subjects – Sir Arthur Conan Doyle, creator of Sherlock Holmes, and Dashiell Hammett, founding father of hard-boiled detective fiction – seem choices almost as inevitable as Poe. And Symons has said that he would never have undertaken the commissioned biographies if he had not felt a strong personal involvement with the subjects.

Introducing his *Conan Doyle: Portrait of an Artist* (1979), Symons promises to look at Doyle's life rather differently from the way it is generally seen today and to provide a balanced view of Doyle as a writer, by encouraging readers to look beyond the usual obsession with Sherlock Holmes at the range and variety of Doyle's work. Just what is different about Symons's view of the life is not spelled out, nor is it necessarily clear to a reader familiar with the biographical and critical studies of Doyle that preceded this one. For Symons, Doyle is an "ideal representative of the Victorian era." Symons's concern is to convey to a probably skeptical reader of the late twentieth century that a representative of the Victorian era may be an attractive human being. There is no question of uncovering new material. Rather, Symons interprets the available material in the light of the attitudes he supposes his readers will bring to the book. Thus, while conceding that in matters such as his hostility to modern art, Doyle manifests the limitations of a middle-class man of his time, he also emphasizes Doyle's eminently Victorian idealism, which most of us can still admire, and his principled and practical application of his ideals. Symons's Doyle is a patriot who can support the cause of Roger Casement, accused of treason against the Crown, and an embodiment of middle-class morality who yet refuses to be distracted or swayed by allegations of Casement's homosexuality.

Symons reserves most of his critical discussion of Doyle as a literary artist to one, largely self-contained, chapter. While he does make sound and specific points about some of Doyle's lesser-known works, there is little reason to suppose that Symons's efforts will have any significant practical effect on Doyle's reputation. It is for the Sherlock Holmes stories that he will be remembered.

Dashiell Hammett had already been the subject of several biographies by the time Symons's book on him appeared in 1985; as in the past, Symons drew heavily on the scholarly research of his predecessors. Symons's book appeared in the HBJ Album Biography series, which, on the account of the publisher, "provides generously illustrated and compact yet thorough studies of modern American writers, intended primarily for readers who may not be familiar with the fuller biographies." The readers for whom Symons's book is intended will find it a clear, uncluttered, and finally fascinating account of the life of the man who may be the finest American writer of crime fiction. To readers who are familiar with the fuller biographies, Symons tells little that is not already known. But the story is a compelling one, and Symons's development of this material is sharp and economical. This is an intensely readable book, perhaps the best introduction to Hammett available.

As an interpretation of Hammett's life, Symons's account has limitations of the sort that have by this time become characteristic of his work. Unwilling to engage in irresponsible speculation, he too often fails to probe even when the material demands it. Why did Hammett fail to produce any substantial work during the last quarter century of his life? Was alcohol responsible? (Here, as in his life of Poe, Symons's understanding of alcoholism seems uninformed.) Had Hammett written himself out? And what would that mean, in this case? In fairness, none of Hammett's biographers to that point could claim to have found fully satisfactory answers to these questions. But it is characteristic of Symons that questions like these are not merely unanswered; they are unasked.

Symons does not separate Hammett's work from the life quite so rigorously as he did in his studies of Dickens and Poe. Yet his critical analyses remain largely self-contained. As usual, Symons proves suspicious of close reading. "With Hammett," he says, "the most straightforward, least high-flown view . . . is likely to be the one he had in mind." Symons's critical analysis of Hammett's work remains of very high value as the commentary of one excellent writer of crime fiction on the work of another. Always sensitive to craft, Symons offers a detailed and perceptive account of Hammett's mastery of language and of the strategies of fictional structure. On balance, Symons's book is an excellent general study of an underappreciated American writer. *Dashiell Hammett* is not the most ambitious of Symons's literary biographies but it may be the most successful of them.

Julian Symons produced no work of literary biography that can be considered a definitive account of the life of a major figure. As a biographer, he is most effective and persuasive when his gifts as a novelist are assigned the congenial task of placing a character in a social environment. As a critic, he has most to tell us when attending most closely to matters of style and craft. That the biographer and the critic can be so easily separated must be regarded as a serious limitation, if the mutual illumination of life and work is what we seek in literary biography. On the other hand, Symons's biographies deserve genuine respect as readable and accessible interpretations of the lives of their subjects in contemporary terms. They arise out of an intelligent and informed enthusiasm for life, for literature, for ideas, that sustained Symons through a long and admirable career.

Reference:

Julian Symons at Eighty: A Tribute, edited by Patricia Craig (Helsinki: Eurographica, 1992).

Papers:

Symons's papers are held at the Humanities Research Center, University of Texas at Austin.

Claire Tomalin

(20 June 1933 –   )

James King
McMaster University

BOOKS: *The Life and Death of Mary Wollstonecraft* (London: Weidenfeld & Nicolson, 1974; New York: Harcourt Brace Jovanovich, 1974);

Shelley and His World (London: Thames & Hudson, 1980);

Katherine Mansfield: A Secret Life (London: Viking, 1987; New York: Knopf, 1987);

The Invisible Woman: The Story of Nelly Ternan and Charles Dickens (London: Viking, 1990; New York: Knopf, 1990);

The Winter Wife (London: Nick Hern Books, 1991);

Mrs. Jordan's Profession: The Story of a Great Actress and a Future King (London: Viking, 1994); published as *Mrs. Jordan's Profession: The Actress and the Prince* (New York: Knopf, 1995).

PLAY PRODUCTION: *The Winter Wife,* Nuffield Theatre, Sheffield, 1991.

Claire Tomalin is best known for the highly acclaimed biographies of three women, each from a different century: Mary Wollstonecraft, Katherine Mansfield, and the actress Nelly Ternan. Central to these books is a concern with how the experience of females is fundamentally different from that of men. However, she does not see herself as a doctrinaire feminist. Rather, she perceives herself as someone concerned with the political and social repercussions of being female. In particular, she writes with great force and precision on how male laws, customs, and practices have imposed themselves on her female subjects.

According to Tomalin, women's experience is often *said* to be more centered on the private and the detailed than men's. Whether this is true or not, Tomalin feels that those characteristics have been useful tools for her in the construction of her books. In the foreword to *Katherine Mansfield: A Secret Life* (1987) she makes a statement that holds true for her two other lives of women: "Yet I can't help feeling that any woman who fights her way through life on two fronts – taking a traditional female role, but

also seeking male privileges – may have a special sympathy for such a pioneer as Katherine, and find some of her actions and attitudes less baffling than even the most understanding of men." As well, Tomalin rejects the label of "literary biographer." She envisions herself as someone who drops an anchor in the past, a historian who searches for new perspectives.

Born in London on 20 June 1933 to Emile Delavenay and Muriel Herbert Delavenay, Tomalin was educated at Hitchins Girls' Grammar School, Dartington Hall School, and Newnham College, Cambridge. From 1955 – the year of her marriage to journalist Nick Tomalin – to 1967 she worked as a reader and editor for three firms, Heinemann, Hutchinson, and Cape. In 1967 she began work for the *Evening Standard*; in 1968 she became assistant literary editor of the *New Statesman* and was literary editor from 1974 until 1977; from 1979 she was literary editor of the *Sunday Times,* a position she resigned in 1986.

Tomalin became a biographer by chance when, following the appearance of her essay on Wollstonecraft in a series of *New Statesman* "Revaluations" in the early 1970s, she was invited by several publishers to write a full-length biography. Tomalin and her husband discussed this matter at length before the invitation from Weidenfeld and Nicolson was accepted.

Wollstonecraft, the author of *The Vindication of the Rights of Women* (1792), has long been a feminist icon, but the strength of Tomalin's book resides in its refusal to add to the accretion of mythologies surrounding the life of her subject. For example, in 1784 Wollstonecraft played a large part in disrupting her sister Eliza's marriage. Tomalin alerts the reader to the fact that Wollstonecraft's arrogant and high-handed behavior in this instance led to tragedy, not salvation. Tomalin also points out the many inconsistencies in her subject's writings. Yet, at the heart of this book, which won the Whitbread Prize, is a great deal of admiration for Wollstone-

Claire Tomalin (photograph by Mark Ellidge)

craft's defiant courage. This becomes quite clear in Tomalin's description of the septicemia that claimed her subject's life. Tomalin recognizes the tragedy that this great pioneer of the rights of women was felled by a disease associated with childbirth.

In her review in the *Spectator* (14 September 1974) Margaret Drabble praised the manner in which the subject's gender is treated: "Claire Tomalin has read widely round her subject, and her book is full of illuminating comments on the history of birth control and changing attitudes to female sexuality. She leaves the conclusions to her readers, but it is impossible to read this book without feeling an overwhelming sympathy for the suffering – not only mental, but the sheer physical suffering that generations of women endured." Tomalin's ability to write about the privations endured by women is constantly balanced by an unsentimental attitude toward her subjects. As Drabble points out, Tomalin is a biographer who invites her readers to form their own judgments.

Shortly before her husband's death in 1973 while covering the Yom Kippur War, Tomalin began work on her biography of Katherine Mansfield. This book, a joint commission from Oxford

University Press and Weidenfeld and Nicolson, was put aside when he died. Much later, she determined to scrap this project and write instead a short book on Mansfield. A friend advised her against this move and urged her to complete the full-length book. In the meantime two biographies of the New Zealand–born writer came out: in 1978 Jeffrey Meyers's life of Mansfield was released and in 1980 Anthony Alpers published a revised, exhaustively researched version of his 1953 biography.

Despite the existence of these books, Tomalin's projected life of Mansfield remained an albatross, even though she had canceled the contract with Oxford and Weidenfeld. She realized that Alpers and Meyers had written good books, but she nevertheless felt that it might still be possible to say something new about Mansfield. As in the case of Wollstonecraft, Tomalin became more and more certain of the validity of this hunch when she reflected on Mansfield's torturous medical history. As a result, after a hiatus of more than ten years, she resumed work on Mansfield's biography.

The "secret" in this biography centers on Tomalin's conviction that it was not tuberculosis that brought Mansfield's life to an early end. Rather, she argues, Mansfield may have actually

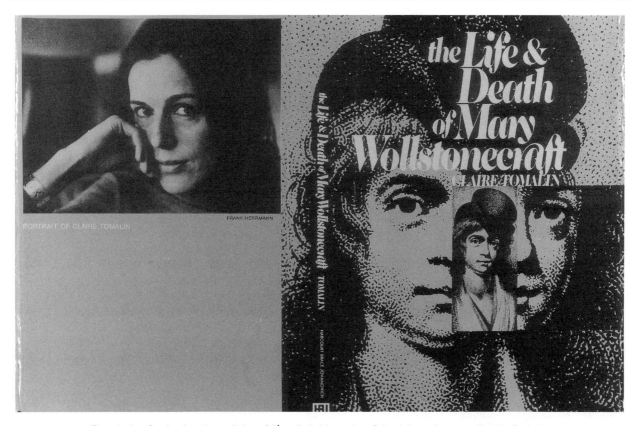

Dust jacket for the American edition of Tomalin's biography of the eighteenth-century British feminist

suffered from the effects of gonorrhea. Like Wollstonecraft, Mansfield was a woman betrayed by her body and by the medical establishment. In writing *Katherine Mansfield: A Secret Life* Tomalin's originality also consists in constructing a series of chapters in each of which the reader sees the subject from the viewpoint of a different friend, notably D. H. Lawrence and Virginia Woolf. Through this kaleidoscope the story of Katherine Mansfield emerges with remarkable clarity. In the *Spectator* (31 October 1987) Frances Partridge speaks warmly of this book's "cool, detached but faithful" portrayal of the subject, one that is "like a fine black and white photograph of a highly coloured, ever-moving subject." Not the least of this book's accomplishments is to show Mansfield in all her vital complexity. Indeed, Tomalin has no hesitation in showing the unpleasant sides of her subject: "Seen through different eyes, her image trembles and blurs: now ambitious and reckless, now vulnerable and wounded; now a simple seeker after purity and truth in life and art, now tarnished and false."

After finishing her biography of Mansfield, Tomalin wrote a play centering on Ida Baker's

motherly friendship with Katherine Mansfield, *The Winter Wife*. The play was first produced at the Nuffield Theatre, Southampton, in 1991 and subsequently transferred to the Nuffield Theatre, Hammersmith. One of the main objects in writing the play, Tomalin reflects in the book's introduction, "was to restore to Ida her due as the true friend and enabler; another, of course, is to celebrate the genius and the torment of Katherine who remains . . . the most liberated, dazzling and modern of modern women." In many ways this play, which allowed Tomalin to explore further the intricacies of Mansfield's personality, was the fitting conclusion to an interest of many years' standing. She brought her subject to life.

Percy Bysshe Shelley was a rebel in the Wollstonecraft and Mansfield mode. Although Tomalin's interest in political and social change is very much in evidence in her elegant, crisp biographical essay on him (undertaken for a series of short, illustrated lives), *Shelley and His World* (1980) asserts that "Shelley's achievement lies . . . in giving us faith in the processes of poetry itself . . . there is a real sense in which the most powerful myth created by Shelley is the myth of himself."

Dust jacket for the American edition of Tomalin's book on actress Nelly Ternan's mysterious relationship with novelist Charles Dickens

The actress Ellen (Nelly) Lawless Ternan (later Mrs. G. Wharton Robinson), the subject of *The Invisible Woman* (1990), led a much quieter and sedate life than either Wollstonecraft or Mansfield, but, like them, she did not accept society's view of herself as a fallen woman. Although Ternan may not have been a conscious heroine, she refused to accept stereotypes imposed by others. This biography, which won the NCR Book Award, the Hawthornden Prize, and the James Tait Black Memorial Prize, differs from those of Wollstonecraft and Mansfield in that the reader, very much in the manner of A. J. A. Symons's *The Quest for Corvo* (1934), is asked to participate in the investigation of a mystery and to become involved in the actual process employed by Tomalin to bring her subject to life: "This is the story of someone who — almost — wasn't there; who vanished into thin air. Her name, dates, family, and experiences very nearly disappeared from the record for good. What's more, she connived at her own obliteration; during her lifetime her children were quite ignorant of her history. Why and how this happened is the theme; and how — by a hair's breadth — she was reclaimed from oblivion despite strenuous efforts to keep her there."

Ternan was born to a family of actors, and, right from the start, her existence was tarnished by the dubious status often accorded to members of the theatrical profession. She met Charles Dickens when he engaged her to take part in *The Frozen Deep,* a melodrama he had written with Wilkie Collins. Ternan and Dickens had a close relationship, but the precise nature of their alliance remains a mystery. In his recent biography of Dickens, Peter Ackroyd takes the position that this was a chaste affair, but Tomalin, on much firmer evidence, disputes this. To an extent Dickens has been exonerated by some biographers: he placed Ternan on a pedestal and cannot, therefore, be said to have mistreated either his wife or Ternan. In direct contrast, Tomalin asks the reader to confront the reality of Dickens's behavior, which was secretive and which helped to make Ternan an invisible woman, a conspiracy in which Ternan herself conspired. In writing her book about Ternan, Tomalin removed the layers of Victorian propriety in which her subject had long been covered. In so doing, she dropped her anchor into a part of history that had been distorted and, in large part, erased.

In "A Postscript: The Death of Dickens" (available only in the 1991 paperback version of *The*

Invisible Woman) Tomalin writes about her pursuit of some new information concerning the possibility that Dickens died in Ternan's house and not — as recorded in all accounts of his life — at his home, Gad's Hill. The clues were supplied by a reader of the biography who subsequently told Tomalin a curious family story: "Charles Dickens did not die at Gad's Hill, as was generally supposed, but at another house 'in compromising circumstances.' " According to the story, the reader's grandfather was involved in the secret removal of the great man's corpse from this house; later, the reader had become aware that his pastor grandfather's church at Peckham was opposite Ternan's house at Windsor Lodge. Armed with equal amounts of scholarly enthusiasm and skepticism, Tomalin investigated the matter fully. The result is that she demonstrates the possibility that the family legend is accurate. This is imaginative biographical research that seeks to base itself in the facts that can be recovered from time's mist.

Tomalin's most recent biography, *Mrs. Jordan's Profession: The Story of a Great Actress and a Future King* (1994), is in some ways a continuation of *The Invisible Woman* especially in that the central figure, Dora Jordan, played a prominent role in *The Invisible Woman*. *Mrs. Jordan* is a study centered on a group of Regency and Victorian actresses, although the emphasis is on Jordan, mistress of the duke of Clarence, by whom she bore ten children. Jordan, who invented her own name, was the foremost comedienne of her day. Her success did not save her from being cast rudely aside when the duke had to marry a rich wife. At that point she also became an invisible woman, a person whose sexuality and fecundity had to be concealed from public view.

Claire Tomalin writes books where, as she says in a personal interview, "my fancy takes me." She has always followed her own route and pursued what others might consider "wayward projects." Her writing is characterized by a warm but never overly idealized relation with her subjects. She accepts the conflicted states in which they lived and thus gives her readers a wonderful sense of their flesh-and-blood existences.

John Wain

(14 March 1925 – 24 May 1994)

Emily A. Hipchen
University of Georgia

See also the Wain entries in *DLB 15: British Novelists, 1930–1959* and *DLB 27: Poets of Great Britain and Ireland, 1945–1960*.

BOOKS: *Mixed Feelings: Nineteen Poems* (Reading, Berkshire: Reading University School of Art, 1951);

Hurry on Down (London: Secker & Warburg, 1953); published as *Born in Captivity* (New York: Knopf, 1954);

Living in the Present (London: Secker & Warburg, 1955; New York: Putnam, 1960);

A Word Carved on a Sill (London: Routledge, 1956; New York: St. Martin's Press, 1956);

Preliminary Essays (London: Macmillan, 1957; New York: St. Martin's Press, 1957);

The Contenders (London: Macmillan, 1958; New York: St. Martin's Press, 1958);

A Travelling Woman (London: Macmillan, 1959; New York: St. Martin's Press, 1959);

Gerard Manley Hopkins: An Idiom of Desperation, British Academy Chatterton Lecture, 1959 (London: Oxford University Press, 1959; Folcroft, Pa.: Folcroft Editions, 1974);

Nuncle and Other Stories (London: Macmillan, 1960; New York: St. Martin's Press, 1961);

A Song about Major Eatherly (Iowa City: Quara Press, 1961);

Weep Before God: Poems (London: Macmillan, 1961; New York: St. Martin's Press, 1961);

Strike the Father Dead (London: Macmillan, 1962; New York: St. Martin's Press, 1962);

Sprightly Running: Part of an Autobiography (London: Macmillan, 1962; New York: St. Martin's Press, 1963);

Essays on Literature and Ideas (London: Macmillan, 1963; New York: St. Martin's Press, 1963);

The Living World of Shakespeare: A Playgoer's Guide (London: Macmillan, 1964; New York: St. Martin's Press, 1964);

Wildtrack: A Poem (London: Macmillan, 1965; New York: Viking, 1965);

The Young Visitors (London: Macmillan, 1965; New York: Viking, 1965);

Death of the Hind Legs and Other Stories (London: Macmillan, 1966; New York: Viking, 1966);

The Smaller Sky (London: Macmillan, 1967);

Arnold Bennett (New York: Columbia University Press, 1967);

Letters to Five Artists (London: Macmillan, 1969; New York: Viking, 1970);

A Winter in the Hills (London: Macmillan, 1970; New York: Viking, 1970);

The Life Guard (London: Macmillan, 1971);

The Shape of Feng (London: Covent Garden Press, 1972);

A House for the Truth: Critical Essays (London: Macmillan, 1972; New York: Viking, 1973);

Samuel Johnson (London: Macmillan, 1974; New York: Viking, 1975; revised edition, London: Papermac, 1988);

Feng (New York: Viking, 1975; London: Macmillan, 1975);

A John Wain Selection, edited by Geoffrey Halson (London: Longman, 1977);

Professing Poetry (London: Macmillan, 1977; abridged edition, New York: Viking, 1978);

The Pardoner's Tale (London: Macmillan, 1978; New York: Viking, 1979);

King Caliban and Other Stories (London: Macmillan, 1978);

Thinking about Mr. Person (Beckenham U.K.: Chimaera Press, 1980);

Lizzie's Floating Shop (London: Bodley Head, 1981);

The Twofold (Frome: Bran's Head, 1981);

Poems: 1949–1979 (London: Macmillan, 1982);

Young Shoulders (London: Macmillan, 1982); published as *The Free Zone Starts Here* (New York: Delacorte, 1982);

Mid-week Period Return: home thoughts of a native (Stratford-upon-Avon: Celandine Press, 1982);

Frank (Oxford: Amber Lane Press, 1984);

Dear Shadows: Portraits from Memory (London: John Murray, 1986);

John Wain

Open Country (London: Hutchinson, 1987);

Where the Rivers Meet (London: Hutchinson, 1988; Philadelphia: Coronet, 1989);

Comedies (London: Hutchinson, 1990; Philadelphia: Coronet, 1991);

Johnson is Leaving: A Monodrama (London: Pisces, 1994);

Hungry Generations (London: Hutchinson, 1994).

OTHER: *Contemporary Reviews of Romantic Poetry,* edited by Wain (London: Harrap, 1953; New York: Barnes & Noble, 1953);

Interpretations: Essays on Twelve English Poems, edited by Wain (London: Routledge, 1955; New York: Hillary House, 1957);

Fanny Burney, *Fanny Burney's Diary,* edited, with an introduction, by Wain (London: Folio Society, 1961);

Samuel Johnson, *Johnson as Critic,* edited by Wain (London: Routledge & Kegan Paul, 1973);

Johnson, *The Lives of English Poets: A Selection,* edited, with an introduction, by Wain (London: Dent, 1975; New York: Dutton, 1976);

Johnson, *Johnson on Johnson: A Selection of the Personal and Autobiographical Writings of Samuel Johnson (1709–1784),* selected, with an introduction and commentary, by Wain (London: Dent, 1976);

An Edmund Wilson Celebration, edited by Wain (Oxford: Phaidon, 1978);

Personal Choice: A Poetry Anthology, edited by Wain (Newton Abbey: David Charles, 1978);

Thomas Hardy, *The New Wessex Selection of Thomas Hardy's Poetry,* edited by Wain and Eirian Wain (London: Macmillan, 1978);

Anthology of Contemporary Poetry, Post-War to the Present, edited by Wain (London: Hutchinson, 1979);

The Seafarer, translated from the Anglo-Saxon by Wain (Warwick: Grenville Press, 1980);

Everyman's Book of English Verse, edited by Wain (London: Dent, 1981);

Arnold Bennett, *The Old Wives' Tale,* introduction and notes by Wain (Harmondsworth: Penguin, 1983);

The Oxford Anthology of English Poetry, chosen and edited by Wain (Oxford & New York: Oxford University Press, 1986);

Wain and his second wife, Eirian, who died in 1987 (Hulton Deutsch)

The Oxford Library of English Poetry, chosen and edited by Wain (Oxford & New York: Oxford University Press, 1986);

James Hogg, *The Private Memoirs and Confessions of a Justified Sinner,* edited and introduced by Wain (Harmondsworth & New York: Penguin, 1986);

Bennett, *Buried Alive,* with an introduction by Wain (Oxford: Inky Parrot Press, 1987);

Jane Austen, *Emma,* edited by Wain (London: Macmillan, 1990);

The Oxford Library of Short Novels, chosen and introduced by Wain (Oxford: Clarendon Press, 1990; New York: Oxford University Press, 1990);

James Boswell, *The Journals of James Boswell 1760–1795,* selected and introduced by Wain (London: Heinemann, 1991; New Haven: Yale University Press, 1991);

John Milton, *Paradise Lost: A Poem in Twelve Books,* with an introduction by Wain (London: Folio Society, 1991);

Geoffrey Chaucer, *The Canterbury Tales,* translated by Neville Coghill, foreword by Melvyn

Bragg, introduction by Wain (London: Cresset Press, 1992).

Perhaps best known as a prolific novelist and poet, John Wain also gained acclaim as a critic and, within the last two decades, as a literary biographer. Wain's first volume of poetry, *Mixed Feelings: Nineteen Poems* (1951), was "the conventional limited edition of a 'slim volume,' " as Wain himself called it, and it was followed fairly rapidly by his appearance on *First Readings,* a BBC program highlighting modern writers. But poetic acclaim came with his later volumes, especially *Weep Before God: Poems* (1961).

Wain's first published novel, *Hurry on Down* (1953), garnered him a position among the up-and-coming young novelists of the 1950s: critics early grouped him with "The Angry Young Men," an array of authors that included Kingsley Amis, John Braine, and John Osborne. After this Wain wrote nearly a dozen novels, including *The Contenders* (1958), *The Young Visitors* (1965), *A Winter in the Hills* (1970), and *The Pardoner's Tale* (1978). He also published several volumes of poetry, collections of short stories, radio and stage dramas, and critical works. His *Preliminary Essays* (1957) won him the W.

Somerset Maugham Award in 1958. For his literary contributions he was awarded the title of Commander of the Order of the British Empire in 1984.

Though Wain was clearly a successful novelist and poet, including him among literary biographers might, on the surface, seem hasty. He wrote only two full-length biographies of literary figures, and the first, his *Sprightly Running: Part of an Autobiography* (1962), received little attention. It was the success of *Samuel Johnson* (1974) that undoubtedly granted him his reputation as a foremost literary biographer: it won both the James Tait Black Memorial Book Prize and the Heinemann Award in 1975. John Wain long interested himself in the biographies of writers. He edited several volumes of personal papers, permeated his critical analyses with reconstructions of the subject's life and mind, and composed, mostly recently, short pieces of reminiscence about writers he knew, designed to give readers a sense of the person.

John Barrington Wain was born 14 March 1925 at Stoke on Trent in Staffordshire, the son of Arnold A. Wain, a dentist, and Anne Turner Wain. He was educated in a dame school there, then went to Froebel Preparatory School, and then went to Newcastle-on-Lyme High School in North Staffordshire. After graduation he attended Saint John's College, Oxford, where he earned a B.A. in 1946, and then became a Fereday Fellow at Saint John's until 1949. From 1947 to 1955 Wain taught at Reading University. The steady employment, Wain writes in *Sprightly Running: Part of an Autobiography,* increased Wain's "settled, middle-aged pessimism, [his] conviction that the hordes of barbarians were already within the gates and that the only thing left was to guard the few fragments in one's possession and accept a backward-looking, stoical melancholy as one's portion in life," created the necessity for marriage. In 1947 he married Marianne Urmstrom and was divorced from her in 1956. The success of *Hurry on Down* combined with his distaste for academic life encouraged Wain to quit his lectureship and pursue writing full-time in 1955. In 1960 Wain married Eirian James, with whom he edited *The New Wessex Selection of Thomas Hardy's Poetry* (1978). As a Welsh woman, she introduced him to "a situation where [he] was very often in places and among people that [he] would have just not got in or among as an English visitor," which gave him some of the insights he needed to write *A Winter in the Hills*. They had three children. Eirian James Wain died in 1987, and Wain married Patricia Dunn in 1988.

More often than not, Wain explored in his fiction and poetry themes that reveal both his connect-

edness to and his distance from the "Angry Young Men" with whom critics frequently tend to group him. Like Amis, Braine, and many of the others, Wain rejected style for style's sake (he believed it was "Style" that destroyed Fanny Burney's writing); he was also something of an iconoclast. "Some of the most talented writers of this century," Wain writes, "have blemished their work, robbed it of its full truthfulness and value, by having programmes." He relished, despite his elders' disapprobation, the "experimental," that which is different, which changes and surprises. Even recently, Wain expressed his disappointment in the conventional. For Wain, Marshall McLuhan's attraction lay in the surprises of his thought patterns, in the nonconformity of his mind, but when McLuhan became famous, Wain lamented his reification: "I felt myself beginning to lose interest in Marshall's ideas because they seemed to me to be hardening into a framework, predictable and inflexible." Like McLuhan, Wain's heroes both fictional and biographical tend to be outsiders, critical of staid thought and behavior. However, Wain wrote both with greater hope and greater pessimism than many of his contemporaries, especially in his later works. As he said, Amis's "novels deal with people who are fairly gay and don't have sores, and mine deal with people who are gay and have sores." Ultimately, Wain was interested in the struggles of the individual to remain an individual and not be absorbed into the establishment, and yet still to find connection with other people.

The result is the kind of analysis of character one finds in Wain's first important foray into biography, *Gerard Manley Hopkins: An Idiom of Desperation* (1959). For Wain the details of Hopkins's life, and more exactly his attachment to the Society of Jesus, is fundamental to both the man and his poetry. The Jesuits allowed Hopkins the seclusion he needed, the separation from society that freed him to write the experimental poetry that gained him his reputation. Hopkins, Wain states, "*was* isolated. He felt keenly that he was considered eccentric and that he could count on no support . . . [he] had no dealings with the nineteenth-century except that for forty-five years he drew breath in it." Hopkins was Wain's cloistered nonconformist, a Catholic in a Protestant land, a Jesuit among Catholics, a poet among Jesuits. But for Wain, in fiction as in life, no gift was completely painless. Hopkins's ability and inclination to absent himself from his culture becomes the foundation not only of his poetry but also of his desperation: "His isolation removed him from the hubbub of the market-place and enabled him to

Wain in the 1980s (photograph © Jerry Bauer)

"overcome the idle habit" of writing that endears her to Wain; once she conformed to her gender roles and married Alexandre Jean-Baptiste Piochard d'Arblay, "she was never again a successful writer." Once she became an "established authoress, she thought it her duty to develop a Style," and for Wain this is the ruin of her talent. "[H]er work," he writes, "grew steadily less interesting, finally ending up in the unreadable quagmire of the Memoir of her father . . . [o]nce that youthful informality and freshness are lost, as a writer she disappears completely."

The introduction to *Fanny Burney's Diary* shows the hallmarks of Wain's biographical style. Inset in his discussion of Burney's life are carefully drawn vignettes of other characters, long bits of their lives, and sometimes deep analysis of character that are frequently only tangentially relevant to the subject at hand. A case in point is Wain's digression on Johnson, which begins with a quote taken from Katherine Mansfield. The center of his aside is Fanny Burney, who, like Mansfield, reacts strongly to Dr. Johnson in her diaries: "She, too," Wain tells us, "took him in immensely." But Wain goes further than just this note. The man to whom Burney responds, the reader is told, is a different Johnson than James Boswell's – and here Wain gives a distillation of the Johnson on whom his later biography expands, one that reacts against Boswell's depiction of "the violently masculine side of his hero; the gravity, the conviviality, the roaring conversational barrages against dullness or affectation." Not only does Wain provide the reader with a relatively detailed sketch of Johnson in the midst of Burney's biography; he also signals his abiding interest in Johnson, one which more than a decade later would flower into *Samuel Johnson.*

Wain finished his autobiography at the end of perhaps the most difficult part of his life. In 1956 he and Marianne Urmstrom Wain were divorced, and probably soon afterward Wain began *Sprightly Running.* He finished the book late in 1960, the same year he married Eirian James, but the book was not published for another two years. *Sprightly Running* grew out of Wain's unhappiness during the last years of his marriage and his four-year bachelorhood. The chapter on his first marriage is both the shortest and the most poignant in the book. The chapters on Oxford and "A Literary Chapter," which include on the one hand vibrant portraits of the people Wain knew at Oxford and on the other many of his philosophies about literature, is most informative. As David Gerard writes, "Portraits rendered with unsentimental clarity, yet with toler-

listen in silence to the messages which came from the real spirit of his age. Yet the deep-seated inability to trade in that market-place also involved him in disappointment, humiliation and weariness." In *Gerard Manley Hopkins: An Idiom of Desperation* Wain's interest in the individual outside, and in some ways at war with, his society is as evident as his growing understanding of, and sensitivity toward, the contradictions inherent in human nature.

With the publication of *Fanny Burney's Diary* (1961) Wain continued choosing subjects and exploring themes he had been working on all along. Burney, like many of Wain's fictional heroes, refused to fit in: in her large, "tumultuous family," Wain writes, Fanny was "a quiet one . . . small, timid, with a myopic poke of the head and hunch of the shoulders." Unlike her siblings Burney was kept home and became something of an autodidact. While Hetty and Susey, her sisters, gained continental polish in France, Fanny sat in the parlor, "shy and silent like a fly on the wall, [and] took in everything that happened." Such, according to Wain, was her education, and he felt that any other learning would have harmed the burgeoning authoress. It is her refusal to be "a good girl" and

ance and acuity, this is the genre in which Wain shines; fraternal understanding of men and women is what counts for him," and the Oxford chapter is memorable for the exercise of just this talent. E. H. W. Meyerstein, an elderly scholar living at Gray's Inn while Wain was at Oxford, is probably his most carefully drawn image, and the portrait of him is itself a short literary biography.

Wain in this chapter shows Meyerstein in all his humanity – dirty, surrounded by manuscripts and books, teeth out and set on the floor beside the chair in danger of being crushed while he paced, absorbed in talking. Like Burney and Hopkins, Meyerstein was an outsider: "It was Meyerstein's peculiar misfortune to be born on the *fringe* of the Establishment." But he was also a prototype for Wain's Samuel Johnson. Meyerstein had Johnson's physical peculiarities. "He was," Wain writes, "a big, thick-set man, dressed in the ruin of what had been a well-cut grey suit, augmented by a dark-blue jersey of which the sleeves poked out over his wrists. The first thing one noticed about him, inevitably, was that one side of his face was tightly screwed up by some kind of nervous seizure which had happened a few years previously. . . . His right eye . . . was almost hidden, and I could never tell how much he was able to see with it. His mouth, too, was drawn upwards on that side. . . . He looked, in short, like a gargoyle." Meyerstein also had something like Johnson's mental disorders. While he worked Meyerstein made noises – "it wasn't singing, or shouting, but an unearthly blend of the two. . . . On his good days, he would be silent except when actually writing; but when the bad fits were on him, he started to perform as soon as he opened his eyes in the morning." And Meyerstein, like Johnson, read broadly and worked compulsively.

"A Literary Chapter" sums up Wain's attitudes toward his critics, the trends he saw in literature, and his own work. He began writing at age nine (detective stories with a hero named "Smellum Oute" and a bang-'em-up magazine called *Hot Stuff,* copies of which were stolen and burned in later years), published his first volume of poetry without having any "ambition to be 'a writer' in the conventional sense," then produced *Hurry on Down* in his spare time, with the "avowed aims . . . [only] to get the book published and to make a hundred pounds from it." Ill health and personal problems suggested a rest, and Wain took one in late 1953, going to the Swiss Alps and writing *Living in the Present* (1955), after which he resigned from his "academic post and launch[ed] out as a free-lance author," despite

the fact that Wain himself believed the novel to have been a failure. He realized the drudgery of academic life, adjudged himself only a second-rate scholar, and with the memory of Meyerstein's fight for acceptance and resulting insanity in front of him he decided that "it was saner and healthier to give up teaching."

Literary trends in the late 1950s seem to have distressed Wain – of them he writes that "[t]he last thirty years have been the hey-day of the poetic charlatan." For Wain it was advertising, publicity, the authorial personality that ruined much contemporary literature. Poetry is, and Wain believed it should be, difficult work: it is "hesitant gropings in the dark cupboard of imagination, which may lead to picking up a jewel – or just as probably, to picking up an old slipper which the dog has carried in to chew in peace." But poets popular when Wain wrote *Sprightly Running* – such as Allen Ginsberg, whose *Howl* (1956) Wain says is "chiefly remarkable for its badness" – "produce the poetic output of three years in one evening at a cafe table . . . [and] nobody will notice it's worthless." The state of criticism in the modern world is almost as bad, and the critics take something of a pounding for their carelessness, for the slapdashery of their work, for their tendency to label and their need to pigeonhole. But Wain always, even when he found fault, attempted to understand. Critics in general do a poor job because "[t]hey are too frightened. Every reviewer of poetry knows in his bones that the time is going to come when he will make a fatal mistake . . . [and] dismiss some new rising star as Keats and Hopkins were dismissed by their contemporaries"; because "[t]he typical consumer . . . is so stuffed with 'famous' names that he has long since abandoned any idea of taking pleasure in the skills and achievements that these people are supposed to be famous *for*. In fact the mess of names in his head is so thick that he can very rarely fish out anything precise when he gropes about in it."

Wain's discussion of his early life reveals the foundation of his love for the outsider: he himself was one, or felt himself one. Wain's description of his youth also shows some of the reasons why Wain's worldview seems full of pain and struggle – his school days culminated in typical childhood "games" infamous for cruelty and pain (the sheer detail of Wain's memory of these events highlights their importance in the development of his thinking); his reminiscences also show the sensitivity and generosity of the man, if not the boy, to those who ill used him as a child. Wain believed pain is the way of the world, and blaming the children and adults who frightened him for his fear would have been useless. But *Sprightly Running* is not so dark that it hides what the element for which Wain, especially in his earlier works, is noted: a highly developed sense of humor. In one anecdote Wain's nurse hurdles him past the local run-down lavatories, and Wain tells us that they "were just one more of the dangers; dirt, in our neighborhood, wasn't ordinary dirt, of the kind that dirtied you if you played about in it, but ravening, prowling dirt ready to jump out at you as you went past."

Wain's interest in Arnold Bennett stemmed from sources similar to those for his interest in Hopkins, Burney, and ultimately Johnson: Bennett's life and work exemplify both the familiar and the desirable. Like Wain, Bennett came from "the chain of six industrial towns lying along the valley of the Trent in North Staffordshire." Bennett was also attractively antiestablishment. Not only was Bennett's sexual life unorthodox (he was married to his French secretary six months after employing her, and fourteen years later he separated from her, though she would not grant him a divorce; five years later he fathered an illegitimate child with his common-law wife); his ideas are equally nonconformist. Like Wain, in his fiction Bennett constantly questions the values of his society and ultimately concludes that "[p]erhaps the only really crucial question about any society is 'Could a decent, good-hearted person, who was also gifted and intelligent, be happy there?' By this test, most societies fail," except for Bennett's fictionalization of his provincial home. But even here, Bennett, like Wain, cannot be "without ironies . . . without critical reservations": the human condition necessitates suffering, and any happiness Bennett might postulate exists in provincial England is mitigated by his sense, according to Wain, that "[i]t was a happiness that became, for him personally, increasingly unattainable." Wain also admired Bennett's energy. He wrote prolifically: while churning out a "stream of newspaper and magazine articles," he was "pelting the as yet indifferent British public with a shower of novels. . . . Two . . . in 1903, two in 1904, one in 1905, three in 1906, three in 1907." He was also both physically imposing and physically eccentric. Bennett, as Wain quotes from a contemporary description, "was stoutly built, and . . . held himself very erect with his shoulders very rigid, so that his body had no natural swing as he walked, but rather swayed stiffly from side to side." In addition, Bennett had a strange hairdo and a stammer, both of which Wain duly notes. When Wain came to write about Johnson, many

of these qualities belonged to him. There is the sexual unconventionality, the energy, the doubts, the huge peculiar physique and unusual manners, the gifted intellect struggling with his humanity.

Samuel Johnson is unquestionably Wain's masterwork. In 1973 Wain was awarded the prestigious Professorship of Poetry at Oxford, and it was there he finally began the project he had been considering for a long time. Wain had "been going about for years saying that one of these days I shall write a book on Johnson." When his agent suggested Wain write out a plan and negotiated a hefty advance, Wain began the actual composition of the book. Perhaps the most niggling of doubts one has about *Samuel Johnson* is the need for it. Boswell, of course, and James L. Clifford and Joseph Wood Krutch, among many others, have written serviceable and sometimes readable Johnson biographies. Many reviewers of *Samuel Johnson* begin with just this question, and almost all conclude that, though they would never have said so before opening *Samuel Johnson,* they believe Wain's book adds something to the genre: David Williams writes in his *Punch* review (7 May 1980) that "[o]f course you might say that Boswell did this particular job definitely and gloriously in 1791, so why go trying to outwrite the greatest biographical masterpiece in English? . . . Wain gives the whole 75 years of [Johnson's] life their right perspective." Wain's biography of Johnson is not the collection of brilliant anecdotes that Boswell's is; neither is it like Clifford's scholarly and well-known *Young Samuel Johnson* (1955), and some reviewers found fault with Wain's acknowledged distance from academic speculation. In his note on sources Wain states outright that "There is no research in this book. Every fact it contains was previously known to scholars and to any reader who kept abreast of scholarship." Carey McIntosh in a review for *Philological Quarterly* (Fall 1976) suggests that both Wain's "crypto-romantic bias" and his lacking "a more wide-ranging acquaintance with contemporary scholarship" mar what is "[b]y and large . . . a highly respectable biography."

But, as Wain writes in his preface, his book "is addressed to the intelligent general reader," not the scholar. It is written, at least in part, to correct what Wain saw as popular bias against Johnson, especially among readers, who he says, "still think of Johnson, when they think of him at all, as a stupid old reactionary." And Wain felt that Boswell is at the root of part of this bias, since "[t]he average reader's picture of Johnson is still very much the one he gets from Boswell." The difficulty with accepting Boswell's version of Johnson is, in Wain's opinion, Boswell's personality and politics: he "was a sentimental-romantic Tory of a very different stripe [than Johnson]. Being a Scot, he yearned over the Stuarts . . . being the son of a laird and a bit of a snob, he deferred to titled people where Johnson . . . was just as likely to growl at them. . . . Boswell naturally highlights those moods and opinions of Johnson's that match his own. What we lose in his portrait is the deeply humanitarian Johnson, the man who from first to last rooted his life among the poor and outcast."

It is just this human and humanitarian Johnson Wain gives the reader in *Samuel Johnson,* a man who kept his house in Fleet Street while living with the Thrales, so that he had a place to keep his luckless friends. "Every Saturday," Wain tells his readers, Johnson "left Streatham, gritted his teeth and entered the dingy, gloomy house, to preside there until Monday. In this way he saw to it that his pensioners had three good dinners in seven days. The rest of the week they got by on a fixed allowance that he left with them." In fact, Johnson was often helping those who needed it. Frank Barber, his servant, "was a worry; he ran away and joined the navy, and Johnson had to write a letter to one of the Lords of the Admiralty begging for his discharge; he went with Johnson into the country one winter, and cut such a swath among the rustic beauties that one of them followed him back to London and made difficulties." If Boswell concentrates on Johnson's verbal acidity, roarings, and mental inflexibilities, Wain, while never ignoring these, refocuses on Johnson's benevolence. "Wain's characterization of Johnson as 'one of the most benevolent men who ever lived' is startling, but the evidence he recounts is conclusive," John J. Roberts writes in his review for *Modern Age* (Spring 1976): "the word Wain repeatedly falls back on in examining Johnson's varied dealings with people is *compassion.*"

Wain also takes another look at the physical Johnson: in Wain's hands the dirty, bumbling Johnson, whose scrofula-scarred face, imposing size, and nervous palsies Boswell and his contemporaries noted well, becomes the Johnson infected with scrofula as a helpless infant by careless parenting; dirty and badly clothed from grinding poverty coupled with the kind of pride that would cause him to refuse a pair of new shoes offered when his were worn through enough that his toes stuck out; large from both genetic disposition and hardy provincial upbringing; and nervous from both acute self-consciousness and early emotional suffering. "Wain lays much stress on Johnson's size," writes Martin Green in his review for *Commentary* (August 1975),

"his huge limbs and weight, to start with, then his awkwardness and grossness and ugliness . . . then his gross appetites and angers; all of which lead on to the theme of his emotional and moral and intellectual size." Green goes on expressing reservations about Wain's delight in Johnson's physical size and power: "it is disturbing that it is an admiration that focuses so much on Johnson's force; on his knocking men down." Anecdotes about, and enjoyment of, Johnson's fist-work aside, Wain gives the reader the other part of the equation as well. If Johnson could and did knock people down, the bulk and ugliness that gave him that power had an equally great emotional impact on him. Johnson was a "raw-boned country youth, ugly in appearance and startling in his odd habits and gestures," and "until he was past thirty, he never tried to make a good impression on anyone, 'considering the matter as hopeless.' He expected everyone he met to be disgusted or terrified by his looks and his nervous mannerisms, his convulsive starts and twitches." Wain also notes, as Boswell does, Johnson's speech habits, especially his Staffordshire way of pronouncing the *u* in such words as *hush* and *punch.* But for Wain, such a retention of dialect is almost admirable – it separates Johnson from other Londoners, makes him in a way an outsider and an individual.

As Wain seemed to understand it, biography violates individualism when it seeks to make smooth and consistent any human behavior; therefore, his Johnson is a man of violent contradictions. For example, Johnson was an avid Christian who, according to Wain, was as tempted as any other man would be who invited streetwalkers to supper with him, but who also seldom succumbed. Wain also writes that though not promiscuous, Johnson's sexual habits seemed to tend toward the unconventional. Wain suggests that the reason for Johnson's predilection for celibacy after his wife's death "may lie in what we know of his sexual fantasies. These, apparently, were of a masochistic tendency." Intellectually, Johnson was both forward thinking (*A Dictionary of the English Language* [1755] being the prime example of this) and obtuse (he consistently underestimated the future of the novel form). Perhaps the best symbol of Wain's understanding of Johnson's character is the repeated description of his working habits. Johnson, according to Wain, could concentrate well enough to shut out the understanding of a simple clock face and yet was subject to sometimes long periods of vagueness and lethargy equally as complete. Wain "sees Johnson as a product of two widely separate contexts," notes Lionel Basney for the *Western Humanities Review* (Autumn 1975), and he "isolates this *discordia concors* . . . find[ing] in it the secret of Johnson's strength." For Wain, Johnson is human and therefore a bundle of contradictory thoughts, habits, and behaviors; and *Samuel Johnson* emphasizes this.

Wain's biographical style is clear throughout the book. *Samuel Johnson* contains a multitude of inset portraits, much like the description of Johnson in *Fanny Burney's Diary* and the picture of Meyerstein in *Sprightly Running*. There are shorter sketches, such as the one of Edward Cave in chapter 6, which discusses at some length his two surviving portraits and what they reveal about his character: "The face is smooth, bland, confident; the painter is working hard to show the self-made man as he wished to see himself," writes Wain about the formal painting. In the other, more relaxed one, Cave's "eyes are watchful and slightly shifty. . . . One hand holds what looks like an invoice; the other is held out . . . as if Cave were saying 'Hand it over.' " The longer portraits — like that of Richard Savage, which is interlaced with Wain's discussion of Johnson's *Life of Savage* (1744), and that of Hester Lynch [Thrale] Piozzi, which takes up the vast majority of chapter 21 — are finely done and often moving. Wain's writing style is also apparent — his refrain, whenever he brings up the standard prejudices and stories about Johnson, is "everybody knows." It is "his good natured signal," writes Christopher Ricks in *The New York Times Book Review* (16 March 1975); "he reminds us of what we somewhat know, and then he [turns] it so that the old fact catches new light." After several repetitions it takes on the ironic flavor, the deep preceding sigh Wain seems to intend it to have. Wain's linguistic strengths are the strengths of many good poets: *Samuel Johnson* is full of startlingly good images and clever turns of phrase. In describing *Rasselas* (1759) for instance, Wain notes that "When most writers of prose fiction were turning to realistic action in credible settings, and cultivating a representational style of dialogue . . . *Rasselas* turns resolutely away from these tendencies." But even so, Johnson's masterpiece of fiction is powerful and indefinitely mobile; it "puts one in mind of a dragonfly — a purposeful and powerful body moving on wings of gauze."

"[W]e come away from Boswell with a store of marvelous anecdotes," writes John J. Roberts in *Modern Age* (Spring 1976), "but from Wain with a sense of kinship and empathy." Wain's ability to make us intimate with Johnson is perhaps the greatest strength of *Samuel Johnson*. Wain's empathy with Johnson stems from Wain's sense of connection with his subject. "Perhaps more than most," Wain

writes in his introduction to the book, "I am in a position to see his life from the inside. I was born in the same district as Johnson — some thirty miles away — and in much the same social *milieu*. I went to the same university, and since then have lived the same life of Grub Street, chance employment, and the unremitting struggle to write enduring books against the background of an unstable existence." Wain, more often than not, found himself in his subjects, and this position, he feels, is intrinsic to his writing: "if you invent something, the mere fact that you invent that story and not some other, the mere fact that you write about people of a certain kind and not some other — all these things tell a great deal about yourself." The people about whom Wain chose to write and the stories he told are the stories he lived or wished to live, and this intimacy, this emotional investment, is for many reviewers the reason to value Wain's *Samuel Johnson*.

Some of the projects that followed *Samuel Johnson* seem to have been spun from it. Not only did Wain write a drama about Frank Barber, Johnson's servant — *Frank* (1984) — but he selected and published in 1975 a version of Johnson's *Lives of the Poets* (1781). Wain's introduction to *Lives of the Poets: A Selection* is not simply a condensation of his *Samuel Johnson;* it is that, of course, but it is also a directional marker. If it is not, as Wain says *Lives of the Poets* is of Johnson, "a work of [his] old age," it is certainly one that Wain produced as he approached his fifth decade, and that precedes what is in a small sense Wain's own *Lives,* the *Dear Shadows: Portraits from Memory* (1986) he wrote some ten years later. *Dear Shadows* is less a strict biography (there are no birth dates, for instance, and little speculation about childhood experiences) than a lengthening of the vignettes typical of Wain's biographical style. They harken back to his treatment of characters in his autobiography, not only because both Neville Coghill and Marshall McLuhan (the two literary subjects in the book) are part of that period of Wain's life but because the vignettes retain the tonal sadness of Wain's memories of his friends and teachers at Oxford especially. "Neville Coghill" is less complete than "Incidental Thoughts of Marshall McLuhan," mostly because Wain had less contact with the former, but what he remembers etches out Coghill's character in fine lines. Coghill offended the establishment at Oxford by pursuing dramatics and was in a way ostracized by the old guard — he is Wain's familiar outsider. Instead of trying to find a place to fit in among the undergraduates with whom he worked, however, he kept himself aloof, even in the "hideous discomfort [of a] bunk-room" when he took Wain and some others on a field trip to Stratford. Marshall McLuhan was also a misfit, an intellectual whiz whose "ceaselessly active mind . . . [which sent] up a shower of comparisons, analogies, wisecracks, sudden satiric jabs at people and attitudes he disliked and equally sudden excursions into scholastic philosophy or modern advertising practice" alienated most of the staid intellectuals with whom he came into contact. With both men, as with Johnson, as with himself and all of his subjects, Wain is kind as well as honest, ameliorating their failings without ignoring them.

If Wain were only to be known for *Samuel Johnson,* he would still have made a significant contribution to literature. But Wain was a writer who, like Johnson, wrote across genres and wrote well. First acclaim came for his fiction and poetry, first prizes for his critical work; and the breadth of his mind and talents would have ensured him continued attention. In 1982 he won the Whitbread Award for *Young Shoulders* (1982), one of at least two works of juvenile fiction he wrote. "He is able," writes Christopher Ricks in *The New York Times Book Review* (16 March 1975), "to write as a man of letters about the greatest man of letters," and this is most assuredly an admirable feat. He was, after all, in love with writing: "Being a writer," Wain believed, is not a profession. "It's a condition. And that's the condition that I'm in."

Wain died of a stroke on 24 May 1994 at John Radcliffe Hospital in Oxford. He had suffered from diabetes and failing eyesight for many years, and writing his Oxford trilogy – *Where the Rivers Meet* (1988), *Comedies* (1990), and *Hungry Generations* (1994) – required "an act of unusual personal courage" given his increasing disability, observes Peter Levi in Wain's obituary for the *Guardian* (25 May 1994). Critics often differ when they focus on any of Wain's single works, but critical opinion has always been remarkably unified when it addresses the man and his career. "He had an alarming capability of turning his hand to novels, to the theatre, to criticism and high-level teaching, and to serious biography," writes Levi, but "[n]one of his work was ever shallow or pretentious or factitious." To the end Wain was a writer, as he said of Johnson – living the "life of Grub Street, chance employment, and the remitting struggle to write enduring books against the background of an unstable existence."

Bibliography:

David Gerard, *John Wain: A Bibliography* (New York: Meckler, 1987).

Interview:

Dale Salwak, *Interviews with . . . Britain's Angry Young Men,* Literary Voices #2: The Mitford Series of Popular Writers of Today, volume 39 (San Bernardino, Cal.: Borgo Press, 1984).

Reference:

Dale Salwak, *John Wain* (Boston: G. K. Hall, 1981).

A. N. Wilson

(27 October 1950 –)

Brian Murray
Loyola College in Maryland

See also the Wilson entry in *DLB 14: British Novelists Since 1960.*

BOOKS: *The Sweets of Pimlico* (London: Secker & Warburg, 1977; New York: Penguin, 1983);

Unguarded Hours (London: Secker & Warburg, 1978);

Kindly Light (London: Secker & Warburg, 1979);

The Laird of Abbotsford: A View of Sir Walter Scott (Oxford & New York: Oxford University Press, 1980);

The Healing Art (London: Secker & Warburg, 1980; New York: Penguin, 1988);

Who Was Oswald Fish? (London: Secker & Warburg, 1981; New York: Penguin, 1988);

The Life of John Milton (Oxford & New York: Oxford University Press, 1983);

Hilaire Belloc (London: Hamish Hamilton, 1984; New York: Atheneum, 1984);

How Can We Know? (London: Hamish Hamilton, 1985; New York: Atheneum, 1985);

Gentlemen in England: A Vision (London: Hamish Hamilton, 1985; New York: Viking, 1986);

Love Unknown (London: Hamish Hamilton, 1986; New York: Viking, 1987);

Tolstoy: A Biography (London: Hamish Hamilton, 1988; New York: Norton, 1988);

Incline Our Hearts (London: Hamish Hamilton, 1988; New York: Viking, 1989);

A Bottle in the Smoke (London: Sinclair-Stevenson, 1989; New York: Viking, 1990);

Eminent Victorians (London: BBC Publications, 1989; New York: Norton, 1990);

C. S. Lewis: A Biography (London: Collins, 1990; New York: Norton, 1990);

Against Religion (London: Chatto & Windus, 1990);

Daughters of Albion (London: Sinclair-Stevenson, 1991; New York: Viking, 1991);

Jesus (London: Sinclair-Stevenson, 1992; New York: Norton, 1992);

A. N. Wilson

The Rise and Fall of the House of Windsor (London: Sinclair-Stevenson, 1993; New York: Norton, 1993);

The Vicar of Sorrows (London: Sinclair-Stevenson, 1993; New York: Norton, 1994).

OTHER: Sir Walter Scott, *Ivanhoe,* edited, with an introduction, by Wilson (London: Penguin, 1982);

Bram Stoker, *Dracula,* edited, with an introduction, by Wilson (Oxford: Oxford University Press, 1983);

Essays by Divers Hand 44, edited by Wilson (Woodbridge, Suffolk: Boydell & Brewer, 1986);

Leo Tolstoy, *The Lion and the Honeycomb: The Religious Writings of Tolstoy,* edited, with an introduction, by Wilson (London: Collins, 1987; New York: Harper, 1987);

John Henry Newman, *John Henry Newman: Prayers, Poems, and Meditations,* edited, with an introduction, by Wilson (London: SPCK, 1989; New York: Crossroad, 1990);

The Faber Book of Church and Clergy, edited, with an introduction, by Wilson (London: Faber & Faber, 1992);

Tolstoy, *How Much Land Does a Man Need? and Other Stories,* translated by Ronald Wilks, with an introduction by Wilson (London & New York: Penguin, 1993);

The Faber Book of London, edited by Wilson (London: Faber, 1993); published as *The Norton Book of London* (New York: Norton, 1995).

A. N. Wilson, one of Britain's most prolific and visible literary figures, has in the past decade attracted much attention as both a novelist and biographer. Wilson's work in both genres demonstrates that he is an erudite, witty, and often provocative writer much interested in literary, political, and religious issues. Indeed, as a biographer, Wilson has shown himself particularly attracted to writers well known for their own intense religious views. He is certainly ambitious. Wilson's *Tolstoy: A Biography* (1988) and *C. S. Lewis: A Biography* (1990), his most important works of nonfiction to date, show him willing to look comprehensively – and controversially – at two of the century's most widely studied and influential literary figures.

Andrew Norman Wilson was born in Stone, Staffordshire, on 27 October 1950 to Norman and Jean Dorothy Crowder Wilson; he was the youngest of three children. His father's working career included a stint as managing director of Wedgwoods, the venerable pottery firm. When he was seven, Wilson was enrolled at Hillstone, a Welsh boarding school he came to loathe. In 1964 he entered Rugby, the prestigious school founded in the sixteenth century and made particularly famous as the setting for Thomas Hughes's novel *Tom Brown's Schooldays* (1857). From Rugby, Wilson went to New College, Oxford, where he studied medieval literature as well as linguistics and where, in 1971, he won the Chancellor's Essay Prize. In the same year Wilson married Katherine Duncan-Jones, a

Renaissance scholar; they had two daughters during their marriage which ended in divorce in 1990.

Soon after completing his university studies in 1972, Wilson decided to train for the priesthood, entering Saint Stephen's, an Anglican seminary near Oxford. Wilson found seminary life dispiriting and withdrew after a year. He then spent a year teaching at a London prep school before assuming a lectureship in English at Saint Hugh's College, Oxford, a post he held until 1982. Wilson also began to publish fiction; his first novel, *The Sweets of Pimlico* (1977), was hailed in the *Daily Telegraph* as "a witty novel of manners" and won the Rhys Memorial Prize for fiction. Wilson's next two novels, *Unguarded Hours* (1978) and *Kindly Light* (1979), follow the same hapless protagonist as he muddles his way through the worlds of academe and organized religion, encountering several well-drawn eccentrics and comic types along the way. Wilson's early novels won wide notice as reviewers praised their tight pacing and deft use of farce. But at least one critic, Paul Ableman, writing in the *Spectator* (2 June 1979), suggested that Wilson, not yet thirty, was still clearly developing his style. "The trouble is," wrote Ableman, "it's not really his style at all. It's partly P. G. Wodehouse's and partly early Aldous Huxley's and preeminently Evelyn Waugh's."

Wilson's continuing interest in nineteenth-century Britain is signaled in *The Laird of Abbotsford: A View of Sir Walter Scott* (1980), a rather brief but impressively fresh critical study with a strong biographical base. Here, as elsewhere, Wilson chose a subject he strongly admires, insisting at the outset that Scott "was not only a great writer; he was also a great man." Wilson aims "to read Scott's life and work as complementary to one another"; moreover, he seeks to rekindle interest in a figure he considers unjustly neglected. Wilson not only discusses Scott's major works, including the influential *Waverly* (1814), but his poetry as well, making a strong case for the forgotten artistry of, for example, *The Lady of the Lake* (1810). One reviewer, Hilary Corke, noted in the *Listener* (24 July 1980) that, as a critic, Wilson "has the fragrance of the Senior Common Room about him": he is, in other words, a bit pedantic – eager to display the breadth of his learning and to voice strong views. Indeed, as a biographer, Wilson has proven himself to be not only widely learned but also deliberately provocative, turning to the first person occasionally and brightening his lucid prose by bluntly airing his biases and peeves. Thus, in *The Laird of Abbotsford,* Wilson manages to allude disparagingly to D. H. Lawrence's "orgiastic fantasies" and to "the intensely embarrassing sugary mind" of the later Evelyn Waugh. He calls E. M. Forster – who found little in Scott – "rather unintelligent." Wilson's tone shows his sympathy for Scott's political views, which he at one point terms Toryism "not of an unreasoning kind." On Scott himself Wilson is similarly frank and certain. "We encounter in Scott's novels," he concludes, "the greatest diversity of realistic human characters outside Shakespeare; we discover from reading his biography one of the most genial men who ever lived. It really requires no further comment."

Wilson's *The Life of John Milton* (1983) shows further the link between his fiction and his intellectual pursuits, particularly his keen interest in the evolution of Christian concepts and ideas. Again, Wilson connects Milton's work with central events in the poet's life; his account of Milton's own legendary misfortunes – including the blindness that marked his final years – is not only impressively erudite but recounted in a lively, rather informal style. Much of Wilson's fiction does not exude orthodox Christian thought, seeming less hopeful than bleak. But Wilson's earlier critical writing, including *The Life of John Milton,* is more clearly the work of an author willing to display conservative religious and political views. At one point, for example, Wilson defends Milton's "traditional" view of marriage and the sexes and thus of his acceptance of "the general rule that God has crowned man with 'an indelible character of priority.' " "This is simply orthodox Christian teaching," Wilson writes, "and only crackpots in Milton's lifetime would have found anything offensive in it."

Wilson's next biography, *Hilaire Belloc* (1984), focuses on a far more marginal literary figure – and "one of the most restless beings who ever crashed about the surface of the earth." Indeed, Wilson's decision to examine closely the now largely forgotten Belloc shows particularly well his continuing fondness for challenging expectations and going against the grain. Belloc was, as Wilson's biography ably reveals, an odd and difficult man of strong political and religious views who, during the first decades of the twentieth century, produced more than one hundred books on a wide range of political and literary subjects, including his own *Milton* (1935). With the exception of *The Bad Child's Book of Beasts* (1896), a collection of nonsense verse, and *The Servile State* (1912), a work of political theory, few of these are widely read today. Belloc, a Roman Catholic, is often linked with his contemporary and ally G. K. Chesterton: both wrote spiritedly in defense of Christianity at a time of growing disbelief; both

also found frequent occasion to express anti-Semitic views. Belloc's own anti-Semitism appeared at times to be particularly virulent, surfacing not only in his talk but in both his published and unpublished writings.

Critics generally agreed that Wilson was fair and perceptive in his appraisal of Belloc's life and work, although Stanley Weintraub, for one, faulted Wilson not only for appearing too willing to dismiss Belloc's anti-Semitism as an "aberration" roughly akin to Yeats's interest in the occult but for seeking to place Belloc on an inappropriately high literary plane. Similarly, John Gross, in the *Observer* (22 April 1984), remained unconvinced that Belloc was, as Wilson suggests, an unusually gifted artist and thinker whose neuroses and quirks kept him from producing work of more lasting distinction ("Belloc is a figure analogous to Doctor Johnson," Wilson argues, "in so far as the power of his personality and the force of his conversational presence – attested by innumerable friends – are never quite lived up to in his work"). "There is a gap between the claims that are made and the evidence that is put forward," wrote Gross. "[T]he details are vivid, but they do not add up a coherent picture – not, at least, on the terms that Mr. Wilson proposes."

Wilson is exceptionally well-read, but he is no longer an academic, and the biographies he writes are, like his novels, aimed at a wide range of literate general readers. Readers with little interest in Belloc's own work are still likely to find Wilson's biography of Belloc worthwhile, for it sheds much light on Belloc's eventful era while chronicling in detail Belloc's curious, curmudgeonly, and often poisonous life. For here, as elsewhere, Wilson again shows himself to be a particularly sound cultural historian capable of effectively illuminating – within a few paragraphs or pages – many of the more consequential ideas and controversies of the past two centuries. His discussion, for example, of Belloc's famous dispute with H. G. Wells over the latter's *Outline of History* (1920) reminds one anew of the intensity of the debate between some conservative Christians and Charles Darwin's more ardent champions – a debate that of course continues to rage, in a host of ways, with profound cultural and social implications.

Wilson's description of Belloc as a "compulsive pen pusher" applies just as well to Wilson himself. By the middle of the 1980s Wilson was not only appearing regularly on British chat shows but writing a television column for the *Sunday Telegraph* and often irreverent opinion pieces for the *Evening Standard.* At the same time Wilson's essays appeared in the *Independent* and the *Spectator,* where — between 1981 and 1983 — he also served as literary editor. In 1990 Wilson, writing for the *Spectator,* sparked a furor when he aired rather unflattering details of his private conversations with members of the royal family, including the Queen Mother. But he has also mocked or teased in print countless other prominent figures ranging from Salman Rushdie to Robert Runcie, the former archbishop of Canterbury. During the 1980s Wilson cultivated a rather dandified persona and showed support for the conservative social and economic policies of Margaret Thatcher, easily the most polarizing British politician in half a century. Wilson, not surprisingly, found himself the target of barbs and denunciations, becoming — for example — "Wilson" in Britain's satiric magazine *Private Eye.*

Wilson has continued to publish novels, including "The Lampitt Papers" sequence, which now includes *Incline Our Hearts* (1988), *A Bottle in the Smoke* (1989), and *Daughters of Albion* (1991). These works feature an ambitious biographer assumed by many in London's literary circles to be modeled, at least in part, on Michael Holroyd. The trilogy also deals directly with many key moral and aesthetic issues related to the practice of biography, as James Atlas noted in a lengthy profile of Wilson published in *The New York Times Magazine* (18 October 1992). "What distinguishes Wilson as a biographer," observed Atlas, "is his willingness to acknowledge the provisional nature of evidence. As he puts it in *Incline Our Hearts:* 'Of all liars the most arrogant are biographers: those who would have us believe, having surveyed a few boxes full of letters, diaries, bank statements and photographs, that they can play at the recording angel and tell the whole truth about another human life.'" Indeed, Wilson's narrator in that novel often ponders the limits of biography and its relationship to the facts of time and human psychology:

When we say "it isn't like him," we betray not so much our imperception about an individual . . . as our general incomprehension of human personality. Pronouns are themselves just shorthand, since when we say "I" or "you" we really mean only that part of ourselves revealed for the time being to the other and seen through the other's eyes. We speak of the mad as people who aren't all there. But none of us are all there all of the time, that is, there is present in none of us at each moment of the day all the different modes of personality which might occasionally overtake us or be, for the time being, the most convenient mode of expressing ourselves. If we are not there to ourselves, still less are we all there to others, presenting to the other every disparate particle of our consciousness, as it were, as fixed

and artificially moulded as a "character" in fiction or biography.

Life, in other words, is not the same as biography; biography, by its very nature, can provide but a flawed and narrow picture of any one life. "In actual lives," continues the narrator of *Incline Our Hearts,* "lives, that is to say, which are lived rather than constructed by biographers — the past recedes and becomes a barely noticeable haze in the background. Things which seemed important in one particular week are shown, by the mere fact of their being forgotten, to be ultimately insignificant. Faces drift in and out of focus." But in biography, "everything, by virtue of being printed on the page in the same typeface, is given the same weight — friendships of enduring importance, encounters which strictly speaking made no imaginative impact at all, social chitchat scribbled on a postcard, hasty judgements of another person scribbled in a secret diary." Significantly, he adds: "hurling all the material at the reader with no sense of its unimportance, may in its own clumsy fashion be less distorting than some right-minded attempt to view a human life 'seriously'; for then the criterion of selection sets the focus and the picture becomes like one of those strange productions of artistic photographers where everything in the foreground is out of focus and all attention is fixed on some small detail in the middle distance."

In his next biography Wilson turned to one of literature's most complex and demanding figures. Wilson's *Tolstoy* is, he writes, "the history of a great genius whose art grew out of his three uneasy and irresolvable relationships: his relationship with God, his relationship with women, and his relationship with Russia. In all cases the relationships were stormy, full of contradictions. They were love-hate relationships, and the hate was sometimes rather hard to distinguish from the love." Wilson shows how these relationships informed Tolstoy's fiction — how, perhaps most notably, his intense sexuality tended to trigger raging bouts of religious guilt. Wilson well documents "the violent contradictions" between Tolstoy's "animal appetites and his sense of spiritual revulsion against the sexual act"; he demonstrates convincingly that, in fact, "few artists have had a more exaggerated sense of sexual guilt; few have been more clumsy of their handling of it in private life, or more creative in their literary use of it." Wilson is not, of course, the first writer on Tolstoy to examine the links between his sexual attitudes and practices and the content of his art, but — as the *Slavic Review* notes — he is particularly good at placing those attitudes and practices within "the general context of sexual mores and attitudes in Russia in his time": a time when, for example, venereal disease was rampant in the nation's provinces.

Wilson's biography is also strengthened by the astute readings it gives to *The Cossacks* (1863), *War and Peace* (1863–1869), and *Anna Karenina* (1875–1877), for he acutely understands that – whatever its links to an author's life – fiction does not equal autobiography, and he carefully shows how Tolstoy transformed the events of his life into the more timeless events of his art. "Almost every particle of *War and Peace* bears a relation to something in Tolstoy's personal experience," Wilson notes. "There is in the whole book hardly an incident, conversation or character which the commentators are not able to tell us is 'autobiographical.' " And yet, Wilson stresses, as one reads *War and Peace* – particularly for the first time – one is simply not interested in the revelations of these "wiseacres." "If we could tear our eyes from the page to talk to the commentators," he writes, "we would rather say, what do you mean by saying that Prince Andrey's chilling thoughts about his wife, or his ruminations on the fields of Austerlitz, or his love for Natasha or his cynicism or his heroism are *based on* such and such an instance in real life? For everyone who has enjoyed the experience of being completely lost in the world of *War and Peace,* such scenes *are* real life. Putting down the novel and returning to the everyday concerns of 'real life' is, in the experience of almost all readers of the book, a turning to something paler, less true than Tolstoy's art itself."

In *Tolstoy* Wilson again shows himself willing to stop the flow of his narrative long enough to comment frankly not only on the function of biography but its relationship to other literary forms. In a particularly insightful passage, Wilson focuses particularly on the connection between biography and the novel, noting that – in both – a writer aims to "comprehend or impose a shape on the inchoate business of existence"; indeed, it is "only by telling the tale that we create the illusion that there is a tale to tell." "The rise of the novel in literature," he notes, "which came with a great resurrection in the art of biography, a passion for journals, letter writing, personal confessions and memoirs, all of which happened shortly before or during the lifetime of Rousseau, gave to articulate beings the means of creating a shape, of holding on to words and moments which would otherwise be forgotten, of creating a barricade against death." Tolstoy himself recognized that – at least in their essential aims – "the

novel and the biography are not really all that different." Tolstoy "loved Rousseau's *Emile* and *The Confessions* equally; and not because they were so wonderfully distant from himself, but because to all serious purposes, he thought they were about himself. Dickens made a similar impression, influencing not merely the novels which [Tolstoy] was to write, but the way in which he was to record his own life in the diaries."

Wilson did come on a whim to this massive project. His "excitement" for Tolstoy began in the late 1960s, he explains, when at Oxford he studied literature with "the man who has written the best critical study on Tolstoy in English, John Bayley." (Wilson dedicated *The Sweets of Pimlico* to Bayley and his wife, the novelist Iris Murdoch.) This interest in Tolstoy remained so strong that, over the next two decades, Wilson acquired a "reading knowledge" of Russian and, at various times, conducted research, in libraries and archives in both Britain and the former Soviet Union. Anna Tavis Tolstoy in the *Slavic Review* (Summer 1990) advised that Wilson "interprets Tolstoy's life and work for well-educated, but amateur readers" and suggested that "the boldness of a fiction writer works well against the rigid hagiographic tradition." But Wilson's work "pales" when compared with more narrow and knowledgeable works of criticism. Still, Wilson's "intuitions on the significance of certain events and situations for Tolstoy's creative work are refreshingly original and in most cases persuasive." Moreover, noted Tavis, both Tolstoy and Wilson share an "abiding capacity to irritate the reader. One of the wittiest British novelists, Wilson knows how to derive humor from the gloomiest situations in Tolstoi's life."

The *Economist* (23 July 1988) hailed *Tolstoy* as "among the most impressively intelligent biographies ever written." James Atlas called the work "brilliant in patches" but suggested that it "will seem like a rehash to anyone familiar with the earlier Tolstoy biographies by Henri Troyat and Aylmer Maude" (*The New York Times Magazine,* 18 October 1992). R. F. Christian, reviewing *Tolstoy* in the *Times Literary Supplement* (20–26 May 1988), took an even harsher stand. Christian found the book marred not only by "factual errors" but also "incorrect references" and "unacknowledged quotations." "As befits a former literary editor of the *Spectator*," fired Christian, Wilson "writes fluently but is also slipshod and colloquial." Michael Holroyd praised the "engaged intimacy of tone" he found in *Tolstoy,* as well as its "wonderful readability." But many readers who prefer literary criticism and biography to be cast in a more formal style are not likely to warm to the informed – but often highly informal – tone that Wilson here sustains for more than eight hundred pages. (Wilson refers to Tolstoy's "midlife crisis," for example, and his "tomfool attempts to be like the peasants.") Some are likely to leave *Tolstoy* under the impression that, in the end, the author of *Anna Karenina* and *War and Peace* was – particularly when it came to women – just another "mixed up guy." Something of the flavor of the book can be found in one of its final paragraphs, where Wilson notes that photographs of Tolstoy in death appear to show a man "completely at peace." "But the sense of peace and stillness in the dead Tolstoy's face," he adds, "which seems so spiritual, so calm, and so grand, can probably be attributed to a cunning bit of facial massage by those who laid out the corpse and a judicious use of formaldehyde."

Wilson's next biography, *C. S. Lewis,* won high praise in some noteworthy quarters: Leon Edel, for one, called it "an astonishing book. I know of no modern biographer who equals Wilson's delicacy of touch and sensitivity to human quandries." It also sparked a wide and somewhat heated debate. Wilson, in his preface, asserts that "this book is not intended to be iconoclastic, but I will try to be realistic, not only because reality is more interesting than fantasy, but also because we do Lewis no honour to make him into a plaster saint. And he deserves our honour." Still, as that comment suggests, Wilson clearly sensed that a new account of the life of one of the century's most widely revered Christian intellectuals would ignite a sharp response – particularly among those he calls "conservative-minded believers."

Wilson, obviously, respects Lewis and much of his work – especially his literary scholarship and criticism. "For me," he writes, "the most attractive Lewis is the author of *English Literature in the Sixteenth Century,* a fluent, highly intelligent man talking about books in a manner which is always engaging." But it is also clear that Wilson wants to debunk the growing Lewis "myth" that he traces, in large part, to American evangelical circles. Wilson claims that "some of Lewis's American publishers actually ask for references to drinking and smoking to be removed from his work," for they recognize that "Lewis's Protestant devotees" require "a Lewis who was, against all evidence, a non-smoker and a lemonade drinker." Since his death in 1963, Lewis, Wilson writes, has become "something very like a saint in the minds of conservative-minded believers."

Front cover for the paperback edition of Wilson's biography of the literary scholar and Christian apologist that Leon Edel praised as "an astonishing book"

Wilson recognizes, then, that Lewis's large appeal comes not from his "wide-ranging erudition," not from his books and lectures on medieval and Renaissance literature; it is not "the rational Lewis" who "speaks to the present generation" but the Lewis who – in the *Chronicles of Narnia* and elsewhere – "plumbed the irrational depths of childhood and religion." Wilson thus does what no other Lewis biographer has attempted before: he takes a strong psychological approach. "Though all Freud's theories about the origins of consciousness may be disavowed," he writes, "this remains the century of Freud. We have learnt that our lives are profoundly affected by what happened to us when we were very young children, and that wherever we travel in mind or body we are compelled to repeat or work out the drama of early years." For Wilson, "the catastrophe" of Lewis's life took place when he was nine. His mother died of cancer. And though this loss was something Lewis managed for years to keep "bottled up within himself," it marked him in significant ways. "More than most men," Wilson suggests, Lewis "was the product of his upbringing and ancestry"; he would remain "constantly preoccupied with his own childhood." His mother's death drove Lewis increasingly into the realm of fantasy and books; it affected, too, his relationships with women.

Wilson's Lewis, he contends, is the Lewis Oxford really knew. Wilson does not deny that Lewis was "a kind and patient teacher." He does not question the depth of sincerity of Lewis's faith. But he clearly delights in depicting a man who – between pipes – smoked two or three packs of cigarettes a day and "liked to drink deep" in Oxford's pubs, where he would roar "out his unfashionable views." Wilson believes that Lewis and his forceful, fussy, and matronly landlady – a widow called Mrs. Moore – were in fact lovers for many years; he suggests that, in later years, Lewis and his wife-to-be, Joy Davidman, were sexually intimate before being legally wed. Both of these claims – particularly the latter – provoked a strong response in critical circles. One reviewer, George Sayer, noted that "if it is true," Wilson's depiction of Lewis's premarital relationship with Davidman "shatters Lewis's credibility as an honest man and a Christian moralist." Writing in the *Bulletin of the New York C. S. Lewis Society,* Sayer – himself a respected Lewis biographer – offered sound evidence against Wilson's claim. He suggested that, at least occasionally, Wilson appears unwilling to let the facts get in the way of a good story – a charge occasionally made by other critics of Wilson's work. Wilson asserts, for example, that at the Wade Center at Wheaton College – where much Lewis material is stored – one may also view the portable typewriter used by the well-known Christian journalist Malcolm Muggeridge, "kept, like the body of Lenin, in a glass case." Sayer asserted that Muggeridge's typewriter "is not and has never been there. Does this inaccuracy matter? If you think it does, perhaps you had better avoid books by biographers of the Wilson school."

Still, Sayer also agreed that Wilson's biography "has great merits," calling it "a good piece of narrative, enlivened by sharp observation, neat vignettes of character, bizarre incidents, and quite a lot of humor." Similarly, in the same publication, Lewis scholar Eugene McGovern called Wilson's book "worth reading" and praised its use of sources largely untapped by previous writers on Lewis's life. But McGovern also faulted Wilson for his "patronizing" attitude toward Lewis's longtime executor, Walter Hooper; he observed that Wilson "has a

weakness for the snide remark." More substantively, he – like Sayer – found evidence of "misjudgments" and "carelessness" in *C. S. Lewis: A Biography* on textual and biographical matters great and small; and, like other critics, he was uneasy with where Wilson's "psychologizing" leads – with, for example, the contention that Lewis's "quest for his lost mother dominated his relations with women." "Except for the trifling fact that she was a loud, foul-mouthed, divorced American," McGovern observed – drawing on Wilson's own portrayal – "Joy Davidman was just like the mother Lewis had lost in 1908."

In 1989 Wilson produced *Eminent Victorians,* a lively biographical and critical study of several figures – including William Gladstone, John Henry Newman, Josephine Butler, and Charlotte Brontë – who made major contributions to British political and cultural life. Again, this is an attractively readable volume aimed at a wide range of educated readers; it aims, Wilson explains, to amend the impression – made especially influential by Lytton Strachey, in his own *Eminent Victorians* (1920) – that the Victorian age was a most peculiar period of British history; that its most influential figures were both "ridiculous" and "absurd." Wilson's treatment of this culturally complex and intellectually robust period served as the basis for a six-part documentary for the BBC, hosted by Wilson himself. Wilson's *Eminent Victorians* is, then, sympathetic but by no means nostalgic; for, as Wilson notes about the era: "Men's clothes were nicer, but children were starving, and worse on the streets of London. On the whole, I have come to echo Lucky Jim in his definitive lecture on the Middle Ages, 'Thank God for the twentieth century.' "

The late 1980s brought significant changes in Wilson's life. In 1990 his first marriage ended in divorce; he is now married to Ruth Guilding. Wilson also reexamined his religious belief. In 1985, in *How Can We Know?,* Wilson had openly championed Christianity and seemed set to become a more contemporary version of Belloc or Lewis or even Muggeridge – the wide-ranging writer eager to make an impassioned case for a Christian worldview at a time when, at least among intellectuals, other more secular ideologies reigned supreme. But just seven years later, in his preface to *Jesus* (1992), Wilson announced that it was no longer "honest to call myself a Christian" – although his interest in the figure of Jesus of history had, if anything, grown. Wilson does not share "the sceptics' view that we could know nothing about Jesus"; his book – much influenced by the writings of Geza

Vermes – seeks to understand Jesus within the particular context of his culture and his times. "For Vermes," Wilson writes, "and those who think like him, Jesus comes alive again as a recognizable Jew of the first-century. I may as well start by confessing that this is the Jesus in whom I have come to believe. I believe that Jesus was a Galilean *hasid* or holy man. A *hasid* was an heir of the prophetic tradition. He had peculiar insights into man's relationship with God, and he had charismatic powers of healing."

Wilson's *Jesus* is not, he stresses "a spiritual autobiography"; much of it deals knowledgeably with rather complex textual and cultural issues relating to Christianity's earliest days. But Wilson's *Jesus* is also, in its way, a biography; indeed, as Adam Gopnik in *The New Yorker* (26 October 1992) put it, this study shows a strong sense that, in the Gospels, "there is a distinct human being in there somewhere, and Wilson is determined to fish him out." Wilson depicts a Jesus who is in many ways unique but not wholly unexpected, given Wilson's current skeptical stance; indeed, as Gopnik notes, Wilson depicts "a wide-ranging Jewish intellectual and wit who also happened to be a reluctant, charismatic national leader – a sort of combination of Jonathan Miller and Gandhi." Writing in the *Times Literary Supplement* (25 September 1992), J. Leslie Houlden observed that readers already familiar with a fair sampling of the material surrounding the historical Jesus will find relatively little that is new – or startling – in Wilson's well-researched and briskly written book. "Wilson's version of Jesus' story is in general pretty predictable and has been presented many times before," Houlden wrote. "It is distilled from the Gospels with the miraculous element sifted out. Inevitably, then, Jesus appears as 'the great apocalyptic prophet, the visionary teacher, the widely popular healer and exorcist.' As such, he is found admirable and inspiring. The rest is faith, initiated conceptually (as it were, despite Jesus) by Paul the apostle, and leading ultimately to the dogmatic formulations of the fourth and fifth centuries."

Wilson's most recent works reveal his continuing interest in religion – and the royals. He has edited *The Faber Book of Church and Clergy* (1992), an anthology of pieces on the clerical life that draws richly and heavily from Victorian sources. More recently, he has charted *The Rise and Fall of the House of Windsor* (1993).

Reference:

Bulletin of the New York C. S. Lewis Society, special issue on the Wilson biography (June–July 1990).

Angus Wilson

(11 August 1913 – 31 May 1991)

Valerie Grosvenor Myer
Cambridge University

See also the Wilson entries in *DLB 15: British Novelists, 1930–1959* and *DLB 139: British Short Fiction Writers, 1945–1980.*

BOOKS: *The Wrong Set and Other Stories* (London: Secker & Warburg, 1949; New York: Morrow, 1950);

Such Darling Dodos and Other Stories (London: Secker & Warburg, 1950; New York: Morrow, 1951);

Emile Zola: An Introductory Study of His Novels (London: Secker & Warburg, 1952; New York: Morrow, 1952);

Hemlock and After (London: Secker & Warburg, 1952; New York: Viking, 1952);

For Whom the Cloche Tolls (London: Methuen, 1953; New York: Viking, 1973);

Anglo-Saxon Attitudes (London: Secker & Warburg, 1956; New York: Viking, 1956);

The Mulberry Bush, (London: Secker & Warburg, 1956);

A Bit Off the May and Other Stories (London: Secker & Warburg, 1957; New York: Viking, 1957);

The Middle Age of Mrs. Eliot (London: Secker & Warburg, 1958; New York: Viking, 1959);

The Old Men at the Zoo (London: Secker & Warburg, 1961; New York; Viking, 1961);

The Wild Garden (London: Secker & Warburg, 1963);

Late Call (London: Secker & Warburg, 1964; New York: Viking, 1965);

Tempo: The Impact of Television on the Arts (London: Studio Vista, 1964; Chester Springs, Pa.: Dufour, 1966);

No Laughing Matter (London: Secker & Warburg, 1967; New York: Viking, 1967);

Death Dance: Twenty-five Stories (New York: Viking, 1969);

The World of Charles Dickens (London: Secker & Warburg, 1970; New York: Viking, 1970);

England (London: Thames & Hudson, 1971);

As If By Magic (London: Secker & Warburg, 1973; New York: Viking, 1973);

The Naughty Nineties (London: Eyre Methuen, 1976);

The Strange Ride of Rudyard Kipling (London: Secker & Warburg, 1977; New York: Viking, 1978);

Setting the World on Fire (London: Secker & Warburg, 1980; New York: Viking, 1980);

Diversity and Depth in Fiction: Selected Critical Writings by Angus Wilson (London: Secker & Warburg, 1983; New York: Viking, 1984);

Reflections in a Writer's Eye: Travel Pieces by Angus Wilson (London: Secker & Warburg, 1986; New York: Viking, 1986).

OTHER: Emile Zola, *Restless House,* introduction by Wilson (London: Weidenfeld & Nicolson, 1953; New York: Farrar, Straus & Young, 1953);

Zola, *Earth,* preface by Wilson (London: Elek, 1954; New York: Grove, 1955);

Zola, *The Kill,* introduction by Wilson (London: Weidenfeld & Nicolson, 1954; New York: Farrar, Straus & Young, 1954);

Zola, *Zest for Life,* preface by Wilson (London: Elek, 1955; Bloomington: Indiana University Press, 1986);

Gremaine Brée, *Marcel Proust and Deliverance from Time,* introduction by Wilson (London: Chatto & Windus, 1956);

"Charles Dickens: A Haunting," in *The Dickens Critics,* edited by George H. Ford and Lauriat Lane (Ithaca: Cornell University Press, 1961; London: Oxford University Press, 1962); reprinted in *Diversity and Depth in Fiction: Selected Critical Writings by Angus Wilson* (London: Secker & Warburg, 1983; New York: Viking, 1984);

Zola, *L'Assommoir,* afterword by Wilson (New York: New American Library: Signet, 1962); reprinted in *Diversity and Depth in Fiction: Selected Critical Writings by Angus Wilson* (London: Secker & Warburg, 1983; New York: Viking, 1984);

Angus Wilson (photograph by Tony Garrett)

"The Heroes and Heroines of Dickens," in *Dickens and the Twentieth Century*, edited by John Gross and Gabriel Pearson (London: Routledge & Kegan Paul, 1962); reprinted in *British Victorian Literature: Recent Revaluations*, edited by Shiv K. Kumar (London: University of London Press, 1969; New York: New York University Press, 1969);

George Meredith, *The Egoist*, afterword by Wilson (New York: New American Library: Signet, 1963);

Charles Dickens, *Oliver Twist*, introduction by Wilson (Harmondsworth: Penguin, 1966);

"The Neighbourhood of Tombuctoo: Conflicts in Jane Austen's Novels," in *Critical Essays on Jane Austen*, edited by B. C. Southam (London: Routledge & Kegan Paul, 1968); reprinted in *Diversity and Depth in Fiction: Selected Critical Writings of Angus Wilson* (London: Secker & Warburg, 1983; New York: Viking, 1984);

"Dickens and Dostoevsky," (London: Dickens Fellowship, 1970);

"Ivy Compton-Burnett," in *The Art of Ivy Compton-Burnett: A Collection of Critical Essays*, edited by Charles Burkhart (London: Gollancz, 1972);

John Cowper Powys, *Weymouth Sands*, introduction by Wilson (Cambridge: Rivers Press, 1973); reprinted in *Diversity and Depth in Fiction: Selected Critical Writings by Angus Wilson* (London: Secker & Warburg, 1983; New York: Viking, 1984);

Dickens, *The Mystery of Edwin Drood*, introduction by Wilson (Harmondsworth: Penguin, 1974);

Sir Arthur Conan Doyle, *The Return of Sherlock Holmes*, introduction by Wilson (London: John Murray/Jonathan Cape, 1974);

Writers of East Anglia, edited with an introduction by Wilson (London: Secker & Warburg, 1977);

"Edmund Wilson, The Man and His Work," in *An Edmund Wilson Celebration*, edited by John Wain (Oxford: Phaidon Press, 1978; New York: New York University Press, 1978);

Iain Mackintosh, *Pit, Boxes and Gallery: The Story of the Theatre Royal, Bury St Edmunds 1819–1971,* foreword by Wilson (London: National Trust, 1979);

The Collected Stories of Elizabeth Bowen, introduction by Wilson (London: Cape, 1980; New York: Knopf, 1980);

"John Cowper Powys," in *Recollections of the Powys Brothers: Lewellyn, Theodore and John Cowper,* edited by Belinda Humfrey (London: Peter Owen, 1980);

Rudyard Kipling, *Kim,* introduction by Wilson (London: Macmillan, 1981); reprinted in *Diversity and Depth in Fiction: Selected Critical Writings by Angus Wilson* (London: Secker & Warburg, 1983; New York: Viking, 1984);

The Portable Dickens, edited with an introduction by Wilson (New York: Viking / Harmondsworth: Penguin, 1983);

"The New and the Old Isherwood," in *Twentieth Century British Literature* (New York: Chelsea House, 1986).

PLAY PRODUCTION: *The Mulberry Bush,* Theatre Royal, Bristol, 1955; Royal Court Theatre, London, 1956.

Angus Frank Johnstone Wilson was born on 11 August 1913 in Sussex, the sixth son of William Johnstone Wilson and Maude Caney Wilson, of Durban, South Africa. His father, a raffish sporting man who never forgot his social position, belonged to the Scottish gentry and had a private income. This became inadequate, so the family lived in genteel poverty in a succession of private hotels, a style of life that provided backgrounds for much of Wilson's work. He spent several years in South Africa, though only one short story, "Union Reunion," deals with this period. He returned to England and attended, first, a private preparatory school where his brother was headmaster, and then Westminster, a distinguished public school. He studied history at Merton College, Oxford, where he also enjoyed reading English and European literature.

A lonely child, he had escaped from the family philistinism by reading fantasy and doing mimicry. His mother died when he was fifteen. Wilson was imbued with the family snobbery, which a Marxist-influenced training at Oxford converted to active socialism. After university he did various odd jobs and in 1936 joined the British Museum as a cataloguer of books. During this period he was politically active, mixing with intellectuals of the Left, who recur in his work. This experience, as well as his education, made him interested in the use and

abuse of power. Wilson's relationship with his father seems to have been affectionate, yet the seedy gamblers and con men who recur in the fictions reflect aspects of him. Wilson's fictional world is peopled with academics, administrators, fat women, affected women with a horror of being thought "common," aesthetes, homosexuals, and the underworld of "rough trade": this was new territory for mainstream fiction and was courageous at a time when homosexual relations, even between consenting adults, were illegal in Britain.

Wilson, by his own account, fell in love and suffered a nervous breakdown. His therapist suggested writing might bring relief, and Wilson started writing short stories, which were soon published, though it is unusual to get stories published before a reputation is established with a novel. *Such Darling Dodos and Other Stories* (1950) reflected postwar social readjustments and family tensions: the "camp" wit and malice were enjoyed.

His *Emile Zola: An Introductory Study of His Novels* appeared in 1952 and, like his later biographies of Charles Dickens and Rudyard Kipling, helped to revive esteem for authors then out of critical fashion. Wilson was a penetrating critic, uncorrupted by fashionable prejudices. Wilson's study of Zola broke fresh ground: it was the first book in English on this then-neglected author in twenty years, and it stimulated new translations of the novels. Wilson's own fame lay in the future, but his characteristic concern for the social and psychological roots of imaginative creation, his demand that the novelist present a picture of his society and his time, were already present and were to remain constant. The book opens: "The form in which an artist's creative impulses are ultimately expressed is frequently moulded by the stresses placed on his emotions in childhood and early adolescence; stresses produced by the gradual realisation of the dreadful gulf that lies between his fantasy world, often protected and nurtured by parental affection, and the vast uncomforting desert of the society in which he must live. Artistic creation, it would seem, represents such fragments of this fantasy world as he is able to retain and to impose upon society." With hindsight this seems obvious, yet Wilson helped the notion to become general. He pursued this idea through his later biographies and in his own artistic autobiography, *The Wild Garden* (1963).

His approach to evaluation is firmly biographical, and with all his subjects he considers childhood crucial: all three authors had, like Wilson himself, disrupted and stressful childhood years. Of Zola's hated job as a bookshop clerk he writes, "Like

Dickens's work in the blacking factory, it symbolised all the horrors of his childhood conflicts . . . beneath the fierce attack on society, the novels had their roots in deep personal aspects of the author's life – aspects which could find their answer in social analysis, because his own inner conflicts were directly related to the social conflicts of the time. . . . In . . . mistrust of mass action, he resembles Dickens, whose early life and education led him to a similar view of society, veering from a vague political radicalism to a sort of pessimistic anarchism . . . the neurotic obsessions of artists are often a clue to their greatest gifts. . . . In that curious combination of prurience, sexuality and Puritan horror . . . Zola far outstripped Charles Dickens. Zola's attack upon contemporary society was no more fierce than that of Dickens, but the pill was not sugared. In the purely emotional and moral source of his work, in the lack of abstraction or intellectualism of all the greater of his novels, Zola was more in key with the English tradition than with that of his own country."

He pleads for Zola's reputation to be rescued from the "dusty cupboard" to which it had been consigned, noting that while his work had been directly influential, this had affected generally writers of the second rank. Wilson characteristically displays his cosmopolitan reading when he writes: "to be largely responsible for George Moore and Arnold Bennett in England, Frank Norris and Dreiser in America, Heinrich Mann in Germany, Jules Romains in France, is an equivocal honour."

Wilson estimates that without these followers, the "embarrassingly naive" theories of *Le Roman Experimental* might have swamped Zola's reputation, so he might only appear as one of the "great, cumbrous pithecanthropi of nineteenth-century literature." For Wilson, Zola's was "a wonderful and enveloping world." Wilson attacks unnamed critics for unfairly extending ridicule of Zola's materialist philosophy and the "vulgarity" of his home to his works, which offer "a pattern of great complexity" stemming from "deep despairs and doubts." The scientific material on which he worked so hard provided a framework for his overflowing emotions and creative powers: the Rougon Macquart novels offer a total picture of Second Empire society. The facts of Zola's life were scrutinized as a means of appreciating his art, a lifelong preoccupation with Wilson and the drive behind all his biographical studies.

In 1955 Wilson resigned his job at the British Library to become a full-time writer. Wilson's 1955 play, *The Mulberry Bush,* was performed successfully

Wilson marching in a demonstration at Belgrave Square in 1975 (Hulton Deutsch)

in Bristol but failed in London. A political play, *The Mulberry Bush* was before its time: its themes were developed by later writers.

The nonfiction work *The Wild Garden* originated as the 1960 Ewing Lectures at the University of California and constitutes the best commentary on Wilson's own work: in it he describes the sources of his imaginative world, the Freudian conflict between instinct, symbolized by the wild garden, and civilization. Wilson also writes of influences on him: "As a child I was much with my brother next in age – thirteen years old when I was born. He was a youth of exceptional histrionic powers, strangely combining sharpness of wit and tenderness of heart, extremely effeminate, with deep powers of creation that were never fulfilled. His wit and his fantasy have both strongly influenced the texture of my free imagination, giving it an unusual quality of severely moral chi-chi and camp. To him also I owe the pervasiveness of the feminine in my work – the strength of the female characters, their invasion of every part of my books, the affectionate mockery with which this invasion is treated. For the rest — the grotesque, the macabre, the purely absurd, the sadistic and the compensatingly pathetic — I can find no influences."

In 1963 Wilson started lecturing on literature at the University of East Anglia, where he eventually became a part-time professor. In 1968 he was awarded a CBE (Commander of the British Empire) and was chairman of the Arts Council literary panel.

The World of Charles Dickens was *Yorkshire Post* Book of the Year in 1970. It was popular in presentation, so its important insights were not immediately recognized by literary scholars. What Wilson wrote of Dickens's background applied to his own life and art: "class consciousness would have been the more acute because the Dickens family only just qualified for . . . [genteel] status. In this social respect Charles Dickens was born on to the outer edge of the world he wished to belong to. . . . The financial ups and downs of his expansive, impecunious father, even before the inevitable crash, must have made the assertions of gentility more strident. . . . It became his aim, like that of most other nineteenth-century novelists, to encompass the whole of society . . . [a] wonderful gallery of snobs and hangers-on . . . early concern with the seedy and down-at-heel." Although separated from his book on Zola by nearly twenty years, Wilson's concerns remain the same: an interest in the world of genteel poverty (like his own) and childhood traumas, conflicts as sources of imaginative energy.

Rarely has Dickens's art been so profoundly, yet simply, understood and analyzed: Wilson observes that Dickens's favorite moral was that in an increasingly utilitarian, industrial world we needed to cultivate the imagination, the fancy of childhood; that his writing is intuitive at one level, rational and didactic at the next, but finally imparting the lesson; that only the intuitive life can make a deadened, materialistic world flower again. Wilson asserts that "[h]is ordinary readers no doubt responded to it directly and unconsciously in his lifetime. It is not easy for us to do so."

There follows a brief history of Dickens criticism in the twentieth century, illuminated by historical understanding. Wilson concludes that both the intellectuals who "seek clear shapes and patterns" and the general reader who is unworried by a mixed response are both right, because "the perpetual child with a strange, sensitive, ludicrous apprehension of life co-existed with the parent, active, impatient, competent, witty, compassionate reformer and man of the world." This passage was written when scholars did seek conclusive answers to critical problems, and Wilson's demand for a more sym-

pathetic acceptance of what had been deemed Dickens's "sentimentality" and "vulgarity" was, in the long term, effective. Wilson's insights have become the commonplaces of Dickens criticism but were original with him.

A chronological account follows this critical analysis, and throughout this is a *critical* biography, one in which the events of the life are interpreted in relation to the output. Dickens's political and social attitudes are considered, and his development charted. Of *Dombey and Son* Wilson writes that "All classes . . . are represented in this novel and none are treated with that innate petty bourgeois prejudice which had lingered in his humour from his *Sketches by Boz* days . . . for the first time every character is fully related to the theme of the novel." The biography is written in Wilson's usual crisp and fastidious prose. When he became a professor of English literature at the University of East Anglia, he refused to teach "creative writing," but his students remember him as the most stimulating and humane of critics. In 1971 Wilson was a council member of the Society of Authors, a vice president of the Royal Society of Literature, and a vice president of the Eastern Arts Association. In 1975 he became president of the Dickens Fellowship.

Wilson has linked his veneration for Kipling with his fear of anarchy. Wilson, unlike Kipling biographer Charles Carrington, did not have access to the Kipling family papers while writing *The Strange Ride of Rudyard Kipling* (1977), but he did go to India. There he observed that Kipling could not have seen the Saint Martiniére school at Lucknow, the model for Saint Xavier's in *Kim*: he argues that the monstrous lions on the building, originally the rococo home of a rich Frenchman, would have stimulated Kipling's visual imagination and drawn Kim's attention. There had been previous biographies of Kipling, but the originality of this one lay in its relation of the life to the writings: as always, Wilson was preoccupied with the roots of imaginative creation.

Wilson compares the experience of exile from India endured by the six-year-old Kipling and his three-year-old sister, Trix, with the short story "Baa, Baa, Black Sheep." Wilson explains the colonial background, then the experience of so many British people, now so remote and accessible only through imaginative re-creation. Wilson cites Edmund Wilson's famous essay, "The Kipling that Nobody Read," and comments that although it is now seen as "somewhat naively Freudian" it was probably "the beginning of the critical resuscitation of Kipling's work in academic and intellectual circles; and this essay took these miserable years of childhood as crucial to Kipling's imaginative development."

Adults in "Baa, Baa, Black Sheep" practiced a grim, life-denying religion. The religious background, so important in the period, is ably presented by Wilson. The complicated network of Kipling's relatives is charted, and their importance in his development assessed: Stanley Baldwin, later to become Conservative prime minister, was a cousin, and Kipling's Aunt Georgie was married to the painter and designer of Victorian stained glass Sir Edward Burne-Jones, who influenced Kipling profoundly. From him, writes Wilson, Kipling inherited an "almost hypnotic sense of a dream kingdom," but in Wilson's view Kipling's strength comes from the testing of dreams by reality. "Where Burne-Jones used his dreams to exclude, Kipling uses them with courage to test his capacity to bear reality. Only . . . in Kipling's treatment of women does he inherit something of that weakening absolute separation of the ideal from the sensual which makes so much of Burne-Jones's painting null."

Kipling's imperialism, which has alienated so many modern readers, is analyzed as befits a novelist who is also a trained historian; Wilson points out that Kipling feared that because tropical countries were unsuitable for the English to settle in, eventually the empire would collapse. While not accepting Kipling's imperial vision, Wilson argues that Kipling's "political and imperial concepts spring from his own agonising sense of personal isolation, of man's lonely, futile-seeming journey from childhood's wonder to death's eclipse. But that, again, is only to say that he was an artist, not a thinker."

Wilson is a gifted biographer because his literary and psychological insights are always informed with lightly carried historical knowledge. The biographies, together with *The Wild Garden*, offer important clues to understanding Wilson himself. Wilson characterizes Kipling as a "gentle-violent man" but avoids an overly Freudian interpretation. He prefers to look at a "social-historical description of long generations of Evangelical belief ending in post-Darwinian doubt," acknowledging that "the mystery of human personality defies all explanations." The book is illustrated with photographs of India in the early 1970s by Tony Garrett, Wilson's companion.

After his retirement in 1978 Wilson held various visiting professorships and in 1985 moved to Provence. *Diversity and Depth in Fiction* (1983) is a collection of critical writings that demonstrates his range and penetration: among them, "Evil in the English Novel" casts light on his own work and that

of others. He traveled widely, and *Reflections in a Writer's Eye* (1986) is a collection of travel pieces.

Wilson's works were out of fashion at the time of his death in 1991, but already there is a revival of interest, and his books are being reissued in paperback. The television version of *Anglo-Saxon Attitudes* (1956) put the book on the best-seller lists, where it had never been during Wilson's lifetime. He responded to the modern world from the standpoint of his Edwardian childhood, his public-school and Oxford education, and the traditional European culture and homosexual subculture, modified by the influences of Karl Marx and Sigmund Freud. Intensely individual, he interpreted the postwar generation to itself. The inner conflicts between cruelty and tenderness, the cultivated and the natural, the decent socialism of the head and the camp, and the snobbish malice of the laughing heart make his work always entertaining, disturbing, and, at its best, profound.

Bibliography:

J. H. Stape and Anne N. Thomas, *Angus Wilson: A Bibliography 1947–1987* (London & New York: Hamell, 1988).

Biography:

Margaret Drabble, *Angus Wilson* (London: Viking, 1995).

References:

Peter Faulkner, *Angus Wilson: Mimic and Moralist* (London: Secker & Warburg, 1980);

Averil Gardner, *Angus Wilson* (Boston: Twayne, 1985);

Jan L. Halio, *Angus Wilson* (Edinburgh: Oliver & Boyd, 1964);

Halio, ed., *Critical Essays on Angus Wilson* (Boston: G. K. Hall, 1985).

Papers:

Collections of Wilson's papers are in the British Library, Reference Division; the Brotherton Library, Leeds; Christ's College, Cambridge; Columbia University, New York; Eton College; the Hall-Carpenter archives, King's College, Cambridge; the Berg Collection, New York Public Library; Northamptonshire Public Record Office; the Bodleian Library, Oxford University; the Royal Society of Literature; Secker and Warburg, publishers; Thames Television; University College, London University; Durham University; the University of East Anglia; the University of Iowa; Reading University; the University of Sussex; and Viking/Penguin publishers.

Tom Winnifrith

(5 April 1938 –)

Margaret D. Sullivan
Hunter College of the City University of New York

BOOKS: *The Brontës and Their Background: Romance and Reality* (London: Macmillan, 1973; New York: Barnes & Noble, 1973);

The Brontës (London & New York: Macmillan, 1977);

Brontë Facts and Brontë Problems, by Winnifrith and Edward Chitham (Atlantic Highlands, N.J.: Humanities Press, 1983; London: Macmillan, 1984);

1984 and All's Well?, by Winnifrith and William V. Whitehead (London: Macmillan, 1984);

The Vlachs: The History of the Balkan People (London: Duckworth, 1987; New York: St. Martin's Press, 1987);

A New Life of Charlotte Brontë (London: Macmillan, 1988; New York: St. Martin's Press, 1988);

Charlotte and Emily Brontë: A Literary Life, by Winnifrith and Chitham (London: Macmillan, 1989; New York: St. Martin's Press, 1989);

Fallen Women in the Nineteenth Century Novel (London: Macmillan, 1994; New York: St. Martin's Press, 1994).

OTHER: "David Benedictus," in *Dictionary of Literary Biography, volume 14: British Novelists Since 1960* (Detroit: Gale Research, 1983), pp. 86–90;

"Emily Brontë," in *Dictionary of Literary Biography, volume 21: Victorian Novelists Before 1885* (Detroit: Gale Research, 1983), pp. 55–65;

"J. G. Farrell," in *Dictionary of Literary Biography, volume 14: British Novelists Since 1960* (Detroit: Gale Research, 1983), pp. 288–292;

Greece Old and New, edited by Winnifrith and Penelope Murray, with an introduction by Winnifrith (London: Macmillan, 1983);

"Henry Kingsley," in *Dictionary of Literary Biography, volume 21: Victorian Novelists Before 1885* (Detroit: Gale Research, 1983), pp. 208–210;

"Lawrence Oliphant and Margaret Oliphant," in *Dictionary of Literary Biography, volume 18: Victo-*

rian Novelists After 1885 (Detroit: Gale Research, 1983), pp. 231–238;

The Poems of Patrick Branwell Brontë, edited, with an introduction, by Winnifrith (London: Blackwell, 1983; New York: New York University Press, 1983);

The Poems of Charlotte Brontë, edited by Winnifrith (Oxford & New York: Blackwell, 1984);

Aspects of the Epic, edited by Winifrith, Murray, and K. W. Gransden (London: Macmillan, 1984; New York: St. Martin's Press, 1984);

Selected Brontë Poems, edited by Winnifrith and Edward Chitham (Oxford & New York: Blackwell, 1985);

The Philosophy of Leisure, edited by Winnifrith and Cyril Barrett (London: Macmillan, 1989; New York: St. Martin's Press, 1989);

Leisure in Art and Literature, edited by Winnifrith and Barrett (London: Macmillan, 1992);

Perspectives on Albania, edited, with an introduction, by Winnifrith (London: Macmillan, 1992; New York: St. Martin's Press, 1992).

SELECTED PERIODICAL PUBLICATIONS – UNCOLLECTED: "Charlotte Brontë's Letters to Ellen Nussey," *Durham University Journal,* 63 (1970): 16–18;

"Matthew Arnold and Clough," *Notes and Queries,* 18 (1971): 249–250;

"Miss Scatcherd's Identity," *Brontë Society Transactions,* 16 (1974): 364;

"Jane Austen's Adulteress," *Notes and Queries,* 37 (March 1990): 19–20.

Thomas John Winnifrith, respected Brontë biographer, scholar, historian, editor, and literary critic, was born 5 April 1938 in London to John Digby Winnifrith and Lesbia Margaret Cochrane Winnifrith. He was educated at Christ Church, Oxford, and became assistant master at Eton College in 1961. At Eton he taught Latin and Greek as well as English and Divinity. "It was perhaps Divinity teaching that first drew me to the Brontës with their strongly religious background and the religious imagery that pervades their novels," Winnifrith has remarked in an unpublished letter. He was E. K. Chambers Student at Corpus Christi College, Oxford, from 1966 to 1968, receiving a master of philosophy degree in 1968. From 1968 until 1970 Winnifrith was William Noble Fellow at the University of Liverpool, where he earned a doctorate in 1970. The Brontës were one of his subjects for the M.Phil. at Oxford and his main subject for the Ph.D. at Liverpool. In 1970 he became lecturer in the Department of English at the University of Warwick and senior lecturer in 1977. Winnifrith has remained at the University of Warwick until the present, teaching most periods of English literature with special emphasis on the eighteenth and nineteenth centuries.

While he was visiting research fellow at All Souls College, Oxford, in 1984, Winnifrith wrote up the research he had done on the Vlachs, dwellers in the mountains of the Central Balkans who speak a dialect derived from Latin. *The Vlachs: The History of the Balkan People* was published in 1987. Another book in this field, *Balkan Fragments,* is scheduled for publication in 1995. In addition to his teaching, research, and writing, Winnifrith has held numerous administrative positions at the University of Warwick. In recent years Winnifrith has lectured in America, Australia, Japan, Italy, Spain, Poland, Romania, Bulgaria, Albania, and Greece. Despite his current diversity, the English Brontës provided his first subject of scholarship and biography.

The Brontës and Their Background: Romance and Reality was published in 1973. The book grew out of Winnifrith's doctoral thesis at Liverpool University and is, perhaps, one of the earliest attempts to separate factual information about the Brontës from myth and lore in a scholarly and critical manner. Winnifrith begins by confronting the primary obstacles in approaching a study of the Brontës: the unreliability of both primary and secondary sources. His first two chapters, "Biographers and Critics" and "Texts and Transmission," are concerned with these issues. As he states in his introduction, "the second task of this book [is] to examine some of the religious, literary and social ideas of the Brontës, and to criticise the way they expressed these ideas in their novels." The remainder of the book is devoted to discussing religious and moral issues, examining each of the Brontës as authors and analyzing the likely influences exerted on them by some of the social issues of their time.

Winnifrith appends four sections to his study: "T. J. Wise and the Brontës," "The Needham Copies of Charlotte Brontë's Letters to Ellen Nussey," "Contemporary Reviews of the Brontë Novels," and "Ellen Nussey's Family Tree," supplying pertinent information in a highly readable format. He also includes detailed notes and a bibliography. Although there is no doubt that this is a work of excellent scholarship, Winnifrith's clear organization and prose style make the book one that also appeals to a more general audience. He succeeds admirably in distinguishing for the reader the difference between "Romance and Reality," his book's subtitle, in the lives and the works of the Brontës.

In 1977 Winnifrith published *The Brontës,* a volume in the Masters of World Literature series. In his introduction he notes some of the problems confronting a biographer of the Brontës: a lack of proper editing of the juvenilia, the poetry, most of the letters, and even some of the novels. In addition, "there are problems of texts, dates, and even authorship to be faced . . . amateurs have rushed in where scholars have feared to tread," so that in "trying to write something new about the Brontës we are faced with a formidable array of old hypotheses masquerading as truths."

Because the popular cult of the Brontës (as well as some earlier biographers) all too often tend to read the novels and poems as thinly veiled autobiography, Winnifrith takes pains to distinguish the lives from the works: "My main aim in spending so much time on the biography has been to show that the lives of the Brontës are different from their books." He devotes his first chapter, "Biography," to a careful discussion of the known facts, distinguishing them clearly from speculation, before moving on to a discussion of the juvenilia and the poetry. He then devotes a chapter to each of the major novels: *Wuthering Heights* (1847), *Agnes Grey* (1847), *The Tenant of Wildfell Hall* (1848), *The Professor* (1857), *Jane Eyre* (1847), *Shirley* (1849), and *Villette* (1853). In each case Winnifrith supplies the reader with publishing history, a brief review of the book's critical success (or lack thereof) over time, and his own critical assessment of the work. He notes in his concluding chapter that the reader should not forget the fact that the Brontës were novelists of the 1840s even though "in their experiments with different levels of narrative, in their exploration of dual personalities, and in their refusal to be tied down by conventional realism" he believes "the Brontës do remind us of their eighteenth-century predecessors as well as twentieth-century innovators in the novel."

Winnifrith also cautions the reader against critics who, finding it difficult to reconcile the Brontë novels with the nineteenth-century realist novel, have tried to consider their work in isolation from their background or, worse, have relegated the novels to the category of "ephemeral escapist fiction which flourished in the middle of Victoria's reign." He suggests that, "sometimes, especially in *Jane Eyre* and *Wuthering Heights,* where realism seems to have been subordinated to cosmic allegory, we seem to have moved far away from the novel as a genre into the realm of romance." Far from using the label "romance" in a pejorative sense, Winnifrith asserts that, "to say that the Brontës are writing romances can mean that we should be comparing their novels with the works of Shakespeare, Spenser, and Sidney," and it is his belief that "they can, unlike the great nineteenth-century realist novels, stand this comparison."

In 1983 Winnifrith published *The Poems of Patrick Branwell Brontë,* a new edition of the *Shakespeare Head Brontë,* enlarged and annotated. The notoriously flawed and unreliable three-volume edition of fifty years earlier, containing much of Charlotte's and Branwell's prose and verse, had been produced by J. A. Symington and T. J. Wise. The latter was exposed after his death as a thief and a forger, a man who, as Winnifrith notes, "acquired many manuscripts dishonestly, copied them inaccurately, and then edited them in a slovenly fashion."

Winnifrith acknowledges that Branwell's poetry is inferior to Emily's, but he nonetheless saw, as he states in the general introduction to his volume, there was "a need to produce an edition that is accurate, available and readable. Branwell was the second best poet in the Brontë family and some of his poems are worth studying in their own right." Winnifrith devotes the first section of his new edition to the poems published in the previous *Shakespeare Head Brontë* and a second section to the poems (mostly Angrian) that Branwell revised in 1837 and copied into a notebook. A third section contains other poems not previously published in the *Shakespeare Head Edition.* The notes to the text attest to the enormity of the task and to Winnifrith's meticulous editing skills, although preserving the format of the *Shakespeare Head Edition* was a handicap to this edition and the subsequent edition of Charlotte's poems.

Brontë Facts and Brontë Problems, which Winnifrith wrote with Edward Chitham, an editor and biographer of Anne and Emily, was published in 1983. The book consists of five chapters written by Winnifrith, and, as one can readily see from the titles, he addresses a broad range of issues: "Charlotte Brontë and Mr. Rochester," "Texts and Transmission," "Branwell Brontë and Ponden Hall," "*Wuthering Heights:* One Volume or Two?," and "Ellen Nussey and the Brontës." As the authors note in their introduction, their aim is to view the Brontës "from many angles, considering poetry as well as prose, biography as well as criticism, Branwell and Anne as well as Emily and Charlotte." Chitham's chapters round out the exploration: "Early Brontë Chronology," "The Inspiration for Emily's Poetry," "Gondal's Queen: Saga or Myth?," "Emily Brontë and Shelley," "Diverging Twins: Some Clues to Wildfell Hall," and "The Development of 'Vision' in Emily Brontë's Poems."

Winnifrith's edition of *The Poems of Charlotte Brontë,* a new enlarged and annotated edition of the *Shakespeare Head Brontë,* was published in 1984. In compiling and editing Charlotte's poems, Winnifrith notes in his general introduction that he faced somewhat different problems from those he encountered in editing Branwell's poetry. Editing the poems Charlotte published in her lifetime is, he claims, "not a difficult task." But when it comes to the poems published after her death, many by T. J. Wise in private editions, the problems of inaccurate copying arises. In addition, "Charlotte wrote more on loose sheets of paper than in notebooks, and it is less easy than with Branwell to date a poem by reason of its proximity to another poem."

The Poems of Charlotte Brontë provides scholars and general readers alike with an accurate edition that is divided into sections containing the poems published in Charlotte's lifetime from the earlier *Shakespeare Head Edition,* those in that edition published after her death, and other poems not published in the earlier edition. In addition to his general introduction, Winnifrith provides a biographical note, a textual introduction, extensive notes, and an appendix listing other poems not in this edition.

Winnifrith collaborated with Chitham on a second volume, *Selected Brontë Poems,* which was published in 1985. This volume, while an example of excellent scholarship, is aimed at a more general readership. Because the collection does not attempt to be comprehensive, Winnifrith and Chitham are able to pick the poems that represent the best efforts of each of the sisters and Branwell, rather than, as they note in their introduction, feeling compelled to include "the large number of poems of indifferent quality which disfigure the poetry of all four Brontës, and especially that of Charlotte." Choosing to assemble such a selection also allows the scholars to eliminate "the dense critical apparatus necessary to establish a correct text," which the note says may make "the complete editions we have produced, or are endeavouring to produce . . . rather forbidding for the general reader."

In 1988 Winnifrith published *A New Life of Charlotte Brontë,* stating in the introduction that "the twisting paths and the complexities of Charlotte's life have been well covered, but seem still to be insufficiently appreciated." He warns the reader with a touch of droll humor (and perhaps a gentle poke at earlier biographers) that "the Charlotte that emerges from the following pages is an admirable but not a particularly attractive figure. The tendency to turn biography into hagiography must be resisted." And, indeed, Winnifrith's Charlotte is both "admirable and pitiable."

The simple chapter headings belie the depth of Winnifrith's analysis and presentation: "Origins," "Pupil," "Writer," "Teacher," "Belgium," "Author," "*Jane Eyre,*" "*Shirley,*" "*Villette,*" and "Wife." Yet the progression as well as the intertwining of the images the titles suggest work extremely well in underscoring what Winnifrith is setting out to do: "This book has no axe to grind, but aims to see Charlotte Brontë and to see her whole." The work fulfills its aim as its author paints the portrait of his subject who, "like many of us . . . was muddled by the conflicting claims of reason and emotion, duty and inclination, religion and passion." Through the vehicles of Winnifrith's lucid prose and careful presentation, the reader is led to understand that, "unlike most of us she was – in her books, if not in her life – capable of resolving these conflicts. This book explores both the conflicts and the resolutions," and it does so in ways and with depths of insight earlier biographies have not.

A less scholarly, but nonetheless intriguing, approach to the lives of the two most famous Brontë sisters can be found in *Charlotte and Emily Brontë: A Literary Life* (1989), the third work of collaboration between Winnifrith and Chitham. The volume is part of a series entitled Literary Lives, and the purpose of the series, as general editor Richard Dutton of the University of Lancaster notes, is to present "stimulating accounts of the literary careers of the most widely read British and Irish authors." To this end, the series will look at "the writers' working lives, not in the spirit of traditional biography, but aiming to trace the professional, publishing and social contexts which shaped their writing." This, of course, brings up the "vexed issue in current critical theory" of the "role and status of 'the author' as the creator of literary texts." Yet the editor believes that "an understanding of writers' careers can promote,

for students and general readers alike, a more informed historical reading of their works." And Winnifrith's and Chitham's volume does just that. In clear and flowing prose the scholars make the difficulties in interpreting the lives and the works clear to their readers while guiding them past the pitfalls of interpreting the works as autobiography.

In addition to his work on the Brontës, Winnifrith has also published collections of essays that were adapted from papers read by various scholars at conferences at the University of Warwick. Some of these lectures were given under the auspices of the European Humanities Research Centre, founded to promote interdisciplinary and comparative research in the European humanities, and the Joint School of Classics. Two conferences were sponsored by the Greek Embassy. *Greece Old and New* (1983), which collects papers given in 1978 and 1979, was edited with Penelope Murray and contains two pieces by Winnifrith, "Greeks and Romans," and "Greece Old and New." A second volume, *Aspects of the Epic* (1984), Winnifrith edited with Murray and K. W. Gransden. This collection of six essays from a conference in 1980 explores various aspects of the European epic tradition ranging from the works of Homer to those of contemporary Greek writers. Winnifrith's essay "Homer in Byzantine Dress" is included in the collection. A third volume edited by Winnifrith is entitled *Perspectives on Albania* (1992) and is derived from a conference held in April 1988. He is responsible for the introduction and contributed "Albania and the Ottoman Empire."

Winnifrith has traveled extensively in the Balkans, and his research into the history of the Latin-speaking people living in the high mountains led to his publication of *The Vlachs.* Additional books of Winnifrith's include a work on George Orwell, *1984 and All's Well?* (1984), with William V. Whitehead; and *The Philosophy of Leisure* (1989) and *Leisure in Art and Literature* (1992), which Winnifrith edited with Cyril Barrett and which contain publications deriving from the European Humanities Research Centre lectures. Winnifrith's paper is "Funeral Games in Homer and Virgil."

Winnifrith's most recent publication is *Fallen Women in the Nineteenth Century Novel* (1994), which examines issues in the lives of Jane Austen, Charlotte Brontë, George Eliot, William Makepeace Thackeray, Charles Dickens, and Thomas Hardy as they may relate to the various writers' treatments of Victorian social, religious, and sexual codes in their novels.

Winnifrith resides in Warwickshire. In 1967 he married Joanna Victoria Lee Booker. She died in 1976, and for the next twelve years, like Mr. Brontë, Winnifrith brought up his three children on his own. None have written any novels, but all three have graduated from Oxford or Cambridge Universities. In 1988, like Mr. Nicholls after Charlotte Brontë's death, Winnifrith married his cousin, Helen Mary Young, and acquired three stepchildren.

Checklist of Further Readings

Aaron, Daniel, ed. *Studies in Biography*. Cambridge, Mass.: Harvard University Press, 1978.

Alter, Robert. *Motives for Fiction*. Cambridge, Mass.: Harvard University Press, 1984.

Altick, Richard Daniel. *The Art of Literary Research*. New York: Norton, 1963.

Altick. *Lives and Letters: A History of Literary Biography in England and America*. New York: Knopf, 1965.

Altick. *The Scholar Adventurers*. New York: Macmillan, 1950.

Anderson, James William. "The Methodology of Psychological Biography," *Journal of Interdisciplinary History*, 11 (Winter 1981): 455–475.

Atlas, James. "Literary Biography," *American Scholar*, 45 (Summer 1976): 448–460.

Barzun, Jacques. "Biography and Criticism – a Misalliance Disputed," *Critical Inquiry*, 1 (March 1975): 479–496.

Bell, Susan Groag, and Marilyn Yalom, eds. *Revealing Lives: Autobiography, Biography, and Gender*. Albany: State University of New York Press, 1990.

Berry, Thomas Elliott, ed. *The Biographer's Craft*. New York: Odyssey Press, 1967.

Birkets, Sven. *An Artificial Wilderness: Essays on 20th-Century Literature*. New York: Morrow, 1987.

Bloom, Harold, ed. *Dr. Samuel Johnson and James Boswell*. New York: Chelsea House, 1986.

Bloom, ed. *James Boswell's Life of Johnson*. New York: Chelsea House, 1986.

Bowen, Catherine Drinker. *Adventures of a Biographer*. Boston: Little, Brown, 1959.

Bowen. *Biography: The Craft and the Calling*. Boston: Little, Brown, 1969.

Brady, Frank, John Palmer, and Martin Price, eds. *Literary Theory and Structure: Essays in Honor of William K. Wimsatt*. New Haven: Yale University Press, 1973.

Britt, Albert. *The Great Biographers*. New York: McGraw-Hill, 1936; London: Whittlesey House, 1936.

Bromwich, David. *Choice of Inheritance: Self and Community from Edmund Burke to Robert Frost*. Cambridge, Mass.: Harvard University Press, 1989.

Browning, J. D., ed. *Biography in the 18th Century*. New York & London: Garland, 1980.

Cafarelli, Annette. *Prose in the Age of Poets: Romanticism and Biographical Narrative from Johnson to De Quincey*. Philadelphia: University of Pennsylvania Press, 1990.

Clifford, James Lowry. *From Puzzles to Portraits: Problems of a Literary Biographer.* Chapel Hill: University of North Carolina Press, 1970.

Clifford, ed. *Biography as an Art: Selected Criticism, 1560–1960.* New York: Oxford University Press, 1962.

Clingham, Greg. *James Boswell: The Life of Johnson.* New York & Cambridge: Cambridge University Press, 1992.

Clingham, ed. *New Light on Boswell: Critical and Historical Essays on the Occasion of the Bicentenary of* The Life of Johnson. New York & Cambridge: Cambridge University Press, 1991.

Cockshut, A. O. J. *Truth to Life: The Art of Biography in the Nineteenth Century.* London: Collins, 1974; New York: Harcourt Brace Jovanovich, 1974.

Connely, Willard. *Adventures in Biography: A Chronicle of Encounters and Findings.* London: W. Laurie, 1956; New York: Horizon, 1960.

Daghlian, Philip B., ed. *Essays in Eighteenth-Century Biography.* Bloomington: Indiana University Press, 1968.

Daiches, David. *Critical Approaches to Literature.* Englewood Cliffs, N. J.: Prentice-Hall, 1956.

Davenport, William H., and Ben Siegel, eds. *Biography Past and Present.* New York: Scribners, 1965.

Denzin, Norman K. *Interpretive Biography.* Newbury Park, Cal.: Sage, 1989.

Dowling, William C. *Language and Logos in Boswell's Life of Johnson.* Princeton: Princeton University Press, 1981.

Dunn, Waldo H. *English Biography.* London: Dent, 1916; New York: Dutton, 1916.

Durling, Dwight, and William Watt, eds. *Biography: Varieties and Parallels.* New York: Dryden, 1941.

Edel, Leon. *Literary Biography.* Toronto: University of Toronto Press, 1957; London: Hart-Davis, 1957; revised edition, Garden City, N.Y.: Doubleday, 1959; revised again, Bloomington: Indiana University Press, 1973; revised and enlarged as *Writing Lives: Principia Biographica.* New York & London: Norton, 1984.

Edel. *Stuff of Sleep and Dreams: Experiments in Literary Psychology.* New York: Harper & Row, 1982.

Ellmann, Richard. *Golden Codgers: Biographical Speculations.* New York & London: Oxford University Press, 1973.

Ellmann. *Literary Biography: An Inaugural Lecture Delivered Before the University of Oxford on 4 May 1971.* Oxford: Clarendon Press, 1971.

Epstein, William H. *Recognizing Biography.* Philadelphia: University of Pennsylvania Press, 1987.

Epstein, ed. *Contesting the Subject: Essays in the Postmodern Theory and Practice of Biography and Biographical Criticism.* West Lafayette, Ind.: Purdue University Press, 1991.

Flanagan, Thomas. "Problems of Psychobiography," *Queen's Quarterly,* 89 (Autumn 1982): 596–610.

Folkenflik, Robert. *Samuel Johnson, Biographer.* Ithaca, N.Y.: Cornell University Press, 1978.

Fowler, Alastair. *Kinds of Literature: An Introduction to the Theory of Genres and Modes.* Cambridge, Mass.: Harvard University Press, 1982.

Frank, Katherine. "Writing Lives: Theory and Practice of Literary Biography," *Genre,* 13 (Winter 1980): 499–516.

Friedson, Anthony M., ed. *New Directions in Biography: Essays.* Honolulu: Published for the Biographical Research Center by the University of Hawaii Press, 1981.

Fromm, Gloria G., ed. *Essaying Biography: A Celebration for Leon Edel.* Honolulu: Published for the Biographical Research Center by the University of Hawaii Press, 1986.

Frye, Northrop. *Anatomy of Criticism: Four Essays.* Princeton: Princeton University Press, 1957.

Frye. *The Well-Tempered Critic.* Bloomington: Indiana University Press, 1963.

Gardner, Helen Louise, Dame. *In Defence of the Imagination.* Cambridge, Mass.: Harvard University Press, 1982.

Garraty, John Arthur. *The Nature of Biography.* New York: Knopf, 1957.

Gittings, Robert. *The Nature of Biography.* London: Heinemann, 1978; Seattle: University of Washington Press, 1978.

Greene, Donald. " 'Tis a Pretty Book, Mr. Boswell, But – , " *Georgia Review,* 32 (Spring 1978): 17–43.

Hamilton, Ian. *Keepers of the Flame: The Making and Unmaking of Literary Reputations from John Donne to Sylvia Plath.* New York: Paragon House, 1993.

Hampshire, Stuart N. *Modern Writers and Other Essays.* London: Chatto & Windus, 1969; New York: Knopf, 1970.

Havlice, Patricia Pate. *Index to Literary Biography,* 2 volumes. Metuchen, N.J.: Scarecrow Press, 1975.

Heilbrun, Carolyn G. *Hamlet's Mother and Other Women.* New York: Columbia University Press, 1990.

Heilbrun. *Writing a Woman's Life.* New York: Norton, 1988.

Hoberman, Ruth. *Modernizing Lives: Experiments in English Biography, 1918–1939.* Carbondale: Southern Illinois University Press, 1987.

Holland, Norman Norwood. *The Dynamics of Literary Response.* New York: Oxford University Press, 1968.

Holland. *Poems in Persons: An Introduction to the Psychoanalysis of Literature.* New York: Norton, 1973.

Holmes, Richard. *Footsteps: Adventures of a Romantic Biographer.* New York: Viking, 1985.

Homberger, Eric, and John Charmley, eds. *The Troubled Face of Biography.* New York: St. Martin's Press, 1988.

Honan, Park. *Authors' Lives: On Literary Biography and the Arts of Language.* New York: St. Martin's Press, 1990.

Honan. "The Theory of Biography," *Novel,* 13 (Fall 1979): 109–120.

Horden, Peregrine, ed. *Freud and the Humanities*. New York: St. Martin's Press, 1985; London: Duckworth, 1985.

Hough, Graham. *Style and Stylistics*. London: Routledge & Kegan Paul, 1969; New York: Humanities, 1969.

Hyde, Marietta Adelaide, ed. *Modern Biography*. New York: Harcourt, Brace, 1926.

Johnson, Edgar. *One Mighty Torrent: The Drama of Biography*. New York: Stackpole, 1937.

Johnson, ed. *A Treasury of Biography*. New York: Howell, Soskin, 1941.

Kaplan, Justin. "In Pursuit of the Ultimate Fiction," *New York Times Book Review,* 19 April 1987, pp. 1, 24–25.

Kazin, Alfred. *The Inmost Leaf: A Selection of Essays*. New York: Harcourt, Brace, 1955.

Kendall, Paul Murray. *The Art of Biography*. New York: Norton, 1965.

Kenner, Hugh. *Historical Fictions: Essays*. San Francisco: North Point, 1990.

Kermode, Frank. *The Art of Telling: Essays on Fiction*. Cambridge, Mass.: Harvard University Press, 1983.

Kermode. *The Genesis of Secrecy. On the Interpretation of Narrative*. Cambridge, Mass.: Harvard University Press, 1979.

Kermode. *The Sense of an Ending: Studies in the Theory of Fiction*. New York: Oxford University Press, 1967.

Krupnick, Mark L. "The Sanctuary of Imagination," *Nation,* 209 (14 July 1969): 55–56.

Levin, David. *In Defense of Historical Literature: Essays on American History, Autobiography, Drama, and Fiction*. New York: Hill & Wang, 1967.

Levin, Harry. *Contexts of Criticism*. Cambridge, Mass.: Harvard University Press, 1957.

Lomask, Milton. *The Biographer's Craft*. New York: Harper & Row, 1986.

Longaker, Mark. *English Biography in the Eighteenth Century*. Philadelphia: University of Pennsylvania Press, 1931.

Mandell, Gail Porter. *Life into Art: Conversations with Seven Contemporary Biographers*. Fayetteville: University of Arkansas Press, 1991.

Maner, Martin. *The Philosophical Biographer: Doubt and Dialectic in Johnson's Lives of the Poets*. Athens: University of Georgia Press, 1988.

Mariani, Paul L. *A Usable Past: Essays on Modern and Contemporary Poetry*. Amherst: University of Massachusetts Press, 1984.

Marquess, William Henry. *Lives of the Poet: The First Century of Keats Biography*. University Park: Pennsylvania State University Press, 1985.

Maurois, Andre. *Aspects of Biography*. New York: Appleton, 1929.

Meyers, Jeffrey. *The Spirit of Biography*. Ann Arbor, Mich.: UMI Research Press, 1989.

Meyers, ed. *The Biographer's Art: New Essays.* New York: New Amsterdam, 1989.

Meyers, ed. *The Craft of Literary Biography.* New York: Schocken, 1985.

Mintz, Samuel T., Alica Chandler, and Christopher Mulvey, eds. *From Smollett to James: Studies in the Novel and Other Essays Presented to Edgar Johnson.* Charlottesville: University Press of Virginia, 1981.

Nadel, Ira Bruce. *Biography: Fiction, Fact and Form.* New York: St. Martin's Press, 1984.

Nagourney, Peter. "The Basic Assumptions of Literary Biography," *Biography,* 1 (Spring 1978): 86–104.

Nicolson, Harold George, Sir. *The Development of English Biography.* London: Hogarth, 1928; New York: Harcourt, Brace, 1928.

Noland, Richard. "Psychohistory, Theory and Practice," *Massachusetts Review,* 18 (Summer 1977): 295–322.

Novarr, David. *The Lines of Life: Theories of Biography, 1880–1970.* West Lafayette, Ind.: Purdue University Press, 1986.

Oates, Stephen B., ed. *Biography as High Adventure: Life-Writers Speak on Their Art.* Amherst: University of Massachusetts Press, 1986.

Pachter, Marc, ed. *Telling Lives, The Biographer's Art.* Washington, D.C.: New Republic Books, 1979.

Pascal, Roy. *Design and Truth in Autobiography.* Cambridge, Mass.: Harvard University Press, 1960.

Passler, David L. *Time, Form, and Style in Boswell's Life of Johnson.* New Haven: Yale University Press, 1971.

Pearson, Hesketh. *Ventilations: Being Biographical Asides.* Philadelphia & London: Lippincott, 1930.

Plagens, Peter. "Biography," *Art in America,* 68 (October 1980): 13–15.

Powers, Lyall H., ed. *Leon Edel and Literary Art.* Ann Arbor, Mich.: UMI Research Press, 1987.

Quilligan, Maureen. "Rewriting History: The Difference of Feminist Biography," *Yale Review,* 77 (Winter 1988): 259–286.

Reed, Joseph W. *English Biography in the Early Nineteenth Century, 1801–1838.* New Haven: Yale University Press, 1966.

Reid, B. L. *Necessary Lives: Biographical Reflections.* Columbia: University of Missouri Press, 1990.

Rose, Phyllis. *Writing of Women: Essays in a Renaissance.* Middletown, Conn.: Wesleyan University Press, 1985.

Runyan, William McKinley. *Life Histories and Psychobiography: Explorations in Theory and Method.* New York: Oxford University Press, 1982.

Said, Edward W. *Beginnings: Intention and Method.* New York: Basic Books, 1975.

Schaber, Ina. "Fictional Biography, Factual Biography and Their Contaminations," *Biography,* 5 (Winter 1982): 1–16.

Scholes, Robert E. *Structuralism in Literature: An Introduction.* New Haven: Yale University Press, 1974.

Shelston, Alan. *Biography*. London: Methuen, 1977.

Siebenschuh, William R. *Fictional Techniques and Factual Works*. Athens: University of Georgia Press, 1983.

Smith, Barbara Herrnstein. *On the Margins of Discourses: The Relation of Literature to Language*. Chicago: University of Chicago Press, 1978.

Sontag, Susan. "On Style," *Partisan Review,* 32 (Fall 1965): 543–560.

Spence, Donald Pond. *Narrative Truth and Historical Truth: Meaning and Interpretation in Psychoanalysis*. New York: Norton, 1982.

Stauffer, Donald A. *The Art of Biography in Eighteenth-Century England*. Princeton: Princeton University Press, 1941; London: H. Milford, Oxford University Press, 1941.

Stauffer. *English Biography before 1700*. Cambridge, Mass.: Harvard University Press, 1930.

Thayer, William Roscoe. *The Art of Biography*. New York: Scribners, 1920.

Vance, John A., ed. *Boswell's Life of Johnson: New Questions, New Answers*. Athens: University of Georgia Press, 1985.

Veninga, James F., ed. *The Biographer's Gift: Life Histories and Humanism*. College Station: Published for the Texas Committee for the Humanities by Texas A&M University Press, 1983.

Vernoff, Edward, and Rima Shore. *The International Dictionary of 20th Century Biography*. London: Sidgwick & Jackson, 1987; New York: New American Library, 1987.

Weintraub, Stanley, ed. *Biography and Truth*. Indianapolis: Bobbs-Merrill, 1967.

Wendorf, Richard. *The Elements of Life: Biography and Portrait-Painting in Stuart and Georgian England*. Oxford: Clarendon Press, 1990; New York: Oxford University Press, 1990.

Wheeler, David, ed. *Domestick Privacies: Samuel Johnson and the Art of Biography*. Lexington: University Press of Kentucky, 1987.

Whittemore, Reed. *Pure Lives: The Early Biographers*. Baltimore: Johns Hopkins University Press, 1988.

Whittemore. *Whole Lives: Shapers of Modern Biography*. Baltimore: Johns Hopkins University Press, 1989.

Winslow, Donald J. *Life-Writing: A Glossary of Terms in Biography, Autobiography, and Related Forms*. Honolulu: Published for the Biographical Research Center by the University of Hawaii Press, 1980.

Woolf, Virginia. *Collected Essays*. London: Hogarth, 1967; New York: Harcourt, Brace & World, 1967.

Contributors

Douglas W. Alden.. *University of Virginia*
Jason Berner .... *Marymount College*
Robert G. Blake ....*Elon College*
David Bordelon .... *Queens College, City University of New York*
Gillian E. Boughton .... *St. John's College, University of Durham*
Marika Brussel..*Sarah Lawrence College*
Charles Calder...*University of Aberdeen*
Robert Calder .... *University of Saskatchewan*
Ethan Casey ....*Bangkok, Thailand*
Richard Greene.. *University of Toronto*
Elizabeth Haddrell.......................... *Graduate Center of the City University of New York*
Michael Herbert.. *University of Saint Andrews*
Emily A. Hipchen.. *University of Georgia*
David Hopkinson ....*Elstead, England*
Vicki K. Janik.................................... *State University of New York at Farmingdale*
Glen M. Johnson .... *Catholic University of America*
A. R. Jones...*University of Wales*
W. P. Kenney...*Manhattan College*
James King ....*McMaster University*
Barbara Mitchell...*University of Leeds*
Brian Murray ....*Loyola College in Maryland*
Valerie Grosvenor Myer...*Cambridge University*
William Over ....*Saint John's University*
Dennis Paoli .... *Hunter College of the City University of New York*
John Henry Raleigh .... *University of California, Berkeley*
Tracy Seeley..*University of San Francisco*
Angus Somerville...*Brock University*
Fiona Stafford...*Somerville College, Oxford*
Margaret D. Sullivan .... *Hunter College of the City University of New York*
Lisa Tolhurst...*New York University*

Cumulative Index

Dictionary of Literary Biography, Volumes 1-155
Dictionary of Literary Biography Yearbook, 1980-1994
Dictionary of Literary Biography Documentary Series, Volumes 1-12

Cumulative Index

DLB before number: *Dictionary of Literary Biography,* Volumes 1-155
Y before number: *Dictionary of Literary Biography Yearbook,* 1980-1994
DS before number: *Dictionary of Literary Biography Documentary Series,* Volumes 1-12

G

H

Q

ISBN 0-8103-5716-X